OECD Factbook 2008

FOREWORD

In 2006, OECD member countries called on the Organisation to "help its members fully reap the benefits and respond to the challenges of globalisation", becoming a hub for discussion of global issues. In 2007, OECD member countries agreed on a strategy for enlargement (five countries were selected, Chile, Estonia, Israel, Russian Federation and Slovenia) and for enhanced engagement with key "global players with a view to Membership" (such as Brazil, China, India, Indonesia and South Africa). These major steps imply a substantial change in the way we operate to better respond: the OECD must be *more open*. At a time when national governments are losing the monopoly of policy decisions, the OECD needs to reach out to society as a whole. Thus, it must be:

- *More representative*: The OECD's platform needs to be more inclusive, bringing in new players in the global economy and new policy issues in the OECD agenda.
- *More supportive of the reform efforts*: The Organisation needs to move beyond proposing best practices, to helping countries put them into operation.
- *Better connected*: The OECD will continue to strengthen its dialogue with a widening circle of interlocutors to help countries better deal with the challenges posed by globalisation.

To underpin these processes at least three elements seem fundamental: good statistical evidence about the overall progress of societies and globalisation-related phenomena; sound analytical tools and the use of a long-term perspective. However, one of the paradoxes of our world today is that people often have too much information. We are bombarded with both relevant and irrelevant information from all sides. What is often missing is an ability to focus on the information that really matters. This can have serious negative consequences for democracy. It can lead to confusion and fragmentation in voting, a withdrawal from political participation, or a reliance on ideology rather than facts or evidence-based knowledge as the basis for public policy choices.

The *OECD Factbook* helps in addressing these issues. It provides, through comparable statistics, a picture of long-term trends of key economic, social and environmental phenomena in member countries and selected non-member economies. It helps the reader put current developments of the country where he/she is living in both a historical perspective and, through international comparisons, in a wider context.

The *OECD Factbook* is part of the strategic agenda of the OECD to support well informed policy decisions, and to achieve a better measurement of the overall progress in societies. The success of the second OECD World Forum on "Statistics, Knowledge and Policy", held in Istanbul (Turkey) in June 2007 and attended by 1 200 people from 130 countries, confirmed the enormous interest in these issues and led to the "Istanbul Declaration" originally signed by the OECD, the European Commission, the Organisation of the Islamic Conference, the United Nations, the United Nations Development Programme and the World Bank, and then agreed by many other organisations, such as UNESCO and UNICEF.

The Istanbul Declaration calls, among other things, for action to stimulate international debate, based on solid statistical data and indicators, on both world issues and comparisons of societal progress and to produce a broader, shared, public understanding of changing conditions. The *OECD Factbook* can contribute to reach these goals and confirm the Organisation's role as a key global knowledge builder to help citizens to better understand the world they are living in. By doing that, the OECD can help to build a better world.

Angel Gurría
Secretary-General

OECD FACTBOOK 2008 – ISBN 978-92-64-04054-0 – © OECD 2008

PREFACE

The *OECD Factbook* is the most comprehensive horizontal statistical publication published by the Organisation. It is a tool to evaluate the long-term trends of economic, social and environmental variables in OECD countries using solid and comparable statistical data. It draws on the full range of data available within the Organisation, including data from three agencies affiliated to the OECD – the *International Energy Agency (IEA)*, the *Nuclear Energy Agency (NEA)* and the *European Conference of Ministers of Transport (ECMT)*.

The *OECD Factbook* is written in non-technical language and aims to:
- provide a wide range of users with a one-stop resource, containing comparative, country-based economic, social and environmental data;
- help users to assess the position and the performance of a single country, looking at a wide range of domains;
- encourage readers to go deeper in the goldmine of OECD statistics by linking to sources and further readings;
- enhance the visibility of the OECD, particularly for non-experts, both in OECD and non-OECD countries;
- highlight measurement issues and underline areas where the comparability of statistics across countries is still weak.

The tables of the *OECD Factbook* are available on line at *www.sourceoecd.org/factbook*. The online version also contains longer time series and more metadata than the paper version. The data included in the *OECD Factbook* are also used to produce the "Country Statistical Profiles" available in the country pages at *www.oecd.org*.

Thanks to the closer co-operation with non-member economies, the *OECD Factbook 2008* includes many more time series concerning key non-OECD countries (Brazil, China, India, Russian Federation and South Africa), while "Country Statistical Profiles" have been developed also for Chile, Israel and Slovenia. The special section in this year's volume deals with productivity, to which the Organisation is paying special attention, notably from the statistical point of view.

The *OECD Factbook* reflects the work of statistical staff throughout the Organisation and was developed in co-operation with the Directorate for Public Affairs and Communications. The Statistics Directorate, which has co-ordinated the project, is grateful for the co-operation of the many staff members involved, but also, of course, for the concerted efforts of statisticians from all OECD countries who have worked, over many years, to develop the wide range of statistics shown here.

Lars Thygesen has co-ordinated the editorial work, co-operating with colleagues from various Directorates in designing the tables, helping to draft many of the texts, checking the quality of data and ensuring the overall coherence of the volume. Jérome Cukier, Ingrid Herrbach, Nobuko Miyachiyo and Katia Sarrazin had overall responsibility for technical work on the manuscript.

Enrico Giovannini
Chief Statistician
and Director of the Statistics Directorate

TABLE OF CONTENTS

Foreword   4
Preface   5
Reader's guide   8

Population and migration

TOTAL POPULATION   12
Evolution of the population   12
Regional population   16
ELDERLY POPULATION   18
Ageing societies   18
Elderly population by region   20
INTERNATIONAL MIGRATION   22
Trends in migration   22
Immigrant population   24
Migration and unemployment   26
Educational attainment of recent
immigrants   28

Macroeconomic trends

GROSS DOMESTIC PRODUCT (GDP)   32
Size of GDP   32
National income per capita   36
Regional GDP   38
ECONOMIC GROWTH   40
Evolution of GDP   40
Household saving   42
Investment rates   44
Inflation   48
Steel production   50
ECONOMIC STRUCTURE   52
Value added by activity   52
Evolution of value added by activity   56
Small and medium-sized enterprises   60

Economic globalisation

TRADE   64
Share of trade in GDP   64
Trade in goods   66
Trade in services   70
Trading partners   74
Balance of payments   78
FOREIGN DIRECT INVESTMENT (FDI)   80
FDI flows and stocks   80
Activities of multinationals   84

Prices

PRICES AND INTEREST RATES   88
Consumer price indices (CPI)   88
Producer price indices (PPI)   92
Long-term interest rates   94
PURCHASING POWER AND EXCHANGE RATES   96
Rates of conversion   96
Effective exchange rates   100

Energy

ENERGY SUPPLY   106
Energy supply   106
Energy supply and economic growth   108
Energy supply per capita   110
Electricity generation   112
Nuclear energy   114
Renewable energy   116
ENERGY PRODUCTION AND PRICES   118
Energy production   118
Oil production   120
Oil prices   122

Labour

EMPLOYMENT   126
Employment rates by gender   126
Employment rates by age group   130
Part-time employment   134
Self-employment   136
UNEMPLOYMENT   140
Unemployment rates   140
Long-term unemployment   144
Regional unemployment   146
LABOUR COMPENSATION
AND HOURS WORKED   148
Labour compensation   148
Hours worked   152

Science and technology

RESEARCH AND DEVELOPMENT (R&D)   156
Expenditure on R&D   156
Investment in knowledge   158
Researchers   160
Patents   162

OECD FACTBOOK 2008 – ISBN 978-92-64-04054-0 – © OECD 2008

⊗ Science and technology

ICT	164
Size of the ICT sector	164
Investment in ICT	166
Computer and Internet access by households	168
COMMUNICATIONS	170
Exports of information and communications equipment	170
Telephone access	172

☼ Environment

WATER AND NATURAL RESOURCES	176
Water consumption	176
Fisheries	178
AIR AND LAND	180
Emissions of carbon dioxide (CO_2)	180
Municipal waste	182
Nutrient use in agriculture	184

◎ Education

OUTCOMES	188
International student assessment	188
Trends in tertiary graduation rates	192
Tertiary attainment	194
EXPENDITURE ON EDUCATION	198
Expenditure on tertiary education	198
Relative earnings of graduates	200
Public and private education expenditure	202

→ Public finance

GOVERNMENT DEFICITS AND DEBT	206
Government deficits	206
Government debt	208
PUBLIC EXPENDITURE	210
Health expenditure	210
Social expenditure	212
Law, order and defence expenditure	214
SUPPORT AND AID	216
Agricultural support estimates	216
Government support for fishing	218
Official development assistance	220
TAXES	224
Total tax revenue	224
Taxes on the average worker	228

❀ Quality of life

HEALTH	232
Life expectancy	232
Infant mortality	236
Obesity	238
LEISURE	240
Tourism: Hotel nights	240
Recreation and culture	242
SOCIETY	246
Youth inactivity	246
Income inequality	248
Prison population	250
TRANSPORT	252
Road network	252
Road motor vehicles and road fatalities	254

Focus on:
Productivity

Introduction	260
ECONOMY-WIDE INDICATORS OF PRODUCTIVITY GROWTH	262
Growth in GDP per capita	262
Labour productivity growth	264
Multi-factor productivity	266
Growth accounts for OECD countries	268
PRODUCTIVITY LEVELS	270
Income and productivity levels	270
Historical income and productivity levels	272
Labour productivity and firm-size heterogeneity	274
PRODUCTIVITY GROWTH BY INDUSTRY	276
Contribution of key activities to aggregate productivity growth	276
Productivity growth in manufacturing	278
Productivity growth in services	280
IMPACT OF LABOUR PRODUCTIVITY ON UNIT LABOUR COSTS	282
Unit labour costs, labour productivity and labour compensation	282
Analytical index	286

READER'S GUIDE

Main features:

- Tables or groups of tables are preceded by a short text that explains how the statistics are defined (**Definition**) and identifies any problems there may be in comparing the performance of one country with another (**Comparability**). To avoid misunderstandings, the tables must be read in conjunction with the texts that accompany them.

- Tables and graphs are also available as files (see below). In their electronic version, tables may feature longer time series and data for Chile, Estonia, Israel and Slovenia are added for many indicators. When appropriate, footnotes may provide additional information.

- While media comment on statistics usually focuses on the short term – what has happened to employment, prices, GDP and so on in the last few months – the *OECD Factbook* takes a longer view; the text and graphs mostly describe developments during the fourteen year period from 1993 to 2006. This long-term perspective provides a good basis for comparing the successes and failures of policies in raising living standards and social conditions in countries.

- Many Factbook indicators have been standardised by relating them to each country's gross domestic product (GDP). In cases where GDP needs to be converted to a common currency, *purchasing power parities* (PPPs) have been used rather than exchange rates. When PPPs are used, differences in GDP levels reflect only differences in the volume of goods and services and differences in price levels are eliminated.

Conventions

Unless otherwise specified:

- *OECD total* refers to all the OECD countries listed in a table as a whole; when the indicator is a ratio or mean, OECD total is the weighted average.

- *OECD average* refers to the unweighted, arithmetic average of the listed OECD countries.

- For each country, average over periods only take into account the years for which data are available. The *average annual growth rate* of a value over a period is the geometric average of the growth rates of that value across the period (the annual compound growth rate).

- Each table and graph specifies the period covered. The mention, *XXXX or latest year available* (where XXXX is a year) means that data for later years are not taken into account.

Signs, abbreviations and acronyms

..	Missing value, not applicable or not available	**DAC**	Development Assistance Committee
0	Less than half of the unit precision level of the observation	**ILO**	International Labor Organisation
-	Absolute zero	**IMF**	International Monetary Fund
|	Break in series	**ITU**	International Telecommunications Union
		UN	United Nations
		UNCTAD	United Nations Conference on Trade and Development
USD	US dollars	**UNECE**	United Nations Economic Commission for Europe
		UNODC	United Nations Office on Drugs and Crime
		WTO	World Trade Organisation
		UNWTO	World Tourism Organisation

OECD FACTBOOK 2008 – ISBN 978-92-64-04054-0 – © OECD 2008

StatLinks

This book includes OECD's unique *StatLink* service, which enables you to download Excel® versions of tables and graphs. Look for the *StatLinks* at the foot of each one of them. *StatLinks* behave like Internet addresses. Simply type the *StatLink* in your Internet browser to obtain the corresponding data in Excel® format.

For more information about OECD's *StatLinks*, please visit: *www.oecd.org/statistics/statlink*.

Accessing OECD publications

- OECD publications cited in the Factbook are available through SourceOECD (*www.sourceoecd.org*), the OECD electronic library.
- All the OECD working papers can be downloaded from SourceOECD.
- All OECD databases mentioned in the book can also be accessed through SourceOECD.
- In addition, print editions of all OECD books can be purchased via the OECD online bookshop (*www.oecdbookshop.org*).

Glossary of Statistical Terms

The online *OECD Glossary of Statistical Terms* (available at *www.oecd.org/statistics/glossary*) is the perfect companion for the *OECD Factbook*. It contains close to 7 000 definitions of terms, acronyms and concepts in an easy to use format. These definitions are primarily drawn from existing international statistical guidelines and recommendations that have been prepared over the last two or three decades by organisations such as the United Nations, ILO, OECD, Eurostat, IMF and national statistical institutes.

POPULATION AND MIGRATION

TOTAL POPULATION
EVOLUTION OF THE POPULATION
REGIONAL POPULATION

ELDERLY POPULATION
AGEING SOCIETIES
ELDERLY POPULATION BY REGION

INTERNATIONAL MIGRATION
TRENDS IN MIGRATION
IMMIGRANT POPULATION
MIGRATION AND UNEMPLOYMENT
EDUCATIONAL ATTAINMENT OF RECENT IMMIGRANTS

EVOLUTION OF THE POPULATION

The size and growth of a country's population are both causes and effects of economic and social developments. The natural increase in population (births minus deaths) has slowed in all OECD countries, resulting in a rise in the average age of populations. In several countries, falling rates of natural increase have been partly offset by immigration from outside the OECD area.

Definition

The tables refer to the resident population. For countries such as France, the United Kingdom and the United States which have overseas colonies, protectorates or other territorial possessions, their populations are generally excluded. For full details, see Sources below.

Growth rates are the annual changes in the population and are the result of births, deaths and net migration during the year.

The total fertility rate is the total number of children that would be born to each woman if she were to live to the end of her child-bearing years and give birth to children in that period in agreement with the prevailing age-specific fertility rates.

Comparability

For most OECD countries, population data are based on regular, ten-yearly censuses, with estimates for intercensal years being derived from administrative data such as population registers, notified births and deaths and migration records. In several European countries, population estimates are based entirely on administrative records. In general, the population data for OECD countries are reliable, although, for some countries, there are breaks in the series as indicated by vertical lines in the tables.

Note that for some countries the population figures shown here are not those used for calculating GDP and other economic statistics on a "per head" basis. There are several reasons for this, but the differences between the two data sets are normally small.

Population projections are taken from national sources where these are available, but for some countries they are based on UN or Eurostat projections; the projection for the world comes from UN. All population projections require assumptions about future trends in life expectancy, fertility rates and migration. Often, a range of projections is produced using different assumptions about these future trends. The estimates shown here correspond to the median or central variants.

Long-term trends

In 2006, OECD countries accounted for 18% of the world's population of 6.5 billion. China accounted for 20% and India for 17%. Within OECD, the United States accounted for 25% of the OECD total, followed by Japan (11%), Mexico (9%), Germany (7%) and Turkey (6%).

Between 1993 and 2006, the population growth rate for all OECD countries averaged 0.7% per annum. Growth rates much higher than this were recorded for Mexico and Turkey (high birth rate countries) and for Australia, Canada, Luxembourg, Ireland, New Zealand and United States (high net immigration). In the Czech Republic, Hungary and Poland, populations declined from a combination of low birth rates and net emigration. Growth rates were very low, although still positive, in Germany and the Slovak Republic.

The population growth of OECD countries is expected to slow down in the coming decennia. Until the middle of this century, the population of OECD countries is expected to grow by less than 0.3 per cent per annum.

Total fertility rates have declined dramatically over the past few decades, falling on average from 2.7 in 1970 to 1.6 children per woman of childbearing age in 2005. By 2005, the total fertility rate was below its replacement level of 2.1 in all OECD countries except Mexico and Turkey. In all OECD countries, fertility rates have declined for young women and increased at older ages, because women are postponing the age at which they start their families.

Sources

- For member countries: OECD (2007), *Labour Force Statistics*, OECD, Paris.
- For Brazil: Instituto Brasileiro de Geografia e Estatistica.
- For China: National Bureau of Statistics.
- For India, Russian Federation and South Africa: UN (2005), Demographic Yearbook 2002, United Nations, New York.
- Fertility rates: OECD (2007), *OECD Health Data 2007*, OECD, Paris.

Further information

Analytical publications
- OECD (2007), *OECD Employment Outlook*, OECD, Paris.

Statistical publications
- Maddison, Angus (2003), The World Economy: Historical Perspectives, OECD, Paris, also available on CD-ROM, *www.theworldeconomy.org*.
- OECD (2004), *Quarterly Labour Force Statistics*, OECD, Paris.
- OECD (2007), *Society at a Glance: OECD Social Indicators – 2006 Edition*, OECD, Paris.

Methodological publications
- d'Addio, A. C. and M. Mira d'Ercole (2005), *Trends and Determinants of Fertility Rates: The Role of Policies*, OECD Social Employment and Migration Working Papers, No. 27, OECD, Paris.
- OECD (2007), *Labour Force Statistics*, OECD, Paris.

Online databases
- *Employment Statistics*.

Websites
- World Population Prospects: The 2002 Revision Population Database, *http://esa.un.org/unpp*.

Total population
Thousands

	1995	1996	1997	1998	1999	2000	2001	2002	2003	2004	2005	2006	2020	2050
Australia	18 072	18 311	18 518	18 711	18 926	19 153	19 413	19 641	19 873	20 092	20 340	20 605	23 663	28 081
Austria	7 948	7 959	7 968	7 977	7 992	8 012	8 043	8 084	8 118	8 175	8 233	8 263	8 651	8 986
Belgium	10 137	10 157	10 181	10 203	10 226	10 251	10 287	10 333	10 376	10 421	10 479	10 465	10 801	10 897
Canada	29 302	29 611	29 907	30 157	30 404	30 689	31 021	31 373	31 676	31 989	32 299	32 623	36 344	41 896
Czech Republic	10 331	10 315	10 304	10 295	10 283	10 273	10 224	10 201	10 202	10 207	10 234	10 241	10 287	9 457
Denmark	5 228	5 262	5 284	5 301	5 319	5 337	5 355	5 374	5 387	5 401	5 416	5 435	5 582	5 621
Finland	5 108	5 125	5 140	5 153	5 165	5 176	5 188	5 201	5 213	5 228	5 246	5 266	5 538	5 747
France	57 844	58 026	58 207	58 398	58 661	59 013	59 393	59 778	60 155	60 521	60 873	61 203	65 102	69 993
Germany	81 678	81 915	82 035	82 047	82 100	82 212	82 350	82 488	82 534	82 516	82 469	82 683	82 635	74 422
Greece	10 634	10 709	10 777	10 835	10 883	10 917	10 950	10 988	11 024	11 062	11 104	11 143	11 426	10 605
Hungary	10 229	10 193	10 155	10 114	10 068	10 122	10 188	10 159	10 130	10 107	10 087	10 066	9 856	8 718
Iceland	267	269	271	274	277	281	285	288	289	293	296	297	327	355
Ireland	3 601	3 626	3 664	3 703	3 742	3 790	3 847	3 917	3 979	4 044	4 131	4 151	4 774	5 482
Italy	56 843	56 859	56 890	56 907	56 917	56 943	56 975	57 151	57 597	58 167	58 597	58 643	59 001	55 710
Japan	125 570	125 864	126 166	126 486	126 686	126 926	127 291	127 435	127 619	127 687	127 757	127 762	122 735	95 152
Korea	45 093	45 525	45 954	46 287	46 617	47 008	47 357	47 622	47 859	48 039	48 138	48 297	49 326	42 343
Luxembourg	409	414	419	425	430	436	442	446	450	453	457	463	523	644
Mexico	91 725	93 130	94 478	95 790	97 115	98 439	99 716	100 909	102 000	103 002	103 947	104 874	115 762	121 856
Netherlands	15 459	15 531	15 611	15 707	15 812	15 926	16 046	16 149	16 225	16 282	16 321	16 344	16 762	16 789
New Zealand	3 673	3 732	3 781	3 815	3 835	3 858	3 881	3 939	4 009	4 061	4 099	4 140	4 565	5 046
Norway	4 359	4 381	4 405	4 431	4 462	4 491	4 514	4 538	4 565	4 592	4 623	4 651	5 061	5 854
Poland	38 275	38 289	38 292	38 284	38 270	38 258	38 248	38 232	38 195	38 180	38 161	38 049	37 038	33 576
Portugal	10 030	10 058	10 091	10 129	10 172	10 226	10 293	10 368	10 441	10 502	10 549	10 578	10 501	9 332
Slovak Republic	5 364	5 374	5 383	5 391	5 395	5 401	5 380	5 379	5 379	5 383	5 387	5 386	5 417	4 880
Spain	39 388	39 479	39 583	39 722	39 927	40 264	40 721	41 314	42 005	42 640	43 210	43 696	45 568	42 703
Sweden	8 827	8 841	8 846	8 851	8 858	8 872	8 896	8 925	8 958	8 994	9 030	9 074	9 658	10 490
Switzerland	7 041	7 072	7 089	7 110	7 144	7 184	7 230	7 285	7 339	7 390	7 437	7 490	7 993	8 067
Turkey	63 070	64 131	65 181	66 221	67 254	67 420	68 365	69 301	70 231	71 152	72 065	72 974	84 301	96 498
United Kingdom	58 025	58 164	58 314	58 475	58 684	58 886	59 113	59 322	59 554	59 835	60 210	60 533	64 449	69 177
United States	266 557	269 667	272 912	276 115	279 295	282 430	285 454	288 427	291 289	294 056	296 940	299 801	336 032	420 081
EU27 total	476 486	477 251	477 918	478 525	479 385	480 578	481 992	483 749	485 738	487 819	489 792	491 094	500 487	484 603
OECD total	1 090 086	1 097 989	1 105 806	1 113 314	1 120 919	1 128 193	1 136 466	1 144 566	1 152 670	1 160 470	1 168 136	1 175 198	1 249 678	1 318 459
Brazil	161 615	164 073	166 566	169 087	171 622	174 161	176 702	179 246	181 787	184 318	186 831	189 323	219 992	254 085
China	1 213 732	1 225 680	1 237 431	1 248 852	1 259 740	1 269 962	1 279 486	1 288 401	1 296 838	1 304 983	1 312 979	1 320 864	1 421 260	1 408 846
India	954 282	972 968	991 513	1 009 905	1 028 145	1 046 235	1 064 156	1 081 899	1 099 494	1 116 985	1 134 403	1 151 751	1 379 198	1 658 270
Russian Federation	149 124	148 926	148 667	148 339	147 927	147 423	146 828	146 159	145 438	144 696	143 953	143 221	132 407	107 832
South Africa	41 505	42 401	43 236	44 009	44 729	45 398	46 017	46 581	47 089	47 541	47 939	48 282	51 281	55 590
World	5 719 045	5 801 566	5 883 316	5 964 308	6 044 563	6 124 123	6 202 979	6 281 209	6 359 055	6 436 826	6 514 751	6 592 900	7 667 090	9 191 287

StatLink http://dx.doi.org/10.1787/272317250164

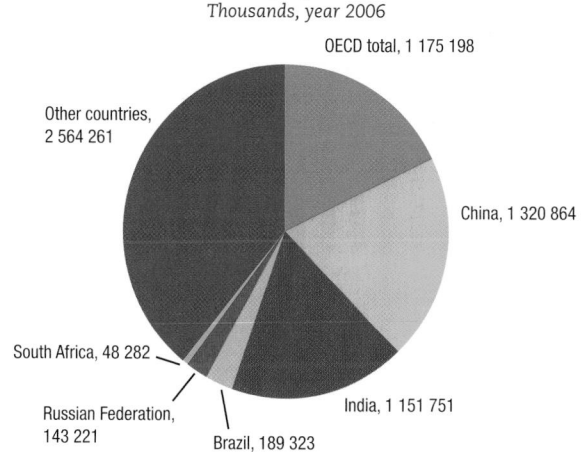

World population
Thousands, year 2006

OECD total, 1 175 198

Other countries, 2 564 261

China, 1 320 864

South Africa, 48 282

Russian Federation, 143 221

Brazil, 189 323

India, 1 151 751

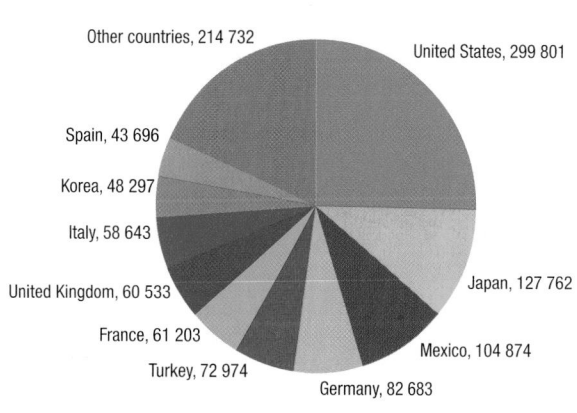

OECD population
Thousands, year 2006

Other countries, 214 732

United States, 299 801

Spain, 43 696

Korea, 48 297

Italy, 58 643

United Kingdom, 60 533

France, 61 203

Turkey, 72 974

Germany, 82 683

Japan, 127 762

Mexico, 104 874

StatLink http://dx.doi.org/10.1787/266215507720

EVOLUTION OF THE POPULATION

Population growth rates
Annual growth in percentage

	1993	1994	1995	1996	1997	1998	1999	2000	2001	2002	2003	2004	2005	2006
Australia	0.99	1.06	1.22	1.32	1.13	1.05	1.15	1.20	1.36	1.17	1.18	1.10	1.24	1.31
Austria	0.83	0.39	0.15	0.14	0.11	0.11	0.19	0.24	0.39	0.51	0.42	0.70	0.72	0.36
Belgium	0.39	0.31	0.21	0.20	0.24	0.21	0.23	0.24	0.34	0.45	0.42	0.43	0.55	-0.13
Canada	1.11	1.11	1.05	1.05	1.00	0.84	0.82	0.94	1.08	1.13	0.97	0.99	0.97	1.00
Czech Republic	0.12	0.05	-0.05	-0.15	-0.11	-0.08	-0.12	-0.10	-0.47	-0.23	0.01	0.05	0.27	0.07
Denmark	0.35	0.30	0.44	0.64	0.43	0.32	0.34	0.34	0.33	0.36	0.24	0.26	0.27	0.34
Finland	0.49	0.43	0.38	0.33	0.30	0.27	0.23	0.21	0.23	0.24	0.24	0.29	0.34	0.38
France	0.40	0.33	0.32	0.31	0.31	0.33	0.45	0.60	0.64	0.65	0.63	0.61	0.58	0.54
Germany	0.66	0.35	0.29	0.29	0.15	0.02	0.06	0.14	0.17	0.17	0.06	-0.02	-0.06	0.26
Greece	0.92	0.84	0.77	0.70	0.63	0.54	0.44	0.32	0.30	0.34	0.33	0.35	0.38	0.35
Hungary	-0.29	-0.31	-0.32	-0.35	-0.38	-0.41	-0.46	0.54	0.65	-0.28	-0.29	-0.22	-0.20	-0.21
Iceland	1.03	0.84	0.52	0.58	0.74	1.06	1.24	1.43	1.39	0.88	0.60	1.15	1.12	0.30
Ireland	0.55	0.33	0.43	0.69	1.05	1.06	1.04	1.28	1.52	1.82	1.58	1.63	2.15	0.50
Italy	0.06	0.02	0.00	0.03	0.05	0.03	0.02	0.05	0.06	0.31	0.78	0.99	0.74	0.08
Japan	0.30	0.26	0.24	0.23	0.24	0.25	0.16	0.19	0.29	0.11	0.14	0.05	0.05	0.00
Korea	1.02	1.01	1.01	0.96	0.94	0.72	0.71	0.84	0.74	0.56	0.50	0.38	0.21	0.33
Luxembourg	1.35	1.37	1.41	1.37	1.26	1.25	1.36	1.35	1.20	1.05	0.85	0.74	0.87	1.15
Mexico	1.80	1.71	1.62	1.53	1.45	1.39	1.38	1.36	1.30	1.20	1.08	0.98	0.92	0.89
Netherlands	0.70	0.60	0.50	0.46	0.52	0.62	0.67	0.72	0.76	0.64	0.47	0.35	0.24	0.14
New Zealand	1.15	1.34	1.47	1.60	1.32	0.89	0.53	0.59	0.59	1.51	1.78	1.30	0.92	0.99
Norway	0.60	0.57	0.52	0.51	0.54	0.60	0.69	0.65	0.51	0.54	0.59	0.59	0.68	0.60
Poland	0.12	0.08	0.06	0.04	0.01	-0.02	-0.04	-0.03	-0.03	-0.04	-0.10	-0.04	-0.05	-0.29
Portugal	0.13	0.22	0.26	0.27	0.33	0.38	0.42	0.53	0.66	0.73	0.70	0.58	0.45	0.28
Slovak Republic	0.34	0.43	0.30	0.19	0.18	0.14	0.08	0.10	-0.39	-0.02	0.00	0.07	0.09	-0.02
Spain	0.31	0.27	0.23	0.23	0.26	0.35	0.52	0.84	1.14	1.46	1.67	1.51	1.34	1.13
Sweden	0.58	0.71	0.53	0.16	0.06	0.06	0.08	0.16	0.27	0.33	0.37	0.39	0.40	0.49
Switzerland	0.91	0.80	0.67	0.44	0.24	0.30	0.48	0.56	0.63	0.76	0.74	0.69	0.64	0.71
Turkey	1.83	1.78	1.73	1.68	1.64	1.60	1.56	0.25	1.40	1.37	1.34	1.31	1.28	1.26
United Kingdom	0.22	0.26	0.28	0.24	0.26	0.28	0.36	0.34	0.39	0.35	0.39	0.47	0.63	0.54
United States	1.31	1.22	1.18	1.17	1.20	1.17	1.15	1.12	1.07	1.04	0.99	0.95	0.98	0.96
EU27 total	0.28	0.21	0.18	0.16	0.14	0.13	0.18	0.25	0.29	0.36	0.41	0.43	0.40	0.27
OECD total	0.84	0.78	0.75	0.72	0.71	0.68	0.68	0.65	0.73	0.71	0.71	0.68	0.66	0.60
Brazil	1.54	1.52	1.52	1.52	1.52	1.51	1.50	1.48	1.46	1.44	1.42	1.39	1.36	1.33
China	1.07	1.02	1.00	0.98	0.96	0.92	0.87	0.81	0.75	0.70	0.65	0.63	0.61	0.60
India	2.11	2.06	2.01	1.96	1.91	1.85	1.81	1.76	1.71	1.67	1.63	1.59	1.56	1.53
Russian Federation	0.02	-0.06	-0.10	-0.13	-0.17	-0.22	-0.28	-0.34	-0.40	-0.46	-0.49	-0.51	-0.51	-0.51
South Africa	2.69	2.58	2.38	2.16	1.97	1.79	1.63	1.50	1.36	1.22	1.09	0.96	0.84	0.72
World	1.55	1.51	1.48	1.44	1.41	1.38	1.35	1.32	1.29	1.26	1.24	1.22	1.21	1.20

StatLink ᴍ𝔰🔗 http://dx.doi.org/10.1787/272324178223

Population growth rates
Average annual growth in percentage, 1993-2006 or latest available period

StatLink ᴍ𝔰🔗 http://dx.doi.org/10.1787/266252532287

OECD FACTBOOK 2008 – ISBN 978-92-64-04054-0 – © OECD 2008

Total fertility rates

Number of children born to women aged 15 to 49

	1992	1993	1994	1995	1996	1997	1998	1999	2000	2001	2002	2003	2004	2005
Australia	1.85	1.89	1.87	1.85	1.82	1.80	1.78	1.76	1.76	1.73	1.76	1.75	1.77	1.81
Austria	1.49	1.48	1.44	1.40	1.42	1.37	1.34	1.32	1.34	1.31	1.40	1.38	1.42	1.41
Belgium	1.65	1.61	1.55	1.55	1.55	1.55	1.53	1.61	1.66	1.64	1.62	1.64	1.64	1.72
Canada	1.69	1.66	1.62	1.62	1.62	1.58	1.54	1.51	1.49	1.51	1.50	1.53	1.53	1.53
Czech Republic	1.72	1.67	1.44	1.28	1.18	1.19	1.16	1.13	1.14	1.14	1.17	1.18	1.22	1.28
Denmark	1.76	1.75	1.81	1.80	1.75	1.75	1.72	1.73	1.77	1.74	1.72	1.76	1.78	1.80
Finland	1.85	1.81	1.85	1.81	1.76	1.75	1.70	1.74	1.73	1.73	1.72	1.76	1.80	1.80
France	1.73	1.65	1.66	1.70	1.72	1.71	1.76	1.79	1.88	1.89	1.87	1.88	1.91	1.94
Germany	1.30	1.28	1.24	1.25	1.32	1.37	1.36	1.36	1.38	1.35	1.31	1.34	1.36	1.34
Greece	1.38	1.34	1.35	1.32	1.30	1.31	1.29	1.28	1.27	1.27	1.27	1.28	1.29	1.28
Hungary	1.77	1.69	1.64	1.57	1.46	1.38	1.33	1.29	1.32	1.31	1.30	1.27	1.28	1.32
Iceland	2.21	2.22	2.14	2.08	2.12	2.04	2.04	1.99	2.08	1.95	1.93	1.99	2.04	2.05
Ireland	1.99	1.91	1.85	1.83	1.89	1.92	1.93	1.88	1.89	1.97	1.97	1.96	1.93	1.88
Italy	1.31	1.25	1.21	1.18	1.20	1.22	1.20	1.23	1.23	1.25	1.25	1.26	1.33	1.34
Japan	1.50	1.46	1.50	1.42	1.44	1.44	1.38	1.34	1.36	1.33	1.32	1.29	1.29	1.26
Korea	1.78	1.67	1.67	1.65	1.58	1.54	1.47	1.42	1.47	1.30	1.17	1.19	1.16	1.08
Luxembourg	1.64	1.70	1.72	1.69	1.76	1.71	1.68	1.73	1.76	1.66	1.63	1.63	1.69	1.70
Mexico	3.20	3.20	3.10	3.00	2.90	2.80	2.70	2.70	2.70	2.60	2.50	2.40	2.30	2.20
Netherlands	1.59	1.57	1.57	1.53	1.53	1.56	1.63	1.65	1.72	1.71	1.73	1.75	1.73	1.73
New Zealand	2.10	2.07	2.05	1.99	1.99	1.96	1.89	1.97	1.98	1.97	1.90	1.95	2.01	2.00
Norway	1.88	1.86	1.86	1.87	1.89	1.86	1.81	1.84	1.85	1.78	1.75	1.80	1.83	1.84
Poland	1.93	1.85	1.80	1.61	1.58	1.51	1.44	1.37	1.34	1.29	1.24	1.22	1.23	1.24
Portugal	1.54	1.52	1.44	1.40	1.43	1.46	1.46	1.50	1.55	1.46	1.47	1.44	1.40	1.40
Slovak Republic	1.86	1.75	1.63	1.52	1.47	1.43	1.38	1.33	1.29	1.20	1.18	1.20	1.24	1.25
Spain	1.32	1.27	1.21	1.18	1.17	1.19	1.16	1.20	1.24	1.26	1.26	1.31	1.32	1.34
Sweden	2.09	1.99	1.88	1.73	1.60	1.52	1.50	1.50	1.54	1.57	1.65	1.71	1.75	1.77
Switzerland	1.58	1.51	1.49	1.48	1.50	1.51	1.47	1.48	1.50	1.41	1.39	1.39	1.42	1.42
Turkey	2.93	2.87	2.81	2.75	2.69	2.63	2.56	2.48	2.27	2.25	2.24	2.22	2.21	2.19
United Kingdom	1.79	1.75	1.74	1.70	1.72	1.72	1.71	1.68	1.65	1.63	1.64	1.71	1.76	1.80
United States	2.07	2.05	2.04	2.02	2.04	2.06	2.00	2.01	2.06	2.03	2.01	2.04	2.05	2.05
OECD average	1.82	1.78	1.74	1.69	1.68	1.66	1.63	1.63	1.64	1.61	1.60	1.61	1.62	1.63
Brazil	2.60	2.57	2.54	2.51	2.48	2.45	2.43	2.41	2.39	2.36	2.35	2.33	2.31	2.29
China	1.95	1.94	1.93	1.92	1.91	1.90	1.90	1.89	1.89	1.89	1.88	1.88	1.85	1.81
India	3.54	3.49	3.45	3.40	3.35	3.30	3.22	3.15	3.07	3.00	2.92	2.92	2.88	2.84
Russian Federation	..	..	..	1.34	1.27	1.22	1.23	1.16	1.19	1.22	1.29	1.32	1.34	1.29
South Africa	3.20	3.16	3.12	3.08	3.04	3.00	2.97	2.93	2.90	2.86	2.84	2.82	2.80	2.78

StatLink http://dx.doi.org/10.1787/272332670175

Total fertility rates

Number of children born to women aged 15 to 49, 2005

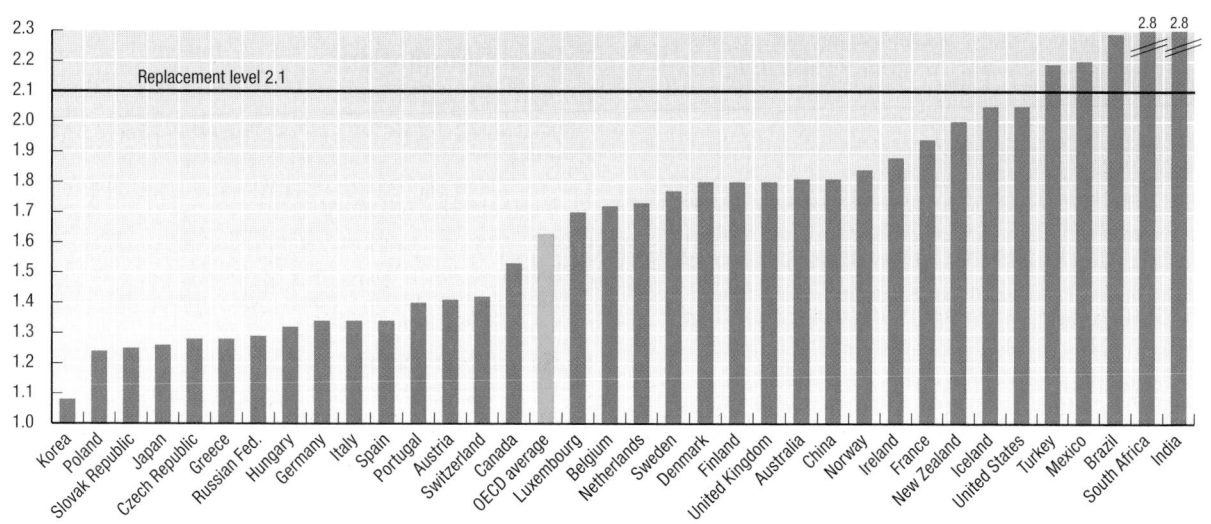

StatLink http://dx.doi.org/10.1787/266322702532

REGIONAL POPULATION

Population is unevenly distributed among regions within countries. Differences in climatic and environmental conditions discourage human settlement in some areas and favour concentration of the population around a few urban centres. This pattern is reinforced by the higher economic opportunities and wider availability of services stemming from urbanisation itself.

Definition

The number of inhabitants of a given region, the total population, can be either the average annual population or the population at a specific date during the year considered. The average population during a calendar year is generally calculated as the arithmetic mean of the population on 1 January of two consecutive years (it is also referred to as the mean population). However, some countries estimate it on a date close to 1 July (mid-year population).

The index of geographic concentration offers an accurate picture of the spatial distribution of the population, as it takes into account the area of each region.

The index compares the economic weight and the geographic weight over all regions in a given country and is constructed to account for both within- and between-country differences in the size of all regions. It lies between 0 (no concentration) and 100 (maximum concentration) in all countries and is suitable for international comparisons.

Comparability

The main problem with economic analysis at the sub-national level is the unit of analysis, *i.e.* the region. The word "region" can mean very different things both within and among countries, with significant differences in area and population.

The smallest OECD region (Melilla, Spain) has an area of 13 square kilometres whereas the largest (Northwest Territories and Nunavut, Canada) has over 3 million square kilometres. Similarly, the population in OECD regions ranges from about 400 inhabitants in Balance ACT (Australia) to more than 47 million in Kanto (Japan).

To address this issue, the OECD has classified regions within each member country. The classification is based on two territorial levels. The higher level (Territorial Level 2) consists of 335 macro regions and the lower level (Territorial Level 3) is composed of 1 679 micro regions. Territorial Level 0 indicates the territory of the whole country while Level 1 denotes groups of macro regions. This classification which, for European Union countries, is largely consistent with the Eurostat NUTS classification facilitates greater comparability of regions at the same territorial level. Indeed, these two levels, which are officially established and relatively stable in all member countries, are used by many as a framework for implementing regional policies.

Overview

The concentration of population is highest in Australia, Canada, Iceland, the United States, and Mexico where 10% of regions account for no less than 47% of their population. In contrast, the territorial distribution appears more balanced, according to this statistic, in the Slovak Republic, the Czech Republic, Belgium and Denmark.

For the OECD as a whole, regional population density ranges from close to zero in Kitikmeot Region (Canada) to 20 504 persons per km^2 in Paris (France). The variation is particularly large in France, Korea and the United Kingdom. In these countries, there is a sharp contrast between predominantly urban regions which record densities of more than 6 000 inhabitants per km^2 and predominantly rural regions where population densities do not exceed 100 inhabitants per km^2 (for a definition of regional typology, see chapter on Regional GDP).

In all OECD counties, almost half (47%) of the population live in predominantly urban regions. In the Netherlands, Belgium, the United Kingdom, Japan, Australia, the United States, Italy, Canada and Korea, urban regions account for more that 50% of the national population.

The index of geographic concentration shows that Canada, Australia and Iceland are the countries with the most uneven population distribution; in contrast, geographic concentration is lowest in the Slovak Republic, the Czech Republic, Hungary, Belgium, the Netherlands and Poland.

Source

- OECD (2007), *OECD Regions at a Glance: 2007 Edition*, OECD, Paris.

Further information
Analytical publications

- OECD (2001), *OECD Territorial Outlook, 2001 Edition*, OECD, Paris.
- OECD (2006), *OECD Territorial Reviews – Competitive Cities in the Global Economy*, OECD, Paris.
- OECD (2007), *OECD Territorial Reviews*, OECD, Paris.
- Spiezia, V. (2003), "Measuring Regional Economies", OECD Statistics Brief, No. 6, October, OECD, Paris, *www.oecd.org/std/statisticsbrief*.

Statistical publications

- OECD (2007), *Labour Force Statistics*, OECD, Paris.

Online databases

- *OECD Regional Database*.

Share of national population in the 10% of regions with the largest population

Percentage, 2004

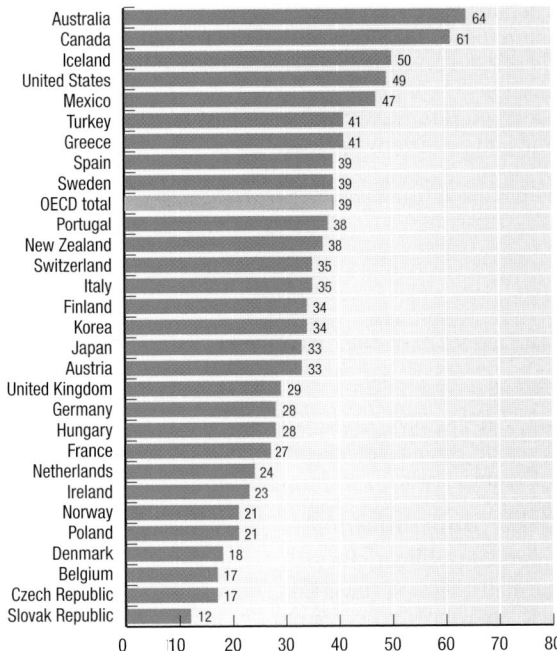

Range of variation in regional population density

Maximum – minimum number of persons per km², 2004

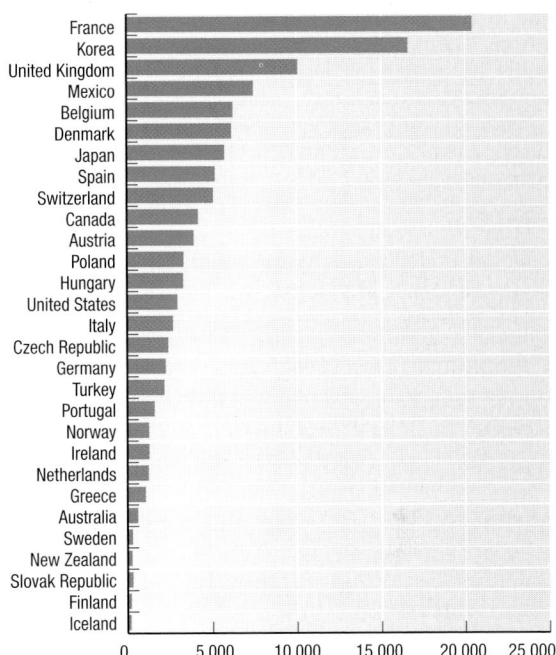

Distribution of the national population into urban, intermediate and rural regions

Percentage, 2004

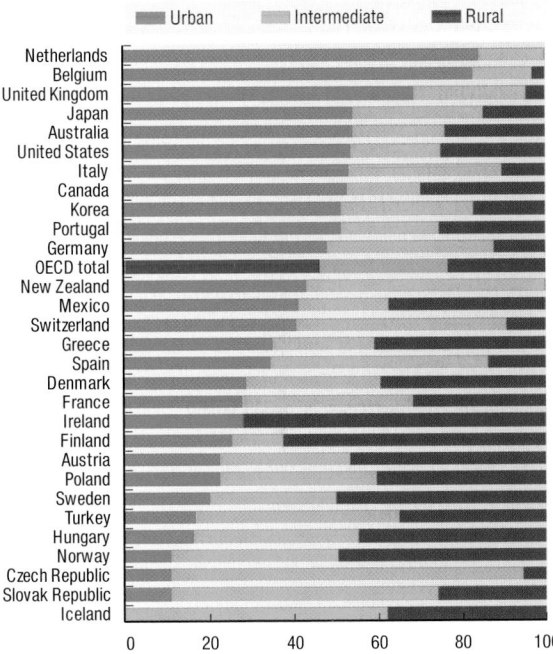

Index of geographic concentration of population

Year 2004

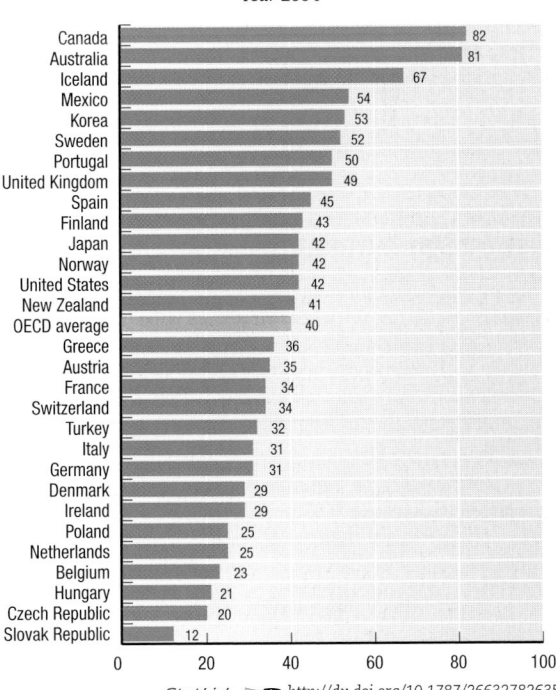

StatLink http://dx.doi.org/10.1787/266327826357

AGEING SOCIETIES

The percentage of the population that is 65 years or older is rising in all OECD countries and is expected to continue doing so. The number of inactive elderly as a ratio of the number in the total labour force is also increasing throughout OECD countries. These trends have a number of implications for government and private spending on pensions and health care and, more generally, for economic growth and welfare.

Definition

Population is defined as the resident population, *i.e.* all persons, regardless of citizenship, who have a permanent place of residence in the country. The labour force is defined according to the ILO Guidelines and consists of those in employment plus persons who are available for work and who are actively seeking employment. Population projections are taken from national sources where these are available, but for some countries they are based on Eurostat and UN projections.

Comparability

Almost all OECD countries now follow the ILO Guidelines for defining the labour force, so there is good comparability between countries.

All population projections require assumptions about future trends in life expectancy, fertility rates and migration. Often, a range of projections is produced using different assumptions about these future trends. The estimates shown here correspond to the median or central variant.

Long-term trends

The youngest populations (low shares of population aged 65 or over) are either in countries with high birth rates such as Mexico, Iceland and Turkey or in countries with high immigration, such as Australia, Canada and New Zealand. All these countries will, however, experience significant ageing over the next 50 years.

The dependency ratio (*i.e.* the ratio of inactive elderly to the total labour force, right panel of the table) is projected to be above 50% in Finland, Italy and Japan by 2020. This means that, for each elderly inactive person, there will be fewer than two persons in the labour force. The lowest dependency ratios by 2020, under 30%, are projected for Iceland, Mexico and Turkey.

All countries will experience a further sharp increase in the dependency ratio over the period 2020 to 2050.

The labour force projections start from the population projections described above but then require additional assumptions about the future labour force participation rates of men and women in different age groups. For the projections shown here, particular care has been taken in modeling future trends in the labour force participation of women and of elderly persons.

Sources

* OECD (2007), *Labour Force Statistics*, OECD, Paris.
* Eurostat, United Nations, national sources and OECD estimates.

Further information
Analytical publications

* Burniaux, J.-M., R. Duval and F. Jaumotte (2004), *Coping with Ageing*, OECD Economics Department Working Papers, No. 371, OECD, Paris.
* OECD (2000), *Reforms for an Ageing Society*, OECD, Paris.
* OECD (2001), *Ageing and Income Financial Resources and Retirement in 9 OECD Countries*, OECD, Paris.
* OECD (2001), *Ageing and Transport Mobility Needs and Safety Issues*, OECD, Paris.
* OECD (2003), *Ageing, Housing and Urban Development*, OECD, Paris.
* OECD (2006), *Ageing and Employment Policies*, series, OECD, Paris.
* OECD (2007), *Ageing and the Public Service: Human Resource Challenges*, OECD, Paris.
* OECD (2007), *OECD Employment Outlook*, OECD, Paris.
* OECD (2007), *Pensions at a Glance: Public Policies across OECD Countries 2007 Edition*, OECD, Paris.
* Oliveira Martins J., F. Gonand, P. Antolin, C. de la Maisonneuve and K.-Y. Yoo (2005), *The Impact of Ageing on Demand, Factor Markets and Growth*, OECD Economics Department Working Papers, No. 420, OECD, Paris.

Statistical publications

* OECD (2004), *Quarterly Labour Force Statistics*, OECD, Paris.
* OECD (2007), *Main Economic Indicators*, OECD, Paris.

Methodological publications

* OECD (1997), "Sources and Methods – Labour and Wage Statistics", *Main Economic Indicators: April Volume 1997 Issue 4*, OECD, Paris.

Online databases

* *Employment Statistics.*
* *Main Economic Indicators.*

Population aged 65 and over

Percentage

	Ratio to the total population							Ratio of inactive elderly to the total labour force						
	2000	2005	2010	2020	2030	2040	2050	2000	2005	2010	2020	2030	2040	2050
Australia	12.5	13.1	14.3	18.3	22.1	24.4	25.7	24.8	25.3	27.2	35.3	44.2	49.9	53.5
Austria	15.4	15.8	17.2	19.4	23.5	26.6	27.5	32.1	31.7	34.1	39.7	51.3	59.7	62.6
Belgium	16.8	17.2	17.5	20.7	24.9	27.4	27.7	38.9	39.4	40.0	49.3	63.5	72.1	73.5
Canada	12.0	12.5	13.8	18.4	23.3	25.1	26.3	22.5	22.6	24.6	33.7	44.6	49.0	52.2
Czech Republic	13.8	14.1	15.4	20.2	22.7	26.5	31.2	27.4	27.9	30.7	41.9	49.5	63.3	80.0
Denmark	15.2	15.4	16.8	20.9	24.1	26.3	25.5	28.5	29.0	32.2	41.7	52.2	59.8	57.3
Finland	15.0	16.0	17.2	22.8	26.1	27.0	27.6	29.9	32.0	35.5	51.1	62.6	66.6	70.2
France	16.1	16.7	16.9	20.4	23.5	25.5	26.1	36.2	37.1	37.9	47.6	56.8	62.8	65.0
Germany	16.7	18.7	20.3	23.0	27.9	30.9	31.5	34.5	37.3	40.3	47.4	62.1	71.1	73.9
Greece	19.1	18.5	19.3	21.8	25.3	29.9	32.3	45.1	40.6	41.9	47.9	58.3	73.2	82.0
Hungary	15.2	15.9	16.7	20.3	21.6	24.0	26.8	37.0	37.6	39.3	48.8	53.9	63.2	73.1
Iceland	11.8	12.3	13.0	16.2	20.2	21.6	21.7	20.2	20.9	22.0	28.6	37.5	40.8	40.8
Ireland	11.2	11.2	11.9	14.9	18.5	22.4	26.3	24.3	22.9	24.2	30.5	38.2	48.2	60.2
Italy	17.7	19.3	20.4	23.2	27.1	32.1	33.7	42.7	45.9	48.5	56.7	71.0	90.9	98.5
Japan	17.2	20.0	23.1	29.2	31.8	36.4	39.5	32.2	38.3	46.4	61.2	68.6	83.1	94.9
Korea	7.4	9.6	11.4	16.4	25.0	33.3	37.6	15.3	19.1	22.8	32.1	51.8	75.5	91.4
Luxembourg	14.0	13.6	14.2	16.7	20.1	22.5	22.2	32.3	30.1	31.0	36.6	46.4	53.1	52.1
Mexico	5.3	6.3	7.1	9.4	12.8	16.8	20.2	13.5	15.6	16.9	20.4	27.0	35.5	43.5
Netherlands	12.9	13.5	15.0	19.6	23.5	25.1	23.6	25.1	26.1	29.3	39.5	50.3	54.7	50.7
New Zealand	11.2	11.6	12.9	17.1	22.0	25.3	26.2	22.2	21.7	23.6	31.3	41.5	49.7	52.0
Norway	15.5	14.9	15.6	18.6	21.2	23.4	23.7	29.4	28.3	30.1	37.5	45.4	51.5	52.3
Poland	12.8	13.8	14.0	19.3	23.2	25.6	29.9	28.1	30.1	30.7	44.3	57.1	67.6	83.1
Portugal	16.4	17.0	17.4	20.0	23.9	28.1	31.8	32.0	32.4	32.7	37.5	45.5	56.5	67.2
Slovak Republic	11.5	11.6	12.7	16.9	21.5	24.9	30.0	23.8	23.6	25.5	35.6	48.4	61.5	81.3
Spain	16.8	16.7	17.4	20.3	25.4	32.1	36.5	36.7	34.0	35.2	42.0	54.6	75.7	91.3
Sweden	17.6	17.5	18.8	21.7	23.4	24.6	24.3	34.3	32.9	35.5	42.4	47.1	49.8	48.7
Switzerland	8.9	15.9	17.1	20.1	24.0	27.0	28.0	14.7	28.2	30.3	36.2	45.7	53.3	55.9
Turkey	5.5	5.9	6.3	7.8	10.6	14.4	17.3	15.6	17.1	18.4	22.9	32.0	44.8	55.2
United Kingdom	15.6	15.9	16.9	20.2	23.4	25.6	25.8	30.8	31.0	33.2	41.7	51.1	57.4	58.1
United States	12.4	12.3	13.2	16.8	20.4	21.1	21.2	23.5	23.5	26.0	35.9	46.5	49.8	50.3
Brazil	5.4	6.1	6.8	9.1	12.5	15.7	19.4	11.3	12.5	13.6	17.9	24.4	31.0	39.2
China	6.8	7.6	8.3	12.0	16.3	22.3	23.8	11.7	12.8	13.9	20.8	30.2	43.1	48.0
India	4.9	5.3	5.7	6.9	9.1	11.7	14.6	12.6	13.3	13.9	16.2	20.6	26.0	32.6
Russian Federation	12.3	13.8	12.5	14.9	18.9	20.1	23.7	25.4	26.9	23.8	28.9	37.4	41.8	52.9

StatLink http://dx.doi.org/10.1787/272346577787

Ratio of the inactive elderly population aged 65 and over to the labour force

Percentage

■ 2000   ■ 2050

StatLink http://dx.doi.org/10.1787/266404458420

ELDERLY POPULATION BY REGION

In all OECD countries, populations aged 65 years and over have dramatically increased over the last 30 years, both in size and as a percentage of total population. As elderly people tend to be concentrated in few areas within each country, a small number of regions will have to face the social and economic challenges raised by ageing population.

Definition

The elderly population is the number of inhabitants of a given region aged 65 or older. The population can be either the average annual population or the population at a specific date during the year considered. The average population during a calendar year is generally calculated as the arithmetic mean of the population on 1 January of two consecutive years (it is also referred to as the mean population).

The geographic concentration index offers an accurate picture of the spatial distribution of elderly population, as it takes into account the area of each region and reveals large international differences in the degree of geographic concentration of elderly people.

The geographic concentration index compares the economic weight and the geographic weight over all regions in a given country and is constructed to account for both within- and between-country differences in the size of all regions. The index lies between 0 (no concentration) and 100 (maximum concentration) in all countries and is suitable for international comparisons of geographic concentration.

Comparability

As for the other regional statistics, the comparability of elderly population is affected by differences in the definition of the regions (see Regional population) and the different geography of rural and urban communities (see Regional GDP) both within and among countries.

Overview

About 35% of elderly people within the OECD live in only 10% of regions. The concentration is much higher in Australia, Canada and Iceland, where 10% of regions account for more than half of the elderly population of these countries.

About 46% of the elderly population in the OECD live in predominantly urban regions. In the Netherlands, Belgium, the United Kingdom and the United States predominantly urban regions account for at least 54% of the total elderly population. In Iceland, Norway, the Slovak Republic, the Czech Republic, Turkey, Sweden, Finland, Hungary, Austria, France and Poland, no less than 75% of the elderly population live in predominantly rural or intermediate regions (see Regional GDP).

According to the geographic concentration index, Canada, Australia and Iceland are the countries with the highest concentration of elderly population. Mexico, Sweden and the United Kingdom have a significantly higher concentration of elderly population than the OECD average (38). In contrast, geographic concentration of elderly people appears much lower in the Slovak Republic, the Czech Republic, Hungary, the Netherlands, Belgium and Ireland.

Source

- OECD (2007), *OECD Regions at a Glance: 2007 Edition*, OECD, Paris.

Further information

Analytical publications

- OECD (2001), *OECD Territorial Outlook, 2001 Edition*, OECD, Paris.
- OECD (2007), *Labour Force Statistics*, OECD, Paris.
- OECD (2007), *OECD Territorial Reviews*, OECD, Paris.
- Oliveira Martins J., F. Gonand, P. Antolin, C. de la Maisonneuve and K.-Y. Yoo (2005), *The Impact of Ageing on Demand, Factor Markets and Growth*, OECD Economics Department Working Papers, No. 420, OECD, Paris.
- Spiezia, V. (2003), "Measuring Regional Economies", OECD Statistics Brief, No. 6, October, OECD, Paris, *www.oecd.org/std/statisticsbrief*.

Statistical publications

- OECD (2007), *Labour Force Statistics*, OECD, Paris.

Online databases

- *OECD Regional Database*.

Percentage of elderly population by country

Percentage, 2004 or latest available year

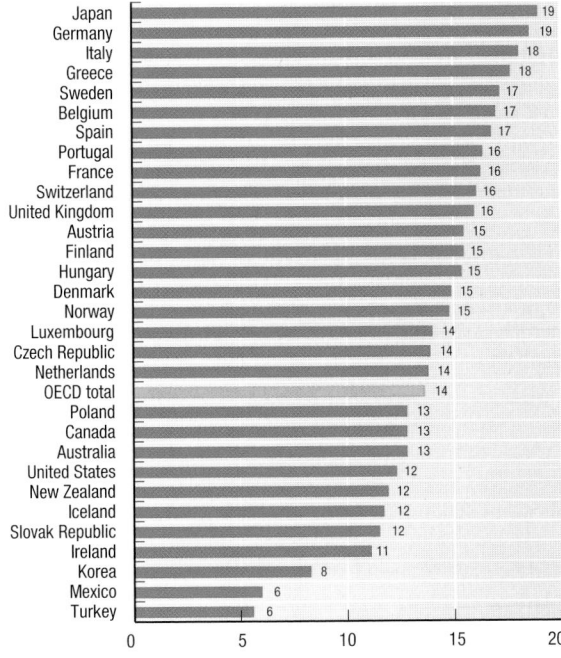

Japan	19
Germany	19
Italy	18
Greece	18
Sweden	17
Belgium	17
Spain	17
Portugal	16
France	16
Switzerland	16
United Kingdom	16
Austria	15
Finland	15
Hungary	15
Denmark	15
Norway	15
Luxembourg	14
Czech Republic	14
Netherlands	14
OECD total	14
Poland	13
Canada	13
Australia	13
United States	12
New Zealand	12
Iceland	12
Slovak Republic	12
Ireland	11
Korea	8
Mexico	6
Turkey	6

Share of national elderly population in the 10% of regions with the largest elderly population

Percentage, 2004 or latest available year

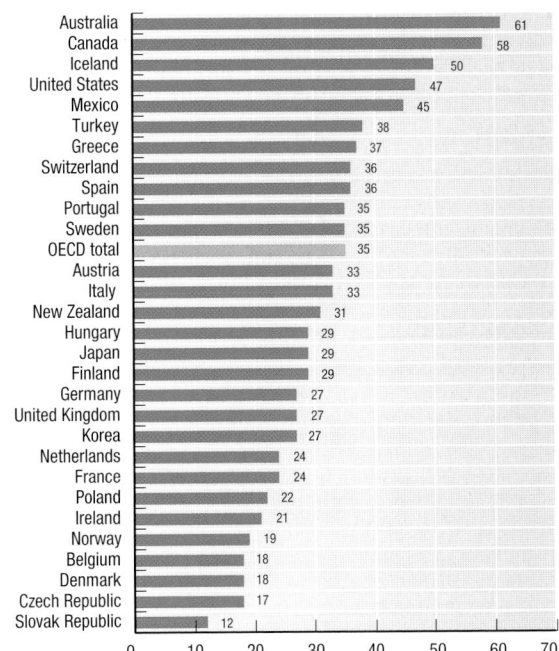

Australia	61
Canada	58
Iceland	50
United States	47
Mexico	45
Turkey	38
Greece	37
Switzerland	36
Spain	36
Portugal	35
Sweden	35
OECD total	35
Austria	33
Italy	33
New Zealand	31
Hungary	29
Japan	29
Finland	29
Germany	27
United Kingdom	27
Korea	27
Netherlands	24
France	24
Poland	22
Ireland	21
Norway	19
Belgium	18
Denmark	18
Czech Republic	17
Slovak Republic	12

Distribution of elderly population into urban, intermediate and rural regions

Percentage, 2004 or latest available year

■ Urban ■ Intermediate ■ Rural

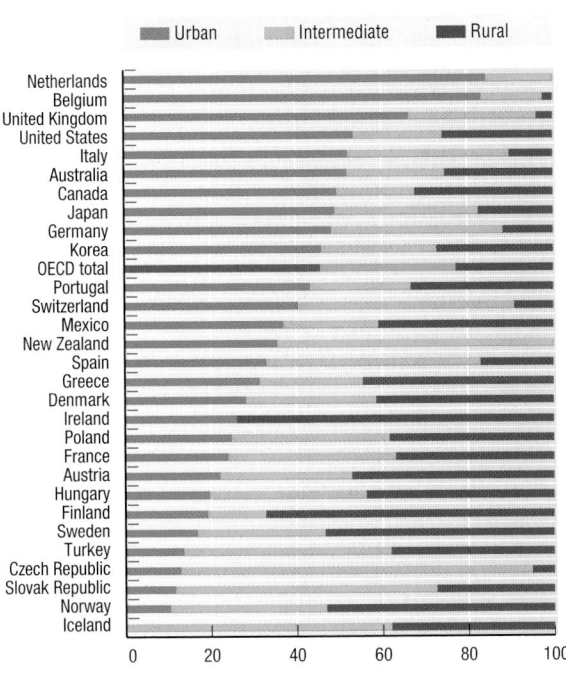

Netherlands, Belgium, United Kingdom, United States, Italy, Australia, Canada, Japan, Germany, Korea, OECD total, Portugal, Switzerland, Mexico, New Zealand, Spain, Greece, Denmark, Ireland, Poland, France, Austria, Hungary, Finland, Sweden, Turkey, Czech Republic, Slovak Republic, Norway, Iceland

Index of geographic concentration of elderly population

2004 or latest available year

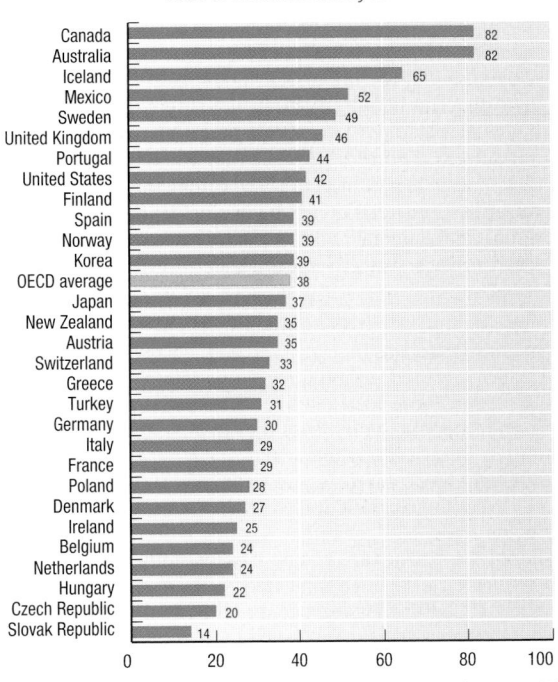

Canada	82
Australia	82
Iceland	65
Mexico	52
Sweden	49
United Kingdom	46
Portugal	44
United States	42
Finland	41
Spain	39
Norway	39
Korea	39
OECD average	38
Japan	37
New Zealand	35
Austria	35
Switzerland	33
Greece	32
Turkey	31
Germany	30
Italy	29
France	29
Poland	28
Denmark	27
Ireland	25
Belgium	24
Netherlands	24
Hungary	22
Czech Republic	20
Slovak Republic	14

StatLink ⌨ http://dx.doi.org/10.1787/266454386504

TRENDS IN MIGRATION

Migration movements include not only entries of persons of foreign nationality, on which public attention tends to be focused; they also include movements of nationals and emigrants. Net migration summarises the overall effect of these movements. It is in more and more OECD countries the main source of increases in population.

Definition

Net migration is defined as the total number of immigrant nationals and foreigners minus the total of emigrant foreigners and nationals. Arrivals and departures for purposes such as tourism and business travel are not included in the statistics.

Comparability

The main sources of information on migration vary across countries, which poses problems for the comparability of available data on inflows and outflows. However, since the comparability problems generally relate to the extent to which short-term movements are covered, taking the difference between arrivals and departures tends to eliminate the movements that are the main source of non-comparability. The net migration data, however, are subject to caution, because unauthorised movements are not taken into account in the inflows and these are significant in some OECD countries. In addition, the data on outflows are of uneven quality, with departures being only partially recorded in many countries or having to be estimated in others.

Net migration rate is used in demographic accounting to describe the contribution of international migration to population increase, the other component being natural increase, the difference between births and deaths in a given year.

Long-term trends

Since 1993 Poland is the only OECD country among the countries shown in the table that has shown negative net migration on a systematic basis. Among countries showing significant increases in population (> 0.5% per year) over the 1995-1999 period as a result of international migration are Australia, Canada, Spain, Ireland and Luxembourg. Since then Iceland, Italy and Switzerland have joined the list. Former emigration countries (Ireland, Italy, Portugal and Spain) thus figure prominently among high net migration countries, a trend which is likely to continue.

There are nonetheless a number of countries where net migration is currently contributing less to population increase than was the case five to ten years ago. These include Greece, Denmark, the Netherlands and Germany. Those where it is contributing more are the four former emigration countries Ireland, Italy, Portugal and Spain as well as Austria and Switzerland. Indeed, all but eight OECD countries are showing a larger contribution to population growth from net migration in recent years. With the retirement of baby-boomers in the near future, to be replaced by smaller entering labour force cohorts, labour supply needs may well increase and OECD countries see a continuing rise in net migration.

Source

- OECD (2007), *Labour Force Statistics*, OECD, Paris.

Further information

Analytical publications

- OECD (2001), *Migration Policies and EU Enlargement: The Case of Central and Eastern Europe*, OECD, Paris.
- OECD (2003), *Migration and the Labour Market in Asia: Recent Trends and Policies – 2002 Edition*, OECD, Paris.
- OECD (2004), *Migration for Employment: Bilateral Agreements at a Crossroads*, OECD, Paris.
- OECD (2004), *Trade and Migration: Building Bridges for Global Labour Mobility*, OECD, Paris.
- OECD (2006), *Local Economic and Employment Development (LEED) – From Immigration to Integration: Local Solutions to a Global Challenge*, OECD, Paris.
- OECD (2007), *International Migration Outlook: SOPEMI – 2007 Edition*, OECD, Paris.
- OECD (2008), *A Profile of Immigrant Populations in the 21st Century: Data from OECD Countries*, OECD, Paris.

Statistical publications

- OECD (2007), *OECD Employment Outlook* , OECD, Paris.

Methodological publications

- Dumont, J.-C. and G. Lemaître (2005), *Counting Immigrants and Expatriates in OECD Countries: A New Perspective*, OECD Social Employment and Migration Working Papers, No. 25, OECD, Paris.

Online databases

- *International Migration Statistics*.

Net migration rate
Per 1 000 inhabitants

	1993	1994	1995	1996	1997	1998	1999	2000	2001	2002	2003	2004	2005	2006
Australia	2.0	3.1	5.9	5.3	3.9	4.8	5.5	5.8	7.0	5.6	5.5	5.3	6.7	7.1
Austria	4.2	0.4	0.3	0.5	0.2	1.1	2.5	2.2	4.1	4.2	4.4	6.2	5.9	3.3
Belgium	2.9	2.9	2.7	2.4	1.9	2.1	2.7	2.5	3.4	4.0	3.9	4.2	4.5	4.8
Canada	5.0	5.2	5.5	5.6	5.2	3.9	5.2	6.5	7.9	6.9	6.4	6.4	6.6	..
Czech Republic	0.5	1.0	1.0	1.0	1.2	0.9	0.9	0.6	-0.8	1.2	2.5	1.8	3.5	3.4
Denmark	2.1	1.9	5.5	3.2	2.3	2.1	1.7	1.7	2.2	1.7	1.1	0.9	1.2	1.8
Finland	1.6	0.6	0.6	0.6	0.8	0.6	0.6	0.4	1.2	1.0	1.2	1.3	1.7	1.9
France	1.2	0.9	0.7	0.6	0.7	0.8	1.0	1.2	1.4	1.6	1.7	1.7	1.6	1.5
Germany	5.7	3.9	4.9	3.4	1.1	0.6	2.5	2.0	3.3	2.7	1.7	1.0	1.0	0.3
Greece	8.3	7.4	7.3	6.6	5.7	5.1	4.1	2.7	3.5	3.5	3.3	3.7	3.5	3.6
Hungary	1.7	1.7	1.7	1.7	1.7	1.7	1.7	1.7	1.0	0.4	1.6	1.8	1.7	1.9
Iceland	-0.4	-2.6	-2.6	-2.6	0.3	3.2	4.0	6.1	3.4	-1.0	-0.5	1.8	13.0	17.3
Ireland	-0.9	-0.8	1.6	4.6	5.1	4.5	6.4	8.4	10.0	8.4	7.8	11.6	15.9	..
Italy	3.2	2.6	1.6	2.6	2.2	1.6	1.8	3.1	2.2	6.1	10.6	9.6	5.2	6.4
Japan	-0.1	-0.7	-0.4	-0.1	0.1	0.3	-0.1	0.3	1.1	-0.4	0.5	-0.3	-0.4	..
Luxembourg	10.6	9.9	11.2	8.9	9.0	9.5	10.9	8.3	2.5	5.9	4.6	3.5	5.8	..
Netherlands	3.9	2.4	2.1	2.8	3.1	3.9	3.8	4.5	4.3	3.4	2.2	1.2	0.6	0.6
New Zealand	3.9	5.5	7.7	6.6	2.0	-1.7	-2.3	-2.9	2.5	9.7	8.7	3.7	1.7	3.6
Norway	3.0	1.6	1.4	1.4	2.5	3.2	4.3	2.0	1.8	3.7	2.4	2.8	3.9	5.1
Poland	-0.4	-0.5	-0.5	-0.3	-0.3	-0.3	-0.4	-0.5	-0.4	-0.5	-0.4	-0.2	-0.3	-0.9
Portugal	1.6	1.7	2.2	2.6	2.9	3.2	3.7	4.6	6.3	6.8	6.1	4.5	3.6	..
Slovak Republic	0.3	0.9	0.5	0.4	0.3	0.2	0.3	0.3	0.2	0.2	0.3	0.5	0.6	0.7
Spain	0.9	0.9	0.9	1.3	1.6	3.1	4.9	8.9	10.1	15.7	14.5	14.7	15.0	..
Sweden	3.7	5.8	1.2	0.7	0.7	1.2	1.6	2.8	3.3	3.5	3.2	2.8	3.0	5.6
Switzerland	5.7	4.4	2.1	-0.8	-1.0	0.2	2.3	2.8	5.8	6.7	5.9	5.4	4.8	4.7
Turkey	1.7	1.7	1.6	1.6	1.6	1.5	1.5	..	..	..	..	..	..	..
United Kingdom	0.3	0.8	1.0	0.9	0.9	1.7	2.3	2.5	2.5	2.5	..	..	..	..
United States	4.5	4.2	4.4	4.6	4.8	4.2	4.4	4.6	4.6	4.5	3.7	3.8	4.0	4.0
Russian Federation	..	..	4.4	3.5	3.5	2.9	1.8	2.5	1.9	1.6	0.6	0.7	0.9	1.1

StatLink ᴪᶳᴸ http://dx.doi.org/10.1787/272370046012

Net migration rate
Per 1 000 inhabitants, annual average 2000-2006 or latest available period

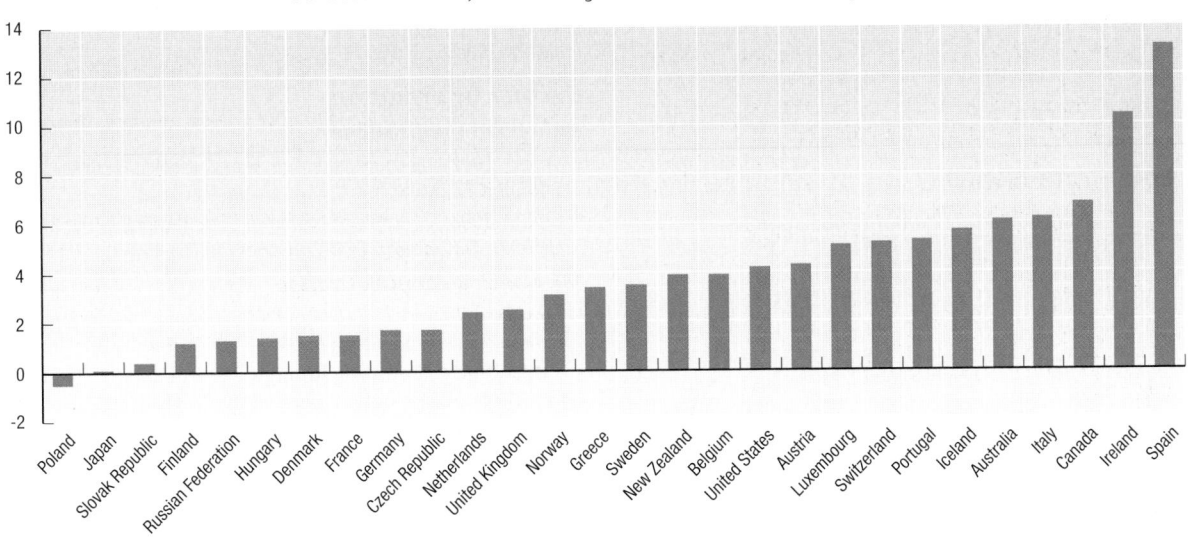

StatLink ᴪᶳᴸ http://dx.doi.org/10.1787/266480748744

IMMIGRANT POPULATION

National views on the appropriate definition of the immigrant population vary from country to country. Despite this, it is now possible to provide an internationally comparable picture of the size of the immigrant population, based either on nationality or on country-of-birth criteria. Strictly speaking, the immigrant population consists of persons residing in a country but born in another country. The definition based on nationality is commonly used in a certain number of countries and reflects a legal view of immigration.

Definition

Nationality and place of birth are the two criteria most commonly used to define the "immigrant" population. The foreign-born population covers all persons who have ever migrated from their country of birth to their current country of residence. The foreign population consists of persons who still have the nationality of their home country. It may include persons born in the host country.

Comparability

The difference across countries between the size of the foreign-born population and that of the foreign population depends on the rules governing the acquisition of citizenship in each country. In some countries, children born in the country automatically acquire the citizenship of their country of birth (*jus solis*, the right of soil) while in other countries, they retain the nationality of their parents (*jus sanguinis*, the right of blood). In others, they retain the nationality of their parents at birth but receive that of the host country at their majority. Differences in the ease with which immigrants may acquire the citizenship of the host country explain part of the gap between the two series. For example, residency requirements vary from as little as three years in Canada to as much as ten years in some countries.

The naturalisation rate is high in settlement countries such as Australia, Canada, New Zealand and in some European countries including Belgium, Sweden and the Netherlands. In general, the foreign-born criterion gives substantially higher percentages for the immigrant population than the definition based on nationality. This is because many foreign-born persons acquire the nationality of the host country and no longer appear as foreign nationals. The place of birth, however, does not change, except when there are changes in country borders.

The data shown for the year 2000 come from a special census data collection covering almost all OECD countries. Note that the foreign-born here include persons born abroad as nationals of their current country of residence. The prevalence of such persons among the foreign-born can be significant in some countries, in particular France and Portugal (repatriations from former colonies).

For a number of countries, reliable data on the foreign-born population are available only at time of census. To make up for this deficiency, the OECD has developed data series for a certain number of countries, applying two estimation methods, the choice of which depends on the auxiliary information available for estimation. These methods are described and evaluated at *www.oecd.org/els/migration/foreignborn*.

For the foreign-born population the data year shown under the 2000 column is 1999 for France; 2001 for Greece, Italy, the Slovak Republic, Spain; 2002 for Poland; under the 2005 column is 2003 for Germany and 2004 for the Slovak Republic. For the foreign population the data year shown as 2000 is 1999 for France; 2001 for Australia, Canada, Greece; 2002 for Poland.

Long-term trends

Not surprisingly, the foreign-born population has increased in the past decade in all countries for which data are available. It is especially high in Australia, Canada, Luxembourg, New Zealand and Switzerland. This increase is likely to continue into the future, with further immigration needs. By contrast, the foreign population tends to increase more slowly, because inflows of foreign nationals tend to be counterbalanced by persons acquiring the nationality of the host country. It thus gives a partial view of the evolution of immigration trends.

Source

- OECD (2007), *International Migration Outlook: SOPEMI – 2007 Edition*, OECD, Paris.

Further information

Analytical publications

- OECD (2007), *International Migration Outlook: SOPEMI – 2007 Edition*, OECD, Paris.
- OECD (2008), *A Profile of Immigrant Populations in the 21st Century: Data from OECD Countries*, OECD, Paris.

Methodological publications

- Lemaître, G. and C. Thoreau (2006), *Estimating the foreign-born population on a current basis*, OECD, Paris.
- OECD (2005), "Counting immigrants and expatriates in OECD countries – a new perspective", *Trends in International Migration: SOPEMI – 2004 Edition*, OECD, Paris.

Online database

- Database on immigrants in OECD countries, *www.oecd.org/els/migration/censusdatabase*.

Foreign-born and foreign populations

As a percentage of the total population

As a percentage of all foreign-born

	Foreign-born population			Foreign population			Foreign-born nationals
	1995	2000	2005	1995	2000	2005	2000
Australia	23.0	23.0	23.8	..	7.4	..	68.4
Austria	..	10.5	13.5	8.5	8.8	9.7	40.9
Belgium	9.7	10.3	12.1	9.0	8.4	8.6	40.8
Canada	17.2	18.1	19.1	..	5.3	..	72.6
Czech Republic	..	4.2	5.1	1.5	1.9	2.7	79.8
Denmark	4.8	5.8	6.5	4.2	4.8	5.0	40.3
Finland	2.0	2.6	3.4	1.3	1.8	2.2	41.6
France	..	7.3	8.1	..	5.6	5.8	53.1
Germany	11.5	12.5	12.9	8.8	8.9	8.8	
Greece	..	10.3	..	..	7.0	..	41.5
Hungary	2.8	2.9	3.3	1.4	1.1	1.5	71.1
Ireland	..	8.7	11.0	2.7	3.3	6.3	45.2
Italy	..	2.5	..	1.7	2.4	4.6	47.5
Japan	..	..	..	1.1	1.3	1.6	..
Korea	..	..	..	0.2	0.4	1.0	..
Luxembourg	..	..	..	33.4	37.3	39.6	13.0
Mexico	0.4	0.5	0.4	..	..	..	..
Netherlands	9.1	10.1	10.6	4.7	4.2	4.2	65.0
New Zealand	..	17.2	19.4	..	..	..	..
Norway	5.5	6.8	8.2	3.8	4.0	4.8	47.6
Poland	..	1.6	..	..	0.1	..	96.1
Portugal	5.4	5.1	6.3	1.7	2.1	4.1	66.3
Slovak Republic	..	2.5	3.9	0.4	0.5	0.5	84.2
Spain	..	5.3	..	1.3	2.2	6.2	30.9
Sweden	10.5	11.3	12.4	6.0	5.4	5.3	62.5
Switzerland	21.4	21.9	23.8	18.9	19.3	20.3	29.3
Turkey	..	1.9	..	..	..	..	79.2
United Kingdom	6.9	7.9	9.7	3.4	4.0	5.2	..
United States	9.3	11.0	12.9	..	6.6	..	46.4

StatLink http://dx.doi.org/10.1787/272383730066

Foreign-born population

As a percentage of total population, 2005

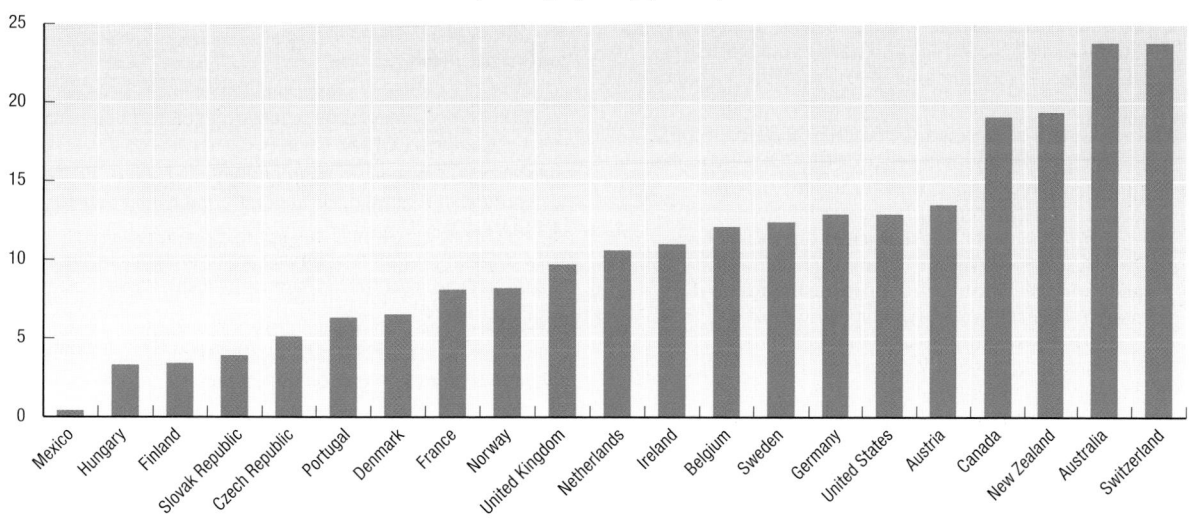

StatLink http://dx.doi.org/10.1787/266484230878

MIGRATION AND UNEMPLOYMENT

Immigrant workers are more affected by unemployment in older European immigration countries while in North America, in Australia and to a lesser extent in Southern Europe, the unemployment rate tends to depend less on the place of birth. Some groups, such as young immigrants, women or older immigrants have particular difficulties finding jobs.

Definition

The unemployment rate is calculated as the share of the unemployed in the total labour force (employed and unemployed persons). In accordance with the ILO standards, unemployed persons consist of those persons who report that they are without work during the reference week, that they are available for work and that they have taken active steps to find work during the four preceding weeks.

Comparability

All data for the European countries are from the European Union Labour Force Survey (second quarter). The national labour force survey, the Survey of Labour and Income Dynamics and the Current Population Survey (March supplement) are used respectively for Australia, Canada and the United States. Even if unemployment levels can at times be affected by changes in the survey design (this is the case for France since 2004) and by survey implementation problems (*e.g.* non-response), the unemployment rates are generally consistent over time.

Long-term trends

In 2005, immigrants in the majority of European OECD countries were relatively more affected by unemployment than was the native population. In the Slovak Republic, in Finland, Germany, and Belgium, the unemployment rate of immigrants is higher than 15%. The rate is more than twice the level observed for the native-born in Finland, Belgium Denmark, Norway, Austria, the Netherlands and Switzerland. In other countries, however, especially the main settlement countries (Australia, Canada, the United States) and recent immigration countries (Italy, Spain, Greece), the unemployment rate does not vary much by birth status.

The period since 1995 has seen some sizable declines in the unemployment rates of the foreign-born, both men and women, in a number of countries, among them Australia, Denmark and Sweden, Greece, Ireland, the Netherlands, Spain and the United Kingdom. At the same time, labour market conditions have stagnated in a number of other countries and have had adverse consequences for immigrants in Austria, Germany and Portugal.

More than 15% of immigrant women in the labour force are seeking employment in Belgium, the Czech Republic, Germany, Finland, France, Greece, and the Slovak Republic. In relative terms, the unemployment rate of immigrant women is at least twice as high as that of natives in Austria, Belgium, Denmark, Finland, and Switzerland. The difference in absolute values *vis-à-vis* the native-born is systematically positive, but does not generally increase with the level of qualifications.

Source

* OECD (2007), *International Migration Outlook: SOPEMI – 2007 Edition*, OECD, Paris.

Further information

Analytical publications

* OECD (2006), *Local Economic and Employment Development (LEED) – From Immigration to Integration: Local Solutions to a Global Challenge*, OECD, Paris.
* OECD (2007), *Jobs for Immigrants (Vol. 1): Labour Market Integration in Australia, Denmark, Germany and Sweden*, OECD, Paris.
* OECD (2008), *A Profile of Immigrant Populations in the 21st Century: Data from OECD Countries*, OECD, Paris.

Websites

* OECD International Migration Statistics, *www.oecd.org/els/migration/statistics*.

Unemployment rates of foreign-and native-born populations
As a percentage of total labour force

| | Men | | | | | | Women | | | | | |
| | Native | | | Foreign-born | | | Native | | | Foreign-born | | |
	1995	2000	2005	1995	2000	2005	1995	2000	2005	1995	2000	2005
Australia	8.4	6.6	4.7	10.6	6.5	5.0	7.7	5.8	5.0	9.6	7.0	5.2
Austria	3.6	4.3	4.1	6.6	8.7	11.8	4.6	4.2	4.4	7.3	7.2	9.8
Belgium	6.3	4.2	6.3	16.9	14.7	14.8	11.2	7.4	7.5	23.8	17.5	20.3
Canada	8.6	5.7	..	10.4	6.1	..	9.8	6.2	..	13.3	8.7	..
Czech Republic	..	..	6.2	..	..	10.4	..	..	9.7	..	..	16.5
Denmark	6.4	3.4 |	4.0	20.5	9.5 |	7.2	8.4	4.3 |	5.0	20.7	9.6 |	12.4
Finland	17.7	10.3	8.0	..	..	16.6	16.1	12.0	8.3	..	..	20.2
France	9.1	7.7	8.1	16.6	14.5	13.3	13.6	11.3	9.2	19.0	19.7	16.5
Germany	..	6.9	10.6	..	12.9	17.5	..	8.0	10.2	..	12.1	16.3
Greece	6.1	7.4	5.9	14.0	9.5	6.4	13.7	16.6	15.3	20.8	21.1	15.9
Hungary	..	7.3	7.0	..	..	..	..	5.8	7.4	..	..	7.3
Ireland	12.0	4.4	4.5	16.8	..	6.0	11.9	4.2	3.5	15.4	..	6.0
Italy	9.3	8.4	6.2	..	6.5	6.1	16.3	14.9	9.2	23.5	21.2	14.6
Luxembourg	..	..	3.0	..	..	4.2	..	..	4.5	..	..	7.5
Netherlands	4.9	1.8	3.6	19.5	5.4	11.9	7.7	3.0	4.5	19.8	7.6	9.5
Norway	..	3.4	4.2	..	6.8	12.5	..	3.2	4.3	..	..	8.5
Portugal	6.6	3.1	6.8	..	3.9	8.5	7.8	4.9	8.4	..	5.4	9.7
Slovak Republic	..	..	15.7	..	..	23.0	..	..	17.0	..	..	28.6
Spain	18.0	9.5	7.0	24.4	12.4	9.5	30.5	20.5	12.0	30.5	20.7	13.5
Sweden	7.9	5.1	7.9	24.8	12.3	15.6	6.6	4.2	7.9	18.5	10.8	14.1
Switzerland	..	..	2.7	..	..	7.7	..	..	3.7	..	..	9.7
United Kingdom	9.9	5.9	4.7	14.2	9.6	7.4	6.7	4.6	3.8	10.9	7.8	7.1
United States	6.2	4.5	6.3	7.9	4.5	5.1	5.3	4.2	5.2	8.2	5.5	5.2
EU15 average	9.9	6.9	7.1	15.9	11.7	12.1	13.2	9.8	8.4	16.6	13.0	13.6
OECD average	8.8	5.8	6.3	15.6	9.0	10.5	11.1	7.7	7.5	17.2	12.1	12.5

StatLink ᴍᴤ http://dx.doi.org/10.1787/272400686475

Foreign-born unemployment rate relative to native-born unemployment rate
Ratio, 2005

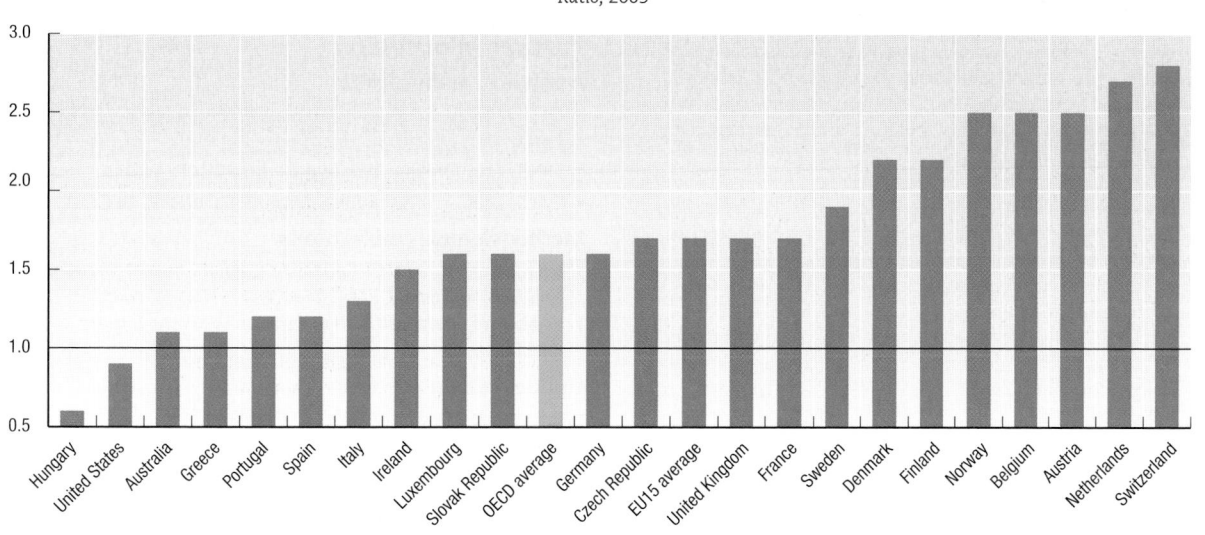

StatLink ᴍᴤ http://dx.doi.org/10.1787/266485760153

EDUCATIONAL ATTAINMENT OF RECENT IMMIGRANTS

In most but not all OECD countries, proportionally fewer recent immigrants have a tertiary qualification than young native-born entrants to the labour force.

Definition

The educational classification shown is a regrouping of the International Standard Classification of Education (ISCED) categories. Generally speaking, "low" corresponds to less than upper secondary education, "intermediate" to upper secondary education and "high" to tertiary education. The latter includes high-level vocational education feeding into technical or semi-professional occupations.

Comparability

All data for the European countries are from the European Union Labour Force Survey (second quarter). The Current Population Survey is used for the United States. The comparability of education levels between immigrants and the native-born and across countries is approximate. The educational qualifications of other countries may not fit exactly into national educational categories because the duration of study or the programme content for ostensibly equivalent qualifications may not be the same. Likewise, the reduction of the ISCED classification into three categories represents some loss of information regarding the duration of study, the programme orientation, etc. For example, high-education qualifications can involve programmes of durations varying from two (some short, university-level technical programmes) to seven years or more (PhDs).

Overview

In many emigration countries, emigrants tend to be of higher educational attainment than the general population. This is because emigration involves certain costs, which are more easily borne by persons with higher education and presumably higher incomes, and because highly educated persons are more "tuned in" to opportunities abroad. Whether or not emigrants are more highly educated than the native-born populations of the countries they are moving to, however, depends in part on the history of immigration in these countries, the needs of their labour markets and the returns to different levels of education in destination countries relative to those in the countries of origin.

Recent arrivals to OECD countries who are in the labour force are in some countries more and in others less educated than the native-born labour force. Immigrants to southern Europe, Finland, the Netherlands and the United States in particular tend to show lower levels of tertiary attainment than both the native-born labour force and younger (25-34) native-born recent entrants to the labour force. In France, Belgium and Scandinavia, on the other hand, recent arrivals tend to have relatively more persons with tertiary education in the labour force than the native-born, but less than native-born persons 25-34. Finally, in Austria, Luxembourg and Switzerland and in Central Europe and Ireland, the percentage of persons with tertiary education is higher among recent immigrants than among both the native-born labour force and native-born recent entrants to the labour force. Migration to these countries and in particular to Ireland, Luxembourg and Switzerland, is especially highly educated.

Source

• *International Migration Statistics.*

Further information

Analytical publications

• OECD (2006), *Migration and Student Performance*, OECD, Paris.
• OECD (2007), *Education at a Glance*, OECD, Paris.
• OECD (2007), *International Migration Outlook*, OECD, Paris.

Methodological publications

• Dumont, J.-C. and G. Lemaître (2005), *Counting Immigrants and Expatriates in OECD Countries: A New Perspective*, OECD Social Employment and Migration Working Papers, No. 25, OECD, Paris.

Online databases

• *Education at a Glance – OECD Database.*
• *International Migration Statistics.*

Educational attainment of recent immigrants compared with that of native-born aged 25-34 and 25-64

Percentage, 2005

| | Foreign-born labour force | | | Native-born labour force | | | | | |
| | Present in the country for 10 years or less | | | Aged 25-34 years | | | Aged 25-64 years | | |
	Low education	Intermediate education	High education	Low education	Intermediate education	High education	Low education	Intermediate education	High education
Austria	25.5	51.4	23.1	7.3	71.2	21.5	12.1	67.1	20.8
Belgium	32.2	24.9	42.9	14.9	41.6	43.5	24.8	38.7	36.6
Czech Republic	11.6	62.8	25.6	4.7	80.9	14.4	6.8	78.8	14.4
Denmark	27.3	33.5	39.2	8.1	50.7	41.2	13.3	51.1	35.6
Finland	30.5	51.0	18.5	9.4	49.9	40.7	18.0	44.3	37.8
France	40.7	25.6	33.7	15.9	43.1	41.0	26.6	45.2	28.3
Germany	32.7	41.0	26.3	9.8	64.9	25.3	10.1	61.6	28.2
Greece	48.3	39.3	12.4	18.8	53.2	27.9	33.9	40.8	25.3
Hungary	8.2	69.7	22.0	12.0	66.6	21.5	15.3	64.0	20.7
Ireland	14.6	37.7	47.7	15.7	42.2	42.1	30.3	37.5	32.2
Italy	45.5	43.6	10.8	30.6	52.7	16.7	40.7	43.9	15.3
Luxembourg	21.2	27.2	51.6	11.7	54.5	33.9	16.8	57.3	25.9
Netherlands	25.9	45.4	28.7	14.7	46.1	39.2	22.6	42.5	34.9
Norway	17.5	46.5	36.0	2.6	55.0	42.4	8.0	56.4	35.6
Poland	14.4	55.8	29.8	7.2	65.7	27.1	11.0	69.1	19.9
Portugal	55.9	27.5	16.6	59.5	21.5	19.0	73.1	13.3	13.6
Slovak Republic	..	..	..	5.8	77.3	16.9	8.2	76.4	15.5
Spain	42.3	35.9	21.8	33.5	22.2	44.4	45.4	20.8	33.9
Sweden	21.4	40.3	38.3	7.1	54.6	38.4	13.1	55.4	31.4
Switzerland	23.9	33.9	42.2	2.4	64.5	33.2	5.3	63.0	31.8
United States	34.1	35.1	30.8	6.5	49.3	44.2	6.3	50.2	43.5
EU15 average	33.8	41.9	24.3	19.0	48.0	33.1	25.2	46.9	27.9
OECD average	28.7	41.4	29.9	14.2	53.7	32.1	21.0	51.3	27.7

StatLink http://dx.doi.org/10.1787/272458580233

Percentage of foreign-born labour force and of the native-born labour force aged 25-34 and 25-64 with a tertiary qualification

Year 2005

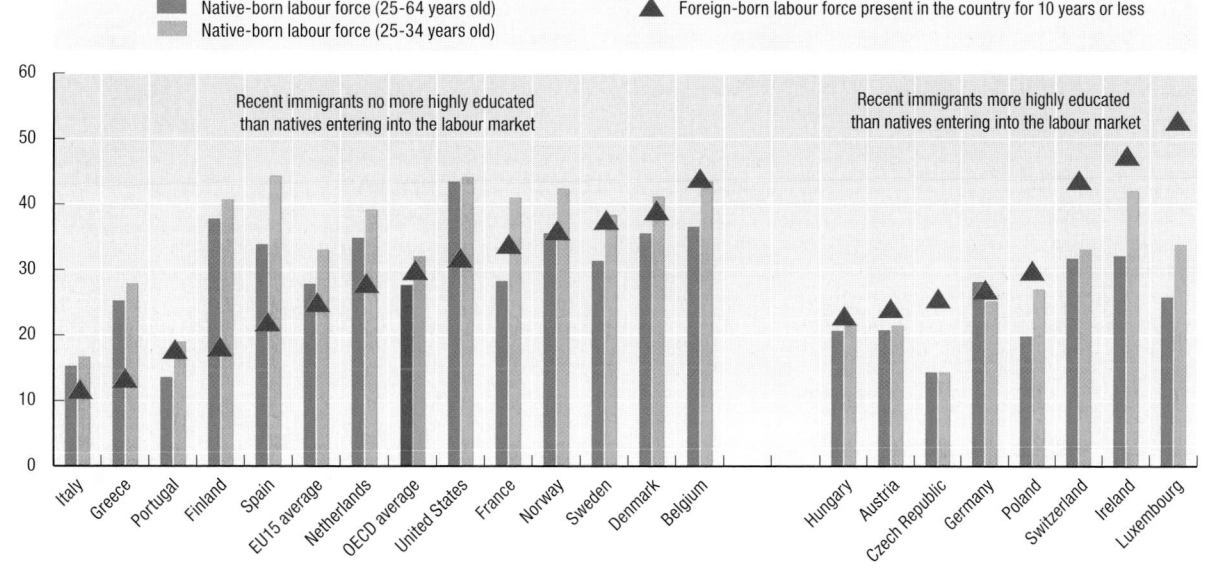

StatLink http://dx.doi.org/10.1787/266511300368

MACROECONOMIC TRENDS

GROSS DOMESTIC PRODUCT (GDP)
SIZE OF GDP
NATIONAL INCOME PER CAPITA
REGIONAL GDP

ECONOMIC GROWTH
EVOLUTION OF GDP
HOUSEHOLD SAVING
INVESTMENT RATES
INFLATION
STEEL PRODUCTION

ECONOMIC STRUCTURE
VALUE ADDED BY ACTIVITY
EVOLUTION OF VALUE ADDED BY ACTIVITY
SMALL AND MEDIUM-SIZED ENTERPRISES

SIZE OF GDP

Gross domestic product (GDP) is the standard measure of the value of the goods and services produced by a country during a period. Per capita GDP is a broad indicator of economic living standards.

Each country calculates GDP in its own currency and, in order to compare countries, these estimates have to be converted into a common currency. Often, the conversion is made using exchange rates, but these give a misleading comparison of the real volumes of goods and services in the GDP. Comparisons of real GDP between countries can best be made using purchasing power parities (PPPs) to convert each country's GDP into a common currency. PPPs are currency converters that equalise the purchasing power of the different currencies (see also Rates of conversion).

Definition

What does gross domestic product mean? "Gross" signifies that no deduction has been made for the depreciation of machinery, buildings and other capital products used in production. "Domestic" means that it is production by the resident institutional units of the country. As many products are used to produce other products it is necessary to define production in terms of value added.

GDP can be measured in three different ways: as output less intermediate consumption (*i.e.* value added) plus taxes less subsidies on products (such as VAT); as the income earned from production by summing employee compensation, the gross operating surplus of enterprises and government, the gross mixed income of unincorporated enterprises and net taxes on production and imports (VAT, payroll tax, import duties, etc, less subsidies); or as the expenditure on the goods and services produced by summing consumption expenditures, gross fixed capital formation, changes in inventories and exports less imports.

Comparability

Virtually all OECD countries now follow the 1993 System of National Accounts. However, since Luxembourg and, to a lesser extent, Switzerland have a relatively large number of frontier workers, their GDP per capita is overstated compared with other countries. Such workers contribute to the GDP but are excluded from the population figures.

For some countries, the latest year has been estimated by the Secretariat. For several countries, the historical data have also been estimated by the OECD; if countries revise their methodologies but only supply revised data for recent years, the historical data have been estimated by mechanically linking the new and old series.

Note that in the tables, the OECD total excludes the Czech Republic, Hungary, Poland and the Slovak Republic.

Long-term trends

In terms of total GDP, the United States is, by far, the largest member country. Japan is the second largest economy followed, at some distance, by the four large EU members – Germany, United Kingdom, France and Italy. The next four are Spain, Mexico, Canada and Korea. These rankings have not changed significantly over the period shown.

Per capita GDP for the OECD as a whole was 31 500 US dollars per head in 2006. Four OECD countries had per capita GDP in excess of 40 000 US dollars – Luxembourg, Norway, United States and Ireland. About half of the 30 OECD members had per capita GDP between 30 000 and 40 000 US dollars, while 12 countries had per capita GDP below 30 000 US dollars. Turkey, Mexico and Poland had the lowest per capita GDP. Note that both GDP and PPPs contain statistical errors, and differences between countries in per capita GDP of 5% or less are not significant.

Source

- OECD (2007), *National Accounts of OECD Countries*, OECD, Paris.

Further information
Analytical publications

- OECD (2003), *The Sources of Economic Growth in OECD Countries*, OECD, Paris.
- OECD (2007), *OECD Economic Outlook: December No. 82 – Volume 2007 Issue 2*, OECD, Paris.

Statistical publications

- Maddison, Angus (2003), *The World Economy: Historical Perspectives*, OECD, Paris, also available on CD-ROM, *www.theworldeconomy.org*.
- OECD, African Development Bank (2007), *African Economic Outlook 2006/2007*, OECD, Paris, also available on CD-ROM, *www.sourceoecd.org/9789264025103*.
- OECD (2007), *Latin American Economic Outlook 2008*, OECD, Paris, also available on CD-ROM, *www.sourceoecd.org/9789264038264*.

Methodological publications

- OECD (2000), *OECD Glossaries, System of National Accounts, 1993 – Glossary*, OECD, Paris.
- UN, OECD, IMF, Eurostat (eds.) (1993), *System of National Accounts 1993*, United Nations, Geneva, *http://unstats.un.org/unsd/sna1993*.

Online databases

- *National Accounts.*
- *OECD Economic Outlook Statistics.*

Websites

- OECD Economic Outlook – Sources and Methods, *www.oecd.org/eco/sources-and-methods*.

SIZE OF GDP

Gross domestic product

Billion US dollars, current prices and PPPs

	1993	1994	1995	1996	1997	1998	1999	2000	2001	2002	2003	2004	2005	2006
Australia	342.6	366.8	392.8	412.4	437.0	464.3	497.4	524.6	552.4	584.9	621.3	656.5	695.8	735.3
Austria	172.7	181.0	188.2	195.8	200.4	209.7	218.1	233.4	235.4	246.6	255.9	270.4	280.8	295.6
Belgium	207.3	218.5	228.3	232.0	242.7	248.3	258.6	282.2	292.4	309.3	312.9	323.6	336.0	353.5
Canada	594.3	636.0	667.2	690.9	732.2	770.6	825.0	872.9	909.9	937.8	987.7	1 049.8	1 133.0	1 201.0
Czech Republic	117.6	122.7	132.7	141.0	142.6	143.8	147.2	153.8	165.5	172.1	183.8	197.2	207.6	226.0
Denmark	106.4	114.6	120.5	126.8	133.6	138.6	143.3	153.7	157.8	165.3	164.2	173.9	182.2	191.5
Finland	85.7	90.6	96.1	99.0	108.0	116.8	122.4	132.8	138.3	143.5	144.5	156.4	159.8	172.4
France	1 107.4	1 155.8	1 204.4	1 243.1	1 301.8	1 369.0	1 425.2	1 533.0	1 630.6	1 711.2	1 701.7	1 768.7	1 862.2	1 962.1
Germany	1 689.3	1 770.8	1 841.1	1 892.0	1 935.7	1 989.6	2 063.8	2 130.3	2 212.6	2 275.4	2 360.0	2 469.7	2 514.8	2 631.6
Greece	144.2	150.2	156.5	162.9	173.0	178.9	185.4	200.8	218.1	238.8	248.8	266.7	282.8	303.6
Hungary	86.1	90.5	93.7	96.9	103.2	110.0	115.8	125.2	138.1	149.6	157.3	164.3	171.6	182.8
Iceland	5.8	6.1	6.2	6.5	7.1	7.6	7.9	8.1	8.7	8.9	8.9	9.8	10.5	10.9
Ireland	53.5	57.8	64.7	71.1	79.8	89.2	97.5	108.6	117.8	129.7	137.6	147.8	157.9	173.2
Italy	1 099.1	1 146.4	1 202.9	1 242.1	1 285.4	1 350.4	1 377.2	1 455.8	1 546.6	1 532.0	1 565.0	1 595.4	1 626.3	1 699.2
Japan	2 636.0	2 721.2	2 831.1	2 964.2	3 061.1	3 031.7	3 071.1	3 246.3	3 330.6	3 417.2	3 509.9	3 709.8	3 870.3	4 077.8
Korea	468.2	518.9	578.0	630.2	670.5	631.5	701.4	772.8	821.7	888.9	910.9	981.4	1 027.4	1 112.7
Luxembourg	14.5	15.4	16.0	16.7	17.1	18.4	21.1	23.4	23.8	25.7	27.3	29.8	32.6	36.9
Mexico	614.5	655.1	627.3	672.1	729.6	774.9	815.6	899.3	920.6	955.7	1 010.4	1 082.7	1 173.2	1 267.9
Netherlands	301.9	317.4	334.0	352.2	376.2	400.2	425.8	467.7	494.2	515.8	514.9	541.1	566.6	597.2
New Zealand	55.6	60.2	63.8	66.5	69.9	71.3	76.4	80.1	84.6	89.2	93.2	98.7	102.0	107.3
Norway	90.4	97.0	103.1	114.3	123.2	121.5	133.0	162.1	167.5	168.2	175.0	194.2	220.1	242.6
Poland	244.7	263.1	287.1	311.5	339.9	362.5	382.6	403.8	419.1	442.1	458.3	497.4	518.0	558.3
Portugal	119.8	123.5	131.4	137.3	145.8	153.7	163.9	174.5	183.3	191.3	196.4	201.5	210.6	220.6
Slovak Republic	38.4	41.6	45.0	49.1	52.9	55.8	56.5	59.4	65.0	69.9	72.6	78.7	85.6	94.8
Spain	575.9	602.0	631.2	660.8	700.8	750.5	791.5	857.5	920.5	994.3	1 040.7	1 109.3	1 183.5	1 294.8
Sweden	171.7	182.2	193.5	200.5	207.3	214.8	228.5	246.0	248.9	258.9	269.6	288.7	295.9	316.7
Switzerland	178.6	184.5	189.0	194.5	202.7	210.4	215.2	227.7	234.0	245.2	246.6	257.7	266.3	285.3
Turkey	300.7	290.3	317.5	347.1	380.2	398.4	383.2	440.0	416.9	453.1	465.5	530.8	561.1	639.7
United Kingdom	1 010.6	1 076.5	1 130.8	1 200.3	1 285.8	1 342.2	1 397.3	1 505.9	1 601.6	1 682.2	1 746.1	1 875.0	1 901.7	1 997.0
United States	6 604.3	7 017.5	7 342.3	7 762.3	8 250.9	8 694.6	9 216.2	9 764.8	10 075.9	10 417.6	10 908.0	11 630.9	12 376.1	13 132.9
EU15 total	6 860.1	7 202.8	7 539.4	7 832.5	8 193.2	8 570.4	8 919.6	9 505.4	10 022.0	10 420.0	10 685.7	11 218.1	11 593.8	12 245.8
OECD total	18 751.0	19 756.5	20 657.7	21 693.7	22 857.7	23 747.2	24 862.0	26 504.0	27 544.9	28 586.6	29 623.2	31 420.6	33 029.5	35 059.1
Brazil	..	..	..	..	..	..	..	..	..	..	..	..	1 585.1	..
China	..	..	..	..	..	..	..	..	..	..	..	..	5 333.2	..
India	..	..	..	..	..	..	..	..	..	..	..	..	2 341.0	..
Russian Federation	..	..	..	..	..	..	..	..	..	..	..	..	1 697.5	..
South Africa	..	..	..	..	..	..	..	..	..	..	..	..	397.5	..

StatLink http://dx.doi.org/10.1787/272500610544

Gross domestic product

Billion US dollars, current prices and PPPs, 2006 or latest available year

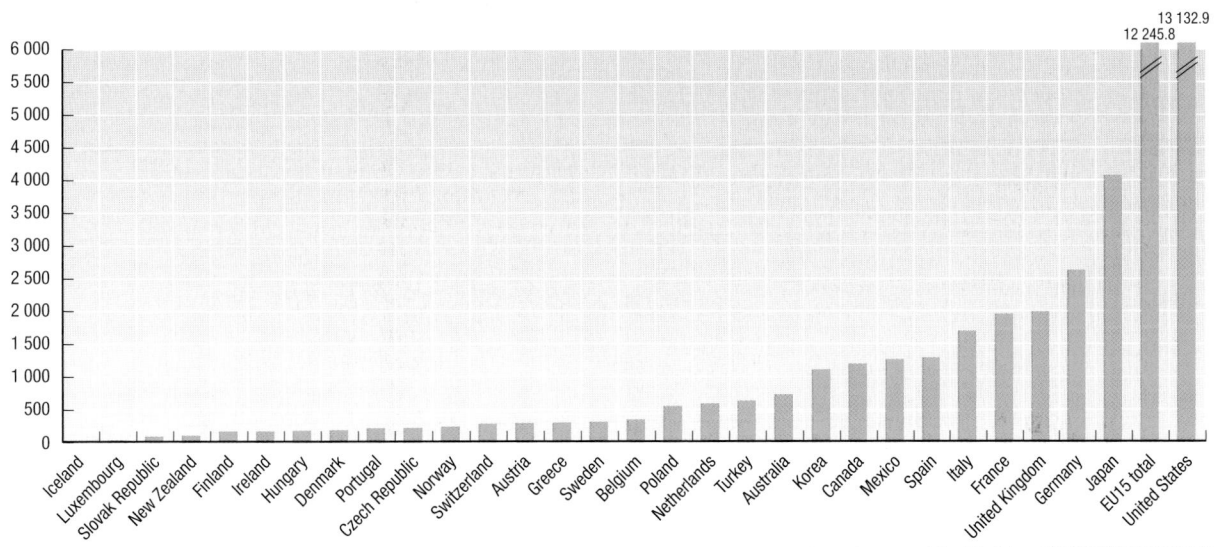

StatLink http://dx.doi.org/10.1787/266601003440

SIZE OF GDP

GDP per capita
US dollars, current prices and PPPs

	1993	1994	1995	1996	1997	1998	1999	2000	2001	2002	2003	2004	2005	2006
Australia	19 293	20 437	21 591	22 391	23 487	24 680	26 128	27 224	28 289	29 611	31 096	32 496	33 983	35 453
Austria	21 841	22 807	23 680	24 598	25 151	26 290	27 290	29 134	29 272	30 500	31 518	33 082	34 107	35 695
Belgium	20 551	21 597	22 517	22 843	23 837	24 341	25 299	27 542	28 445	29 946	30 167	31 062	32 077	33 527
Canada	20 722	21 933	22 771	23 334	24 481	25 554	27 135	28 444	29 331	29 893	31 182	32 818	35 078	36 813
Czech Republic	11 383	11 875	12 843	13 671	13 836	13 965	14 312	14 976	16 183	16 872	18 012	19 324	20 280	22 009
Denmark	20 498	22 015	23 046	24 099	25 272	26 145	26 926	28 790	29 455	30 756	30 462	32 185	33 626	35 217
Finland	16 917	17 811	18 817	19 320	21 006	22 665	23 698	25 654	26 662	27 592	27 722	29 925	30 468	32 736
France	18 771	19 521	20 269	20 849	21 758	22 799	23 615	25 233	26 652	27 772	27 429	28 324	29 644	31 048
Germany	20 810	21 748	22 545	23 102	23 591	24 255	25 142	25 920	26 871	27 587	28 599	29 936	30 496	31 950
Greece	13 658	14 160	14 713	15 207	16 051	16 509	17 032	18 390	19 918	21 732	22 573	24 108	25 472	27 233
Hungary	8 359	8 816	9 069	9 401	10 031	10 719	11 309	12 265	13 552	14 722	15 526	16 251	17 014	18 154
Iceland	21 829	22 900	23 275	24 212	26 108	27 756	28 556	28 739	30 379	30 925	30 744	33 644	35 571	35 749
Ireland	14 978	16 120	17 957	19 620	21 796	24 042	25 990	28 587	30 531	33 036	34 469	36 416	38 061	40 716
Italy	19 340	20 169	21 161	21 845	22 594	23 730	24 196	25 566	27 143	26 804	27 168	27 425	27 750	28 866
Japan	21 117	21 739	22 564	23 571	24 283	23 985	24 252	25 593	26 195	26 814	27 482	29 037	30 290	31 919
Korea	10 594	11 623	12 818	13 843	14 592	13 644	15 047	16 439	17 352	18 666	19 033	20 429	21 342	23 038
Luxembourg	36 527	38 166	38 933	40 175	40 733	43 081	48 845	53 317	53 940	57 546	60 510	65 006	69 984	78 138
Mexico	6 999	7 332	6 884	7 263	7 770	8 136	8 447	9 152	9 247	9 484	9 919	10 525	11 299	12 104
Netherlands	19 746	20 636	21 603	22 686	24 108	25 484	26 933	29 373	30 806	31 943	31 738	33 243	34 724	36 548
New Zealand	15 565	16 631	17 369	17 818	18 474	18 689	19 914	20 754	21 774	22 620	23 237	24 299	24 882	25 910
Norway	20 962	22 356	23 652	26 094	27 976	27 419	29 800	36 085	37 114	37 052	38 342	42 301	47 620	52 047
Poland	6 402	6 877	7 501	8 137	8 875	9 470	9 996	10 555	10 957	11 563	11 998	13 028	13 573	14 641
Portugal	12 011	12 353	13 102	13 646	14 445	15 175	16 113	17 068	17 811	18 447	18 812	19 191	19 967	20 839
Slovak Republic	7 212	7 789	8 386	9 142	9 830	10 346	10 473	10 992	12 077	12 997	13 493	14 617	15 881	17 585
Spain	14 668	15 307	16 026	16 738	17 705	18 895	19 824	21 296	22 605	24 067	24 776	25 985	27 270	29 382
Sweden	19 693	20 748	21 919	22 677	23 430	24 267	25 801	27 727	27 980	29 004	30 097	32 099	32 770	34 870
Switzerland	25 554	26 223	26 685	27 373	28 501	29 507	30 028	31 583	32 122	33 391	33 304	34 572	35 500	37 747
Turkey	5 055	4 793	5 151	5 536	6 086	6 278	5 955	6 522	6 076	6 508	6 583	7 394	7 786	8 766
United Kingdom	17 511	18 604	19 488	20 636	22 049	22 954	23 811	25 573	27 094	28 357	29 320	31 336	31 580	32 990
United States	25 374	26 636	27 542	28 780	30 228	31 485	32 994	34 571	35 293	36 116	37 445	39 548	41 674	43 801
EU15 total	18 504	19 374	20 228	20 959	21 869	22 826	23 686	25 148	26 396	27 300	27 834	29 046	29 843	31 364
OECD total	18 585	19 423	20 144	20 991	21 977	22 668	23 561	24 868	25 638	26 400	27 145	28 581	31 469
Brazil	..	..	..	..	..	..	..	..	..	..	..	..	8 606	..
China	..	..	..	..	..	..	..	..	..	..	..	..	4 091	..
India	..	..	..	..	..	..	..	..	..	..	..	..	2 126	..
Russian Federation	..	..	..	..	..	..	..	..	..	..	..	..	11 861	..
South Africa	..	..	..	..	..	..	..	..	..	..	..	..	8 477	..

StatLink http://dx.doi.org/10.1787/272508632043

GDP per capita
US dollars, current prices and PPPs, 2006 or latest available year

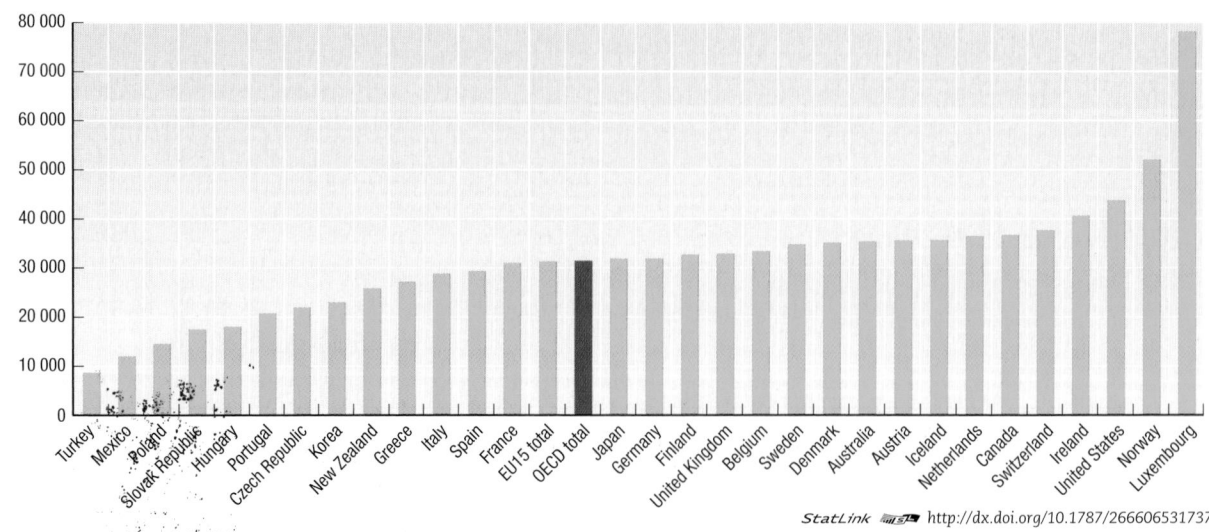

StatLink http://dx.doi.org/10.1787/266606531737

OECD FACTBOOK 2008 – ISBN 978-92-64-04054-0 – © OECD 2008

Volume index of GDP per capita

OECD = 100 in 2000, at 2000 price levels and PPPs

	1993	1994	1995	1996	1997	1998	1999	2000	2001	2002	2003	2004	2005	2006
Australia	90.2	93.3	95.8	98.3	101.7	105.8	108.7	109.5	112.1	114.3	117.6	119.4	121.1	122.5
Austria	98.2	100.4	102.2	104.7	106.5	110.2	113.6	117.2	117.7	118.1	119.0	120.9	122.5	125.8
Belgium	93.2	95.9	98.0	99.0	102.2	103.7	107.0	110.8	111.3	112.4	113.0	115.9	117.2	119.8
Canada	92.8	96.2	97.8	98.4	101.5	104.8	109.7	114.4	115.2	117.2	118.3	120.7	123.2	125.4
Czech Republic	51.4	52.5	55.6	58.0	57.6	57.2	58.0	60.2	62.0	63.3	65.6	68.5	72.7	77.0
Denmark	95.1	100.1	102.6	104.9	107.8	109.8	112.2	115.8	116.2	116.3	116.4	118.6	121.9	125.8
Finland	77.6	80.0	82.8	85.6	90.5	95.0	98.4	103.2	105.6	107.1	108.8	112.5	115.4	120.7
France	87.2	88.8	90.3	91.0	92.7	95.6	98.3	101.5	102.6	102.9	103.4	105.2	106.4	107.9
Germany	91.3	93.5	95.0	95.7	97.2	99.2	101.1	104.2	105.3	105.1	104.9	106.0	106.9	110.1
Greece	62.0	62.9	64.1	65.1	67.1	69.0	71.0	74.0	77.0	79.8	83.5	87.0	90.0	93.4
Hungary	38.5	39.7	40.1	40.7	42.6	44.8	46.8	49.3	51.4	53.9	56.3	59.1	61.7	64.2
Iceland	93.5	96.1	95.7	99.7	103.7	109.2	112.3	115.6	118.4	117.3	119.8	127.5	135.1	134.7
Ireland	67.1	70.7	77.2	82.9	91.5	97.5	106.5	115.0	120.1	125.8	129.3	132.6	137.6	141.9
Italy	89.2	91.1	93.7	94.4	96.1	97.4	99.3	102.8	104.6	104.6	103.8	104.1	103.4	104.9
Japan	96.6	97.4	99.1	101.6	102.9	100.5	100.2	102.9	102.9	102.9	104.1	106.9	109.0	111.4
Korea	47.9	51.5	55.6	59.0	61.1	56.5	61.4	66.1	68.1	72.5	74.4	77.6	80.7	84.4
Luxembourg	166.6	170.5	170.4	170.6	178.4	187.5	200.5	214.4	218.3	224.9	226.8	234.5	242.6	253.3
Mexico	32.2	33.1	30.4	31.5	33.2	34.3	35.1	36.8	36.3	36.2	36.3	37.4	38.1	39.6
Netherlands	95.0	97.2	99.8	102.7	106.6	110.1	114.5	118.1	119.5	118.8	118.6	120.9	122.4	125.9
New Zealand	72.4	75.2	77.2	78.7	78.9	78.5	82.2	83.5	85.9	88.5	90.0	92.1	93.1	93.9
Norway	115.2	120.4	124.8	130.5	136.8	139.6	141.5	145.1	147.3	148.6	149.3	154.2	157.3	159.4
Poland	29.0	30.5	32.6	34.6	37.1	38.9	40.7	42.4	43.0	43.6	45.3	47.8	49.5	52.6
Portugal	54.7	55.1	57.3	59.2	61.5	64.2	66.4	68.6	69.6	69.6	68.5	69.2	69.4	70.0
Slovak Republic	33.7	35.6	37.6	40.1	42.3	43.8	43.9	44.2	45.8	47.7	49.7	52.3	55.5	60.0
Spain	68.3	69.8	71.6	73.2	75.8	78.9	82.2	85.6	87.8	88.8	90.1	91.5	93.3	95.4
Sweden	89.1	91.9	95.1	96.3	98.6	102.3	107.0	111.5	112.4	114.7	116.5	120.8	124.3	128.6
Switzerland	116.6	117.2	116.9	117.2	119.5	122.3	123.3	127.0	127.1	126.7	125.4	127.7	130.0	133.2
Turkey	24.2	22.5	23.7	24.9	26.9	27.3	25.6	26.2	23.9	25.4	26.4	28.4	30.3	31.8
United Kingdom	83.4	86.8	89.1	91.3	93.9	96.8	99.4	102.8	104.9	106.6	109.2	112.2	113.5	116.2
United States	115.4	118.7	120.3	123.3	127.4	131.2	135.6	139.0	138.6	139.4	141.5	145.3	148.3	151.1
EU15 total	84.9	87.0	89.0	90.4	92.6	95.1	97.7	101.1	102.7	103.3	103.9	105.7	106.8	109.2
OECD total	85.1	87.0	88.5	90.4	93.0	94.7	97.2	100.0	100.4	101.1	102.3	104.7	106.7	109.1

StatLink ⟨⟩ http://dx.doi.org/10.1787/272524056685

Change in relative volume indices of GDP per capita

Absolute differences between the 2006 and 1993 indices

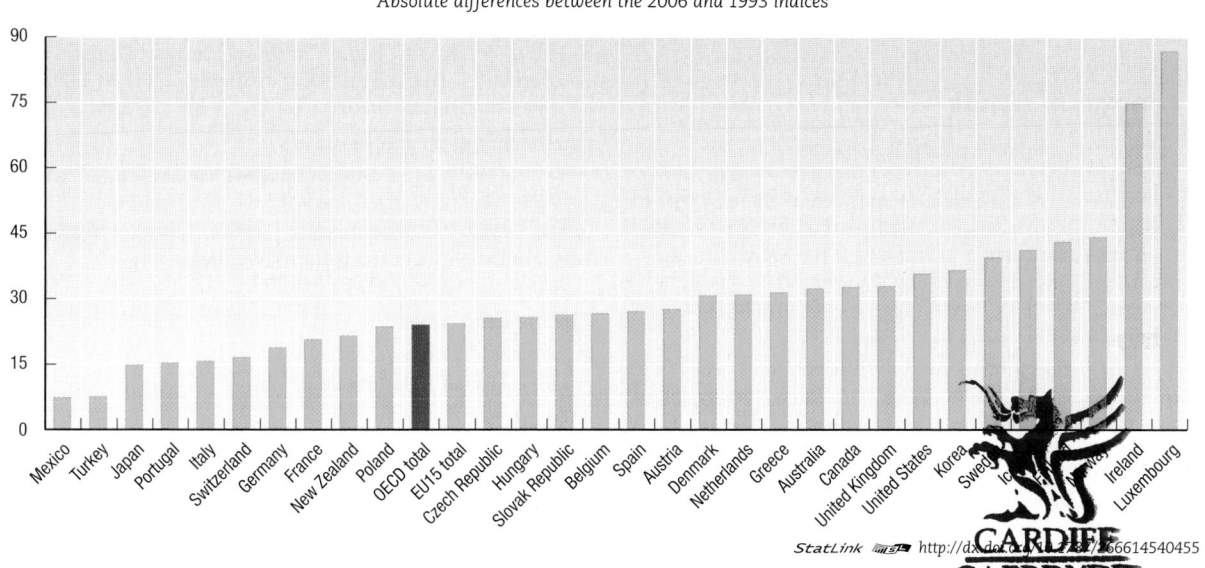

StatLink ⟨⟩ http://dx.doi.org/10.1787/266614540455

NATIONAL INCOME PER CAPITA

While per capita gross domestic product is the indicator most commonly used to compare income levels, two other measures are preferred by many analysts. These are per capita gross national income (GNI) and net national income (NNI).

Definition

GNI is defined as GDP plus net receipts from abroad of wages and salaries and of property income.

Wages and salaries from abroad are those that are earned by residents, that is, by persons who essentially live and consume inside the economic territory but work abroad (this happens in border areas on a regular basis) or for persons that live and work abroad for only short periods (seasonal workers) and whose centre of economic interest thus remains in their home country. Guest-workers and other migrant workers who live abroad for twelve months or more are considered to be resident in the country where they are working. Such persons may send part of their earnings to relatives at home, but these remittances are treated as transfers between resident and non-resident households and do not enter into net receipts from abroad of wages and salaries.

Property income from abroad includes interest, dividends and all or part of the retained earnings of foreign enterprises owned fully or in part by residents. In most countries, net receipts of property income account for most of the difference between GDP and GNI. Note that retained earnings of foreign enterprises owned by residents may not actually return to the residents concerned, and, in some countries, there are restrictions on the repatriation of profits. Receipt of retained earnings is an imputation, and, since there is no actual transaction, it is necessary to impute an outflow of the same amount. The imputed outflow is treated as a financial transaction (a reinvestment of earnings abroad) and not as an outflow of property income.

Countries with large stocks of outward foreign direct investment may be shown as having large receipts of property income from abroad and therefore high GNI even though much of the property income may never actually be returned to the country, but instead add to the foreign direct investment.

Depreciation, which is deducted from GNI to obtain NNI, is the decline in the market value of fixed capital assets – dwellings, buildings, machinery, transport equipment and physical infrastructure – through wear and tear and obsolescence.

Comparability

Both measures are compiled according to the definitions of the 1993 *System of National Accounts*. There are, however, practical difficulties in the measurement both of international flows of wages and salaries and property income and of depreciation. It is for that reason that GDP per capita is the most widely used indicator of income or welfare, even though it is theoretically inferior to either GNI or NNI.

Source

- OECD (2007), *National Accounts of OECD Countries*, OECD, Paris.

Further information

Analytical publications

- OECD (2003), *The Sources of Economic Growth in OECD Countries*, OECD, Paris.
- OECD (2007), *OECD Economic Outlook: December No. 82 – Volume 2007 Issue 2*, OECD, Paris.

Statistical publications

- Maddison, Angus (2003), *The World Economy: Historical Perspectives*, OECD, Paris, also available on CD-ROM, *www.theworldeconomy.org*.

Methodological publications

- OECD (2000), *OECD Glossaries, System of National Accounts, 1993 – Glossary*, OECD, Paris.
- UN, OECD, IMF, Eurostat (eds.) (1993), *System of National Accounts 1993*, United Nations, Geneva, *http://unstats.un.org/unsd/sna1993*.

Online databases

- *National Accounts*.
- *OECD Economic Outlook Statistics*.

Websites

- OECD Economic Outlook – Sources and Methods, *www.oecd.org/eco/sources-and-methods*.

Long-term trends

In the chart, countries are ranked according to GNI, which is usually around 16 or 17% higher than NNI. Note that the country rankings are not much affected by the choice of income measure; countries that would be more than one place lower in the ranking if NNI were used are Japan, and Denmark, and those that would be more than one place higher in the ranking are Germany, Iceland Sweden and the United Kingdom.

Over the period shown, the growth of per capita GNI mirrors that of per capita GDP, with Ireland, Norway, the Slovak Republic and Poland at the top end and Germany, Iceland, Italy and Japan with the lowest rates of growth.

Gross national income per capita
US dollars, current prices and PPPs

	1993	1994	1995	1996	1997	1998	1999	2000	2001	2002	2003	2004	2005	2006
Australia	18 757	19 676	20 777	21 605	22 751	23 931	25 388	26 484	27 532	28 770	30 225	31 320	32 617	..
Austria	21 627	22 551	23 274	24 349	24 777	25 877	26 713	28 574	28 570	30 123	31 235	32 779	33 756	35 241
Belgium	20 799	22 027	22 907	23 292	24 331	24 783	25 795	28 165	28 876	30 325	30 585	31 340	32 255	33 937
Canada	20 005	21 137	21 968	22 544	23 713	24 704	26 217	27 703	28 501	29 145	30 447	32 150	34 452	36 539
Czech Republic	11 371	11 903	12 817	13 482	13 620	13 705	13 975	14 637	15 640	16 103	17 236	18 262	19 287	20 821
Denmark	20 173	21 691	22 800	23 792	24 914	25 849	26 699	28 181	29 039	30 393	30 275	32 334	33 911	35 704
Finland	15 980	17 055	18 185	18 789	20 592	22 122	23 347	25 399	26 539	27 651	27 331	30 109	30 590	32 906
France	18 922	19 600	20 307	20 957	21 901	22 970	23 977	25 580	26 968	27 848	27 601	28 548	29 878	31 288
Germany	20 842	21 631	22 378	22 980	23 420	24 003	24 873	25 677	26 604	27 246	28 399	30 140	30 773	32 255
Greece	13 989	14 509	15 079	15 535	16 401	16 862	17 160	18 439	19 946	21 666	22 350	23 829	24 961	26 735
Hungary	7 944	8 344	8 448	8 726	9 191	9 797	10 440	11 612	12 834	13 912	14 748	15 295	16 010	16 852
Iceland	21 302	22 196	22 623	23 656	25 513	27 156	27 995	27 942	29 422	30 874	30 261	32 274	34 324	32 662
Ireland	13 685	14 796	16 206	17 812	19 471	21 325	22 384	24 629	25 809	27 410	29 452	31 082	32 412	35 072
Italy	19 013	19 791	20 835	21 569	22 448	23 567	24 091	25 374	26 964	26 594	26 945	27 267	27 629	28 788
Japan	21 212	21 818	22 637	23 827	24 602	24 314	24 564	25 920	26 632	27 261	27 960	29 598	31 006	32 826
Korea	10 572	11 593	12 774	13 790	14 512	13 422	14 872	16 368	17 321	18 688	19 053	20 476	21 310	23 038
Luxembourg	34 050	34 275	36 054	37 399	39 202	39 631	43 887	46 458	47 913	47 726	45 893	56 465	58 277	63 945
Mexico	6 799	7 114	6 569	6 963	7 528	7 881	8 229	8 932	9 049	9 311	9 737	10 364	..	..
Netherlands	19 746	20 776	21 923	22 889	24 429	25 220	27 226	30 007	31 039	32 236	32 099	34 133	34 942	37 149
New Zealand	14 473	15 505	16 254	16 497	17 311	17 789	18 714	19 397	20 535	21 404	22 038	22 713	23 105	..
Norway	20 485	21 980	23 365	25 797	27 683	27 110	29 550	35 599	37 147	37 166	38 580	42 383	47 950	51 915
Poland	6 149	6 818	7 393	8 081	8 809	9 405	9 940	10 472	10 885	11 475	11 817	12 501	13 112	..
Portugal	11 980	12 268	13 076	13 572	14 271	14 957	15 843	16 647	17 285	18 065	18 560	18 888	19 554	20 170
Slovak Republic	7 151	7 727	8 423	9 208	9 844	10 354	10 415	10 956	12 086	12 960	13 386	14 674	15 475	17 051
Spain	14 584	15 020	15 932	16 579	17 544	18 708	19 638	21 117	22 240	23 703	24 489	25 639	26 888	28 882
Sweden	18 910	20 240	21 405	22 171	22 919	23 924	25 546	27 489	27 708	28 905	30 368	32 029	32 721	35 023
Switzerland	26 272	26 735	27 441	28 246	29 931	31 116	31 961	33 904	33 602	34 469	35 818	37 039	38 841	41 226
Turkey	5 094	4 817	5 212	5 614	6 203	6 433	6 022	6 575	6 010	6 448	6 527	7 367	7 773	8 758
United Kingdom	17 384	18 612	19 413	20 575	22 066	23 190	23 763	25 593	27 319	28 923	29 914	32 012	32 214	33 424
United States	24 960	26 195	27 296	28 562	30 090	31 615	33 243	35 159	35 760	36 295	37 472	39 742	41 887	44 055

StatLink http://dx.doi.org/10.1787/272524436267

Gross and net national income per capita
US dollars, current prices and PPPs, 2006 or latest available year

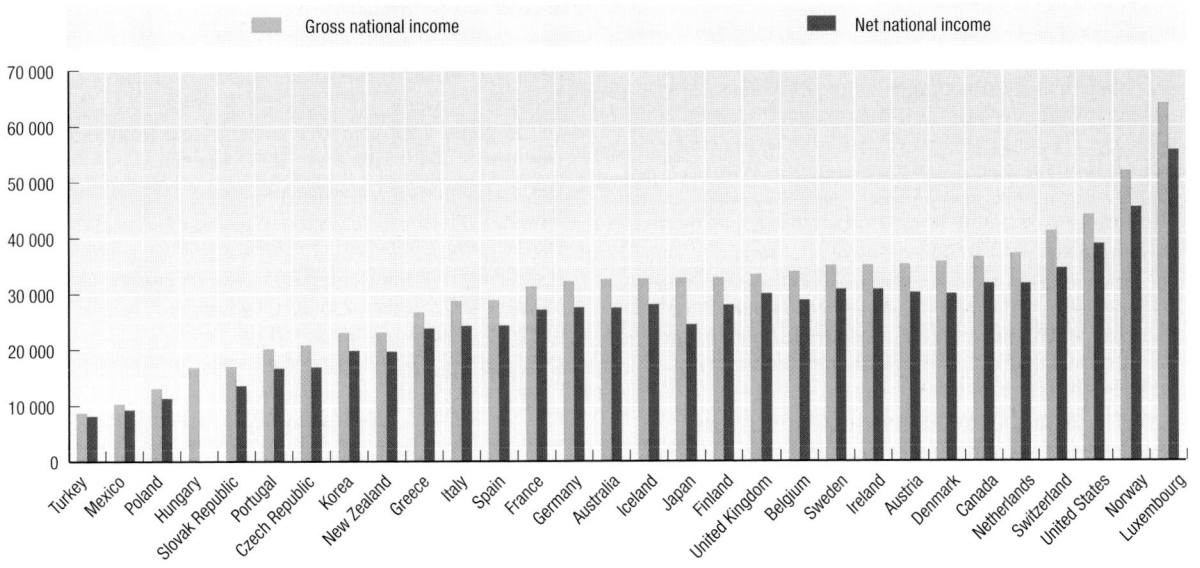

StatLink http://dx.doi.org/10.1787/266663722333

REGIONAL GDP

GDP per capita varies significantly among OECD countries, but international disparities in GDP per capita are often smaller than differences among regions within countries. In 2004, GDP per capita in the richest region was twice as large as the poorest one in 85% of OECD countries.

Definition

Regional GDP is measured according to the definitions of the 1993 System of National Accounts. GDP per capita is calculated by dividing the GDP of a country or region by the population (number of inhabitants) living there.

The Gini index offers an accurate picture of regional disparities. It looks not only at the regions with the highest and the lowest GDP per capita but also at the differences among all regions. The index ranges between 0 and 1: the higher its value, the larger the regional disparities. Regional disparities tend to be underestimated when the size of regions is large. This may be the case for Australia, Canada, Mexico and the United States, where GDP figures are only available for Territorial Level 2 regions (see Regional population).

Comparability

As for the other regional statistics, the comparability of regional GDP per capita is affected by differences in the meaning of the word "region" (see Regional population). In addition, different regional type – urban or rural – can affect the comparability of regional GDP per capita. For instance, in the United Kingdom, one might question the relevance of comparing the highly urbanised area of London to the rural region of the Shetland Islands, despite the fact that both regions belong to the same territorial level. To take account of these differences, the OECD has established a regional typology according to which regions have been classified as *predominantly urban*, *predominantly rural* and *intermediate*. This typology, based on the percentage of regional population living in rural communities, enables meaningful comparisons between regions belonging to the same type.

The OECD regional typology is based on two criteria. The first identifies rural communities according to their population density. A community is defined as rural if its population density is below 150 inhabitants per square kilometers (500 inhabitants for Japan because its national population density exceeds 300 inhabitants per square kilometers). The second classifies regions according to the percentage of population living in rural communities. Thus a region is classified as:

- *Predominantly rural*, if more than 50% of its population lives in rural communities.

- *Predominantly urban*, if less than 15% of the population lives in rural communities.

- *Intermediate*, if the percentage of population living in rural communities is between 15 and 50%.

Overview

Differences in GDP per capita among regions of the same country are often substantial. In Turkey, for instance, GDP per capita in the region of Kocaeli is almost 11 times higher than in Agri. In the United Kingdom, GDP per capita in Inner London West is almost 8 times higher than in the Isle of Anglesey.

Part of the observed differences in regional GDP per capita may be due to commuting. By working in one area and living in another, commuters tend to increase GDP per capita in the region where they are employed and decrease GDP per capita in the region where they reside. In several urban regions (*e.g.* Inner London – West, District of Columbia, Paris), GDP per capita appears significantly overstated owing to commuting.

More than half (53%) of the population in OECD countries reside in regions with a level of GDP per capita below the national average. In the Slovak Republic, the Czech Republic, Mexico, Poland, Denmark, Belgium and Korea, no less than 60% of the population lives in regions with low GDP per capita.

According to the Gini index, Turkey, Mexico and the Slovak Republic recorded the largest disparities in GDP per capita. In contrast, the lowest disparities were present in Sweden, Japan, the Netherlands, Finland and Australia.

Source

- *OECD Regional Database*.

Further information

Analytical publications

- OECD (2001), *OECD Territorial Outlook, 2001 Edition*, OECD, Paris.
- OECD (2003), *Geographic Concentration and Territorial Disparity in OECD Countries*, OECD, Paris.
- OECD (2005), *Local Governance and the Drivers of Growth*, OECD, Paris.
- OECD (2006), *OECD Territorial Reviews – Competitive Cities in the Global Economy*, OECD, Paris.
- OECD (2007), *Higher Education and Regions: Globally Competitive, Locally Engaged*, OECD, Paris.
- OECD (2007), *OECD Regions at a Glance: 2007 Edition*, OECD, Paris.
- Spiezia, V. (2003), "Measuring Regional Economies", OECD Statistics Brief, No. 6, October, OECD, Paris, *www.oecd.org/std/statisticsbrief*.

Websites

- OECD Regional Database, *www.oecd.org/gov/territorialindicators*.

National GDP per capita
US dollars, current prices and PPPs, 2004

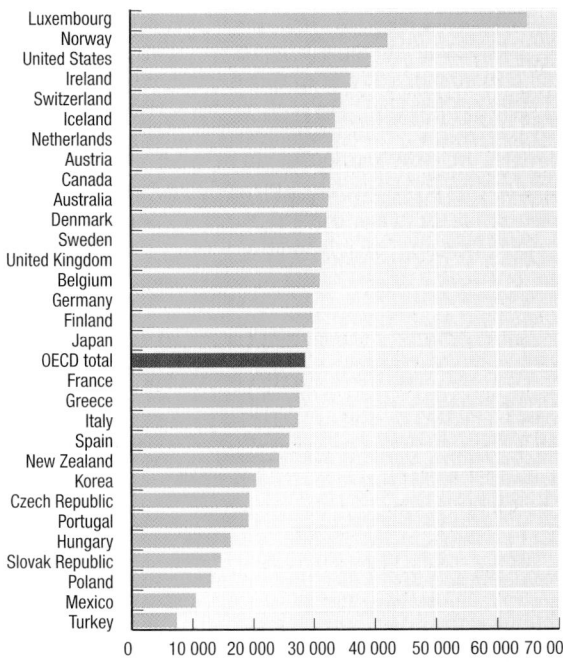

Share of total population living in regions with a GDP per capita below the national average
Percentage, 2004 or latest available year

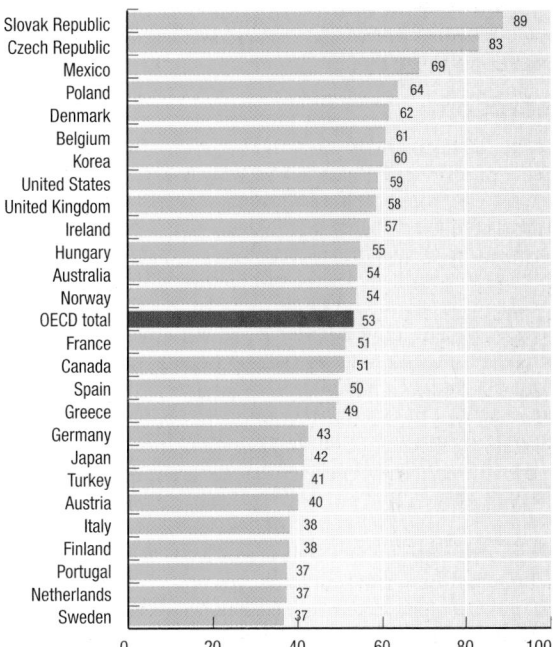

Variation of regional GDP per capita
As a percentage of of national GDP per capita, 2004

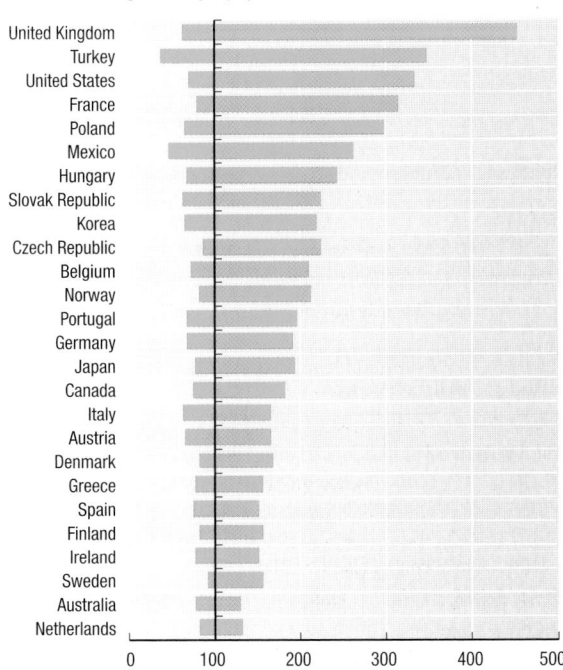

Gini index of regional disparities in GDP
2004 or latest available year

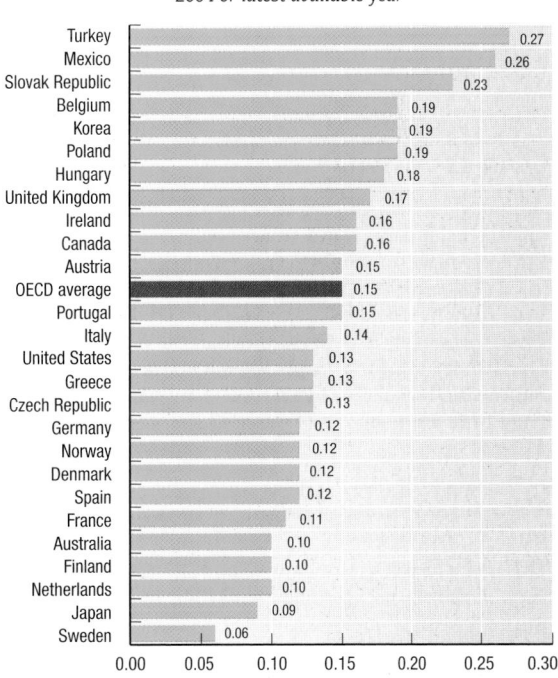

StatLink http://dx.doi.org/10.1787/266668620750

EVOLUTION OF GDP

Gross domestic product (GDP) is a standard measure of the value of production by a country during a period. For the definition refer to Size of GDP. Growth of real GDP, *i.e.* ignoring price changes, is widely used to assess governments' performance in managing their economies.

Definition

In order to calculate the growth rate of GDP free of the direct effects of inflation, data at fixed, or constant, prices should be used. Price relativities change over time, and the *1993 System of National Accounts* recommends that the fixed prices used should be representative of the periods for which the growth rates are calculated, which means that new fixed prices should be introduced frequently, typically every year. The growth rates of GDP between successive periods are linked together to form chain volume indices. All OECD countries derive their "volume" estimates in this way, except for Korea, Mexico, Turkey and the Slovak Republic. These four, like many non-OECD countries, only revise their fixed weights every five or ten years. Such practices tend to lead to biased growth rates, usually upward.

The growth rates for OECD total and Euro area are averages of the growth rates of individual countries weighted by the relative size of each country's GDP in US dollars. Conversion to US dollars is done using purchasing power parities so that each country is weighted by the relative size of its real GDP. Note that OECD total GDP excludes the Czech Republic, Hungary, Poland and the Slovak Republic because growth rates for these countries are not available for the full period.

Comparability

The GDP statistics used for these growth rates have been compiled according to the 1993 System of National Accounts, except for Turkey which still uses the 1968 SNA, and GDP estimates at current prices are generally regarded as highly comparable between countries. However, there is more variability in how countries calculate their volume estimates of GDP, particularly in respect of government consumption and some types of capital expenditures.

Note that in the table, the OECD total excludes the Czech Republic, Hungary, Poland and the Slovak Republic.

Long-term trends

Annual growth for OECD total averaged 2.6% from 1993 to 2006. Ireland and Korea substantially outperformed the average with annual growth of over 5%. Growth rates in Ireland were particularly impressive between 1995 and 2000 – the so-called Celtic Tiger period. Korea's growth was badly affected by the financial crisis in Asia; real GDP fell by nearly 7% in 1998 but Korea has since returned to high rates of growth. Luxembourg, Poland and the Slovak Republic all recorded growth of close to 4.5% per year.

At the other end of the scale, Germany, Italy Japan and Switzerland- recorded average growth rates of 1.5% or less over the period.

The Czech Republic, Hungary, Poland and the Slovak Republic all experienced substantial falls in real GDP in the early years of their transition to market-based economies but generally began to achieve positive rates of growth during the second half of the 1990s. Their growth rates have been among the highest of all OECD countries in recent years.

Sources

- OECD (2007), *National Accounts of OECD Countries*, OECD, Paris, *www.sourceOECD.org/nationalaccounts*.
- For non-member countries: *national sources*.

Further information
Analytical publications

- OECD (2006), *Development Centre Studies – The Rise of China and India: What's in it for Africa?*, OECD, Paris.
- OECD (2007), *Economic Policy Reforms: Going for Growth, 2007 Edition*, OECD, Paris.
- OECD (2007), *OECD Economic Outlook: December No. 82 – Volume 2007 Issue 2*, OECD, Paris.

Online databases

- *National Accounts*.
- *OECD Economic Outlook Statistics*.

Websites

- OECD Economic Outlook – Sources and Methods, *www.oecd.org/eco/sources-and-methods*.

EVOLUTION OF GDP

Real GDP growth
Annual growth in percentage

	1993	1994	1995	1996	1997	1998	1999	2000	2001	2002	2003	2004	2005	2006
Australia	4.1	4.5	4.1	3.9	4.5	5.2	4.0	1.9	3.8	3.2	4.1	2.7	2.8	2.5
Austria	0.3	2.7	1.9	2.6	1.8	3.6	3.3	3.4	0.8	0.9	1.2	2.3	2.0	3.3
Belgium	-1.0	3.2	2.4	1.2	3.5	1.7	3.4	3.7	0.8	1.5	1.0	3.0	1.7	2.8
Canada	2.3	4.8	2.8	1.6	4.2	4.1	5.5	5.2	1.8	2.9	1.9	3.1	3.1	2.8
Czech Republic	0.1	2.2	5.9	4.0	-0.7	-0.8	1.3	3.6	2.5	1.9	3.6	4.5	6.4	6.4
Denmark	-0.1	5.5	3.1	2.8	3.2	2.2	2.6	3.5	0.7	0.5	0.4	2.1	3.1	3.5
Finland	-0.9	3.6	3.9	3.7	6.1	5.2	3.9	5.0	2.6	1.6	1.8	3.7	2.9	5.0
France	-0.9	2.2	2.1	1.1	2.2	3.5	3.3	3.9	1.9	1.0	1.1	2.5	1.7	2.0
Germany	-0.8	2.7	1.9	1.0	1.8	2.0	2.0	3.2	1.2	0.0	-0.2	1.1	0.8	2.9
Greece	-1.6	2.0	2.1	2.4	3.6	3.4	3.4	4.5	4.5	3.9	5.0	4.6	3.8	4.2
Hungary	-0.6	2.9	1.5	1.3	4.6	4.9	4.2	5.2	4.1	4.4	4.2	4.8	4.1	3.9
Iceland	1.3	3.6	0.1	4.8	4.8	6.4	4.1	4.3	3.9	-0.1	2.7	7.6	7.2	2.6
Ireland	2.7	5.8	9.6	8.2	11.3	8.0	10.4	9.4	6.1	6.6	4.5	4.4	6.0	5.7
Italy	-0.9	2.2	2.8	0.7	1.9	1.4	1.9	3.6	1.8	0.3	0.0	1.2	0.1	1.9
Japan	0.2	1.1	2.0	2.7	1.6	-2.0	-0.1	2.9	0.2	0.3	1.4	2.7	1.9	2.2
Korea	6.1	8.5	9.2	7.0	4.7	-6.9	9.5	8.5	3.8	7.0	3.1	4.7	4.2	5.0
Luxembourg	4.2	3.8	1.4	1.5	5.9	6.5	8.4	8.4	2.5	4.1	2.1	4.9	5.0	6.1
Mexico	2.0	4.4	-6.2	5.2	6.8	5.0	3.8	6.6	0.0	0.8	1.4	4.2	2.8	4.8
Netherlands	1.3	3.0	3.1	3.4	4.3	3.9	4.7	3.9	1.9	0.1	0.3	2.2	1.5	3.0
New Zealand	6.4	5.3	4.2	3.5	1.5	0.4	5.3	2.1	3.6	4.6	3.4	3.7	2.0	1.9
Norway	2.8	5.1	4.2	5.1	5.4	2.7	2.0	3.3	2.0	1.5	1.0	3.9	2.7	2.2
Poland	3.7	5.3	7.0	6.2	7.1	5.0	4.5	4.3	1.2	1.4	3.9	5.3	3.6	6.1
Portugal	-2.0	1.0	4.3	3.6	4.2	4.9	3.8	3.9	2.0	0.8	-0.8	1.5	0.7	1.2
Slovak Republic	1.9	6.2	5.8	6.9	5.7	3.7	0.3	0.7	3.2	4.1	4.2	5.4	6.0	8.3
Spain	-1.0	2.4	2.8	2.4	3.9	4.5	4.7	5.0	3.6	2.7	3.1	3.3	3.6	3.9
Sweden	-2.0	3.9	4.0	1.5	2.5	3.8	4.6	4.4	1.1	2.4	1.9	4.1	3.3	4.1
Switzerland	-0.2	1.2	0.4	0.6	2.1	2.6	1.3	3.6	1.2	0.4	-0.2	2.5	2.4	3.2
Turkey	8.0	-5.5	7.2	7.0	7.5	3.1	-4.7	7.4	-7.5	7.9	5.8	8.9	7.4	6.1
United Kingdom	2.3	4.3	2.9	2.8	3.1	3.4	3.0	3.8	2.4	2.1	2.8	3.3	1.8	2.8
United States	2.7	4.1	2.5	3.7	4.5	4.2	4.5	3.7	0.8	1.6	2.5	3.6	3.1	2.9
Euro area	-0.7	2.5	2.4	1.5	2.6	2.8	3.0	3.8	1.9	0.9	0.8	2.0	1.5	2.8
OECD total	1.4	3.2	2.5	3.0	3.6	2.6	3.3	3.9	1.2	1.6	1.9	3.2	2.5	2.9
Brazil	4.9	5.9	4.2	2.2	3.4	0.0	0.3	4.3	1.3	2.7	1.1	5.7	2.9	..
China	13.9	13.1	10.9	10.0	9.3	7.8	7.6	8.4	8.3	9.1	10.0	10.1	10.4	11.1
India	..	..	..	..	..	..	..	..	3.9	4.5	6.9	7.9	9.0	9.7
Russian Federation	..	..	-4.1	-3.6	1.4	-5.3	6.4	10.0	5.1	4.7	7.3	7.2	6.4	6.7
South Africa	1.2	3.2	3.1	4.3	2.6	0.5	2.4	4.2	2.7	3.7	3.1	4.9	5.0	5.4

StatLink http://dx.doi.org/10.1787/272530778260

Real GDP growth
Average annual growth in percentage

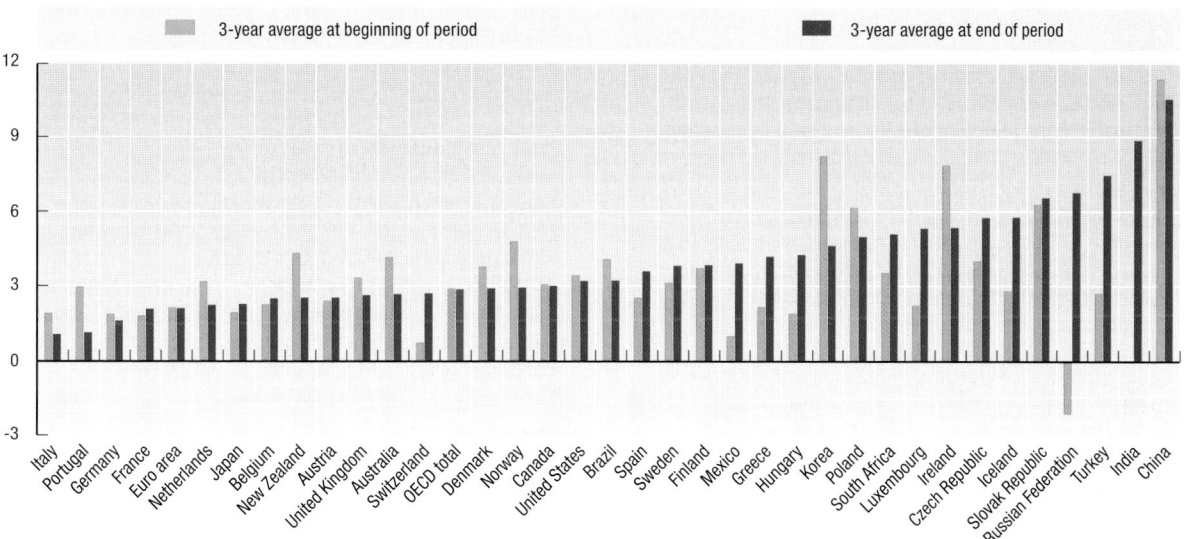

StatLink http://dx.doi.org/10.1787/266710014804

HOUSEHOLD SAVING

Household saving is the main domestic source of funds to finance capital investment, which is a major impetus for long-term economic growth.

Definition

In the national accounts, saving is estimated by subtracting household consumption expenditure from household disposable income.

The latter consists essentially of income from employment and from the operation of unincorporated enterprises, plus receipts of interest, dividends and social benefits minus payments of income taxes, interest and social security contributions. Note that enterprise income includes imputed rents paid by owner-occupiers of dwellings.

Household consumption expenditure consists mainly of cash outlays for consumer goods and services but it also includes the imputed expenditures that owner occupiers pay, as occupiers, to themselves as owners of their dwellings.

Households include households plus non-profit institutions serving households.

The household saving rate is calculated as the ratio of household saving to household disposable income.

Comparability

Saving rates may be measured on either a net or a gross basis. Net saving rates are measured after deducting consumption of fixed capital (depreciation) in respect of assets used in enterprises operated by households and in respect of owner-occupied dwellings from saving and from the disposable income of households, so that both saving and disposable income are shown on a net basis. Sometimes, countries have difficulties in estimating consumption of fixed capital for the household sector. The international system of accounts therefore provides for both disposable income and saving to be shown on a gross basis, i.e. with both aggregates including consumption of fixed capital. All figures are shown on a net basis.

Because saving is a residual between two large aggregates – disposable income and household consumption expenditure – both of which are subject to estimation errors, estimates of savings are subject to large relative errors and revisions over time.

Long-term trends

Household saving rates are very variable between countries. This is partly due to institutional differences between countries such as the extent to which old-age pensions are funded by government rather than through personal saving and the extent to which governments provide insurance against sickness and unemployment. The age composition of the population is also relevant because the elderly tend to run down financial assets acquired during their working life, so that a country with a high share of retired persons will usually have a low saving rate.

Over the period covered in the table, saving rates have been stable or rising in Austria, France, Italy, Norway and Portugal but have been falling in the other countries. Particularly sharp declines occurred in Australia, Canada, Japan, the United Kingdom and the United States. Negative saving – which means that consumption expenditures by households exceeded their income – was recorded in some countries, in particular in Australia, Denmark, Greece and New Zealand.

Source

• OECD (2007), *OECD Economic Outlook: December No. 82 – Volume 2007 Issue 2*, OECD, Paris.

Further information
Analytical publications

• Cotis, J.-P., J. Coppel and L. de Mello (2004), *Is the US Prone to Over-consumption?*, paper presented at The Macroeconomics of Fiscal Policy Federal Reserve Bank of Boston Economic Conference, Cape Cod, 14-16 June, *www.oecd.org/eco/speeches*.
• Harvey, R. (2004), "Comparison of Household Saving Ratios: Euro Area/United States/Japan", OECD Statistics Brief, No. 8, June, OECD, Paris, *www.oecd.org/std/statisticsbrief*.
• Kohl, R. and P. O'Brien (1998), *The Macroeconomics of Ageing, Pensions and Savings*, OECD Economics Department Working Papers, No. 200, OECD, Paris.
• de Serres, A. and F. Pelgrin (2003), "The Decline of Private Saving Rates in the 1990s in OECD Countries: How Much Can Be Explained by Non-wealth Determinants?", OECD Economic Studies, No. 36, 2003/1, OECD, Paris, *www.oecd.org/oecdeconomicstudies*.

Websites

• OECD Economic Outlook – Sources and Methods, *www.oecd.org/eco/sources-and-methods*.

Household net saving rates
As a percentage of household disposable income

	1993	1994	1995	1996	1997	1998	1999	2000	2001	2002	2003	2004	2005	2006
Australia	6.3	5.9	6.4	6.2	2.9	1.9	1.7	2.2	1.1	-2.7	-2.8	-1.9	-0.7	..
Austria	..	..	11.0	8.6	7.3	8.2	8.8	8.5	7.5	7.6	8.8	8.9	9.4	9.7
Belgium	..	..	16.3	14.5	13.6	12.7	12.8	11.0	12.0	11.2	9.7	8.3	7.1	7.6
Canada	12.1	9.6	9.4	7.2	5.0	4.9	4.1	4.8	5.3	3.5	2.8	2.7	1.2	..
Czech Republic	..	..	10.0	6.2	6.1	4.1	3.4	3.3	2.2	3.0	2.4	-0.5	0.6	0.0
Denmark	2.7	-1.8	1.3	1.0	-1.7	0.0	-3.6	-2.0	4.1	4.6	4.7	1.2	-2.7	..
Finland	7.5	1.1	3.9	0.4	2.0	0.5	2.1	-0.1	0.1	0.6	1.4	2.5	0.6	-2.0
France	12.2	11.4	12.7	11.7	12.6	12.2	11.9	11.8	12.5	13.7	12.5	12.4	11.8	12.0
Germany	12.1	11.5	11.1	10.6	10.2	10.2	9.5	9.3	9.5	10.1	10.4	10.5	10.7	10.6
Greece	..	..	..	..	..	..	..	-6.0	-7.5	-8.0	-7.3	-7.2	-8.0	-7.3
Hungary	..	..	..	..	..	..	..	..	..	..	..	7.0	6.7	..
Italy	..	..	..	..	..	..	10.4	8.6	10.6	11.4	10.4	10.5	10.1	8.8
Japan	..	..	..	11.5	11.0	11.8	10.3	8.9	5.2	5.1	3.9	3.6	3.1	..
Korea	21.8	20.6	17.5	17.5	16.1	24.8	17.4	10.7	6.4	2.2	3.9	6.3	4.7	3.9
Mexico	4.9	3.4	2.4	5.8	10.0	7.3	7.1	10.6	7.7	7.9	7.6	7.0	..	..
Netherlands	15.6	15.8	15.7	13.9	14.5	13.5	9.9	7.5	10.5	9.4	8.4	8.1	6.9	7.0
New Zealand	-0.6	-3.8	-3.6	-2.6	-4.6	-4.2	-5.3	-3.8	..	..	..	..	..	..
Poland	..	..	14.6	11.7	11.7	12.1	10.6	8.4	9.9	6.0	5.2	4.7	4.7	..
Portugal	..	..	..	..	..	..	..	3.6	4.5	4.0	4.4	4.0	2.5	..
Slovak Republic	..	..	5.2	8.9	9.3	7.7	6.3	6.1	3.9	3.6	1.4	0.7	1.8	1.2
Spain	..	..	..	..	..	..	..	5.9	5.6	5.6	5.9	5.0	3.8	3.1
United Kingdom	7.6	5.9	6.7	5.9	5.8	2.1	0.5	0.5	2.0	0.5	0.7	-0.7	-0.1	..
United States	6.1	5.3	5.1	4.2	3.7	4.5	2.5	2.4	1.8	2.5	2.4	2.0	0.6	0.5
Euro area	10.7	9.9	10.8	10.0	10.1	9.8	9.3	8.9	9.6	10.0	9.6	9.6	9.3	..
Brazil	..	..	..	..	..	..	..	7.8	8.2	8.8	8.6	..	7.0	..
Russian Federation	..	..	16.2	20.4	15.3	6.1	-2.3	6.7	7.5	14.0	14.6	12.6	11.2	..

StatLink http://dx.doi.org/10.1787/272560812251

Household net saving rates
As a percentage of household disposable income

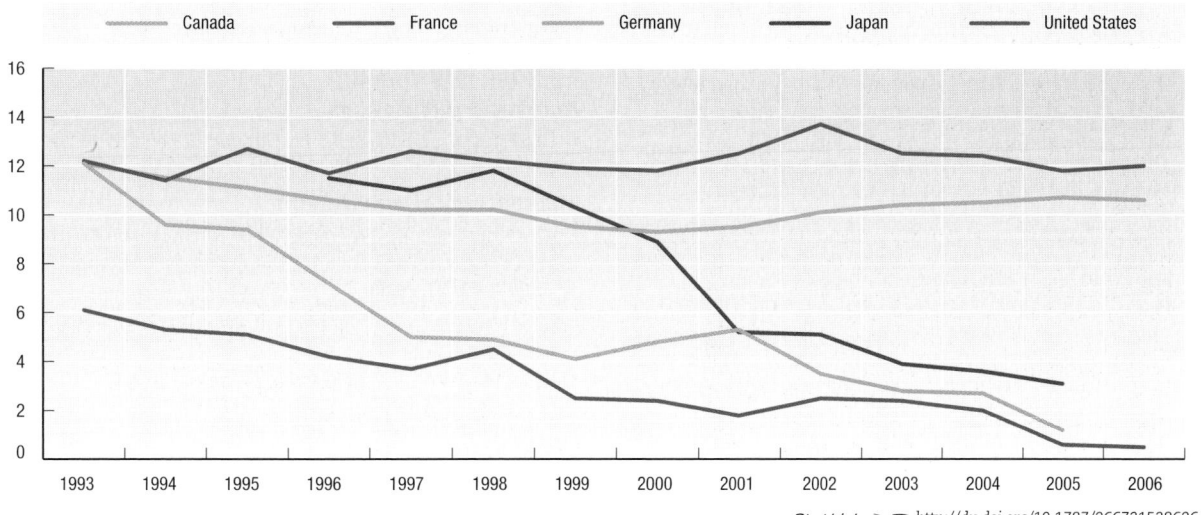

StatLink http://dx.doi.org/10.1787/266731538626

INVESTMENT RATES

The share of total GDP that is devoted to investment in fixed assets is an important indicator of future economic growth, although not all types of investment contribute to future growth in the same way. The following tables show the total of gross fixed capital formation (investment or GFCF) as a share of GDP and two of the main components – *dwellings* and *machinery and equipment*.

Definition

Gross fixed capital formation (GFCF) is the acquisition, less disposal, of fixed assets, *i.e.* products which are expected to be used in production for several years. *Acquisitions* include both purchases of assets (new or second-hand) and the construction of assets by producers for their own use. Disposals include sales of assets for scrap as well as sales of used assets in a working condition to other producers: New Zealand, Mexico and some Central European countries import substantial quantities of used assets.

Fixed assets consist of machinery and equipment; dwellings and other buildings; roads, bridges, airfields and dams; orchards and tree plantations; improvements to land such as fencing, leveling and draining; draught animals and other animals that are kept for the milk and wool that they produce; computer software and databases; entertainment, literacy or artistic originals, and expenditures on mineral exploration. What all these things have in common is that they contribute to future production. This may not be obvious in the case of dwellings but, in the national accounts, flats and houses are considered to produce housing services which are consumed by owners or tenants over the life of the building.

In calculating the shares, gross fixed capital formation and GDP are both valued at current market prices.

Comparability

When the *System of National Accounts* was revised in 1993, the scope of GFCF was widened to include mineral exploration, computer software and entertainment, literary and artistic originals. In several countries these three items are only partially covered. In the case of Turkey, which still adheres to the 1968 version of SNA, they are not included at all.

Note that in the table, OECD total excludes the Czech Republic, Hungary, Poland and the Slovak Republic.

Long-term trends

The total investment rate now averages 21% for the OECD as a whole but rates are substantially higher than this in Korea, Spain, Iceland and Australia and well below 20% in Sweden, United Kingdom, Germany and Norway. For the OECD as a whole, total investment rates are largely unchanged compared to 1993-1995. Particularly sharp falls occurred in Korea, Turkey, Japan and Germany, although in Korea and Japan, investment rates remain well above the OECD average. Total investment rates are now much higher than at the beginning of the 1990s in Ireland, Iceland, Spain and Greece.

Investment in machinery and equipment accounts for more than 30% of GFCF in most OECD countries, but investment rates tend to be higher than this in countries with a significant manufacturing base, such as Japan and Switzerland. Over the period shown, the machinery investment rates have fallen in most countries, with particularly sharp falls in Luxembourg, Korea, Ireland and the Netherlands, reflecting higher growth of service activities. Rates grew most in Greece and Iceland.

Investment rates in dwellings were particularly high at both the beginning and the end of the period in Norway and Portugal. Ireland, Spain and the Slovak Republic recorded substantial increases over the period, but a number of countries recorded large falls: Turkey, Luxembourg, Germany, Japan and Austria. In the short term, rates of investment in dwellings are sensitive to the business cycle, but, over the long run, investment rates in dwellings reflect population growth rates either through natural growth or immigration, and rising affluence, as is evident for Ireland and Norway.

Sources

- OECD (2007), *National Accounts of OECD Countries*, OECD, Paris.
- For Brazil, Russian Federation and South Africa: OECD (2007), *Main Economic Indicators*, OECD, Paris.
- For China: National Bureau of Statistics.

Further information

Analytical publications

- OECD (2007), *OECD Economic Outlook: December No. 82 – Volume 2007 Issue 2*, OECD, Paris.

Methodological publications

- Ahmad, N. (2004), "Towards More Harmonised Estimates of Investment in Software", *OECD Economic Studies*, No. 37, 2003/2, OECD, Paris.
- OECD (2000), *OECD Glossaries, System of National Accounts, 1993 – Glossary*, OECD, Paris.
- UN, OECD, IMF, Eurostat (eds.) (1993), *System of National Accounts 1993*, United Nations, Geneva, *http://unstats.un.org/unsd/sna1993*.

Websites

- OECD Economic Outlook – Sources and Methods, *www.oecd.org/eco/sources-and-methods*.

Gross fixed capital formation
As a percentage of GDP

	1993	1994	1995	1996	1997	1998	1999	2000	2001	2002	2003	2004	2005	2006
Australia	22.7	23.9	22.9	22.9	24.0	24.2	24.8	22.0	22.9	24.8	25.4	25.8	26.5	26.9
Austria	22.5	22.9	22.1	22.1	22.3	22.4	22.1	22.8	22.1	20.4	21.3	20.7	20.4	20.6
Belgium	19.4	18.9	19.3	19.4	20.0	20.2	20.6	20.8	20.4	19.2	18.8	19.6	20.3	20.7
Canada	18.0	18.8	17.6	17.9	19.8	19.9	19.8	19.2	19.6	19.5	19.6	20.3	21.0	22.0
Czech Republic	27.9	28.2	31.5	32.1	29.9	28.2	27.0	28.0	28.0	27.5	26.7	25.8	25.0	24.6
Denmark	16.9	17.2	18.4	18.6	19.6	20.4	19.8	20.2	19.8	19.6	19.3	19.4	20.4	22.4
Finland	16.4	15.6	16.6	17.1	18.3	19.0	19.0	19.4	19.5	17.9	18.1	18.2	18.9	19.1
France	18.7	18.4	18.1	17.9	17.5	17.9	18.8	19.5	19.5	18.8	18.8	19.3	19.8	20.4
Germany	22.5	22.6	21.9	21.3	21.0	21.1	21.3	21.5	20.0	18.3	17.9	17.5	17.4	18.0
Greece	18.5	17.1	17.0	17.8	18.1	19.4	20.8	21.6	21.5	22.4	24.3	24.4	23.4	25.8
Hungary	18.4	19.6	19.6	20.9	21.7	23.1	23.3	23.0	23.0	23.0	22.1	22.4	22.7	21.8
Iceland	16.4	15.9	15.7	18.9	19.7	24.0	21.8	22.9	21.6	18.1	20.0	23.6	28.2	32.0
Ireland	15.2	16.3	17.3	18.8	20.2	21.7	23.3	23.4	22.6	21.7	22.3	23.6	26.0	26.3
Italy	18.8	18.5	19.1	18.9	18.9	19.3	19.6	20.3	20.3	20.9	20.4	20.5	20.6	20.8
Japan	29.5	28.5	28.0	28.3	27.7	25.9	25.5	25.2	24.7	23.3	23.2	22.7	23.1	23.8
Korea	36.3	36.4	37.3	37.5	35.6	30.3	29.7	31.1	29.5	29.1	29.9	29.5	29.3	29.0
Luxembourg	21.9	20.6	19.9	20.1	21.7	21.8	23.5	20.8	22.6	22.6	21.6	20.8	20.0	18.4
Mexico	18.6	19.4	16.2	17.9	19.5	20.9	21.2	21.4	20.0	19.3	18.9	19.6	19.3	20.4
Netherlands	21.1	20.6	20.8	21.6	21.9	22.2	22.9	21.9	21.1	20.0	19.5	18.8	19.0	19.7
New Zealand	19.0	20.9	22.1	22.0	21.1	20.1	20.9	20.4	20.8	21.4	22.6	23.4	23.8	23.0
Norway	19.6	19.8	19.8	20.2	22.0	25.0	21.9	18.4	18.1	17.9	17.3	18.0	18.8	18.9
Poland	15.1	17.1	17.7	19.8	22.4	24.1	24.4	23.7	20.7	18.7	18.2	18.1	18.2	19.9
Portugal	21.9	21.9	22.5	23.0	25.2	26.5	26.8	27.1	26.5	25.0	22.9	22.6	21.7	21.0
Slovak Republic	29.5	26.2	24.6	31.4	33.6	35.7	29.3	25.7	28.5	27.3	25.0	24.1	26.8	26.4
Spain	20.8	20.7	21.5	21.4	21.8	23.0	24.6	25.8	26.0	26.3	27.2	28.0	29.3	30.4
Sweden	15.4	15.3	15.7	15.9	15.5	16.3	17.0	17.6	17.5	16.8	16.3	16.4	17.4	18.1
Switzerland	23.1	23.5	23.3	22.1	21.6	22.2	22.2	22.7	21.9	21.3	20.5	20.8	21.2	21.3
Turkey	26.5	24.6	23.8	25.1	26.4	24.6	21.9	22.4	18.2	16.6	15.5	17.8	19.6	21.0
United Kingdom	16.1	16.3	16.8	17.0	17.0	18.0	17.7	17.4	17.1	17.1	16.7	17.1	17.2	17.9
United States	16.7	17.2	17.7	18.2	18.6	19.1	19.6	19.9	19.2	17.9	17.9	18.5	19.2	19.3
EU15 total	19.6	19.4	19.5	19.4	19.4	20.0	20.4	20.7	20.3	19.7	19.6	19.7	20.1	20.7
OECD total	20.5	20.5	20.5	20.8	21.0	20.9	21.1	21.3	20.7	19.8	19.7	20.0	20.5	21.0
Brazil	..	..	18.3	16.9	17.4	17.0	15.7	16.8	17.0	16.4	15.3	16.1	15.9	..
China	36.0	34.5	33.0	32.4	31.8	33.0	33.6	34.3	34.6	36.3	39.2	40.6	41.5	..
India	..	..	..	..	..	..	..	23.0	22.8	23.6	24.3	25.9	27.7	29.1
Russian Federation	..	..	21.1	20.0	18.3	16.1	14.4	16.9	18.9	17.9	18.4	18.4	17.8	17.9
South Africa	14.7	15.2	15.9	16.3	16.5	17.1	15.5	15.1	15.1	15.5	15.0	15.9	16.1	18.7

StatLink http://dx.doi.org/10.1787/272576005608

Gross fixed capital formation
As a percentage of GDP

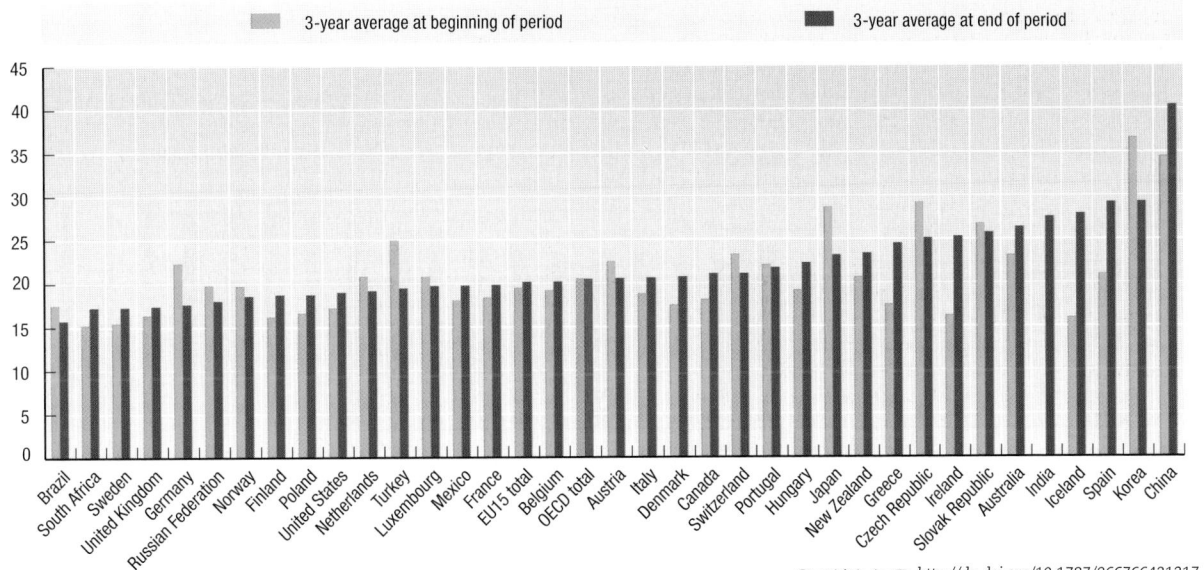

3-year average at beginning of period   3-year average at end of period

StatLink http://dx.doi.org/10.1787/266766431317

Gross fixed capital formation in machinery and equipment

As a percentage of GDP

	1993	1994	1995	1996	1997	1998	1999	2000	2001	2002	2003	2004	2005	2006
Australia	7.6	8.5	8.3	8.1	8.4	8.1	8.3	7.9	7.7	8.1	7.9	8.1	8.2	..
Austria	8.3	8.2	8.0	8.1	8.3	8.4	8.5	9.2	9.1	8.1	8.6	8.1	8.0	7.8
Canada	5.6	5.9	6.1	6.1	7.2	7.6	7.7	7.4	7.0	6.6	6.3	6.3	6.3	6.2
Denmark	7.0	7.4	8.0	7.3	7.8	8.3	7.8	8.1	8.0	7.6	7.1	7.0	7.5	8.4
Finland	5.8	5.7	6.3	6.7	7.1	6.9	6.3	6.1	6.3	5.5	5.5	5.4	5.2	5.1
France	5.5	5.5	5.6	5.6	5.4	5.7	6.1	6.3	6.2	5.6	5.5	5.4	5.4	5.6
Germany	7.7	7.2	7.0	7.0	7.2	7.6	7.9	8.6	7.9	7.1	6.9	7.0	7.2	7.5
Greece	..	..	4.9	5.7	5.5	6.2	7.1	7.6	7.4	8.4	9.5	9.6	9.1	9.2
Hungary	..	..	..	..	..	..	..	10.7	10.0	9.2	9.2	9.4	9.1	..
Iceland	4.3	4.6	5.0	7.3	7.1	8.8	6.9	8.5	6.9	4.9	4.6	5.9	10.1	..
Ireland	5.9	6.2	6.7	6.8	6.6	7.3	7.6	7.2	6.0	5.4	4.7	4.6	5.2	4.5
Italy	7.2	7.6	8.2	8.2	8.4	8.9	9.1	9.5	9.3	9.3	8.6	8.6	8.5	8.6
Japan	10.0	9.3	10.0	10.7	10.7	10.0	10.0	10.0	9.9	8.9	8.9	9.0	9.5	..
Korea	12.4	13.6	14.1	14.1	12.2	8.4	10.3	12.8	11.0	10.4	9.6	9.2	9.0	8.9
Luxembourg	9.9	8.1	7.9	7.5	9.3	8.6	10.5	8.0	8.9	7.5	5.8	6.2	5.7	5.1
Mexico	8.6	8.9	7.6	8.9	10.0	11.1	11.0	10.8	9.7	8.9	8.5	8.7	..	..
Netherlands	7.3	7.0	7.3	7.5	7.6	7.4	7.7	6.9	6.3	5.7	5.7	5.4	5.3	5.8
New Zealand	9.1	9.8	9.8	9.4	8.4	8.2	8.2	8.7	9.3	8.8	8.9	8.8	8.9	..
Norway	5.4	6.1	6.0	6.3	6.9	8.0	7.3	6.4	5.9	5.7	5.2	5.5	5.5	5.0
Poland	..	..	7.6	8.7	9.7	10.4	10.2	9.7	8.2	7.3	7.0	7.1	7.2	..
Portugal	7.4	7.6	7.4	7.7	8.6	9.3	9.4	9.5	8.9	7.8	7.1	7.1	6.8	6.7
Slovak Republic	13.4	12.1	11.4	14.1	16.8	17.8	12.9	11.0	13.5	13.3	12.4	11.4	13.3	14.1
Spain	5.3	5.6	6.0	6.3	6.8	7.5	7.9	8.1	7.6	7.0	6.9	6.9	7.1	7.5
Sweden	5.8	6.6	7.4	7.6	7.6	7.9	8.5	8.6	8.0	7.4	7.2	6.9	7.4	7.4
Switzerland	10.5	10.2	10.6	10.6	10.6	11.1	11.3	11.6	10.9	10.1	9.5	9.5	9.7	..
United Kingdom	6.8	7.2	7.7	8.1	7.7	8.7	8.2	8.0	7.5	6.8	6.1	5.8	5.8	5.8
United States	6.4	6.7	7.1	7.2	7.2	7.3	7.4	7.4	6.6	5.8	5.6	5.6	5.8	5.8
Brazil	..	..	8.8	7.4	7.5	6.9	6.1	7.2	7.8	7.3	7.2	7.7	7.9	..

StatLink http://dx.doi.org/10.1787/272584530027

Gross fixed capital formation in machinery and equipment

As a percentage of GDP

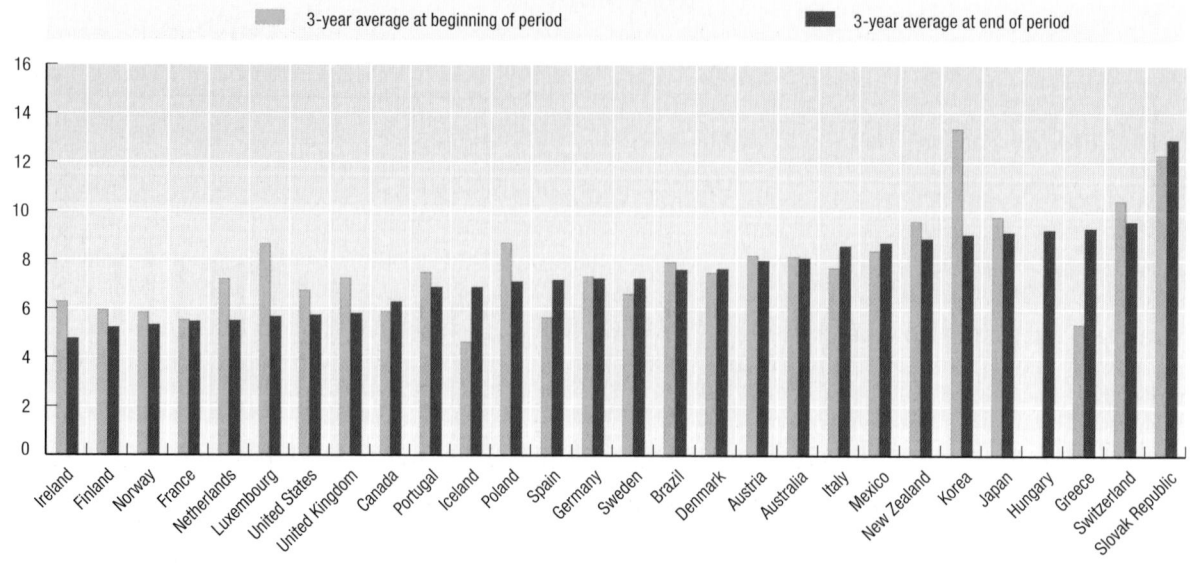

StatLink http://dx.doi.org/10.1787/266822583878

OECD FACTBOOK 2008 – ISBN 978-92-64-04054-0 – © OECD 2008

Gross fixed capital formation in housing
As a percentage of GDP

	1993	1994	1995	1996	1997	1998	1999	2000	2001	2002	2003	2004	2005	2006
Australia	6.7	6.8	5.7	5.5	6.1	6.3	7.1	5.9	6.7	7.6	8.0	7.6	7.1	..
Austria	5.8	6.1	6.6	6.6	6.5	6.1	5.8	5.3	4.9	4.6	4.4	4.4	4.4	4.5
Canada	5.5	5.5	4.5	4.8	5.0	4.7	4.6	4.5	5.0	5.7	6.0	6.5	6.6	6.8
Denmark	3.0	3.2	3.5	3.6	3.9	3.9	4.0	4.2	3.9	3.8	4.3	4.7	5.3	5.8
Finland	4.0	3.9	3.7	3.7	4.4	4.7	5.2	5.3	4.7	4.5	4.9	5.2	5.6	5.8
France	4.3	4.4	4.3	4.2	4.1	4.1	4.2	4.1	4.1	4.1	4.2	4.3	4.6	4.9
Germany	7.1	7.8	7.7	7.6	7.4	7.2	7.2	6.8	6.3	5.8	5.7	5.5	5.2	5.4
Greece	8.4	7.2	7.1	6.8	7.0	7.4	7.5	6.8	6.8	6.7	7.1	7.0	6.7	7.8
Hungary	..	..	..	..	..	..	..	3.5	4.4	4.8	5.0	5.3	4.6	..
Iceland	6.6	6.4	6.1	6.7	6.9	7.0	7.5	7.7	7.3	7.7	8.3	9.1	9.8	..
Ireland	4.1	5.0	5.3	6.0	6.7	7.2	8.0	8.4	8.6	8.8	10.6	12.2	14.0	14.6
Italy	4.7	4.5	4.3	4.1	3.9	3.7	3.7	3.8	3.8	3.8	3.9	4.0	4.3	4.4
Japan	5.2	5.5	5.2	5.7	5.0	4.3	4.3	4.3	4.0	3.9	3.8	3.8	3.8	..
Korea	8.1	7.3	7.3	7.0	6.5	6.0	5.1	4.3	4.7	5.0	5.5	5.7	5.8	5.6
Luxembourg	4.3	3.5	3.3	2.9	2.9	3.0	2.6	2.4	2.8	2.3	2.6	2.5	2.3	2.1
Mexico	5.0	5.1	4.8	4.6	4.6	4.6	4.7	4.8	4.7	4.7	4.6	4.7	..	..
Netherlands	5.5	5.7	5.6	5.7	5.8	5.8	5.9	5.9	6.1	5.8	5.7	5.9	6.2	6.4
New Zealand	4.7	5.5	5.6	5.8	5.9	5.0	5.7	4.8	4.6	5.7	6.6	6.9	6.7	..
Norway	13.6	13.2	13.4	13.5	14.3	16.4	14.3	11.7	11.9	11.9	11.9	12.3	12.9	13.3
Poland	..	..	2.2	2.2	2.4	2.6	2.8	3.0	2.8	2.8	2.7	2.6	2.8	..
Portugal	11.9	11.7	12.3	12.4	13.6	13.8	13.6	13.8	14.0	13.4	12.2	12.0	11.4	10.8
Slovak Republic	..	..	1.2	1.4	1.8	3.0	3.8	4.4	3.5	3.3	3.1	3.0	3.0	2.6
Spain	4.2	4.2	4.4	4.8	4.7	5.0	5.5	6.1	6.5	7.1	7.8	8.4	8.9	9.3
Sweden	3.3	2.0	1.5	1.6	1.4	1.4	1.5	1.7	1.9	2.1	2.1	2.5	2.8	3.2
Switzerland	4.8	5.6	5.6	4.8	4.4	4.4	4.2	4.1	4.0	3.9	4.4	4.8	5.0	..
Turkey	8.6	9.5	8.4	7.8	7.6	7.0	6.6	5.3	5.2	3.8	3.2	3.5	4.9	6.6
United Kingdom	3.1	3.1	3.1	2.9	2.9	2.9	2.8	2.9	3.0	3.3	3.4	3.7	3.9	4.2
United States	4.0	4.3	4.1	4.3	4.2	4.5	4.6	4.6	4.7	4.9	5.3	5.8	6.2	5.8
Brazil	..	..	8.0	8.2	8.6	8.8	8.3	8.3	7.9	7.7	6.8	7.0	6.7	..

StatLink http://dx.doi.org/10.1787/272610430086

Gross fixed capital formation in housing
As a percentage of GDP

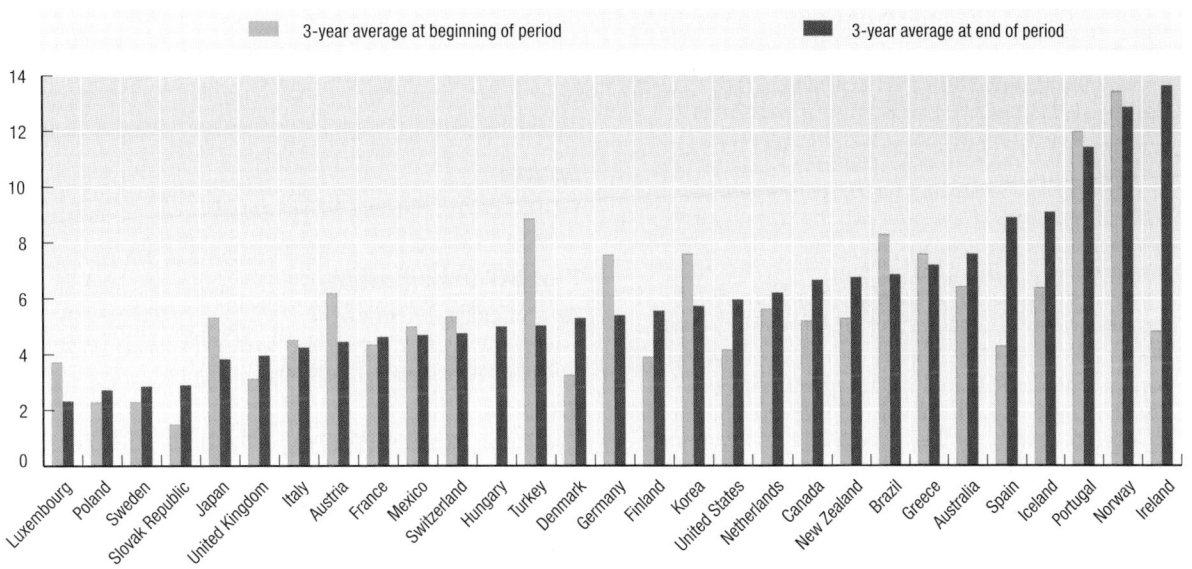

StatLink http://dx.doi.org/10.1787/266862878511

INFLATION

There are several ways in which inflation can be measured. The most common is by reference to a consumer price index (CPI) which measures the changes in prices of a basket of goods and services purchased by a representative set of households. The CPI is a narrow measure of inflation and does not measure changes in the prices of other goods and services, such as those used for intermediate consumption or the prices of capital products. A much broader indicator of inflation is provided by the GDP deflator, and this is the inflation measure shown here.

Definition

The GDP deflator is an implicit, not an explicit deflator. It is derived by dividing an index of GDP measured in current prices by a chain volume index of GDP (see Evolution of GDP), both derived using the expenditure approach (see Size of GDP). It is therefore a weighted average of the price indices of:

- goods and services consumed by households;
- expenditure by government on goods, services and salaries;
- fixed capital assets;
- changes in inventories;
- exports of goods and services;
- imports of goods and services (minus).

While the CPI measures the price changes of goods and services consumed by households, the GDP deflator measures the price changes of the goods and services produced by a country. Hence, the treatment of exports and imports merits special attention. The GDP deflator will go up, indicating more inflation, if the prices of exports rise; although higher inflation is usually thought of as a bad thing, it may actually be beneficial to a country if the prices of its exports rise, since it is non-residents who pay the higher prices. Final expenditures include imports and they need to be subtracted to measure expenditures on GDP. It follows that price changes in imports need to be subtracted from price changes in final expenditures to measure price changes in GDP. However, changes in import prices may not be directly reflected in the prices of final expenditures; they may be absorbed by domestic producers, such as manufacturers, wholesalers or retailers, for a period of time.

Comparability

The comparability of the inflation rates shown here depends on the methods used to calculate in volume terms the expenditure components of GDP. Most countries use similar methods for consumer goods and imports and exports, but there are clear differences in the methods used to derive volume estimates for government consumption.

Some countries calculate their volume estimates of government consumption by deflating their current price estimates using representative input price indexes, while others weight together output indicators for services provided by hospitals, schools, etc.

Note that in the table, OECD total excludes the Czech Republic, Hungary, Poland and the Slovak Republic.

Long-term trends

During the period 1993-2006, inflation in the OECD area fell to a record low of 1.2% in 1999. It then gradually increased to 2.5% in 2006.

The average annual rate of inflation over the last three years was below 5% for all OECD countries, except Norway, Mexico and Turkey. The volatility in the Norwegian GDP deflator is mostly due to variations in the export prices of petroleum, and these grew very strongly over the last few years. The strong growth in the GDP deflator for Mexico and Turkey reflects general domestic inflation. These latter two countries have, however, drastically reduced their inflation rates over the period 1993-2006. At the other extreme, Finland, Germany, Korea, Japan, Sweden and Switzerland recorded average annual rates of inflation over the last three years of below 1%.

Several countries (Canada, Czech Republic, Finland, Germany, Luxembourg, Norway and Switzerland) recorded deflation over the period 1993-2006 for one or more years, but Japan is the only country where this has been sustained over a number of years.

Source
- OECD (2007), *National Accounts of OECD Countries*, OECD, Paris.

Further information
Analytical publications
- OECD (2007), *OECD Economic Outlook: December No. 82 – Volume 2007 Issue 2*, OECD, Paris.

Websites
- Inflation Measures: Too High – Too Low – Internationally Comparable? Documents for the meeting held at the OECD, 21-22 June 2005, *www.oecd.org/std/price-indices*.
- OECD Purchasing Power Parities, *www.oecd.org/std/ppp*.

OECD FACTBOOK 2008 – ISBN 978-92-64-04054-0 – © OECD 2008

GDP deflator

Annual growth in percentage

	1993	1994	1995	1996	1997	1998	1999	2000	2001	2002	2003	2004	2005	2006
Australia	0.9	1.2	2.3	1.3	1.3	0.1	2.1	4.8	2.9	3.0	3.3	3.9	4.8	4.9
Austria	2.7	2.7	1.9	1.0	0.0	0.3	0.6	1.8	1.8	1.4	1.2	2.1	1.8	1.8
Belgium	4.0	2.1	1.2	0.5	1.1	2.1	0.4	1.8	2.0	1.9	1.6	2.4	2.5	2.0
Canada	1.4	1.1	2.3	1.6	1.2	-0.4	1.7	4.1	1.1	1.1	3.3	3.2	3.4	2.4
Czech Republic	21.0	13.4	10.2	10.3	8.4	11.1	2.8	1.5	4.9	2.8	0.9	4.5	-0.2	1.7
Denmark	0.7	1.5	1.3	2.0	2.0	1.2	1.7	3.0	2.5	2.3	1.6	2.0	3.2	2.2
Finland	2.0	1.4	4.8	-0.2	2.2	3.4	0.9	2.6	3.0	1.3	-0.4	0.6	0.2	1.2
France	1.5	1.3	1.3	1.6	1.0	0.9	0.0	1.4	2.0	2.4	1.9	1.6	1.7	2.3
Germany	3.7	2.4	1.9	0.5	0.3	0.6	0.4	-0.7	1.2	1.4	1.2	1.1	0.7	0.6
Greece	14.4	11.2	9.8	7.3	6.8	5.2	3.0	3.4	2.7	3.7	3.5	3.4	3.3	3.4
Hungary	21.3	19.5	26.7	21.2	18.5	12.6	8.4	9.9	8.5	7.8	5.8	4.4	2.2	3.7
Iceland	1.8	2.6	3.0	2.5	3.0	4.8	3.2	3.6	8.6	5.6	0.6	2.5	2.9	8.9
Ireland	5.2	1.7	3.0	2.3	3.9	7.0	4.4	5.5	5.4	4.5	2.5	2.1	2.6	2.3
Italy	3.9	3.6	5.0	5.2	2.5	2.6	1.3	2.0	3.0	3.4	3.1	2.9	2.2	1.8
Japan	0.5	0.1	-0.5	-0.6	0.6	0.0	-1.3	-1.7	-1.2	-1.5	-1.6	-1.1	-1.3	-0.9
Korea	6.3	7.8	7.4	5.1	4.6	5.8	-0.1	0.7	3.5	2.8	2.7	2.7	-0.2	-0.4
Luxembourg	6.0	3.5	2.3	3.0	-1.9	-0.4	5.3	2.0	0.1	2.1	5.0	1.7	4.2	6.2
Mexico	9.5	8.3	37.9	30.7	17.7	15.4	15.1	12.1	5.8	7.0	8.5	7.4	5.5	4.5
Netherlands	1.6	2.1	2.1	1.3	2.6	1.9	1.8	4.1	5.1	3.8	2.2	0.7	2.1	1.9
New Zealand	1.6	1.8	2.0	1.3	2.2	1.3	0.7	3.5	3.8	0.5	3.2	2.9	3.0	2.4
Norway	2.3	-0.2	3.0	4.2	2.8	-0.8	6.6	15.7	1.7	-1.8	3.0	5.3	8.7	8.5
Poland	30.6	37.2	28.0	17.9	13.9	11.1	6.0	7.3	3.5	2.2	0.4	4.1	2.6	1.4
Portugal	7.4	7.3	3.4	2.6	3.8	3.8	3.3	3.0	3.7	3.9	3.2	2.4	2.6	2.9
Slovak Republic	15.4	13.4	9.9	4.6	4.6	5.1	7.5	9.7	5.0	4.6	4.7	6.0	2.4	2.7
Spain	4.5	3.9	4.9	3.5	2.4	2.5	2.6	3.5	4.2	4.3	4.1	4.0	4.2	4.0
Sweden	3.0	2.7	3.7	0.9	1.5	0.6	0.9	1.5	2.3	1.6	1.9	0.2	0.9	1.8
Switzerland	2.4	1.3	0.7	0.2	-0.1	0.3	0.6	1.1	0.8	0.5	1.0	0.6	0.3	1.6
Turkey	67.8	106.5	87.2	77.8	81.5	75.7	55.6	49.9	54.8	44.1	22.5	9.9	5.4	11.5
United Kingdom	2.7	1.6	2.7	3.5	2.9	2.7	2.2	1.3	2.2	3.1	3.1	2.6	2.3	2.6
United States	2.3	2.1	2.0	1.9	1.7	1.1	1.4	2.2	2.4	1.8	2.1	2.9	3.2	3.2
Euro area	3.5	2.7	2.7	2.0	1.4	1.6	0.9	1.4	2.4	2.6	2.1	2.0	1.9	1.9
EU15 total	3.2	2.4	2.7	2.2	1.7	1.7	1.2	1.4	2.4	2.6	2.3	2.1	2.0	2.0
OECD total	2.1	1.8	2.1	1.7	1.7	1.4	1.2	1.8	2.2	2.1	2.2	2.3	2.3	2.5
Brazil	..	..	..	17.1	7.6	4.2	8.5	6.2	9.0	10.6	13.7	8.0	7.5	4.3
Russian Federation	..	..	178.2	45.8	15.1	18.6	72.5	37.6	16.5	15.5	14.0	20.1	19.2	16.1
South Africa	..	9.6	10.3	8.0	8.1	7.7	7.1	8.8	7.7	10.5	4.6	5.5	5.2	7.2

StatLink http://dx.doi.org/10.1787/272648160131

GDP deflator

Average annual growth in percentage

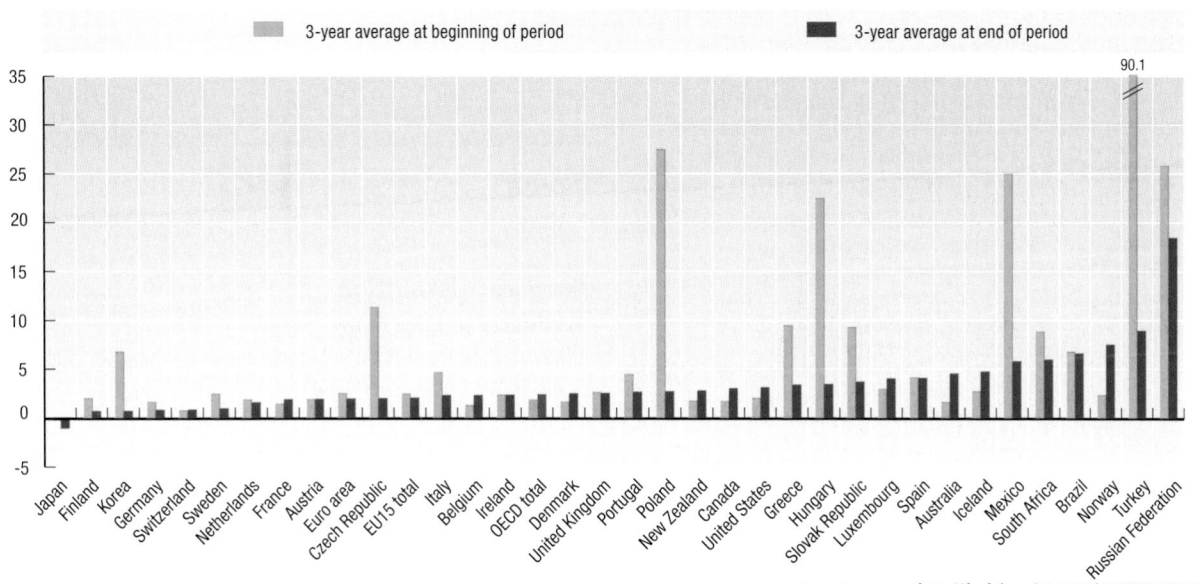

StatLink http://dx.doi.org/10.1787/266887772736

STEEL PRODUCTION

Steel is a core commodity in industrial societies. The OECD regularly monitors capacity, production, consumption, trade and employment in steel for its member countries as well as for all other major steel producing countries and areas.

The table omits production by minor steel producing countries (those with less than 2 million tonnes of production per year).

Definition

Steel production is here measured in tonnes of crude steel. Total crude steel is defined as the total output of usable ingots, continuously cast semi-finished products, and liquid steel for castings.

Comparability

The data on crude steel production are compiled by the International Iron and Steel Institute and are compatible across countries. The data comprise figures submitted by steel companies and associations in more than 70 countries which account for more than 99.5% of total world crude steel production. Non-reporting countries are estimated using independent sources.

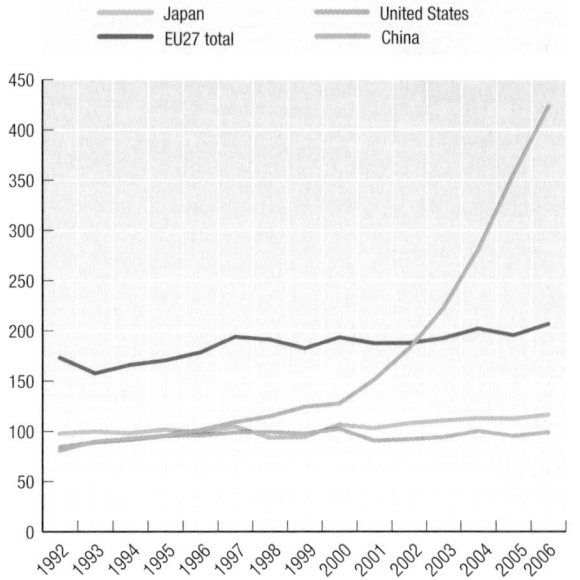

Steel production in selected countries
Million tonnes

Japan — United States — EU27 total — China

StatLink http://dx.doi.org/10.1787/267011772358

Long-term trends

Since 1992, world steel production has grown at an average rate of 3.9% per year. Annual production growth in the OECD countries averaged only 1.6%. Experience within the OECD has been mixed with falling production in the United Kingdom, Luxembourg, and the Czech Republic, while strong growth has been observed in Korea, Mexico, Turkey and, from a low base, in Austria and Finland.

Among the non-OECD countries, steel production in China has been growing at an average of almost 13% per year, more than 7% in India and 2% in Brazil. In the Russian Federation, growth has averaged only 0.4% per annum, though production levels have been recovering well in the latter half of the period.

By the end of the period, China had extended its position as the world's largest steel producer. Its production in 2006 of 423 million tonnes was more than three and half times that of the second largest producing country, Japan. The next largest producers were the United States, Russian Federation, and Korea.

Source

- OECD (2006), *Iron and Steel Industry in 2004: 2006 Edition*, OECD, Paris.

Further information
Statistical publications

- OECD (2005), *Developments in Steelmaking Capacity of Non-OECD Economies, 2003 Edition*, OECD, Paris.

Steel production

Million tonnes

	1993	1994	1995	1996	1997	1998	1999	2000	2001	2002	2003	2004	2005	2006
Australia	7.7	8.4	8.5	8.4	8.8	8.9	8.2	7.1	7.0	7.5	7.5	7.4	7.8	7.9
Austria	4.2	4.4	5.0	4.4	5.2	5.3	5.2	5.7	5.9	6.2	6.3	6.5	7.0	7.1
Belgium	10.2	11.3	11.6	10.8	10.7	11.4	10.9	11.6	10.7	11.3	11.1	11.7	10.4	11.6
Canada	14.4	13.9	14.4	14.7	15.6	15.9	16.2	16.6	15.3	16.0	15.9	16.3	15.3	15.5
Czech Republic	6.8	7.1	7.2	6.5	6.8	6.5	5.6	6.2	6.3	6.5	6.8	7.0	6.2	6.9
Finland	3.3	3.4	3.2	3.3	3.7	4.0	4.0	4.1	3.9	4.0	4.8	4.8	4.7	5.1
France	17.1	18.0	18.1	17.6	19.8	20.1	20.2	21.0	19.3	20.3	19.8	20.8	19.5	19.6
Germany	37.6	40.8	42.0	39.8	45.0	44.0	42.1	46.4	44.8	45.0	44.8	46.4	44.5	47.2
Italy	25.7	26.2	27.8	23.9	25.8	25.7	24.9	26.8	26.5	26.1	27.1	28.6	29.4	31.6
Japan	99.6	98.3	101.6	98.8	104.6	93.6	94.2	106.4	102.9	107.8	110.5	112.7	112.5	116.2
Korea	33.0	33.8	36.8	38.9	42.6	39.9	41.0	43.1	43.9	45.4	46.3	47.5	47.8	48.5
Luxembourg	3.3	3.1	2.6	2.5	2.6	2.5	2.6	2.6	2.7	2.7	2.7	2.7	2.2	2.8
Mexico	9.2	10.3	12.2	13.2	14.2	14.2	15.3	15.6	13.3	14.0	15.2	16.7	16.2	16.3
Netherlands	6.0	6.2	6.4	6.3	6.6	6.4	6.1	5.7	6.0	6.1	6.6	6.8	6.9	6.4
Poland	9.9	11.1	11.9	10.4	11.6	9.9	8.8	10.5	8.8	8.4	9.1	10.6	8.4	10.0
Slovak Republic	3.9	4.0	4.0	3.6	3.8	3.4	3.6	3.7	4.0	4.3	4.6	4.5	4.5	5.1
Spain	13.0	13.4	13.8	12.2	13.7	14.8	14.9	15.9	16.5	16.4	16.3	17.6	17.8	18.4
Sweden	4.6	5.0	5.0	4.9	..	5.2	5.1	5.2	5.5	5.8	5.7	6.0	5.7	5.5
Turkey	11.5	12.6	13.2	13.6	14.5	14.1	14.3	14.3	15.0	16.5	18.3	20.5	21.0	23.3
United Kingdom	16.6	17.3	17.6	18.0	18.5	17.3	16.3	15.2	13.5	11.7	13.3	13.8	13.2	13.9
United States	88.8	91.2	95.2	95.5	98.5	98.7	97.4	101.8	90.1	91.6	93.7	99.7	94.9	98.6
EU27 total	157.5	165.9	170.3	178.2	193.9	191.0	182.2	193.4	187.4	187.7	192.5	202.0	195.5	206.6
OECD total	433.1	446.2	464.3	453.4	478.9	468.4	463.1	492.4	468.7	480.6	493.0	515.9	503.7	525.5
Brazil	25.2	25.7	25.1	25.2	26.2	25.8	25.0	27.9	26.7	29.6	31.1	32.9	31.6	30.9
China	89.5	92.6	95.4	101.2	108.9	114.6	124.0	127.2	150.9	182.2	222.4	280.5	355.8	422.7
India	18.2	19.3	22.0	23.8	24.4	23.5	24.3	26.9	27.3	28.8	31.8	32.6	38.1	49.5
Russian Federation	58.4	48.8	51.6	49.3	48.5	43.8	51.5	59.1	59.0	59.8	61.5	65.6	66.1	70.8
World	730.1	726.0	752.2	750.1	798.9	777.3	789.0	847.7	850.4	903.9	969.7	1 068.6	1 138.8	1 230.0

StatLink ⬛ᵐˢˡ *http://dx.doi.org/10.1787/272653518664*

World steel production
Million tonnes

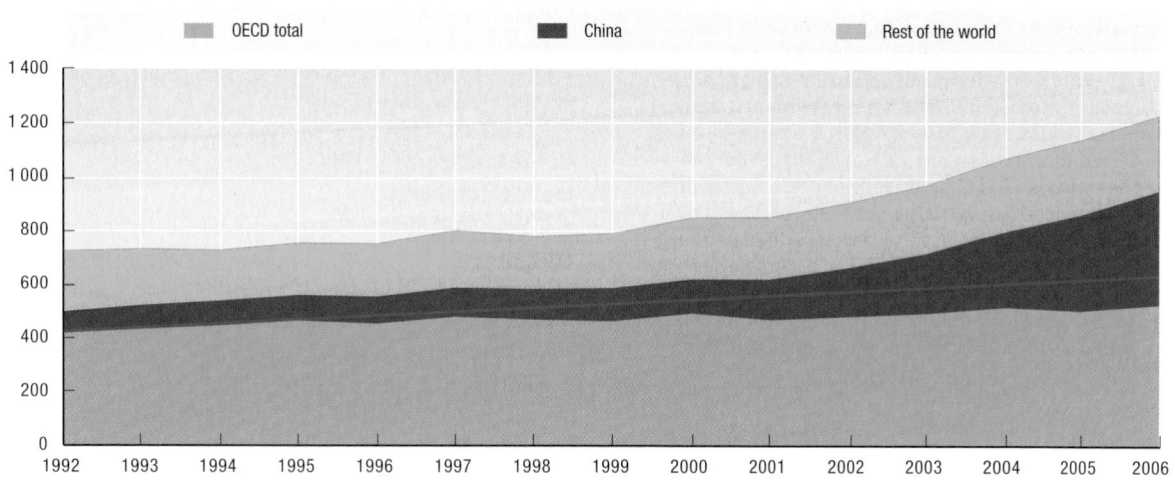

StatLink ⬛ᵐˢˡ *http://dx.doi.org/10.1787/267003332132*

VALUE ADDED BY ACTIVITY

The contributions of primary, secondary and tertiary activities to total value added have changed sharply over recent decades. Agriculture, fishing and forestry are now relatively small in almost all OECD countries. The share of manufacturing has also fallen while services now account for well over 60% of total gross value added in most OECD countries.

Definition

Gross value added is defined as output minus intermediate consumption and equals the sum of employee compensation, gross operating surplus of government and corporations, gross mixed income of unincorporated enterprises and taxes less subsidies on production and imports, except for net taxes on products. The shares of each sector are calculated by dividing the value added in each sector by total value added. Total value added is less than GDP because it excludes value-added tax (VAT) and other product taxes.

In the following analysis, tables and graphs for some industry branches are grouped together as follows: "industry" consists of mining and quarrying, manufacturing, and production and distribution of electricity, gas and water; "trade" consists of retail and wholesale trade and repair services; "real estate" covers rents for dwellings including the imputed rents of owner-occupiers; "government" includes public administration, law and order and defence.

Comparability

All OECD member countries, except for Turkey, follow the international 1993 System of National Accounts, so there is good comparability between countries as regards the definitions of value added and the coverage of the six sectors. However, the decline of industry and the rise of service activities are overstated to some extent because of the move in the last decade towards outsourcing by industrial enterprises of service activities that were previously carried out internally. For example, if cleaning and security services were earlier provided by employees of a manufacturing enterprise, their salaries would have formed part of value added by industry, but if these services are now purchased from specialised producers, the salaries of the employees will form part of the value added of "other business services". There will appear to have been a decline in the share of industry and a rise in the share of services although there may have been no change in the quantity of cleaning and security services actually produced.

Long-term trends

The share of agriculture, etc. has been declining throughout the period in almost all countries and, towards the end of the period, makes a significant contribution only in Iceland (fishing), New Zealand and Turkey. Shares in industry have also been falling throughout the period. Manufacturing is the most important activity within industry except in Norway, where oil and gas production are more important.

All service activities account for around 70% of total gross value added for the OECD countries as a whole, with very high shares in France, Luxembourg and the United Kingdom and rather low shares in the Czech Republic, Korea, Norway and Turkey. It should be noted, however, that, in most countries, the largest part of service value added is goods-related and consists of trade, transport and business services purchased by industry. A high share of service value added does not necessarily mean that a country has become a service economy; the production, transport and distribution of goods remain the predominant activities in most OECD countries in terms of employment and value added.

Source
- OECD (2007), National Accounts of OECD Countries, OECD, Paris.

Further information
Analytical publications
- Lal, K. (2003), Measurement of Output, Value Added, GDP in Canada and the United States, OECD Statistics Working Papers, No. 2003/4, OECD, Paris.
- OECD (1996), Services: Measuring Real Annual Value Added, OECD, Paris.
- OECD (2002), Measuring the Non-Observed Economy: A Handbook, OECD, Paris.

Online databases
- STAN: OECD Structural Analysis Statistics – online database.

Websites
- OECD National Accounts, www.oecd.org/std/national-accounts.
- OECD National Accounts Archive, www.oecd.org/std/national-accounts/papers.

Value added in agriculture and industry
As percentage of total value added

	Agriculture, hunting, forestry and fishing							Industry, including energy						
	1990	1995	2000	2003	2004	2005	2006	1990	1995	2000	2003	2004	2005	2006
Australia	3.6	3.8	4.0	3.5	3.3	3.1	..	23.4	22.4	20.7	19.3	19.8	21.0	..
Austria	4.0	2.7	2.1	1.9	1.9	1.6	1.7	24.9	22.5	23.0	22.2	22.1	22.2	23.0
Belgium	2.1	1.5	1.4	1.1	1.1	0.9	0.9	26.0	23.2	22.0	19.9	19.7	19.3	19.2
Canada	2.9	2.9	2.3	2.1	..	..	..	24.5	25.8	28.2	25.8	..	..	..
Czech Republic	8.7	5.0	3.9	3.1	3.3	2.9	2.6	34.9	31.7	31.6	29.5	32.1	31.4	31.7
Denmark	4.0	3.5	2.6	2.0	1.9	1.5	1.6	20.5	20.4	21.3	19.6	19.4	19.9	20.0
Finland	6.3	4.3	3.5	3.2	3.0	2.9	2.5	25.0	28.4	28.2	26.7	26.1	25.5	26.3
France	3.8	3.4	2.8	2.5	2.5	2.3	2.0	20.1	18.7	17.7	15.9	15.4	14.9	14.4
Germany	1.5	1.3	1.3	1.0	1.1	0.9	0.9	31.3	25.4	25.1	24.5	25.0	25.0	25.4
Greece	9.0	8.9	6.6	5.4	4.7	4.3	3.7	18.1	15.4	13.9	14.8	14.2	15.0	15.7
Hungary	..	8.5	5.4	4.3	4.8	4.3	4.2	..	25.6	27.2	25.1	25.4	25.3	25.4
Iceland	11.2	11.1	8.6	7.5	6.5	5.8	..	20.6	22.4	17.5	16.9	16.5	14.2	..
Ireland	8.9	7.0	3.4	2.5	2.4	2.0	1.7	29.6	32.6	34.7	30.5	27.9	26.2	25.0
Italy	3.5	3.3	2.8	2.5	2.5	2.2	2.1	25.9	25.0	23.4	21.4	21.2	20.6	20.5
Japan	2.5	1.9	1.7	1.6	1.6	1.4	..	28.9	25.2	24.0	22.7	22.9	22.6	..
Korea	8.9	6.3	4.9	3.8	3.8	3.4	3.2	30.2	30.3	32.4	29.4	31.3	31.1	30.5
Luxembourg	1.5	1.0	0.7	0.6	0.6	0.4	0.4	22.3	15.3	12.6	11.0	10.6	9.7	9.3
Mexico	7.8	5.2	4.0	3.8	3.8	..	..	24.2	22.6	22.6	20.3	20.6	..	..
Netherlands	4.4	3.5	2.6	2.3	2.2	2.1	2.2	23.7	21.9	19.3	18.3	18.5	18.5	18.6
New Zealand	6.7	7.2	8.6	6.5	..	..	..	22.7	21.8	20.1	19.1	..	..	..
Norway	3.4	3.1	2.1	1.5	1.6	1.5	1.5	29.3	29.7	37.8	33.4	35.3	38.4	40.5
Poland	..	8.0	5.0	4.4	5.1	4.5	4.4	..	28.4	24.0	23.7	25.2	24.7	25.1
Portugal	9.1	5.8	3.8	3.2	3.2	2.8	2.9	22.4	21.9	20.0	18.8	18.3	17.9	18.1
Slovak Republic	..	5.9	4.5	4.5	4.5	4.3	4.0	..	32.7	29.2	29.0	29.0	28.9	28.1
Spain	5.5	4.5	4.4	4.0	3.6	3.2	2.9	24.4	21.9	20.9	19.0	18.6	18.4	18.2
Sweden	3.6	2.9	2.0	1.9	1.8	1.1	1.3	23.9	26.1	24.6	22.9	23.1	23.1	23.7
Switzerland	2.9	2.1	1.6	1.3	1.4	1.3	1.2	23.6	23.6	21.8	21.2	21.1	21.4	21.9
Turkey	17.6	15.7	14.2	11.9	11.5	10.5	9.4	25.8	26.4	23.5	25.1	25.3	25.9	26.1
United Kingdom	1.8	1.8	1.0	1.0	0.9	0.9	0.9	27.3	25.7	21.9	17.7	17.0	17.4	17.5
United States	2.1	1.6	1.2	1.2	1.4	1.2	..	23.5	22.2	19.4	17.2	17.2	17.6	..
Brazil	..	5.8	5.6	7.4	6.9	5.7	..	..	22.0	22.2	23.2	25.0	24.4	..
Russian Federation	..	..	..	6.7	6.0	5.4	4.8	..	..	..	26.9	30.8	33.1	32.6
South Africa	..	3.9	3.3	3.6	3.2	2.7	2.8	..	31.7	29.3	29.2	28.5	28.4	28.6

StatLink ⬛ http://dx.doi.org/10.1787/272684715810

Value added in industry
As a percentage of total value added, 2006 or latest available year

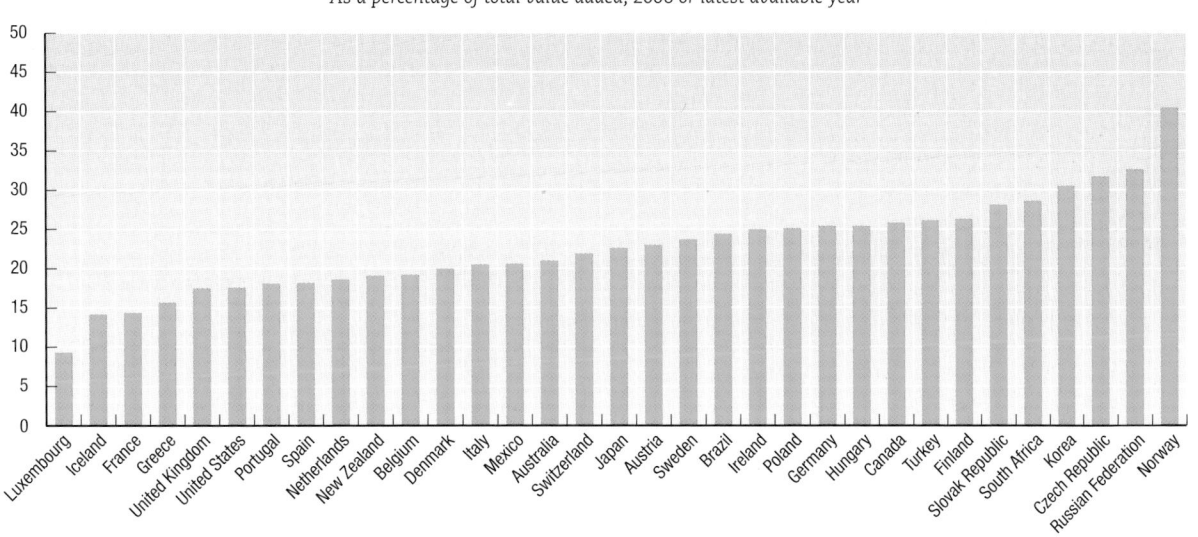

StatLink ⬛ http://dx.doi.org/10.1787/267032354114

Value added in construction and in transport, trade, hotels and restaurants
As percentage of total value added

	Construction							Transport, trade, hotels and restaurants						
	1990	1995	2000	2003	2004	2005	2006	1990	1995	2000	2003	2004	2005	2006
Australia	6.8	6.0	5.4	6.8	6.9	7.0	..	22.8	23.5	22.1	22.3	22.0	21.0	..
Austria	6.9	7.8	7.9	7.7	7.6	7.6	7.7	25.7	24.2	24.4	24.8	24.7	24.2	23.6
Belgium	5.4	5.1	5.0	4.9	4.8	4.8	5.0	22.5	21.9	21.1	22.6	22.9	23.1	23.1
Canada	6.8	4.9	5.0	5.4	..	..	..	21.7	20.7	20.3	21.0	..	..	..
Czech Republic	8.2	6.6	6.5	6.4	6.5	6.7	6.4	16.8	24.4	25.8	26.7	24.4	24.7	25.5
Denmark	5.1	4.7	5.5	5.3	5.5	5.6	6.1	21.9	22.3	21.8	22.0	21.8	22.0	21.5
Finland	8.3	4.4	5.5	5.3	5.4	5.9	6.1	21.8	20.8	21.5	22.9	22.8	22.6	22.3
France	6.6	6.1	5.2	5.3	5.5	5.8	6.3	19.9	19.3	18.9	19.7	19.5	19.2	18.6
Germany	6.1	6.8	5.2	4.4	4.2	3.9	4.0	17.4	18.0	18.2	17.8	17.7	17.7	17.9
Greece	7.1	6.0	7.0	7.9	7.7	7.2	8.6	26.5	27.8	30.1	30.4	31.5	31.0	30.1
Hungary	..	4.5	5.0	4.8	4.9	4.9	4.8	..	22.0	20.8	20.9	20.7	20.4	20.6
Iceland	9.7	8.0	8.6	7.6	8.5	9.5	..	21.8	22.5	21.6	19.4	19.8	18.5	..
Ireland	5.4	5.3	7.5	8.1	8.9	9.5	9.9	20.5	17.3	18.0	17.7	17.5	17.4	16.8
Italy	6.2	5.3	5.0	5.6	5.8	6.0	6.1	23.5	24.2	23.9	23.4	23.4	23.3	23.0
Japan	9.7	8.0	7.1	6.3	6.4	6.1	..	19.1	21.3	20.2	19.6	19.7	19.9	..
Korea	11.3	11.6	8.4	9.6	9.3	9.2	9.1	20.2	18.2	18.2	17.8	17.1	17.0	17.0
Luxembourg	7.1	6.5	5.7	6.5	6.2	6.1	5.3	23.6	21.3	21.8	21.6	21.9	21.3	21.0
Mexico	3.9	3.9	5.1	5.2	5.4	..	..	33.4	29.4	32.2	30.3	30.9	..	..
Netherlands	5.7	5.4	5.6	5.5	5.4	5.4	5.5	21.9	21.7	23.1	22.6	22.5	21.9	21.9
New Zealand	4.1	4.1	4.3	4.9	..	..	..	24.5	24.5	22.1	23.1	..	..	..
Norway	4.6	4.5	4.1	4.4	4.6	4.4	4.6	23.4	22.3	18.8	18.7	17.9	17.1	16.0
Poland	..	6.7	7.7	5.8	5.5	6.0	6.6	..	25.7	27.3	27.6	27.4	27.4	27.6
Portugal	5.7	6.4	7.6	7.1	7.1	6.9	6.5	24.9	24.2	24.1	24.3	24.6	24.7	24.8
Slovak Republic	..	5.1	7.1	6.1	6.3	6.8	6.9	..	24.6	25.1	25.1	25.1	26.1	26.8
Spain	8.6	7.5	8.3	9.9	10.6	11.6	12.2	25.1	26.9	26.1	25.8	25.6	25.1	24.6
Sweden	6.8	4.5	4.0	4.3	4.5	4.6	4.8	19.3	19.1	19.0	19.3	19.3	19.5	19.5
Switzerland	8.3	6.7	5.5	5.7	5.6	5.7	5.6	23.9	22.4	21.4	22.6	22.6	22.4	22.1
Turkey	6.4	5.5	5.2	3.6	3.6	4.5	5.4	31.2	33.2	34.4	35.4	35.7	35.9	35.2
United Kingdom	6.7	5.0	5.3	5.8	5.9	5.7	5.5	21.6	21.4	22.8	22.1	21.9	21.6	21.3
United States	4.6	4.2	4.7	4.8	4.9	5.2	..	21.9	22.2	19.7	19.3	19.1	18.8	..
Brazil	..	5.5	5.5	4.7	5.1	4.9	..	..	..	17.2	16.8	17.3	17.8	..
Russian Federation	..	..	..	6.0	5.7	5.4	5.8	..	..	..	33.3	31.9	30.0	29.8
South Africa	..	3.2	2.5	2.4	2.4	2.5	2.6	..	23.2	24.3	23.4	23.8	23.8	23.6

StatLink ⏩ http://dx.doi.org/10.1787/272752766453

Value added in transport, trade, hotels and restaurants
As a percentage of total value added, 2006 or latest available year

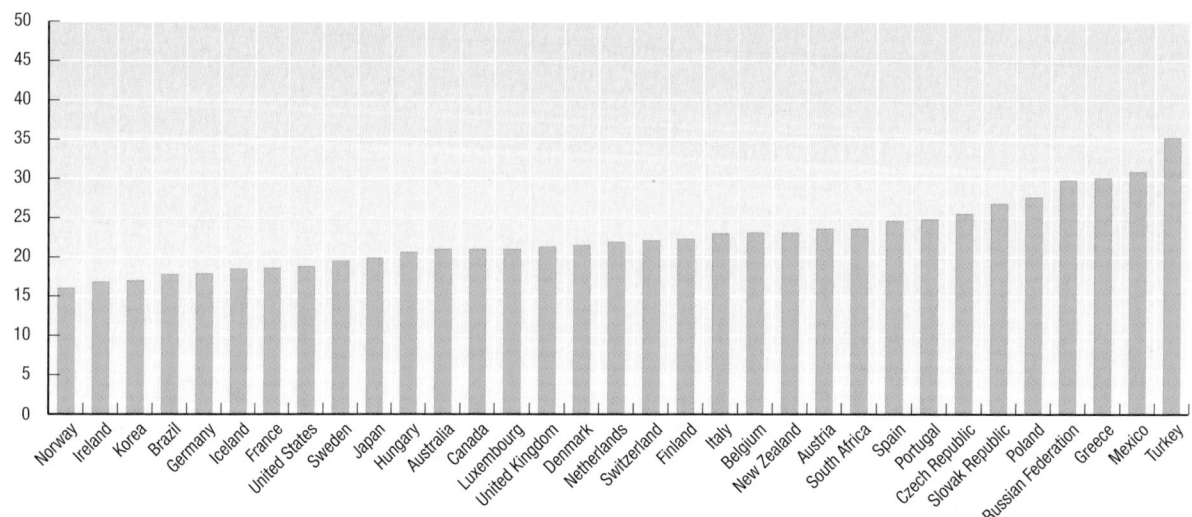

StatLink ⏩ http://dx.doi.org/10.1787/267045458408

OECD FACTBOOK 2008 – ISBN 978-92-64-04054-0 – © OECD 2008

Value added in business services and in government and personal services
As percentage of total value added

	Banks, insurance, real estate and other business services							Government, health, education and other and personal services						
	1990	1995	2000	2003	2004	2005	2006	1990	1995	2000	2003	2004	2005	2006
Australia	25.2	25.9	29.3	29.2	29.0	28.7	..	18.3	18.5	18.5	18.9	18.9	19.2	..
Austria	17.7	19.9	21.7	22.3	23.1	23.5	23.4	20.8	22.8	20.9	20.9	20.7	21.0	20.7
Belgium	22.6	25.6	27.8	27.8	28.0	28.3	28.4	21.5	22.7	22.6	23.7	23.4	23.6	23.4
Canada	22.7	24.2	25.0	25.7	..	..	..	21.4	21.4	19.2	20.0	..	..	..
Czech Republic	16.9	16.8	16.2	16.7	16.5	17.0	16.8	13.4	15.5	16.0	17.6	17.2	17.2	17.0
Denmark	21.5	22.2	22.3	23.5	23.8	23.8	24.1	27.0	26.9	26.4	27.6	27.7	27.1	26.7
Finland	16.2	18.8	20.5	20.0	20.6	20.7	20.9	22.3	23.2	20.8	22.0	22.0	22.4	21.9
France	27.1	28.2	30.7	31.1	31.5	32.0	32.8	22.6	25.1	24.7	25.5	25.6	25.8	25.8
Germany	23.0	26.4	27.5	29.3	29.2	29.7	29.5	20.8	22.2	22.8	23.2	22.9	22.8	22.3
Greece	16.7	20.3	20.6	18.5	18.2	18.4	18.2	20.2	21.3	21.7	23.1	23.7	24.0	23.7
Hungary	..	18.9	20.1	20.9	20.9	21.8	22.3	..	21.3	21.6	24.0	23.3	23.4	22.7
Iceland	16.7	16.3	20.0	22.9	23.9	26.2	..	20.0	21.8	23.6	25.7	24.8	25.8	..
Ireland	16.3	17.3	20.5	23.3	24.2	25.5	26.4	19.2	20.3	15.9	17.8	19.0	19.4	20.2
Italy	20.1	22.4	24.7	26.5	26.6	26.9	27.1	20.7	19.8	20.1	20.5	20.5	21.0	21.3
Japan	20.7	23.1	24.9	26.5	26.2	26.6	..	19.2	20.5	22.1	23.3	23.2	23.4	..
Korea	14.9	18.3	20.1	21.6	20.6	20.9	21.2	14.4	15.3	16.1	17.8	17.8	18.3	18.9
Luxembourg	28.5	39.2	43.8	43.5	43.1	45.7	48.5	17.3	16.7	15.4	16.8	17.5	16.8	15.6
Mexico	13.1	17.4	12.0	13.0	12.8	..	..	17.6	21.5	24.1	27.3	26.5	..	..
Netherlands	20.7	24.2	27.3	26.6	27.0	27.7	27.7	23.6	23.2	22.1	24.5	24.6	24.4	24.1
New Zealand	25.4	25.8	27.1	28.2	..	..	..	16.7	16.5	17.7	18.1	..	..	..
Norway	17.4	17.5	16.9	19.2	18.7	17.9	17.5	21.8	23.0	20.3	22.9	21.9	20.6	19.9
Poland	..	12.6	18.1	18.2	17.6	18.1	17.6	..	18.6	18.0	20.2	19.1	19.2	18.7
Portugal	20.2	19.8	20.6	21.1	20.9	20.9	21.4	18.3	21.9	24.0	25.6	25.9	26.8	26.3
Slovak Republic	..	17.5	17.1	18.0	19.4	18.6	18.9	..	14.3	17.0	17.4	15.7	15.3	15.4
Spain	17.2	17.9	19.5	20.6	20.7	20.9	21.3	19.1	21.3	20.8	20.7	20.8	20.9	20.9
Sweden	20.3	22.9	25.0	24.4	24.4	24.9	24.2	26.3	24.6	25.4	27.2	26.9	26.8	26.5
Switzerland	16.2	18.5	24.0	22.3	22.6	22.6	23.0	25.0	26.7	25.7	26.9	26.8	26.7	26.1
Turkey	6.6	7.4	8.5	9.2	9.5	9.2	9.6	12.4	11.9	14.2	14.9	14.4	14.2	14.1
United Kingdom	21.9	24.5	27.5	30.9	31.5	32.0	32.7	20.6	21.5	21.5	22.5	22.7	22.5	22.3
United States	24.8	26.3	31.6	32.2	32.4	32.4	..	23.2	23.4	23.2	25.3	25.0	24.8	..
Brazil	..	..	26.8	25.9	24.2	25.6	..	..	..	22.6	22.0	21.4	21.7	..
Russian Federation	..	..	..	14.0	12.7	13.6	13.9	..	..	..	13.2	12.9	12.5	13.1
South Africa	..	16.4	18.6	20.0	20.8	21.4	21.7	..	21.7	22.0	21.4	21.4	21.2	20.7

StatLink http://dx.doi.org/10.1787/272763624226

Value added in banks, insurance, real estate and other business services
As a percentage of total value added, 2006 or latest available year

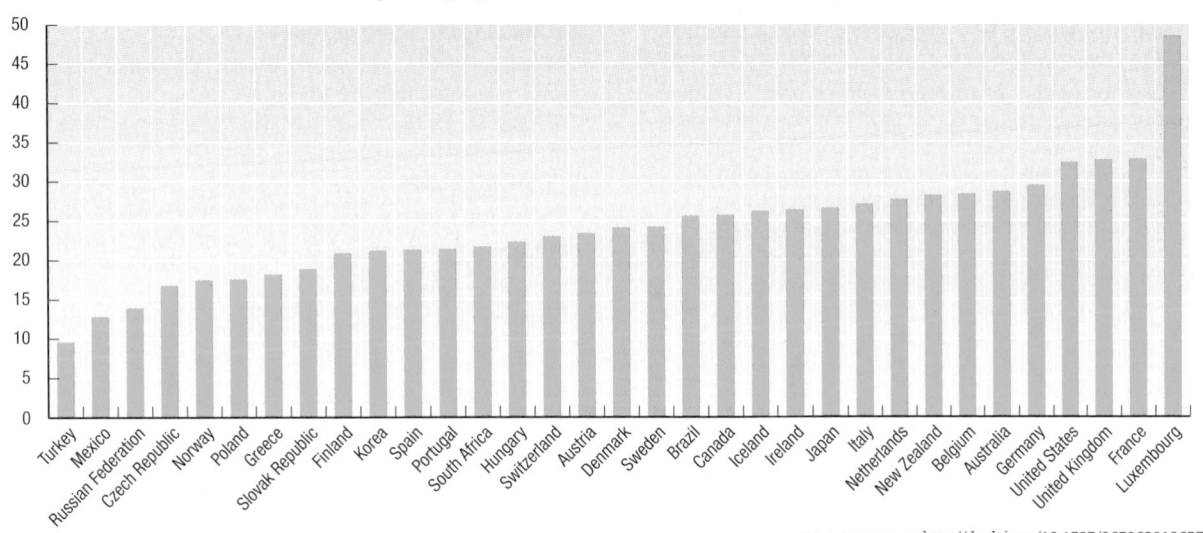

StatLink http://dx.doi.org/10.1787/267062013657

EVOLUTION OF VALUE ADDED BY ACTIVITY

While total GDP has been growing in all OECD countries in most years since 1990, that growth is not evenly spread over all the different kinds of economic activities. Some economic activities have grown faster than others and some have tended to decline in importance. A convenient way to show how the patterns of growth are changing is to divide the economy into primary, secondary and tertiary sectors – agriculture, industry and services, respectively.

Definition

Gross value added is defined as output minus intermediate consumption and equals employee compensation, net operating surplus, net mixed income and depreciation of capital assets. The growth rates shown here refer to volume estimates of gross value added.

Industry consists of mining and quarrying; manufacturing; production and distribution of electricity, gas and water; and construction. Services consists of retail and wholesale trade; transport and communications; real estate, finance, insurance and business services; education, health and other personal services; public administration; and defence.

Comparability

All OECD member countries, except for Turkey, follow the international *System of National Accounts*, so there is good comparability between countries as regards the definitions and coverage. However, the decline of industry and the rise of service activities are overstated to some extent because of the move in the last decade towards outsourcing of service activities that were previously carried out internally within industrial enterprises. For example, if cleaning and security services were earlier provided by employees of a manufacturing enterprise, their salaries would have formed part of value added by industry but if these services are now purchased from specialised producers, the salaries of the employees will form part of the value added of the service sector. No change in the quantity of cleaning and security services produced may have occurred.

Source

- OECD (2007), *National Accounts of OECD Countries*, OECD, Paris.

Further information

Analytical publications

- OECD (2007), *OECD Economic Outlook: December No. 82 – Volume 2007 Issue 2*, OECD, Paris.

Statistical publications

- Maddison, Angus (2003), *The World Economy: Historical Perspectives*, OECD, Paris, also available on CD-ROM, *www.theworldeconomy.org*.
- OECD (2007), *Quaterly National Accounts*, OECD, Paris.

Methodological publications

- OECD (2000), *OECD Glossaries, System of National Accounts, 1993 – Glossary*, OECD, Paris.
- UN, OECD, IMF, Eurostat (eds.) (1993), *System of National Accounts 1993*, United Nations, Geneva.

Online databases

- STAN: OECD Structural Analysis Statistics – online database.

Websites

- OECD National Accounts, *www.oecd.org/std/national-accounts*.

Long-term trends

For OECD countries as a whole, agriculture has been growing by about 1% per year since 1992, industry by 2.6% per year and services by 3% per year.

Annual growth in agriculture is generally very uneven, with changes from year to year of 10% or more being quite common. Growth in industry is somewhat smoother in most countries, while year-to-year growth in services tends to be very smooth in all countries, one reason being that services include government services.

The graphs show growth rates averaged over the three latest years for which data are available. Over this recent period, agriculture declined in eight countries – most pronounced in Ireland, Luxembourg, Japan, Spain and Belgium. Industry grew in most countries, although there was decline in Portugal. The service sector, however, grew in all countries with particularly sharp increases in Iceland, Ireland, Luxembourg and Turkey.

OECD FACTBOOK 2008 – ISBN 978-92-64-04054-0 – © OECD 2008

Real value added in agriculture, forestry and fishing
Annual growth in percentage

	1993	1994	1995	1996	1997	1998	1999	2000	2001	2002	2003	2004	2005	2006
Australia	3.4	-16.9	23.2	7.5	-0.5	10.2	5.2	4.0	3.2	-23.5	31.4	-0.7	3.7	..
Austria	-1.0	5.6	-1.1	-0.1	3.7	6.4	3.7	-3.0	0.3	-3.1	-2.0	4.0	-1.9	-0.3
Belgium	6.2	-6.8	2.2	-0.2	2.8	2.9	2.9	4.2	-5.5	4.3	-7.6	5.3	-5.4	-5.9
Canada	6.7	1.3	1.4	0.1	-3.4	6.2	7.5	-1.8	-9.1	-5.2	9.7	6.5	3.2	..
Czech Republic	51.7	-17.3	-4.9	-3.1	-13.4	6.1	5.3	4.1	-2.8	3.4	3.8	7.8	5.0	-5.3
Denmark	23.5	3.7	5.2	2.2	2.1	2.4	-3.5	8.3	3.8	-3.7	1.0	3.2	9.7	5.2
Finland	5.0	-2.2	-3.8	-2.9	8.9	-9.0	-1.3	8.7	1.9	2.0	-7.0	1.5	3.2	-0.7
France	-4.7	1.5	3.6	5.1	1.7	1.7	3.7	-1.4	-2.8	5.0	-15.3	20.5	-5.8	-2.2
Germany	-1.6	-9.4	5.2	4.0	3.4	-6.0	12.7	-0.4	3.8	-7.0	-5.5	20.7	-10.6	-3.2
Greece	-1.4	5.9	-4.0	-3.3	0.4	2.3	3.5	-3.7	-5.5	-5.6	-5.2	6.8	-2.5	-5.6
Hungary	-7.9	-0.4	2.7	4.2	-0.2	-1.4	0.9	-7.4	16.4	-9.8	0.0	53.4	-1.4	-7.0
Iceland	5.8	-4.8	-0.7	3.8	-0.6	-4.6	-2.3	-1.8	1.5	2.5	-2.9	3.9	-2.4	..
Ireland	..	..	..	7.0	2.0	-1.1	-1.2	-0.4	1.1	-1.0	-1.4	0.9	-21.8	1.1
Italy	-0.6	1.3	1.5	1.5	2.8	2.4	6.0	-2.3	-2.5	-3.1	-4.9	13.1	-4.4	-3.1
Japan	-9.1	2.4	-6.0	2.4	-1.2	2.0	1.0	2.1	-2.4	6.0	-5.9	-7.1	2.3	..
Korea	-6.0	0.4	5.3	2.3	4.6	-6.4	5.9	1.2	1.1	-3.5	-5.3	9.2	0.7	-2.6
Luxembourg	2.9	-5.8	9.4	-3.2	-16.3	15.2	14.4	-13.0	-14.3	11.3	-11.8	-6.2	-7.7	-5.3
Mexico	3.1	0.2	1.8	3.8	0.2	3.0	1.5	0.4	5.9	-0.9	3.8	3.2	..	..
Netherlands	2.8	2.6	2.0	-2.4	7.4	-5.6	5.8	2.1	-4.5	-1.5	4.1	5.8	0.4	-1.9
New Zealand	16.9	0.6	7.4	7.7	0.7	-4.2	4.4	2.5	1.6	-1.5	0.7	0.0	1.4	..
Norway	14.9	2.8	6.7	-0.3	-1.3	1.6	-0.2	-2.7	-2.7	9.0	0.5	12.4	-4.4	0.0
Poland	6.0	-14.9	10.2	1.7	0.2	3.6	-0.5	-4.1	6.6	1.0	2.7	6.8	-1.0	6.7
Portugal	2.3	-2.1	-1.1	4.5	-8.3	-3.5	4.8	-4.2	-3.2	2.3	-2.3	5.8	-7.9	10.1
Slovak Republic	..	8.1	-3.6	-4.1	12.6	-0.9	-8.7	2.3	12.5	16.8	0.9	11.9	15.7	2.6
Spain	2.8	-4.7	-6.1	20.6	7.1	3.1	-1.0	7.3	-2.0	0.4	-0.5	-2.3	-8.6	2.4
Sweden	2.1	-3.7	0.2	-1.0	1.8	-5.6	2.3	2.7	4.9	0.5	0.9	7.7	-5.0	11.6
Switzerland	-4.6	-5.6	4.9	-0.6	-4.9	2.9	-1.7	7.8	-8.2	1.6	-9.2	11.4	-2.7	-2.2
Turkey	-1.3	-0.7	2.0	4.4	-2.3	8.4	-5.0	3.9	-6.5	6.9	-2.5	2.0	5.6	2.9
United Kingdom	-8.1	-1.2	-1.3	-3.3	3.4	2.2	3.3	-0.8	-9.4	12.3	-2.1	-1.0	4.4	2.8
United States	-3.0	6.0	-10.0	5.8	10.3	4.7	11.7	12.7	-7.5	-2.9	11.6	2.0	7.3	..
Brazil	..	..	..	3.0	0.8	3.4	6.5	2.7	6.1	6.6	5.8	2.3	1.0	..
Russian Federation	..	..	..	..	..	..	..	..	..	..	5.3	2.8	1.2	2.4
South Africa	..	7.5	-19.0	22.7	0.6	-5.3	6.2	4.7	-3.3	6.5	-2.1	1.4	5.4	-7.9

StatLink http://dx.doi.org/10.1787/272782202070

Real value added in agriculture, forestry and fishing
Annual growth in percentage averaged over the latest three available years

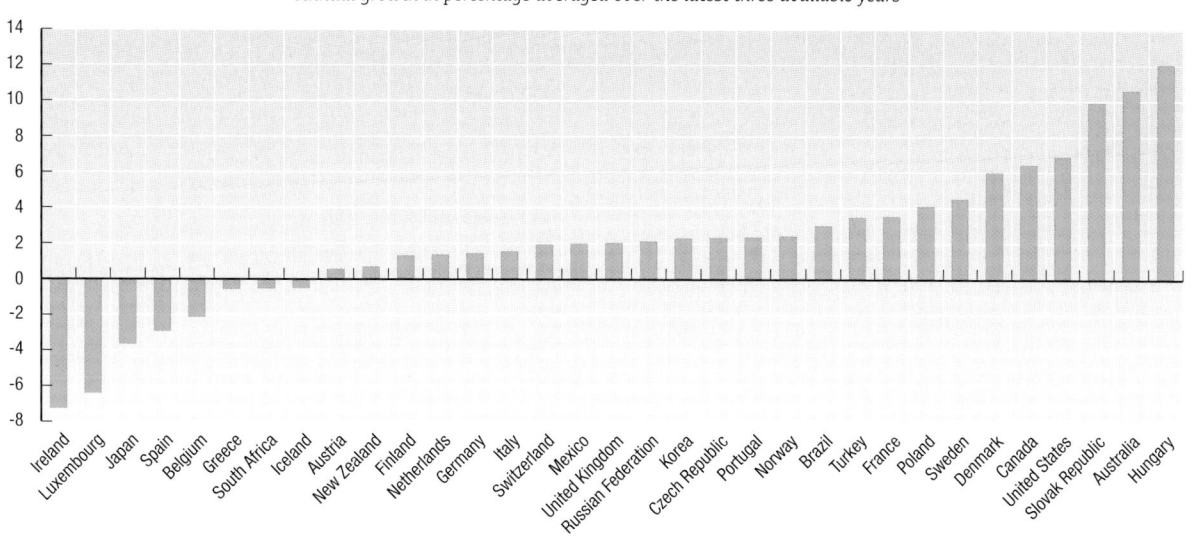

StatLink http://dx.doi.org/10.1787/267067558425

Real value added in industry
Annual growth in percentage

	1993	1994	1995	1996	1997	1998	1999	2000	2001	2002	2003	2004	2005	2006
Australia	4.2	3.7	2.7	1.8	4.6	3.2	3.0	-0.8	3.4	5.4	1.5	1.6	1.7	..
Austria	-0.4	4.0	3.1	2.3	2.8	3.9	4.3	5.0	1.3	1.0	1.9	2.2	2.5	7.8
Belgium	-3.9	3.4	3.4	1.2	6.0	1.6	1.4	5.0	0.2	-1.0	-0.8	3.1	0.6	4.4
Canada	3.2	5.6	3.2	1.5	5.1	3.4	5.5	7.9	-2.1	2.2	1.0	2.6	2.0	..
Czech Republic	-11.7	4.0	10.2	10.8	-5.0	-5.1	2.2	7.1	-1.8	2.8	-0.5	11.6	9.5	13.6
Denmark	-5.0	8.1	5.5	-0.5	5.2	1.9	2.9	3.3	-1.6	-1.9	-1.2	3.7	1.1	4.7
Finland	0.8	6.7	2.8	5.4	8.9	8.2	5.5	9.6	3.6	3.0	2.6	4.6	3.7	9.6
France	-6.0	2.8	3.4	-1.0	-0.4	3.9	2.8	4.4	2.4	0.1	1.2	1.2	1.7	1.9
Germany	-6.2	3.2	-1.0	-2.4	2.4	0.5	0.8	4.5	-0.1	-1.8	-0.4	3.4	0.3	5.3
Greece	-2.3	0.0	0.3	2.2	-1.1	7.4	2.3	5.4	11.8	2.2	7.7	-0.8	4.0	11.4
Hungary	1.4	5.7	5.7	1.3	10.8	7.5	6.7	8.2	1.7	3.6	4.1	3.7	3.6	4.9
Iceland	-1.6	1.0	-0.6	6.8	6.5	3.6	2.8	6.8	4.2	-4.3	4.6	8.4	7.4	..
Ireland	..	..	..	8.7	16.3	13.6	12.9	9.3	6.6	9.3	2.2	4.3	3.9	4.7
Italy	-3.2	4.2	3.8	-0.6	0.7	0.2	0.3	2.5	0.7	-0.2	-1.3	-0.5	-1.3	2.3
Japan	-2.6	-2.3	0.7	3.2	1.4	-4.5	-0.6	2.7	-4.2	-1.8	2.4	4.8	1.8	..
Korea	6.6	9.5	9.8	7.2	4.5	-8.2	12.2	11.7	3.1	6.4	6.1	8.8	5.7	6.5
Luxembourg	4.9	3.7	2.2	-0.4	5.1	5.0	7.0	6.0	-0.1	6.1	0.8	5.3	2.1	-0.1
Mexico	0.4	5.0	-8.7	10.1	9.3	6.2	4.7	6.0	-3.6	0.0	0.0	4.3	..	..
Netherlands	-0.6	3.6	2.0	1.6	0.1	2.2	3.6	4.9	1.2	0.0	-2.3	2.7	-0.3	1.8
New Zealand	7.0	6.2	2.8	3.6	0.2	-3.7	5.7	0.6	0.9	9.2	1.9	3.2	-1.1	..
Norway	1.3	8.3	5.3	5.3	5.5	-1.8	-1.1	3.5	1.1	0.8	0.2	2.3	0.5	-1.8
Poland	4.9	7.8	9.2	6.4	10.4	4.8	3.0	4.6	-2.4	-2.4	5.5	8.8	4.3	10.3
Portugal	-2.8	3.5	6.1	6.8	6.9	3.7	1.2	3.8	2.1	-1.5	-2.2	0.4	-1.8	0.2
Slovak Republic	..	8.3	5.5	16.6	-5.8	8.4	-3.7	1.5	3.2	5.1	14.4	7.8	14.1	10.5
Spain	-4.4	1.6	4.2	1.6	4.7	5.3	5.9	4.7	4.8	1.8	2.6	2.3	2.9	3.4
Sweden	-1.4	9.8	10.4	1.8	4.9	5.8	7.6	6.5	-0.8	4.4	2.8	8.7	4.2	4.3
Switzerland	-0.9	3.4	-0.2	-2.0	0.8	0.8	0.3	0.5	2.7	0.1	-0.1	1.3	3.5	4.5
Turkey	8.1	-4.8	8.1	6.9	9.3	1.8	-6.5	5.7	-7.1	6.6	5.0	8.7	8.5	9.3
United Kingdom	1.5	5.1	1.5	1.7	1.6	1.1	1.1	1.6	-0.7	-0.9	0.7	1.5	-1.2	0.3
United States	3.1	6.7	5.2	2.8	4.1	4.1	4.8	4.0	-4.1	0.8	1.1	5.4	3.0	..
Brazil	..	..	..	1.1	4.2	-2.6	-1.9	4.8	-0.6	2.1	1.3	7.9	2.2	..
Russian Federation	..	..	..	..	..	..	..	..	..	..	9.4	7.1	4.7	5.1
South Africa	..	2.6	3.5	1.3	2.6	-1.2	-0.2	5.1	1.9	2.7	0.8	4.3	4.5	4.8

StatLink http://dx.doi.org/10.1787/272803006522

Real value added in industry
Annual growth in percentage averaged over the latest three available years

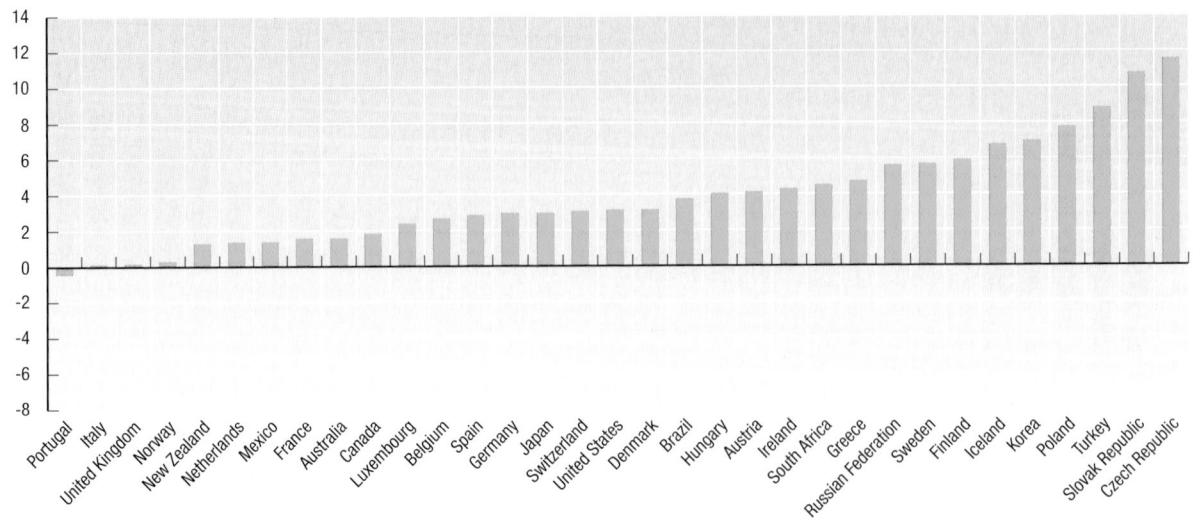

StatLink http://dx.doi.org/10.1787/267076224882

OECD FACTBOOK 2008 – ISBN 978-92-64-04054-0 – © OECD 2008

Real value added in services

Annual growth in percentage

	1993	1994	1995	1996	1997	1998	1999	2000	2001	2002	2003	2004	2005	2006
Australia	3.7	5.8	3.9	4.8	4.2	5.9	4.4	3.5	3.8	3.7	3.9	3.2	3.5	..
Austria	0.9	2.1	2.0	2.2	1.4	3.8	2.3	3.5	0.7	0.7	1.4	2.5	2.3	2.2
Belgium	-0.4	2.7	2.9	0.5	2.1	1.5	3.8	3.1	1.9	2.2	2.0	2.1	2.4	2.4
Canada	2.1	4.1	2.5	1.3	4.0	4.1	5.5	4.7	3.6	3.0	2.4	3.3	3.2	..
Czech Republic	8.5	3.3	2.5	-0.7	1.5	2.1	0.3	1.5	5.7	2.4	5.0	0.1	4.8	3.2
Denmark	1.5	3.6	2.2	3.4	2.3	1.9	3.0	4.6	1.5	1.3	0.9	0.4	2.9	3.1
Finland	-1.7	2.6	4.6	3.6	4.5	4.2	3.5	3.3	2.5	0.4	0.5	3.4	2.5	3.6
France	0.9	1.2	0.4	1.5	1.9	2.8	2.9	3.7	1.7	1.1	1.5	2.4	1.8	1.9
Germany	1.9	2.2	3.7	3.1	1.6	2.9	2.2	3.4	2.1	1.3	0.1	0.4	1.4	1.9
Greece	0.8	0.8	3.9	2.4	5.0	3.0	1.9	5.0	2.9	5.2	4.9	5.3	3.7	1.7
Hungary	1.5	4.5	-3.3	2.4	2.5	3.8	3.2	4.0	3.8	5.3	4.1	2.7	4.8	4.6
Iceland	0.4	3.7	2.6	5.6	5.1	9.1	7.3	6.9	4.8	0.0	4.3	7.5	10.6	..
Ireland	..	..	..	8.2	8.0	5.6	7.2	8.6	7.8	4.3	4.3	5.2	7.2	6.9
Italy	0.7	1.3	2.2	1.2	2.1	1.7	2.2	4.3	2.4	1.0	0.3	1.1	1.0	1.6
Japan	2.5	2.6	3.2	3.0	1.9	-0.5	0.6	1.9	2.1	1.7	1.2	1.1	2.3	..
Korea	6.8	7.7	8.1	6.2	5.1	-3.9	6.6	6.1	4.8	7.8	1.6	1.9	3.4	4.2
Luxembourg	5.6	5.0	2.5	2.0	5.4	6.4	8.2	8.1	4.2	3.4	2.4	4.3	5.8	8.5
Mexico	2.8	4.6	-6.4	2.9	6.4	4.6	3.5	7.1	1.0	1.4	1.8	4.2	..	..
Netherlands	1.9	2.4	3.3	3.8	5.6	4.7	4.8	3.7	2.3	0.3	1.3	2.2	2.1	3.6
New Zealand	4.8	4.8	4.4	3.4	2.5	2.4	4.7	2.7	5.0	3.5	4.0	4.2	3.3	..
Norway	2.7	3.5	2.8	4.4	5.4	4.8	3.8	3.5	2.4	1.2	1.5	3.6	3.9	4.6
Poland	0.6	4.7	4.5	5.4	4.6	4.6	5.3	4.4	2.7	3.0	2.9	3.6	3.3	4.3
Portugal	-0.2	-2.4	3.0	2.1	3.8	4.7	3.9	4.4	2.9	1.6	0.4	2.0	1.4	1.3
Slovak Republic	..	-1.0	6.9	2.3	14.0	0.1	3.3	-0.7	5.3	1.3	-1.2	0.2	-3.4	11.8
Spain	-0.5	2.0	2.6	1.4	2.9	3.8	4.3	5.1	3.6	3.0	3.0	3.8	4.1	4.1
Sweden	0.4	2.0	2.4	1.5	1.7	3.1	3.4	4.2	1.4	1.6	1.7	2.8	3.1	4.1
Switzerland	0.4	0.3	0.4	1.9	2.2	3.3	0.9	4.3	0.7	0.7	-0.3	2.7	2.0	2.8
Turkey	7.5	-3.2	6.5	5.7	7.0	3.4	-2.4	6.5	-5.5	5.9	5.4	7.6	5.9	4.2
United Kingdom	2.9	4.6	3.4	3.8	4.0	4.8	3.9	5.0	3.6	2.7	3.6	4.4	3.2	4.2
United States	1.8	2.5	2.8	4.0	5.0	5.3	4.4	3.5	2.6	1.5	2.8	3.5	3.2	..
Brazil	..	..	..	2.2	2.6	1.1	1.2	3.6	1.9	3.2	0.8	5.0	3.4	..
Russian Federation	..	..	..	..	..	..	..	..	..	..	6.6	7.2	7.5	7.7
South Africa	..	2.8	4.3	4.3	2.6	2.0	3.9	4.1	3.6	4.2	4.5	5.2	5.2	6.1

StatLink http://dx.doi.org/10.1787/272820560477

Real value added in services

Annual growth in percentage averaged over the latest three available years

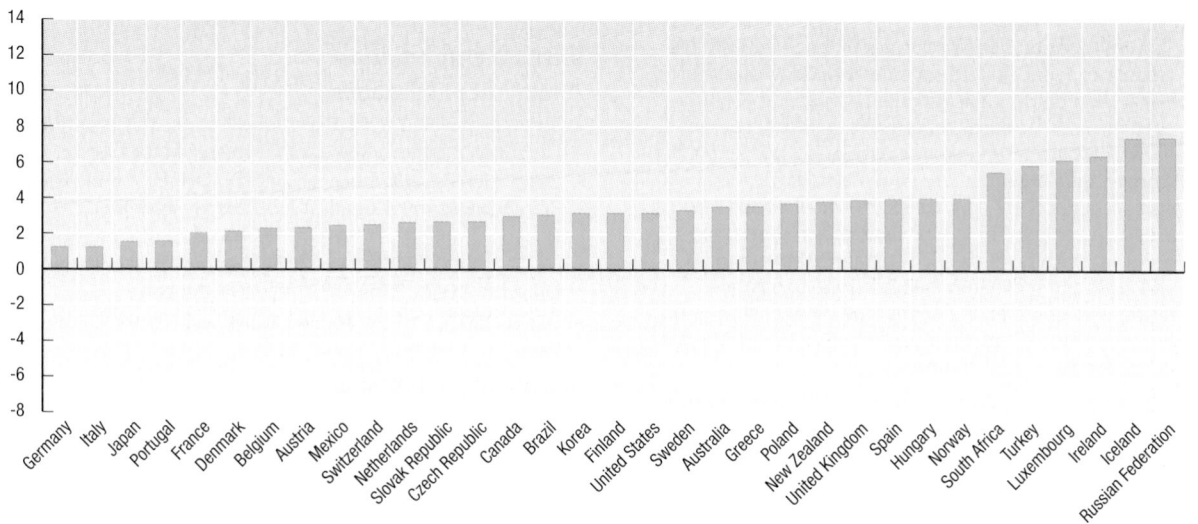

StatLink http://dx.doi.org/10.1787/267087716221

SMALL AND MEDIUM-SIZED ENTERPRISES

Statistics showing the distribution of enterprises by size class are important in illustrating the potential contribution of small enterprises to economic growth. Of particular relevance in the context of the tables presented here is that small firms are often the most dynamic and innovative, reflecting the fact that many of them are recent start-ups. Note, however, that because they are not longitudinal, the data do not show the contribution that small enterprises make to economic and employment growth over time as they move from the start-up phase to some optimal size. Many studies have used longitudinal datasets to establish their important contribution in this context.

Definition

An *enterprise* is a legal entity possessing the right to conduct business on its own; for example to enter into contracts, own property, incur liabilities for debts, and establish bank accounts. It may consist of one or more local units or establishments corresponding to production units situated in a geographically separate place and in which one or more persons work for the enterprise to which they belong.

The *number of employees* includes all persons, workers and employees, covered by a contractual arrangement and working in the enterprise and who receive compensation for their work, whether full-time or part-time. In particular, the following are considered as employees: salaried managers, students who have a formal commitment whereby they contribute to the unit's process of production in return for remuneration and/or education services, employees engaged under a contract specifically designed to encourage the recruitment of unemployed persons. This category includes persons on sick leave, paid leave or vacation. It excludes working proprietors, active business partners, unpaid family workers and home-workers, irrespective of whether or not they are on the payroll.

Overview

The contribution and importance of small enterprises across economies varies considerably. Generally, the larger the economy the lower the proportion of small enterprises. This partly reflects the greater scope for growth in larger markets, where there is a greater pool of workers and larger demand, but it also partly reflects a statistical phenomenon. For example, when an enterprise opens a new establishment in the same economy within which it is registered, the enterprise will grow and move from being a small to a large enterprise. However, if it opens a new establishment in another country, this will be recorded as the creation of an enterprise in that country.

In most economies, the percentage of businesses with less than 10 persons employed is over 70%. The reverse is true where the number of employees is concerned, where businesses with more than 20 employees contribute around 70% or more.

Comparability

All countries present information using the enterprise as the statistical unit except Japan, Korea, Mexico and Turkey, which use establishments. This may create some incomparability but, because most enterprises are also establishments, this is not expected to be significant. An area where considerable differences can and do arise, however, concerns the coverage of data on enterprises/establishments. In many countries, this information is based on business registers, economic censuses or surveys that may have a size-class cut off. Indeed, all countries have thresholds of one sort or another, depending, often, on the tax legislation and permissible business burdens in place across countries. For Ireland, only enterprises with 3 or more persons engaged are reflected, while the data for Japan, Korea and Turkey do not include establishments with fewer than 4, 5 and 10 persons engaged respectively. Enterprises that operate purely in the underground economy will naturally be very difficult, if not impossible, to capture, and these are most likely to be small. However, despite these differences, it is possible to make sensible comparisons across countries.

Employment data for Australia and Switzerland refer to the *total number* of persons engaged rather than the *number of employees*.

Data for the Czech Republic, Greece, Japan, Norway (employment), Portugal (number of enterprises), the United Kingdom (employment) and the United States are for 2004, data for Mexico and Norway (number of enterprises) are for 2003, while data for Switzerland and Turkey are for 2001.

Finally, data in the "Less than 10" and "Less than 20" size classes for Mexico and New Zealand include statistical units with no persons engaged.

Source
- OECD (2005), *OECD SME and Entrepreneurship Outlook – 2005 Edition*, OECD, Paris.

Further information
Analytical publications
- Birch, D. (1979), *The Job Generation Process*, MIT Program on Neighborhood and Regional Change, Cambridge.
- OECD (2005), *Local Economic and Employment Development Entrepreneurship: A Catalyst for Urban Regeneration*, OECD, Paris.
- OECD (2006), *The SME Financing Gap (Vol. I): Theory and Evidence*, OECD, Paris.
- OECD (2007), *SMEs in Mexico: Issues and Policies*, OECD, Paris.

Statistical publications
- OECD (2006), *Structural and Demographic Business Statistics: 1996-2003, 2006 Edition*, OECD, Paris.

Methodological publications
- Eurostat, OECD (2007), *Eurostat-OECD Manual on Business Demography Statistics*, OECD, Paris.

Number of employees and number of enterprises in manufacturing
Breakdown by size-class of enterprise, 2005 or latest available year

Number of persons engaged	As percentage of total number of employees in manufacturing							As a percentage of total number of enterprises in manufacturing					
	Less than 20	20 or more	Less than 10	10-19	20-49	50-249	250 or more	less than 20	20 or more	Less than 10	10-19	20-49	50-249	250 or more
Australia	29.3	70.7	19.4	9.8	13.9	..	..	94.2	5.8	88.2	6.0	3.8	..	..
Austria	14.8	85.2	7.7	7.1	11.4	27.2	46.6	85.4	14.6	73.9	11.5	7.9	5.2	1.5
Belgium	13.7	86.3	7.1	6.6	13.1	25.2	48.0	88.3	11.7	80.0	8.4	6.9	3.8	1.0
Czech Republic	11.5	88.5	5.6	5.9	10.8	29.4	48.3	94.2	5.8	90.4	3.7	3.0	2.3	0.6
Denmark	13.1	86.9	6.0	7.0	13.1	27.3	46.5	83.7	16.3	72.4	11.2	9.3	5.7	1.3
Finland	12.7	87.3	7.4	5.3	10.4	23.7	53.1	90.0	10.0	83.7	6.3	5.3	3.6	1.0
France	17.0	83.0	10.2	6.8	12.7	22.6	47.7	90.4	9.6	83.3	7.2	5.7	3.0	0.8
Germany	14.1	85.9	5.3	8.8	7.6	24.3	54.0	82.0	18.0	59.9	22.1	8.1	8.0	2.0
Greece	33.1	66.9	28.3	4.7	11.0	24.9	31.0	97.8	2.2	96.6	1.3	1.2	0.8	0.2
Hungary	16.4	83.6	9.7	6.8	11.5	25.9	46.2	92.1	7.9	86.2	5.8	4.3	2.9	0.7
Iceland	..	..	..	..	..	..	..	88.9	11.1	80.2	8.7	6.7	3.8	0.7
Ireland	9.3	90.7	3.7	5.7	12.6	30.9	47.2	60.1	39.9	38.1	22.0	20.7	15.2	4.0
Italy	30.7	69.3	14.9	15.8	18.0	25.0	26.3	93.1	6.9	82.9	10.1	4.7	1.9	0.3
Japan	20.6	79.4	9.5	11.2	17.9	31.0	30.4	71.6	28.4	48.0	23.6	17.5	9.4	1.5
Korea	25.6	74.4	11.4	14.2	20.6	24.3	29.4	76.5	23.5	50.5	25.9	16.1	6.4	1.1
Luxembourg	8.1	91.9	4.3	3.9	8.3	21.7	61.8	78.2	21.8	67.3	10.9	10.5	8.2	3.1
Mexico	13.7	86.3	9.4	4.3	7.3	21.6	57.3	92.8	7.2	89.7	3.1	2.2	1.8	0.7
Netherlands	19.5	80.5	10.3	9.2	14.9	29.8	35.8	86.8	13.2	77.1	9.7	7.4	4.8	1.1
New Zealand	22.7	81.4	12.0	10.6	15.4	12.0	54.1	90.2	9.8	80.9	9.3	6.0	2.0	1.7
Norway	17.2	82.8	8.7	8.5	14.4	28.4	40.1	77.8	22.2	60.5	17.2	12.9	7.7	1.6
Poland	14.9	85.1	10.5	4.3	10.1	32.1	43.0	91.8	8.2	88.1	3.7	3.9	3.5	0.8
Portugal	31.3	68.7	19.7	11.6	18.5	29.7	20.4	89.8	10.2	80.3	9.4	6.5	3.3	0.4
Slovak Republic	8.5	91.5	3.7	4.8	7.0	27.4	57.2	68.6	31.4	48.0	20.7	11.7	15.0	4.7
Spain	27.8	72.2	15.3	12.5	20.5	24.5	27.1	89.1	10.9	78.3	10.8	7.7	2.8	0.5
Sweden	14.5	85.5	8.5	6.0	10.1	23.3	52.1	92.7	7.3	87.5	5.2	3.9	2.7	0.7
Switzerland	22.7	77.3	14.9	7.8	13.0	29.2	35.1	87.8	12.2	79.1	8.7	6.7	4.5	0.9
Turkey	3.7	96.3	..	3.7	13.0	31.3	51.9	25.3	74.7	..	25.3	38.9	27.7	8.0
United Kingdom	16.2	83.8	9.2	7.0	11.7	26.2	45.8	85.1	14.9	73.6	11.5	8.2	5.4	1.3
United States	11.1	88.9	5.7	5.4	..	..	..	76.7	23.3	62.6	14.2	..	..	..

StatLink http://dx.doi.org/10.1787/272838112214

Enterprises with less than 20 persons engaged
As a percentage of total number of employees or total number of enterprises, 2005 or latest available year

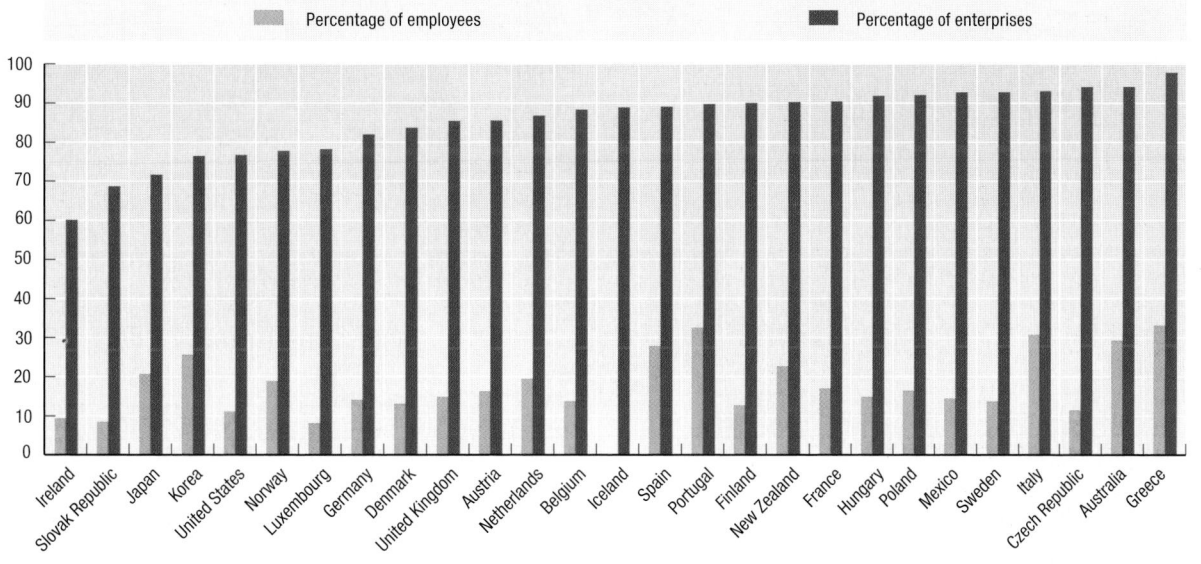

StatLink http://dx.doi.org/10.1787/267127807553

ECONOMIC GLOBALISATION

TRADE
SHARE OF TRADE IN GDP
TRADE IN GOODS
TRADE IN SERVICES
TRADING PARTNERS
BALANCE OF PAYMENTS

FOREIGN DIRECT INVESTMENT (FDI)
FDI FLOWS AND STOCKS
ACTIVITIES OF MULTINATIONALS

SHARE OF TRADE IN GDP

International trade in goods and services is a principal channel of economic integration. A convenient way to measure the importance of international trade is to calculate the share of trade in GDP.

International trade tends to be more important for countries that are small (in terms of geographic size or population) and surrounded by neighboring countries with open trade regimes than for large, relatively self-sufficient countries or those that are geographically isolated and thus penalised by high transport costs. Other factors also play a role and help explain differences in trade-to-GDP ratios across countries, such as history, culture, trade policy, the structure of the economy (especially the weight of non-tradable services in GDP), re-exports and the presence of multinational firms, which leads to much intra-firm trade.

Definition

The rates shown in this table correspond to the average of imports and exports (of both goods and services) at current prices as a percentage of GDP. The data are taken from national accounts statistics compiled according to the *1993 System of National Accounts*, except for Turkey, which still uses the 1968 SNA. Goods consist of merchandise imports and exports. Services cover transport, travel, communications, construction, IT, financial, other business, personal and government services, as well as royalties and license fees.

Comparability

The ratios shown in this table are compiled using common standards and definitions and are highly comparable.

The trade-to-GDP ratio is often called the "trade openness ratio". However, the term openness may be somewhat misleading. In fact, a low ratio for a country does not necessarily imply high tariff or non-tariff obstacles to foreign trade, but may be due to the factors mentioned above, especially size and geographic remoteness from potential trading partners.

Please note that the trade-to-GDP ratio shown by WTO, IMF and OECD trade indicators refers to the sum of the imports and exports and not to the average, as is the case here. Also note that OECD total GDP excludes the Czech Republic, Hungary, Poland and the Slovak Republic because growth rates for these countries are not available for the full period.

Long-term trends

In 2006, the trade-to-GDP ratio for OECD countries was 26%, while the rate for the EU15 was 38%. For the reasons noted above, there were large differences in these ratios across countries. The ratios exceeded 50% for small countries – Austria, Belgium, the Czech Republic, Denmark, Hungary, Ireland, Luxembourg, the Netherlands and the Slovak Republic – but were under 20% for the two largest OECD countries – Japan and the United States.

Between 1993 and 2006, trade-to-GDP ratios for the OECD as a whole increased by 9 percentage points, and the EU15 increased by 13 points. Substantial increases in trade-to-GDP ratios were recorded for Luxembourg, Hungary and the Slovak Republic.

Source

- OECD (2007), *National Accounts of OECD Countries*, OECD, Paris.

Further information

Statistical publications

- OECD (2007), *International Trade by Commodity Statistics*, OECD, Paris.
- OECD (2007), *Main Economic Indicators*, OECD, Paris.
- OECD (2007), *Monthly Statistics of International Trade*, OECD, Paris.
- OECD (2007), *Statistics on International Trade in Services*, OECD, Paris.

Methodological publications

- Lindner, A., *et al.* (2001), "Trade in Goods and Services: Statistical Trends and Measurement Challenges", OECD Statistics Brief, No. 1, October, OECD, Paris, *www.oecd.org/std/statisticsbrief*.
- UN, EC, IMF, OECD, UNCTAD and the WTO (2002), *Manual on Statistics of International Trade in Services*, United Nations, New York.

Websites

- OECD International Trade Statistics, *www.oecd.org/std/its*.

Trade in goods and services
As a percentage of GDP

	1993	1994	1995	1996	1997	1998	1999	2000	2001	2002	2003	2004	2005	2006
Australia	18.3	19.1	19.4	19.3	20.3	19.9	20.9	22.5	21.1	20.4	18.8	20.0	21.0	22.3
Austria	32.8	34.0	35.2	36.3	39.6	41.0	41.8	44.7	46.6	46.4	46.9	48.9	51.0	53.3
Belgium	61.5	63.8	65.6	67.7	71.8	72.5	73.2	83.2	83.0	80.2	78.8	81.6	84.8	86.1
Canada	30.2	33.4	35.7	36.4	38.5	40.4	41.4	42.7	40.7	39.4	36.2	36.3	35.9	35.0
Czech Republic	51.4	48.9	52.9	51.8	54.7	54.8	56.0	64.9	66.6	61.3	62.9	70.1	70.6	74.2
Denmark	34.0	35.1	35.6	35.5	37.0	37.2	38.2	43.6	44.0	44.4	42.3	43.3	46.4	50.5
Finland	29.4	31.9	32.6	33.4	34.7	34.0	33.7	38.4	36.1	35.0	34.4	35.9	39.0	41.9
France	20.6	21.4	22.2	22.4	24.3	25.0	25.1	28.1	27.5	26.3	25.1	25.7	26.5	27.6
Germany	22.3	23.0	23.7	24.4	26.8	28.0	29.0	33.2	33.8	33.4	33.7	35.8	38.4	42.3
Greece	21.8	21.3	21.8	22.1	24.0	24.6	27.4	31.6	29.8	27.0	26.7	28.0	27.4	28.2
Hungary	29.5	31.1	43.1	46.6	52.8	60.5	63.5	73.9	71.7	64.0	62.6	64.9	66.8	77.5
Iceland	31.2	33.2	33.7	36.0	36.0	37.0	36.0	37.3	39.4	36.9	35.9	37.0	38.0	41.5
Ireland	60.2	65.3	70.3	71.2	72.8	80.8	82.0	91.6	92.2	85.4	75.8	76.5	75.7	74.6
Italy	19.8	21.1	23.8	22.4	23.3	23.6	23.5	26.6	26.4	25.2	24.3	25.0	26.1	28.2
Japan	8.1	8.1	8.5	9.6	10.3	10.0	9.5	10.3	10.2	10.7	11.2	12.3	13.6	15.5
Korea	26.3	27.0	29.4	29.6	32.7	39.7	35.7	39.2	36.7	34.6	36.8	41.9	41.1	42.7
Luxembourg	91.7	93.9	95.8	101.0	112.2	119.3	124.6	139.5	137.8	130.9	124.4	137.5	144.5	151.3
Mexico	17.2	19.2	29.1	31.1	30.4	31.8	31.6	32.0	28.7	27.8	28.6	30.6	30.8	32.6
Netherlands	51.9	54.0	56.5	57.0	60.5	60.2	60.9	67.3	64.4	60.9	59.9	62.7	65.8	69.5
New Zealand	29.1	29.7	28.6	27.8	27.9	29.2	31.0	34.7	33.9	31.5	28.8	29.3	29.0	30.0
Norway	34.7	35.1	34.9	36.3	37.3	36.7	35.7	38.0	37.3	34.4	33.8	35.3	36.4	37.5
Poland	20.5	20.6	22.1	23.0	25.4	28.4	27.1	30.3	28.9	30.3	34.6	38.5	37.3	40.8
Portugal	28.8	30.3	31.8	31.7	32.6	33.4	33.0	35.2	33.9	32.1	31.3	32.3	32.8	35.0
Slovak Republic	58.1	56.3	56.3	58.1	60.6	64.4	63.0	71.5	76.7	74.5	77.4	76.5	79.8	88.0
Spain	18.5	20.8	22.4	23.4	25.9	26.8	27.6	30.6	29.8	28.4	27.5	27.9	28.3	29.1
Sweden	30.9	33.9	36.4	35.3	38.4	39.8	39.9	43.4	43.2	41.2	40.4	42.2	44.9	47.3
Switzerland	33.6	33.5	33.4	34.1	37.5	38.2	39.3	43.6	43.5	41.1	40.8	42.9	45.6	48.7
Turkey	16.5	20.9	22.1	24.7	27.5	26.1	25.0	27.8	32.5	30.0	29.0	31.8	30.7	32.0
United Kingdom	25.9	26.8	28.4	29.4	28.6	27.2	27.1	28.9	28.6	27.7	26.8	26.7	28.3	30.2
United States	10.4	10.9	11.7	11.8	12.2	11.9	12.2	13.2	12.1	11.7	11.8	12.8	13.5	14.1
EU15 total	25.7	27.0	28.6	28.9	30.6	31.2	31.7	35.4	35.2	34.0	33.2	34.4	36.0	38.3
OECD total	16.9	17.7	19.1	19.8	20.7	20.9	20.8	22.3	21.7	21.5	22.0	23.5	24.7	26.3

StatLink ⚡ http://dx.doi.org/10.1787/272874373823

Trade to GDP ratios
Difference between 2006 and 1993 ratios in percentage points

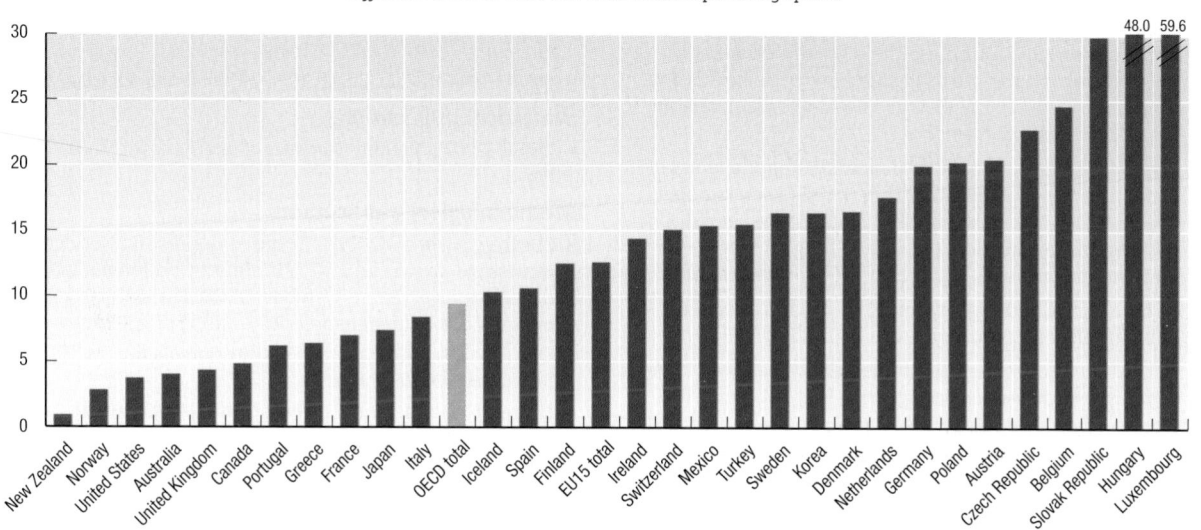

StatLink ⚡ http://dx.doi.org/10.1787/267130224184

OECD FACTBOOK 2008 – ISBN 978-92-64-04054-0 – © OECD 2008

TRADE IN GOODS

Since its creation, the OECD has sought to promote international trade, considering it an effective way of enhancing economic growth and raising living standards. Member countries benefit from increased trade as do OECD's trade partners in the rest of the world.

Definition

According to United Nations guidelines, international merchandise trade statistics record all goods which add to or subtract from the stock of material resources of a country by entering (imports) or leaving (exports) its economic territory. Goods simply being transported through a country or goods temporarily admitted or withdrawn (except for goods for inward or outward processing) are not included in the international merchandise trade statistics.

Comparability

All OECD countries use the United Nations guidelines so far as their data sources allow. There are some, generally minor, differences across countries in the coverage of certain types of transactions such as postal trade, imports and exports of military equipment under defence agreements, sea products traded by domestic vessels on the high seas and goods entering or leaving bonded customs areas.

Exports are usually valued free on board (f.o.b.), with the exception of the United States which values exports free alongside ship (f.a.s.), which is lower than f.o.b. by the cost of loading the goods on board. Imports are valued by most countries at cost, insurance and freight (c.i.f.) i.e. the cost of the goods plus the costs of insurance and freight to bring the goods to the borders of the importing country. The following countries, however, report their imports at f.o.b. values: Australia, Canada, the Czech Republic, Mexico and the Slovak Republic. The trade balances shown in the table are, therefore, not strictly comparable because imports are not valued in the same way by all countries.

The introduction by the European Union of the single market in 1993 resulted in some loss of accuracy for intra-EU trade because customs documents were no longer available to record all imports and exports. Note that while the OECD data mostly follow the UN recommendations, trade statistics reported by Eurostat follow the Community definitions. As a result, OECD trade statistics for European Union countries are not strictly comparable with those reported by Eurostat.

OECD total includes Mexico from 1990, Hungary and Poland from 1992, the Czech Republic from 1993, Korea from 1994 and the Slovak Republic from 1997.

Long-term trends

Over the ten-year period from 1996 to 2006, relative import growth (i.e. growth in a single country divided by growth for all OECD countries) was low in Japan, New Zealand, Norway and Switzerland while relative import growth in some new member countries – Hungary, the Czech Republic and Poland – was particularly high. Concerning BRIC countries, China continued to show high relative import growth while growth for the Russian Federation was about OECD average and Brazil's relative import growth was very low.

Over the same period, relative growth rates of exports of goods were again high for Hungary, the Czech Republic, Poland, and Turkey. Japan, New Zealand, the United States, France, Italy and the United Kingdom were among the countries with below average growth rates.

China, again, had higher growth in imports as well as exports than any country in this comparison.

The United States' negative trade balance has been large throughout the period and growing in most years. The United Kingdom, Spain, Turkey and France also recorded high negative trade balances for goods, while Germany had by far the largest trade surpluses for an OECD country. The Russian Federation and China had significant trade surpluses, similar to Germany, too.

Sources

- UN Commodity Trade Statistics Database.
- OECD (2007), *International Trade by Commodity Statistics*, OECD, Paris.

Further information

Analytical publications

- OECD (2005), *Trade and Structural Adjustment: Embracing Globalisation*, OECD, Paris.
- OECD (2006), *The Development Dimension – Aid for Trade: Making it Effective*, OECD, Paris.
- OECD (2006), *Trade Based Money Laundering*, OECD, Paris.

Statistical publications

- OECD (2007), *Monthly Statistics of International Trade*, OECD, Paris.

Methodological publications

- Lindner, A., *et al.* (2001), "Trade in Goods and Services: Statistical Trends and Measurement Challenges", OECD Statistics Brief, No. 1, October, OECD, Paris, *www.oecd.org/std/statisticsbrief*.
- OECD (2004), *International Trade by Commodity Statistics – Definitions*, OECD, Paris.
- United Nations (1998), International Merchandise Trade Statistics: Compilers Manual, United Nations, New York, *http://unstats.un.org/unsd/trade/methodology.htm*.

Online databases

- ITCS International Trade by Commodity Statistics.
- Monthly International Trade.

Trade balance: exports of goods minus imports of goods
Billion US dollars

	1993	1994	1995	1996	1997	1998	1999	2000	2001	2002	2003	2004	2005	2006
Australia	0.1	-2.7	-4.4	-1.2	1.0	-5.0	-9.5	-4.0	2.4	-4.5	-14.6	-17.3	-13.1	-9.3
Austria	-8.7	-10.2	-8.5	-10.1	-6.9	-6.2	-6.2	-5.2	-4.4	-0.1	-2.3	-0.3	-2.2	-0.2
Belgium	11.4	13.3	15.4	11.4	12.3	14.4	14.3	13.5	11.6	17.7	20.7	21.0	13.8	15.5
Canada	5.9	7.7	16.5	19.2	18.1	13.3	23.2	37.6	39.4	30.2	31.8	43.4	45.7	38.1
Czech Republic	0.2	-0.9	-3.9	-5.8	-4.4	-2.2	-2.0	-3.2	-3.1	-2.2	-2.5	-0.9	1.7	1.7
Denmark	6.5	5.8	4.7	5.7	3.7	1.7	4.7	5.2	5.8	6.4	8.4	7.9	8.3	5.6
Finland	5.5	6.4	10.9	9.7	10.0	10.8	10.2	11.7	10.7	11.0	10.9	10.7	6.8	7.8
France	6.2	5.0	10.6	6.2	16.8	14.7	9.5	-8.5	-4.4	1.1	-4.5	-20.5	-41.6	-50.9
Germany	37.4	45.6	59.6	68.3	67.1	72.3	69.3	54.8	85.7	125.6	146.8	193.6	200.4	206.8
Greece	-14.0	-11.7	-15.0	-15.7	-15.8	-19.4	-18.8	-18.8	-17.9	-21.8	-31.2	-37.6	-37.4	-42.8
Hungary	-3.6	-4.2	-2.6	-3.1	-2.1	-2.7	-3.0	-4.0	-3.2	-3.3	-4.7	-4.8	-3.6	-2.9
Iceland	..	0.1	..	-0.1	-0.2	-0.6	-0.5	-0.7	-0.3	..	-0.4	-0.8	-1.9	-2.1
Ireland	7.2	8.2	11.5	12.4	14.4	19.9	24.0	25.6	26.4	36.0	38.7	42.0	39.7	32.5
Italy	22.2	22.1	27.2	43.9	29.9	26.5	14.7	1.8	8.1	7.7	2.0	-1.9	-12.7	-5.1
Japan	120.6	121.6	107.1	61.8	82.2	107.5	107.2	99.6	54.0	79.1	88.5	110.5	79.1	67.7
Korea	..	-6.5	-10.4	-19.6	-8.5	39.0	23.9	11.8	9.3	10.4	15.0	29.4	23.2	16.1
Luxembourg	..	..	..	..	..	..	-2.8	-2.8	-2.9	-2.9	-3.7	-4.6	-4.9	-5.9
Mexico	-13.6	-18.7	6.8	6.2	0.5	-8.0	-5.7	-5.8	-7.6	-5.7	-5.6	-8.8	-7.6	-6.1
Netherlands	17.2	15.3	19.6	16.5	15.5	10.9	2.7	5.4	5.6	11.9	18.3	32.8	36.9	38.7
New Zealand	0.6	-0.1	-0.7	-0.6	-0.8	-0.6	-2.4	-1.2	-	-1.2	-2.0	-2.8	-4.5	-4.0
Norway	7.9	7.3	9.0	14.0	12.8	2.9	11.3	25.5	26.0	24.7	29.0	33.8	48.3	58.0
Poland	-4.7	-4.4	-6.1	-12.7	-16.5	-18.8	-18.5	-17.3	-14.2	-14.1	-14.4	-14.4	-12.2	-16.2
Portugal	-8.8	-9.1	-10.2	-10.6	-11.1	-12.8	-15.3	-15.6	-15.4	-14.2	-15.3	-19.2	-23.1	-23.8
Slovak Republic	..	..	..	..	-2.1	-2.4	-1.1	-0.9	-2.1	-2.2	-0.7	-1.5	-2.4	-2.7
Spain	-18.7	-19.0	-23.0	-21.0	-18.2	-25.8	-36.4	-39.5	-38.8	-40.0	-53.4	-76.5	-96.8	-115.9
Sweden	7.5	9.4	15.8	18.9	18.3	16.4	16.3	14.2	12.8	15.9	18.2	22.8	18.9	20.3
Switzerland	2.5	2.4	1.5	1.5	0.2	-1.2	0.4	-2.0	-2.1	4.2	4.2	6.8	4.4	6.5
Turkey	-14.1	-5.2	-14.1	-20.4	-22.3	-19.0	-14.1	-26.7	-10.1	-15.5	-22.1	-34.4	-43.3	-52.1
United Kingdom	-28.0	-31.3	-25.9	-28.7	-26.3	-46.9	-53.2	-56.6	-65.4	-78.8	-85.8	-113.1	-131.4	-162.0
United States	-138.4	-176.7	-187.9	-194.8	-210.5	-263.9	-366.4	-477.7	-449.1	-509.1	-581.4	-707.4	-828.0	-882.0
EU15 total	42.8	49.7	92.7	106.8	109.8	76.4	33.0	-14.7	17.4	75.5	67.9	57.0	-25.3	-86.4
OECD total	6.2	-30.4	3.7	-48.7	-43.0	-85.1	-224.0	-383.7	-343.0	-333.8	-411.9	-512.2	-739.3	-875.9
Brazil	11.4	8.0	-7.2	-9.0	-12.1	-9.7	-3.7	-3.6	-0.3	10.6	22.1	29.7	39.7	46.1
China	-12.2	5.4	16.7	12.2	40.4	43.6	29.2	24.1	22.5	30.4	25.5	32.1	102.0	177.5
India	-1.1	-2.3	-4.9	-5.6	-6.6	-9.2	-13.0	-6.1	-7.6	-8.6	-14.2	-28.4	-46.3	..
Russian Federation	..	..	..	27.6	19.7	28.6	42.6	69.2	58.8	60.5	76.3	106.1	142.7	163.8
South Africa	..	..	..	..	..	..	..	3.4	3.7	-3.1	-2.9	-7.5	-8.0	-16.0

StatLink ⬛️ http://dx.doi.org/10.1787/273000336708

Trade balance: exports of goods minus imports of goods
Billion US dollars, average 2004-2006

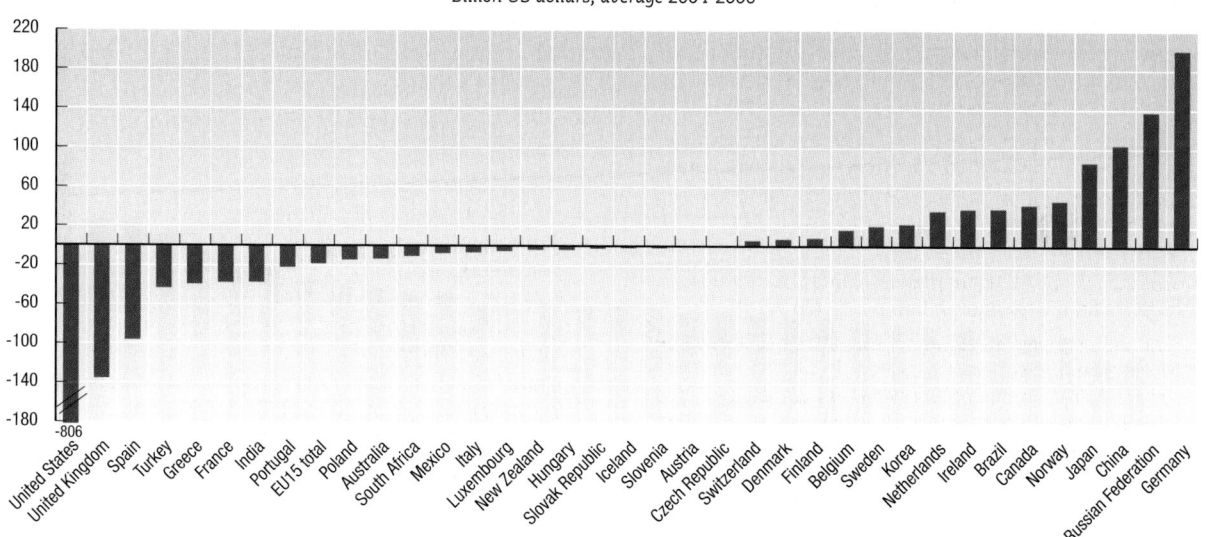

StatLink ⬛️ http://dx.doi.org/10.1787/267144834066

Imports of goods
Billion US dollars

	1993	1994	1995	1996	1997	1998	1999	2000	2001	2002	2003	2004	2005	2006
Australia	42.4	49.9	57.4	61.4	61.8	60.8	65.5	67.8	60.9	69.5	84.8	103.8	118.9	132.7
Austria	50.4	55.2	66.3	67.1	63.6	67.1	68.7	67.4	69.0	71.4	91.5	111.2	120.0	134.2
Belgium	114.8	127.6	152.3	159.4	158.3	164.9	164.6	171.7	178.7	198.1	234.8	285.5	320.2	353.7
Canada	131.7	148.4	164.5	171.0	197.1	201.3	215.6	240.0	221.6	222.4	240.2	273.4	314.4	349.9
Czech Republic	12.7	14.9	20.8	27.4	27.2	30.5	28.8	32.2	36.5	40.7	51.2	68.1	76.5	93.4
Denmark	31.0	36.5	45.6	45.0	44.5	46.2	44.3	44.4	44.3	49.3	56.2	66.9	75.0	84.5
Finland	18.0	23.3	29.5	30.9	31.0	32.4	31.6	34.1	32.2	33.6	41.6	50.1	58.5	69.5
France	210.1	228.3	273.5	277.7	266.6	285.8	292.8	304.0	304.2	303.8	362.4	434.4	476.0	529.9
Germany	342.6	381.7	464.3	444.4	445.3	471.6	473.5	495.4	486.3	490.1	601.8	718.2	777.4	919.0
Greece	22.8	20.9	25.9	27.0	27.0	30.3	29.5	29.8	28.2	32.5	44.9	52.8	54.9	63.7
Hungary	12.5	14.9	15.5	16.2	21.2	25.7	28.0	32.1	33.7	37.6	47.7	60.2	65.9	77.0
Iceland	1.4	1.5	1.8	2.0	2.0	2.5	2.5	2.6	2.3	2.3	2.8	3.6	5.0	5.6
Ireland	21.8	25.9	32.3	35.8	39.2	44.4	46.5	50.7	51.1	52.3	54.2	62.3	70.3	76.4
Italy	157.6	167.9	204.0	208.2	208.1	215.6	220.3	237.3	236.1	246.6	297.4	351.1	380.6	405.7
Japan	241.7	276.1	336.1	349.2	338.8	280.6	309.9	379.7	348.6	337.6	383.5	455.2	515.9	579.1
Korea	..	103.1	137.9	144.1	144.6	93.3	119.8	160.5	141.1	152.1	178.8	224.5	261.2	309.4
Luxembourg	..	..	..	..	..	..	..	10.6	10.6	11.2	11.5	13.6	16.8	17.6	19.5
Mexico	65.3	79.3	72.5	89.5	109.8	125.3	142.0	171.1	165.1	165.7	170.5	196.8	221.8	256.1
Netherlands	129.8	130.5	157.7	162.5	158.3	156.8	167.9	174.7	169.9	163.4	209.0	257.7	283.2	331.5
New Zealand	9.3	11.9	13.9	14.7	14.5	12.5	14.3	13.9	13.3	15.0	18.6	23.2	26.2	26.4
Norway	24.0	27.4	33.0	35.6	35.8	37.5	34.2	34.4	33.0	34.9	41.2	48.5	55.5	64.2
Poland	18.8	21.6	28.9	37.1	42.3	47.0	45.9	48.9	50.2	55.1	68.0	88.2	101.5	125.6
Portugal	24.2	27.1	33.6	35.2	35.1	37.0	39.8	39.9	39.5	40.0	47.1	54.9	61.2	65.9
Slovak Republic	..	..	..	..	11.7	13.1	11.1	12.7	14.7	16.6	22.6	29.1	34.2	44.4
Spain	79.7	91.0	116.5	123.6	124.4	137.2	147.9	152.9	155.0	165.9	209.7	259.3	289.6	330.0
Sweden	46.7	52.0	61.6	64.0	63.2	68.6	68.5	73.1	63.5	67.1	84.2	100.5	111.4	127.1
Switzerland	62.0	67.9	80.2	78.2	75.9	80.1	79.9	82.5	84.2	83.7	96.4	110.0	126.6	141.4
Turkey	29.4	23.3	35.7	43.6	48.6	45.9	40.7	54.5	41.4	51.3	69.3	97.5	116.8	137.4
United Kingdom	209.4	234.0	268.2	287.6	307.5	320.3	323.8	339.4	338.0	359.4	393.5	461.3	515.8	606.4
United States	603.2	689.0	770.8	817.6	898.0	944.4	1 059.2	1 258.1	1 180.1	1 202.3	1 305.1	1 525.3	1 732.3	1 919.0
EU15 total	1 458.8	1 601.7	1 931.3	1 968.4	1 972.0	2 078.1	2 130.3	2 225.6	2 207.1	2 285.0	2 741.8	3 282.8	3 611.5	4 120.2
OECD total	2 713.3	3 130.9	3 700.2	3 856.2	4 001.4	4 078.5	4 327.7	4 816.4	4 633.7	4 771.8	5 522.7	6 590.3	7 384.3	8 381.7
Brazil	27.3	35.5	53.7	56.7	65.1	60.8	51.7	58.9	58.5	49.7	49.8	65.3	76.4	91.4
China	104.0	115.6	132.1	138.8	142.4	140.2	165.7	225.1	243.6	295.2	412.8	561.2	660.0	791.5
India	23.3	28.7	36.6	39.1	41.4	42.4	49.7	51.4	51.9	61.1	77.2	108.2	149.7	..
Russian Federation	..	..	..	61.1	67.6	43.7	30.3	33.9	41.9	46.2	57.3	75.6	98.6	137.7
South Africa	..	..	..	..	..	..	..	26.8	24.2	26.2	34.5	47.7	55.0	69.2

StatLink ⬛🌐 http://dx.doi.org/10.1787/273003170707

Relative annual growth of imports of goods
Growth over the period 1996-2006, OECD total = 1

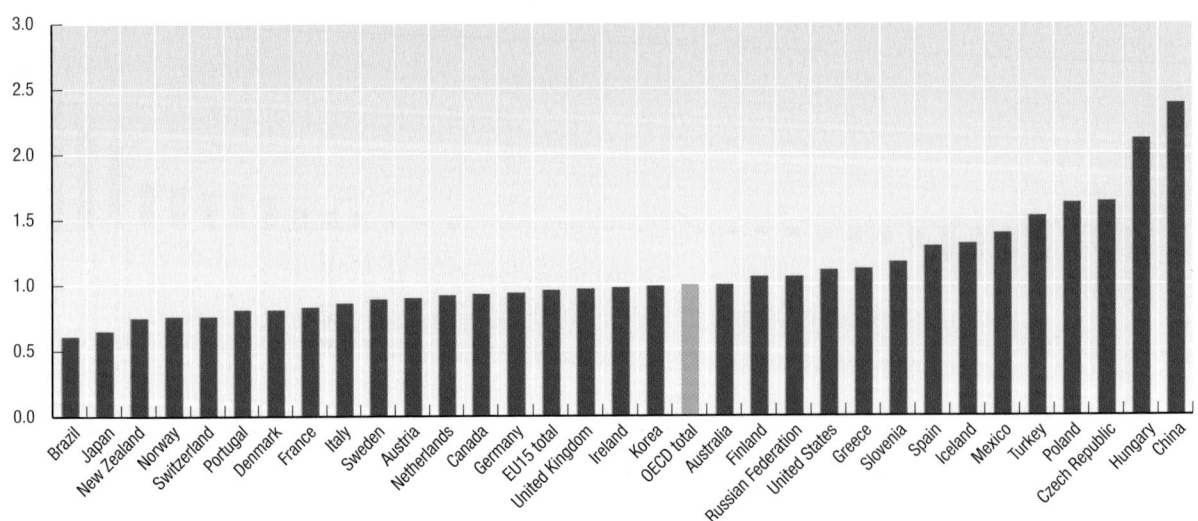

StatLink ⬛🌐 http://dx.doi.org/10.1787/267154257336

OECD FACTBOOK 2008 – ISBN 978-92-64-04054-0 – © OECD 2008

Exports of goods
Billion US dollars

	1993	1994	1995	1996	1997	1998	1999	2000	2001	2002	2003	2004	2005	2006
Australia	42.5	47.3	53.0	60.2	62.8	55.8	56.0	63.8	63.3	65.0	70.2	86.4	105.8	123.3
Austria	41.6	45.0	57.8	57.1	56.7	60.9	62.4	62.3	64.7	71.3	89.2	110.8	117.7	134.1
Belgium	126.1	140.9	167.7	170.8	170.7	179.3	178.9	185.2	190.3	215.8	255.5	306.5	334.0	369.2
Canada	137.6	156.1	181.0	190.2	215.1	214.6	238.9	277.6	261.1	252.6	272.1	316.9	360.1	388.0
Czech Republic	12.9	14.0	16.8	21.7	22.7	28.3	26.8	29.1	33.4	38.5	48.7	67.2	78.2	95.1
Denmark	37.5	42.3	50.3	50.7	48.2	47.9	49.0	49.6	50.1	55.7	64.6	74.8	83.3	90.1
Finland	23.5	29.8	40.4	40.6	41.0	43.2	41.8	45.8	42.8	44.7	52.5	60.8	65.2	77.3
France	216.2	233.3	284.1	283.9	283.4	300.5	302.3	295.6	299.8	304.9	357.9	413.9	434.4	479.0
Germany	380.0	427.3	523.9	512.7	512.4	543.8	542.8	550.2	572.0	615.6	748.5	911.8	977.8	1 125.8
Greece	8.8	9.2	11.0	11.3	11.2	10.9	10.7	11.0	10.3	10.8	13.7	15.2	17.5	20.9
Hungary	8.9	10.7	12.9	13.1	19.1	23.0	25.0	28.1	30.5	34.3	43.0	55.5	62.3	74.1
Iceland	1.5	1.6	1.8	1.9	1.9	1.9	2.0	1.9	2.0	2.2	2.4	2.8	3.1	3.5
Ireland	29.0	34.1	43.8	48.2	53.6	64.2	70.5	76.3	77.4	88.3	92.9	104.3	110.0	108.9
Italy	179.8	190.0	231.3	252.1	238.0	242.1	235.1	239.1	244.2	254.3	299.4	349.1	367.9	400.6
Japan	362.3	397.7	443.3	410.9	421.0	388.1	417.1	479.2	402.6	416.7	472.0	565.7	594.9	646.7
Korea	..	96.6	127.5	124.5	136.2	132.3	143.7	172.3	150.4	162.5	193.8	253.8	284.4	325.5
Luxembourg	..	..	..	..	..	..	7.8	7.9	8.3	8.6	10.0	12.2	12.7	13.6
Mexico	51.7	60.6	79.3	95.7	110.2	117.3	136.3	165.3	157.5	160.0	164.9	188.0	214.2	250.0
Netherlands	147.0	145.8	177.4	179.0	173.8	167.6	170.5	180.1	175.5	175.3	227.3	290.5	320.1	370.3
New Zealand	9.9	11.8	13.3	14.2	13.7	11.9	11.9	12.7	13.3	13.8	16.5	20.3	21.7	22.4
Norway	31.9	34.8	42.0	49.6	48.5	40.4	45.5	59.9	59.0	59.6	70.3	82.2	103.8	122.2
Poland	14.1	17.2	22.9	24.4	25.7	28.2	27.4	31.6	36.1	41.0	53.5	73.8	89.4	109.3
Portugal	15.4	18.0	23.4	24.6	24.0	24.2	24.5	24.4	24.1	25.8	31.8	35.7	38.1	42.1
Slovak Republic	..	..	..	..	9.6	10.7	10.1	11.8	12.6	14.5	22.0	27.6	31.9	41.7
Spain	61.1	71.9	93.5	102.6	106.2	111.4	111.5	113.3	116.1	125.9	156.3	182.7	192.8	214.1
Sweden	54.1	61.3	77.4	82.9	81.5	85.0	84.8	87.4	76.3	82.9	102.4	123.2	130.3	147.4
Switzerland	64.5	70.3	81.6	79.7	76.2	78.9	80.3	80.5	82.1	87.9	100.7	116.8	130.9	147.9
Turkey	15.3	18.1	21.6	23.2	26.2	27.0	26.6	27.8	31.3	35.8	47.3	63.1	73.5	85.3
United Kingdom	181.4	202.7	242.2	258.9	281.2	273.4	270.7	282.9	272.6	280.6	307.7	348.2	384.4	444.4
United States	464.8	512.3	583.0	622.8	687.5	680.4	692.8	780.3	731.0	693.2	723.7	817.9	904.3	1 037.0
EU15 total	1 501.6	1 651.4	2 024.0	2 075.2	2 081.8	2 154.5	2 163.4	2 210.9	2 224.5	2 360.5	2 809.8	3 339.8	3 586.2	4 033.9
OECD total	2 719.5	3 100.5	3 703.9	3 807.5	3 958.4	3 993.4	4 103.7	4 432.7	4 290.7	4 438.0	5 110.9	6 078.0	6 645.0	7 505.9
Brazil	38.7	43.6	46.5	47.7	53.0	51.1	48.0	55.3	58.2	60.4	71.9	95.0	116.1	137.5
China	91.7	121.0	148.8	151.0	182.8	183.8	194.9	249.2	266.1	325.6	438.2	593.3	762.0	968.9
India	22.2	26.3	31.7	33.5	34.8	33.2	36.7	45.2	44.3	52.5	63.0	79.8	103.4	..
Russian Federation	..	..	..	88.7	87.4	72.3	72.9	103.1	100.7	106.7	133.7	181.6	241.2	301.6
South Africa	..	..	..	..	..	..	..	30.2	27.9	23.1	31.6	40.3	47.0	53.2

StatLink http://dx.doi.org/10.1787/273008628204

Relative annual growth of exports of goods
Growth over the period 1996-2006, OECD total = 1

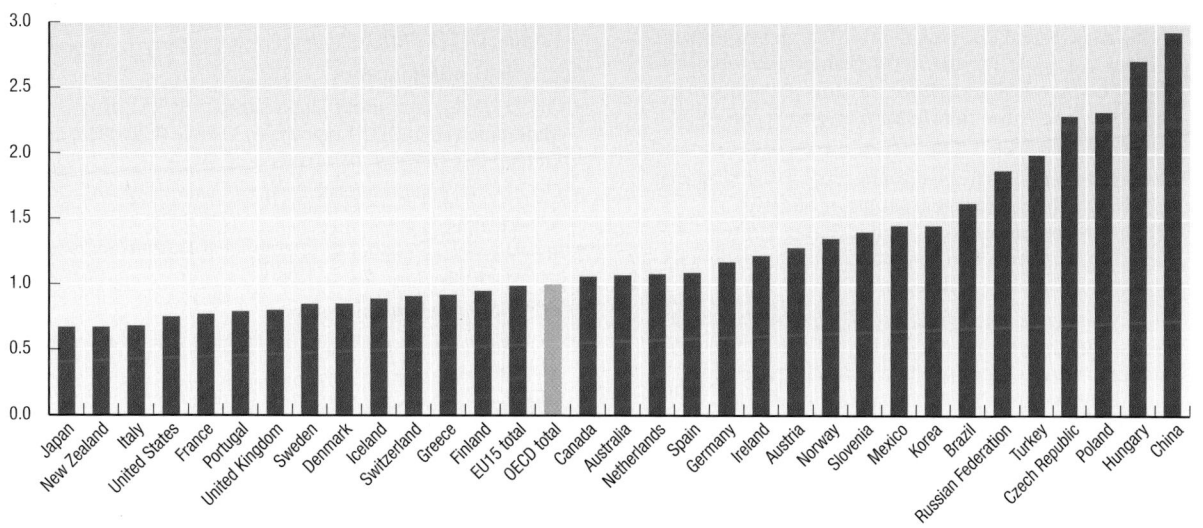

StatLink http://dx.doi.org/10.1787/267160057464

TRADE IN SERVICES

International trade in services is growing in importance both among OECD countries and with the rest of the world. Traditional services – transport, insurance on merchandise trade, and travel – account for about half of total international trade in services, but trade in newer types of services, particularly those that can be conducted via the Internet, is growing rapidly.

Definition

International trade in services is defined according to the 5th edition of the IMF Balance of Payments Manual (BPM5). Services include transport (both freight and passengers), travel (mainly expenditure on goods and services by tourists and business travellers), communications services (postal, telephone, satellite, etc.), construction services, insurance and financial services, computer and information services, royalties and license fees, other business services (merchanting, operational leasing, technical and professional services, etc.), cultural and recreational services (rents for films, fees for actors and other performers, but excluding purchases of films, recorded music, books, etc.) and government services not included in the list above.

Long-term trends

Between 1997 and 2006, growth among OECD member countries of service imports was highest in Ireland and was also well above average in Greece, Luxembourg and Iceland. Imports of services grew relatively slowly in Japan.

In the same period, the growth rate of service exports for Ireland was again well above the average and relatively high growth was also recorded for India, Luxembourg and Denmark. Rather low relative growth occurred in Turkey, Mexico and France.

Averaged over the last three years, trade in services was relatively balanced for most countries but large surpluses were recorded for United States, United Kingdom, Euro Area and Spain and substantial deficits occurred in Germany and Japan.

The fastest growing services in OECD exports are now insurance and computer and information services, and for imports insurance and government services not included elsewhere. The slowest growing export category has been construction services.

Comparability

BPM5 was issued in 1993 and countries began to implement it in the next two or three years. Prior to that, services were defined according to BPM4. All OECD countries now report international trade in services broadly according to the BPM5 framework, and BPM4 is of interest principally for some historic series that have not been revised. The main difference between them is that BPM5 makes a clear distinction between transactions in services and payments of income. In BPM4, labour and non-financial property incomes were included with services. Countries have tried to preserve continuity by revising earlier figures in line with BPM5 but this has not always been possible.

Sources

- OECD (2007), *Main Economic Indicators*, OECD, Paris.
- OECD (2007), *Statistics on International Trade in Services*, OECD, Paris.

Further information

Analytical publications

- OECD (2004), *Promoting Trade in Services: Experience of the Baltic States*, OECD, Paris.
- OECD (2005), *Trade and Structural Adjustment: Embracing Globalisation*, OECD, Paris.
- OECD (2006), *Export Credit Financing Systems in OECD Member Countries and Non-Member Economies*, OECD, Paris.
- OECD (2006), *OECD Trade Policy Studies – Liberalisation and Universal Access to Basic Services: Telecommunications, Water and Sanitation, Financial Services, and Electricity*, OECD, Paris.
- OECD (2007), *Infrastructure to 2030 (Vol.2): Preparing the Future* , OECD, Paris.

Statistical publications

- OECD (2002), *Measuring Globalisation: The Role of Multinationals in OECD Economies, Volume II: Services 2001 Edition*, OECD, Paris.
- OECD (2007), *International Trade by Commodity Statistics*, OECD, Paris.
- OECD (2007), *Statistics on International Trade in Services*, OECD, Paris.

Methodological publications

- IMF (1993), *Balance of Payments Manual*, 5th edition, IMF, Washington, DC.

Websites

- OECD International Trade in Services, *www.oecd.org/std/trade-services*.

Services trade balance: exports of services minus imports of services
Billion US dollars

	1993	1994	1995	1996	1997	1998	1999	2000	2001	2002	2003	2004	2005	2006
Australia	-1.5	-1.3	-0.9	0.2	0.2	-0.9	0.1	0.9	0.7	1.2	1.8	0.5	0.5	0.8
Austria	7.5	7.4	4.6	4.6	1.0	2.4	1.8	1.6	1.8	0.6	1.9	8.8	11.5	13.9
Belgium	..	..	-0.1	0.2	1.3	0.8	1.4	2.1	1.8	1.8	1.7	3.6	5.0	6.3
Canada	-10.5	-8.5	-7.4	-6.7	-6.4	-4.3	-4.5	-3.9	-5.0	-4.6	-8.2	-9.2	-10.0	-13.4
Czech Republic	1.0	0.5	1.8	1.9	1.8	1.9	1.2	1.4	1.5	0.7	0.5	0.6	1.5	1.5
Denmark	1.6	0.5	0.7	1.3	0.1	-0.3	2.0	2.4	3.4	2.0	3.5	3.3	6.4	6.7
Finland	-2.2	-1.8	-2.2	-1.7	-1.6	-1.1	-1.1	-0.7	1.1	2.4	1.5	2.9	1.8	0.5
France	..	..	14.3	15.1	16.7	17.3	18.6	19.8	17.8	17.1	15.8	14.6	13.2	10.4
Germany	-38.3	-46.1	-53.4	-51.7	-48.1	-51.6	-57.9	-55.0	-54.1	-43.2	-50.7	-51.2	-52.0	-47.9
Greece	..	..	..	..	7.2	7.0	7.6	8.2	7.9	9.7	13.0	19.2	19.5	19.3
Hungary	0.2	0.2	0.6	1.5	1.7	1.7	1.3	0.8	1.1	-	-1.2	-0.3	1.3	1.6
Iceland	-	-	-	-	-	-	-0.1	-0.1	-	-	-0.1	-0.2	-0.5	-0.7
Ireland	-3.0	-4.1	-6.3	-7.7	-9.0	-9.9	-10.8	-12.8	-11.9	-13.0	-12.5	-12.7	-11.6	-9.3
Italy	3.3	5.2	6.3	7.2	7.8	4.9	1.2	1.1	-	-2.9	-2.7	1.5	-0.6	-1.9
Japan	-43.0	-47.9	-57.3	-62.3	-54.1	-49.3	-54.0	-47.6	-43.7	-42.0	-35.5	-39.0	-27.9	-20.1
Korea	-2.1	-1.8	-3.0	-6.2	-3.2	1.0	-0.7	-2.8	-3.9	-8.2	-7.4	-8.0	-13.7	-18.8
Luxembourg	..	..	3.2	3.5	4.0	4.2	5.4	6.8	6.4	8.0	9.8	12.9	16.3	20.7
Mexico	-2.1	-2.0	0.7	0.4	-0.7	-0.9	-1.8	-2.3	-3.6	-4.0	-4.6	-4.6	-4.7	-5.7
Netherlands	-0.1	0.2	1.1	2.0	3.3	2.5	2.6	-2.1	-2.5	-1.0	-0.7	4.3	6.8	2.8
New Zealand	-0.6	-0.3	-0.2	-0.2	-0.6	-0.7	-0.2	-0.1	0.1	0.6	1.1	0.9	0.4	0.3
Norway	..	0.2	0.5	1.4	1.4	0.7	1.0	2.7	2.6	1.6	1.1	1.0	-0.2	1.5
Poland	..	2.8	3.5	3.4	3.2	4.2	1.4	1.4	0.8	0.8	0.5	1.0	1.9	2.2
Portugal	..	..	..	1.4	1.5	1.9	2.0	2.0	2.6	3.1	4.0	5.0	4.8	6.1
Slovak Republic	0.3	0.8	0.7	0.2	0.2	0.2	0.2	0.4	0.5	0.5	0.2	0.3	0.3	0.7
Spain	11.7	14.8	17.4	19.0	18.2	19.7	20.5	19.4	20.6	21.1	26.2	26.9	27.7	27.7
Sweden	0.1	0.2	-0.4	-0.9	-1.3	-1.6	-1.3	-1.5	-0.6	-0.8	2.0	5.8	7.8	9.8
Switzerland	12.0	11.9	13.3	13.1	13.7	14.3	15.2	15.9	14.2	15.3	18.3	20.6	22.7	26.4
Turkey	6.7	7.1	9.6	6.7	10.9	13.5	7.5	11.4	9.1	7.9	10.5	12.8	15.3	13.4
United Kingdom	10.1	9.9	14.1	17.4	23.1	24.3	22.1	20.8	20.8	24.9	31.3	47.5	44.8	53.4
United States	62.1	67.3	77.8	86.9	90.2	82.1	82.7	74.9	64.4	61.2	54.0	57.5	72.8	79.7
Euro area	..	..	..	..	5.0	0.7	-10.1	-9.1	-2.7	16.6	25.6	35.7	39.2	44.1
OECD total	..	..	..	..	82.1	84.0	63.1	64.4	53.7	61.6	77.5	120.6	154.2	188.1
Brazil	-5.6	-5.3	-7.5	-8.1	-9.3	-9.0	-7.0	-7.2	-7.8	-5.0	-4.9	-4.7	-8.1	-9.7
China	-0.8	0.3	-6.1	-2.0	-3.4	-2.8	-5.3	-5.6	-5.9	-6.8	-8.6	-9.7	-9.4	..
India	0.8	0.6	0.2	0.3	1.3	2.1	2.2	3.4	2.9	4.4	6.4	13.0	22.2	29.0
Russian Federation	..	-7.0	-9.6	-5.4	-5.9	-4.1	-4.3	-6.7	-9.1	-9.9	-10.9	-12.7	-13.9	-13.8
South Africa	-1.4	-1.3	-1.4	-0.7	-0.6	-0.3	-0.5	-0.8	-0.4	-0.5	0.3	-0.6	-1.0	-2.3

StatLink http://dx.doi.org/10.1787/273056150274

Services trade balance: exports of services minus imports of services
Billion US dollars, average 2004-2006

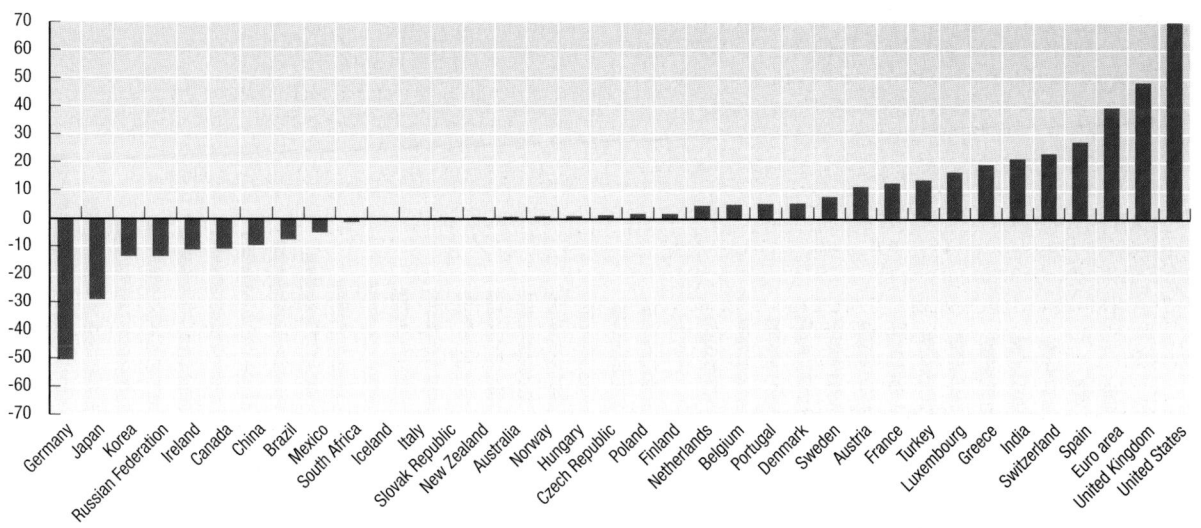

StatLink http://dx.doi.org/10.1787/267231516586

Imports of services
Billion US dollars

	1993	1994	1995	1996	1997	1998	1999	2000	2001	2002	2003	2004	2005	2006
Australia	13.4	15.4	17.4	18.9	19.2	18.0	18.8	18.9	17.3	18.3	21.8	27.9	30.4	32.2
Austria	19.2	20.6	24.6	25.4	26.7	27.1	29.5	29.8	31.5	34.8	41.1	28.0	29.5	32.5
Belgium	..	..	29.7	29.0	27.8	30.0		31.2	32.3	33.6	35.9	42.9	49.1	51.1	53.1
Canada	32.4	32.5	33.5	35.9	38.0	38.1	40.6	44.1	43.8	45.0	52.3	58.9	65.3	72.6
Czech Republic	3.7	4.7	4.9	6.3	5.4	5.7	5.9	5.4	5.6	6.4	7.3	9.0	10.2	11.8
Denmark	10.6	11.8	13.2	13.9	14.2	15.6	18.4	22.1	23.5	25.1	27.9	33.3	37.3	45.3
Finland	6.6	7.3	9.6	8.8	8.2	7.8		7.6	8.4	8.1	8.1	10.0	12.3	15.2	15.6
France	..	..	64.5	66.8	64.2	67.5		63.1	60.8	62.4	68.7	82.9	98.4	105.6	107.9
Germany	102.0	111.6	133.4	135.3	130.7	135.6		141.9	138.2	142.7	145.5	173.8	196.6	209.2	221.8
Greece	..	..	..	..	4.1	4.5		9.7	11.5		11.6	9.6	11.2	14.0	14.7	16.4
Hungary	2.6	3.0	3.6	3.5	4.1	4.2		4.4	4.8	5.6	6.8	9.2	10.6	11.5	11.7
Iceland	0.6	0.6	0.6	0.7	0.8	1.0	1.0	1.2	1.1	1.1	1.5	1.8	2.6	2.6
Ireland	6.7	8.4	11.3	13.4	15.2		23.9		27.7	32.8	37.5	42.8	54.5	65.4	71.5	78.4
Italy	45.6	45.7	51.1	53.4	54.2	59.1		57.7	55.6	57.8	63.0	74.3	83.3	90.0	100.3
Japan	96.2	106.2	122.8	130.0	123.4	111.7	114.9	116.8	108.2	107.8	108.8	133.7	134.0	134.5
Korea	15.1	18.6	25.8	29.6	29.5	24.5	27.2	33.4	32.9	36.6	40.4	49.9	58.8	70.6
Luxembourg	..	..	7.5	8.5	8.7	9.9		11.5	13.2	13.3	12.3	15.4	20.8	24.6	30.2
Mexico	11.5	12.3	9.0	10.2	11.8	12.4	13.5	16.0	16.2	16.7	17.1	18.6	20.8	22.0
Netherlands	38.0	41.1	44.8	45.3	45.8	47.2		49.5	51.4	53.8	57.0	63.9	69.5	73.3	79.4
New Zealand	3.5	4.0	4.7	4.9	4.8	4.4	4.5	4.5	4.3	4.8	5.7	7.2	8.2	7.8
Norway	..	12.0	13.1	13.4	14.3	14.8	15.4	15.0	15.8	17.8	20.6	24.3	29.6	31.4
Poland	..	3.9	7.1	6.3	5.7	6.6	7.0	9.0	9.0	9.2	10.6	12.5	14.3	18.4
Portugal	..	..	..	6.5	6.2	6.9		7.3	7.1	6.8	7.2	8.3	9.8	10.5	11.6
Slovak Republic	1.7	1.6	1.8	2.0	2.1	2.3	1.8	1.8	2.0	2.3	3.0	3.4	4.1	4.7
Spain	18.9	18.9	22.9	25.5	25.6	28.6		32.0	33.2	35.2	38.8	48.0	59.2	67.1	78.4
Sweden	12.7	14.0	16.8	18.4	19.7	21.4	23.0	24.2	23.6	24.0	28.7	33.1	35.3	39.8
Switzerland	9.2	10.3	12.1	12.7	11.2	12.3	13.1	12.8	13.5	14.2	16.3	21.3	24.5	25.5
Turkey	4.2	4.0	5.3		6.7	8.8	10.2	9.3	9.0	6.9	6.9	8.5	11.3	11.4	11.1
United Kingdom	52.4	60.0	65.7	73.0	78.6	88.3	97.0	99.8	100.3	110.1	127.3	150.0	164.5	175.9
United States	123.8	133.1	141.4	152.6	165.9	180.7	199.2	223.7	221.8	231.1	250.4	292.2	315.7	342.8
Euro area	..	..	..	..	241.4	262.8		279.6	281.9	290.4	298.7	352.4	416.5	457.6	490.7
OECD total	..	..	..	..	975.1		1 020.5		1 083.9	1 137.3		1 146.0	1 209.6	1 384.8	1 623.2	1 756.3	1 887.2
Brazil	9.6	10.3	13.6	12.7	15.3	16.7	14.2	16.7	17.1	14.5	15.4	17.3	24.2	29.1
China	12.0	16.3	25.2	22.6	28.0	26.7	31.6	36.0	39.3	46.5	55.3	72.1	83.8	..
India	4.3	5.5	6.7	7.1	7.8	9.6	12.3	13.3	14.5	15.0	17.5	25.2	33.5	45.5
Russian Federation	..	15.4	20.2	18.7	20.0	16.5	13.4	16.2	20.6	23.5	27.1	33.3	38.9	44.7
South Africa	4.7	5.1	6.0	5.7	6.0	5.7	5.8	5.8	5.2	5.5	8.0	10.3	12.2	14.3

StatLink http://dx.doi.org/10.1787/273063146718

Relative annual growth in imports of services
Growth over the period 1997-2006, OECD total = 1

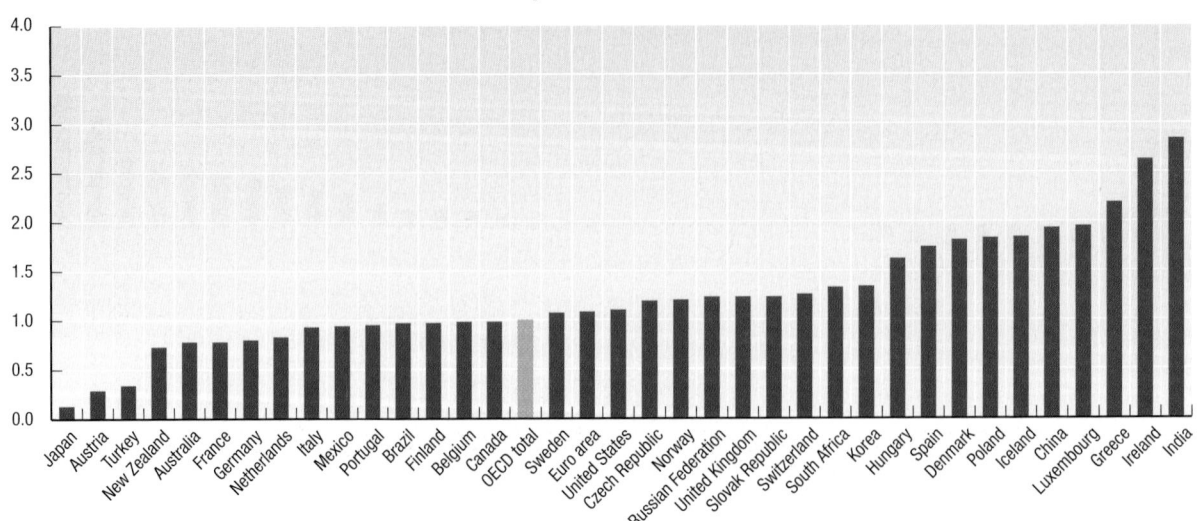

StatLink http://dx.doi.org/10.1787/267240035354

OECD FACTBOOK 2008 – ISBN 978-92-64-04054-0 – © OECD 2008

Exports of services
Billion US dollars

	1993	1994	1995	1996	1997	1998	1999	2000	2001	2002	2003	2004	2005	2006
Australia	11.9	14.2	16.5	19.1	19.3	17.2	18.9	19.9	18.1	19.6	23.6	28.5	31.0	33.1
Austria	26.7	28.0	29.2	30.0	27.7	29.5	31.3	31.4	33.3	35.3	43.0	36.7	41.0	46.4
Belgium	..	..	29.6	29.3	29.1	30.8		32.6	34.3	35.4	37.7	44.6	52.7	56.1	59.4
Canada	21.9	24.0	26.1	29.2	31.6	33.9	36.1	40.2	38.8	40.4	44.1	49.7	55.3	59.3
Czech Republic	4.7	5.2	6.7	8.2	7.2	7.6	7.1	6.9	7.1	7.1	7.8	9.6	11.8	13.3
Denmark	12.2	12.3	13.9	15.1	14.3	15.3	20.4	24.5	26.9	27.1	31.4	36.6	43.6	52.0
Finland	4.4	5.5	7.4	7.1	6.7	6.7	6.5	7.7	9.2	10.4	11.5	15.2	17.0	16.1
France	..	..	78.9	81.9	80.9	84.8	81.7	80.6	80.2	85.8	98.7	112.9	118.8	118.3
Germany	63.7	65.5	79.9	83.6	82.6	84.0	84.0	83.2	88.6	102.3	123.1	145.5	157.2	173.9
Greece	..	..	..	..	11.2	11.5	17.4	19.6	19.5	19.2	24.2	33.2	34.3	35.6
Hungary	2.8	3.1	4.3	5.0	5.7	5.9	5.6	5.6	6.6	6.9	8.0	10.4	12.8	13.3
Iceland	0.6	0.6	0.7	0.8	0.8	1.0	0.9	1.0	1.1	1.1	1.4	1.6	2.0	1.8
Ireland	3.8	4.3	5.0	5.7	6.2	14.1	16.9	20.0	25.6	29.8	42.0	52.7	59.9	69.1
Italy	48.9	50.9	57.5	60.6	62.0	64.0	58.9	56.7	57.9	60.1	71.6	84.7	89.3	98.4
Japan	53.2	58.3	65.5	67.7	69.3	62.4	60.9	69.2	64.5	65.7	73.3	94.7	106.1	114.4
Korea	12.9	16.8	22.8	23.4	26.3	25.6	26.5	30.5	29.1	28.4	33.0	41.9	45.1	51.9
Luxembourg	..	..	10.7	12.0	12.7	14.2	16.9	20.0	19.8	20.3	25.2	33.7	40.9	51.0
Mexico	9.4	10.3	9.7	10.6	11.1	11.5	11.7	13.7	12.7	12.7	12.5	14.0	16.1	16.2
Netherlands	37.9	41.4	45.9	47.2	49.0	49.7	52.1	49.3	51.3	56.0	63.2	73.7	80.1	82.2
New Zealand	2.9	3.7	4.5	4.7	4.2	3.8	4.3	4.4	4.4	5.4	6.8	8.1	8.6	8.1
Norway	..	12.2	13.7	14.8	15.7	15.5	16.4	17.8	18.4	19.4	21.7	25.2	29.3	32.9
Poland	..	6.7	10.7	9.7	8.9	10.8	8.4	10.4	9.8	10.0	11.2	13.5	16.3	20.6
Portugal	..	..	..	7.9	7.7	8.8	9.3	9.0	9.4	10.3	12.3	14.7	15.2	17.7
Slovak Republic	2.0	2.3	2.5	2.2	2.3	2.4	2.1	2.2	2.5	2.8	3.3	3.7	4.4	5.4
Spain	30.6	33.6	40.3	44.5	43.9	48.4	52.5	52.6	55.8	59.9	74.2	86.2	94.8	106.0
Sweden	12.8	14.2	16.4	17.5	18.4	19.7	21.7	22.7	23.0	23.3	30.7	38.9	43.1	49.6
Switzerland	21.2	22.2	25.5	25.8	25.0	26.5	28.2	28.7	27.7	29.6	34.6	41.9	47.2	52.0
Turkey	10.9	11.1	14.9	13.4	19.7	23.7	16.8	20.4	16.0	14.8	19.0	24.0	26.6	24.5
United Kingdom	62.4	69.8	79.8	90.5	101.7	112.6	119.1	120.6	121.1	135.0	158.5	197.6	209.4	229.3
United States	185.9	200.4	219.2	239.5	256.1	262.8	281.9	298.6	286.2	292.3	304.3	349.7	388.4	422.6
Euro area	..	..	..	..	246.4	263.5	269.5	272.9	287.7	315.4	377.9	452.1	496.8	534.8
OECD total	..	..	..	..	1 057.2	1 104.4	1 147.0	1 201.6	1 199.7	1 271.2	1 462.3	1 743.8	1 910.5	2 075.3
Brazil	4.0	4.9	6.1	4.7	6.0	7.6	7.2	9.5	9.3	9.6	10.4	12.6	16.1	19.5
China	11.2	16.6	19.1	20.6	24.6	23.9	26.2	30.4	33.3	39.7	46.7	62.4	74.4	..
India	5.1	6.1	6.9	7.5	9.1	11.7	14.5	16.7	17.3	19.5	23.9	38.3	55.7	74.6
Russian Federation	..	8.4	10.6	13.3	14.1	12.4	9.1	9.6	11.4	13.6	16.2	20.6	25.0	30.9
South Africa	3.3	3.8	4.6	5.1	5.4	5.4	5.2	5.0	4.8	5.0	8.3	9.7	11.2	12.0

StatLink http://dx.doi.org/10.1787/273132650802

Relative annual growth in exports of services
Growth over the period 1997-2006, OECD total = 1

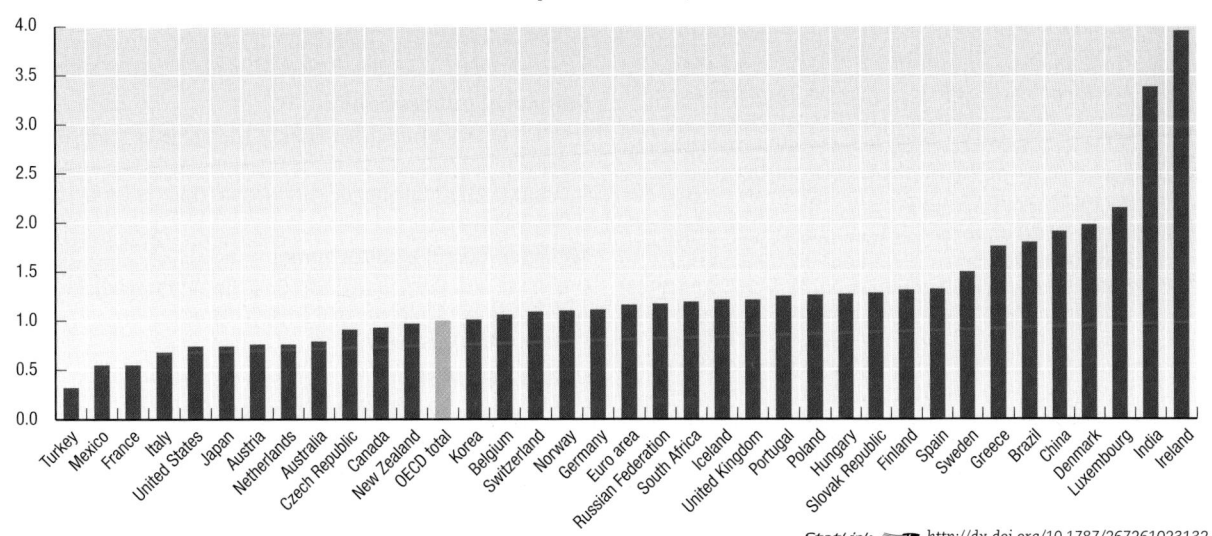

StatLink http://dx.doi.org/10.1787/267261023132

TRADING PARTNERS

The pattern of OECD merchandise trade – where imports come from and where exports go to – has undergone significant shifts over the last decade. These are in response to changes in the distribution of global income and to globalisation – in particular, the outsourcing of manufacturing from OECD countries to the rest of the world.

These tables refer to total OECD imports and exports and show merchandise trade both within the OECD area and with countries in the rest of the world.

Definition

NAFTA is the North American Free Trade Area and consists of Canada, Mexico and the United States. OECD Asia and Oceania includes Australia and New Zealand as well as Japan and Korea. Non-OECD America covers the Caribbean, South America and Central America, except Mexico. Non-OECD Asia covers Central Asia, China, the Indian sub continent and South East. Middle East covers the Gulf Arabian Countries, Iran, Israel, Jordan, Lebanon, the Occupied Palestinian territory and the Syrian Arab Republic.

The definitions of merchandise imports and exports are explained under "Trade in goods".

Comparability

OECD countries follow common definitions and procedures in compiling their merchandise trade statistics which are comparable and of good quality. The removal of customs frontiers following the creation of a common market in Europe required EU countries to adopt a system of recording trade flows through sample surveys of exporters and importers. This led to some fall in the reliability of merchandise trade statistics for trade between the EU countries. Statistics on trade between EU countries and non-EU countries, however, were not affected.

Source

- OECD (2007), *International Trade by Commodity Statistics*, OECD, Paris.

Further information

Analytical publications

- OECD, IOM and the World Bank (eds.) (2004), *Trade and Migration: Building Bridges for Global Labour Mobility*, OECD, Paris.
- OECD (2004), *Agriculture, Trade and the Environment: The Dairy Sector*, OECD, Paris.
- OECD (2004), *Internationalisation and Trade in Higher Education: Opportunities and Challenges*, OECD, Paris.
- OECD (2004), *The Impact of Regulations on Agro-Food Trade: The Technical Barriers to Trade (TBT) and Sanitary and Phytosanitary Measures (SPS) Agreements*, OECD, Paris.
- OECD (2004), *Trade and Competitiveness in Argentina, Brazil and Chile Not as Easy as A-B-C*, OECD, Paris.
- OECD (2005), *OECD Trade Policy Studies – Environmental Requirements and Market Access*, OECD, Paris.
- OECD (2005), *Trade and Structural Adjustment: Embracing Globalisation*, OECD, Paris.
- OECD (2006), *The Development Dimension – Aid for Trade: Making it Effective*, OECD, Paris.
- OECD (2006), *Trade Based Money Laundering*, OECD, Paris.

Statistical publications

- OECD (2007), *Monthly Statistics of International Trade*, OECD, Paris.
- OECD (2007), *Statistics in International Trade in Services*, OECD, Paris.

Methodological publications

- UN, EC, IMF, OECD, UNCTAD and the WTO (2002), *Manual on Statistics of International Trade in Services*, United Nations, New York.

Online databases

- *ITCS International Trade by Commodity Statistics*.
- *Monthly International Trade*.

Websites

- OECD International Trade Statistics, *www.oecd.org/std/its*.

Long-term trends

Since 1988, there has been a steady decline in the share of OECD imports and exports among OECD member countries. In 1988, imports from OECD countries accounted for 80% of total OECD imports but by 2006 this had fallen to 65%. For exports the fall in intra-OECD trade was less marked – down from 81% in 1988 to 75% in 2006.

Outside the OECD area, the low trade shares with Africa have been overtaken by trade with non-OECD America and the Middle East. OECD imports from Non-OECD Asia have risen from 7% to 18% over the period and exports to them from 7.5% to 12%. A large change occurred in trade between OECD and China. In 1988 China supplied a little over 1% of total OECD imports but by 2006 this had risen to 10%. China's importance as a destination for OECD countries has increased less sharply, rising from 1% in 1988 to 4% in 2006.

Partner countries and regions of OECD merchandise trade

As a percentage of total OECD merchandise trade

	1988	1994	1995	1996	1997	1998	1999	2000	2001	2002	2003	2004	2005	2006
OECD	**80.4**	**76.1**	**76.1**	**75.7**	**75.6**	**77.4**	**77.7**	**75.9**	**75.9**	**75.6**	**74.2**	**73.5**	**71.0**	**69.6**
G7	**52.3**	**50.4**	**49.7**	**49.0**	**49.1**	**50.1**	**50.4**	**49.2**	**48.8**	**47.8**	**45.0**	**44.9**	**42.9**	**41.9**
NAFTA	16.3	20.2	19.0	19.7	21.2	21.7	22.7	23.8	23.1	22.2	18.1	18.9	18.6	18.0
Canada	1.3	4.8	4.5	4.6	4.8	4.9	5.1	5.3	5.1	4.8	4.5	4.2	4.3	4.1
Mexico	0.3	2.0	1.8	2.0	2.3	2.5	2.7	3.2	3.1	3.0	2.7	2.5	2.5	2.6
United States	14.7	13.5	12.7	13.1	14.0	14.3	14.9	15.4	14.8	14.3	10.8	12.1	11.7	11.3
OECD Asia Oceania	6.5	9.1	8.9	8.4	8.1	7.4	7.7	8.0	7.3	7.1	6.9	6.8	6.5	6.3
Japan	3.6	6.0	5.7	5.3	5.1	4.7	4.9	4.9	4.5	4.2	4.0	3.8	3.6	3.4
Korea	1.5	1.8	2.0	1.9	1.7	1.4	1.7	1.9	1.7	1.7	1.8	1.8	1.8	1.8
OECD Europe	57.8	46.7	48.1	47.5	46.4	48.3	47.2	44.1	45.5	46.1	49.4	47.8	45.9	45.3
Switzerland	2.6	1.9	2.0	1.9	1.8	1.9	1.8	1.6	1.7	1.6	1.7	1.6	1.3	1.5
EU15	52.8	42.1	43.2	42.4	41.1	42.8	42.0	39.0	40.1	40.5	43.2	41.7	39.9	38.8
Austria	1.7	1.4	1.3	1.3	1.3	1.4	1.3	1.2	1.3	1.3	1.4	1.4	1.3	1.4
Belgium-Luxembourg	4.7	3.5	3.6	3.4	3.2	3.3	3.1	2.9	3.1	3.2	3.4	3.4	2.9	3.4
France	8.0	6.3	6.3	6.1	5.9	6.2	6.1	5.5	5.7	5.7	6.0	5.8	5.5	5.3
Germany	12.7	10.2	10.6	10.3	9.6	10.1	9.8	9.0	9.3	9.4	10.1	10.0	9.6	9.3
Italy	5.5	4.1	4.3	4.2	4.0	4.2	4.0	3.7	3.8	3.9	4.2	4.0	3.3	3.7
Netherlands	5.1	3.9	4.1	4.0	4.0	4.0	3.9	3.7	3.7	3.7	3.9	3.8	3.8	3.2
Spain	2.1	2.1	2.3	2.3	2.3	2.5	2.6	2.4	2.4	2.6	2.8	2.8	2.7	2.6
Sweden	2.2	1.5	1.6	1.6	1.5	1.6	1.6	1.5	1.4	1.4	1.5	1.5	1.5	1.4
United Kingdom	6.6	5.5	5.5	5.6	5.7	5.8	5.7	5.4	5.5	5.4	5.4	5.0	4.8	4.7
Non-OECD	**17.6**	**22.4**	**22.5**	**22.9**	**23.4**	**21.6**	**21.3**	**23.1**	**23.1**	**23.4**	**24.8**	**25.7**	**27.3**	**28.4**
Africa	3.3	2.4	2.3	2.4	2.3	2.2	2.1	2.2	2.3	2.2	2.3	2.4	3.1	3.3
South Africa	0.8	0.4	0.5	0.5	0.5	0.5	0.4	0.4	0.5	0.4	0.5	0.5	0.5	0.5
America	2.1	3.1	3.1	3.1	3.3	3.2	3.0	3.0	3.0	2.8	2.6	2.8	3.0	3.6
South America	1.6	2.3	2.3	2.3	2.4	2.3	2.0	2.1	2.1	1.9	1.8	2.0	2.2	2.3
Brazil	0.7	0.8	0.9	0.9	0.9	0.9	0.8	0.8	0.9	0.8	0.8	0.8	0.8	0.8
Asia	7.2	12.1	12.4	12.4	12.6	11.5	11.8	12.8	12.5	13.0	13.8	14.2	14.6	14.9
China	1.3	2.7	2.8	2.9	3.1	3.2	3.4	3.9	4.2	4.9	5.8	6.3	6.8	7.2
India	0.5	0.6	0.6	0.6	0.6	0.6	0.5	0.5	0.5	0.6	0.6	0.7	0.7	0.8
Chinese Taipei	1.4	1.9	1.9	1.8	1.8	1.8	1.8	2.0	1.7	1.6	1.5	1.6	1.4	1.4
Europe	2.2	2.0	2.1	2.2	2.3	2.2	1.9	2.2	2.4	2.5	2.9	3.1	3.6	3.7
Russian Federation	0.2	1.0	1.0	1.1	1.1	1.0	0.8	1.0	1.1	1.1	1.3	1.5	1.7	1.7
Middle East	2.6	2.7	2.5	2.6	2.8	2.4	2.4	2.9	2.9	2.7	2.9	3.0	3.4	3.4

StatLink http://dx.doi.org/10.1787/273172474460

Partner countries and regions of OECD merchandise trade

As a percentage of total OECD merchandise trade

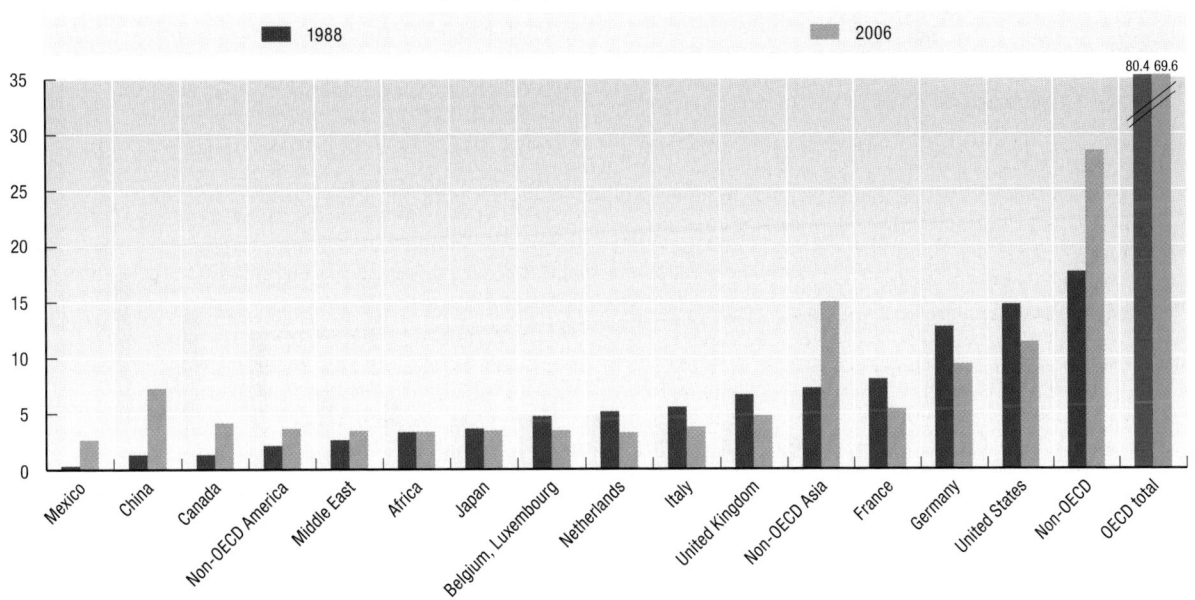

StatLink http://dx.doi.org/10.1787/267266880251

Partner countries and regions of OECD merchandise imports

As a percentage of total OECD merchandise imports

	1988	1994	1995	1996	1997	1998	1999	2000	2001	2002	2003	2004	2005	2006
OECD	**80.2**	**75.9**	**76.3**	**75.6**	**75.4**	**76.8**	**75.9**	**73.1**	**73.3**	**72.9**	**71.3**	**70.3**	**67.0**	**65.2**
G7	**52.5**	**51.3**	**50.8**	**50.2**	**50.0**	**50.5**	**49.8**	**47.5**	**47.0**	**45.9**	**43.1**	**42.7**	**40.1**	**39.0**
NAFTA	14.7	19.4	18.9	19.7	20.8	20.7	21.1	21.7	21.1	19.9	16.1	16.5	16.0	15.6
Canada	1.3	5.1	5.0	5.0	5.1	5.2	5.4	5.6	5.5	5.2	4.8	4.6	4.6	4.3
Mexico	0.4	1.9	2.0	2.2	2.5	2.6	2.9	3.3	3.3	3.3	3.0	2.7	2.7	2.8
United States	13.0	12.3	11.9	12.4	13.1	12.9	12.8	12.8	12.2	11.5	8.3	9.2	8.7	8.5
OECD Asia Oceania	7.8	10.8	10.2	9.2	9.2	9.0	9.3	9.4	8.5	8.2	7.9	7.9	7.5	7.2
Japan	4.7	7.9	7.2	6.4	6.4	6.2	6.4	6.3	5.6	5.4	5.1	4.9	4.6	4.3
Korea	1.6	1.6	1.7	1.6	1.6	1.6	1.9	2.0	1.8	1.8	1.8	1.9	1.8	1.8
OECD Europe	58.0	45.8	47.3	46.7	45.5	47.1	45.6	42.0	43.6	44.5	47.6	45.9	43.5	42.4
Switzerland	2.3	1.9	1.9	1.8	1.7	1.7	1.6	1.4	1.5	1.5	1.5	1.5	1.1	1.4
EU15	53.3	41.3	42.5	41.8	40.6	42.1	40.6	37.1	38.3	39.0	41.4	39.9	37.8	36.3
Austria	1.5	1.3	1.2	1.1	1.1	1.2	1.2	1.0	1.1	1.2	1.3	1.2	1.2	1.2
Belgium-Luxembourg	4.6	3.3	3.4	3.2	3.0	3.0	2.9	2.6	2.8	2.9	3.1	3.1	2.6	3.0
France	7.6	6.1	6.1	5.9	5.8	6.1	5.8	5.1	5.3	5.3	5.6	5.3	4.9	4.7
Germany	14.6	10.4	10.9	10.6	10.0	10.5	10.2	9.2	9.6	10.0	10.8	10.7	10.2	9.8
Italy	5.6	4.5	4.6	4.6	4.3	4.5	4.2	3.7	3.8	3.9	4.1	3.9	3.1	3.5
Netherlands	5.3	3.8	4.0	3.9	3.9	4.0	3.7	3.5	3.5	3.5	3.8	3.8	3.8	3.1
Spain	1.8	1.9	2.0	2.1	2.1	2.2	2.1	1.9	2.0	2.1	2.3	2.2	2.1	2.1
Sweden	2.3	1.7	1.7	1.7	1.7	1.7	1.6	1.5	1.4	1.4	1.5	1.5	1.5	1.5
United Kingdom	5.6	5.0	5.1	5.2	5.2	5.2	5.1	4.9	4.8	4.6	4.5	4.1	4.0	3.8
Non-OECD	**18.0**	**22.8**	**22.6**	**23.3**	**23.9**	**22.4**	**23.2**	**26.0**	**25.7**	**25.9**	**27.6**	**28.9**	**31.3**	**32.7**
Africa	3.6	2.5	2.4	2.6	2.5	2.2	2.1	2.4	2.5	2.3	2.6	2.7	3.5	3.8
South Africa	1.0	0.4	0.5	0.5	0.5	0.5	0.5	0.5	0.5	0.5	0.5	0.5	0.5	0.5
America	2.5	3.1	2.9	3.0	3.0	2.8	2.8	3.0	2.9	3.0	2.9	3.2	3.4	4.0
South America	2.1	2.4	2.3	2.3	2.3	2.1	2.1	2.2	2.2	2.2	2.2	2.5	2.7	2.8
Brazil	1.0	1.0	0.9	0.8	0.8	0.8	0.8	0.8	0.9	0.9	0.9	1.0	1.0	1.0
Asia	6.9	12.3	12.4	12.8	13.2	13.2	13.7	14.6	14.5	15.2	16.0	16.6	17.2	17.8
China	1.3	3.6	3.7	4.0	4.4	4.5	4.9	5.5	5.9	6.8	7.7	8.5	9.3	9.8
India	0.4	0.6	0.6	0.6	0.6	0.6	0.6	0.6	0.6	0.7	0.7	0.7	0.7	0.8
Chinese Taipei	1.5	2.0	1.9	1.9	1.9	1.9	1.9	2.1	1.8	1.7	1.6	1.6	1.3	1.4
Europe	2.2	2.0	2.1	2.1	2.1	2.0	2.0	2.4	2.4	2.5	2.8	3.1	3.7	3.6
Russian Federation	0.2	1.2	1.2	1.2	1.2	1.1	1.1	1.4	1.4	1.4	1.6	1.8	2.1	2.2
Middle East	2.7	2.7	2.6	2.7	2.9	2.2	2.5	3.5	3.3	2.9	3.2	3.3	3.9	4.1

StatLink http://dx.doi.org/10.1787/273255355332

Partners countries and regions of OECD merchandise imports

As a percentage of total OECD merchandise imports

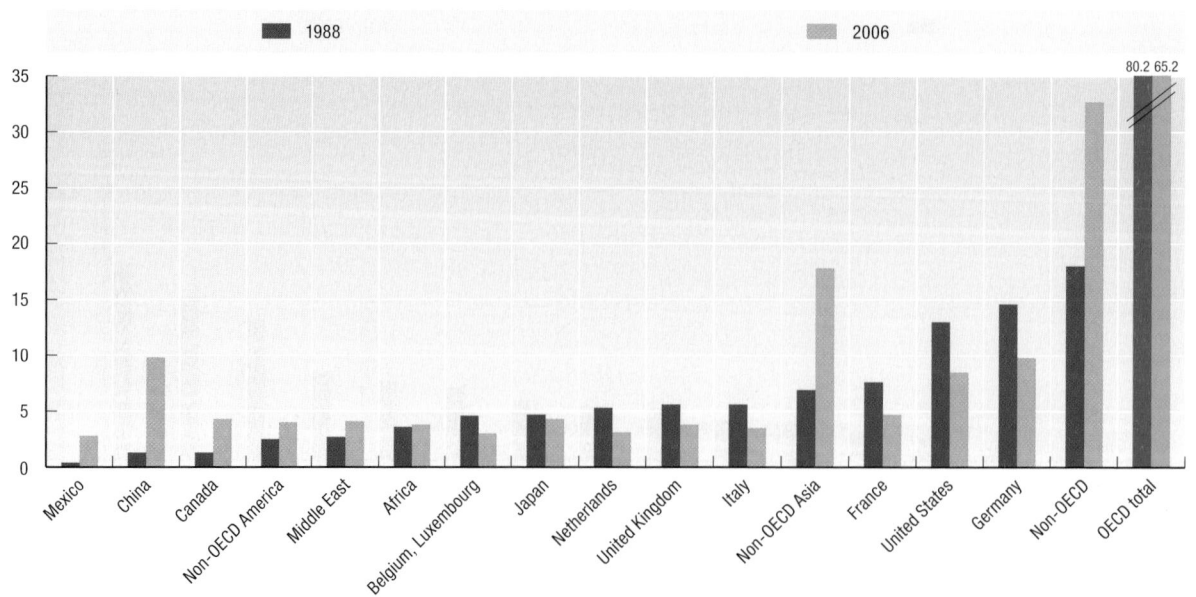

StatLink http://dx.doi.org/10.1787/267275266665

OECD FACTBOOK 2008 – ISBN 978-92-64-04054-0 – © OECD 2008

Partner countries and regions of OECD merchandise exports

As a percentage of total OECD merchandise exports

	1988	1994	1995	1996	1997	1998	1999	2000	2001	2002	2003	2004	2005	2006
OECD	**80.5**	**76.3**	**75.9**	**75.7**	**75.8**	**77.9**	**79.6**	**79.0**	**78.8**	**78.5**	**77.4**	**77.0**	**75.4**	**74.6**
G7	**52.2**	**49.5**	**48.6**	**47.9**	**48.2**	**49.7**	**51.1**	**51.0**	**50.8**	**49.9**	**47.1**	**47.4**	**46.1**	**45.0**
NAFTA	17.9	21.1	19.2	19.7	21.6	22.6	24.5	26.1	25.2	24.6	20.2	21.4	21.5	20.7
Canada	1.3	4.5	4.1	4.2	4.5	4.6	4.8	4.8	4.6	4.5	4.2	3.9	4.0	3.9
Mexico	0.3	2.1	1.6	1.8	2.2	2.4	2.6	3.0	2.9	2.7	2.5	2.3	2.3	2.4
United States	16.3	14.6	13.5	13.7	14.8	15.6	17.1	18.3	17.6	17.4	13.5	15.2	15.1	14.5
OECD Asia Oceania	5.3	7.5	7.6	7.6	7.0	5.7	6.1	6.5	6.0	5.9	5.9	5.6	5.4	5.2
Japan	2.5	4.1	4.1	4.1	3.8	3.2	3.3	3.4	3.2	2.9	2.8	2.6	2.5	2.4
Korea	1.4	2.0	2.2	2.2	1.9	1.2	1.6	1.8	1.6	1.7	1.7	1.7	1.7	1.7
OECD Europe	57.5	47.7	49.0	48.4	47.2	49.6	49.0	46.4	47.6	47.9	51.4	50.0	48.5	48.6
Switzerland	2.9	2.0	2.0	2.0	1.8	2.0	1.9	1.7	1.8	1.8	1.8	1.7	1.4	1.7
EU15	52.4	43.0	43.9	42.9	41.6	43.7	43.4	41.0	42.1	42.1	45.1	43.6	42.3	41.6
Austria	1.8	1.5	1.5	1.5	1.4	1.5	1.5	1.4	1.4	1.4	1.6	1.6	1.5	1.5
Belgium-Luxembourg	4.7	3.8	3.8	3.6	3.4	3.5	3.4	3.2	3.4	3.5	3.8	3.8	3.2	3.8
France	8.4	6.6	6.6	6.2	5.9	6.3	6.3	6.0	6.2	6.1	6.5	6.3	6.2	6.0
Germany	10.7	10.0	10.3	9.9	9.3	9.7	9.4	8.8	9.0	8.8	9.5	9.2	9.0	8.8
Italy	5.4	3.8	4.0	3.8	3.7	3.9	3.9	3.7	3.8	3.9	4.3	4.1	3.5	3.8
Netherlands	4.9	4.1	4.2	4.1	4.1	4.1	4.1	3.9	3.8	3.8	4.0	3.8	3.7	3.4
Spain	2.4	2.3	2.5	2.5	2.5	2.8	3.0	2.8	2.9	3.0	3.4	3.4	3.4	3.3
Sweden	2.1	1.3	1.5	1.5	1.4	1.4	1.4	1.4	1.3	1.3	1.5	1.4	1.4	1.4
United Kingdom	7.6	6.0	5.9	6.0	6.2	6.4	6.3	6.1	6.3	6.3	6.3	6.0	5.7	5.6
Non-OECD	**17.2**	**22.0**	**22.5**	**22.4**	**23.0**	**20.8**	**19.3**	**20.1**	**20.4**	**20.6**	**21.7**	**22.1**	**22.7**	**23.6**
Africa	3.1	2.3	2.2	2.2	2.1	2.3	2.0	1.9	2.0	2.0	2.1	2.1	2.6	2.7
South Africa	0.6	0.4	0.5	0.5	0.4	0.5	0.4	0.4	0.4	0.4	0.4	0.5	0.5	0.5
America	1.7	3.2	3.3	3.3	3.7	3.7	3.1	3.0	3.1	2.7	2.3	2.5	2.6	3.2
South America	1.1	2.1	2.3	2.3	2.6	2.6	2.0	1.9	2.0	1.6	1.3	1.4	1.6	1.7
Brazil	0.3	0.7	0.9	0.9	1.0	1.0	0.8	0.8	0.9	0.7	0.6	0.6	0.7	0.7
Asia	7.5	11.8	12.4	12.0	12.0	9.8	9.9	10.9	10.3	10.7	11.5	11.7	11.7	11.7
China	1.2	1.8	1.8	1.8	1.8	1.8	1.9	2.2	2.4	2.9	3.6	3.9	4.0	4.3
India	0.6	0.5	0.6	0.6	0.5	0.5	0.5	0.5	0.5	0.5	0.6	0.7	0.8	0.7
Chinese Taipei	1.4	1.9	1.9	1.7	1.8	1.7	1.7	2.0	1.5	1.5	1.5	1.6	1.5	1.4
Europe	2.2	1.9	2.1	2.3	2.5	2.4	1.9	1.9	2.4	2.6	3.0	3.1	3.4	3.8
Russian Federation	0.2	0.8	0.8	0.9	1.1	0.9	0.5	0.6	0.8	0.8	1.0	1.1	1.2	1.4
Middle East	2.6	2.6	2.4	2.5	2.6	2.6	2.3	2.2	2.4	2.5	2.6	2.6	2.8	2.6

StatLink http://dx.doi.org/10.1787/273267418181

Partner countries and regions of OECD merchandise exports

As a percentage of total OECD merchandise exports

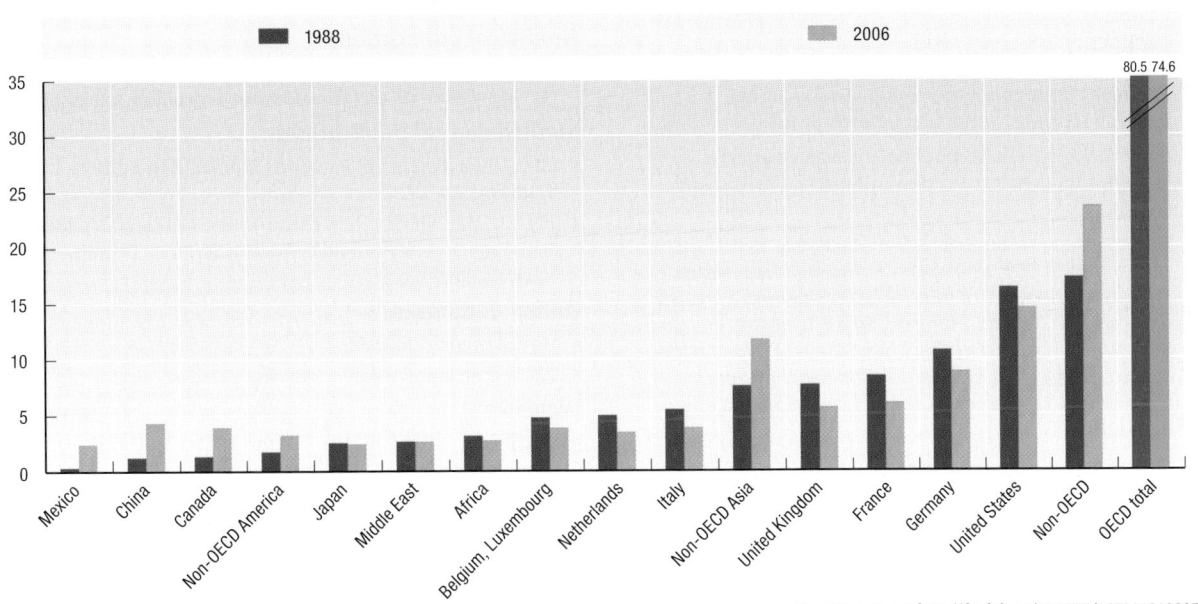

StatLink http://dx.doi.org/10.1787/267311813207

BALANCE OF PAYMENTS

The current account balance is the difference between current receipts from abroad and current payments to abroad. When the current account of the balance of payments is positive, the country can use the surplus to repay foreign debts or to lend to the rest of the world. When the current account balance is negative, the deficit will be financed by borrowing from abroad or by liquidating foreign assets acquired in earlier periods.

Definition

The current account balance is the difference between a country's current receipts from and its current payments to the rest of the world. These current transactions consist of exports and imports of goods; exports and imports of services such as tourism, international freight and passenger transport, insurance and financial services; income consisting of wages and salaries, dividends, interest and other property income; and transfers.

Note that property income includes retained earnings of foreign-owned subsidiaries. All earnings of foreign-owned subsidiaries are treated as if they were remitted abroad and the part which is actually retained in the country where the subsidiary is located is then shown as a re-investment flow in the capital account.

Long-term trends

Current account balances have been negative throughout the period since 1993 in Australia, Hungary, Mexico, New Zealand, Spain, the United States and the United Kingdom; this is partly due to the way in which earnings of foreign owned-subsidiaries are treated. Countries which have recorded current account surpluses throughout the period include Japan, Luxembourg, the Netherlands, Norway and Switzerland.

Since 1993, current account balances have generally moved from deficit to surplus in Austria, Canada and Germany.

The chart shows current account balances as a percentage of GDP, averaged over the last three years. Deficits averaged 5% or more of GDP in Iceland, Portugal, Greece, New Zealand, Hungary, Spain, the Slovak Republic, Turkey, the United States and Australia. Surpluses in excess of 5% were recorded by Norway, Switzerland, Luxembourg, Netherlands, Sweden and Finland.

Comparability

The data in this table are taken from balance of payments statistics compiled according to the International Monetary Fund (IMF) *Balance of Payments Manual* (BPM5). The IMF closely monitors balance of payments statistics reported by its member countries through regular meetings of balance of payments compilers. As a result, there is relatively good comparability across countries.

Because all earnings of foreign-owned subsidiaries are treated as though they are remitted even though a large part may in practice be retained by the subsidiaries in the countries where they are located, the existence of foreign-owned subsidiaries in an economy will tend to reduce its current account balance.

Sources

- For member countries and South Africa: OECD (2007), *Main Economic Indicators*, OECD, Paris.
- For Brazil, China, India and Russian Federation: National sources.

Further information
Analytical publications

- OECD (2006), *Export Credit Financing Systems in OECD Member Countries and Non-Member Economies*, OECD, Paris.

Methodological publications

- IMF (1993), *Balance of Payments Manual*, 5th edition, IMF, Washington, DC.
- UN, EC, IMF, OECD, UNCTAD and the WTO (2002), *Manual on Statistics of International Trade in Services*, United Nations, New York.

Online databases

- *Main Economic Indicators*.
- *OECD Economic Outlook Statistics*.

Websites

- OECD Economic Outlook – Sources and Methods, *www.oecd.org/eco/sources-and-methods*.

Current account balance of payments
As a percentage of GDP

	1993	1994	1995	1996	1997	1998	1999	2000	2001	2002	2003	2004	2005	2006
Australia	-3.1	-4.8	-5.0	-3.6	-2.8	-4.7	-5.1	-3.6	-1.9	-3.7	-5.2	-5.9	-5.5	-5.3
Austria	-0.8	-1.6	-2.6	-2.3	-3.1	-2.4	-3.2	-2.5	-1.9	0.3	-0.2	1.7	2.1	2.8
Belgium	..	..	5.4	5.0	5.5	5.2	5.1	4.0	3.4	4.6	4.1	3.5	2.6	2.7
Canada	-3.9	-2.3	-0.8	0.5	-1.3	-1.2	0.3	2.7	2.3	1.7	1.2	2.3	2.0	1.6
Czech Republic	1.2	-1.8	-2.5	-6.6	-6.2	-2.0	-2.4	-4.8	-5.3	-5.5	-6.3	-5.2	-1.6	-3.1
Denmark	2.8	1.5	0.7	1.4	0.4	-0.9	1.9	1.6	2.6	2.9	3.5	2.4	3.8	2.4
Finland	-1.3	1.1	4.1	4.0	5.6	5.6	6.2	8.7	9.6	10.2	6.5	7.8	4.9	5.2
France	..	..	0.7	1.3	2.7	2.6	3.1	1.6	1.9	1.4	0.8	0.5	-0.9	-1.3
Germany	-0.9	-1.4	-1.2	-0.6	-0.5	-0.7	-1.3	-1.7	-	2.0	1.9	4.3	4.6	4.9
Greece	..	..	..	..	-3.9	-2.7	-3.8	-7.8	-7.3	-6.8	-6.6	-5.9	-7.2	-11.0
Hungary	-8.7	-9.2	-3.3	-3.8	-4.3	-7.0	-7.6	-8.4	-6.0	-6.9	-7.9	-8.4	-6.8	-6.5
Iceland	0.7	1.9	0.7	-1.8	-1.7	-6.7	-6.7	-10.2	-4.3	1.5	-4.8	-9.8	-16.2	-25.7
Ireland	3.5	2.8	2.6	2.8	2.3	0.8	0.2	-0.4	-0.7	-0.9	-	-0.6	-3.6	-4.2
Italy	0.8	1.2	2.2	3.1	2.8	1.9	0.7	-0.5	-0.1	-0.8	-1.3	-0.9	-1.6	-2.6
Japan	3.1	2.7	2.1	1.4	2.3	3.1	2.6	2.6	2.1	2.9	3.2	3.7	3.6	3.9
Korea	0.2	-1.0	-1.7	-4.1	-1.6	11.7	5.5	2.4	1.7	1.0	2.0	4.1	1.9	0.7
Luxembourg	..	..	12.1	11.2	10.4	9.2	8.4	13.2	8.8	11.7	8.0	11.6	10.9	10.3
Mexico	-5.8	-7.0	-0.6	-0.8	-1.9	-3.8	-2.9	-3.2	-2.8	-2.2	-1.3	-1.0	-0.7	-0.2
Netherlands	4.1	4.9	6.1	5.1	6.5	3.2	3.8	1.9	2.4	2.5	5.5	7.5	7.2	8.3
New Zealand	-3.7	-3.8	-5.0	-5.7	-6.3	-3.9	-6.2	-5.2	-2.7	-3.8	-4.2	-6.3	-8.5	-8.6
Norway	..	3.0	3.5	6.8	6.3	-	5.6	15.0	16.1	12.5	12.3	12.7	15.5	16.4
Poland	..	0.9	0.6	-2.1	-3.7	-4.0	-7.4	-5.8	-2.8	-2.5	-1.9	-4.2	-1.6	-3.3
Portugal	..	..	..	-4.2	-5.9	-7.0	-8.5	-10.2	-9.9	-8.1	-6.1	-7.7	-9.7	-9.4
Slovak Republic	-4.4	4.8	2.6	-9.2	-8.4	-8.8	-4.8	-3.4	-8.3	-7.9	-0.8	-3.4	-8.6	-8.3
Spain	-1.1	-1.2	-0.3	-0.2	-0.1	-1.2	-2.9	-4.0	-3.9	-3.3	-3.5	-5.3	-7.4	-8.6
Sweden	-1.3	1.1	3.3	3.5	4.1	3.8	4.1	3.8	3.8	4.0	7.2	6.7	6.8	7.0
Switzerland	7.7	6.3	6.5	7.0	9.3	9.2	10.8	12.1	7.7	8.4	12.9	12.9	13.5	15.1
Turkey	-3.6	2.0	-1.4	-1.3	-1.4	1.0	-0.7	-4.9	2.3	-0.8	-3.4	-5.1	-6.2	-8.1
United Kingdom	-1.8	-1.0	-1.2	-0.9	-0.1	-0.4	-2.4	-2.6	-2.2	-1.6	-1.3	-1.6	-2.5	-3.2
United States	-1.3	-1.7	-1.5	-1.6	-1.7	-2.5	-3.3	-4.3	-3.8	-4.4	-4.8	-5.5	-6.1	-6.2
Brazil	-	-0.2	-2.4	-2.8	-3.5	-4.0	-4.3	-3.8	-4.2	-1.5	0.8	1.8	1.6	1.2
China	-1.9	1.2	0.2	0.8	3.9	3.1	1.9	1.7	1.3	2.4	2.8	3.6	7.2	..
India	..	..	..	..	..	..	..	-1.0	0.3	1.4	1.5	0.1	-1.0	-1.2
Russian Federation	..	..	2.3	2.8	-	0.1	12.6	18.0	11.1	8.4	8.2	10.1	11.0	9.7
South Africa	2.1	-	-1.6	-1.2	-1.5	-1.6	-0.5	-0.1	0.3	0.8	-1.1	-3.2	-4.0	-6.5

StatLink ⬛ http://dx.doi.org/10.1787/273288250851

Current account balance of payments
As a percentage of GDP, average 2004-2006

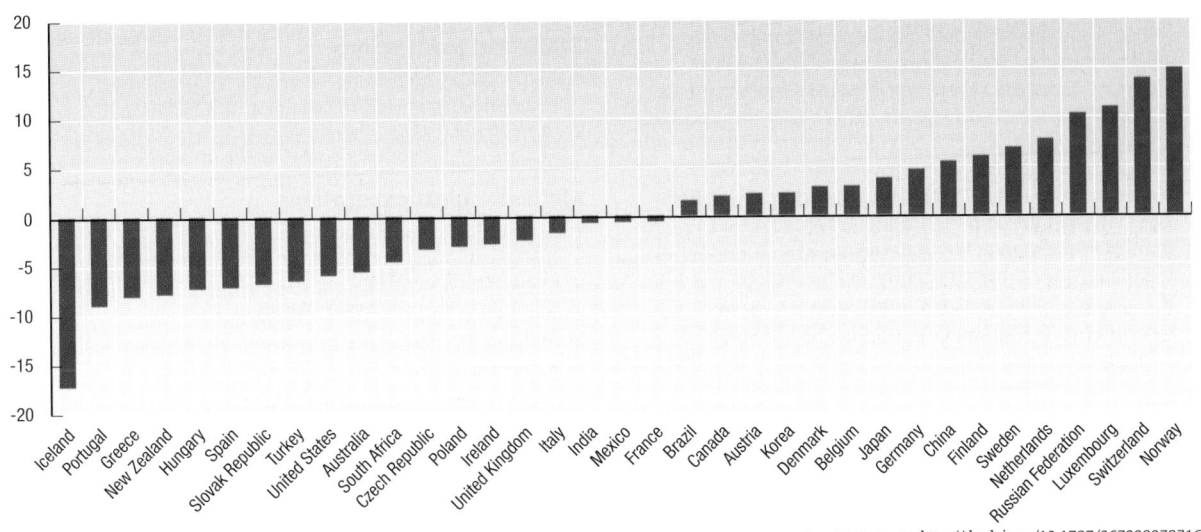

StatLink ⬛ http://dx.doi.org/10.1787/267328378716

FDI FLOWS AND STOCKS

Foreign direct investment (FDI) is a key element in the rapidly evolving process of international economic integration. FDI creates direct, stable and long-lasting links between economies. FDI encourages the transfer of technology and know-how between countries, and it allows the host economy to promote its products more widely in international markets. Finally, FDI is an additional source of funding for capital investment and under right policy environment it can serve as an important vehicle for enterprise development.

Definition

Foreign direct investment (FDI) is defined as investment by a resident entity in one economy with the objective of obtaining a lasting interest in an enterprise resident in another economy. The lasting interest means the existence of a long-term relationship between the direct investor and the enterprise and a significant degree of influence by the direct investor on the management of the direct investment enterprise. The ownership of at least 10% of the voting power, representing the influence by the investor, is the criterion used. Hence, control by the foreign investor is not required

Inward stocks are the direct investments held by non-residents; outward stocks are the investments held in other economies.

The stock tables also show the distribution of stocks according to broad sectors of the industry (manufacturing) and services.

Negative flows may generally indicate disinvestments or the impact of substantial reimbursements of inter-company loans.

Comparability

International standards call for FDI stocks to be valued at market prices but most OECD countries report their FDI stocks using book values as recorded in the balance sheets of enterprises. Book values may be very different from market values and the rules for estimating book values also vary between countries.

Despite improvements in recent years, there are also methodological differences between countries as regards the inward and outward flow of FDI. For more details, see the joint IMF/OECD analysis of how countries apply the international standards (see the methodological publications below).

Totals for OECD and EU are only for the countries for which data are available. Data for 2005 and 2006 are provisional.

Long-term trends

Both inflows and outflows of FDI worldwide dropped drastically in 2001 following the spectacular investment boom of the late 1990s. FDI into the OECD area continued to decline until 2004 when inflows picked up timidly by 6% and outflows more significantly by 29%. The global environment for FDI further improved in 2006 while at the same time macro-economic growth continued, stock prices remained firm and corporate profitability was generally strong. Multinational enterprises based in emerging economies were active to acquire enterprises in the OECD area. Also, large amounts of investments by financial investors such as private equity companies were recorded in 2006. Direct investment into OECD picked up in 2006 by 27% reaching 948 billion US dollars. The United States and the United Kingdom were the main destinations for FDI in the OECD. Investment flows to EU countries dropped slightly by 20 billion to 538 billion US dollars. Investments into China, amongst the foremost destinations of FDI in 2005, declined by 3 billion US dollars in 2006. FDI outflows from the OECD increased further by 30% to 1 128 billion US dollars in 2006. The OECD area continued to be significant net outward investor at around historically high 180 billion US dollars in 2006, (55 billion US dollars higher than in the previous year).

Source

- OECD (2005), *International Direct Investment Statistics Yearbook*, OECD, Paris.

Further information

Analytical publications

- OECD (2006), *Reviews of Foreign Direct Investment*, OECD, Paris.
- OECD (2006), *Policy Framework for Investment: A Review of Good Practices*, OECD, Paris.
- OECD (2007), *International Investment Perspectives 2007: Freedom of Investment in a Changing World*, OECD, Paris.

Statistical publications

- OECD (2002), *Measuring Globalisation: The Role of Multinationals in OECD Economies*, OECD, Paris.
- OECD (2005), *Measuring Globalisation: OECD Economic Globalisation Indicators*, OECD, Paris.

Methodological publications

- IMF, OECD (1999), *Report on the Survey of Implementation of Methodological Standards for Direct Investment*.
- OECD (1996), *OECD Benchmark Definition of Foreign Direct Investment*, Third edition, OECD, Paris.
- OECD (2001), *Non-Tariff Measures in the ICT Sector: A Survey*, OECD, Paris.
- OECD (2005), *Measuring Globalisation: OECD Handbook on Economic Globalisation Indicators*, OECD, Paris.

Websites

- OECD International Investment, *www.oecd.org/daf/investment*.

Outward and inward FDI stocks
Million US dollars

	Outward direct investment stocks							Inward direct investment stocks						
	1990	1995	2000	2002	2003	2004	2005	1990	1995	2000	2002	2003	2004	2005
Australia	30 495	53 009	85 385	114 848	161 887	204 197	178 335	73 615	104 074	111 138	141 086	198 420	259 145	206 348
Austria	4 747	11 832	24 820	42 483	55 961	67 785	68 187	10 972	19 721	30 431	43 507	53 844	62 337	62 524
Canada	84 813	118 106	237 647	275 711	318 974	373 008	394 681	112 850	123 182	212 723	225 902	289 157	318 610	350 030
Czech Republic	..	345	738	1 473	2 284	3 759	3 610	..	7 350	21 647	38 672	45 286	57 246	60 662
Denmark	..	24 703	73 074	86 697	102 587	123 147	127 101	..	23 801	73 573	82 743	100 236	115 190	115 495
Finland	11 227	14 993	52 109	63 931	76 050	85 023	81 369	5 132	8 465	24 272	33 986	50 257	57 363	54 308
France	110 121	204 430	445 087	586 307	724 445	845 451	882 287	84 931	191 433	259 773	385 187	527 625	641 807	627 931
Germany	130 760	233 107	486 750	602 780	720 718	810 622	801 351	74 067	104 367	462 529	529 323	666 174	709 433	660 428
Greece	..	..	5 852	9 001	12 337	13 791	13 602	..	..	14 113	15 560	22 454	28 482	29 189
Hungary	..	278	1 279	2 166	3 509	6 022	7 993	569	11 304	22 856	36 213	48 345	62 624	61 886
Iceland	75	177	663	1 255	1 733	4 025	10 085	147	149	491	797	1 190	1 998	4 696
Ireland	..	..	27 925	58 880	74 490	106 042	102 865	..	..	127 088	182 890	222 960	209 675	166 230
Italy	60 195	106 319	180 274	194 488	238 888	280 481	293 475	60 009	65 347	121 169	130 814	180 891	220 720	224 079
Japan	201 440	238 452	278 441	304 237	335 500	370 544	386 581	9 850	33 508	50 322	78 140	89 729	96 984	100 899
Korea	..	..	..	20 735	24 986	32 165	38 638	..	..	..	62 658	66 070	87 766	104 879
Luxembourg	..	4 703	7 927	18 139	21 355	27 883	33 410	..	18 503	23 492	34 970	41 730	49 733	43 721
Mexico	..	..	..	12 869	16 587	22 219	28 040	22 424	41 130	97 170	158 651	172 834	191 509	209 564
Netherlands	106 896	172 675	305 459	396 514	523 207	597 887	629 941	68 729	116 051	243 730	349 955	426 611	469 936	447 121
New Zealand	..	7 676	6 065	9 162	11 458	12 495	12 592	..	25 728	28 070	29 502	38 155	49 518	49 997
Norway	10 889	22 521	46 302	72 487	82 787	89 980	..	12 404	19 836	30 261	42 649	48 967	76 110	..
Poland	..	539	1 018	1 456	2 146	3 224	6 439	109	7 843	34 233	47 900	57 841	85 506	89 544
Portugal	..	..	19 793	21 324	36 060	46 114	44 072	..	18 973	32 043	44 635	62 200	69 144	65 598
Slovak Republic	..	..	139	379	486	633	583	617	..	1 297	4 679	8 531	11 284	14 504	15 796
Spain	..	36 547	167 718	233 937	292 464	370 931	372 944	..	110 291	156 347	257 095	339 652	395 984	371 451
Sweden	50 720	73 143	123 234	146 510	183 631	214 826	208 836	12 636	31 089	93 972	119 315	157 084	196 369	171 768
Switzerland	66 087	142 481	232 176	292 210	341 384	399 297	426 195	34 245	57 064	86 810	124 808	162 238	197 672	168 989
Turkey	..	..	3 668	5 847	6 138	7 060	8 315	..	..	19 209	18 795	33 536	38 519	64 433
United Kingdom	229 307	304 865	897 845	994 136	1 187 045	1 247 190	1 228 326	203 905	199 772	848 631	523 319	606 157	701 913	831 357
United States	616 655	885 506	1 531 607	1 867 043	2 059 850	2 399 224	2 453 933	505 346	680 066	1 421 017	1 499 952	1 576 983	1 727 062	1 874 263
OECD total	1 714 426	2 656 546	5 243 234	6 437 112	7 619 095	8 764 975	8 843 821	1 291 940	2 020 343	4 241 790	5 247 557	6 297 910	7 192 858	7 233 187
of which:														
Manufacturing	39%	39%	25%	22%	23%	22%	..	39%	33%	28%	24%	24%	25%	..
Services	49%	52%	55%	58%	60%	58%	..	44%	49%	57%	56%	57%	57%	..
Brazil	..	..	..	54 423	54 892	69 196	69 196	..	..	..	100 847	132 799	161 259	195 562
China	..	..	..	..	..	52 704	52 704	..	..	..	..	..	368 970	471 549
India	..	..	2 615	5 825	7 079	9 568	9 568	..	..	20 326	31 221	39 104	44 511	50 260
Russian Federation	..	2 420	20 141	62 349	90 873	107 291	107 291	..	345	32 204	70 884	96 729	122 295	180 313
Slovenia	..	490	768	1 505	2 350	3 025	3 025	..	1 763	2 893	4 112	6 308	7 590	7 077
South Africa	15 010	23 301	32 325	21 980	27 185	38 483	38 483	9 210	15 014	43 451	29 611	45 715	63 071	77 362

StatLink http://dx.doi.org/10.1787/273336788171

FDI stocks
As a percentage of GDP, 2005 or latest available year

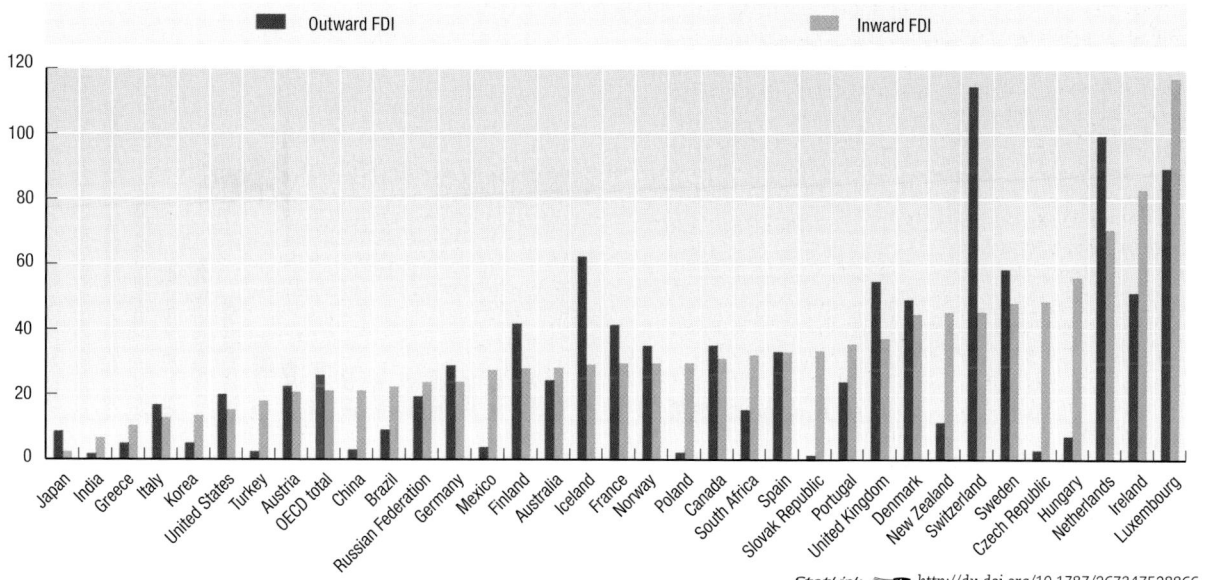

StatLink http://dx.doi.org/10.1787/267347528866

Inflows of foreign direct investment
Million US dollars

	1993	1994	1995	1996	1997	1998	1999	2000	2001	2002	2003	2004	2005	2006
Australia	4 282	5 025	11 963	6 111	7 633	6 003	3 268	13 950	8 297	16 996	7 981	35 963	-34 967	24 547
Austria	1 137	2 103	1 904	4 429	2 656	4 534	2 975	8 842	5 921	357	7 151	3 892	9 039	249
Belgium	..	..	..	..	..	..	..	..	..	15 641	32 127	43 583	33 950	71 519
Canada	4 730	8 204	9 255	9 633	11 522	22 803	24 747	66 796	27 670	22 146	7 619	1 533	33 824	66 605
Czech Republic	653	868	2 562	1 428	1 301	3 716	6 326	4 980	5 645	8 483	2 109	4 975	11 654	5 963
Denmark	1 669	4 898	4 180	768	2 799	7 726	14 657	31 306	11 525	6 633	2 597	-10 721	13 109	7 033
Finland	864	1 578	1 063	1 109	2 116	12 141	4 610	8 836	3 732	8 053	3 322	3 005	4 504	3 708
France	16 443	15 574	23 679	21 960	23 171	30 984	46 546	43 258	50 485	49 079	42 538	32 585	81 007	81 121
Germany	368	7 134	12 025	6 573	12 243	24 597	56 077	198 313	26 419	53 571	32 398	-9 201	35 845	42 891
Greece	1 244	1 166	1 198	1 196	1 089	72	561	1 108	1 589	50	1 276	2 103	606	5 366
Hungary	2 446	1 144	5 102	3 300	4 171	3 337	3 313	2 763	3 936	2 994	2 137	4 508	7 621	6 097
Iceland	..	-2	9	83	148	148	67	170	173	91	328	654	3 075	3 233
Ireland	1 068	856	1 442	2 616	2 710	8 856	18 211	25 784	9 653	29 350	22 803	-10 614	-31 114	12 818
Italy	3 751	2 236	4 816	3 535	4 962	4 280	6 911	13 377	14 873	14 558	16 430	16 824	19 959	16 587
Japan	210	888	41	228	3 224	3 193	12 743	8 318	6 244	9 239	6 324	7 819	2 778	-6 503
Korea	588	809	1 776	2 325	2 844	5 412	9 333	9 283	3 528	2 392	3 526	9 246	6 309	36 456
Luxembourg	..	..	..	..	..	..	..	..	..	115 276	89 290	79 126	116 304	97 013
Mexico	4 389	15 069	9 679	10 087	14 165	12 409	13 631	17 588	27 151	18 275	14 184	22 301	19 643	19 037
Netherlands	6 443	7 158	12 307	16 660	11 137	36 925	41 206	63 866	51 937	25 060	21 063	2 124	41 432	4 373
New Zealand	2 212	2 616	2 850	3 922	1 917	1 826	940	1 344	4 590	-1 251	2 041	2 851	3 140	1 570
Norway	1 461	2 778	2 408	3 168	3 946	4 354	7 062	6 908	2 232	670	3 701	2 547	5 053	6 773
Poland	1 716	1 875	3 658	4 500	4 914	6 368	7 276	9 446	5 697	4 121	4 867	12 484	9 542	13 860
Portugal	1 516	1 255	660	1 344	2 362	3 005	1 157	6 637	6 232	1 801	8 601	2 328	3 962	7 375
Slovak Republic	179	273	241	396	231	707	429	2 383	1 584	4 127	594	1 107	1 907	4 232
Spain	9 572	9 276	6 285	6 821	6 388	11 798	18 744	39 582	28 347	39 249	25 844	24 775	25 005	20 027
Sweden	3 845	6 350	14 447	5 437	10 967	19 843	60 964	23 431	10 905	12 157	4 990	11 669	10 170	27 837
Switzerland	-83	3 368	2 224	3 078	6 642	8 942	11 714	19 266	8 859	6 284	16 505	1 373	-1 263	25 101
Turkey	636	608	885	722	805	940	783	982	3 352	1 137	1 752	2 883	9 801	20 165
United Kingdom	14 821	9 255	19 968	24 441	33 245	74 349	87 973	118 824	52 650	24 052	16 846	56 002	193 658	139 566
United States	51 362	46 121	57 776	86 502	105 603	179 045	289 444	321 274	167 021	84 372	63 961	133 162	109 754	183 571
EU15 total	62 742	68 837	103 974	96 887	115 844	239 109	360 592	583 163	274 269	394 887	327 277	247 481	557 435	537 482
OECD total	137 524	158 480	214 404	232 371	284 910	498 311	751 669	1 068 614	550 246	574 962	464 905	490 887	745 307	948 191
Brazil	1 292	3 072	4 859	11 200	19 650	31 913	28 576	32 779	22 457	16 590	10 144	18 166	15 193	18 782
China	27 515	33 767	37 521	41 726	45 257	45 463	40 319	40 715	46 878	52 743	53 505	60 630	72 406	69 468
India	550	973	2 144	2 426	3 577	2 635	2 169	4 031	6 125	5 036	4 322	5 987	7 661	19 442
Russian Federation	..	690	2 065	2 579	4 865	2 761	3 309	2 714	2 748	3 461	7 958	15 444	12 886	30 827
South Africa	11	374	1 248	816	3 811	550	1 503	969	7 270	735	783	701	6 133	-11

StatLink http://dx.doi.org/10.1787/273373015068

Inflows of foreign direct investment
Million US dollars, average 2004-2006

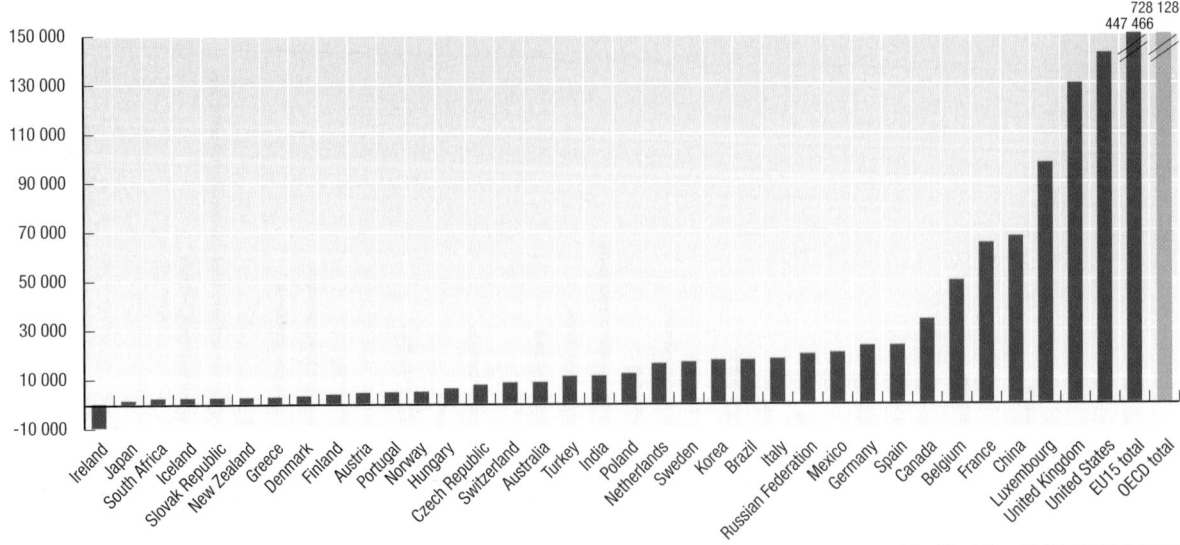

StatLink http://dx.doi.org/10.1787/267348560151

OECD FACTBOOK 2008 – ISBN 978-92-64-04054-0 – © OECD 2008

Outflows of foreign direct investment
Million US dollars

	1993	1994	1995	1996	1997	1998	1999	2000	2001	2002	2003	2004	2005	2006
Australia	1 947	2 817	3 282	7 088	6 428	3 345	-421	3 158	11 962	7 852	16 185	10 800	-34 289	20 987
Austria	1 190	1 257	1 131	1 935	1 988	2 745	3 301	5 741	3 138	5 812	7 143	8 305	10 017	4 089
Belgium	..	..	..	..	..	..	..	..	..	12 705	36 933	34 038	31 761	62 587
Canada	5 700	9 294	11 462	13 094	23 059	34 349	17 250	44 678	36 037	26 761	21 526	43 248	34 084	42 134
Czech Republic	90	120	37	153	25	127	90	43	165	206	207	1 014	-19	1 345
Denmark	1 261	3 955	3 063	2 519	4 207	4 477	16 434	23 093	13 376	5 695	1 124	-10 371	15 026	8 195
Finland	1 407	4 298	1 497	3 597	5 292	18 642	6 616	24 035	8 372	7 378	-2 282	-1 080	4 475	9
France	19 736	24 372	15 758	30 419	35 581	48 613	126 859	177 482	86 783	50 486	53 197	56 762	120 891	115 101
Germany	17 196	18 858	39 052	50 806	41 794	88 837	108 692	56 567	39 691	18 963	5 827	14 837	55 481	79 466
Greece	..	..	..	..	..	-276	552	2 137	616	655	413	1 030	1 450	4 169
Hungary	11	48	59	-4	462	278	250	620	368	278	1 644	1 119	2 327	3 015
Iceland	14	24	25	63	56	74	123	393	342	320	373	2 553	7 063	4 160
Ireland	218	436	820	728	1 014	3 902	6 109	4 630	4 066	11 035	5 555	18 079	13 560	22 114
Italy	7 231	5 109	5 731	6 465	12 245	16 078	6 722	12 318	21 476	17 138	9 079	19 273	41 795	42 060
Japan	13 915	18 117	22 628	23 419	25 991	24 155	22 747	31 539	38 349	32 280	28 799	30 963	45 830	50 244
Korea	1 340	2 461	3 552	4 670	4 449	4 740	4 198	4 999	2 420	2 617	3 426	4 658	4 298	7 129
Luxembourg	..	..	..	..	..	..	..	..	..	125 945	99 861	84 089	123 955	81 552
Mexico	..	..	..	..	..	..	..	..	4 404	891	1 253	4 432	6 474	5 758
Netherlands	10 063	17 554	20 176	32 098	24 522	36 475	57 611	75 649	50 602	32 046	44 076	26 586	142 840	22 705
New Zealand	-1 389	2 008	1 783	-1 240	-1 566	401	1 073	609	408	-1 133	195	1 083	-315	-1 641
Norway	933	2 172	2 856	5 892	5 015	3 201	5 504	8 621	539	4 622	2 655	3 526	21 830	20 476
Poland	18	29	42	53	45	316	31	17	-89	229	305	770	3 070	4 134
Portugal	107	283	685	729	2 092	4 029	3 191	8 134	6 263	-149	8 035	7 850	2 077	3 509
Slovak Republic	13	18	43	63	95	147	-377	29	65	11	13	152	146	369
Spain	3 174	4 111	4 158	5 590	12 547	18 938	44 384	58 224	33 113	32 744	28 745	60 567	41 804	89 728
Sweden	1 358	6 701	11 214	5 025	12 648	24 379	21 929	40 976	7 328	10 596	21 121	20 758	26 544	24 146
Switzerland	8 765	10 797	12 214	16 150	17 748	18 769	33 264	44 698	18 326	8 212	15 443	26 287	54 178	81 547
Turkey	14	49	113	110	251	367	645	870	497	175	499	859	1 078	934
United Kingdom	26 063	32 206	43 560	34 056	61 620	122 861	201 437	233 488	58 885	50 347	62 439	91 083	83 692	79 470
United States	83 950	80 167	98 750	91 885	104 803	142 644	224 934	159 212	142 349	154 460	149 897	244 128	9 072	248 856
EU15 total	89 004	119 139	146 845	173 967	215 548	389 699	603 835	722 473	333 710	381 397	381 266	431 805	715 368	638 901
OECD total	204 325	247 260	303 691	335 365	402 411	622 612	913 145	1 021 958	589 851	619 179	623 686	807 397	870 197	1 128 349
Brazil	491	1 037	1 384	-467	1 042	2 721	1 690	2 282	-2 258	2 482	249	9 471	2 517	28 203
China	4 400	2 000	2 000	2 114	2 563	2 634	1 775	916	6 884	2 518	2 855	5 498	12 261	17 634
India	..	83	117	239	113	48	79	759	1 391	1 819	1 934	2 274	2 931	11 005
Russian Federation	..	281	605	922	3 185	1 270	2 208	3 177	2 533	3 533	9 727	13 782	12 768	22 657
South Africa	292	1 261	2 494	1 048	2 324	1 634	1 584	277	-3 515	-402	553	1 305	909	6 496

StatLink http://dx.doi.org/10.1787/273388003773

Outflows of foreign direct investment
Million US dollars, average 2004-2006

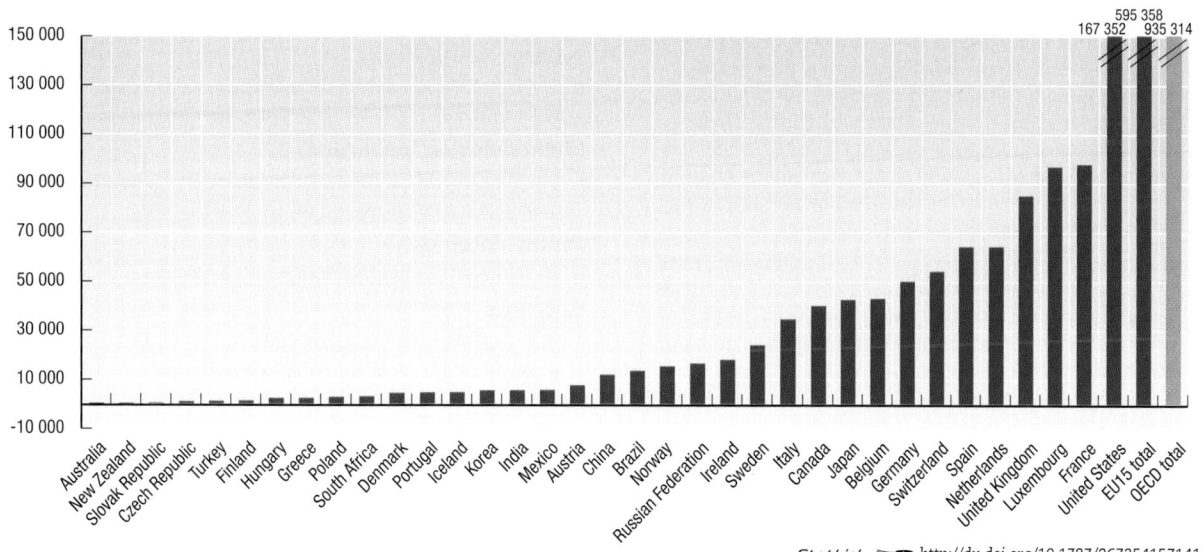

StatLink http://dx.doi.org/10.1787/267354157141

ACTIVITIES OF MULTINATIONALS

Firms in OECD countries increasingly adopt global strategies and establish overseas sales, marketing, production and research units to cope with new competitive pressures. Indicators on the activity of affiliates under foreign control are thus an important complement to information on FDI when analysing the weight and economic contribution of such firms in host countries.

While data on the manufacturing sector have been available since the beginning of the 1980s, the OECD did not start collecting data on the activity of affiliates under foreign control in services until the second half of the 1990s, and data are not yet available for all OECD countries.

Definition

An affiliate under foreign control is defined as one in which a single foreign investor holds more than 50% of the shares with voting rights. The notion of control allows all of a company's activities to be attributed to the controlling investor. This means that variables such as a company's turnover, staff or exports are all attributed to the controlling investor and the country from which he or she comes. Control may be direct or indirect.

Comparability

Fewer countries are able to supply estimates of employment in service affiliates than in manufacturing affiliates because collection of employment data on services began later. For employment in manufacturing, there are breaks in the series for Austria (2001/2002), the Czech Republic (1999/2000), France (2001/2002), Germany (2001/2002), Hungary (2002/2003), Portugal (2002/2003) and for the United States (1996/1997) because of changes to the data collection methods. For employment in services, the main problem in comparability is that financial institutions are excluded by Belgium, Germany, Ireland, Netherlands, Portugal, Spain, Sweden, the United Kingdom and the United States.

Long-term trends

The shares of foreign affiliates in manufacturing employment show considerable variation across OECD countries ranging from under 15% in Denmark, Italy, Portugal, Switzerland, Turkey and the United States to 35% or more in the Czech Republic, Luxembourg, the Slovak Republic and Ireland. Employment in service sector foreign affiliates is lower in all countries although as noted above, comparability is affected in several countries by the exclusion of employment in banking and insurance services.

In the period from 1999 to 2005, employment in foreign-controlled manufacturing affiliates grew or remained stable in all countries for which data are available except Spain and Ireland, where the rate slightly fell and in Belgium, Luxembourg and the United States where the shares have remained fairly stable. Particularly sharp increases were recorded by the Czech Republic, Norway, Poland, Sweden and the United Kingdom.

Over the same period, employment in foreign-controlled service affiliates grew or remained stable in all countries for which data are available, except Belgium. The biggest increases were recorded in the Czech Republic, Ireland, Poland and Sweden.

Source
- OECD (2007), *OECD Science, Technology and Industry: Scoreboard 2007*, OECD, Paris.

Further information
Analytical publications
- OECD (2005), *Measuring Globalisation: OECD Economic Globalisation Indicators*, OECD, Paris.
- OECD (2007), *Annual Report on the OECD Guidelines for Multinational Enterprises 2007: Corporate Responsibility in the Financial Sector*, OECD, Paris.

Statistical publications
- OECD (2007), *Measuring Globalisation: Activities of Multinationals – Volume I: Manufacturing, 2000-2004, 2007 Edition*, OECD, Paris.
- OECD (2008), *Measuring Globalisation: Activities of Multinationals – Volume II: services, 2000-2004*, OECD, Paris.

Methodological publications
- OECD (2005), *Measuring Globalisation: OECD Handbook on Economic Globalisation Indicators*, OECD, Paris.

Online databases
- *Measuring Globalisation Statistics.*

Websites
- OECD Measuring Globalisation, *www.oecd.org/sti/measuring-globalisation*.
- OECD Science, Technology and Industry, *www.oecd.org/sti*.

Employment in affiliates under foreign control

As percentage of total employment

	Share of employment in manufacturing							Share of employment in services						
	1999	2000	2001	2002	2003	2004	2005	1999	2000	2001	2002	2003	2004	2005
Australia	..	22.7	..	..	..	..	..	..	10.5	..	..	..	..	..
Austria	..	19.6	18.0		24.0	22.5	..	..	..	..	9.7	..	..	..	..
Belgium	..	..	..	32.3	34.5	32.8	33.1	..	..	..	17.2	16.2	15.3	14.2
Czech Republic	16.2		25.3	28.9	27.2	32.6	37.2	37.8	..	14.2	..	..	21.1	22.7	..
Denmark	10.2		15.1	14.1	14.4	..	..	..	6.1	..	..	..	..	..	..
Finland	15.9	15.9	17.2	17.4	17.4	16.1	16.5	9.0	11.1	11.9	..	..	..	..
France	28.5		30.1	30.8		26.4	26.8	26.2	26.4	6.1	6.1	5.6	5.2		10.0	10.5	..
Germany	6.2	6.0	5.8		14.8	15.5	15.7	15.2	..	3.2	2.9		7.2	6.1	6.5	..
Hungary	46.5	44.5	45.2	43.6		27.1	32.4	..	..	15.2	15.1	14.8	15.9	..	..
Ireland	49.1	48.1	49.2	48.4	46.7	48.0	..	..	..	..	22.3	..	..	..
Italy	..	..	10.8	13.1	12.5	12.4	..	..	..	5.1	5.4	5.7	6.1	..
Luxembourg	38.9	39.6	40.7	41.5	37.9	39.1	39.3	..	..	..	..	..	..	..
Netherlands	18.9	18.3	21.0	25.7	25.1	..	..	..	8.7	9.1	12.1	8.9	..	..
Norway	19.9	21.4	23.1	22.2	22.3	..	..	..	..	..	..	..	..	..
Poland	18.6	20.9	21.9	24.1	25.4	28.1	29.5	..	..	13.4	15.3	15.3	17.1	..
Portugal	8.9	10.1	9.5	8.9		12.8	12.6	..	3.9	4.0	4.7	..	..	..	..
Slovak Republic	..	..	..	..	34.9	41.4	..	..	..	..	..	..	..	..
Spain	16.5	16.8	16.4	15.9	15.4	15.6	15.6	..	..	..	8.7	10.0	9.5	..
Sweden	24.1	29.1	32.7	34.8	33.2	32.4	33.8	14.0	14.5	..	17.5	20.6	22.4	..
Switzerland	..	..	..	..	12.1	13.0	12.9	..	..	..	..	7.3	7.6	8.2
Turkey	5.4	5.7	7.0	..	..	..	..	..	..	..	..	..	..	..
United Kingdom	17.7	19.6	24.0	24.6	26.1	25.8	27.6	..	..	..	..	11.6	12.0	..
United States	11.2	11.5	11.1	11.3	11.4	11.1	11.2	..	..	..	3.8	..	..	..

StatLink http://dx.doi.org/10.1787/273436866125

Employment in manufacturing and services in affiliates under foreign control

As a percentage of total employment, 2005 or latest available year

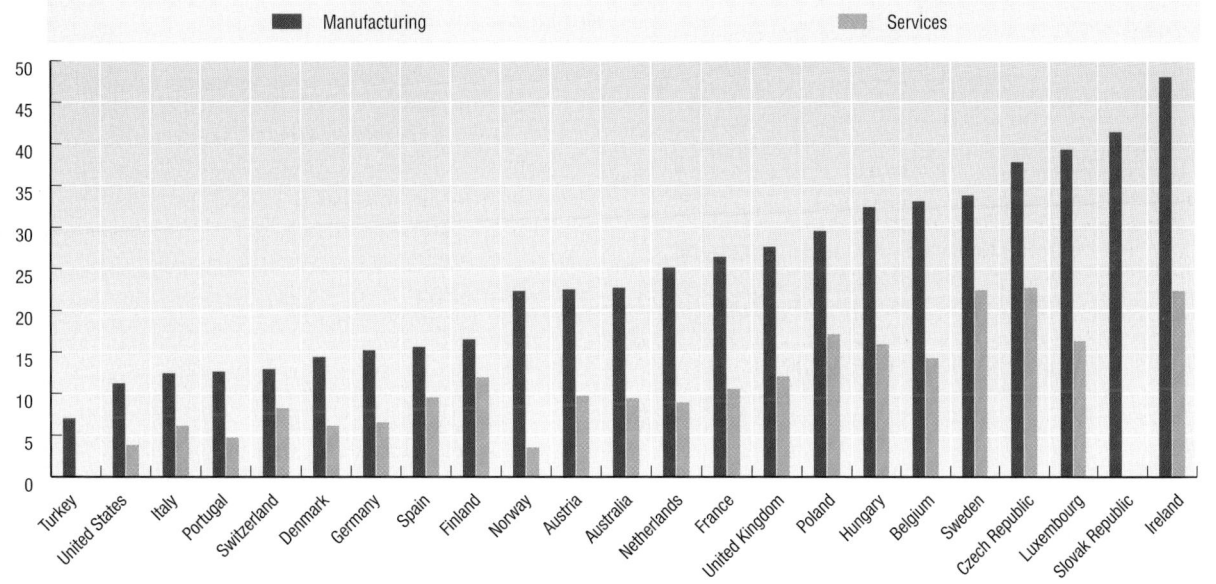

StatLink http://dx.doi.org/10.1787/267402482548

```
                        500,000 •  +
                     85,679,200 •  −
                     43,628,500 •  −
                     36,286,400 •  +
                 34,432,741,064 •  ◇

                 34,432,741,064 •  ✳

                    220,061,246 •  +
                        242,765 •  +
                     54,975,316 •  −
                  3,458,295,462 •  −
                  9,423,290,000 •  +
                    527,646,320 •  −
                    242,347,296 •  +
                        312,759 •  +
                    184,652,108 •  ◇
```

PRICES

PRICES AND INTEREST RATES
CONSUMER PRICE INDICES (CPI)
PRODUCER PRICE INDICES (PPI)
LONG-TERM INTEREST RATES

PURCHASING POWER AND EXCHANGE RATES
RATES OF CONVERSION
EFFECTIVE EXCHANGE RATES

CONSUMER PRICE INDICES (CPI)

Consumer price indices have a long history in official statistics. They measure the erosion of living standards through price inflation and are probably the best known economic statistics among the media and general public.

Definition

Consumer price indices measure the change in the prices of a basket of goods and services that are typically purchased by specific groups of households. For the indices in these tables, the groups of households have been broadly defined and cover virtually all households except for "institutional" households – prisons and military barracks for example – and, in some countries, households in the highest income group.

The index for food covers food and non-alcoholic beverages but excludes purchases in restaurants. The index for energy is intended to cover all forms of energy, including fuels for motor vehicles, heating and other household uses.

Comparability

There are a number of differences in the ways that these indices are calculated. The most important ones concern the treatment of dwelling costs, adjustments for changes in the quality of goods and services, the frequency with which the basket weights are updated and the index formulae used. In particular, country methodologies for the treatment of owner-occupied housing vary significantly. The European Harmonized Indices of Consumer Prices (HICP) exclude owner-occupied housing as do national CPIs for Belgium, France, Greece, Italy, Luxembourg, Poland, Portugal, Spain and the United Kingdom. For the United Kingdom, the national CPI is the same as the HICP. The European Union area CPI refers to the HICP published by Eurostat and covers the twenty seven countries for the entire period of the time series. In addition, there are practical difficulties in measuring consumer prices in countries experiencing very high inflation – such as Hungary, Mexico and Turkey during the period considered here.

Long-term trends

For most OECD countries, consumer price indices have grown only moderately since 1993, with inflation lower in the latter part of the period compared with the years up to 1997. Over the period as a whole, inflation has been exceptionally low in Japan, averaging close to 0% per year but quite substantial in Greece, Mexico, Turkey and the four recent member countries in Central Europe – Czech Republic, Hungary, Poland and Slovak Republic.

As regards the five non-member economies shown, CPIs have risen sharply since 1993 in Brazil, India, Russian Federation and South Africa. In China, however, prices rose sharply up to 1996, but since then have either fallen or increased only moderately.

Food and energy are shown separately because they are important items in the consumer price indices of all countries and because their price movements tend to be more volatile than other goods and services. Food prices have risen over the period by less than total consumer prices, and increases have been moderate in most of the European Union countries. However, substantial increases occurred in 2001 and, except in Europe, between 1996 and 1998. Energy prices have been rather volatile; for example they rose over 10% in 2000 and 2005 but actually fell in 1998 and 2002. Over the period as whole, energy prices have risen faster that the total consumer price indices.

Source

- OECD (2007), *Main Economic Indicators*, OECD, Paris.

Further information

Analytical publications

- Brook, A.M. *et al.* (2004), *Oil Price Developments: Drivers, Economic Consequences and Policy Responses*, OECD Economics Department Working Papers, No. 412, OECD, Paris.
- OECD (2007), *OECD Economic Outlook: December No. 82 – Volume 2007 Issue 2*, OECD, Paris.

Methodological publications

- ILO, IMF, OECD, Eurostat, World Bank (2004), *Consumer Price Index Manual: Theory and Practice*, ILO, Geneva.
- OECD (1999), *Main Economic Indicators: July Volume 1999 Issue 7*, OECD, Paris.
- OECD (2002), "Comparative Methodological Analysis: Consumer and Producer Price Indices", *Main Economic Indicators, Volume 2002, Supplement 2*, OECD, Paris.

Websites

- OECD Main Economic Indicators, *www.oecd.org/std/mei*.

CPI: all items
Year 2000 = 100

	1993	1994	1995	1996	1997	1998	1999	2000	2001	2002	2003	2004	2005	2006
Australia	85.3	86.9	90.9	93.3	93.5	94.3	95.7	100.0	104.4	107.5	110.5	113.1	116.1	120.2
Austria	88.6	91.2	93.3	95.0	96.3	97.2	97.7	100.0	102.7	104.5	105.9	108.1	110.6	112.2
Belgium	88.7	90.8	92.1	94.0	95.5	96.4	97.5	100.0	102.5	104.2	105.8	108.0	111.0	113.0
Canada	89.7	89.9	91.8	93.2	94.7	95.7	97.4	100.0	102.5	104.8	107.7	109.7	112.2	114.4
Czech Republic	60.1	66.2	72.2	78.5	85.2	94.3	96.2	100.0	104.7	106.6	106.8	109.8	111.8	114.7
Denmark	85.7	87.4	89.2	91.1	93.1	94.8	97.2	100.0	102.4	104.8	107.0	108.3	110.2	112.3
Finland	91.2	92.2	92.9	93.5	94.6	95.9	97.0	100.0	102.6	104.2	105.1	105.3	106.0	107.6
France	91.0	92.5	94.2	96.0	97.2	97.8	98.3	100.0	101.6	103.6	105.8	108.0	109.9	111.7
Germany	89.9	92.3	93.9	95.3	97.1	98.0	98.6	100.0	102.0	103.4	104.5	106.2	108.3	110.1
Greece	65.4	72.5	79.0	85.4	90.2	94.5	96.9	100.0	103.4	107.1	110.9	114.1	118.2	122.0
Hungary	32.6	38.7	49.7	61.3	72.5	82.8	91.1	100.0	109.1	114.9	120.2	128.3	132.9	138.1
Iceland	84.3	85.6	87.0	89.0	90.6	92.1	95.1	100.0	106.4	111.9	114.2	117.8	122.5	130.7
Ireland	84.0	86.0	88.2	89.7	91.0	93.2	94.7	100.0	104.9	109.7	113.6	116.1	118.9	123.5
Italy	81.0	84.2	88.7	92.2	94.1	95.9	97.5	100.0	102.8	105.3	108.1	110.5	112.7	115.1
Japan	98.0	98.6	98.5	98.6	100.4	101.1	100.7	100.0	99.2	98.4	98.1	98.1	97.8	98.1
Korea	74.2	78.8	82.3	86.4	90.2	97.0	97.8	100.0	104.1	106.8	110.7	114.7	117.8	120.5
Luxembourg	89.0	91.0	92.7	93.8	95.1	96.0	96.9	100.0	102.7	104.8	106.9	109.3	112.0	115.0
Mexico	28.9	30.9	41.7	56.0	67.6	78.3	91.3	100.0	106.4	111.7	116.8	122.3	127.2	131.8
Netherlands	85.8	88.2	89.9	91.7	93.7	95.6	97.7	100.0	104.2	107.6	109.9	111.2	113.1	114.4
New Zealand	88.2	89.7	93.1	95.2	96.3	97.6	97.5	100.0	102.6	105.4	107.2	109.7	113.0	116.8
Norway	85.9	87.1	89.2	90.4	92.7	94.8	97.0	100.0	103.0	104.3	106.9	107.4	109.1	111.6
Poland	32.5	43.2	55.3	66.2	76.1	84.9	91.0	100.0	105.4	107.4	108.2	111.8	114.3	115.7
Portugal	79.8	84.1	87.6	90.3	92.4	95.0	97.2	100.0	104.4	108.1	111.6	114.2	116.9	120.5
Slovak Republic	54.1	61.4	67.4	71.3	75.7	80.7	89.3	100.0	107.3	110.7	120.2	129.2	132.7	138.7
Spain	80.2	84.0	87.9	91.0	92.8	94.5	96.7	100.0	103.6	106.8	110.0	113.4	117.2	121.3
Sweden	93.4	95.4	97.7	98.3	98.9	98.7	99.1	100.0	102.4	104.6	106.6	107.0	107.5	109.0
Switzerland	93.9	94.7	96.4	97.2	97.7	97.7	98.5	100.0	101.0	101.6	102.3	103.1	104.3	105.4
Turkey	1.6	3.3	6.3	11.4	21.2	39.2	64.6	100.0	154.4	223.8	272.2	295.6	319.8	350.4
United Kingdom	88.3	90.0	92.4	94.7	96.4	97.9	99.2	100.0	101.2	102.5	103.9	105.3	107.5	110.0
United States	83.9	86.1	88.5	91.1	93.2	94.7	96.7	100.0	102.8	104.5	106.8	109.7	113.4	117.1
EU27 total	..	..	..	83.6	89.7	93.9	96.7	100.0	103.2	105.8	108.1	110.5	113.1	115.7
OECD total	74.6	77.8	82.1	86.3	90.0	93.4	96.4	100.0	103.4	105.9	108.4	110.9	113.7	116.6
Brazil	1.9	42.0	69.7	80.7	86.3	89.1	93.4	100.0	106.8	115.9	132.9	141.7	151.4	157.8
China	62.9	78.1	91.5	99.1	101.8	101.0	99.6	100.0	100.7	100.0	101.1	105.1	107.0	108.5
India	57.2	63.0	69.5	75.7	81.1	91.9	96.1	100.0	103.8	108.2	112.4	116.6	121.5	128.6
Russian Federation	1.7	6.9	20.6	30.4	34.9	44.6	82.8	100.0	121.5	140.7	159.9	177.3	199.8	219.2
South Africa	61.2	66.6	72.4	77.8	84.4	90.3	94.9	100.0	105.7	115.4	122.1	123.8	128.1	134.0

StatLink http://dx.doi.org/10.1787/273438112184

CPI: all items
Average annual growth in percentage

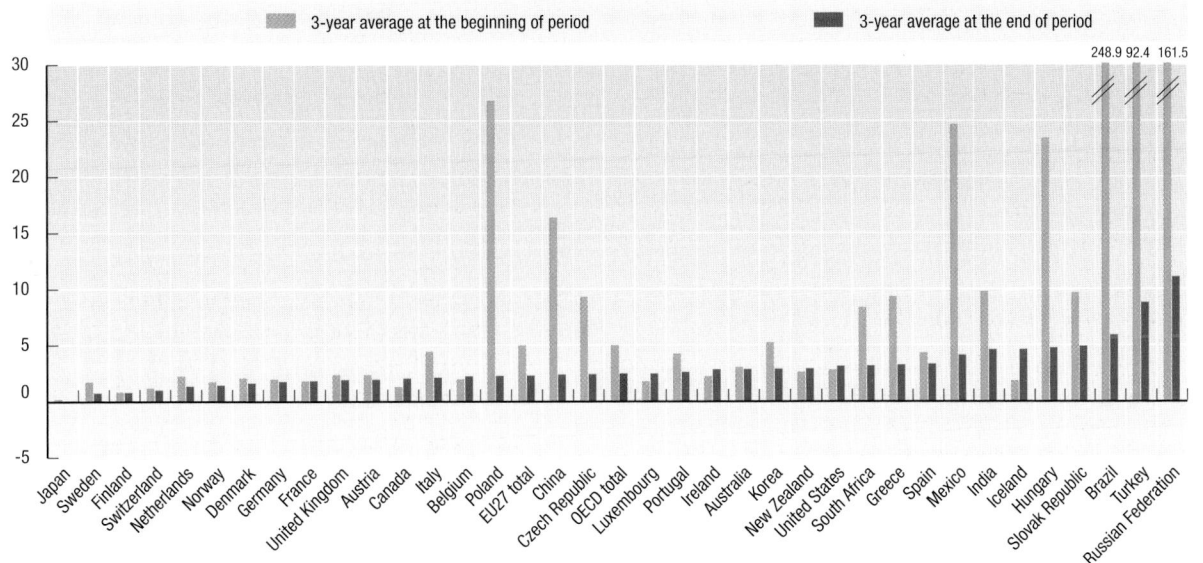

StatLink http://dx.doi.org/10.1787/267436084144

CONSUMER PRICE INDICES (CPI)

CPI: food
Year 2000 = 100

	1993	1994	1995	1996	1997	1998	1999	2000	2001	2002	2003	2004	2005	2006
Australia	82.1	84.0	88.1	90.7	93.2	96.0	99.4	100.0	106.2	110.2	114.3	116.6	118.9	130.2
Austria	96.8	98.2	96.5	96.6	98.1	100.0	99.4	100.0	103.6	105.1	106.9	109.0	111.3	113.3
Belgium	90.9	92.7	93.9	95.2	97.3	99.2	99.1	100.0	104.6	107.0	109.2	110.5	112.5	115.3
Canada	91.5	91.6	94.0	95.1	96.6	97.9	99.0	100.0	104.9	107.5	109.1	111.0	113.6	116.2
Czech Republic	..	79.6	89.0	96.1	100.3	104.7	98.9	100.0	105.0	103.0	100.7	104.2	103.9	104.8
Denmark	85.0	87.5	90.2	91.7	94.9	96.9	97.5	100.0	103.9	106.1	107.7	106.6	107.3	110.2
Finland	106.3	106.5	98.1	96.7	97.1	99.0	98.9	100.0	104.4	107.4	108.1	108.9	109.5	111.0
France	91.2	92.0	93.1	94.1	95.8	97.4	97.8	100.0	105.5	108.4	110.9	111.4	111.6	113.4
Germany	96.4	98.0	99.0	99.6	101.0	102.0	100.7	100.0	104.5	105.3	105.2	104.8	105.2	107.3
Greece	67.1	76.0	82.4	88.2	91.8	95.9	98.1	100.0	105.1	110.7	116.2	116.9	117.6	122.0
Hungary	35.0	43.3	56.6	66.4	77.9	89.0	91.6	100.0	113.6	118.6	120.3	127.1	129.2	139.8
Iceland	84.5	82.6	84.9	87.6	90.5	93.0	96.0	100.0	106.9	111.4	108.5	109.6	106.8	115.3
Ireland	82.5	85.2	87.6	89.1	90.4	94.1	97.0	100.0	106.5	110.2	111.8	111.5	110.7	112.2
Italy	84.6	87.7	93.0	96.7	96.6	97.6	98.5	100.0	104.1	107.9	111.3	113.7	113.7	115.6
Japan	100.7	101.5	99.8	99.7	101.4	103.2	102.4	100.0	99.4	98.3	98.1	99.2	97.9	98.5
Korea	70.5	78.2	80.2	82.5	86.0	94.7	99.1	100.0	105.0	110.0	115.1	124.3	127.6	128.2
Luxembourg	88.8	90.3	92.5	93.3	94.3	96.8	98.0	100.0	104.8	108.9	111.0	113.0	114.8	117.6
Mexico	28.6	29.9	41.7	59.3	70.7	82.0	94.9	100.0	105.1	109.1	115.1	123.5	130.2	134.9
Netherlands	92.7	94.5	94.8	94.8	96.4	98.6	99.7	100.0	107.0	110.5	111.7	107.8	106.5	108.2
New Zealand	91.1	90.4	91.4	92.6	94.7	98.1	99.0	100.0	106.8	109.9	109.3	109.7	111.0	114.3
Norway	84.2	85.4	86.7	88.1	91.1	95.4	98.1	100.0	98.1	96.4	99.7	101.5	103.1	104.5
Poland	..	..	63.3	74.5	83.7	89.6	91.2	100.0	104.6	104.0	102.7	108.8	111.2	111.9
Portugal	85.0	88.1	90.5	92.3	92.6	95.9	97.9	100.0	106.5	108.6	111.4	112.6	112.0	115.0
Slovak Republic	60.3	70.6	79.4	82.7	87.4	92.5	95.0	100.0	106.1	107.6	111.3	116.6	115.0	116.6
Spain	84.3	88.8	93.2	96.3	95.6	96.7	98.0	100.0	105.9	111.2	115.7	120.2	124.0	129.1
Sweden	101.1	102.9	104.3	97.1	97.4	98.5	100.0	100.0	102.9	106.2	106.6	106.1	105.4	106.2
Switzerland	96.5	97.0	97.6	97.1	97.8	98.6	98.5	100.0	102.2	104.6	105.9	106.6	105.9	105.8
Turkey	1.8	3.9	7.6	13.1	25.1	46.2	68.2	100.0	149.1	223.0	273.5	292.2	306.6	336.3
United Kingdom	91.6	92.8	96.4	99.4	99.2	100.2	100.5	100.0	103.8	104.6	105.8	106.5	108.2	110.9
United States	83.4	85.8	88.6	91.9	94.2	96.0	97.8	100.0	103.3	104.6	106.9	110.9	113.0	115.0
EU27 total	..	..	..	78.8	89.2	94.8	96.2	100.0	106.5	109.7	111.9	113.9	115.1	117.9
OECD total	75.8	79.1	83.6	88.1	91.7	95.5	97.9	100.0	104.4	107.1	109.5	112.5	114.0	116.5
Brazil	0.3	7.2	81.3	88.1	89.6	90.7	92.5	100.0	109.6	131.0	140.8	146.2	149.1	150.9
China	..	83.8	103.0	110.8	110.7	107.2	102.7	100.0	100.0	99.4	102.8	113.1	116.4	119.1
Russian Federation	1.8	7.0	21.4	30.0	33.9	43.1	84.9	100.0	121.3	136.2	151.4	167.2	190.2	208.8
South Africa	58.0	66.0	71.7	76.1	83.3	88.4	92.7	100.0	105.4	122.1	131.9	134.9	137.9	147.9

StatLink http://dx.doi.org/10.1787/273511451853

CPI: food
Average annual growth in percentage

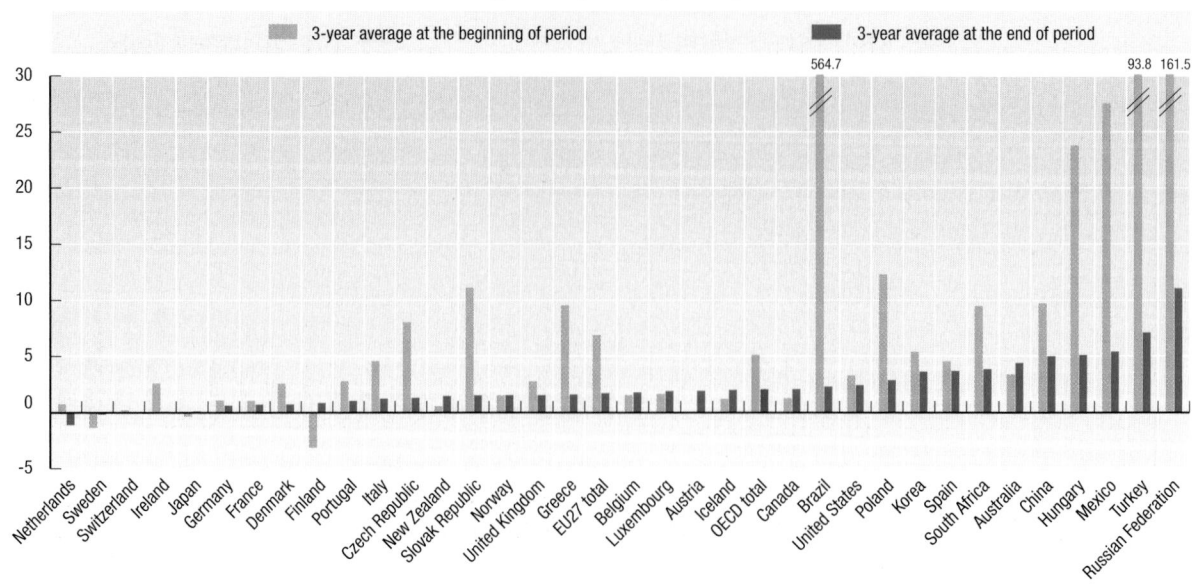

StatLink http://dx.doi.org/10.1787/267484605864

OECD FACTBOOK 2008 – ISBN 978-92-64-04054-0 – © OECD 2008

CPI: energy
Year 2000 = 100

	1993	1994	1995	1996	1997	1998	1999	2000	2001	2002	2003	2004	2005	2006
Australia	81.5	81.7	84.2	85.8	87.3	84.3	85.8	100.0	102.5	103.3	108.6	115.5	126.9	138.8
Austria	80.7	81.9	84.9	90.3	93.0	90.0	90.3	100.0	100.5	98.1	99.1	105.4	115.7	122.9
Belgium	81.4	82.1	81.5	86.1	88.8	85.7	87.4	100.0	100.6	97.4	97.3	103.7	115.7	124.3
Canada	79.0	79.5	80.5	82.9	84.9	81.4	86.0	100.0	103.2	101.2	109.2	116.6	127.8	134.4
Czech Republic	..	..	..	60.8	68.9	82.3	87.4	100.0	104.2	104.6	105.6	110.0	117.2	127.4
Denmark	73.8	73.8	75.2	80.1	82.6	83.7	89.2	100.0	101.5	103.7	104.6	107.0	115.0	121.1
Finland	85.0	83.2	77.3	85.2	86.7	85.6	88.8	100.0	98.2	97.3	102.0	105.9	113.1	119.7
France	82.8	83.9	85.5	89.6	91.4	88.8	89.2	100.0	98.4	96.9	99.2	103.9	114.2	121.5
Germany	81.7	84.5	83.8	84.6	87.0	84.2	87.7	100.0	105.7	106.0	110.2	114.7	126.5	137.2
Greece	81.5	84.5	88.3	95.6	91.8	88.8	85.4	100.0	98.3	98.1	102.0	107.9	123.2	134.2
Hungary	27.3	30.4	41.2	53.0	66.0	75.3	85.3	100.0	104.1	106.4	112.8	124.4	133.8	142.6
Iceland	80.6	80.9	81.4	85.0	88.9	86.9	89.4	100.0	104.1	101.9	103.9	111.7	118.6	128.0
Ireland	80.4	80.9	81.4	84.4	86.9	86.4	88.0	100.0	97.4	100.8	104.8	113.6	128.0	138.5
Italy	90.9	94.5	99.0	88.6	90.2	89.0	89.6	100.0	101.8	99.0	102.2	104.4	113.4	122.8
Japan	106.7	104.9	102.8	100.1	102.9	98.4	96.9	100.0	100.5	98.1	98.2	99.8	103.5	109.6
Korea	53.7	53.7	54.7	60.2	70.5	90.9	91.3	100.0	107.0	103.6	107.4	113.2	119.1	127.5
Luxembourg	81.5	79.2	78.1	82.6	85.7	81.3	83.5	100.0	98.4	94.4	96.6	105.5	121.5	133.6
Mexico	23.3	26.0	37.2	50.5	62.4	71.9	84.9	100.0	108.6	117.4	128.4	138.4	146.9	157.7
Netherlands	71.1	73.8	74.2	79.0	85.2	85.1	87.1	100.0	107.0	109.5	114.5	120.8	135.2	145.4
New Zealand	83.3	83.1	84.9	87.1	89.0	87.4	88.4	100.0	99.1	100.5	104.6	115.1	127.1	143.0
Norway	79.1	79.1	83.6	86.6	91.0	87.4	89.7	100.0	108.2	105.7	126.4	123.1	126.1	148.5
Poland	..	..	50.8	60.5	70.9	81.7	88.5	100.0	107.3	112.6	117.3	122.3	128.7	135.8
Portugal	86.2	88.8	89.8	91.8	95.5	96.1	94.3	100.0	105.1	106.2	111.3	117.3	128.9	139.2
Slovak Republic	..	..	43.2	45.7	47.3	49.0	69.9	100.0	113.9	127.7	153.0	174.9	188.6	211.9
Spain	78.1	80.9	83.7	86.8	88.9	85.5	88.2	100.0	99.0	98.2	99.6	104.4	114.4	123.5
Sweden	81.3	81.7	83.1	88.5	92.9	92.9	92.7	100.0	107.1	108.6	121.8	125.5	132.2	142.3
Switzerland	80.2	79.3	81.5	84.8	87.5	82.4	85.0	100.0	98.7	93.8	95.0	99.4	109.7	117.6
Turkey	..	3.3	5.9	12.2	22.3	36.6	64.0	100.0	192.2	279.9	330.9	346.5	397.5	442.2
United Kingdom	77.8	81.3	84.2	86.4	89.2	89.5	93.4	100.0	97.3	96.5	99.1	105.3	116.9	134.1
United States	83.6	84.0	84.5	88.4	89.5	82.6	85.6	100.0	103.8	97.6	109.5	121.5	142.1	158.0
EU27 total	..	..	..	79.6	85.4	85.5	88.8	100.0	102.8	104.4	108.5	114.4	125.7	136.3
OECD total	70.9	73.4	76.4	80.9	84.9	83.5	87.4	100.0	104.4	103.1	110.6	118.5	132.6	145.0
Brazil	0.2	6.8	44.0	72.7	73.8	81.2	83.4	100.0	117.9	141.4	171.5	188.0	203.1	203.7

StatLink http://dx.doi.org/10.1787/273513344501

CPI: energy
Average annual growth in percentage

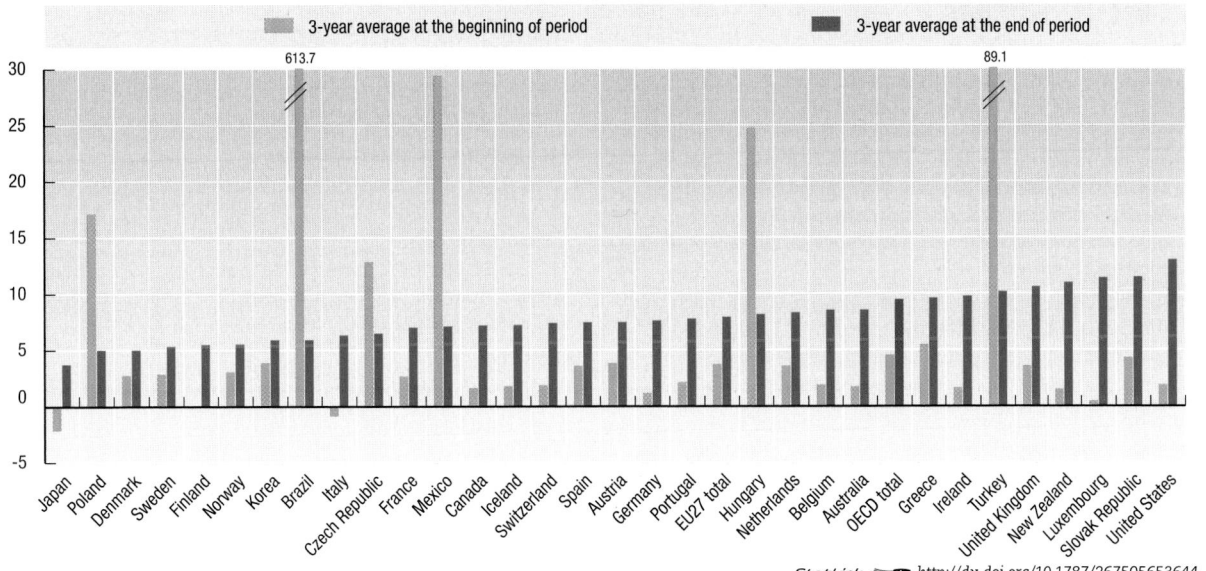

StatLink http://dx.doi.org/10.1787/267505653644

PRODUCER PRICE INDICES (PPI)

A variety of tools are used to measure price changes taking place in an economy. These include consumer price indices (CPI), price indices relating to specific goods and/or services, GDP deflators and producer price indices (PPI). Whereas CPIs are designed to measure changes over time in average retail prices of a fixed basket of goods and services taken as representing the consumption habits of households, the purpose of PPIs is to provide measures of average movements of prices received by the producers of commodities.

Producer price indices measure changes in prices at an early stage in the production process. Because of this, they are often seen as advance indicators of price changes throughout the economy, including changes in the prices of consumer goods and services.

Definition

Producer prices are defined as "ex-factory prices" and exclude any taxes, transport and trade margins that the purchaser may have to pay. Manufacturing covers the production of semi-processed goods and other intermediate goods as well as final products such as consumer goods and capital equipment.

Comparability

The price indices shown here are intended to be producer price indices for manufacturing. In practice many countries do not calculate such indices for the manufacturing sector alone. The indices for Austria, Greece, Italy, Luxembourg, Mexico, Spain, Switzerland and Turkey all have broader coverage, usually including (in addition to manufacturing) mining, electricity, gas and water and, in some countries, agriculture.

An additional problem is that Austria and Turkey calculate wholesale price indices rather than producer price indices. Wholesale prices include taxes and transport and trade margins in addition to the ex-factory cost of the goods.

There are also differences between countries in the ways in which they adjust prices for quality changes, in the frequency with which the weights are updated, and in the price index formulae used.

Long-term trends

Compared with consumer prices, producer prices have risen more slowly throughout the period 1993-2006, for OECD in total by 3 %. More than half of OECD countries recorded average annual increases of under 2.5% and in two countries – Japan, and Switzerland – producer prices were actually lower at the end of the period than in 1993. All countries recorded unusually sharp rises in 1995, 2000 and 2005-2006 due to sharp movements in world commodity prices.

For the Czech Republic, Hungary, Mexico, Poland and Turkey, very high growth rates in the first 3-year period have been replaced by moderate growth in 2003-2006.

Source
- OECD (2007), *Main Economic Indicators*, OECD, Paris.

Further information
Analytical publications
- Brook, A.M. *et al.* (2004), *Oil Price Developments: Drivers, Economic Consequences and Policy Responses*, OECD Economics Department Working Papers, No. 412, OECD, Paris.
- OECD (2007), *OECD Economic Outlook: December No. 82 – Volume 2007 Issue 2*, OECD, Paris.

Methodological publications
- IMF, ILO, OECD, Eurostat, UN, World Bank (2004), *Producer Price Index Manual: Theory and Practice*, IMF, Washington, DC.
- OECD (2002), "Comparative Methodological Analysis: Consumer and Producer Price Indices", *Main Economic Indicators, Volume 2002, Supplement 2*, OECD, Paris.

Websites
- OECD Main Economic Indicators, *www.oecd.org/std/mei*.

PPI: manufacturing

Year 2000 = 100

	1993	1994	1995	1996	1997	1998	1999	2000	2001	2002	2003	2004	2005	2006
Australia	86.4	87.0	90.2	91.0	92.1	92.7	93.3	100.0	103.1	103.3	103.8	107.9	114.3	123.4
Austria	96.1	97.4	97.7	97.7	98.1	97.6	96.7	100.0	101.5	101.1	102.8	107.8	110.1	113.3
Belgium	86.5	88.0	90.0	90.7	92.4	91.0	91.1	100.0	99.5	99.2	98.8	102.9	105.6	110.9
Canada	81.5	86.4	92.8	93.2	93.9	94.2	95.9	100.0	101.0	101.0	99.7	102.8	104.3	106.8
Czech Republic	72.0	75.8	82.2	86.3	90.3	94.5	94.6	100.0	102.6	101.3	101.0	107.0	109.1	109.9
Denmark	90.4	90.7	93.5	94.8	96.3	95.7	96.0	100.0	102.9	103.9	104.0	105.1	108.2	111.6
Finland	91.0	92.4	94.1	92.3	93.3	91.7	91.2	100.0	98.9	96.6	95.5	95.3	98.0	101.5
France	97.6	98.9	103.9	101.1	100.5	99.6	98.0	100.0	101.2	101.0	101.3	102.5	104.3	106.9
Germany	94.0	94.7	96.7	96.8	97.4	97.2	97.0	100.0	101.3	101.5	102.1	103.9	106.8	109.7
Greece	..	..	80.0	85.3	87.9	90.4	92.3	100.0	102.9	104.8	106.3	110.2	116.2	123.6
Hungary	..	..	53.0	64.5	77.3	85.4	89.3	100.0	104.3	101.7	103.2	105.9	110.9	116.5
Ireland	87.3	88.3	89.6	89.2	89.5	91.9	93.6	100.0	101.7	100.5	92.4	90.2	90.1	90.7
Italy	81.8	84.9	91.5	93.2	94.4	94.6	94.3	100.0	101.9	102.1	103.7	106.5	110.8	117.0
Japan	106.5	104.6	103.8	102.1	102.7	101.3	99.9	100.0	97.7	95.6	94.8	95.9	97.8	100.8
Korea	78.4	79.6	83.5	85.3	88.2	101.0	97.7	100.0	97.9	96.4	98.1	105.5	108.8	112.0
Luxembourg	97.1	97.3	100.7	96.5	98.1	99.8	95.0	100.0	99.8	99.0	100.4	109.3	118.1	127.2
Mexico	29.5	31.3	44.3	59.6	69.1	78.6	90.9	100.0	103.3	107.8	115.9	126.7	132.0	140.7
Netherlands	85.6	86.2	88.1	89.4	92.1	89.9	90.1	100.0	101.0	99.8	100.5	104.7	111.2	116.5
New Zealand	93.0	93.7	93.8	93.0	91.7	92.5	93.4	100.0	104.8	105.1	103.8	105.8	109.7	114.6
Norway	81.6	83.3	84.9	86.1	86.8	87.6	90.6	100.0	100.6	97.5	99.2	105.5	112.5	121.5
Poland	..	..	..	76.6	83.1	88.4	92.9	100.0	99.9	99.9	102.3	109.1	108.8	109.6
Portugal	74.5	76.9	80.8	85.5	88.1	83.9	86.9	100.0	102.7	103.1	103.5	106.5	110.3	115.3
Slovak Republic	..	..	78.2	81.9	86.0	88.6	91.6	100.0	105.9	106.7	109.4	113.2	115.6	118.0
Spain	83.2	86.8	92.3	93.9	94.8	94.2	94.8	100.0	101.7	102.4	103.9	107.4	112.7	118.7
Sweden	85.6	89.5	98.3	96.1	96.9	96.4	95.9	100.0	101.5	100.9	99.8	100.7	104.5	108.6
Switzerland	104.5	104.0	103.9	102.0	101.3	100.1	99.1	100.0	100.5	100.0	100.0	101.2	102.0	104.1
Turkey	2.0	4.2	7.8	13.8	25.1	43.1	66.0	100.0	161.6	242.6	304.6	338.4	366.3	402.1
United Kingdom	88.8	91.1	94.8	97.2	98.1	98.1	98.5	100.0	99.7	99.8	101.3	103.8	106.7	109.4
United States	89.2	90.4	93.1	95.2	95.5	94.5	96.1	100.0	100.8	100.1	102.7	107.1	113.0	117.5
EU27 total	88.4	90.3	94.7	95.7	96.3	95.7	95.7	100.0	101.2	101.5	102.8	105.8	109.5	113.3
OECD total	79.9	82.3	87.1	90.0	92.8	93.7	95.4	100.0	101.5	101.9	103.8	107.4	111.7	115.9
Brazil	1.6	38.4	61.0	64.9	70.1	72.6	84.7	100.0	112.6	131.4	167.6	185.1	195.4	197.0
China	..	..	..	104.3	104.0	99.7	97.3	100.0	98.7	96.5	98.8	104.7	109.9	113.2
India	65.0	71.7	78.7	82.2	85.9	90.9	94.1	100.0	105.2	107.8	113.5	121.0	126.7	132.8
Russian Federation	1.6	6.8	23.1	34.9	40.1	42.9	68.3	100.0	118.2	130.5	151.9	187.4	225.9	253.9
South Africa	61.2	66.8	73.4	79.3	85.0	88.3	92.9	100.0	107.1	121.4	127.0	129.5	134.3	142.9

StatLink http://dx.doi.org/10.1787/273524812843

PPI: manufacturing

Average annual growth in percentage

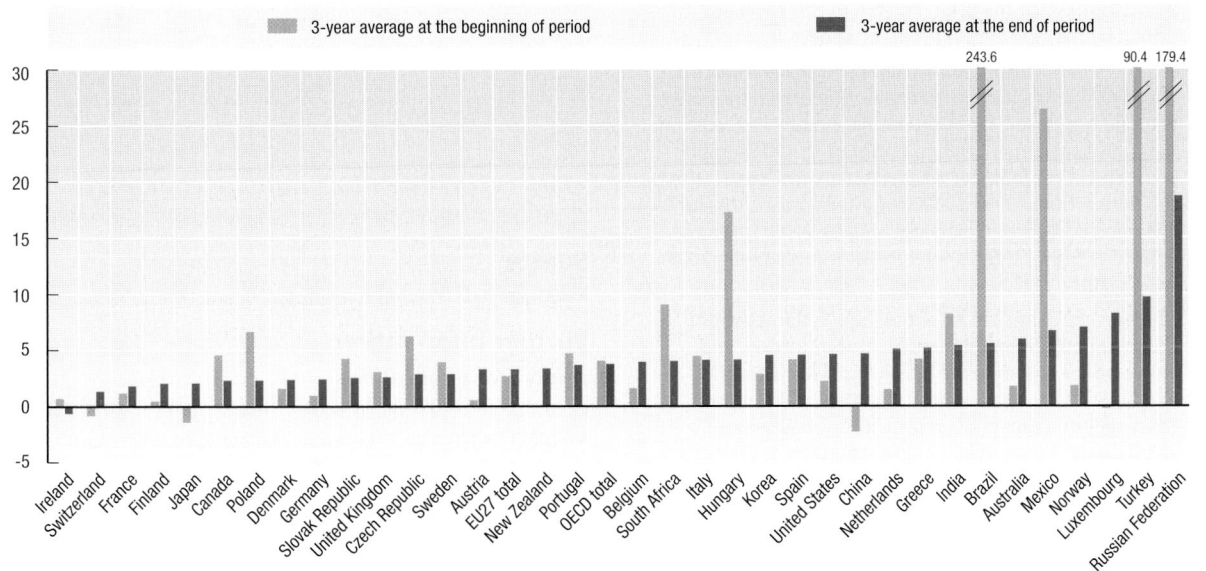

StatLink http://dx.doi.org/10.1787/267518425102

LONG-TERM INTEREST RATES

Long-term interest rates are one of the determinants of business investment. Low interest rates encourage investment in new equipment and high interest rates discourage it. Investment is, in turn, a major source of economic growth.

Definition

These interest rates refer to government bonds with a residual maturity of about ten years. They are not the interest rates at which the loans were issued, but the interest rates implied by the prices at which the bonds are traded on financial markets. For example if a bond was initially bought for 100 with an interest rate of 9%, but the bond is now trading at 90, the interest rate has risen to 10% ([9/90] x 100).

Comparability

The monthly rates shown are, where possible, averages of daily rates. They are in all cases interest rates on bonds whose capital repayment is guaranteed by governments.

Comparability is considered to be high.

Evolution of long-term interest rates
Percentage

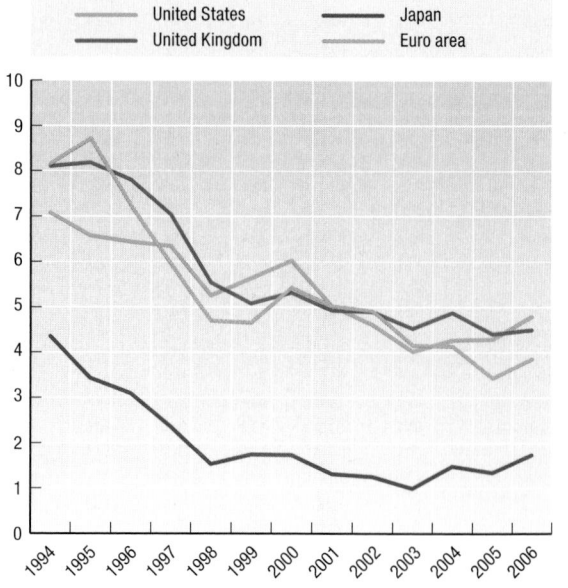

StatLink ⟪⟫ http://dx.doi.org/10.1787/267557374002

Long-term trends

Interest rates are determined by three factors: – the price that lenders charge for postponing consumption, the risk that the borrower may not repay the capital and the fall in the real value of the capital that the lender expects to occur because of inflation during the lifetime of the loan. The interest rates shown here refer to government borrowing and the risk factor is very low. To an important extent the interest rates in this table are driven by the expected rates of inflation.

From 1993 long-term interest rates fell for a few years but edged upwards again in 1994/1995. Since then they have been falling steadily in most member countries, but have starting to rise again in 2006. For the 20 member countries in the table for which data are available for the full period from 1993 to 2006, long-term interest rates averaged 6.9% in 1993 but only 3.8% by 2006. For many countries the long-term interest rates recorded in 2005 were historically low.

The most striking feature of the table is the reduction in the variance of interest rates among countries. The convergence of long-term interest rates is mostly explained by the increasing integration of financial markets – one aspect of globalisation – and was particularly pronounced among members of the euro area. Japan and Switzerland are exceptions; their interest rates have remained low but are not converging to the OECD average.

Source

- OECD (2007), *Main Economic Indicators*, OECD, Paris.

Further information

Analytical publications

- OECD (2007), *Financial Market Trends*, series, OECD, Paris.
- OECD (2007), *OECD Economic Outlook: December No. 82 – Volume 2007 Issue 2*, OECD, Paris.

Methodological publications

- OECD (1998), *Main Economic Indicators – Sources and Methods: Interest Rates and Share Price Indices*, OECD, Paris.

Long-term interest rates
Percentage

	1993	1994	1995	1996	1997	1998	1999	2000	2001	2002	2003	2004	2005	2006
Australia	7.38	8.89	9.21	8.21	6.95	5.49	6.01	6.31	5.62	5.84	5.37	5.59	5.34	5.59
Austria	6.71	7.03	7.13	6.32	5.68	4.71	4.68	5.56	5.08	4.97	4.15	4.15	3.39	3.80
Belgium	7.22	7.70	7.38	6.30	5.59	4.70	4.71	5.57	5.06	4.89	4.15	4.06	3.37	3.81
Canada	7.24	8.36	8.16	7.24	6.14	5.28	5.54	5.93	5.48	5.30	4.80	4.58	4.07	4.21
Czech Republic	..	..	..	..	..	..	..	..	6.31	4.88	4.12	4.75	3.51	3.78
Denmark	7.30	7.83	8.27	7.19	6.26	5.04	4.92	5.66	5.09	5.06	4.31	4.30	3.40	3.81
Finland	8.83	9.04	8.79	7.08	5.96	4.79	4.72	5.48	5.04	4.98	4.14	4.11	3.35	3.78
France	6.78	7.22	7.54	6.31	5.58	4.64	4.61	5.39	4.94	4.86	4.13	4.10	3.41	3.80
Germany	6.52	6.88	6.86	6.23	5.66	4.58	4.50	5.27	4.80	4.78	4.07	4.04	3.35	3.76
Greece	..	..	..	..	..	8.48	6.31	6.11	5.30	5.12	4.27	4.26	3.59	4.07
Iceland	..	6.98	9.65	9.24	8.71	7.66	8.47	11.20	10.36	7.96	6.65	7.49	7.73	9.33
Ireland	7.58	8.04	8.23	7.25	6.26	4.75	4.77	5.48	5.02	4.99	4.13	4.06	3.32	3.79
Italy	11.19	10.52	12.21	9.40	6.86	4.88	4.73	5.58	5.19	5.03	4.30	4.26	3.56	4.05
Japan	4.32	4.36	3.44	3.10	2.37	1.54	1.75	1.74	1.32	1.26	1.00	1.49	1.35	1.74
Korea	..	..	..	..	..	..	..	..	6.86	6.59	5.05	4.73	4.95	5.15
Luxembourg	..	7.15	7.23	6.30	5.60	4.73	4.67	5.52	4.86	4.68	3.32	2.84	2.41	3.30
Netherlands	6.36	6.86	6.90	6.15	5.58	4.63	4.63	5.41	4.96	4.89	4.12	4.10	3.37	3.78
New Zealand	6.93	7.63	7.78	7.89	7.19	6.29	6.41	6.85	6.39	6.53	5.87	6.07	5.88	5.78
Norway	6.88	7.43	7.43	6.77	5.89	5.40	5.50	6.22	6.24	6.38	5.05	4.37	3.75	4.08
Poland	..	..	..	..	..	..	..	..	10.68	7.36	5.78	6.90	5.22	5.23
Portugal	..	10.48	11.47	8.56	6.36	4.88	4.78	5.60	5.16	5.01	4.18	4.14	3.44	3.91
Slovak Republic	..	..	..	..	..	..	..	..	8.06	6.91	4.99	5.02	3.52	4.41
Spain	10.21	10.00	11.27	8.74	6.40	4.83	4.73	5.53	5.12	4.96	4.13	4.10	3.39	3.78
Sweden	8.54 |	9.50 |	10.24	8.03	6.61	4.99	4.98	5.37	5.11	5.30	4.64	4.43	3.38	3.70
Switzerland	4.55	4.96	4.52	4.00	3.36 |	3.04	3.04	3.93	3.38	3.20	2.66	2.74	2.10	2.52
United Kingdom	7.48 |	8.12	8.20	7.81	7.05	5.55	5.09	5.33	4.93	4.90	4.53	4.88	4.41	4.50
United States	5.87	7.08	6.58	6.44	6.35	5.26	5.64	6.03	5.02	4.61	4.02	4.27	4.29	4.79
Euro area	8.42	8.18	8.73	7.23	5.96	4.70 |	4.66	5.44 |	5.03	4.92	4.16	4.14	3.44	3.86
Russian Federation	..	..	..	..	..	..	87.38	35.16	19.38	15.82	8.90	7.79	7.76	6.83
South Africa	13.97	14.83	16.11	15.48	14.70	15.12	14.90	13.79	11.41	11.50	9.62	9.53	8.07	7.94

StatLink ᗰᔕᒪ http://dx.doi.org/10.1787/273562364605

Long-term interest rates
Percentage, 2006

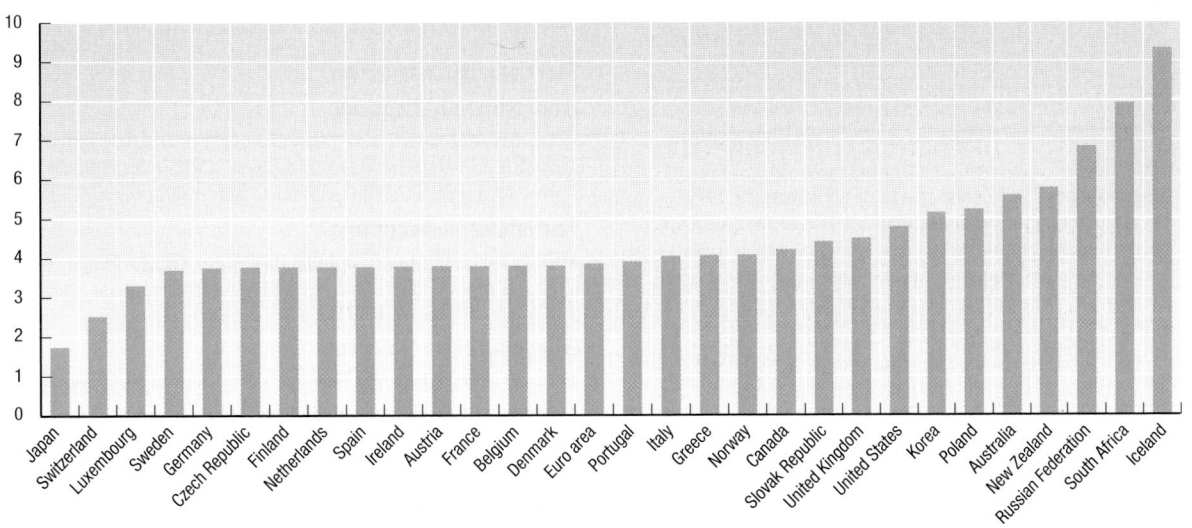

StatLink ᗰᔕᒪ http://dx.doi.org/10.1787/267540725558

RATES OF CONVERSION

To compare a single country's real GDP over a period of years, it is necessary to remove any movements that are due to price changes. In the same way, in order to compare the real GDPs of a group of countries at a single point in time, it is necessary to remove any differences in their GDPs that are due to differences in their price levels. Price indices are used to remove the effects of price changes in a single country over time; purchasing power parities (PPP) are used to remove the effects of the different levels of prices within a group of countries at a single point in time.

Definition

PPPs are currency converters that equalise price levels between countries. The PPPs shown here have been calculated by comparing the prices in OECD countries of a common basket of about 2 500 goods and services. Countries are not required to price all the items in the common basket because some of the items may be hard to find in certain countries, but the common basket has been drawn up in such a way that each country can find prices for a wide range of the goods and services that are representative of their markets.

Long-term trends

Over the period 1993-2006, movements of PPPs and of exchange rates were rarely similar and even when they moved in the same direction they were not of the same magnitude – see for example Ireland and the Czech Republic in the graph on the opposite page.

Exchange rates are sometimes used to convert the GDPs in different currencies to a common currency. However, comparisons of GDP based on exchange rates do not reflect the real volumes of goods and services in the GDPs of the countries being compared. For many of the low income countries, the differences between GDP converted using exchange rates and real GDP converted using PPPs are considerable. The differences are illustrated in the second graph.

For the Slovak Republic, for example, the difference between PPP-converted GDP and exchange rate-converted is over seventy per cent. In general, the use of exchange rates understates the real GDP of low-income countries and overstates the real GDP of high-income countries.

The price level indices in the third table are the PPPs divided by exchange rates, with the OECD set to 100. In general, there is a positive correlation between income levels and price levels; Denmark, Iceland, Norway and Switzerland, four high-income countries, had the highest price levels in 2006 while the Czech Republic, Hungary, Poland, the Slovak Republic and Turkey, five of the poorer OECD countries, had price levels around sixty per cent of the OECD average.

The goods and services to be priced cover all those that enter into final expenditure – household consumption, government services, capital formation and net exports. Prices for the different items are weighted by their shares in total final expenditures to obtain the GDP PPPs shown here.

Comparability

The PPPs shown here have been calculated jointly by the OECD and Eurostat using standard procedures. In consultation with their member countries, OECD and Eurostat keep their methodology under review and improvements are made regularly.

Source

- OECD (2008), *Purchasing Power Parities and Real Expenditures – 2005 Benchmark Year, 2007 Edition*, OECD, Paris.

Further information

Analytical publications

- Schreyer, P. and F. Koechlin (2002), "Purchasing Power Parities – Measurement and Uses", *OECD Statistics Brief*, No. 3, March, OECD, Paris, *www.oecd.org/std/statisticsbrief*.

Statistical publications

- OECD (2007), *Main Economic Indicators*, OECD, Paris.
- OECD (2007), *National Accounts of OECD Countries*, OECD, Paris.

Websites

- Joint World Bank-OECD Seminar on Puchasing Power Parities, 2001, *www.oecd.org/std/ppp/seminar2001*.
- OECD Purchasing Power Parities, *www.oecd.org/std/ppp*.

Purchasing power parities

National currency units per US dollar

	1993	1994	1995	1996	1997	1998	1999	2000	2001	2002	2003	2004	2005	2006
Australia	1.34	1.33	1.32	1.32	1.32	1.31	1.30	1.31	1.33	1.34	1.35	1.37	1.39	1.41
Austria	0.928	0.933	0.933	0.929	0.924	0.917	0.917	0.901	0.917	0.896	0.884	0.873	0.874	0.862
Belgium	0.918	0.918	0.910	0.911	0.911	0.924	0.921	0.892	0.885	0.865	0.878	0.895	0.899	0.889
Canada	1.22	1.21	1.21	1.21	1.21	1.19	1.19	1.23	1.22	1.23	1.23	1.23	1.21	1.20
Czech Republic	9.2	10.2	11.1	11.9	12.7	13.9	14.1	14.2	14.2	14.3	14.0	14.3	14.4	14.2
Denmark	8.57	8.52	8.46	8.43	8.43	8.39	8.47	8.42	8.46	8.30	8.53	8.39	8.52	8.44
Finland	0.979	0.972	0.998	1.002	0.997	1.003	1.003	0.996	1.011	1.003	1.010	0.974	0.983	0.965
France	1.007	0.999	0.992	0.987	0.974	0.967	0.960	0.940	0.918	0.905	0.937	0.939	0.923	0.915
Germany	1.003	1.006	1.004	0.992	0.990	0.988	0.975	0.968	0.955	0.942	0.917	0.895	0.893	0.870
Greece	0.489	0.532	0.572	0.604	0.630	0.662	0.681	0.679	0.671	0.660	0.688	0.695	0.702	0.703
Hungary	42	50	62	73	85	94	101	108	111	115	120	126	129	129
Iceland	71.9	72.3	73.0	74.9	74.4	77.2	79.7	84.4	88.9	91.3	94.4	94.1	97.1	102.5
Ireland	0.82	0.81	0.82	0.83	0.85	0.88	0.93	0.96	0.99	1.00	1.01	1.00	1.02	1.01
Italy	0.755	0.766	0.788	0.808	0.816	0.808	0.818	0.818	0.807	0.845	0.853	0.872	0.875	0.863
Japan	182	179	174	170	168	167	162	155	149	144	140	134	130	124
Korea	621	656	690	712	732	767	755	749	757	770	796	794	789	762
Luxembourg	0.93	0.94	0.95	0.95	0.96	0.95	0.94	0.94	0.95	0.93	0.94	0.92	0.92	0.95
Mexico	2.04	2.17	2.93	3.76	4.35	4.96	5.63	6.11	6.31	6.55	6.82	7.12	7.13	7.22
Netherlands	0.914	0.914	0.914	0.908	0.910	0.906	0.907	0.894	0.906	0.902	0.926	0.908	0.898	0.888
New Zealand	1.47	1.46	1.46	1.47	1.45	1.45	1.43	1.45	1.47	1.47	1.50	1.51	1.54	1.52
Norway	9.27	9.06	9.15	9.04	9.08	9.38	9.33	9.14	9.18	9.11	9.11	8.98	8.84	9.21
Poland	0.70	0.94	1.17	1.36	1.52	1.66	1.74	1.84	1.86	1.83	1.84	1.86	1.90	1.87
Portugal	0.608	0.639	0.648	0.659	0.672	0.693	0.697	0.701	0.705	0.708	0.706	0.715	0.707	0.706
Slovak Republic	10.9	12.1	13.0	13.3	13.7	14.2	15.1	15.9	15.7	15.9	16.7	17.2	17.2	17.1
Spain	0.677	0.689	0.708	0.717	0.719	0.719	0.733	0.735	0.739	0.733	0.752	0.758	0.768	0.774
Sweden	9.16	9.22	9.35	9.24	9.30	9.37	9.29	9.15	9.35	9.35	9.33	9.09	9.24	9.12
Switzerland	2.02	2.00	1.98	1.94	1.89	1.88	1.87	1.85	1.84	1.77	1.77	1.75	1.74	1.71
Turkey	0.007	0.013	0.024	0.043	0.076	0.131	0.202	0.283	0.428	0.613	0.773	0.811	0.868	0.939
United Kingdom	0.639	0.635	0.639	0.641	0.635	0.645	0.653	0.637	0.626	0.628	0.640	0.632	0.649	0.645
United States	1.00	1.00	1.00	1.00	1.00	1.00	1.00	1.00	1.00	1.00	1.00	1.00	1.00	1.00
Brazil	..	..	..	..	..	..	..	..	..	..	..	..	1.36	..
China	..	..	..	..	..	..	..	..	..	..	..	..	3.45	..
India	..	..	..	..	..	..	..	..	..	..	..	..	14.67	..
Russian Federation	..	..	..	..	..	..	..	..	..	..	..	..	12.74	..
South Africa	..	..	..	..	..	..	..	..	..	..	..	..	3.87	..

StatLink http://dx.doi.org/10.1787/273566548038

Changes in exchange rates and purchasing power parities

Average annual growth in percentage, 1993-2006

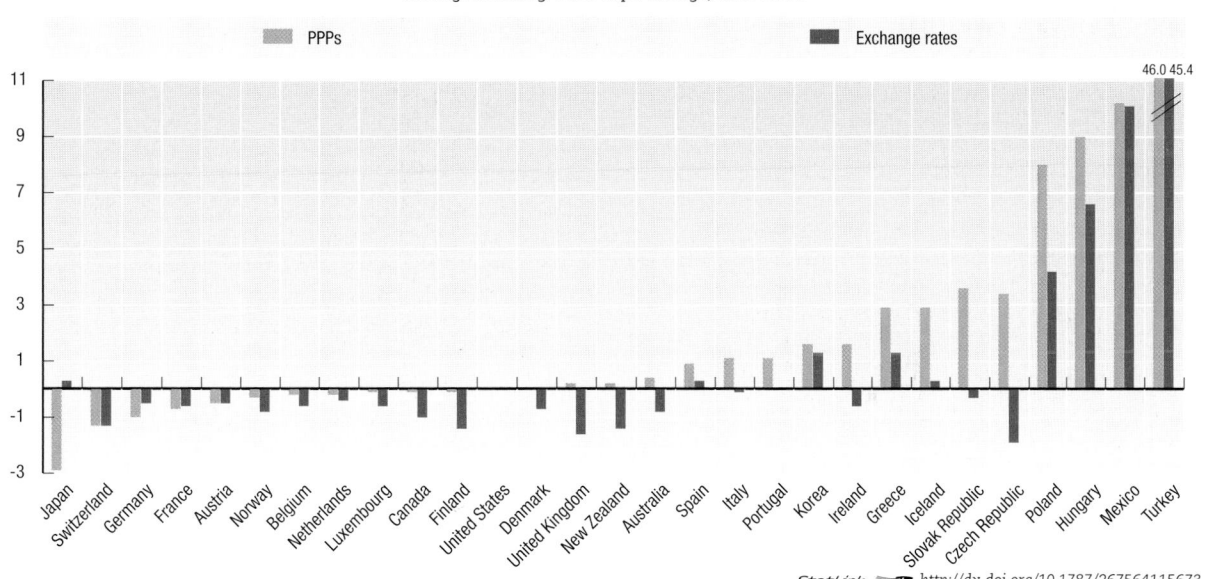

StatLink http://dx.doi.org/10.1787/267564115673

Exchange rates
National currency units per US dollar

	1993	1994	1995	1996	1997	1998	1999	2000	2001	2002	2003	2004	2005	2006
Australia	1.471	1.368	1.349	1.278	1.347	1.592	1.550	1.725	1.933	1.841	1.542	1.360	1.309	1.328
Austria	0.845	0.830	0.733	0.769	0.887	0.900	0.939	1.085	1.118	1.063	0.886	0.805	0.804	0.797
Belgium	0.858	0.829	0.731	0.768	0.887	0.900	0.939	1.085	1.118	1.063	0.886	0.805	0.804	0.797
Canada	1.290	1.366	1.372	1.363	1.385	1.483	1.486	1.485	1.549	1.569	1.401	1.301	1.212	1.134
Czech Republic	29.15	28.79	26.54	27.14	31.70	32.28	34.57	38.60	38.04	32.74	28.21	25.70	23.96	22.60
Denmark	6.484	6.361	5.602	5.799	6.604	6.701	6.976	8.083	8.323	7.895	6.588	5.991	5.997	5.947
Finland	0.961	0.879	0.734	0.773	0.873	0.899	0.939	1.085	1.118	1.063	0.886	0.805	0.804	0.797
France	0.863	0.846	0.761	0.780	0.890	0.899	0.939	1.085	1.118	1.063	0.886	0.805	0.804	0.797
Germany	0.845	0.830	0.733	0.769	0.887	0.900	0.939	1.085	1.118	1.063	0.886	0.805	0.804	0.797
Greece	0.673	0.712	0.680	0.706	0.801	0.867	0.897	1.072	1.118	1.063	0.886	0.805	0.804	0.797
Hungary	91.93	105.16	125.68	152.65	186.79	214.40	237.15	282.18	286.49	257.89	224.31	202.75	199.58	210.39
Iceland	67.60	69.94	64.69	66.50	70.90	70.96	72.34	78.62	97.42	91.66	76.71	70.19	62.98	70.20
Ireland	0.860	0.849	0.792	0.794	0.838	0.892	0.939	1.085	1.118	1.063	0.886	0.805	0.804	0.797
Italy	0.813	0.833	0.841	0.797	0.880	0.897	0.939	1.085	1.118	1.063	0.886	0.805	0.804	0.797
Japan	111.20	102.21	94.06	108.78	120.99	130.91	113.91	107.77	121.53	125.39	115.93	108.19	110.22	116.30
Korea	802.67	803.45	771.27	804.45	951.29	1 401.44	1 188.82	1 130.96	1 290.99	1 251.09	1 191.61	1 145.32	1 024.12	954.79
Luxembourg	0.858	0.829	0.731	0.768	0.887	0.900	0.939	1.085	1.118	1.063	0.886	0.805	0.804	0.797
Mexico	3.116	3.375	6.419	7.599	7.918	9.136	9.560	9.456	9.342	9.656	10.789	11.286	10.898	10.899
Netherlands	0.843	0.826	0.729	0.765	0.885	0.900	0.939	1.085	1.118	1.063	0.886	0.805	0.804	0.797
New Zealand	1.851	1.687	1.524	1.455	1.512	1.868	1.890	2.201	2.379	2.162	1.722	1.509	1.420	1.542
Norway	7.094	7.058	6.335	6.450	7.073	7.545	7.799	8.802	8.992	7.984	7.080	6.741	6.443	6.413
Poland	1.812	2.272	2.425	2.696	3.279	3.475	3.967	4.346	4.094	4.080	3.889	3.658	3.235	3.103
Portugal	0.802	0.828	0.754	0.769	0.874	0.898	0.939	1.085	1.118	1.063	0.886	0.805	0.804	0.797
Slovak Republic	30.77	32.04	29.71	30.65	33.62	35.23	41.36	46.04	48.35	45.33	36.77	32.26	31.02	29.70
Spain	0.765	0.805	0.749	0.761	0.880	0.898	0.939	1.085	1.118	1.063	0.886	0.805	0.804	0.797
Sweden	7.783	7.716	7.133	6.706	7.635	7.950	8.262	9.162	10.329	9.737	8.086	7.349	7.473	7.378
Switzerland	1.478	1.368	1.182	1.236	1.451	1.450	1.502	1.689	1.688	1.559	1.347	1.244	1.245	1.254
Turkey	0.011	0.030	0.046	0.081	0.152	0.261	0.419	0.625	1.226	1.507	1.501	1.426	1.344	1.428
United Kingdom	0.667	0.653	0.634	0.641	0.611	0.604	0.618	0.661	0.695	0.667	0.612	0.546	0.550	0.543
United States	1.000	1.000	1.000	1.000	1.000	1.000	1.000	1.000	1.000	1.000	1.000	1.000	1.000	1.000
Euro area	0.854	0.843	0.765	0.788	0.882	0.894	0.939	1.085	1.117	1.061	0.885	0.805	0.805	0.797
Brazil	0.0322	0.6393	0.9177	1.0051	1.0780	1.1605	1.8147	1.8301	2.3577	2.9208	3.0771	2.9251	2.4344	2.1753
China	5.762	8.619	8.351	8.314	8.290	8.279	8.278	8.279	8.277	8.277	8.277	8.277	8.194	7.973
India	30.49	31.37	32.43	35.43	36.31	41.26	43.06	44.94	47.19	48.61	46.58	45.32	44.10	45.31
Russian Federation	1.0007	2.3915	4.6260	5.1675	5.8375	9.7051	24.6199	28.1292	29.1685	31.3485	30.6920	28.8137	28.2844	27.1910
South Africa	3.268	3.551	3.627	4.299	4.608	5.528	6.109	6.940	8.609	10.541	7.565	6.460	6.359	6.772

StatLink ᵜ️ http://dx.doi.org/10.1787/273610154367

Percentage differences in GDP when converted to US dollars using exchange rates and PPPs
PPP-based GDP minus exchange rate-based GDP as per cent of exchange rate-based GDP, 2006

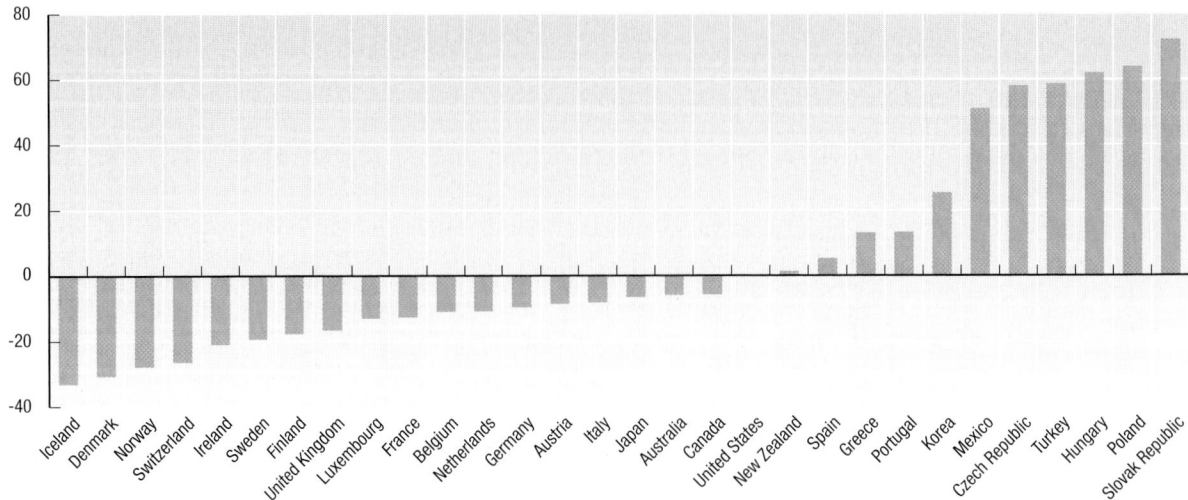

StatLink ᵜ️ http://dx.doi.org/10.1787/267586670181

Indices of price levels
OECD = 100

	1993	1994	1995	1996	1997	1998	1999	2000	2001	2002	2003	2004	2005	2006
Australia	85	89	86	95	96	84	85	81	77	80	89	98	103	104
Austria	103	104	112	111	102	104	99	88	91	93	102	106	106	107
Belgium	100	102	110	109	101	104	99	87	88	90	101	108	109	110
Canada	89	82	78	81	86	81	81	88	88	87	89	92	97	104
Czech Republic	30	33	37	40	39	44	41	39	42	48	51	54	58	62
Denmark	124	123	133	133	126	127	123	111	113	116	132	136	138	142
Finland	95	102	119	119	112	113	108	97	101	104	116	118	119	119
France	109	109	115	116	108	109	103	92	92	94	108	114	112	112
Germany	111	112	120	118	110	112	105	95	95	98	106	108	108	109
Greece	68	69	74	78	77	78	77	67	67	69	79	84	85	87
Hungary	43	43	43	44	45	45	43	41	43	49	55	61	63	61
Iceland	99	95	99	103	103	111	111	114	102	110	126	131	150	147
Ireland	89	88	91	96	100	101	100	94	99	104	117	122	124	124
Italy	87	85	82	93	91	92	88	80	80	88	98	105	106	107
Japan	153	161	163	143	137	129	144	153	137	127	123	121	114	105
Korea	72	75	79	81	76	56	64	70	65	68	68	68	75	78
Luxembourg	102	105	114	113	106	107	101	92	94	97	108	111	112	113
Mexico	61	59	40	45	54	55	60	69	75	75	61	61	64	65
Netherlands	101	102	110	109	101	102	98	87	90	94	107	110	109	110
New Zealand	74	80	84	93	95	79	77	70	69	75	89	98	105	97
Norway	122	118	127	129	126	126	121	110	114	126	131	130	133	136
Poland	36	38	43	46	45	49	44	45	51	50	48	49	57	60
Portugal	71	71	76	79	76	78	75	68	70	74	81	86	86	87
Slovak Republic	33	35	39	40	40	41	37	37	36	39	46	52	54	57
Spain	83	79	83	86	80	81	79	72	74	76	87	92	93	93
Sweden	110	110	115	126	120	120	114	106	101	106	118	121	120	122
Switzerland	128	135	147	144	128	132	126	116	121	126	134	137	136	133
Turkey	56	41	47	48	49	51	49	48	39	45	53	55	63	62
United Kingdom	90	90	89	92	102	109	107	102	100	104	107	113	115	118
United States	94	92	88	92	98	102	101	106	111	111	102	97	97	98
EU15 total	98	98	103	105	101	103	99	90	90	94	103	108	108	109
OECD total	100	100	100	100	100	100	100	100	100	100	100	100	100	100
Brazil	..	..	..	..	..	..	..	..	..	..	..	..	54	..
China	..	..	..	..	..	..	..	..	..	..	..	..	42	..
India	..	..	..	..	..	..	..	..	..	..	..	..	32	..
Russian Federation	..	..	..	..	..	..	..	..	..	..	..	..	45	..
South Africa	..	..	..	..	..	..	..	..	..	..	..	..	59	..

StatLink http://dx.doi.org/10.1787/273627116186

Indices of price levels
OECD = 100, year 2006

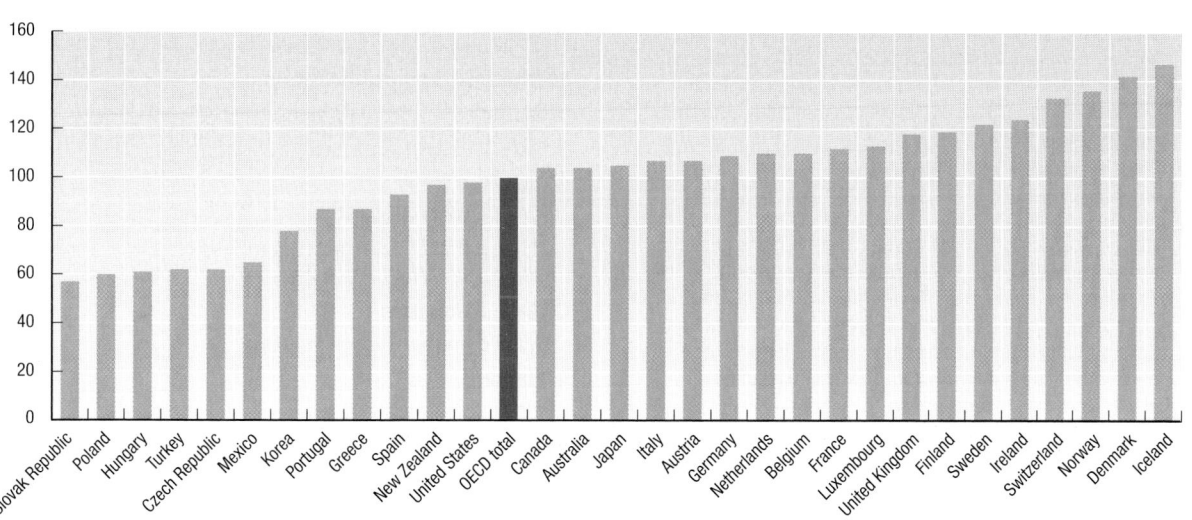

StatLink http://dx.doi.org/10.1787/267624670523

EFFECTIVE EXCHANGE RATES

A broad interpretation of international competitiveness would involve comparison of the success of different countries in raising productivity, fostering innovation and improving living standards. The two competitiveness indicators shown here have a narrower objective – namely to measure changes in a country's price competitiveness in international markets based on changes in that country's exchange rate and price level (either consumer goods prices or unit labour costs in manufacturing) relative to those of its competitors. In addition, we present indices of nominal effective exchange rates. This indicator reflects only variations in market exchange rates, which is just one of the factors that enter the calculation of the two competitiveness indicators mentioned above.

Definition

The nominal effective exchange rate indices are calculated by comparing, for each country, the change in its own exchange rate against the US dollar to a weighted average of changes in its competitors' exchange rates (also against the US dollar), using the weighting matrix for the current year (based on the importance of bilateral trade).

The other two indicators, relative consumer price indices and relative unit labour costs in manufacturing, can be described as indices of real effective exchange rates. Unlike nominal effective exchange rates, they take into account not only changes in market exchange rates, but also variations in relative price levels (using, respectively, consumer prices and unit labour costs in manufacturing), and therefore can be used as indicators of competitiveness. The change in a country's index of relative consumer prices between two years is obtained by comparing the change in the country's consumer price index (converted into US dollars at market exchange rates) to a weighted average of changes in its competitors' consumer price indices (also expressed in US dollars), using the weighting matrix for the current year (based on the importance of bilateral trade). Changes in the index of relative unit labour costs in manufacturing are calculated in the same way.

Comparability

All three indices shown here are constructed using a common procedure.

Long-term trends

A rise in the indices represents a deterioration in that country's competitiveness. Note that the indices only show changes in the international competitiveness of each country over time and that differences between countries in the levels of the indices have no significance.

All three indices are rather variable from year to year, so that it is difficult to detect long-term movements. Between 2000 and 2005, Japan, Sweden and the United States have generally improved their international competitiveness as judged by both relative consumer price indices and unit labour costs in manufacturing, while the competitive positions of Australia, Canada, Hungary and New Zealand have generally deteriorated. For both groups of countries, these changes reflected in large part movements in these countries' nominal effective exchange rates. By contrast, in the case of the United States, the improvement in competitiveness in terms of unit labour costs since 2000 has been significantly larger than the change in their nominal effective exchange rate, and therefore must have been due to favourable developments in unit labour costs in manufacturing, which in turn reflected trends in productivity and wage costs.

Source
- OECD (2007), *OECD Economic Outlook: December No. 82 – Volume 2007 Issue 2*, OECD, Paris.

Further information

Statistical publications
- OECD (2007), *Main Economic Indicators*, OECD, Paris.

Methodological publications
- Durand, M., C. Madaschi and F. Terribile (1998), *Trends in OECD Countries' International Competitiveness*, OECD Economics Department Working Papers, No. 195, OECD, Paris.
- Durand, M., J. Simon and C. Webb (1992), *OECD's Indicators of International Trade and Competitiveness*, OECD Economics Department Working Papers, No. 120, OECD, Paris.

Online databases
- *OECD Economic Outlook Statistics.*

Websites
- OECD Economic Outlook – Sources and Methods, *www.oecd.org/eco/sources-and-methods*.

Nominal effective exchange rates
Year 2000 = 100

	1993	1994	1995	1996	1997	1998	1999	2000	2001	2002	2003	2004	2005	2006
Australia	99.5	107.2	103.9	113.9	115.4	107.4	107.6	100.0	93.7	97.2	108.6	117.1	120.0	118.3
Austria	95.6	97.8	102.5	101.5	99.6	101.6	102.3	100.0	100.4	101.0	104.4	105.5	104.7	104.8
Belgium	97.9	102.2	107.9	106.2	102.0	104.4	104.1	100.0	101.2	103.0	108.3	110.2	109.7	109.8
Canada	107.7	102.8	102.0	103.9	104.3	99.4	99.1	100.0	97.0	95.5	105.5	112.0	119.8	127.7
Czech Republic	94.7	98.1	98.8	100.4	97.4	99.1	98.7	100.0	105.0	117.0	116.7	117.0	124.3	130.5
Denmark	98.2	100.5	105.7	104.7	102.3	104.9	104.2	100.0	101.8	103.3	108.1	109.5	108.6	108.4
Finland	79.5	90.1	103.6	101.1	98.9	101.7	104.7	100.0	102.1	104.2	110.3	112.4	111.5	111.3
France	97.4	100.4	104.5	104.9	102.1	104.5	103.8	100.0	100.9	102.5	107.4	109.0	108.4	108.5
Germany	93.9	98.5	106.0	104.5	100.9	104.6	104.5	100.0	101.2	103.1	109.4	111.6	110.3	110.3
Greece	120.5	115.1	113.8	111.9	109.9	106.6	107.0	100.0	101.0	102.8	107.8	109.5	108.5	108.6
Hungary	214.4	192.8	153.0	130.3	120.7	109.3	105.4	100.0	101.9	108.9	108.3	110.4	111.1	104.0
Iceland	97.1	92.9	93.3	92.8	94.8	97.4	99.0	100.0	85.2	87.9	92.0	93.1	103.5	92.7
Ireland	107.4	109.2	111.2	114.1	113.9	110.5	107.3	100.0	101.2	103.6	112.6	115.1	114.9	115.1
Italy	99.2	99.1	91.3	100.5	101.8	104.0	103.8	100.0	101.3	103.2	108.3	110.1	109.2	109.3
Japan	74.4	86.4	92.5	80.6	77.1	80.0	91.9	100.0	92.3	88.4	91.5	95.3	92.4	85.4
Korea	117.8	119.1	119.5	121.4	112.4	81.3	93.3	100.0	92.4	95.4	94.8	94.8	105.6	113.9
Luxembourg	99.2	102.0	105.4	104.3	102.0	103.0	102.8	100.0	100.4	101.5	104.9	106.1	105.5	105.5
Mexico	272.4	263.8	138.6	117.7	115.5	102.6	97.9	100.0	102.8	99.7	87.1	81.9	84.3	83.8
Netherlands	97.2	101.8	108.8	107.3	102.1	105.7	105.4	100.0	101.4	103.7	110.8	113.4	112.7	112.6
New Zealand	102.0	109.4	116.9	124.3	127.3	114.3	110.3	100.0	98.7	106.8	121.5	129.7	135.8	125.4
Norway	100.0	100.8	104.5	104.6	105.6	102.4	102.2	100.0	103.3	112.1	109.7	106.0	110.6	109.9
Poland	170.5	139.2	122.7	114.4	106.3	104.0	97.0	100.0	110.2	105.4	94.8	92.7	103.6	106.8
Portugal	102.5	101.7	104.9	104.5	103.1	103.0	102.4	100.0	100.9	102.0	104.8	105.5	104.9	105.0
Slovak Republic	98.2	97.1	100.4	101.3	106.0	105.9	98.3	100.0	97.6	98.0	103.6	108.0	110.1	113.4
Spain	111.0	105.7	106.0	107.1	102.8	104.0	103.1	100.0	101.1	102.5	106.3	107.5	106.9	107.0
Sweden	92.5	93.6	94.0	103.5	100.2	99.9	99.7	100.0	91.9	94.1	99.5	101.3	98.7	99.1
Switzerland	86.8	95.6	104.0	102.7	96.9	101.0	101.8	100.0	104.0	109.3	111.1	111.5	110.6	108.9
Turkey	4 239.0	1 719.1	990.8	581.1	345.5	207.8	137.2	100.0	56.3	41.8	36.8	35.9	37.7	35.1
United Kingdom	76.6	79.0	76.4	78.1	91.1	97.0	97.4	100.0	99.0	100.2	96.3	100.8	99.3	99.8
United States	72.7	76.9	78.5	82.9	88.8	98.0	97.6	100.0	105.3	105.8	99.6	95.1	92.6	91.0
Euro area	94.2	100.8	109.5	111.7	104.6	110.8	109.9	100.0	102.5	106.4	119.3	123.8	121.8	121.9
Brazil	..	367.8	165.8	154.8	153.8	149.9	96.7	100.0	80.9	71.7	61.7	61.9	74.2	82.3

StatLink http://dx.doi.org/10.1787/273627564665

Nominal effective exchange rates
Year 1993 = 100

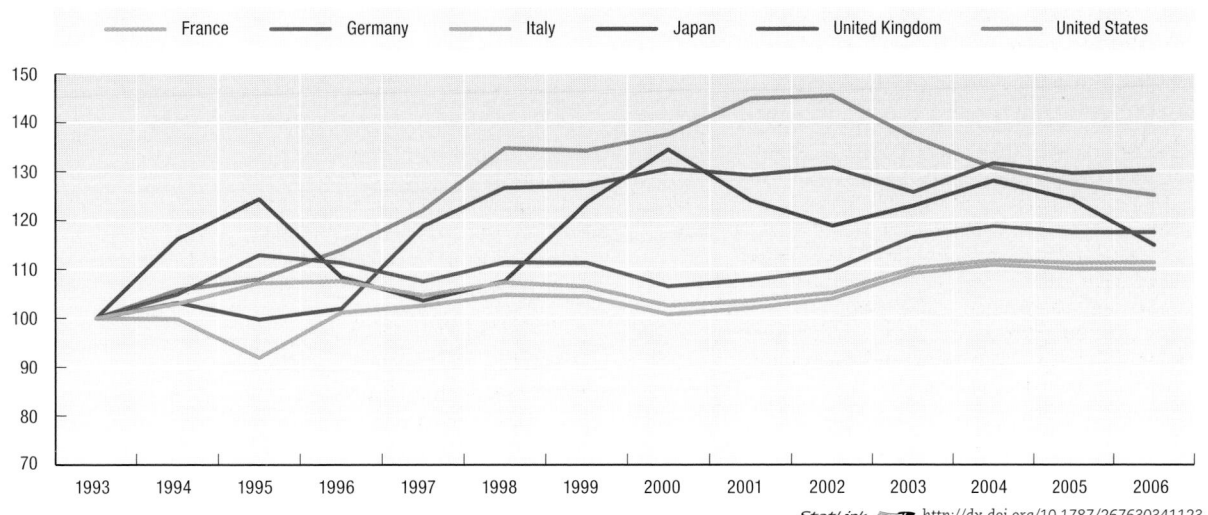

StatLink http://dx.doi.org/10.1787/267630341123

EFFECTIVE EXCHANGE RATES

Relative consumer price indices
Year 2000 = 100

	1993	1994	1995	1996	1997	1998	1999	2000	2001	2002	2003	2004	2005	2006
Australia	101.6	106.7	104.9	114.8	113.8	104.1	104.7	100.0	96.2	101.5	114.8	124.3	128.1	127.8
Austria	106.3	106.4	109.4	107.0	103.4	103.7	102.6	100.0	100.2	100.5	103.3	104.2	103.5	102.9
Belgium	107.1	108.8	112.5	109.8	104.5	105.5	104.0	100.0	100.9	102.1	106.8	108.7	108.8	108.4
Canada	118.7	109.1	106.8	106.8	106.1	100.1	99.4	100.0	96.9	96.0	106.7	112.6	119.4	126.1
Czech Republic	77.0	80.9	83.6	89.1	90.7	99.4	98.0	100.0	106.7	118.5	115.9	116.7	123.6	130.3
Denmark	102.0	101.7	105.4	103.8	101.2	103.5	103.6	100.0	101.5	103.4	108.4	109.1	107.9	107.6
Finland	102.2	106.1	113.9	107.3	103.3	104.6	104.4	100.0	101.4	102.4	106.8	106.6	103.9	102.9
France	108.9	108.8	111.0	110.3	106.0	106.9	104.6	100.0	99.8	101.1	106.0	107.6	106.4	105.9
Germany	112.8	113.5	117.8	113.1	107.7	108.9	106.3	100.0	99.9	100.6	105.5	106.9	105.3	104.6
Greece	99.9	100.8	104.0	106.9	107.7	106.3	106.8	100.0	101.0	103.7	109.8	112.2	112.6	113.6
Hungary	95.7	93.4	88.7	89.6	95.1	95.8	98.6	100.0	108.2	119.2	121.8	129.7	132.2	126.0
Iceland	97.7	91.6	90.3	89.6	91.2	93.6	96.2	100.0	88.8	94.8	99.6	102.3	116.1	108.5
Ireland	108.1	108.0	109.2	111.0	109.9	107.1	103.8	100.0	103.8	109.4	120.8	123.7	123.6	125.9
Italy	102.9	100.0	92.9	102.8	103.4	104.9	103.9	100.0	101.2	103.2	108.9	110.6	109.4	109.2
Japan	96.1	103.8	105.5	88.2	83.4	84.2	94.5	100.0	89.5	83.9	85.0	86.3	81.3	73.4
Korea	106.9	108.1	109.4	113.3	106.9	81.5	92.8	100.0	94.6	99.5	101.2	102.8	115.6	125.2
Luxembourg	104.5	105.7	108.3	105.7	102.6	102.9	102.1	100.0	100.7	101.9	105.7	107.0	106.7	107.4
Mexico	99.6	95.2	64.5	72.0	83.4	84.2	92.1	100.0	106.5	106.7	95.3	91.6	95.0	95.1
Netherlands	107.8	107.9	112.0	109.0	103.3	106.3	105.6	100.0	102.9	106.7	114.2	115.9	114.3	113.0
New Zealand	106.1	111.8	119.8	127.0	129.5	115.7	110.1	100.0	98.9	108.2	123.0	131.7	139.0	129.4
Norway	103.2	100.6	103.0	101.8	103.1	100.6	101.1	100.0	103.9	112.0	110.2	105.2	109.5	109.3
Poland	73.3	74.0	79.1	84.8	87.8	93.3	90.7	100.0	112.9	107.7	95.6	94.6	105.7	107.9
Portugal	100.4	98.9	102.4	102.3	101.1	101.9	102.0	100.0	102.5	104.8	108.6	109.5	108.6	109.3
Slovak Republic	85.1	84.2	86.1	85.9	90.8	91.8	90.7	100.0	101.2	102.5	115.6	126.6	129.5	136.4
Spain	107.2	102.4	104.0	105.6	101.1	102.1	102.0	100.0	102.1	104.4	109.4	111.6	112.3	113.9
Sweden	106.1	104.6	103.8	111.7	106.3	103.3	101.4	100.0	91.7	94.0	99.4	99.5	95.4	94.9
Switzerland	103.5	108.3	114.8	110.7	102.3	104.1	102.9	100.0	102.2	105.8	106.2	105.2	103.2	100.4
Turkey	89.8	66.0	71.5	72.3	77.3	85.0	89.3	100.0	81.5	88.7	93.4	96.4	107.2	106.6
United Kingdom	84.0	83.9	80.3	81.6	94.3	99.6	99.2	100.0	97.4	97.6	93.2	96.7	95.1	95.5
United States	84.8	84.9	83.7	86.3	90.8	98.1	96.8	100.0	105.7	105.8	99.7	95.6	94.1	93.4
Euro area	119.5	119.1	123.5	122.3	111.8	114.9	110.9	100.0	101.9	105.7	118.4	122.5	120.3	119.9

StatLink ⬛📊 http://dx.doi.org/10.1787/273642853420

Relative consumer price indices
Year 1993 = 100

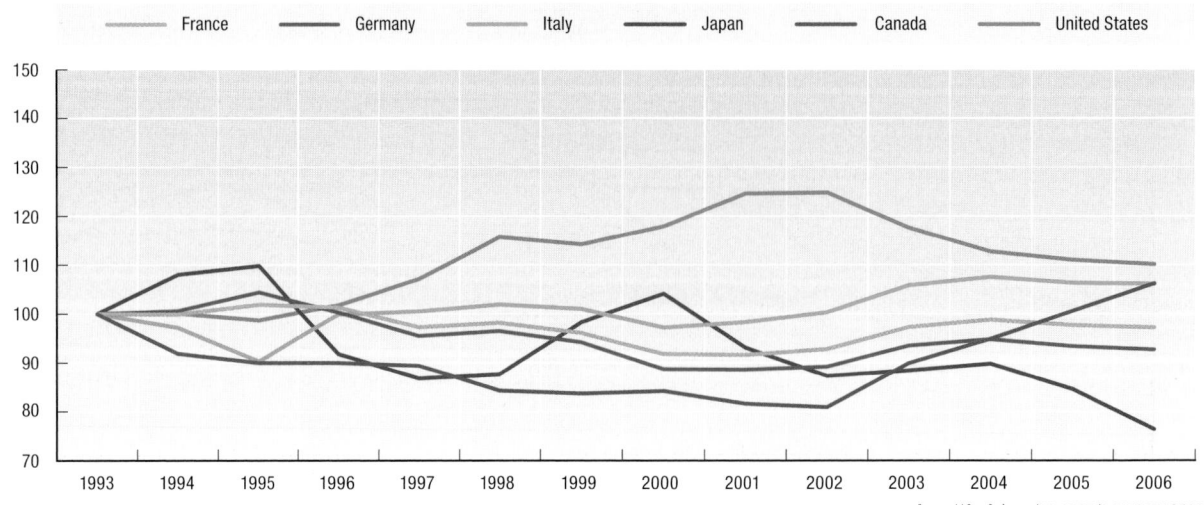

| France | Germany | Italy | Japan | Canada | United States |

StatLink ⬛📊 http://dx.doi.org/10.1787/267708510501

Relative unit labour costs in manufacturing
Year 2000 = 100

	1993	1994	1995	1996	1997	1998	1999	2000	2001	2002	2003	2004	2005	2006
Australia	88.9	92.9	97.7	108.9	110.0	101.1	106.7	100.0	92.5	97.5	111.8	124.8	133.1	133.6
Austria	121.6	122.2	120.6	112.8	109.2	109.4	106.3	100.0	97.8	97.0	101.0	102.9	103.2	100.5
Belgium	111.1	114.1	116.4	111.8	103.7	104.7	106.0	100.0	102.6	104.4	110.4	110.7	111.6	112.1
Canada	110.3	102.8	105.6	109.9	109.7	104.7	104.2	100.0	101.1	103.8	118.5	131.8	142.6	156.1
Czech Republic	88.7	86.3	86.1	94.2	96.3	108.3	100.5	100.0	111.2	124.8	129.1	126.7	127.1	124.2
Denmark	99.7	95.3	99.9	103.2	98.9	103.6	104.2	100.0	102.8	107.5	115.2	115.5	114.6	116.6
Finland	103.0	108.0	124.0	118.1	111.6	111.5	111.4	100.0	98.9	96.8	99.0	99.2	97.6	92.3
France	115.2	115.2	116.0	114.9	109.5	106.6	104.9	100.0	99.0	101.2	103.8	105.7	102.3	103.1
Germany	104.4	104.5	114.4	112.7	104.0	106.8	106.5	100.0	98.6	100.7	105.3	104.9	100.0	96.9
Greece	98.0	100.3	105.4	107.8	115.3	110.8	107.4	100.0	95.7	99.9	106.5	123.6	120.1	122.9
Hungary	141.9	126.7	114.9	106.4	105.0	99.1	95.7	100.0	108.1	112.0	111.2	119.9	121.7	113.0
Iceland	73.5	71.6	72.8	72.4	76.2	83.0	92.1	100.0	87.4	92.9	97.9	101.5	117.9	113.9
Ireland	143.3	141.1	133.6	133.2	126.1	114.1	105.3	100.0	97.8	90.8	99.3	103.4	104.2	104.5
Italy	98.5	93.7	85.5	97.6	101.0	102.7	103.9	100.0	102.1	107.4	118.9	126.8	129.9	131.5
Japan	92.2	104.8	103.8	85.6	81.7	85.4	97.6	100.0	91.7	86.4	81.1	79.6	73.4	64.8
Korea	117.9	120.4	133.9	144.8	128.1	85.6	92.9	100.0	93.1	97.6	96.7	99.0	110.1	113.3
Luxembourg	110.5	111.0	115.0	111.7	107.7	103.8	101.9	100.0	103.5	104.2	109.4	109.4	113.8	117.2
Mexico	96.9	93.9	58.4	62.3	74.4	76.1	86.7	100.0	113.0	114.8	105.7	101.8	105.7	106.1
Netherlands	110.5	107.8	111.2	107.3	104.3	107.9	107.2	100.0	102.2	107.0	116.2	117.5	114.5	113.8
New Zealand	99.3	108.1	114.4	124.9	129.8	117.8	113.1	100.0	101.9	114.1	132.0	145.7	153.0	144.0
Norway	77.7	80.6	85.7	85.7	91.0	93.8	98.6	100.0	102.9	113.8	109.0	105.9	111.4	113.1
Poland	77.4	82.2	88.2	94.5	97.9	104.0	97.6	100.0	105.2	92.4	75.4	70.7	79.3	78.1
Portugal	100.5	100.4	102.5	99.2	97.6	99.7	102.2	100.0	100.1	101.8	103.3	104.3	102.6	100.5
Slovak Republic	78.3	94.1	98.8	98.2	101.9	97.9	91.2	100.0	96.2	101.4	105.8	108.2	100.7	100.1
Spain	98.4	94.0	94.7	96.9	96.2	99.1	100.0	100.0	100.8	103.8	110.8	115.2	117.6	119.0
Sweden	117.9	110.5	108.2	121.2	112.9	106.3	99.7	100.0	95.2	93.2	96.0	92.3	85.7	84.7
Switzerland	90.0	97.2	106.0	102.2	96.3	99.3	100.7	100.0	106.0	112.9	114.9	114.0	114.3	115.2
Turkey	98.4	65.7	57.5	56.9	66.6	72.8	89.0	100.0	77.9	75.5	74.4	77.7	87.3	86.0
United Kingdom	72.5	73.8	69.7	70.3	84.6	95.7	97.4	100.0	97.2	100.1	96.5	101.9	106.1	110.4
United States	91.7	89.9	85.5	86.7	89.8	96.1	95.2	100.0	101.3	97.6	91.4	83.0	79.6	77.1
Euro area	114.9	113.1	119.7	121.1	110.2	112.6	112.0	100.0	99.9	105.7	120.5	127.5	124.0	122.8

StatLink ⬛ http://dx.doi.org/10.1787/273701452710

Relative unit labour costs in manufacturing
Year 1993 = 100

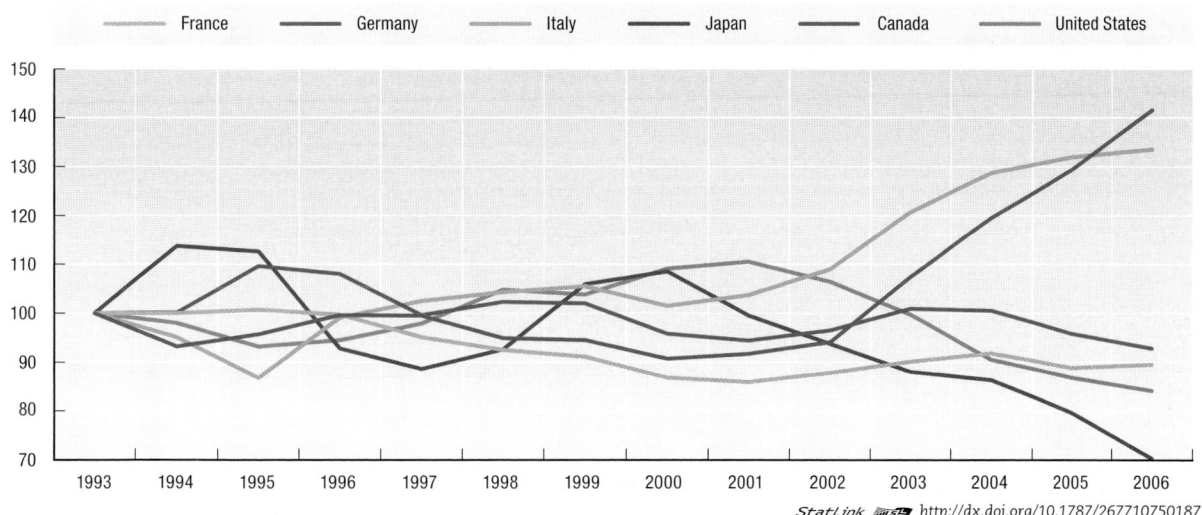

StatLink ⬛ http://dx.doi.org/10.1787/267710750187

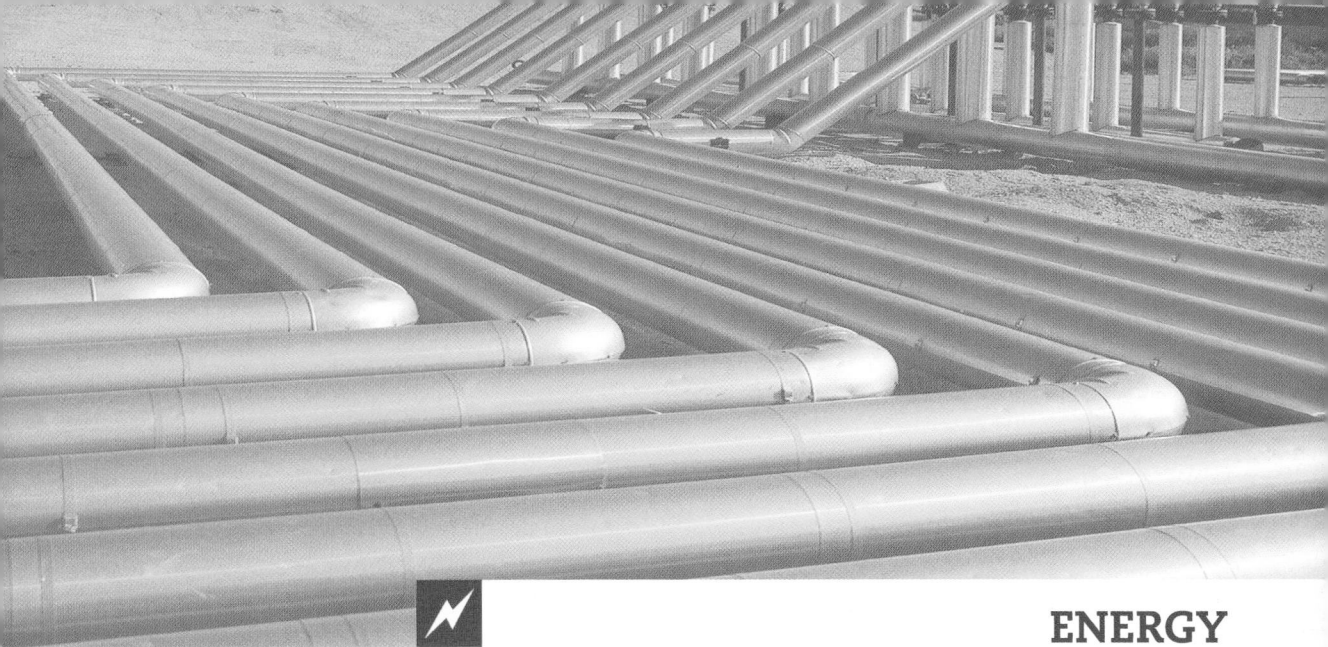

ENERGY

ENERGY SUPPLY
ENERGY SUPPLY
ENERGY SUPPLY AND ECONOMIC GROWTH
ENERGY SUPPLY PER CAPITA
ELECTRICITY GENERATION
NUCLEAR ENERGY
RENEWABLE ENERGY

ENERGY PRODUCTION AND PRICES
ENERGY PRODUCTION
OIL PRODUCTION
OIL PRICES

ENERGY SUPPLY

An analysis of energy problems requires a comprehensive presentation of basic supply and demand data for all fuels in a manner which will allow the easy comparison of the contribution each fuel makes to the economy and their interrelationships through the conversion of one fuel into another. This type of presentation is suitable for the study of energy substitution, energy conservation and forecasting.

Definition

The table refers to total primary energy supply (TPES). TPES equals production plus imports minus exports minus international marine bunkers plus or minus stock changes. The IEA energy balance methodology is based on the calorific content of the energy commodities and a common unit of account. The unit of account adopted by the IEA is the tonne of oil equivalent (toe) which is defined as 10^7 kilocalories (41.868 gigajoules). This quantity of energy is, within a few per cent, equal to the net heat content of 1 tonne of crude oil. The difference between the "net" and the "gross" calorific value for each fuel is the latent heat of vaporisation of the water produced during combustion of the fuel. For coal and oil, net calorific value is about 5% less than gross, for most forms of natural and manufactured gas the difference is 9-10%, while for electricity there is no difference as the concept has no meaning in this case. The IEA balances are calculated using the physical energy content method to calculate the primary energy equivalent. The forecasts provided in the table refer to the Reference Scenario of the *World Energy Outlook*. The Reference Scenario projects supply and demand if present policies were to continue. The *World Energy Outlook* also presents an Alternative Policy Scenario which analyses how the global energy market could evolve if countries were to adopt all of the policies they are currently considering related to energy security and energy-related CO_2 emissions.

Comparability

While every effort is made to ensure the accuracy of the data, quality is not homogeneous for all countries/regions. In some countries data are based on secondary sources, and where incomplete or unavailable, the IEA has made estimates. In general, data are likely to be more accurate for production and trade than for international marine bunkers or stock changes. Moreover, statistics for combustible renewables and waste are less accurate than traditional commercial energy data in most countries.

Long-term trends

Over the 34-year period of 1971 to 2005, the world's total primary energy supply increased by 106%, reaching 11 434 Mtoe (million tonnes of oil equivalent). This equates to a compound growth rate of 2.2% per annum. By comparison, world population grew by 1.6% and gross domestic product by 3.4% per annum in real terms over the same period.

Energy supply growth was fairly constant over the period, except in 1974-1975 and in the early 1980s as a consequence of the first two oil shocks, and in the early 1990s following the dissolution of the Soviet Union.

The share of OECD in world primary energy supply decreased again in 2005. Strong economic development in Asia led to a large increase in the share of Asia (including China) in world energy supply, from 13% in 1971 to 26% in 2005. By contrast, the combined share of the former USSR and non-OECD Europe decreased significantly in the late 1980s.

Sources
- IEA (2007), *Energy Balances of Non-OECD Countries*, IEA, Paris.
- IEA (2007), *Energy Balances of OECD Countries*, IEA, Paris.
- IEA (2007), *World Energy Outlook 2007: China and India Insights*, IEA, Paris.

Further information
Analytical publications
- IEA (2006), *Energy Technology Perspectives: Scenarios and Strategies to 2050*, IEA, Paris.
- IEA (2007), *Energy Policies of IEA Countries*, series, IEA, Paris.
- IEA (2007), *Energy Use in the New Millennium: Trends in IEA Countries*, IEA, Paris.
- IEA (2007), *Mind the Gap: Quantifying Principal-Agent Problems in Energy Efficiency*, IEA, Paris.

Online databases
- *World Energy Statistics and Balances*.

Websites
- International Energy Agency, *www.iea.org*.

Total primary energy supply

Million tonnes of oil equivalent (Mtoe)

	1971	1990	1996	1997	1998	1999	2000	2001	2002	2003	2004	2005	2006	2030
Australia	52.2	87.5	100.9	103.4	106.3	108.6	110.5	108.3	112.0	113.0	113.5	122.0	122.5	..
Austria	19.0	25.1	28.9	28.8	29.2	29.0	29.0	30.9	31.4	33.0	33.3	34.4	34.2	..
Belgium	39.9	49.2	56.4	57.0	58.3	58.5	59.1	58.8	56.8	59.4	58.1	56.7	56.2	..
Canada	141.8	209.4	236.5	240.4	239.6	246.8	249.2	246.1	250.1	262.4	268.7	272.0	269.9	..
Czech Republic	45.6	49.0	42.3	42.5	41.1	38.4	40.4	41.4	42.0	44.6	45.8	45.2	45.4	..
Denmark	19.2	17.9	22.6	21.0	20.7	19.9	19.4	19.9	19.6	20.8	20.2	19.6	20.3	..
Finland	18.4	29.2	31.9	33.1	33.5	33.4	33.0	33.7	35.4	37.6	37.9	35.0	37.7	..
France	162.2	227.8	254.8	247.3	255.4	255.7	258.4	266.9	266.7	271.3	274.9	276.0	273.2	..
Germany	307.9	356.2	353.9	351.2	349.2	341.7	343.6	353.5	345.3	347.2	348.2	344.7	349.2	..
Greece	9.1	22.2	24.2	25.1	26.4	26.6	27.8	28.7	29.0	29.9	30.5	31.0	30.6	..
Hungary	19.1	28.6	26.2	25.8	25.4	25.3	25.0	25.4	25.8	26.3	26.4	27.8	27.6	..
Iceland	1.0	2.2	2.5	2.5	2.7	3.1	3.2	3.4	3.4	3.4	3.5	3.6	4.3	..
Ireland	7.1	10.4	11.7	12.5	13.3	13.8	14.3	15.3	15.6	15.0	15.2	15.3	16.2	..
Italy	114.5	148.0	160.7	162.9	167.5	169.8	173.1	173.5	173.7	180.7	182.8	185.2	183.7	..
Japan	269.6	444.5	513.1	519.0	512.4	519.7	527.6	519.5	519.9	515.3	532.3	530.5	527.1	601.0
Korea	17.0	93.4	161.4	175.5	160.7	177.4	190.1	192.8	202.9	207.4	213.3	213.8	218.5	..
Luxembourg	4.1	3.6	3.4	3.4	3.3	3.5	3.7	3.8	4.0	4.3	4.7	4.8	4.8	..
Mexico	43.5	124.3	136.7	141.4	147.8	149.7	150.3	152.1	155.5	159.8	165.2	176.5	177.5	..
Netherlands	51.3	66.8	75.6	74.2	74.5	73.7	75.9	78.0	78.7	81.0	82.2	81.8	80.5	..
New Zealand	7.2	13.8	16.7	17.2	16.8	17.7	18.0	18.1	17.6	17.1	17.4	16.9	17.5	..
Norway	13.6	21.5	23.2	24.6	25.6	26.9	25.8	26.5	25.1	27.1	28.3	32.1	30.2	..
Poland	86.3	99.9	103.8	102.5	95.8	93.1	89.4	90.0	89.2	91.5	91.8	93.0	98.5	..
Portugal	6.5	17.7	20.5	21.6	23.3	25.1	25.3	25.4	26.5	25.8	26.5	27.2	25.6	..
Slovak Republic	14.2	21.3	18.1	18.1	17.6	17.6	17.7	18.6	18.7	18.6	18.3	18.8	18.6	..
Spain	43.1	91.1	101.4	107.9	113.3	118.8	124.7	127.9	131.6	136.1	142.3	145.2	144.9	..
Sweden	36.5	47.6	52.1	50.8	51.7	50.8	48.2	51.2	52.3	51.1	53.2	52.2	51.3	..
Switzerland	17.1	25.0	25.5	26.1	26.4	26.4	26.2	27.7	26.8	26.9	27.1	27.2	28.3	..
Turkey	19.5	53.0	67.3	71.0	72.2	71.0	77.0	71.0	75.2	78.8	81.9	85.2	85.6	..
United Kingdom	211.0	212.2	233.1	227.1	230.2	231.6	233.9	234.6	228.6	232.3	233.5	233.9	232.5	..
United States	1 593.2	1 927.5	2 143.5	2 165.7	2 185.6	2 242.6	2 306.6	2 259.7	2 289.8	2 282.8	2 328.6	2 340.3	2 322.7	2 925.0
EU27 total	..	1 656.2	1 720.8	1 706.9	1 719.1	1 707.2	1 722.1	1 761.5	1 755.1	1 794.0	1 812.6	1 815.2	..	2 006.0
OECD total	3 390.8	4 525.5	5 048.7	5 099.7	5 125.9	5 216.1	5 326.4	5 302.6	5 349.0	5 400.4	5 505.4	5 547.6	5 535.0	6 800.0
Brazil	69.6	134.0	163.2	171.5	177.3	182.5	185.7	186.9	191.4	193.7	204.8	209.5	..	..
China	391.7	863.2	1 086.5	1 090.1	1 089.6	1 093.6	1 104.9	1 103.1	1 194.9	1 360.4	1 582.6	1 717.2	..	3 819.0
India	157.0	319.9	400.3	416.0	425.1	450.9	459.6	466.2	478.7	490.7	520.6	537.3	..	1 299.0
Russian Federation	..	878.3	622.2	595.1	581.3	603.0	613.9	621.3	617.8	639.7	641.5	646.7	..	871.0
South Africa	45.3	91.2	105.4	106.9	108.4	108.9	111.1	109.2	105.3	118.1	129.3	127.6	..	..
World	5 543.7	8 757.7	9 482.1	9 574.0	9 629.2	9 823.6	10 029.2	10 067.6	10 293.8	10 636.8	11 135.6	11 433.9	..	17 721.0

StatLink 📊 http://dx.doi.org/10.1787/273710224322

Total primary energy supply by region

Million tonnes of oil equivalent (Mtoe)

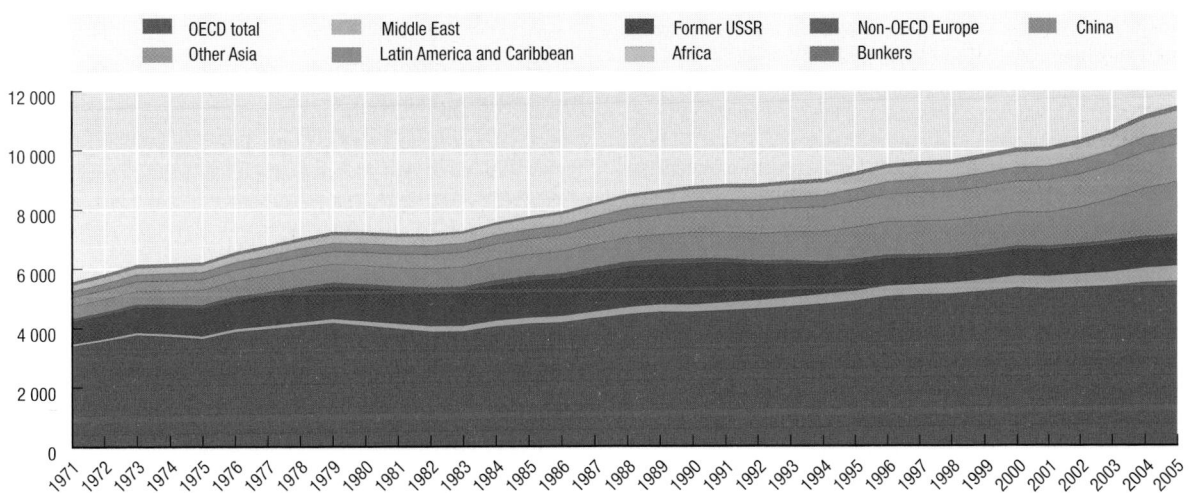

StatLink 📊 http://dx.doi.org/10.1787/267715242324

ENERGY SUPPLY AND ECONOMIC GROWTH

It is not an easy task to monitor the overall trend in energy efficiency of a country, since there are numerous elements to consider such as climate change, outsourcing of goods produced by energy-intensive industries, etc. A common way to measure progress in energy intensity is to look at the changes in the ratio of energy use to GDP. Indeed, some experts look at energy intensity to derive trends of energy efficiency, but such an analysis has many limitations.

Definition

The table shows total primary energy supply (TPES) per thousand US dollars of GDP. The ratios are calculated by dividing each country's annual TPES by each country's annual GDP expressed in constant 2000 prices and converted to US dollars using purchasing power parities (PPPs) for the year 2000.

TPES consists of primary energy production adjusted for net trade and stock changes. Production of secondary energy (*e.g.* oil/coal products, electricity from fossil fuels, etc.) is not included since the "energy equivalent" of the primary fuels used to create the secondary products or electric power has already been counted. TPES is expressed in tonnes of oil equivalent (see the IEA sources below for details on how TPES is calculated).

Comparability

Care should be taken when comparing energy intensities between countries and over time. Different national circumstances such as density of population, country size, average temperatures and economic structure will affect the ratios. A decrease in the TPES/GDP ratio may be partly attributable to a restructuring of the economy by transferring energy-intensive industries such as iron and steel out of the country – *i.e.* by purchasing energy-intensive products from abroad. The harmful effects of such outsourcing may actually increase the damage to the environment if the producers abroad use less energy efficient techniques.

Total primary energy supply per unit of GDP

Tonnes of oil equivalent (toe) per thousand 2000 US dollar of GDP calculated using PPPs, 2005

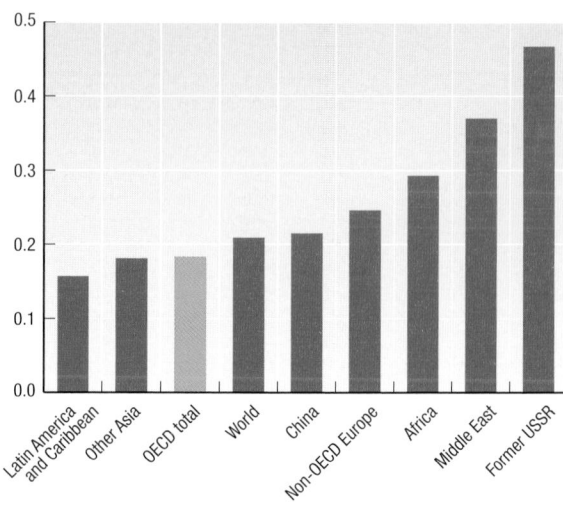

StatLink http://dx.doi.org/10.1787/267758544245

Long-term trends

Sharp improvements in the efficiency of key end uses, shifts to electricity, and some changes in manufacturing output and consumer behaviour have occurred in many OECD countries since 1971. As a consequence, energy supply per unit of GDP fell significantly, particularly in the 1979-1990 period.

Contributing to the trend were higher fuel prices, long-term technological progress, government energy efficiency programmes and regulations. Overall growth in per capita GDP, combined with higher living standards and slow population growth, produced steadily rising demand after 1985.

The ratio of energy supply to GDP (TPES/GDP) fell less than the ratio of energy consumption to GDP (TFC/GDP), because of increased use of electricity. The main reason for this is that losses in electricity generating outweighed intensity improvements achieved in end uses such as household appliances.

Among OECD countries, the ratio of energy consumption to GDP varies considerably. Apart from energy prices, winter weather is a key element in these variations, as are raw materials processing techniques, the distance goods must be shipped, the size of dwellings, use of private rather than public transport and other lifestyle factors.

Sources

- IEA (2007), *Energy Balances of Non-OECD Countries*, IEA, Paris.
- IEA (2007), *Energy Balances of OECD Countries*, IEA, Paris.

Further information

Analytical publications

- IEA (2007), *Energy Policies of IEA Countries*, series, IEA, Paris.
- IEA (2007), *Energy Use in the New Millennium: Trends in IEA Countries*, IEA, Paris.
- IEA (2007), *Mind the Gap: Quantifying Principal-Agent Problems in Energy Efficiency*, IEA, Paris.
- IEA (2007), *World Energy Outlook 2007: China and India Insights*, IEA, Paris.

Online databases

- World Energy Statistics and Balances.

Websites

- International Energy Agency, *www.iea.org*.

Total primary energy supply per unit of GDP

Tonnes of oil equivalent (toe) per thousand 2000 US dollars of GDP calculated using PPPs

	1971	1990	1996	1997	1998	1999	2000	2001	2002	2003	2004	2005	2006
Australia	0.24	0.24	0.22	0.22	0.21	0.21	0.21	0.20	0.20	0.19	0.19	0.20	0.19
Austria	0.18	0.14	0.14	0.14	0.14	0.13	0.13	0.13	0.13	0.14	0.14	0.14	0.13
Belgium	0.30	0.22	0.23	0.23	0.23	0.22	0.22	0.21	0.20	0.21	0.20	0.19	0.19
Canada	0.41	0.32	0.33	0.32	0.30	0.30	0.29	0.28	0.27	0.28	0.28	0.27	0.27
Czech Republic	0.44	0.33	0.29	0.29	0.28	0.26	0.27	0.27	0.26	0.27	0.27	0.25	0.23
Denmark	0.24	0.15	0.16	0.15	0.14	0.13	0.13	0.13	0.13	0.13	0.13	0.12	0.12
Finland	0.31	0.26	0.29	0.28	0.27	0.26	0.24	0.24	0.25	0.26	0.25	0.23	0.23
France	0.22	0.18	0.18	0.17	0.17	0.17	0.16	0.17	0.16	0.17	0.16	0.16	0.16
Germany	0.29	0.21	0.18	0.18	0.17	0.17	0.16	0.17	0.16	0.16	0.16	0.16	0.16
Greece	0.08	0.12	0.12	0.12	0.12	0.12	0.12	0.12	0.12	0.11	0.11	0.11	0.10
Hungary	0.28	0.24	0.25	0.24	0.22	0.21	0.20	0.19	0.19	0.18	0.18	0.18	0.17
Iceland	0.33	0.34	0.37	0.36	0.36	0.40	0.40	0.40	0.40	0.39	0.38	0.36	0.42
Ireland	0.28	0.19	0.16	0.15	0.15	0.14	0.13	0.13	0.13	0.12	0.11	0.11	0.11
Italy	0.16	0.12	0.12	0.12	0.12	0.12	0.12	0.12	0.12	0.12	0.12	0.12	0.12
Japan	0.21	0.16	0.16	0.16	0.16	0.17	0.16	0.16	0.16	0.16	0.16	0.15	0.15
Korea	0.17	0.22	0.24	0.25	0.25	0.25	0.25	0.24	0.24	0.24	0.23	0.22	0.22
Luxembourg	0.62	0.26	0.21	0.19	0.18	0.17	0.17	0.17	0.17	0.18	0.19	0.18	0.17
Mexico	0.15	0.19	0.19	0.18	0.18	0.18	0.17	0.17	0.17	0.17	0.17	0.18	0.17
Netherlands	0.24	0.20	0.20	0.19	0.18	0.17	0.17	0.17	0.17	0.18	0.17	0.17	0.16
New Zealand	0.16	0.23	0.23	0.23	0.23	0.23	0.23	0.22	0.22	0.20	0.19	0.18	0.18
Norway	0.23	0.19	0.16	0.16	0.16	0.17	0.16	0.16	0.15	0.16	0.16	0.18	0.16
Poland	0.40	0.35	0.31	0.29	0.26	0.24	0.22	0.22	0.21	0.21	0.20	0.20	0.20
Portugal	0.09	0.13	0.13	0.13	0.13	0.14	0.13	0.13	0.14	0.13	0.14	0.14	0.13
Slovak Republic	0.39	0.40	0.35	0.33	0.31	0.31	0.30	0.31	0.30	0.28	0.27	0.26	0.23
Spain	0.12	0.14	0.14	0.15	0.15	0.15	0.15	0.15	0.15	0.15	0.15	0.15	0.14
Sweden	0.27	0.24	0.25	0.24	0.23	0.22	0.20	0.21	0.21	0.20	0.20	0.19	0.18
Switzerland	0.12	0.13	0.13	0.13	0.13	0.12	0.12	0.12	0.13	0.12	0.12	0.12	0.12
Turkey	0.14	0.16	0.17	0.16	0.16	0.17	0.17	0.17	0.16	0.16	0.15	0.15	0.14
United Kingdom	0.27	0.18	0.18	0.17	0.16	0.16	0.16	0.15	0.15	0.14	0.14	0.14	0.13
United States	0.41	0.27	0.26	0.25	0.24	0.24	0.24	0.23	0.23	0.22	0.22	0.21	0.20
EU27 total	..	0.19	0.18	0.18	0.17	0.17	0.16	0.16	0.16	0.16	0.16	0.16	..
OECD total	0.30	0.22	0.21	0.21	0.20	0.20	0.20	0.19	0.19	0.19	0.19	0.18	0.18
Brazil	0.17	0.14	0.14	0.14	0.15	0.15	0.15	0.15	0.15	0.15	0.15	0.15	..
China	0.88	0.47	0.30	0.28	0.26	0.24	0.22	0.20	0.20	0.21	0.22	0.22	..
India	0.26	0.23	0.21	0.20	0.20	0.20	0.19	0.18	0.18	0.17	0.17	0.16	..
Russian Federation	..	0.58	0.68	0.64	0.66	0.65	0.60	0.58	0.55	0.53	0.49	0.47	..
South Africa	0.22	0.28	0.30	0.30	0.30	0.29	0.29	0.28	0.26	0.28	0.29	0.28	..
World	0.32	0.26	0.24	0.24	0.23	0.23	0.22	0.22	0.22	0.21	0.21	0.21	..

StatLink ⟋⟍ *http://dx.doi.org/10.1787/273712872411*

Total primary energy supply per unit of GDP

Tonnes of oil equivalent (toe) per thousand 2000 US dollars of GDP calculated using PPPs, 2006

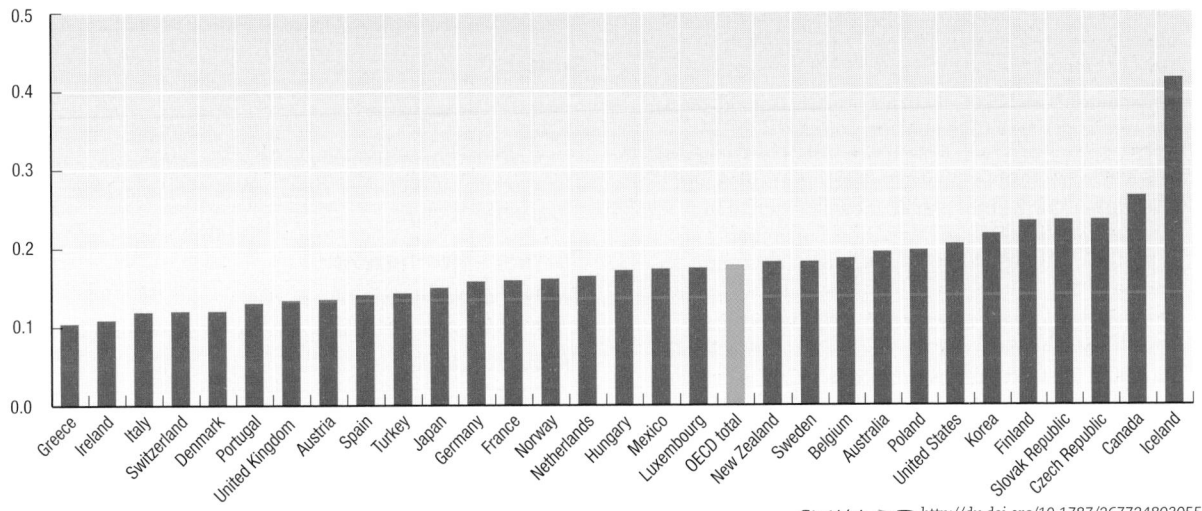

StatLink ⟋⟍ *http://dx.doi.org/10.1787/267724803055*

ENERGY SUPPLY PER CAPITA

Total primary energy supply per capita is a common, albeit an imperfect measure of energy efficiency in a country. For instance, neither the impact of climate on energy use (heating, cooling) nor the size of the country and the density of the population are properly taken into account when comparing countries. Energy analysts usually prefer to compare energy use per unit of output or per unit of GDP. However, the ratio has been presented here since its use is widespread.

Definition

The table refers to total primary energy supply (TPES) per head of population. The ratio is expressed in tonnes of oil equivalent (toe) per person. TPES consists of primary energy production adjusted for net trade and stock changes. Production of secondary energy (*e.g.* oil/coal products, electricity from fossil fuels, etc.) is not included since the "energy equivalent" of the primary fuels used to create the secondary products or electric power has already been

counted. TPES is expressed in tonnes of oil equivalent (see the IEA sources below for details on how TPES is calculated). The forecasts provided in the table refer to the Reference Scenario of the *World Energy Outlook*.

Comparability

Care should be taken when comparing energy supply per capita between countries and over time. Different national circumstances such as density of population, country size, temperatures, economic structure and domestic energy resources affect the ratios.

Total primary energy supply per capita
Tonnes of oil equivalent (toe) per capita, 2005

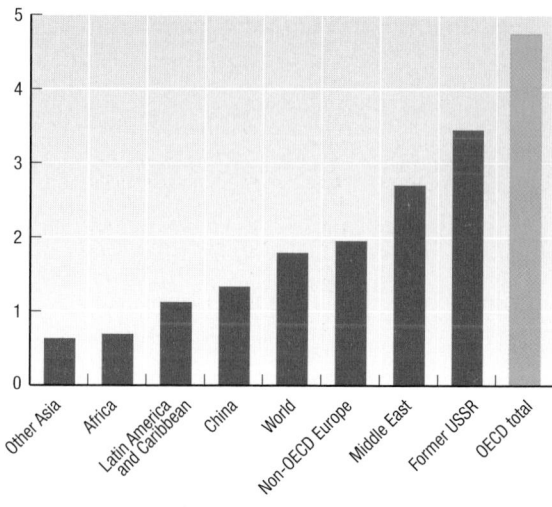

StatLink ⟹ http://dx.doi.org/10.1787/267848160840

Long-term trends

The level of energy supply on a per capita basis varied significantly across OECD countries. The countries with the highest ratios were those countries with the smallest populations. In 2006, the energy supply per capita for Iceland was 14.4 toe/capita and for Luxembourg was 10.4 toe/capita. The high ratio for Iceland is explained partly by the climate but also be the availability of cheap – and non-polluting – thermal energy from hot springs. In the case of Luxembourg, the high ratio is partly due to low sales taxes on petroleum products; motorists and other consumers from neighbouring countries – Belgium, France and Germany – buy their supplies in Luxembourg.

The United States and Canada are also large consumers of energy per capita, with ratios of 7.8 and 8.3 toe/capita in 2006. On the other end of the scale, the countries with the lowest TPES/capita were Turkey (1.2 toe/capita) and Mexico
(1.7 toe/capita).

Between 1971 and 2006, there are striking differences in the trends of the OECD countries. Compared to 1971, TPES/capita in 2006 was eight times higher in Korea and more than doubled in Greece, Iceland, Portugal, Spain and Turkey. On the other hand, the ratio decreased in four OECD countries over this period: Luxembourg (-14%), the Czech Republic (-5%), Denmark (-4%) and Poland (-2%).

In general, the TPES/capita of non-OECD countries is lower than that of the OECD countries. In 2005, the ratio for China (1.3 toe/capita) was twice as much as in 1971. South Africa (2.7 toe/capita), Brazil (1.1 toe/capita) and India (0.5 toe/capita) grew slightly more slowly.

Sources

- IEA (2007), *Energy Balances of Non-OECD Countries*, IEA, Paris.
- IEA (2007), *Energy Balances of OECD Countries*, IEA, Paris.
- IEA (2007), *World Energy Outlook 2007: China and India Insights*, IEA, Paris.

Further information
Analytical publications
- IEA (2007), *Energy Policies of IEA Countries*, series, IEA, Paris.
Online databases
- *World Energy Statistics and Balances*.
Websites
- International Energy Agency, *www.iea.org*.

OECD FACTBOOK 2008 – ISBN 978-92-64-04054-0 – © OECD 2008

Total primary energy supply per capita

Tonnes of oil equivalent (toe) per capita

	1971	1990	1996	1997	1998	1999	2000	2001	2002	2003	2004	2005	2006	2030
Australia	3.96	5.10	5.48	5.56	5.65	5.70	5.73	5.55	5.67	5.66	5.62	5.96	5.93	..
Austria	2.53	3.27	3.63	3.61	3.67	3.63	3.62	3.84	3.88	4.06	4.07	4.17	4.16	..
Belgium	4.13	4.93	5.55	5.60	5.71	5.73	5.77	5.72	5.50	5.73	5.58	5.41	5.36	..
Canada	6.46	7.56	7.99	8.04	7.94	8.12	8.12	7.93	7.97	8.28	8.40	8.43	8.30	..
Czech Republic	4.64	4.73	4.10	4.13	3.99	3.74	3.93	4.05	4.11	4.37	4.48	4.42	4.42	..
Denmark	3.88	3.48	4.29	3.97	3.91	3.75	3.63	3.72	3.65	3.86	3.74	3.62	3.73	..
Finland	4.00	5.85	6.22	6.43	6.49	6.46	6.37	6.49	6.81	7.20	7.24	6.67	7.18	..
France	3.10	3.92	4.27	4.13	4.25	4.24	4.26	4.37	4.33	4.38	4.41	4.40	4.36	..
Germany	3.93	4.49	4.32	4.28	4.26	4.16	4.18	4.29	4.19	4.21	4.22	4.18	4.24	..
Greece	1.02	2.15	2.26	2.32	2.44	2.45	2.55	2.62	2.64	2.71	2.75	2.79	2.74	..
Hungary	1.84	2.76	2.54	2.51	2.47	2.47	2.45	2.50	2.54	2.60	2.61	2.75	2.75	..
Iceland	4.79	8.52	9.23	9.34	9.85	11.15	11.54	11.80	11.79	11.72	11.94	12.25	14.36	..
Ireland	2.37	2.96	3.24	3.43	3.59	3.67	3.76	3.95	3.96	3.76	3.73	3.69	3.89	..
Italy	2.12	2.61	2.83	2.86	2.94	2.98	3.04	3.04	3.04	3.14	3.14	3.16	3.14	..
Japan	2.57	3.60	4.08	4.12	4.05	4.10	4.16	4.09	4.08	4.04	4.17	4.15	4.13	5.09
Korea	0.52	2.18	3.55	3.82	3.47	3.81	4.05	4.07	4.26	4.34	4.44	4.43	4.50	..
Luxembourg	12.03	9.35	8.28	8.09	7.78	8.06	8.39	8.67	9.06	9.47	10.33	10.45	10.35	..
Mexico	0.87	1.53	1.48	1.50	1.54	1.54	1.52	1.52	1.53	1.56	1.59	1.68	1.66	..
Netherlands	3.89	4.47	4.87	4.76	4.75	4.66	4.76	4.86	4.87	4.99	5.05	5.02	4.90	..
New Zealand	2.51	4.09	4.46	4.54	4.41	4.62	4.65	4.65	4.47	4.27	4.29	4.12	4.24	..
Norway	3.49	5.07	5.30	5.59	5.77	6.02	5.75	5.87	5.53	5.95	6.16	6.95	6.51	..
Poland	2.63	2.62	2.69	2.65	2.48	2.41	2.34	2.35	2.33	2.39	2.40	2.44	2.58	..
Portugal	0.75	1.78	2.04	2.14	2.30	2.46	2.47	2.47	2.55	2.47	2.53	2.58	2.43	..
Slovak Republic	3.12	4.02	3.37	3.37	3.26	3.27	3.28	3.44	3.48	3.46	3.41	3.50	3.45	..
Spain	1.26	2.33	2.57	2.72	2.85	2.97	3.10	3.14	3.19	3.24	3.33	3.35	3.29	..
Sweden	4.51	5.56	5.89	5.74	5.85	5.74	5.43	5.76	5.86	5.70	5.91	5.78	5.66	..
Switzerland	2.69	3.68	3.58	3.66	3.70	3.68	3.63	3.80	3.65	3.63	3.64	3.62	3.78	..
Turkey	0.54	0.94	1.07	1.14	1.14	1.10	1.14	1.03	1.08	1.11	1.14	1.18	1.17	..
United Kingdom	3.77	3.71	4.01	3.89	3.94	3.95	3.97	3.97	3.85	3.90	3.90	3.88	3.84	..
United States	7.67	7.70	7.95	7.93	7.91	8.03	8.17	7.92	7.94	7.84	7.92	7.89	7.76	8.08
EU27 total	..	3.50	3.59	3.55	3.57	3.54	3.57	3.64	3.62	3.68	3.70	3.69	..	4.03
OECD total	3.85	4.34	4.60	4.62	4.61	4.66	4.71	4.66	4.66	4.67	4.73	4.74	4.70	5.25
Brazil	0.71	0.90	1.00	1.03	1.05	1.07	1.07	1.06	1.07	1.07	1.11	1.12	..	..
China	0.47	0.76	0.89	0.89	0.88	0.87	0.88	0.87	0.93	1.06	1.22	1.32	..	2.62
India	0.28	0.38	0.42	0.43	0.43	0.45	0.45	0.45	0.46	0.46	0.48	0.49	..	0.89
Russian Federation	..	5.92	4.21	4.04	3.96	4.12	4.20	4.26	4.25	4.42	4.46	4.52	..	7.07
South Africa	2.01	2.59	2.64	2.61	2.59	2.54	2.52	2.44	2.32	2.58	2.79	2.72	..	2.16
World	1.48	1.67	1.65	1.64	1.63	1.64	1.66	1.64	1.66	1.66	1.69	1.75	1.78	..

StatLink http://dx.doi.org/10.1787/273732373885

Total primary energy supply per capita

Tonnes of oil equivalent (toe) per capita, 2006

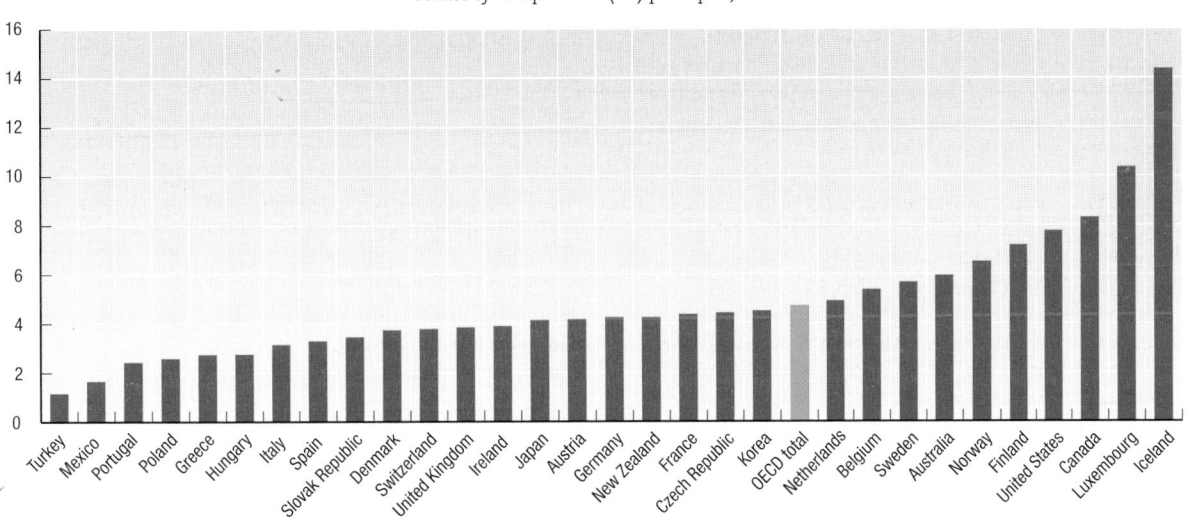

StatLink http://dx.doi.org/10.1787/267843062371

ELECTRICITY GENERATION

The amount of electricity generated by a country and the breakdown of the production by fuel is a reflection of its natural resources, imported energy, national policies on security of energy supply, population, electrification rate and the development and growth of the economy in general.

Definition

The table refers to electricity generation from fossil fuels, nuclear, hydro (excluding pumped storage), geothermal, solar, biomass, etc. It includes electricity produced in electricity-only plants and in combined heat and power plants. Both main activity producer and autoproducer plants have been included, where data are available. Main activity producers generate electricity for sale to third parties as their primary activity. Autoproducer undertakings generate electricity wholly or partly for their own use as an activity which supports their primary activity. Both types of plants may be privately or publicly owned. The forecasts provided in the table refer to the Reference Scenario of the *World Energy Outlook*.

Comparability

Some countries, both OECD and non-OECD, have trouble reporting electricity generation from autoproducer plants. It is also difficult to obtain information on electricity generated by combustible renewables and waste in some non-OECD countries. For example, electricity generated from waste biomass in sugar refing remains largely unreported.

World electricity generation by source of energy
As a percentage of world electricity generation

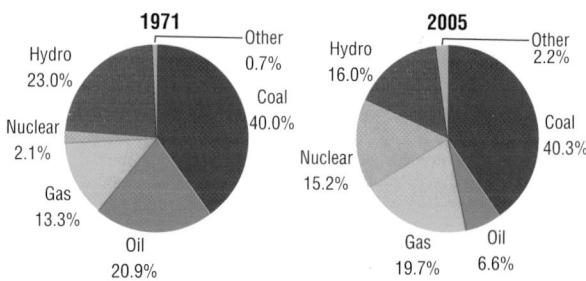

StatLink 〓🔗 http://dx.doi.org/10.1787/267885304876

Long-term trends

World electricity generation rose at an average annual rate of 3.7% from 1971 to 2005, greater than the 2.2% growth in total primary energy supply. This increase was largely due to more electrical appliances, development of electrical heating in several developed countries and rural electrification programmes in developing countries.

The share of electricity production from fossil fuels has gradually fallen, from just under 75% in 1971 to 67% in 2005. This decrease was due to a progressive move away from oil, which fell from 20.9% to 6.6%.

Oil for power generation has been displaced in particular by dramatic growth in nuclear electricity generation, which rose from 2.1% in 1971 to 15.2% in 2005. The share of coal remained stable, at 40% while that of natural gas increased from 13.3% to 19.7%. The share of hydro-electricity decreased from 23.0% to 16.0%. Due to large programmes to develop wind and solar energy in several OECD countries, the share of new and renewable energies, such as solar, wind, geothermal, biomass and waste increased. However, these energy forms remain limited: in 2005, they accounted for only 2.2% of total electricity production.

Sources

- IEA (2007), *Energy Balances of Non-OECD Countries*, IEA, Paris.
- IEA (2007), *Energy Balances of OECD Countries*, IEA, Paris.
- IEA (2007), *World Energy Outlook 2007: China and India Insights*, IEA, Paris.

Further information
Analytical publications

- IEA, NEA (2005), *Projected Costs of Generating Electricity*, OECD, Paris.
- IEA (2005), *Saving Electricity in a Hurry: Dealing with Temporary Shortfalls on Electricity Suppliers*, IEA, Paris.
- IEA (2006), *China's Power Sector Reforms: Where to Next?*, IEA, Paris.
- IEA (2006), *Energy Efficiency Policy Profiles Light's labour's lost: Policies for Energy-Efficient Lighting*, IEA, Paris.
- IEA (2007), *Fossil Fuel-Fired Power Generation: Case Studies of Recently constructed coal- and gas-fired power plants*, IEA, Paris.
- IEA (2007), *Tackling Investment Challenges in Power Generation in IEA Countries*, IEA, Paris.

Statistical publications

- IEA (2007), *Electricity Information: 2007 Edition*, IEA, Paris.

Online databases

- *World Energy Statistics and Balances.*

Websites

- International Energy Agency, *www.iea.org*.

Electricity generation
Terawatt hours (TWh)

	1971	1990	1996	1997	1998	1999	2000	2001	2002	2003	2004	2005	2006	2030
Australia	53.0	154.3	177.3	182.8	195.6	203.0	207.4	216.5	226.2	227.9	238.8	250.9	254.8	..
Austria	28.2	49.3	53.6	55.7	55.9	59.3	60.2	60.7	60.4	57.7	61.6	63.0	60.8	..
Belgium	33.2	70.3	75.1	77.9	82.1	83.4	82.8	78.6	80.9	83.6	84.4	85.7	84.9	..
Canada	221.8	481.9	572.8	573.5	561.5	578.8	605.5	589.6	601.0	589.9	600.1	628.1	616.5	..
Czech Republic	36.4	62.3	63.8	64.2	64.6	64.2	72.9	74.2	76.0	82.8	83.8	81.9	83.6	..
Denmark	18.6	26.0	53.6	44.3	41.1	38.9	36.0	37.7	39.3	46.2	40.4	36.3	45.6	..
Finland	21.7	54.4	69.4	69.2	70.2	69.5	70.0	74.5	74.9	84.2	85.8	70.6	82.2	..
France	155.8	417.2	509.3	501.1	507.3	521.3	536.1	545.7	553.9	561.8	568.6	570.6	569.2	..
Germany	327.2	547.7	550.7	548.0	552.4	550.5	567.1	581.8	566.9	595.6	610.0	613.2	626.3	..
Greece	11.6	34.8	42.4	43.3	46.2	49.4	53.4	53.1	53.9	57.9	58.8	59.4	58.7	..
Hungary	15.0	28.4	35.1	35.4	37.2	37.8	35.2	36.4	36.2	34.1	33.7	35.8	35.9	..
Iceland	1.6	4.5	5.1	5.6	6.3	7.2	7.7	8.0	8.4	8.5	8.6	8.7	9.9	..
Ireland	6.3	14.2	18.9	19.7	20.9	21.8	23.7	24.6	24.8	24.9	25.2	25.6	27.5	..
Italy	123.9	213.1	239.4	246.5	253.7	259.3	269.9	271.9	277.5	283.4	293.0	294.4	308.2	..
Japan	382.9	836.7	983.3	1 006.8	1 012.8	1 030.6	1 051.3	1 033.0	1 052.1	1 041.7	1 071.2	1 094.2	1 063.4	1 411.0
Korea	10.5	105.4	202.6	222.1	216.1	235.6	263.4	281.2	329.8	343.2	366.6	387.9	405.6	..
Luxembourg	1.3	0.6	0.4	0.4	0.4	0.4	0.4	0.5	2.8	2.8	3.4	3.4	3.5	..
Mexico	31.0	124.1	168.2	180.9	181.2	189.9	203.6	209.2	214.6	217.9	224.1	234.9	253.3	..
Netherlands	44.9	71.9	85.2	86.6	91.2	86.9	89.7	93.8	96.1	96.8	100.8	100.2	98.3	..
New Zealand	15.5	32.3	36.3	35.9	36.3	38.2	39.2	39.4	41.1	41.2	42.8	43.0	43.1	..
Norway	63.5	121.6	104.4	110.7	116.1	122.3	139.6	119.2	130.3	106.8	110.2	137.3	121.3	..
Poland	69.5	134.4	141.2	140.9	140.8	140.0	143.2	143.7	142.5	150.0	152.6	155.4	160.7	..
Portugal	7.9	28.4	34.4	34.1	38.9	42.9	43.4	46.2	45.7	46.5	44.8	46.2	48.6	..
Slovak Republic	10.9	25.5	25.5	25.1	25.7	28.1	30.8	31.9	32.2	31.0	30.5	31.4	31.2	..
Spain	61.6	151.2	173.4	189.2	193.4	205.9	222.2	233.2	241.6	257.9	277.1	290.6	298.9	..
Sweden	66.5	146.0	140.6	149.2	158.8	154.8	145.2	161.6	146.7	135.4	151.7	158.4	143.1	..
Switzerland	31.2	55.0	56.3	62.0	62.3	68.7	66.1	71.1	65.5	65.4	63.9	57.8	62.3	..
Turkey	9.8	57.5	94.9	103.3	111.0	116.4	124.9	122.7	129.4	140.6	150.7	162.0	175.9	..
United Kingdom	255.8	317.8	349.3	349.2	361.1	365.3	374.4	382.4	384.6	395.5	392.7	397.6	394.9	..
United States	1 703.4	3 202.8	3 651.2	3 672.2	3 804.5	3 873.5	4 025.7	3 838.6	4 026.1	4 054.4	4 147.7	4 268.4	4 260.4	5 947.0
EU27 total	..	2 567.1	2 810.8	2 825.3	2 886.6	2 911.6	2 991.9	3 076.9	3 084.0	3 178.5	3 252.2	3 274.1	..	4 404.0
OECD total	3 820.7	7 569.6	8 713.7	8 835.7	9 045.5	9 243.5	9 591.1	9 461.0	9 761.5	9 865.4	10 123.6	10 392.5	10 428.3	14 597.0
Brazil	51.6	222.8	291.3	308.1	321.9	334.8	349.2	327.9	345.7	364.9	387.5	403.0	..	..
China	138.4	621.2	1 080.0	1 134.5	1 166.2	1 239.3	1 355.6	1 471.7	1 640.5	1 907.4	2 199.6	2 497.4	..	8 472.0
India	66.4	289.4	436.7	465.8	496.9	537.4	562.2	580.9	598.4	635.1	667.5	699.0	..	2 774.0
Russian Federation	..	1 082.2	846.2	833.2	826.2	845.3	876.5	889.3	889.3	914.3	929.9	951.2	..	1 352.0
South Africa	54.6	165.4	199.5	207.7	203.0	200.4	207.8	208.2	215.7	232.3	242.5	242.9	..	..
World	5 245.5	11 805.6	13 649.5	13 945.8	14 286.7	14 689.2	15 355.3	15 454.2	16 072.1	16 677.1	17 460.6	18 235.1	..	35 384.0

StatLink http://dx.doi.org/10.1787/273751532475

World electricity generation by source of energy
Terawatt hours (TWh)

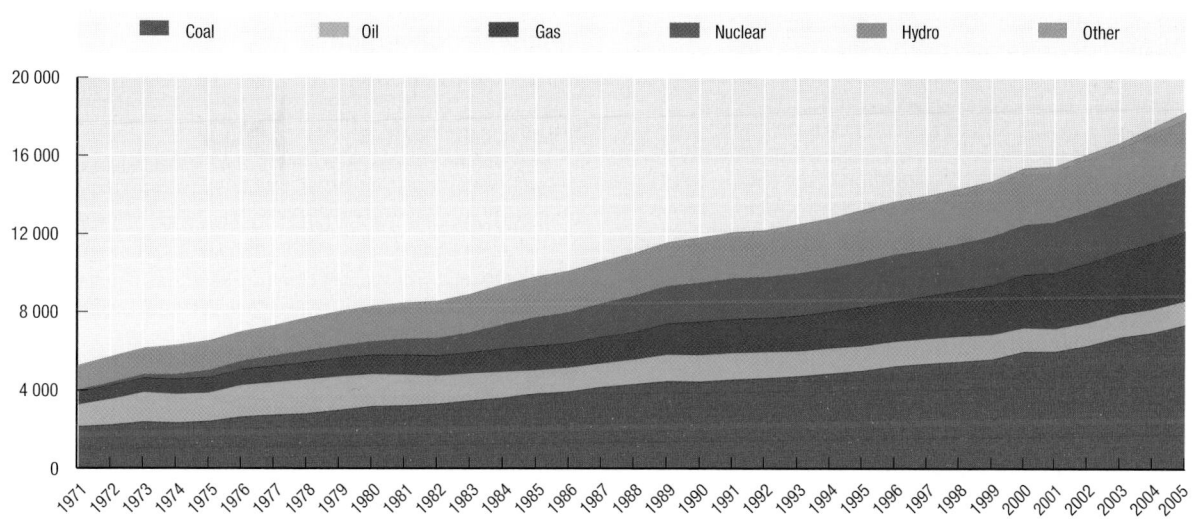

Coal · Oil · Gas · Nuclear · Hydro · Other

StatLink http://dx.doi.org/10.1787/267881553222

NUCLEAR ENERGY

In 2006 nuclear energy provided over 23% of total electricity supply in OECD countries. However, the use of nuclear energy varies widely. In all, 17 of the 30 OECD countries use nuclear energy at present, with eight generating more than one-third of their power from this source. Collectively, OECD countries produce about 85% of the world's nuclear energy. The remainder is produced in 14 non-OECD countries.

Definition

The table gives the net nuclear generation in terawatt hours (TWh) in each of the OECD member countries. The percentage share this represents of total net electricity generation in each country and in the OECD as a whole is also given, and is shown in the chart.

Long-term trends

After growing strongly in the 1970s and 1980s, nuclear energy has since stagnated. Only a few new nuclear power plants have been ordered in the last 20 years, with the Czech Republic, Japan and Korea being the only OECD countries where new nuclear plants have entered in operation since 2000.

However, the role of nuclear energy in reducing greenhouse gas emissions and in increasing energy diversification and security of supply has been increasingly recognised over the last few years. This has led to renewed interest in building new nuclear plants in several countries. As a result, nuclear capacity is now expected to grow more strongly over the next 10 to 20 years and beyond.

Much of this growth is expected to be in non-OECD countries (in particular, China, India and Russia), although OECD members Japan, Korea and the United States are also expected to add significantly to their nuclear capacity. Recent forecasts indicate that worldwide nuclear capacity could grow from 370 GWe (gigawatt electrical) in 2006 (of which, 309 GWe in OECD countries) to about 483 GWe by 2020 (of which, 329 GWe in OECD countries), and to about 533 GWe by 2025 (of which, 360 GWe in OECD countries). This implies world capacity growing at around 2% on average per year, with much of this taking place in non-OECD countries. However, OECD nuclear capacity could grow more strongly after 2020.

Comparability

Data for the UK and Japan exclude autoproduction, and data for Japan is for the fiscal year. Some data is provisional and may be subject to slight revision.

Source

- NEA (2007), *Nuclear Energy Data: 2007 Edition*, OECD, Paris.

Further information

Analytical publications

- IEA (2007), *World Energy Outlook 2007: China and India Insights*, IEA, Paris.
- NEA (2007), *Innovation in Nuclear Energy Technology*, OECD, Paris.
- OECD, NEA and IAEA (2006), *Uranium 2005: Resources, Production and Demand*, OECD, Paris.
- NEA (2006), *Forty Years of Uranium Resources, Production and Demand in Perspective: The Red Book Retrospective*, NEA, Paris.

Websites

- Nuclear Energy Agency, *www.nea.fr*.

Nuclear electricity generation

Year 2006

	Terawatt hours net	As a percentage of total electricity generation
Australia	-	-
Austria	-	-
Belgium	44.3	54.4
Canada	92.5	15.6
Czech Republic	24.5	31.5
Denmark	-	-
Finland	22.3	28.4
France	428.7	78.1
Germany	158.6	27.0
Greece	-	-
Hungary	12.7	38.3
Iceland	-	-
Ireland	-	-
Italy	-	-
Japan	317.2	34.2
Korea	141.2	38.9
Luxembourg	-	-
Mexico	10.9	4.7
Netherlands	3.6	3.1
New Zealand	-	-
Norway	-	-
Poland	-	-
Portugal	-	-
Slovak Republic	16.6	57.6
Spain	57.8	19.8
Sweden	65.0	46.4
Switzerland	26.0	40.6
Turkey	-	-
United Kingdom	69.2	19.5
United States	787.0	19.4
OECD total	2 278.1	23.1

StatLink http://dx.doi.org/10.1787/273765486153

Nuclear electricity generation

As a percentage of total electricity generation, 2006

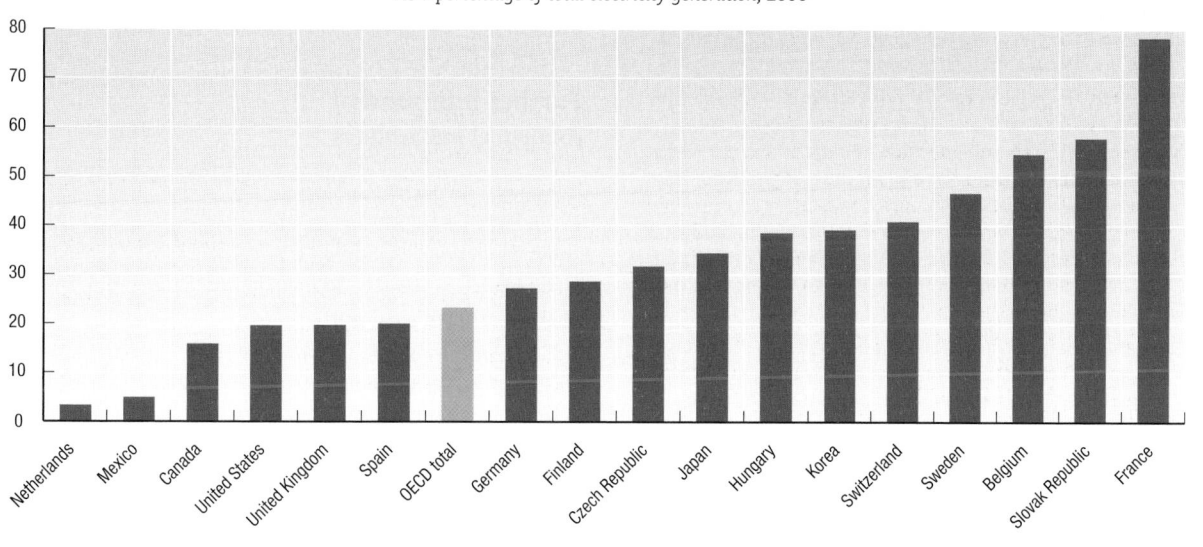

StatLink http://dx.doi.org/10.1787/268005474813

RENEWABLE ENERGY

More and more governments are recognising the importance of promoting sustainable development and combating climate change when setting out their energy policies. As energy use has increased, greenhouse gas emissions have spiraled up and their concentration in the atmosphere has increased. One way to reduce emissions is to replace energy from fossil fuels by energy from renewables.

Definition

The table refers to the contribution of renewables to total primary energy supply (TPES) in OECD countries. Renewables include the primary energy equivalent of hydro (excluding pumped storage), geothermal, solar, wind, tide and wave. It also includes solid biomass, biogasoline, biodiesel, other liquid biofuels, biogas, industrial waste and municipal waste. Biomass is defined as any plant matter used directly as fuel or converted into fuels (e.g. charcoal) or electricity and/or heat. Included here are wood, vegetal waste (including wood waste and crops used for energy production), ethanol, animal materials/wastes and sulphite lyes. Municipal waste comprises wastes produced by the residential, commercial and public service sectors that are collected by local authorities for disposal in a central location for the production of heat and/or power. The forecasts provided in the table refer to the Reference Scenario of the World Energy Outlook.

Comparability

Biomass and waste data are often based on small sample surveys or other incomplete information. Thus, the data give only a broad impression of developments and are not strictly comparable between countries. In some cases, complete categories of vegetal fuel are omitted due to lack of information.

Long-term trends

In OECD countries, total renewables supply grew by 2.3% per annum between 1971 and 2006 as compared to 1.4% per annum for total primary energy supply. Annual growth for hydro (1.1%) was lower than for other renewables such as geothermal (5.8%) and combustible renewables and waste (2.7%). Due to a very low base in 1971, solar and wind experienced the most rapid growth in OECD member countries, especially where government policies have stimulated expansion of these energy sources.

For total OECD, the contribution of renewables to energy supply increased from 4.7% in 1971 to 6.5% in 2006. The contribution of renewables varied greatly by country. On the high end, renewables represented 78% in Iceland and 39% in Norway. On the low end, renewables contributed only 1% to 2% of supply for Korea, Luxembourg and the United Kingdom.

In general, the contribution of renewables to the energy supply in non-OECD countries is higher than in OECD countries. In 2005, renewables contributed 40% to the supply of Brazil, 31% in India, 15% in China, 11% in South Africa and 3% in the Russian Federation.

Sources

- IEA (2007), Energy Balances of Non-OECD Countries, IEA, Paris.
- IEA (2007), Energy Balances of OECD Countries, IEA, Paris.
- IEA (2007), World Energy Outlook 2007: China and India Insights, IEA, Paris.

Further information

Analytical publications

- IEA (2006), Energy Technology Perspectives: Scenarios and Strategies to 2050, IEA, Paris.
- IEA (2006), Renewable Energy RD D Priorities: Insights from IEA Technology Programme, IEA, Paris.
- IEA (2007), Renewables for Heating and Cooling, IEA, Paris.

Statistical publications

- IEA (2007), Renewables Information: 2007 Edition, IEA, Paris.

Online databases

- World Energy Statistics and Balances.

Websites

- International Energy Agency, www.iea.org.

Contribution of renewables to energy supply
As a percentage of total primary energy supply

	1971	1990	1996	1997	1998	1999	2000	2001	2002	2003	2004	2005	2006	2030
Australia	8.7	6.0	6.3	6.4	6.0	6.0	5.9	6.1	6.2	5.9	6.0	5.5	5.2	..
Austria	10.9	20.7	21.0	21.6	21.1	22.9	23.3	22.8	22.5	20.0	21.6	21.3	21.3	..
Belgium	..	1.6	1.6	1.6	1.6	1.8	1.8	2.1	2.1	2.4	2.6	2.9	3.1	..
Canada	15.2	16.1	17.1	16.7	16.3	16.7	17.0	16.1	16.8	15.6	15.5	16.2	16.1	..
Czech Republic	0.2	0.2	1.5	1.7	1.7	2.4	2.0	2.1	2.5	3.7	4.1	4.3	4.5	..
Denmark	1.7	6.6	7.3	8.4	8.8	9.7	11.0	11.5	12.5	13.4	15.1	16.1	15.6	..
Finland	26.9	18.8	19.8	20.9	22.2	22.2	24.1	22.7	22.3	21.4	23.1	23.3	22.6	..
France	8.4	7.2	7.3	7.1	7.0	7.3	7.0	7.1	6.4	6.4	6.3	6.0	6.3	..
Germany	1.2	1.8	2.2	2.5	2.8	2.8	3.1	3.4	3.8	3.9	4.4	4.9	6.3	..
Greece	7.4	5.0	5.8	5.5	5.2	5.6	5.3	4.7	4.9	5.3	5.2	5.3	5.8	..
Hungary	2.9	1.7	1.9	2.0	1.9	1.9	2.1	2.0	3.5	3.5	3.7	4.4	4.3	..
Iceland	42.4	64.5	64.9	66.4	67.0	70.9	71.3	72.9	72.4	72.6	71.7	72.5	77.6	..
Ireland	0.6	1.6	1.5	1.6	1.9	1.8	1.8	1.7	1.9	1.7	2.0	2.6	2.9	..
Italy	5.1	4.5	5.3	5.4	5.5	6.0	6.0	6.2	5.9	6.1	6.8	6.5	6.8	..
Japan	2.7	3.5	3.2	3.4	3.4	3.3	3.3	3.2	3.2	3.5	3.4	3.2	3.4	6.2
Korea	0.6	1.4	0.7	0.7	0.9	0.8	0.9	0.9	0.9	1.1	1.1	1.2	1.3	..
Luxembourg	..	0.8	1.2	1.5	1.5	1.4	1.4	1.6	1.2	1.4	1.5	1.7	1.7	..
Mexico	16.6	11.1	11.3	10.6	10.3	10.5	10.6	10.1	9.5	9.5	9.7	9.7	9.4	..
Netherlands	..	1.5	1.9	2.1	2.2	2.4	2.4	2.5	2.7	2.6	2.9	3.5	3.6	..
New Zealand	30.8	34.7	30.2	28.6	30.9	31.0	30.9	28.9	28.0	27.6	29.4	28.9	30.0	..
Norway	39.9	53.2	43.4	43.4	43.9	44.6	51.6	44.1	50.1	38.5	37.7	40.6	38.5	..
Poland	1.6	2.4	4.4	4.3	4.5	4.5	4.7	5.0	5.2	5.1	5.2	5.3	5.2	..
Portugal	18.8	18.5	18.5	17.4	16.0	13.4	15.2	16.1	13.8	16.8	14.7	13.2	16.9	..
Slovak Republic	2.4	1.5	3.9	3.9	4.0	4.4	4.6	4.4	4.2	3.7	4.2	4.6	4.8	..
Spain	6.4	6.9	7.1	6.4	6.2	5.3	5.7	6.5	5.4	6.9	6.4	6.0	6.6	..
Sweden	20.2	24.7	23.2	27.1	27.6	26.9	31.2	28.4	25.8	25.0	25.5	29.4	29.3	..
Switzerland	14.9	14.2	14.8	16.1	16.0	18.0	17.4	18.1	16.7	17.1	17.5	17.6	17.0	..
Turkey	31.1	18.2	16.7	15.8	15.9	15.1	13.1	13.2	13.4	12.7	13.2	11.9	12.2	..
United Kingdom	0.1	0.5	0.8	0.9	1.0	1.0	1.0	1.2	1.4	1.5	1.7	2.0	2.1	..
United States	3.7	5.2	5.4	5.2	5.1	4.9	4.8	4.3	4.3	4.6	4.6	4.7	5.0	8.7
EU27 total	..	4.5	5.3	5.6	5.7	5.8	6.0	6.1	6.0	6.2	6.5	6.7	..	14.5
OECD total	4.7	6.0	6.2	6.1	6.1	6.1	6.1	5.8	5.9	6.0	6.1	6.2	6.5	10.8
Brazil	56.5	44.3	39.0	37.9	37.8	37.9	37.2	35.6	37.2	39.6	40.0	40.4	..	..
China	40.0	24.5	20.5	20.6	20.8	21.1	21.1	21.8	20.3	17.9	15.9	15.0	..	9.1
India	62.5	43.6	36.8	35.9	35.6	34.1	33.8	33.7	33.1	32.8	31.5	31.1	..	17.3
Russian Federation	..	3.0	3.2	3.4	3.3	3.5	3.4	3.5	3.4	3.1	3.5	3.4	..	3.6
South Africa	10.4	11.5	11.1	11.2	11.2	11.4	11.5	11.9	12.6	11.3	10.3	10.8	..	..
World	13.2	12.8	13.1	13.1	13.2	13.2	13.2	13.1	13.1	13.0	12.8	12.7	..	13.2

StatLink http://dx.doi.org/10.1787/273766530064

OECD renewable energy supply
Million tonnes of oil equivalent (Mtoe)

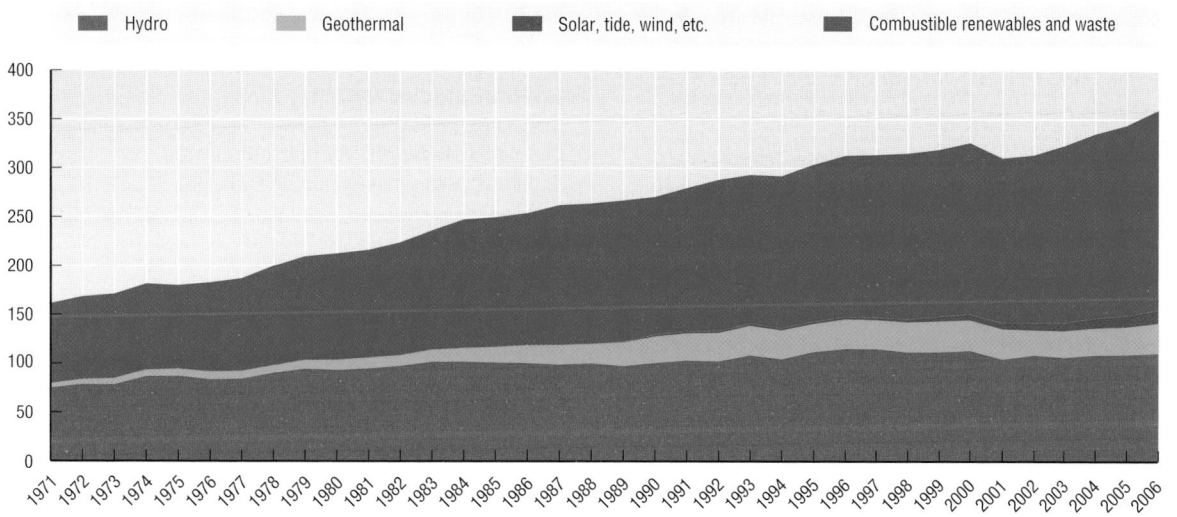

StatLink http://dx.doi.org/10.1787/268021727170

ENERGY PRODUCTION

Energy production is a function of the natural resources of a country and the economic incentives to exploit those resources. Countries will also take into consideration energy security and environmental protection when making decisions on how much and what type of energy to produce.

Definition

Production refers to the quantities of fuels extracted from the ground after the removal of inert matter or impurities (*e.g.* sulphur from natural gas). For non-combusted energy such as nuclear, hydro and solar, the primary energy equivalent is calculated using the physical energy content method.

Comparability

In general, data on energy production are of high quality. In some instances, information has been based on secondary sources or estimated by the IEA.

Total energy production by product

As a percentage of total energy production

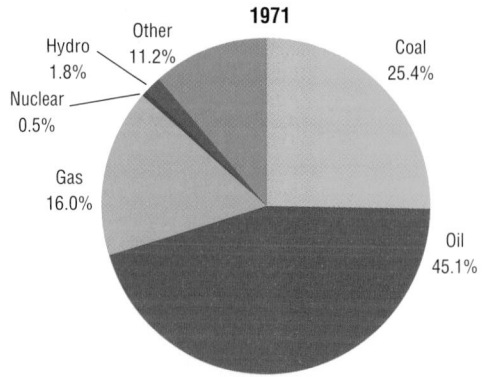

1971

- Other 11.2%
- Hydro 1.8%
- Nuclear 0.5%
- Gas 16.0%
- Coal 25.4%
- Oil 45.1%

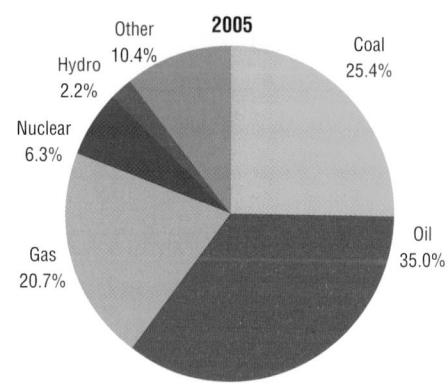

2005

- Other 10.4%
- Hydro 2.2%
- Nuclear 6.3%
- Gas 20.7%
- Coal 25.4%
- Oil 35.0%

StatLink ⟶ http://dx.doi.org/10.1787/268051345162

Long-term trends

World energy production increased by 2.1% per year between 1971 and 2005, reaching 11 468 million tonnes of oil equivalent (Mtoe). The OECD, with a 33% share of the global production, was the main energy producing region in 2005. The United States accounted for 14% of world energy production, China for 14%, the Middle East region for 13% and the Russian Federation for 10%. Since 1971, the shares of the OECD, Middle East and Former USSR decreased, while Latin America and non-OECD Europe remained stable. On the other hand, the share of energy production in China (as well as the rest of Asia) increased dramatically since 1971.

The energy mix has changed significantly between 1971 and 2005. Nuclear energy, which experienced an annual average growth of 10% since 1971, increased its share of production from 0.5% to 6.3%. Renewable energy also experienced a high growth rate over the last 34 years, but its share was very low in 1971, making this growth less meaningful. The share of natural gas in total production increased from 16.0% in 1971 to 20.7% in 2005, causing the share of oil to fall from 44.9% to 35.0%. The share of coal production remained at around 25%.

Sources

- IEA (2007), *Energy Balances of Non-OECD Countries*, IEA, Paris.
- IEA (2007), *Energy Balances of OECD Countries*, IEA, Paris.

Further information

Analytical publications

- IEA (2005), *Resources to Reserves: Oil and Gas Technologies for the Energy Markets of the Future*, IEA, Paris.
- IEA (2007), *Energy Policies of IEA Countries*, series, IEA, Paris.
- NEA (2006), *Forty Years of Uranium Resources, Production and Demand in Perspective: The Red Book Retrospective*, NEA, Paris.

Online databases

- *World Energy Statistics and Balances*.

Websites

- International Energy Agency, *www.iea.org*.

OECD FACTBOOK 2008 – ISBN 978-92-64-04054-0 – © OECD 2008

Total production of energy
Million tonnes of oil equivalent (Mtoe)

	1971	1990	1995	1996	1997	1998	1999	2000	2001	2002	2003	2004	2005	2006
Australia	53.9	157.5	186.9	189.8	201.1	216.5	213.6	233.6	249.2	254.5	253.9	259.0	271.0	273.7
Austria	7.4	8.1	8.7	8.6	8.8	8.9	9.5	9.8	9.9	10.1	9.8	10.0	9.8	9.4
Belgium	6.8	13.1	11.9	12.4	13.4	13.1	13.9	13.7	13.3	13.5	13.7	13.8	13.9	13.6
Canada	155.6	273.7	348.8	358.3	364.9	365.5	366.1	372.5	376.9	384.0	385.9	397.4	401.3	409.5
Czech Republic	39.9	40.1	31.8	32.5	32.8	30.8	28.0	29.9	30.5	30.7	33.4	34.5	32.9	33.5
Denmark	0.3	10.0	15.6	17.7	20.2	20.4	23.8	27.7	27.1	28.6	28.5	31.1	31.3	29.4
Finland	5.0	12.1	13.2	13.6	15.0	13.6	15.4	15.1	15.0	16.0	15.9	15.8	16.6	17.6
France	47.7	112.4	128.5	132.3	129.5	126.5	128.4	132.1	133.4	135.2	136.5	137.3	136.9	137.1
Germany	175.2	186.2	145.0	143.2	143.6	136.0	137.2	135.3	134.7	134.5	134.6	136.2	134.5	138.1
Greece	2.1	9.2	9.3	9.1	9.6	9.8	9.5	10.0	10.0	10.2	9.9	10.3	10.3	9.9
Hungary	11.8	14.3	13.5	13.1	12.8	12.0	11.5	11.3	10.9	11.2	10.4	10.2	10.3	10.3
Iceland	0.4	1.4	1.6	1.6	1.7	1.8	2.2	2.3	2.5	2.5	2.5	2.5	2.6	3.3
Ireland	1.4	3.5	4.1	3.6	2.9	2.5	2.5	2.2	1.8	1.6	1.9	1.9	1.7	1.6
Italy	19.6	25.3	29.4	30.3	30.4	30.3	29.2	28.2	26.9	27.5	27.6	28.2	27.6	27.0
Japan	35.8	75.2	98.6	101.7	106.2	109.1	104.5	105.8	104.7	96.9	84.0	95.0	99.8	100.8
Korea	6.4	22.6	21.1	22.5	23.7	27.1	30.6	32.6	33.2	34.8	37.9	38.3	42.9	43.7
Luxembourg	-	-	-	-	-	0.1	-	0.1	0.1	0.1	0.1	0.1	0.1	0.1
Mexico	43.4	194.8	202.3	213.3	223.2	228.5	223.0	226.1	230.2	229.9	242.3	253.6	259.2	259.1
Netherlands	37.3	60.5	66.2	74.0	65.8	63.0	59.1	57.2	61.0	60.4	58.4	67.7	61.9	60.8
New Zealand	3.4	12.0	13.0	14.0	14.8	13.8	14.5	14.9	14.7	14.4	13.0	12.7	12.2	12.9
Norway	6.0	120.3	186.5	209.7	215.1	208.0	211.7	229.1	226.5	235.2	235.5	238.6	233.7	227.9
Poland	99.2	99.4	99.4	99.0	100.0	87.6	83.9	79.6	80.3	80.2	79.9	78.8	78.6	77.1
Portugal	1.4	3.4	3.3	3.8	3.7	3.7	3.4	3.8	4.1	3.6	4.3	3.9	3.6	4.3
Slovak Republic	2.7	5.3	5.0	5.0	4.9	5.0	5.5	6.3	6.7	6.8	6.6	6.5	6.6	6.6
Spain	10.4	34.6	31.5	32.7	31.7	32.3	30.7	31.7	33.5	31.8	33.0	32.7	30.3	31.5
Sweden	7.4	29.8	31.9	32.1	32.5	34.1	33.3	30.6	34.0	31.9	31.0	34.5	34.8	33.1
Switzerland	2.9	9.7	10.8	10.3	10.8	11.0	11.5	11.5	12.0	11.6	11.8	11.8	10.9	12.1
Turkey	13.8	25.8	26.5	27.1	28.0	29.1	27.5	25.9	24.4	24.1	23.6	24.1	23.6	25.2
United Kingdom	109.8	208.0	257.5	268.9	268.3	271.9	281.6	272.4	262.3	258.3	246.6	225.4	204.3	185.8
United States	1 435.8	1 650.3	1 663.7	1 689.7	1 686.9	1 701.5	1 681.2	1 678.8	1 699.6	1 667.3	1 634.5	1 647.0	1 630.7	1 657.1
EU27 total	..	939.8	959.8	987.7	979.9	953.2	954.6	946.0	946.2	945.1	935.5	931.5	897.9	..
OECD total	2 343.1	3 418.7	3 665.9	3 769.9	3 802.2	3 813.6	3 792.8	3 829.8	3 869.4	3 847.4	3 806.9	3 858.9	3 833.8	3 852.4
Brazil	49.2	98.1	105.6	111.6	118.6	127.0	136.0	143.8	147.7	162.0	171.7	176.3	187.8	..
China	394.1	886.3	1 066.3	1 097.3	1 097.8	1 088.8	1 069.0	1 073.0	1 104.5	1 183.7	1 331.3	1 509.4	1 640.9	..
India	141.5	291.1	334.7	341.1	351.6	350.3	357.4	364.2	372.2	381.3	394.2	408.4	419.0	..
Russian Federation	..	1 280.3	953.9	953.0	921.6	928.4	950.5	966.5	996.1	1 034.5	1 106.9	1 158.4	1 184.9	..
South Africa	37.8	114.5	133.7	133.9	142.4	144.1	144.6	145.3	144.9	143.8	153.5	157.5	158.6	..
World	5 654.5	8 795.3	9 250.1	9 499.9	9 633.0	9 749.6	9 751.7	9 994.8	10 121.7	10 228.1	10 612.0	11 130.3	11 467.7	..

StatLink http://dx.doi.org/10.1787/273776751543

Total energy production by region
Million tonnes of oil equivalent (Mtoe)

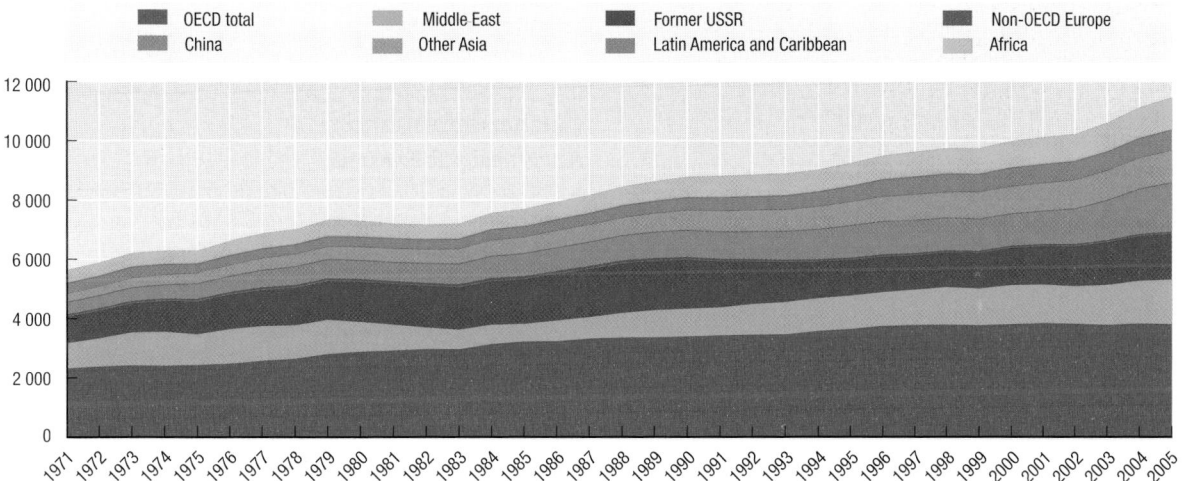

StatLink http://dx.doi.org/10.1787/268044737200

OIL PRODUCTION

The Middle East and North Africa are exceptionally well-endowed with energy resources, holding 66% of the world's proven oil reserves at the end of 2006. Current oil production is relatively low in comparison to these reserves and further development of them will be critical to meeting global energy needs in the coming decades.

Definition

Crude oil production refers to the quantities of oil extracted from the ground after the removal of inert matter or impurities. It includes crude oil, natural gas liquids (NGLs) and additives. Crude oil is a mineral oil consisting of a mixture of hydrocarbons of natural origin, being yellow to black in colour, of variable density and viscosity. NGLs are the liquid or liquefied hydrocarbons produced in the manufacture, purification and stabilisation of natural gas. Additives are non-hydrocarbon substances added to or blended with a product to modify its properties, for example, to improve its combustion characteristics (*e.g.* MTBE and tetraethyl lead).

Refinery production refers to the output of secondary oil products from an oil refinery.

Comparability

In general, data on oil production are of high quality. In some instances, information has been based on secondary sources or estimated by the IEA.

Share of refinery production by product

As a percentage of refinery production

1971

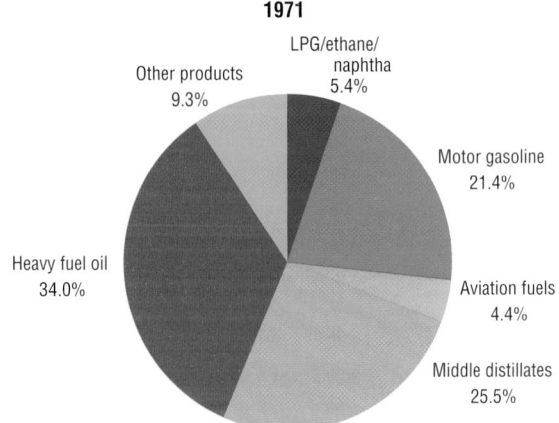

2005

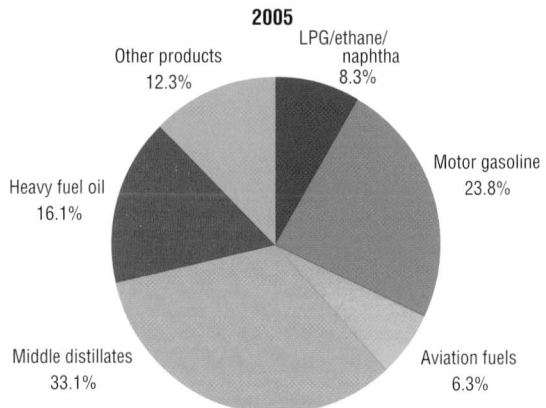

StatLink ⬛⬛ http://dx.doi.org/10.1787/268185726041

Long-term trends

World crude oil production increased by 58% over the 35-year period from 1971 to 2006. In 2006, production reached 3 936 million tonnes or about 82 million barrels per day. Growth was not constant over the period as production declined in the aftermath of two oil shocks.

In 2006, the Middle East region's share of oil production was 31% of the world total. However, both production and share varied significantly over the period, with the Middle East representing 32% in 1971 falling to less than 19% in 1985. Increased production in the 1980s and 1990s put the OECD on par with the Middle East during that period, but by 2006, the share of OECD oil production had fallen to 23%.

Refinery production of secondary oil products changed significantly between 1971 and 2005. The share of heavy fuel oil in the refinery mix fell from 34% in 1971 to 16% in 2005 whereas the share of middle distillates increased from 25% to 33%.

Sources

- IEA (2007), *Energy Balances of Non-OECD Countries*, IEA, Paris.
- IEA (2007), *Energy Balances of OECD Countries*, IEA, Paris.
- IEA (2007), *Oil Information*, IEA, Paris.

Further information

Analytical publications

- IEA (2005), *Resources to Reserves: Oil and Gas Technologies for the Energy Markets of the Future*, IEA, Paris.
- IEA (2005), *Saving Oil in a Hurry*, IEA, Paris.
- IEA (2007), *Energy Policies of IEA Countries*, series, IEA, Paris.
- IEA (2007), *Oil Supply Security: Emergency Response of IEA Countries 2007*, IEA, Paris.

Online databases

- *World Energy Statistics and Balances.*

Websites

- International Energy Agency, *www.iea.org.*

Production of crude oil
Million tonnes

	1971	1990	1995	1996	1997	1998	1999	2000	2001	2002	2003	2004	2005	2006
Australia	14.3	27.5	26.9	26.4	26.7	29.4	23.7	32.1	33.1	31.3	29.1	26.2	22.9	21.1
Austria	2.6	1.2	1.1	1.0	1.0	1.0	1.1	1.1	1.0	1.0	1.0	1.1	1.0	1.0
Canada	70.6	91.6	110.3	113.5	119.0	124.7	119.9	124.8	126.6	132.9	140.4	145.4	143.5	151.2
Czech Republic	..	0.2	0.2	0.2	0.4	0.4	0.4	0.4	0.4	0.4	0.5	0.6	0.6	0.4
Denmark	..	6.0	9.2	10.1	11.1	11.4	14.5	17.8	16.9	18.1	18.1	19.3	18.5	16.8
Finland	..	..	..	..	0.1	0.1	0.1	0.1	0.1	0.1	0.1	0.1	0.1	0.1
France	2.5	3.5	3.0	2.6	2.3	2.1	2.0	1.9	1.6	1.5	1.4	1.4	1.2	1.1
Germany	7.6	5.3	3.9	3.7	3.7	3.8	3.8	4.3	4.3	4.6	4.8	4.9	5.2	5.9
Greece	..	0.8	0.5	0.5	0.5	0.3	-	0.3	0.2	0.2	0.1	0.1	0.1	0.1
Hungary	2.0	2.3	2.3	2.1	2.0	1.8	1.8	1.7	1.5	1.6	1.6	1.6	1.4	1.3
Italy	1.3	4.7	5.5	5.7	6.1	5.8	5.2	4.8	4.2	5.8	5.9	5.7	6.4	6.1
Japan	0.8	0.5	0.7	0.7	0.7	0.6	0.6	0.6	0.6	0.6	0.6	0.7	0.7	0.7
Korea	..	..	..	..	0.5	0.4	0.4	0.4	0.7	0.6	0.5	0.5	0.4	0.5
Mexico	25.4	151.1	153.6	160.4	169.0	171.9	166.9	169.3	175.5	178.3	189.3	191.4	187.6	183.2
Netherlands	1.7	4.0	3.5	3.1	2.9	2.7	2.5	2.4	2.3	3.1	3.1	2.9	2.3	2.0
New Zealand	-	1.9	1.7	2.2	2.8	2.3	2.0	1.8	1.8	1.6	1.2	1.1	1.0	1.0
Norway	0.3	82.1	138.5	156.8	156.5	149.8	149.4	161.0	162.5	157.7	153.6	151.8	140.1	132.5
Poland	0.4	0.2	0.4	0.4	0.4	0.4	0.5	0.7	0.8	0.8	0.8	0.9	0.9	0.8
Slovak Republic	0.2	0.1	0.1	0.1	0.1	0.1	0.1	0.1	0.1	0.1	..	..	..	..
Spain	0.1	1.1	0.8	0.5	0.4	0.5	0.3	0.2	0.3	0.3	0.3	0.3	0.2	0.1
Turkey	3.5	3.7	3.5	3.5	3.4	3.2	2.9	2.8	2.5	2.4	2.4	2.3	2.3	2.2
United Kingdom	0.2	91.6	130.5	130.1	128.4	132.5	137.2	126.4	116.8	116.1	106.2	95.5	84.7	76.6
United States	527.7	413.3	383.3	382.5	380.9	369.8	354.2	353.0	349.9	348.1	338.4	325.9	310.0	309.6
EU27 total	..	129.0	167.9	167.4	166.4	170.1	176.2	168.7	157.3	161.5	151.5	140.4	128.9	118.2
OECD total	661.1	892.7	979.1	1 006.2	1 018.8	1 015.2	989.4	1 008.0	1 003.6	1 007.1	999.6	979.5	931.3	914.5
Brazil	8.4	32.4	35.7	40.3	43.7	50.6	57.2	64.3	67.4	75.6	77.9	77.5	85.5	90.2
China	39.4	138.3	150.0	157.3	160.7	161.2	160.2	163.1	164.1	167.1	169.7	175.9	181.4	184.3
India	7.3	34.6	38.4	36.2	37.4	36.4	36.4	36.4	36.2	37.4	37.7	38.3	36.3	37.0
Russian Federation	..	523.7	305.1	305.1	303.9	301.4	303.2	321.7	345.8	377.2	418.6	456.3	466.4	476.9
South Africa	..	..	0.4	0.4	0.8	0.9	0.8	1.0	0.8	1.0	0.7	1.7	1.5	1.2
World	2 487.1	3 160.5	3 293.9	3 389.1	3 479.8	3 554.5	3 481.2	3 605.9	3 609.1	3 591.1	3 708.0	3 863.0	3 918.9	3 935.7

StatLink http://dx.doi.org/10.1787/273800532531

Production of crude oil by region
Million tonnes

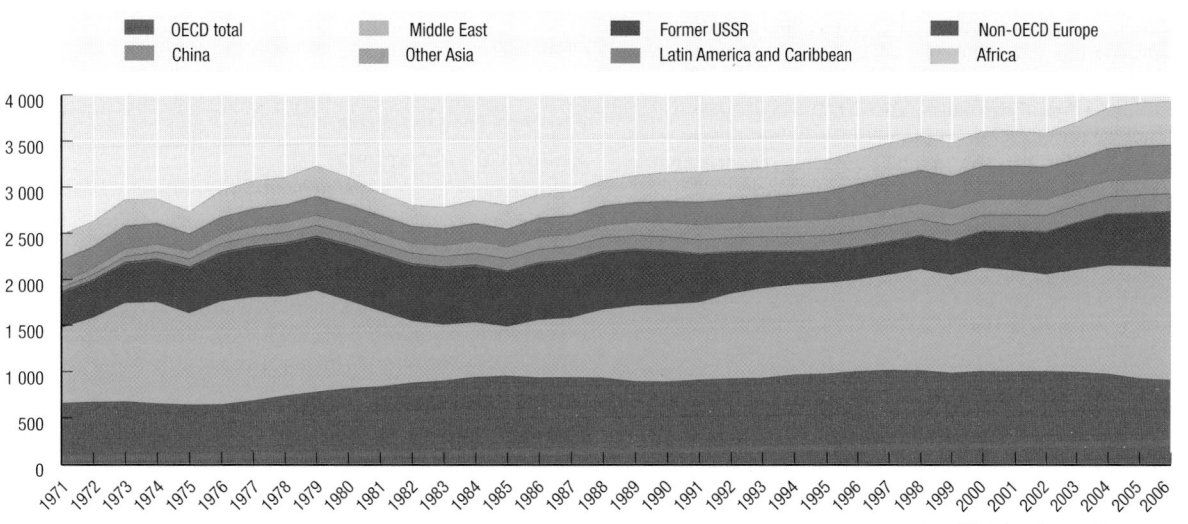

StatLink http://dx.doi.org/10.1787/268177377505

OIL PRICES

The price of crude oil, from which petroleum products such as gasoline are derived, is influenced by a number of factors beyond the traditional movements of supply and demand, notably geopolitics. Some of the lowest cost reserves are located in sensitive areas of the world. There is not one price for crude oil but many. World crude oil prices are established in relation to three market traded benchmarks (West Texas Intermediate [WTI], Brent, Dubai), and are quoted at premiums or discounts to these prices.

Definition

Crude oil import prices come from the Crude Oil Import Register. Information is collected according to type of crude and average prices are obtained by dividing value by volume as recorded by customs administrations for each tariff position. Values are recorded at the time of import and include cost, insurance and freight (CIF) but exclude import duties.

The nominal crude oil spot price from 1985 to 2006 is for Dubai and from 1970 to 1984 for Arabian Light. The real price was calculated using the deflator for GDP at market prices and was rebased with base year 1970 = 100.

Long-term trends

The 1973 Arab oil embargo had a major price impact as Arabian Light prices surged from USD 1.84/barrel in 1972 to USD 10.77 in 1974.

The first spike after 1973 came in 1981, in the wake of the Iranian revolution, when prices rose to a high of nearly USD 40. Prices declined gradually after this crisis. They dropped considerably in 1986 when Saudi Arabia increased its oil production substantially.

The first Gulf crisis in 1990 brought a new peak. In 1997, crude oil prices started to decline due to the impact of the Asian financial crisis.

Prices started to increase again in 1999 with OPEC target reductions and tightening stocks. A dip occurred in 2001 and 2002, but the expectation of war in Iraq raised prices to over USD 30 in the first quarter of 2003. Prices remained high in the latter part of 2003 and in 2004. Crude oil prices increased dramatically in late August 2005 after Hurricane Katrina hit the eastern coast of the US Gulf of Mexico. Prices continued to increase throughout 2006 as the demand for oil in emerging economies, especially China, put pressure on the supply/demand balance, averaging 24 per cent higher than the previous year. In 2007, the increase continued with Dubai hitting USD 88.82/barrel at the beginning of November and WTI climbing to USD 96.50/barrel.

After the 1986 oil price decrease, the real price of crude oil (adjusted for inflation) has remained relatively stable until the sharp increase in crude oil prices in August 2005.

Comparability

Average crude oil import prices are affected by the quality of the crude oil that is imported into a country. High quality crude oils such as UK Forties, Norwegian Oseberg and Venezuelan Light will be more expensive than lower quality crude oils such as Canadian Heavy and Venezuelan Extra Heavy. For a given country, the mix of crude oils imported each month will affect the average monthly price.

Sources

- IEA (2007), *Energy Prices and Taxes*, IEA, Paris.

Further information

Analytical publications

- IEA (2006), *China's Power Sector Reforms: Where to Next?*, IEA, Paris.
- IEA (2006), *Optimising Russian Natural Gas: Reform and Climate Policy*, IEA, Paris.
- IEA (2007), *Energy Policies of IEA Countries*, series, IEA, Paris.
- IEA (2007), *Natural Gas Market Review 2007: Security in a Globalising Market to 2015*, IEA, Paris.

Online databases

- *Energy Prices and Taxes*.

Websites

- International Energy Agency, *www.iea.org*.

Crude oil import prices
US dollars per barrel, average unit value, CIF

	1976	1990	1995	1996	1997	1998	1999	2000	2001	2002	2003	2004	2005	2006
Australia	..	24.21	18.53	21.81	21.78	14.60	18.38	30.79	26.61	25.80	31.24	40.93	56.71	66.71
Austria	12.85	24.58	18.78	22.06	21.31	14.34	17.54	29.39	25.32	24.64	29.59	38.21	53.15	64.44
Belgium	12.64	21.11	16.94	20.53	18.65	11.97	17.33	27.87	24.20	24.35	27.72	35.35	50.06	61.06
Canada	..	24.15	17.76	21.26	20.59	13.15	17.85	29.10	24.87	24.97	29.53	38.13	52.37	64.33
Czech Republic	..	..	15.60	..	..	..	..	26.59	23.74	23.37	28.13	34.82	51.28	62.05
Denmark	12.98	23.18	17.49	21.25	20.15	13.49	17.71	29.66	24.82	24.88	29.68	38.78	54.40	66.92
Finland	..	..	17.83	21.69	19.44	12.80	18.31	28.13	23.49	24.51	27.72	36.09	51.12	63.37
France	..	..	17.14	20.82	18.99	12.43	17.45	28.18	24.13	24.63	28.87	37.61	52.74	63.69
Germany	13.27	23.17	17.07	20.68	19.01	12.48	17.51	28.09	24.15	24.40	28.44	36.65	52.30	63.29
Greece	12.13	22.42	16.54	20.08	18.45	11.66	16.64	26.95	23.22	24.08	27.17	34.53	50.33	60.97
Hungary	..	..	16.08	19.32	16.74	10.77	16.05	26.22	..	..	..	..	..	..
Ireland	..	25.55	17.65	21.19	19.99	13.55	17.14	29.88	25.31	25.52	29.66	39.24	55.24	66.38
Italy	12.41	23.23	16.90	20.53	18.88	12.21	17.10	27.77	23.87	24.34	28.58	36.60	51.33	62.50
Japan	12.59	22.64	18.02	20.55	20.55	13.68	17.38	28.72	25.01	24.96	29.26	36.59	51.57	64.03
Korea	..	..	17.32	20.11	20.34	13.72	16.91	28.22	24.87	24.12	28.80	36.15	50.19	62.82
Netherlands	13.06	21.83	16.92	20.39	18.37	11.98	16.97	27.59	23.48	23.99	27.67	35.02	50.00	61.47
New Zealand	..	21.97	18.73	21.86	21.65	14.63	18.16	29.95	26.14	25.89	31.00	41.71	56.07	67.36
Norway	..	18.46	16.41	21.62	16.71	12.23	17.46	28.91	23.43	24.46	30.41	39.20	53.08	58.83
Portugal	12.14	22.75	17.22	20.35	18.95	12.21	17.38	28.20	24.02	24.27	28.72	37.89	51.94	62.77
Spain	12.54	21.88	16.96	20.45	18.34	11.80	16.99	27.16	23.32	23.95	28.13	36.03	50.54	60.99
Sweden	13.22	23.02	17.23	20.86	18.90	12.61	17.68	28.13	24.03	23.86	28.60	36.47	51.78	62.50
Switzerland	13.87	24.23	17.69	21.71	20.50	13.38	18.35	29.53	25.04	25.34	30.26	38.73	55.81	66.76
Turkey	..	23.11	16.78	20.25	18.79	11.99	16.07	26.61	22.98	23.57	27.05	34.90	50.65	61.48
United Kingdom	12.57	22.92	17.29	21.08	19.32	12.64	18.01	28.45	24.45	24.58	29.13	37.75	53.79	65.00
United States	13.48	21.07	16.74	20.16	18.34	12.02	17.06	27.54	22.07	23.52	27.66	35.86	48.82	59.15

StatLink http://dx.doi.org/10.1787/273815130673

Crude oil spot prices
US dollars per barrel

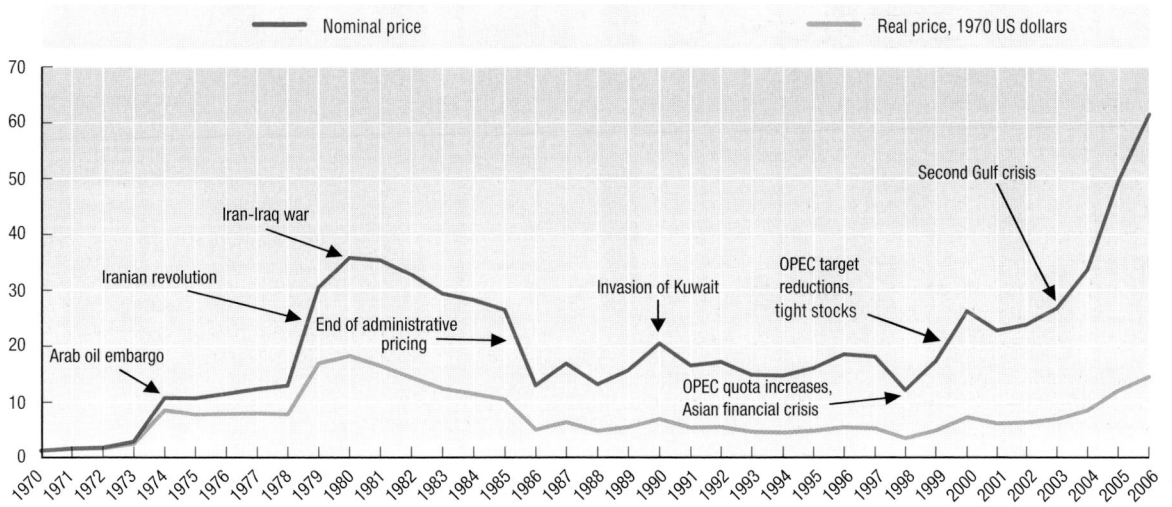

StatLink http://dx.doi.org/10.1787/268201752728

LABOUR

EMPLOYMENT
EMPLOYMENT RATES BY GENDER
EMPLOYMENT RATES BY AGE GROUP
PART-TIME EMPLOYMENT
SELF-EMPLOYMENT

UNEMPLOYMENT
UNEMPLOYMENT RATES
LONG-TERM UNEMPLOYMENT
REGIONAL UNEMPLOYMENT

LABOUR COMPENSATION AND HOURS WORKED
LABOUR COMPENSATION
HOURS WORKED

EMPLOYMENT RATES BY GENDER

Employment rates show the percentage of persons of working age who are in employment. In the short term, these rates are sensitive to the economic cycle, but in the longer term they are significantly affected by government policies with regard to higher education and income support and by policies that facilitate employment of women.

Employment rates for men and women differ both between countries and over time in individual countries. Employment rates are here shown for total employment and for men and women separately.

Definition

Employment rates are calculated as the ratio of the employed to the working age population. To calculate this employment rate, the population of working age is divided into two groups: those who are employed and those who are not. Employment is generally measured through household labour force surveys and, according to the ILO Guidelines, employed persons are defined as those aged 15 or over who report that they have worked in gainful employment for at least one hour in the previous week. Those not in employment consist of persons who are out of work but seeking employment, students and all others who have excluded themselves from the labour force for one reason or another, such as incapacity or the need to look after young children or elderly relatives.

Working age is generally defined as persons in the 15 to 64 age bracket although in some countries working age is defined as 16 to 64.

Long-term trends

Over the period 1993-2006, total employment rates (men and women) have fallen in 4 member countries and risen in 16. Particularly large falls were recorded in Poland, Turkey and the Czech Republic and particularly large increases occurred in Ireland and Spain.

Growth in employment rates was very different for men and women. Employment rates for men decreased in 13 member countries during the period with the strongest decline occurring in Poland, Turkey and the Czech Republic. For women, on the other hand, employment rates grew in 25 member countries with particularly strong increases recorded for Spain, Ireland, the Netherlands, Italy and Greee.

Clearly, these differences in the growth of employment rates are leading to convergence in the rates for women and men although differences remain large in many countries.

Comparability

All OECD countries use the ILO Guidelines for measuring employment, but the operational definitions used in national labour force surveys vary slightly in Iceland and Turkey. Employment levels are also likely to be affected by changes in the survey design and/or the survey conduct, but employment rates are likely to be fairly consistent over time.

Source

- OECD (2007), *OECD Employment Outlook*, OECD, Paris.

Further information

Analytical publications

- Durand, M., J. Simon and C. Webb (1992), *OECD's Indicators of International Trade and Competitiveness*, OECD Economics Department Working Papers, No. 120, OECD, Paris.
- Jeaumotte, F. (2003), *Female Labour Force Participation*, OECD Economics Department Working Papers, No. 376, OECD, Paris.
- OECD (2002-2004), *Babies and Bosses – Reconciling Work and Family Life*, series, OECD, Paris.

Statistical publications

- OECD (2004), *Quarterly Labour Force Statistics*, OECD, Paris.
- OECD (2007), *Labour Force Statistics*, OECD, Paris.

Online databases

- *Employment Statistics*.

Websites

- OECD Labour Statistics Database, *www.oecd.org/statistics/labour*.
- OECD Employment Data, *www.oecd.org/els/employment/data*.
- Putting More Women to Work: A Colloquium on Employment, Child Care and Taxes, *www.oecd.org/employment/colloquium/women*.

Employment rates: total

Share of persons of working age (15 to 64 years) in employment

	1993	1994	1995	1996	1997	1998	1999	2000	2001	2002	2003	2004	2005	2006
Australia	64.7	66.0	67.7	67.6	67.4	67.9	68.4	69.3	69.0	69.4	70.0	70.3	71.6	72.2
Austria	..	68.3	68.6	67.7	67.7	67.7	68.2	68.2	68.0	68.5	68.7	67.8	68.6	70.2
Belgium	56.0	55.7	56.3	56.3	57.0	57.3	58.9	60.9	59.7	59.7	59.3	60.5	61.0	60.4
Canada	66.5	67.0	67.5	67.3	68.0	68.9	70.0	70.9	70.8	71.4	72.2	72.5	72.5	72.9
Czech Republic	69.0	69.2	69.4	69.3	68.7	67.5	65.9	65.2	65.3	65.7	64.9	64.2	64.8	65.3
Denmark	72.4	72.4	73.9	74.0	75.4	75.3	76.5	76.4	75.9	76.4	75.1	76.0	75.5	76.9
Finland	60.6	59.9	61.1	61.9	62.8	64.1	66.1	67.0	67.7	67.7	67.4	67.2	68.0	68.9
France	59.1	58.4	59.1	59.2	58.9	59.4	59.8	61.1	62.0	62.2	62.5	62.4	62.3	62.3
Germany	65.1	64.5	64.6	64.3	63.8	64.7	65.2	65.6	65.8	65.3	64.6	65.0	65.5	67.2
Greece	53.5	54.1	54.5	54.9	54.8	55.6	55.4	55.9	55.6	57.7	58.9	59.6	60.3	61.0
Hungary	54.5	53.5	52.9	52.7	52.7	53.8	55.7	56.0	56.2	56.2	57.0	56.8	56.9	57.3
Iceland	78.2	78.5	80.5	80.4	80.0	82.2	84.2	84.6	84.6	82.8	84.1	82.8	84.4	85.3
Ireland	50.9	51.9	54.1	55.0	56.3	59.6	62.5	64.5	65.0	65.0	65.0	65.5	67.1	68.1
Italy	52.5	51.5	51.2	51.4	51.6	52.2	52.9	53.9	54.9	55.6	56.2	57.4	57.5	58.4
Japan	69.5	69.3	69.2	69.5	70.0	69.5	68.9	68.9	68.8	68.2	68.4	68.7	69.3	70.0
Korea	61.8	62.8	63.5	63.7	63.7	59.2	59.6	61.5	62.1	63.3	63.0	63.6	63.7	63.8
Luxembourg	60.9	60.2	58.5	59.1	59.9	60.2	61.6	62.7	63.0	63.6	62.2	62.5	63.6	..
Mexico	59.3	58.7	57.2	58.1	60.3	60.4	60.4	60.1	59.4	59.3	58.8	59.9	59.6	61.0
Netherlands	63.8	63.9	65.1	66.2	68.1	69.8	71.3	72.1	72.5	72.4	71.8	71.2	71.1	72.4
New Zealand	66.1	68.0	70.1	71.1	70.6	69.6	70.1	70.7	71.8	72.4	72.5	73.5	74.6	75.2
Norway	71.3	72.2	73.5	75.3	77.0	78.3	78.0	77.9	77.5	77.1	75.8	75.6	75.2	75.5
Poland	58.9	58.3	58.1	58.4	58.8	58.9	57.5	55.0	53.5	51.7	51.4	51.9	53.0	54.5
Portugal	64.9	64.0	63.2	63.6	64.7	66.8	67.4	68.3	68.8	68.1	67.1	67.8	67.5	67.9
Slovak Republic	..	59.8	60.2	61.9	61.1	60.5	58.1	56.8	56.9	56.9	57.7	57.0	57.7	59.4
Spain	48.0	47.4	48.3	49.3	50.7	52.4	55.0	57.4	58.8	59.5	60.7	62.0	64.3	65.7
Sweden	72.6	71.5	72.2	71.6	70.7	71.5	72.9	74.2	75.2	74.9	74.3	73.5	73.9	74.5
Switzerland	77.0	75.6	76.4	77.0	76.9	78.0	78.4	78.4	79.2	78.9	77.9	77.4	77.2	77.9
Turkey	50.0	52.4	52.4	52.5	51.3	51.4	50.8	48.9	47.8	46.7	45.5	46.1	45.9	45.9
United Kingdom	68.2	68.7	69.2	69.7	70.6	71.0	71.5	72.2	72.5	72.3	72.6	72.7	72.6	72.5
United States	71.2	72.0	72.5	72.9	73.5	73.8	73.9	74.1	73.1	71.9	71.2	71.2	71.5	72.0
EU15 total	60.2	59.9	60.3	60.5	60.8	61.7	62.5	63.5	64.1	64.2	64.3	64.8	65.2	66.0
OECD total	63.9	64.0	64.2	64.5	65.0	65.1	65.3	65.6	65.4	65.0	64.8	65.1	65.5	66.1
Brazil	67.2	..	67.7	65.1	65.3	64.4	64.6	..	64.3	65.4	65.0	66.4	67.0	67.4
China	..	..	..	..	..	..	..	..	75.6	74.9	74.5	74.2	74.0	73.8
Russian Federation	..	..	59.0	57.7	54.9	53.0	56.8	58.5	58.4	59.8	59.5	60.3	61.1	61.4

StatLink 🔗 http://dx.doi.org/10.1787/273871542812

Employment rates: total

Average annual growth in percentage, 1993-2006 or latest available period

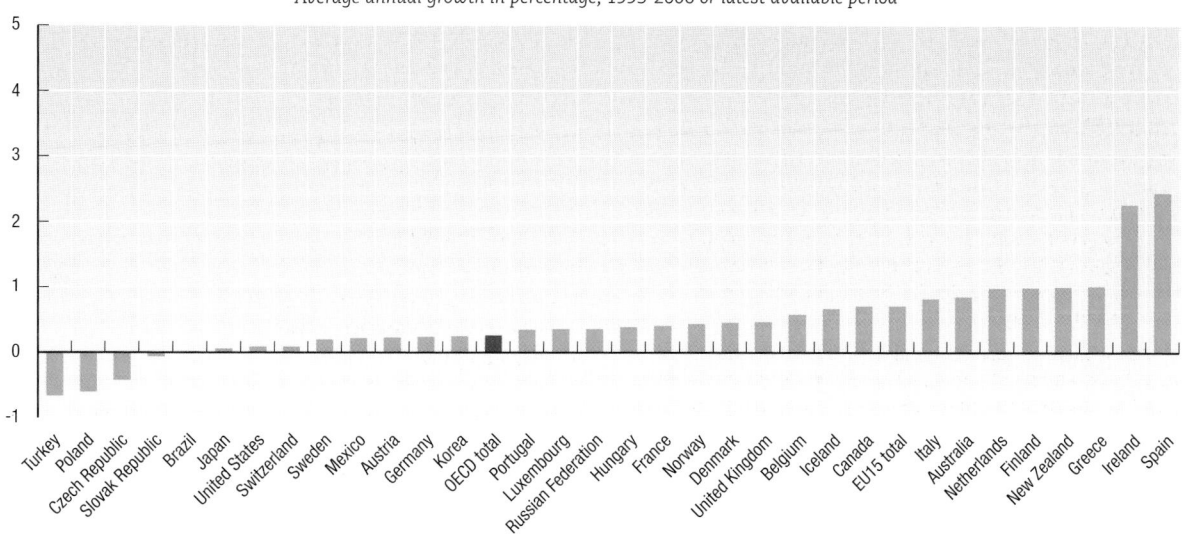

StatLink 🔗 http://dx.doi.org/10.1787/268225167705

Employment rates: men
Share of men of working age (15 to 64 years) in employment

	1993	1994	1995	1996	1997	1998	1999	2000	2001	2002	2003	2004	2005	2006
Australia	73.8	75.0	76.4	76.3	75.8	76.2	76.6	77.1	76.4	76.8	77.1	77.6	78.5	78.8
Austria	..	77.5	78.1	77.0	76.8	76.6	77.0	76.8	76.2	75.9	76.0	74.9	75.4	76.9
Belgium	67.0	66.5	66.9	66.8	67.1	67.0	67.5	69.8	68.5	68.1	67.1	67.9	67.7	67.0
Canada	72.4	73.0	73.4	73.2	73.8	74.3	75.4	76.2	75.7	75.9	76.4	76.7	76.7	76.8
Czech Republic	77.6	77.5	77.9	78.1	77.4	76.3	74.3	73.6	73.6	74.2	73.4	72.4	73.3	73.7
Denmark	75.9	77.6	80.7	80.5	81.3	80.2	81.2	80.7	80.2	80.2	79.7	79.9	80.1	80.6
Finland	61.5	61.1	63.1	64.2	65.2	66.8	68.4	69.4	70.0	69.2	69.0	68.8	69.4	70.5
France	67.2	66.1	66.7	66.8	66.3	66.6	66.8	68.1	69.0	68.6	68.6	68.1	67.8	67.5
Germany	74.9	74.0	73.7	72.8	72.1	72.9	72.8	72.9	72.8	71.7	70.4	70.8	71.4	72.9
Greece	71.7	72.2	72.2	72.6	71.9	71.6	70.9	71.3	70.9	72.5	73.5	74.0	74.5	74.6
Hungary	60.0	59.6	60.2	60.2	60.3	60.6	62.6	62.7	63.0	62.9	63.4	63.1	63.1	63.8
Iceland	82.3	82.4	84.0	84.3	84.2	86.0	88.2	88.2	88.0	85.7	86.8	86.2	87.4	88.7
Ireland	63.5	64.8	66.7	66.6	67.8	71.0	73.5	75.6	76.0	74.7	74.5	75.2	76.2	77.3
Italy	69.3	67.8	67.0	66.9	66.8	67.1	67.6	68.2	68.7	69.2	69.7	69.7	69.7	70.5
Japan	82.3	81.9	81.9	82.1	82.4	81.7	81.0	80.9	80.5	79.9	79.8	80.0	80.4	81.0
Korea	75.2	76.3	76.8	76.7	76.2	71.3	71.3	73.1	73.5	74.9	75.0	75.2	75.0	74.6
Luxembourg	76.6	74.9	74.3	74.4	74.3	74.6	74.4	75.0	74.9	75.5	73.3	72.8	73.3	..
Mexico	84.3	82.9	79.9	81.4	83.7	83.5	83.7	82.8	82.3	81.6	80.8	81.0	80.2	81.6
Netherlands	75.2	74.9	76.0	76.9	78.4	79.9	80.8	81.2	81.1	80.7	79.3	78.0	77.4	78.7
New Zealand	74.4	76.2	78.6	79.0	78.6	77.3	77.4	78.2	79.1	79.8	79.4	80.8	81.5	82.1
Norway	75.8	76.8	78.1	80.0	81.7	82.8	82.1	81.7	81.0	80.2	78.7	78.4	78.3	78.6
Poland	65.9	64.9	64.7	65.2	66.1	65.8	63.6	61.2	59.2	57.0	56.7	57.4	59.0	60.9
Portugal	74.9	73.5	72.1	72.0	72.5	75.6	75.6	76.3	76.5	75.7	73.9	74.1	73.4	73.9
Slovak Republic	..	67.2	67.6	69.2	68.4	67.8	64.3	62.2	62.1	62.5	63.4	63.2	64.6	67.0
Spain	64.4	63.3	64.0	64.7	66.1	68.3	70.8	72.7	73.8	73.9	74.5	74.9	76.4	77.3
Sweden	73.1	72.2	73.5	73.2	72.4	73.6	74.8	76.2	76.9	76.4	75.7	75.0	75.9	76.8
Switzerland	88.0	86.3	87.3	86.8	85.9	87.2	87.1	87.3	87.6	86.2	85.1	84.5	83.9	84.7
Turkey	74.2	74.6	74.6	74.9	74.8	74.3	72.7	71.7	69.3	66.9	65.9	67.9	68.2	68.0
United Kingdom	74.8	75.3	76.1	76.3	77.4	78.0	78.3	78.9	79.1	78.6	78.9	78.9	78.8	78.4
United States	78.7	79.0	79.5	79.7	80.1	80.5	80.5	80.6	79.4	78.0	76.9	77.2	77.6	78.1
EU15 total	71.1	70.5	70.7	70.6	70.8	71.6	72.1	72.9	73.2	72.9	72.6	72.6	72.9	73.5
OECD total	75.6	75.4	75.4	75.6	76.0	76.0	76.0	76.2	75.7	75.0	74.5	74.8	75.0	75.6
Brazil	83.7	..	83.1	80.8	80.7	79.5	78.8	..	78.2	78.7	77.9	79.3	79.4	79.6
China	..	..	..	..	..	..	..	..	81.6	81.2	81.1	81.8	81.4	79.5
Russian Federation	..	..	65.7	64.2	60.9	58.7	62.1	63.8	63.5	64.5	64.1	64.9	65.7	65.7

StatLink http://dx.doi.org/10.1787/273873175687

Employment rates: men
Average annual growth in percentage, 1993-2006 or latest available period

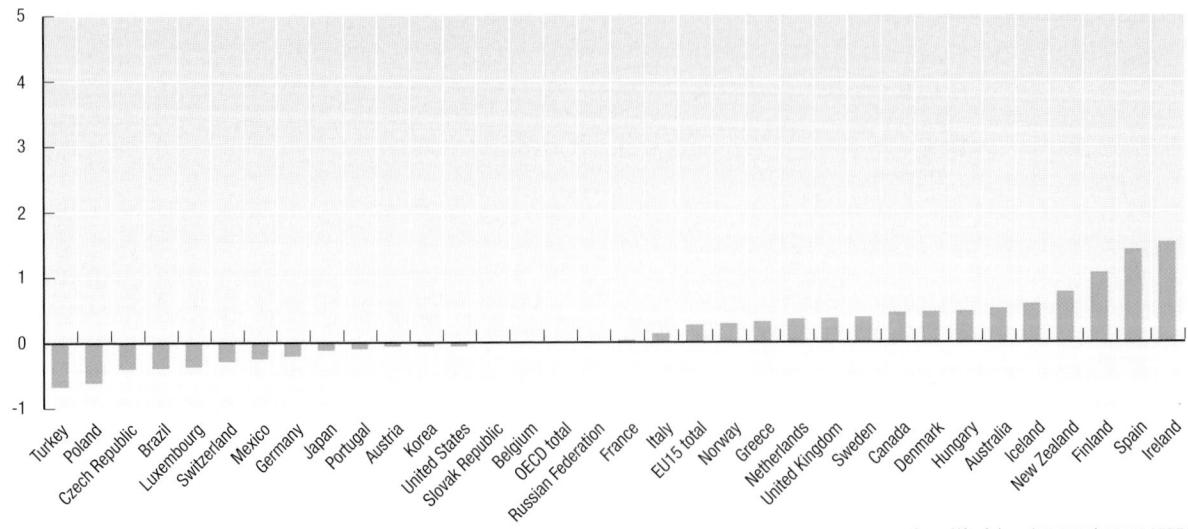

StatLink http://dx.doi.org/10.1787/268231077767

OECD FACTBOOK 2008 – ISBN 978-92-64-04054-0 – © OECD 2008

Employment rates: women

Share of women of working age (15 to 64 years) in employment

	1993	1994	1995	1996	1997	1998	1999	2000	2001	2002	2003	2004	2005	2006
Australia	55.5	56.9	59.0	58.9	58.9	59.6	60.0	61.4	61.7	62.1	62.9	63.1	64.7	65.5
Austria	..	58.8	58.9	58.2	58.4	58.5	59.3	59.4	59.8	61.0	61.5	60.7	62.0	63.5
Belgium	44.9	44.8	45.4	45.6	46.7	47.5	50.2	51.9	50.7	51.1	51.4	53.0	54.1	53.6
Canada	60.5	61.1	61.6	61.5	62.1	63.5	64.6	65.6	65.9	67.0	67.9	68.4	68.3	69.0
Czech Republic	60.4	61.0	61.0	60.6	59.9	58.7	57.4	56.9	57.0	57.1	56.3	56.0	56.3	56.8
Denmark	68.7	67.1	67.0	67.4	69.4	70.3	71.6	72.1	71.4	72.6	70.5	72.0	70.8	73.2
Finland	59.7	58.7	59.0	59.5	60.4	61.3	63.6	64.5	65.4	66.1	65.7	65.5	66.5	67.3
France	51.1	50.8	51.6	51.8	51.7	52.4	53.0	54.3	55.2	55.8	56.4	56.7	56.9	57.1
Germany	55.1	54.7	55.3	55.5	55.3	56.3	57.4	58.1	58.7	58.8	58.7	59.2	59.6	61.5
Greece	36.4	37.1	38.0	38.5	39.1	40.3	40.7	41.3	41.2	43.1	44.5	45.5	46.2	47.5
Hungary	49.3	47.8	45.9	45.5	45.5	47.3	49.0	49.6	49.8	49.8	50.9	50.7	51.0	51.2
Iceland	74.0	74.6	76.8	76.5	75.6	78.3	80.2	81.0	81.1	79.8	81.2	79.4	81.2	81.6
Ireland	38.2	38.9	41.5	43.3	44.7	48.2	51.3	53.3	54.0	55.2	55.4	55.8	58.0	58.8
Italy	35.8	35.4	35.4	36.0	36.4	37.3	38.3	39.6	41.1	42.0	42.7	45.2	45.3	46.3
Japan	56.6	56.5	56.4	56.8	57.6	57.2	56.7	56.7	57.0	56.5	56.8	57.4	58.1	58.8
Korea	48.8	49.8	50.5	51.1	51.6	47.3	48.1	50.0	50.9	52.0	51.1	52.2	52.5	53.1
Luxembourg	44.8	44.9	42.2	43.6	45.4	45.6	48.5	50.0	50.8	51.5	50.9	51.9	53.7	..
Mexico	36.0	36.2	36.0	36.8	39.1	39.3	39.1	39.6	39.0	39.5	39.1	40.9	41.6	42.9
Netherlands	52.0	52.6	53.9	55.2	57.6	59.4	61.6	62.7	63.7	64.0	64.2	64.3	64.8	66.0
New Zealand	58.0	59.9	61.7	63.4	62.8	62.1	63.0	63.5	64.8	65.3	65.7	66.5	68.0	68.4
Norway	66.6	67.5	68.8	70.4	72.2	73.6	73.8	74.0	73.8	73.9	72.7	72.7	72.0	72.3
Poland	52.1	51.9	51.8	51.8	51.8	52.2	51.6	48.9	47.8	46.4	46.2	46.4	47.0	48.2
Portugal	55.3	55.0	54.8	55.6	57.2	58.3	59.5	60.5	61.0	60.8	60.6	61.7	61.7	62.0
Slovak Republic	..	52.6	53.0	54.6	54.0	53.5	52.1	51.5	51.8	51.4	52.2	50.9	50.9	51.9
Spain	31.5	31.5	32.5	33.8	35.2	36.5	39.1	42.0	43.8	44.9	46.8	49.0	51.9	54.0
Sweden	72.1	70.7	70.9	69.9	68.9	69.4	70.9	72.2	73.5	73.4	72.8	71.8	71.8	72.1
Switzerland	66.1	64.9	65.6	67.1	67.8	68.8	69.6	69.4	70.7	71.5	70.7	70.3	70.4	71.1
Turkey	25.8	30.4	30.2	30.3	28.0	28.5	28.9	26.2	26.3	26.6	25.2	24.3	23.7	23.8
United Kingdom	61.8	62.1	62.5	63.3	64.0	64.2	65.0	65.6	66.0	66.3	66.4	66.6	66.7	66.8
United States	64.0	65.2	65.8	66.3	67.1	67.4	67.6	67.8	67.1	66.1	65.7	65.4	65.6	66.1
EU15 total	49.3	49.4	49.9	50.4	50.9	51.8	53.0	54.2	55.0	55.6	56.0	56.9	57.5	58.5
OECD total	52.4	52.9	53.2	53.6	54.2	54.4	54.9	55.2	55.3	55.3	55.3	55.7	56.1	56.8
Brazil	51.6	..	53.1	50.3	50.7	50.1	51.3	..	51.3	52.9	52.9	54.3	55.3	55.9
China	..	..	..	..	..	..	..	..	69.4	68.5	67.8	66.5	66.6	68.2
Russian Federation	..	..	52.9	51.9	49.5	47.9	52.0	53.8	53.9	55.5	55.3	56.1	57.0	57.6

StatLink ⟶ http://dx.doi.org/10.1787/273881774445

Employment rates: women

Average annual growth in percentage, 1993-2006 or latest available period

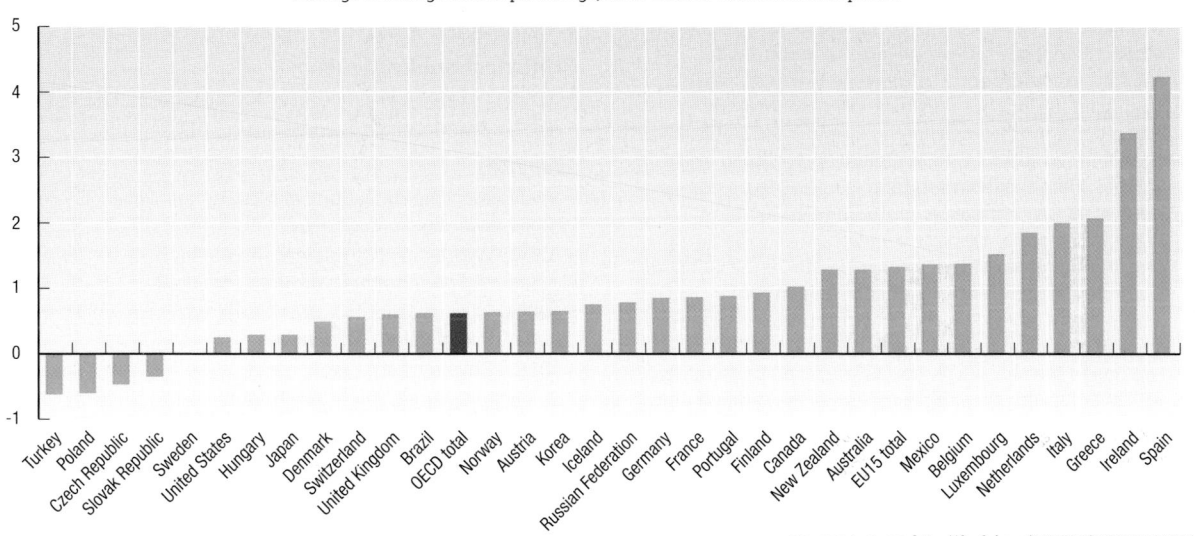

StatLink ⟶ http://dx.doi.org/10.1787/268242684081

EMPLOYMENT RATES BY AGE GROUP

The employment rates in this chapter show the percentage of persons of working age who are in employment, broken down into three age groups. The youngest age group contains persons who are just entering the labour market, the second group those in their prime working lives, and the third group those who are approaching retirement.

Employment rates in these different age groups are significantly affected by government policies with regard to higher education, pensions and retirement age.

Definition

To calculate the employment rate for a given age group, the total population in that age group is divided between those in employment and those who are not. The numbers in employment are then expressed as a percentage of the total numbers in that age group.

Employment is generally measured through household labour force surveys and, in accordance with the ILO Guidelines, employed persons are defined as those aged 15 or over who report that they have worked in gainful employment for at least one hour in the previous week. Those not in employment consist of persons who are out of work but seeking employment, students and all others who have excluded themselves from the labour force for one reason or another, such as incapacity or the need to look after young children or elderly relatives.

Comparability

All OECD countries use the ILO Guidelines for measuring employment, but the operational definitions used in national labour force surveys vary slightly in Iceland and Turkey. Employment levels are also likely to be affected by changes in the survey design and/or the survey conduct, but employment rates are likely to be fairly consistent over time.

Long-term trends

In general, employment rates for those in the prime working age group – 25 to 54 – are relatively similar between countries with ratios for most countries ranging between 70% and 90% in 2006. Rates are most variable between countries for those in the youngest age group where, in 2006, they ranged from under 25% in Hungary, Greece, Poland and Luxembourg to over 60% in the Switzerland, Denmark, Australia Netherlands, and Iceland. Employment rates for the oldest age group also vary considerably between countries, with more than 60% of this age group in employment in 2006 in Iceland, New Zealand, Sweden, Norway, Switzerland, Japan, the United States and Denmark but less than 30% employed in Poland.

Over the period 1993-2006, employment rates for the youngest age group have been falling for the OECD as a whole. This partly reflects government policies to encourage young people to increase their educational qualifications, but the falls have been particularly marked in countries where total employment rates have been falling, such as the Czech Republic, Poland and Turkey; when the labour market is tight, young people have particular difficulties in finding employment. For those in the prime working age group – 25 to 54 – employment rates have remained stable for the OECD as a whole, but there were significant falls in the employment rates for Turkey, Poland and Czech Republic and large gains in Ireland, Spain and the Netherlands. Persons in the oldest age group have fared particularly well overall, with the largest increases in employment rates for New Zealand, the Netherlands, Hungary, Belgium, Slovak republic and Czech Republic.

Source
- OECD (2007), *OECD Employment Outlook*, OECD, Paris.

Further information

Analytical publications
- Burniaux, J.-M., R. Duval and F. Jaumotte (2004), *Coping with Ageing*, OECD Economics Department Working Papers, No. 371, OECD, Paris.
- OECD (2000), *From Initial Education to Working Life: Making Transitions Work*, OECD, Paris.
- OECD (2006), *Ageing and Employment Policies*, OECD, Paris.

Statistical publications
- OECD (2004), *Quarterly Labour Force Statistics*, OECD, Paris.
- OECD (2007), *Labour Force Statistics*, OECD, Paris.

Websites
- NERO Meeting on Labour Market Issues, Paris, 25 June 2004, *www.oecd.org/eco/nero*.
- OECD Ageing and Employment Policies, *www.oecd.org/els/employment/olderworkers*.
- OECD Labour Statistics Database, *www.oecd.org/statistics/labour*.
- OECD Employment Data, *www.oecd.org/els/employment/data*.
- Youth Employment Summit, *www.yesweb.org*.
- OECD Job for Youth project, *www.oecd.org/employment/youth*.

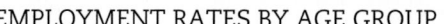

Employment rates for age group 15-24

Persons in employment as a percentage of population in that age group

	1993	1994	1995	1996	1997	1998	1999	2000	2001	2002	2003	2004	2005	2006
Australia	56.0	58.6	60.8	60.5	58.9	59.9	61.0	62.1	61.2	61.1	61.8	62.4	63.6	63.8
Austria	..	59.5	57.3	55.7	54.8	54.1	54.0	53.1	52.0	52.1	51.5	51.9	53.1	54.0
Belgium	28.1	27.5	26.6	26.1	25.2	26.0	25.5	30.3	28.5	28.5	27.1	28.1	26.6	26.2
Canada	53.4	53.8	53.8	52.7	51.5	52.5	54.5	56.3	56.3	57.5	58.3	58.0	57.8	58.7
Czech Republic	46.9	47.5	46.6	45.8	44.2	43.0	40.1	38.3	36.1	33.7	31.4	28.5	27.3	27.7
Denmark	60.3	62.1	65.9	66.0	68.2	66.4	66.0	67.1	61.7	64.0	59.4	61.3	62.0	63.7
Finland	30.1	27.9	29.0	29.8	33.3	34.9	38.8	39.8	40.3	39.4	38.5	38.1	39.2	40.6
France	24.2	22.0	21.8	21.3	19.9	20.8	20.7	23.2	24.3	24.1	27.0	26.4	26.0	25.3
Germany	52.7	51.4	49.1	47.0	45.8	46.7	47.1	47.2	47.0	44.8	42.4	41.9	42.6	43.9
Greece	27.5	26.7	26.5	25.4	24.5	28.1	26.8	26.9	26.0	26.8	26.2	27.4	25.3	24.5
Hungary	31.5	30.8	31.3	30.4	31.3	35.3	35.7	32.5	30.7	28.5	26.7	23.6	21.8	21.7
Iceland	52.4	51.7	54.9	54.8	55.7	61.6	65.1	68.2	66.8	59.4	68.1	66.3	71.6	72.9
Ireland	34.4	33.5	37.3	36.4	38.3	43.0	46.4	48.2	47.0	45.3	45.8	44.8	46.3	48.0
Italy	30.0	28.3	27.3	26.9	27.0	27.2	27.3	27.8	27.4	26.7	26.0	27.2	25.5	25.5
Japan	44.8	45.0	44.7	45.0	45.3	44.6	42.9	42.7	42.0	41.0	40.3	40.0	40.9	41.4
Korea	33.6	34.5	34.6	33.7	32.2	27.1	27.6	29.4	30.1	31.5	30.8	31.2	29.9	27.2
Luxembourg	45.7	42.8	38.2	36.9	34.7	33.1	31.7	31.8	32.3	32.3	27.0	23.3	24.9	..
Mexico	51.6	50.3	48.2	48.2	49.2	50.3	50.3	48.9	47.2	45.4	44.1	44.3	43.7	44.8
Netherlands	55.5	55.4	56.3	58.3	61.1	62.4	66.0	66.5	66.8	66.7	64.9	63.2	61.9	63.9
New Zealand	53.9	56.5	59.4	59.5	58.2	55.7	54.6	54.6	55.8	56.6	56.3	56.8	56.9	58.8
Norway	47.8	48.4	49.2	52.3	55.1	57.9	57.8	58.1	56.5	56.9	55.3	54.4	52.9	53.1
Poland	29.5	28.0	27.3	27.9	28.8	28.6	24.3	24.5	22.1	20.0	19.6	20.0	20.9	24.0
Portugal	43.1	40.5	37.6	37.1	39.2	42.8	42.6	42.0	42.7	41.9	38.4	36.9	36.1	35.8
Slovak Republic	..	34.4	34.8	36.8	36.4	35.0	31.0	29.0	27.9	27.2	27.6	26.5	25.6	25.7
Spain	29.5	28.3	28.6	28.3	29.4	31.0	34.4	36.3	37.1	36.6	36.8	38.4	41.9	43.3
Sweden	42.4	41.3	42.5	40.3	39.7	41.6	43.8	46.1	46.7	46.5	45.1	42.8	42.5	44.0
Switzerland	64.6	60.3	60.1	63.3	62.9	63.2	64.8	65.1	63.9	65.4	63.5	61.9	59.9	63.3
Turkey	39.5	43.0	41.0	42.0	40.3	39.5	39.7	37.0	35.3	33.0	30.5	31.6	31.2	30.8
United Kingdom	58.8	58.8	59.0	60.2	60.8	60.8	60.8	61.5	61.0	60.9	59.7	60.1	58.6	57.3
United States	57.2	58.1	58.3	57.6	58.0	59.0	59.0	59.7	57.7	55.7	53.9	53.9	53.9	54.2
EU15 total	39.8	39.0	38.3	37.8	37.8	38.8	39.5	40.7	40.8	40.2	39.6	39.9	39.9	40.2
OECD total	45.7	45.7	45.1	44.9	45.0	45.3	45.4	45.6	44.7	43.7	42.7	42.9	42.9	43.3
Brazil	58.7	..	57.7	54.7	54.0	52.1	51.7	..	50.8	51.7	50.8	52.4	52.7	52.6
China	..	..	..	..	..	..	..	..	70.1	65.7	61.5	57.1	55.7	52.8
Russian Federation	..	..	41.0	38.0	33.0	29.6	34.4	34.6	33.5	34.2	32.7	32.5	32.9	32.5

StatLink 〰️🖳 http://dx.doi.org/10.1787/274004037286

Employment rates for age group 15-24

Persons in employment as a percentage of population in that age group, 2006 or latest available year

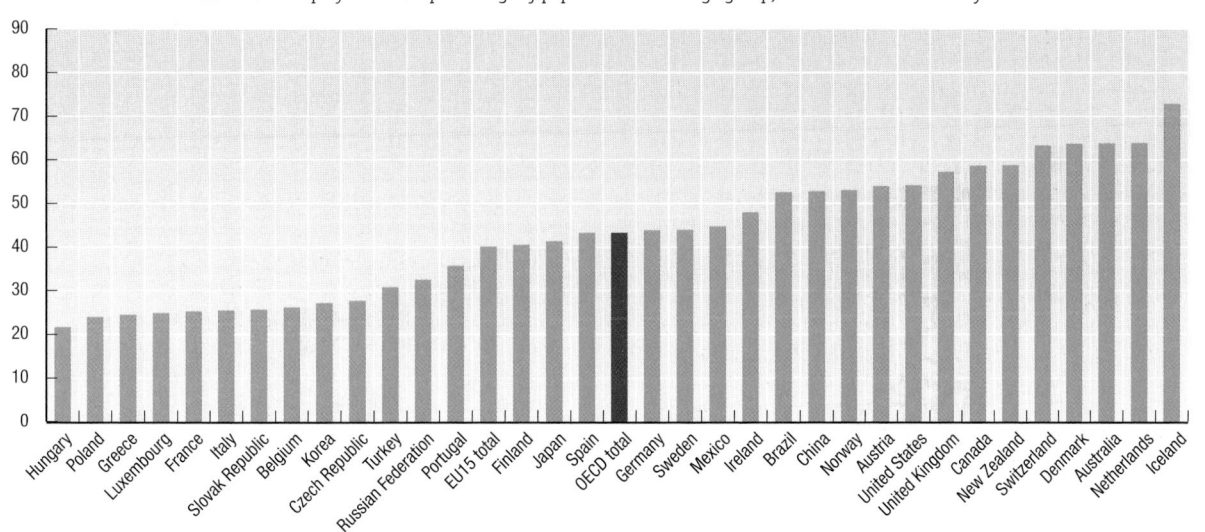

StatLink 〰️🖳 http://dx.doi.org/10.1787/268244816088

Employment rates for age group 25-54

Persons in employment as a percentage of population in that age group

	1993	1994	1995	1996	1997	1998	1999	2000	2001	2002	2003	2004	2005	2006
Australia	72.9	73.6	75.2	74.9	74.9	75.3	75.5	76.3	76.3	76.7	77.2	77.4	78.8	79.2
Austria	..	79.5	80.4	80.1	80.6	80.7	81.6	82.2	82.4	83.2	83.7	82.6	82.6	83.5
Belgium	73.6	73.1	73.8	73.9	74.6	74.4	76.4	77.9	76.6	76.6	76.1	77.3	78.3	78.2
Canada	74.9	75.5	76.2	76.2	77.3	78.3	79.2	79.9	79.8	80.3	80.8	81.3	81.3	81.6
Czech Republic	86.3	86.3	86.3	85.8	85.0	83.7	81.9	81.6	82.1	82.5	81.7	81.4	82.0	82.5
Denmark	80.8	80.5	81.7	82.2	82.8	83.4	84.4	84.3	84.5	84.7	83.5	84.0	83.9	85.5
Finland	75.0	74.9	76.1	76.8	77.5	79.0	80.4	80.9	81.5	81.6	81.1	81.0	81.7	82.5
France	77.0	76.3	77.0	76.9	76.4	76.8	77.0	78.3	79.3	79.4	79.1	79.3	79.6	80.0
Germany	76.8	76.2	76.8	76.8	76.7	78.0	78.7	79.3	79.3	78.8	78.2	78.1	77.4	78.8
Greece	67.8	68.6	68.8	69.5	69.7	69.9	70.0	70.2	70.4	71.9	73.1	73.7	74.3	75.3
Hungary	72.5	71.7	70.7	70.4	70.2	70.3	72.3	73.0	73.1	73.0	73.7	73.6	73.7	74.2
Iceland	87.0	87.5	89.1	89.3	88.2	88.9	90.9	90.6	90.7	90.0	89.2	88.0	88.2	89.1
Ireland	60.9	62.7	64.7	66.3	67.4	70.6	73.2	75.3	76.4	76.6	76.0	76.7	78.0	78.4
Italy	66.7	65.8	65.5	65.7	65.8	66.3	67.1	68.0	69.2	70.1	70.8	72.1	72.2	73.3
Japan	79.8	79.5	79.3	79.6	79.9	79.2	78.7	78.6	78.6	78.0	78.3	78.6	79.0	79.6
Korea	73.0	73.6	74.2	74.7	74.8	70.2	70.3	72.2	72.6	73.4	73.1	73.4	73.4	73.9
Luxembourg	73.3	73.5	71.9	73.2	74.4	74.7	76.7	78.2	78.7	79.1	77.8	79.3	80.7	..
Mexico	65.1	65.0	63.7	65.2	67.6	67.3	66.9	67.4	67.1	67.6	67.3	68.7	68.8	69.9
Netherlands	73.8	73.7	75.0	75.8	77.5	79.3	80.4	81.0	81.6	81.2	81.1	80.6	80.9	82.0
New Zealand	74.9	76.2	77.6	78.4	77.8	76.8	77.6	78.6	79.3	79.6	79.8	80.8	82.0	82.1
Norway	80.7	81.3	82.4	83.7	85.0	85.8	85.5	85.3	85.1	84.4	82.9	83.1	83.2	84.4
Poland	74.4	73.8	74.2	74.6	74.7	75.0	73.7	70.9	69.3	67.5	67.6	68.3	69.5	71.8
Portugal	79.5	78.7	78.7	78.7	79.3	80.1	80.6	81.8	82.2	81.5	81.0	81.1	80.8	81.3
Slovak Republic	..	78.4	78.7	80.3	79.3	78.5	76.1	74.7	74.8	75.1	76.0	74.7	75.3	77.2
Spain	58.7	58.4	59.5	60.6	62.0	63.6	66.1	68.4	69.5	70.1	71.3	72.7	74.4	75.8
Sweden	83.2	81.9	82.6	81.8	80.7	81.3	82.5	83.8	84.6	84.2	83.5	82.9	83.9	84.7
Switzerland	83.8	83.2	84.2	83.6	83.4	85.0	85.1	85.4	86.0	86.0	84.8	84.7	85.1	85.2
Turkey	58.0	59.8	60.5	60.1	59.0	59.2	58.2	56.7	55.5	54.6	54.0	54.1	54.1	54.2
United Kingdom	76.3	76.5	77.1	77.4	78.3	79.0	79.6	80.2	80.5	80.3	80.7	80.7	81.1	81.2
United States	78.5	79.2	79.7	80.2	80.9	81.1	81.4	81.5	80.5	79.3	78.8	79.0	79.3	79.8
EU15 total	72.9	72.7	73.2	73.4	73.7	74.6	75.5	76.4	77.0	77.0	77.1	77.5	77.7	78.6
OECD total	74.4	74.5	74.8	75.1	75.5	75.6	75.7	76.0	75.8	75.4	75.2	75.6	75.8	76.5
Brazil	73.9	..	75.0	72.8	73.3	72.8	73.2	..	73.1	74.2	74.0	75.4	75.9	76.3
China	..	..	..	..	..	..	..	..	88.7	87.7	86.6	85.6	85.2	88.0
Russian Federation	..	..	81.1	80.7	77.9	76.2	77.9	80.2	80.7	81.8	81.4	82.2	82.9	83.1

StatLink ⟨⟨⟨ http://dx.doi.org/10.1787/274008276366

Employment rates for age group 25-54

Persons in employment as a percentage of population in that age group, 2006 or latest available year

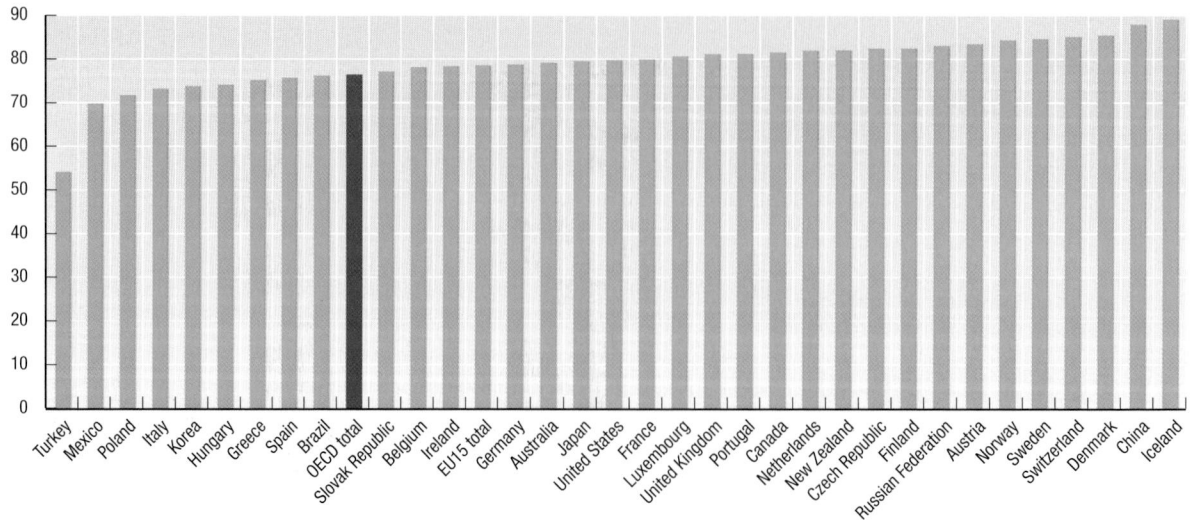

StatLink ⟨⟨⟨ http://dx.doi.org/10.1787/268252280751

OECD FACTBOOK 2008 – ISBN 978-92-64-04054-0 – © OECD 2008

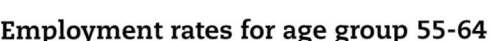

Employment rates for age group 55-64

Persons in employment as a percentage of population in that age group

	1993	1994	1995	1996	1997	1998	1999	2000	2001	2002	2003	2004	2005	2006
Australia	38.9	40.5	41.7	42.4	42.7	43.9	44.3	46.2	46.7	48.7	50.5	52.0	53.7	55.6
Austria	..	28.4	30.4	29.2	28.6	29.0	29.6	28.1	28.2	29.1	30.1	28.8	31.8	35.5
Belgium	21.9	22.4	23.3	21.8	22.0	22.5	24.7	25.0	25.2	25.8	28.1	30.1	32.1	30.4
Canada	43.0	43.6	43.2	43.5	44.4	45.2	46.8	48.1	48.2	50.1	53.0	53.9	54.8	55.6
Czech Republic	31.3	32.3	34.8	37.3	38.3	37.1	37.5	36.3	37.1	40.8	42.3	42.6	44.6	45.2
Denmark	51.3	50.2	49.3	47.5	51.4	50.4	54.2	54.6	56.5	57.3	60.7	61.8	59.8	60.9
Finland	34.8	33.5	34.4	35.6	35.7	36.2	39.2	42.3	45.9	47.8	49.9	51.0	52.6	54.5
France	33.9	33.4	33.5	33.5	33.6	33.0	34.2	34.3	36.5	39.3	40.3	40.6	40.7	40.5
Germany	35.9	35.9	37.4	38.0	38.3	38.4	37.8	37.6	37.9	38.6	39.0	41.8	45.5	48.5
Greece	38.8	39.5	40.5	40.7	40.7	39.1	38.4	39.0	38.0	38.9	41.0	39.4	41.6	42.4
Hungary	19.1	17.0	17.1	17.4	17.3	16.6	19.4	21.9	23.5	25.6	29.0	31.1	33.0	33.6
Iceland	83.2	84.7	85.1	83.8	83.7	86.7	85.9	84.2	85.6	87.2	83.3	82.0	84.8	84.9
Ireland	38.9	39.5	39.4	40.3	40.2	41.6	43.8	45.2	46.6	48.0	49.3	49.5	51.7	53.4
Italy	30.4	29.4	28.4	28.7	28.0	27.9	27.6	27.7	28.0	28.9	30.3	30.5	31.4	32.5
Japan	64.5	63.7	63.7	63.6	64.2	63.8	63.4	62.8	62.0	61.6	62.1	63.0	63.9	64.7
Korea	61.5	62.9	63.6	63.2	63.8	58.7	58.2	57.8	58.3	59.5	57.8	58.5	58.7	59.3
Luxembourg	26.1	23.2	24.0	22.6	23.7	25.0	26.3	27.2	24.8	27.9	30.3	30.4	31.7	..
Mexico	53.8	52.4	50.0	51.3	54.5	52.6	54.1	51.7	51.1	52.2	52.9	53.8	52.6	55.0
Netherlands	28.2	29.0	29.4	30.5	31.7	33.4	35.1	37.6	39.2	42.7	42.9	44.2	44.9	46.9
New Zealand	44.5	47.3	50.4	53.9	54.5	55.7	56.9	57.2	60.7	63.4	64.3	67.2	69.7	70.4
Norway	60.7	61.6	63.1	64.6	66.0	67.2	67.3	67.1	67.4	68.4	68.6	68.0	67.6	67.4
Poland	35.1	34.4	33.8	33.0	33.6	32.3	32.5	28.4	29.0	27.9	28.6	28.0	29.1	28.1
Portugal	44.9	45.9	44.6	46.2	47.1	49.7	50.4	50.8	50.0	50.9	51.1	50.3	50.5	50.1
Slovak Republic	..	21.3	21.7	22.8	21.4	22.8	22.3	21.3	22.3	22.9	24.6	26.8	30.4	33.2
Spain	34.5	32.7	32.4	33.2	34.1	35.1	35.1	37.0	39.2	39.7	40.8	41.3	43.1	44.1
Sweden	63.4	61.9	62.0	63.4	62.7	63.1	64.0	65.1	67.0	68.4	69.0	69.5	69.6	69.8
Switzerland	63.1	61.1	61.7	63.3	63.9	64.4	64.6	63.3	67.3	64.6	65.7	65.2	65.1	65.7
Turkey	37.7	40.8	41.7	41.6	40.5	41.1	39.3	36.4	35.9	35.3	32.7	33.1	30.8	30.1
United Kingdom	46.6	47.4	47.5	47.8	48.5	48.3	49.4	50.4	52.1	53.1	55.4	56.2	56.7	57.4
United States	53.8	54.4	55.1	55.9	57.2	57.7	57.7	57.8	58.6	59.5	59.9	59.9	60.8	61.8
EU15 total	36.5	36.1	36.4	36.8	37.1	37.3	37.7	38.3	39.3	40.7	41.9	42.9	44.4	45.6
OECD total	46.3	46.1	46.4	46.9	47.6	47.6	47.9	47.9	48.4	49.4	50.2	51.0	52.0	53.0
Brazil	52.6	..	53.3	50.7	51.1	51.0	52.2	..	51.2	52.7	52.1	52.5	54.0	54.0
China	..	..	..	..	..	..	..	..	56.5	55.9	54.5	52.6	58.3	64.5
Russian Federation	..	..	33.7	32.6	31.6	29.4	34.8	34.8	31.9	35.2	37.8	40.4	44.6	47.4

StatLink http://dx.doi.org/10.1787/274026503021

Employment rates for age group 55-64

Persons in employment as a percentage of population in that age group, 2006 or latest available year

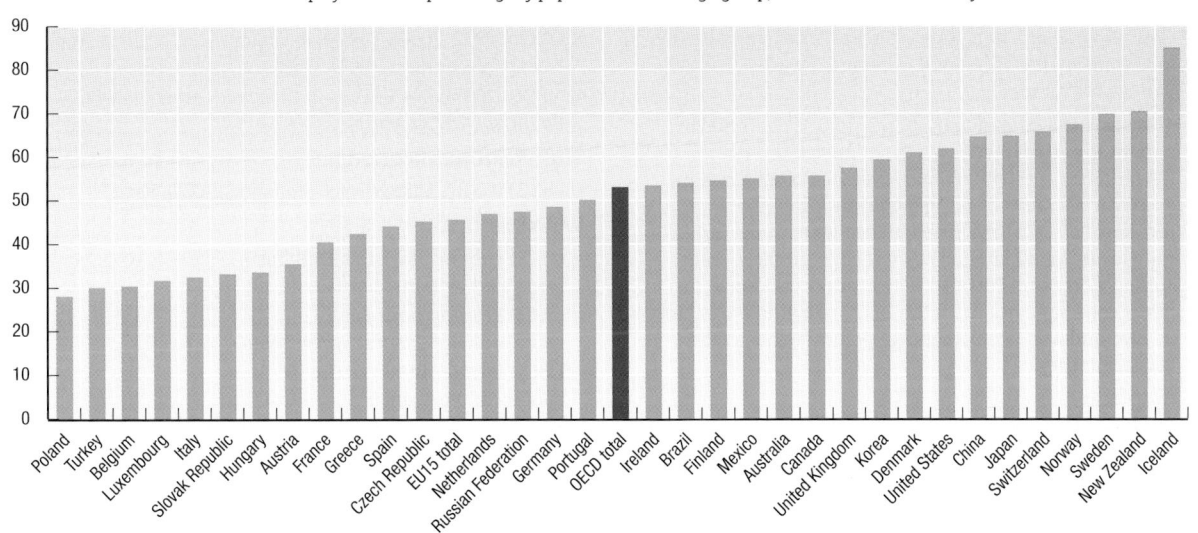

StatLink http://dx.doi.org/10.1787/268264658852

PART-TIME EMPLOYMENT

Part-time work accounted for a substantial share of overall employment growth in many OECD countries between 1993 and 2006. Part-time work has been an important factor behind employment growth of groups that are often under-represented in the labour force, such as women, youths and, to a lesser extent, older workers.

Recent surveys in a large number of OECD countries show that most people who work part-time do so from choice. This suggests that countries with little part-time employment could foster increased employment by policies that promote the availability of part-time positions. This would particularly benefit women with young children.

Definition

Part-time employment refers to persons who usually work less than 30 hours per week in their main job. Both employees and the self-employed may be part-time workers.

Employment is generally measured through household labour force surveys and, according to the ILO Guidelines, employed persons are defined as those aged 15 or over who report that they have worked in gainful employment for at least one hour in the previous week. The rates shown here refer to the numbers of persons who usually work less than 30 hours per week as a percentage of the total number of those in employment.

Comparability

All OECD countries use the ILO Guidelines for measuring employment, but the operational definitions used in national labour force surveys vary slightly in Iceland and Turkey. Employment levels are also likely to be affected by changes in the survey design and/or the survey conduct, but employment rates are likely to be fairly consistent over time. Information on the number of hours worked is collected in household labour force surveys and the rates shown here are considered to be of good comparability.

Long-term trends

For the OECD as a whole, the part-time employment rate increased by 7% between 1993 and 2006. Part-time employment rates grew considerably in Austria, Germany, Ireland, Italy, Korea and Spain but they also fell in several countries including Iceland, Sweden, United States and Turkey.

The chart shows great variation between countries in part-time employment in 2006. In Australia, Japan, Netherlands and Switzerland, over 25% of all those in employment were working part-time while the incidence of part-time employment were under 10% in the Slovak Republic, Hungary, Czech Republic, Greece, Turkey, Korea and Portugal. The average incidence of part-time employment for the OECD as a whole was 16% in 2006 and was two percentage points higher in the EU15 countries.

Source

- OECD (2007), *OECD Employment Outlook*, OECD, Paris.

Further information

Analytical publications

- OECD (1999), *Implementing the OECD Jobs Strategy: Assessing Performance and Policy*, OECD, Paris.
- OECD (2002-2004), *Babies and Bosses – Reconciling Work and Family Life*, series, OECD, Paris.
- OECD (2003), *The Sources of Economic Growth in OECD Countries*, OECD, Paris.

Statistical publications

- OECD (2007), *Labour Force Statistics*, OECD, Paris.

Websites

- OECD Labour Statistics Database, *www.oecd.org/statistics/labour*.
- OECD Employment Data, *www.oecd.org/els/employment/data*.
- OECD Productivity Database, *www.oecd.org/statistics/productivity*.

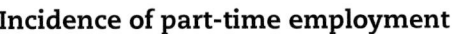
Incidence of part-time employment

As a percentage of total employment

	1993	1994	1995	1996	1997	1998	1999	2000	2001	2002	2003	2004	2005	2006
Australia	24.3	24.4	25.0	25.2	26.0	25.9	26.1	26.2	27.2	27.5	27.9	27.1	27.3	27.1
Austria	..	..	11.1	10.9	10.8	11.5	12.3	12.2	12.4	13.6	13.5	15.4	16.0	17.3
Belgium	14.7	14.6	14.6	14.8	15.0	15.6	19.9	19.0	17.0	17.9	18.0	18.9	18.5	19.3
Canada	19.2	18.9	18.8	19.1	19.1	18.8	18.4	18.1	18.1	18.8	18.9	18.5	18.3	18.1
Czech Republic	3.6	3.6	3.4	3.4	3.4	3.3	3.4	3.2	3.2	2.9	3.2	3.1	3.3	3.3
Denmark	19.0	17.3	16.9	16.6	17.2	17.1	15.3	16.1	14.7	16.0	15.7	17.3	17.6	18.1
Finland	8.9	8.9	8.7	8.5	9.3	9.7	9.9	10.4	10.5	11.0	11.3	11.3	11.2	11.4
France	13.2	13.8	14.2	14.0	14.8	14.7	14.6	14.2	13.8	13.8	12.8	13.2	13.5	13.3
Germany	12.8	13.5	14.2	14.9	15.8	16.6	17.1	17.6	18.3	18.8	19.6	20.1	21.8	21.9
Greece	7.1	7.8	7.8	8.0	8.3	9.1	8.0	5.5	4.9	5.6	5.6	6.0	6.1	7.5
Hungary	..	..	2.8	2.7	2.9	2.9	3.2	2.9	2.5	2.6	3.2	3.3	3.2	2.7
Iceland	22.4	22.6	22.5	20.9	22.4	23.2	21.2	20.4	20.4	20.1	16.0	16.6	16.4	16.0
Ireland	13.1	13.5	14.3	14.2	15.0	17.6	17.9	18.1	17.9	18.6	19.3	19.3	19.6	19.9
Italy	10.0	10.0	10.5	10.5	11.3	11.2	11.8	12.2	12.2	11.9	12.0	14.8	14.6	14.9
Japan	21.1	21.4	20.1	21.8	23.3	23.6	24.1	22.6	24.9	25.1	26.0	25.5	25.8	24.5
Korea	4.5	4.5	4.3	4.3	5.0	6.7	7.7	7.0	7.3	7.6	7.7	8.4	9.0	8.8
Luxembourg	9.8	10.7	11.3	10.4	11.0	12.6	12.1	12.4	13.3	12.5	13.3	13.2	13.9	12.7
Mexico	..	..	16.6	14.9	15.5	15.0	13.7	13.5	13.7	13.5	13.4	15.1	..	..
Netherlands	27.9	28.9	29.4	29.3	29.1	30.0	30.4	32.1	33.0	33.9	34.6	35.0	35.7	35.5
New Zealand	20.8	21.0	20.9	21.9	22.3	22.7	23.0	22.2	22.4	22.6	22.3	22.0	21.7	21.3
Norway	22.0	21.5	21.4	21.6	21.0	20.8	20.7	20.2	20.1	20.6	21.0	21.1	20.8	21.1
Poland	..	..	..	..	11.9	11.8	14.0	12.8	11.6	11.7	11.5	12.0	11.7	10.8
Portugal	8.8	9.5	8.6	9.2	10.2	10.0	9.4	9.4	9.2	9.7	10.0	9.6	9.8	9.3
Slovak Republic	..	2.7	2.3	2.1	2.0	2.0	1.8	1.9	1.9	1.6	2.3	2.8	2.6	2.5
Spain	6.0	6.4	7.0	7.5	7.9	7.7	7.8	7.7	7.8	7.7	8.0	8.5	11.3	11.1
Sweden	15.4	15.8	15.1	14.8	14.2	13.5	14.5	14.0	13.9	13.8	14.1	14.4	13.5	13.4
Switzerland	23.2	23.2	22.9	23.7	24.0	24.2	24.8	24.4	24.8	24.8	25.1	24.9	25.1	25.5
Turkey	8.9	8.8	6.4	5.5	6.1	6.0	7.7	9.4	6.2	6.6	6.0	6.6	5.8	7.9
United Kingdom	22.1	22.4	22.3	22.9	22.9	23.0	22.9	23.0	22.7	23.3	23.7	24.0	23.5	23.4
United States	14.7	14.2	14.0	13.9	13.5	13.4	13.3	12.6	12.8	13.1	13.2	13.2	12.8	12.6
EU15 total	14.1	14.6	14.8	15.1	15.6	15.9	16.1	16.2	16.2	16.5	16.6	17.3	18.0	18.0
OECD total	15.1	15.1	14.8	14.9	15.2	15.3	15.5	15.2	15.4	15.6	15.8	16.1	16.3	16.1
Brazil	16.3	..	16.2	15.3	15.9	16.3	16.9	..	16.0	17.0	17.1	17.3	17.9	18.0

StatLink http://dx.doi.org/10.1787/274035667834

Incidence of part-time employment

As a percentage of total employment, 2006 or latest available year

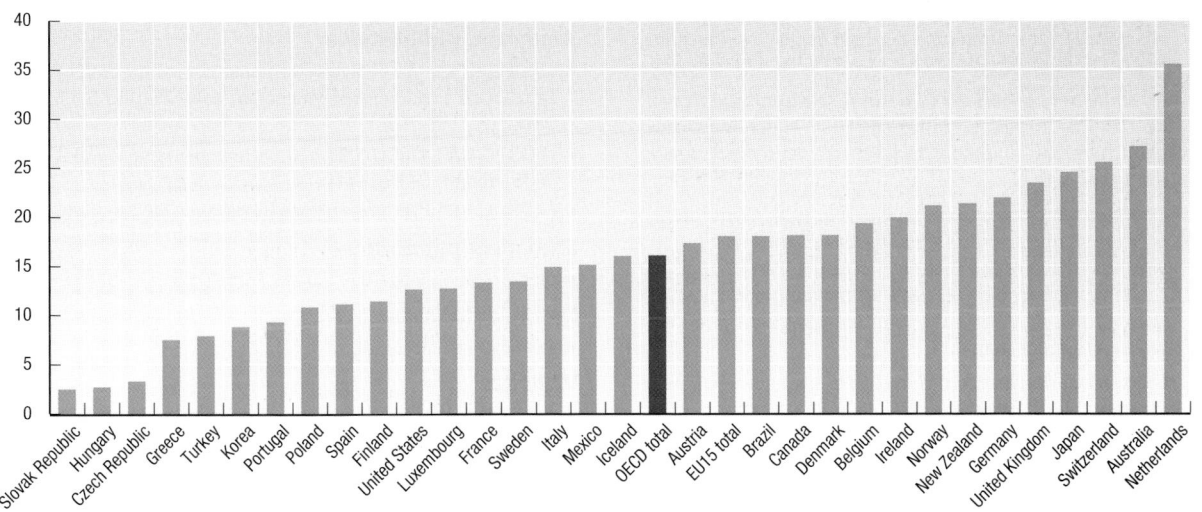

StatLink http://dx.doi.org/10.1787/268310713028

SELF-EMPLOYMENT

Self-employment may be seen either as a survival strategy for those who cannot find any other means of earning an income or as evidence of entrepreneurial spirit and a desire to be one's own boss. The self-employment rates shown in this section reflect these various motives.

Definition

Employment is generally measured through household labour force surveys and, according to the ILO Guidelines, employed persons are defined as those aged 15 or over who report that they have worked in gainful employment for at least one hour in the previous week.

Self-employed persons include employers, own-account workers, members of producers' co-operatives, and unpaid family workers. The last of these are unpaid in the sense that they do not have a formal contract to receive a fixed amount of income at regular intervals, but they share in the income generated by the enterprise; unpaid family workers are particularly important in farming and retail trade. Note that all persons who work in corporate enterprises, including company directors, are considered to be employees.

The rates shown here are the percentages of the self-employed in total civilian employment *i.e.*, total employment less military employees.

Comparability

All OECD countries use the ILO Guidelines for measuring employment, but the operational definitions used in national labour force surveys vary slightly in Iceland and Turkey. Employment levels are also likely to be affected by changes in the survey design and/or the survey conduct, but employment rates are likely to be fairly consistent over time.

Note that the composition of the self-employed with regard to the four categories listed above varies considerably among countries. In particular, countries with relatively large numbers of small farms, Brazil, Mexico and Turkey, for example, will have relatively large numbers of unpaid family workers.

Long-term trends

In 2006, the total self-employment rates (men and women together) ranged from under 9% in Luxembourg, United States, Norway, and Denmark to well over 30% in Korea, Mexico, Brazil, Greece and Turkey. In general, self-employment rates are highest in countries with low per capita income although Italy, with a self-employment rate of 26.7%, is a striking exception. Ireland and Spain are also countries with both high per capita incomes and high self-employment rates.

Over the period 1993-2006, self-employment rates have been falling in most countries although there have been small increases in Austria and Germany and much larger increases in the Czech Republic and the Slovak Republic.

The levels and changes in total self-employment rates conceal significant differences between men and women. In half of the member countries, over 17% of all men in employment were self-employed in 2006; half of the member countries had a self-employment rate for women of more than 10%.

Growth rates have also differed. Self-employment rates for men rose in five countries – Belgium, Austria, Germany, the Slovak Republic and the Czech Republic. For women, self-employment decreased in all countries.

Source
- OECD (2007), *Labour Force Statistics*, OECD, Paris.

Further information
Analytical publications
- OECD (2000), "The Partial Renaissance of the Self-Employed", *OECD Employment Outlook*, Chapter 5, OECD, Paris, pp. 155-199.
- OECD (2005), *OECD SME and Entrepreneurship Outlook – 2005 Edition*, OECD, Paris.
- OECD (2007), *OECD Employment Outlook*, OECD, Paris.

Statistical publications
- OECD (2004), *Quarterly Labour Force Statistics*, OECD, Paris.

Online databases
- *Employment Statistics*.

Websites
- OECD Directorate for Employment, Labour and Social Affairs, *www.oecd.org/els*.
- OECD Entrepreneurship at Local Level, *www.oecd.org/tds/leed/entrepreneurship*.

Self-employment rates: total
As a percentage of total civilian employment

	1993	1994	1995	1996	1997	1998	1999	2000	2001	2002	2003	2004	2005	2006
Australia	16.5	15.9	15.4	15.1	15.1	14.6	14.5	14.1	13.8	13.9	13.5	13.3	13.0	13.0
Austria	13.1	13.8	14.4	14.0	13.6	13.7	13.4	13.1	13.2	13.1	12.8	12.8	13.3	13.6
Belgium	18.9	18.9	18.8	18.8	18.6	18.2	17.8	14.8	15.0	15.0	15.0	14.9	14.7	14.7
Canada	10.7	10.7	10.6	11.1	11.4	11.7	11.3	10.6	9.9	9.8	9.8	9.5	9.4	9.1
Czech Republic	9.4	10.6	12.0	12.2	12.4	13.8	14.5	15.2	15.2	16.1	17.3	16.9	16.1	16.2
Denmark	10.8	10.0	9.6	9.5	9.1	9.4	9.1	8.7	8.9	9.0	8.8	8.7	8.7	8.9
Finland	16.0	16.3	15.6	15.3	14.9	14.3	14.0	13.7	13.0	12.9	12.9	12.8	12.7	12.9
France	11.7	11.3	10.8	10.4	10.1	9.8	9.5	9.2	8.9	8.8	8.8	8.9	9.0	9.0
Germany	10.4	10.6	10.7	10.8	10.9	11.0	10.8	11.0	11.1	11.2	11.4	12.1	12.4	12.2
Greece	46.7	46.7	46.1	45.7	45.2	43.6	42.2	41.9	39.9	39.3	39.0	36.6	36.4	36.3
Hungary	18.1	17.8	18.0	18.1	17.4	16.1	15.7	15.2	14.5	13.9	13.5	13.4	13.8	12.8
Iceland	18.0	18.4	19.7	18.2	17.7	17.9	17.7	18.0	16.9	16.6	13.9	14.1	14.2	14.7
Ireland	23.4	22.7	22.2	20.8	20.8	20.2	19.2	18.9	18.1	17.8	17.5	18.0	17.4	16.5
Italy	28.9	29.0	29.3	29.3	29.1	29.1	28.6	28.5	28.2	27.7	27.5	28.4	27.0	26.7
Japan	19.1	18.7	18.3	17.7	17.5	17.3	17.2	16.6	15.9	15.4	15.1	14.9	14.7	13.8
Korea	37.9	37.1	36.8	36.7	36.8	38.3	37.6	36.8	36.7	36.0	34.9	34.0	33.6	32.8
Luxembourg	8.3	8.4	8.4	8.3	8.2	8.0	7.7	7.4	7.1	6.9	6.8	6.7	6.6	6.4
Mexico	43.8	43.7	41.2	40.1	40.9	38.6	38.0	36.0	36.4	36.8	36.6	36.5	35.5	34.5
Netherlands	11.6	12.3	12.4	12.5	12.6	11.8	11.3	12.0	11.5	11.6	11.5	11.2	11.0	11.0
New Zealand	21.2	21.1	20.9	20.9	20.0	20.4	21.2	20.7	19.9	19.4	19.4	19.2	18.5	17.7
Norway	10.2	9.8	9.3	8.7	8.2	8.3	7.8	7.4	7.2	7.1	7.3	7.4	7.4	8.5
Poland	31.2	30.9	29.7	29.5	28.3	27.2	26.9	27.4	28.0	28.1	27.3	26.7	25.8	24.4
Portugal	26.3	27.7	27.9	28.6	28.9	28.1	27.0	26.1	26.8	26.6	26.7	25.9	25.1	24.1
Slovak Republic	..	6.3	6.5	6.4	6.3	6.8	7.7	7.9	8.4	8.6	9.7	12.0	12.6	12.6
Spain	26.0	25.9	25.2	24.7	23.5	22.7	21.3	20.2	19.8	19.0	18.3	18.1	18.2	17.9
Sweden	10.8	11.1	11.2	11.0	10.8	10.6	10.6	10.3	10.0	9.8	9.6	9.9	9.8	10.0
Switzerland	12.7	12.7	12.7	13.4	13.9	14.0	14.0	13.2	12.9	12.5	11.9	11.4	11.2	11.2
Turkey	57.8	59.1	58.5	57.2	55.4	55.4	55.0	51.4	52.8	50.2	49.4	49.2	45.8	43.5
United Kingdom	15.6	15.7	15.6	14.9	14.5	13.7	13.2	12.8	12.8	12.7	13.2	13.6	13.0	13.2
United States	8.8	8.8	8.5	8.4	8.2	7.9	7.7	7.4	7.4	7.2	7.6	7.6	7.5	7.4
EU15 total	17.2	17.3	17.2	17.0	16.8	16.5	16.0	15.8	15.7	15.5	15.6	15.9	15.6	14.2
OECD total	19.7	19.8	19.4	19.2	19.0	18.6	18.3	17.6	17.5	17.3	17.2	17.3	16.9	16.0
Brazil	37.9	..	38.6	37.0	37.8	37.7	38.5	..	35.6	35.7	35.6	34.9	34.9	34.0
China	..	..	..	..	..	..	..	..	53.4	51.8	48.8	45.8	48.2	52.0
Russian Federation	..	..	1.9	2.1	2.9	2.9	8.0	7.6	6.0	5.9	5.7	5.8	6.1	6.0

StatLink http://dx.doi.org/10.1787/274046608842

Self-employment rates: total
As a percentage of total civilian employment, 2006

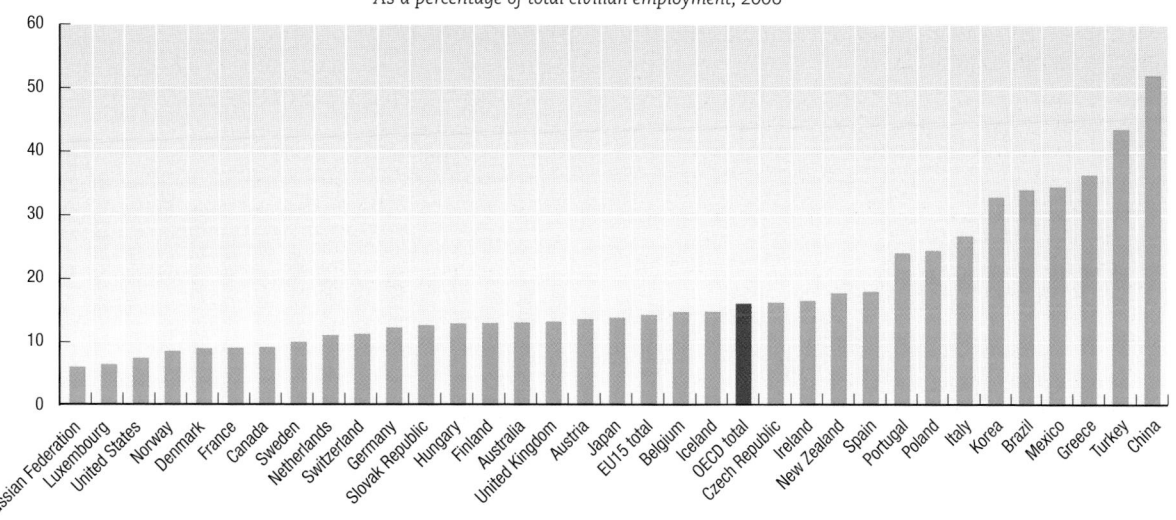

StatLink http://dx.doi.org/10.1787/268324348764

Self-employment rates: men
As a percentage of total male civilian employment

	1993	1994	1995	1996	1997	1998	1999	2000	2001	2002	2003	2004	2005	2006
Australia	19.0	18.3	17.9	17.6	17.4	17.1	17.1	16.7	16.6	16.7	16.3	15.9	15.6	15.6
Austria	..	..	13.9	14.1	14.0	14.2	14.0	13.9	14.1	14.2	14.0	14.8	15.3	15.4
Belgium	19.4	19.6	19.7	19.9	19.9	19.6	19.5	19.2	19.7	19.6	19.8	19.6	19.8	19.9
Canada	12.1	12.0	11.8	12.2	12.5	12.9	12.5	11.7	11.2	10.8	11.0	10.8	10.5	10.2
Czech Republic	12.0	13.7	15.1	15.7	15.9	17.3	18.4	19.1	19.1	20.3	21.7	21.5	20.4	20.3
Denmark	..	..	12.4	12.4	12.4	12.4	12.2	11.7	12.4	12.5	11.9	11.9	11.6	11.7
Finland	21.0	21.1	20.2	19.7	19.0	18.2	18.1	17.8	16.8	16.7	16.7	16.7	16.7	17.1
France	13.7	13.3	12.9	12.6	12.3	11.8	11.5	11.1	10.8	10.5	10.7	10.7	10.9	10.9
Germany	11.9	12.3	12.5	12.7	13.0	13.1	13.2	13.4	13.4	13.6	14.0	14.9	14.9	14.7
Greece	47.7	47.6	47.4	46.9	46.8	44.9	43.8	43.7	42.1	41.4	41.0	39.4	39.1	39.1
Hungary	21.9	21.9	22.1	22.6	21.5	19.9	19.5	19.2	18.1	17.3	17.1	17.9	17.3	16.0
Iceland	24.2	25.6	27.6	23.9	23.2	23.9	23.7	24.0	23.1	23.6	19.2	19.3	20.1	20.8
Ireland	30.9	30.3	29.9	28.2	28.1	27.4	26.1	25.8	25.2	25.2	24.7	25.4	24.8	23.7
Italy	31.4	31.6	32.3	32.5	32.4	32.5	32.1	32.3	32.2	31.7	31.5	32.4	31.2	30.8
Japan	16.6	16.4	16.1	15.8	15.9	15.6	15.8	15.5	15.0	14.8	14.7	14.7	14.5	13.9
Korea	35.4	34.7	34.3	34.4	34.7	36.3	36.1	35.7	36.0	35.7	35.3	34.4	34.0	33.2
Mexico	45.1	44.2	41.6	40.6	40.8	38.7	38.1	36.4	36.9	36.9	36.5	36.2	35.7	34.4
Netherlands	..	..	13.7	13.8	14.0	13.3	12.7	13.4	13.0	13.5	13.5	13.3	13.1	12.9
New Zealand	26.3	25.8	25.4	25.8	24.9	25.5	26.4	25.9	24.9	24.5	24.6	24.0	23.0	22.0
Norway	13.3	12.8	12.1	11.4	10.9	11.0	10.3	9.8	9.4	9.7	10.1	10.3	10.2	11.7
Poland	32.2	32.4	31.4	31.1	30.0	29.1	29.2	29.5	29.9	30.4	29.8	28.9	27.9	26.6
Portugal	27.4	29.0	29.9	30.3	30.0	29.3	28.2	27.5	28.4	28.1	28.3	27.8	26.7	25.5
Slovak Republic	..	8.6	8.7	8.7	8.4	9.1	10.4	10.8	11.3	11.8	13.0	16.0	17.2	16.7
Spain	26.9	27.0	26.2	26.1	25.3	24.4	23.2	22.2	21.9	21.3	20.7	20.5	20.8	20.7
Sweden	15.5	15.7	15.7	15.6	15.3	14.8	14.8	14.5	14.1	14.0	13.9	14.3	14.0	14.2
Switzerland	12.4	12.5	13.3	14.0	14.1	14.6	14.6	13.8	13.6	13.0	12.4	11.9	11.7	11.6
Turkey	52.8	52.7	52.1	50.5	49.8	49.8	48.9	46.5	47.5	45.1	44.5	45.0	42.2	40.1
United Kingdom	20.3	20.6	20.6	19.6	19.1	18.0	17.7	16.7	17.0	17.0	17.6	18.3	17.6	17.7
United States	10.9	10.3	9.9	9.8	9.5	9.2	8.9	8.6	8.5	8.4	8.8	8.9	8.8	8.6
EU15 total	19.8	19.8	20.2	20.1	20.1	19.6	19.2	18.9	18.8	18.8	18.9	19.3	19.0	20.2
OECD total	21.6	21.4	21.0	20.9	20.8	20.4	20.1	19.5	19.5	19.3	19.4	19.5	19.1	19.3
Brazil	37.7	..	38.8	38.2	39.0	39.2	40.0	..	37.4	37.2	37.4	36.7	36.2	35.5
China	..	..	..	..	..	..	..	..	56.0	54.5	51.2	48.8	51.3	54.1
Russian Federation	..	..	2.3	2.5	3.2	3.2	7.5	7.3	5.8	5.8	5.8	6.0	6.3	6.2

StatLink 〰🖩 http://dx.doi.org/10.1787/274047374404

Self-employment rates: men
As a percentage of total male civilian employment, 2006

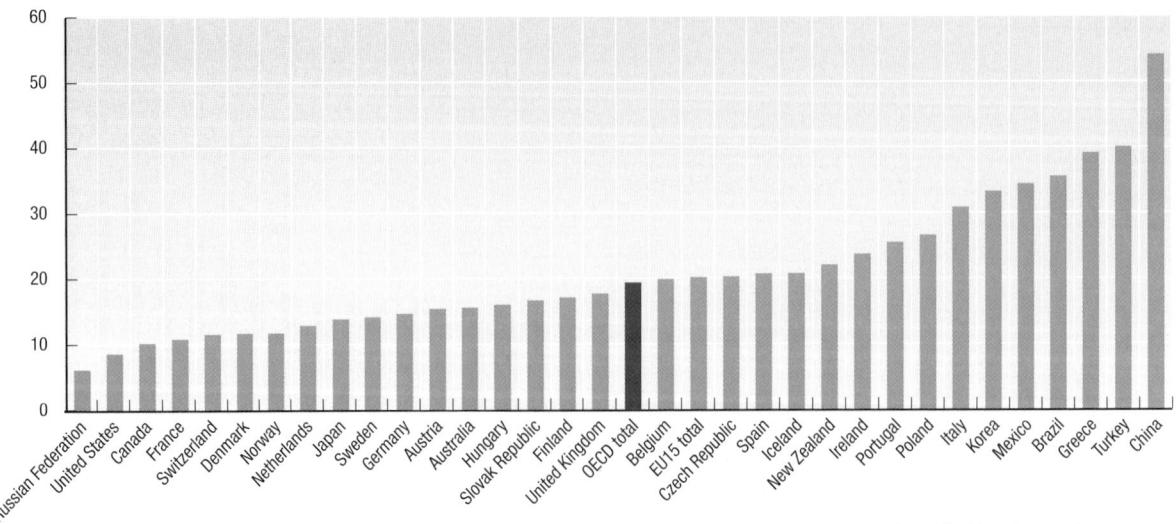

StatLink 〰🖩 http://dx.doi.org/10.1787/268350200571

OECD FACTBOOK 2008 – ISBN 978-92-64-04054-0 – © OECD 2008

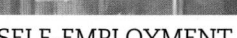
Self-employment rates: women
As a percentage of total female civilian employment

	1993	1994	1995	1996	1997	1998	1999	2000	2001	2002	2003	2004	2005	2006
Australia	13.1	12.6	12.1	11.9	12.2	11.4	11.1	10.7	10.3	10.5	10.0	9.9	9.8	9.8
Austria	..	..	13.7	13.8	13.2	13.1	12.6	12.2	12.1	11.8	11.3	10.3	10.9	11.3
Belgium	18.1	17.7	17.6	17.4	16.9	16.2	15.7	15.3	15.5	15.4	15.2	15.0	14.5	14.6
Canada	9.0	9.2	9.1	9.7	10.2	10.4	9.8	9.2	8.4	8.5	8.4	8.0	8.1	7.9
Czech Republic	6.2	6.8	8.0	7.9	8.0	9.2	9.6	10.2	10.2	10.7	11.5	10.9	10.4	10.9
Denmark	..	..	6.3	6.1	5.9	5.8	5.6	5.5	4.9	5.2	5.3	5.2	5.3	5.8
Finland	10.8	11.1	10.5	10.5	10.2	10.0	9.5	9.2	8.9	8.7	8.8	8.5	8.5	8.4
France	9.2	8.8	8.3	7.9	7.5	7.3	7.1	6.9	6.7	6.8	6.7	6.8	6.9	6.9
Germany	8.2	8.3	8.3	8.1	8.1	8.2	7.8	7.9	8.3	8.2	8.4	8.8	9.4	9.3
Greece	44.9	45.2	43.8	43.7	42.4	41.3	39.3	38.9	36.1	35.7	35.6	32.1	32.0	32.1
Hungary	13.7	13.0	13.0	12.7	12.4	11.6	11.1	10.5	10.2	10.0	9.2	10.1	9.9	9.1
Iceland	10.7	10.4	10.6	11.5	11.4	11.2	10.8	11.0	9.7	8.7	8.0	8.3	7.4	7.6
Ireland	10.8	10.0	9.7	9.6	9.5	9.6	9.2	9.0	8.0	7.5	7.6	7.8	7.4	6.7
Italy	24.3	24.2	23.8	23.6	23.2	23.0	22.6	22.0	21.6	21.2	21.1	22.2	20.6	20.5
Japan	22.8	22.0	21.5	20.4	19.9	19.8	19.3	18.3	17.2	16.3	15.8	15.3	14.9	13.7
Korea	41.7	40.7	40.4	40.1	39.8	41.4	39.7	38.4	37.6	36.5	34.5	33.4	32.9	32.3
Mexico	41.0	42.6	40.5	38.9	41.3	38.4	37.8	35.3	35.6	36.7	36.7	37.1	35.3	34.6
Netherlands	..	..	10.7	10.6	10.7	9.8	9.4	10.2	9.5	9.1	9.1	8.9	8.6	8.6
New Zealand	14.8	15.3	15.3	14.9	14.1	14.3	15.0	14.7	14.0	13.3	13.2	13.6	13.4	12.5
Norway	6.6	5.8	6.1	5.7	5.1	5.3	5.0	4.8	4.7	4.2	4.3	4.3	4.5	4.9
Poland	29.9	29.2	27.7	27.5	26.3	25.0	24.1	24.8	25.7	25.4	24.3	24.1	23.1	21.8
Portugal	25.0	26.0	25.5	26.5	27.5	26.6	25.6	24.4	24.9	24.7	24.8	23.5	23.3	22.4
Slovak Republic	..	3.4	3.8	3.5	3.8	4.0	4.4	4.7	4.9	4.7	5.9	7.1	7.0	7.3
Spain	24.4	23.6	23.2	21.9	20.2	19.6	17.8	16.6	16.2	15.1	14.5	14.3	14.5	13.8
Sweden	5.8	6.3	6.4	6.0	5.9	6.0	6.1	5.7	5.6	5.3	5.1	5.1	5.3	5.4
Switzerland	13.1	13.0	12.0	12.6	13.5	13.1	13.2	12.4	12.0	11.7	11.3	10.7	10.7	10.7
Turkey	72.3	74.6	74.0	73.6	70.0	69.9	70.0	64.7	66.8	63.0	61.9	60.7	56.2	53.3
United Kingdom	10.0	9.8	9.6	9.3	9.1	8.7	8.0	8.3	7.8	7.8	8.2	8.3	7.8	8.0
United States	6.4	7.1	6.9	6.9	6.7	6.4	6.2	6.1	6.1	5.9	6.1	6.1	5.9	6.0
EU15 total	12.3	12.1	13.1	12.9	12.7	12.4	11.8	11.7	11.5	11.3	11.4	11.6	11.4	12.2
OECD total	16.7	17.2	17.1	16.8	16.7	16.2	15.8	15.1	14.9	14.7	14.4	14.4	14.0	14.3
Brazil	38.1	..	38.4	35.3	36.1	35.5	36.3	..	33.0	33.5	33.1	32.5	33.1	31.8
China	..	..	..	..	..	..	..	..	50.7	49.1	46.3	42.7	45.4	49.9
Russian Federation	..	..	1.4	1.6	2.5	2.4	8.5	8.0	6.1	5.9	5.5	5.6	6.0	5.7

StatLink http://dx.doi.org/10.1787/274100685300

Self-employment rates: women
As a percentage of total female civilian employment, 2006

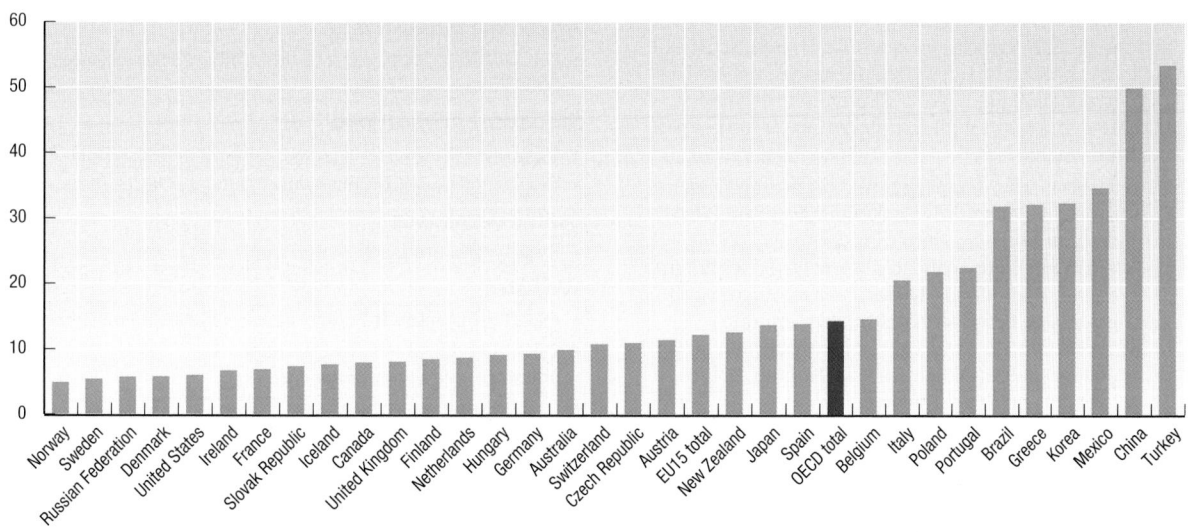

StatLink http://dx.doi.org/10.1787/268356235542

UNEMPLOYMENT RATES

Most OECD countries publish unemployment rates that are based on the numbers of persons who are registered as unemployed at government labour offices. Because they are available soon after the end of the month or quarter to which they refer, the numbers of registered unemployed are treated as the "headline" unemployment figures by many countries. However, the rules for registering at labour offices vary from country to country, so that unemployment statistics based on this source are not comparable between countries. The unemployment rates shown here use ILO Guidelines that provide common definitions of unemployment and of the labour force.

Definition

Unemployed persons are defined as those who report that they are without work, that they are available for work and that they have taken active steps to find work in the last four weeks. The ILO Guidelines specify what actions count as active steps to find work and these include answering vacancy notices, visiting factories, construction sites and other places of work, and placing advertisements in the press as well as registering with labour offices.

The unemployment rate is defined as the number of unemployed persons as a percentage of the civilian labour force, where the latter consists of the unemployed plus those in civilian employment, which are defined as persons who have worked for one hour or more in the last week.

When unemployment is high, some persons become discouraged and stop looking for work. They are then excluded from the labour force so that the unemployment rate may fall, or stop rising, even though there has been no underlying improvement in the labour market.

Comparability

All OECD countries use the ILO Guidelines for measuring unemployment, but the operational definitions used in national labour force surveys vary slightly in Iceland, Mexico and Turkey. Unemployment levels are also likely to be affected by changes in the survey design and/or the survey conduct, but unemployment rates are likely to be fairly consistent over time.

Long-term trends

In almost all OECD countries, unemployment rates rose in the early part of the 1990s but have been falling since then. Falls have been particularly marked in Australia, Finland, Denmark, Ireland and Spain.

There is no obvious pattern in the differences in unemployment rates for men and women. Unemployment rates for women are usually higher than for men, but in several countries unemployment rates for women are lower – Canada, Hungary, Korea, Sweden and the United Kingdom, for example. This is also true in Japan for the recent years. Part of the reason may be that women are more easily discouraged than men and so withdraw in larger numbers from the labour force when unemployment rises.

The charts shows unemployment rates averaged over the last decade. As regards total unemployment rates, countries can be divided into three groups: a low unemployment group with rates below 5% (Luxembourg, Switzerland, Netherlands, Norway, Korea, Austria and Japan); a middle group with unemployment rates between 5% and 10%; and a high unemployment group with average rates of 10% and above (Finland, Greece, Spain, Poland and the Slovak Republic).

Source
- OECD (2007), *Main Economic Indicators*, OECD, Paris.

Further information

Analytical publications
- OECD (2007), *Society at a Glance: OECD Social Indicators – 2006 Edition*, OECD, Paris.

Statistical publications
- OECD (2004), *Quarterly Labour Force Statistics*, OECD, Paris.
- OECD (2007), *OECD Employment Outlook*, OECD, Paris.

Online databases
- *Employment Statistics*.

Websites
- OECD Employment Policy, *www.oecd.org/els/employment*.
- OECD Labour Statistics Database, *www.oecd.org/statistics/labour*.
- OECD Employment Data, *www.oecd.org/els/employment/data*.

Unemployment rates: total

As a percentage of civilian labour force

	1993	1994	1995	1996	1997	1998	1999	2000	2001	2002	2003	2004	2005	2006
Australia	10.6	9.5	8.2	8.2	8.3	7.7	6.9	6.3	6.7	6.4	5.9	5.4	5.1	4.8
Austria	4.0	3.8	3.9	4.3	4.4	4.5	3.9	3.6	3.6	4.2	4.3	4.8	5.2	4.7
Belgium	8.6	9.8	9.7	9.5	9.2	9.3	8.5	6.9	6.6	7.5	8.2	8.4	8.4	8.2
Canada	11.4	10.4	9.5	9.6	9.1	8.3	7.6	6.8	7.2	7.7	7.6	7.2	6.8	6.3
Czech Republic	4.4	4.3	4.1	3.9	4.8		6.4	8.6	8.7	8.0	7.3	7.8	8.3	7.9	7.1
Denmark	9.5	7.7	6.8	6.3	5.2	4.9	5.1	4.3	4.5	4.6	5.4	5.5	4.8	3.9
Finland	16.2	16.8	15.1	14.9	12.7	11.4	10.3	9.6	9.1	9.1	9.1	8.8	8.3	7.7
France	11.1	11.7	11.1	11.6	11.5	11.1	10.5	9.1	8.4	8.7	9.5	9.6	9.7	9.5
Germany	7.6	8.2	8.0	8.7	9.4	9.0	8.2	7.5	7.6	8.3	9.3	9.8	10.6	9.8
Greece	8.6	8.8	9.0	9.7	9.6	11.0	12.0	11.2	10.7	10.3	9.7	10.5	9.9	8.9
Hungary	12.1	11.0	10.4		9.6	9.0	8.4	6.9	6.4	5.7	5.8	5.9	6.1	7.2	7.4
Ireland	15.6	14.3	12.3	11.7	9.9	7.5	5.7	4.3	4.0	4.5	4.7	4.5	4.3	4.4
Italy	9.8	10.6	11.2	11.2	11.3	11.4	10.9	10.1	9.1	8.6	8.4	8.0	7.7	6.8
Japan	2.5	2.9	3.1	3.4	3.4	4.1	4.7	4.7	5.0	5.4	5.3	4.7	4.4	4.1
Korea	2.9	2.5	2.1	2.0	2.6	7.0	6.6		4.4	4.0	3.3	3.6	3.7	3.7	3.5
Luxembourg	2.6	3.2	2.9	2.9	2.7	2.7	2.4	2.3	2.0	2.7	3.7	5.1	4.5	4.7
Netherlands	6.2	6.8	6.6	6.0	4.9	3.8	3.2	2.8	2.2	2.8	3.7	4.6	4.7	3.9
New Zealand	9.5	8.1	6.3	6.1	6.6	7.4	6.8	6.0	5.3	5.2	4.6	3.9	3.7	3.8
Norway	6.6	6.0	5.4	4.8	4.0	3.2	3.2	3.4	3.6	3.9	4.5	4.4	4.6	3.5
Poland	16.3	16.9	15.4	14.1		10.9	10.2	13.4	16.1	18.2	19.9	19.6	19.0	17.7	13.8
Portugal	5.6	6.9	7.3	7.3	6.8		5.1	4.5	4.0	4.0	5.0	6.3	6.7	7.6	7.7
Slovak Republic	..	13.7	13.1	11.3	11.9		12.6	16.3	18.8	19.3	18.6	17.6	18.2	16.3	13.3
Spain	18.3	19.5	18.4	17.8	16.7	15.0	12.5	11.1	10.4	11.1	11.1	10.6	9.2	8.5
Sweden	9.0	9.4	8.8	9.6	9.9	8.2	6.7	5.6	4.9	4.9	5.6	6.3	7.3		7.0
Switzerland	3.9	3.9	3.5	3.9	4.2	3.6	3.0	2.7	2.6	3.2	4.2	4.4	4.5	4.0
United Kingdom	10.2	9.3	8.5	7.9	6.8	6.1	5.9	5.3	5.0	5.1	4.9	4.7	4.8	5.3
United States	6.9		6.1	5.6	5.4	4.9	4.5	4.2		4.0	4.7	5.8	6.0	5.5	5.1	4.6
EU15 total	10.0	10.4	10.0	10.1	9.9	9.3	8.6	7.7	7.2	7.6	8.0	8.1	8.2	7.7
OECD total	7.8		7.6	7.2	7.2	6.9	6.9	6.7	6.2	6.4	6.9	7.1	6.9	6.7	6.1
Russian Federation	..	..	9.4	9.7	11.8	13.3	13.0	10.6	9.0	7.9	8.2	7.8	7.2	7.2

StatLink http://dx.doi.org/10.1787/274172076743

Unemployment rates: total

As a percentage of civilian labour force, average 1996-2006

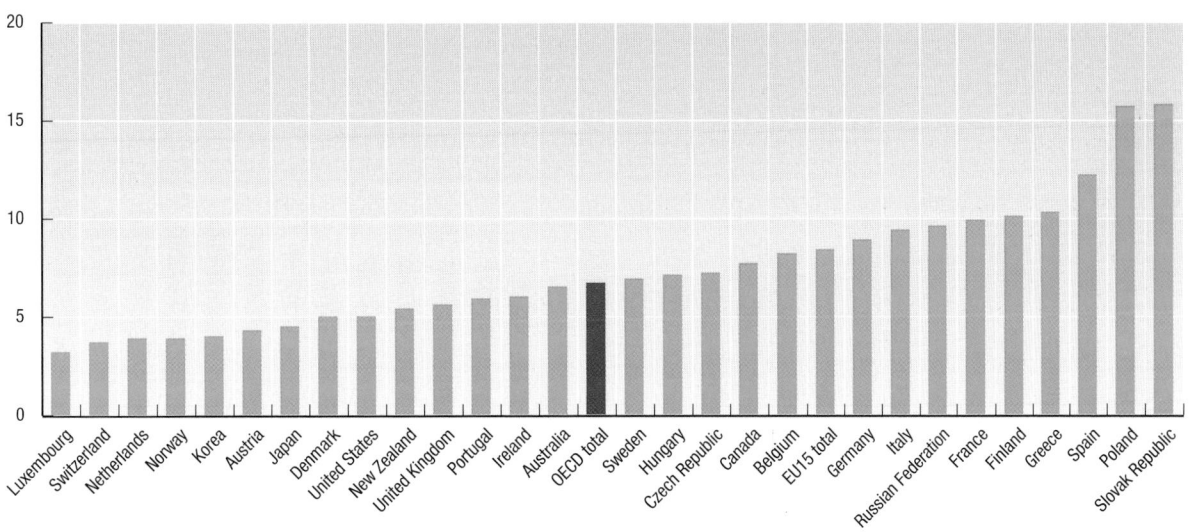

StatLink http://dx.doi.org/10.1787/268437156644

Unemployment rates: men

As a percentage of male civilian labour force

	1993	1994	1995	1996	1997	1998	1999	2000	2001	2002	2003	2004	2005	2006
Australia	11.4	9.9	8.7	8.5	8.6	8.1	7.2	6.5	7.1	6.6	5.9	5.3	4.9	4.7
Austria	3.1	3.0	3.1	3.6	3.6	3.8	3.3	3.1	3.1	4.0	4.0	4.4	4.9	4.3
Belgium	6.7	7.7	7.6	7.4	7.3	7.7	7.2	5.6	5.9	6.6	7.7	7.5	7.6	7.4
Canada	11.9	10.9	9.8	9.9	9.3	8.5	7.8	6.9	7.5	8.1	7.9	7.5	7.0	6.5
Czech Republic	3.5	3.7	3.5	3.4	4.0		5.0	7.3	7.3	6.7	5.9	6.2	7.1	6.5	5.8
Denmark	9.3	7.1	5.7	5.3	4.4	3.9	4.5	3.9	4.1	4.3	4.8	5.1	4.4	3.3
Finland	18.1	18.4	15.2	15.0	12.3	10.9	9.7	8.7	8.7	9.1	9.3	8.7	8.1	7.4
France	9.6	10.1	9.4	10.0	10.1	9.5	9.0	7.6	7.0	7.8	8.5	8.7	8.8	8.7
Germany	6.5	7.2	7.2	8.2	9.0	8.8	8.1	7.5	7.8	8.8	9.8	10.3	11.1	10.2
Greece	5.7	6.0	6.2	6.0	6.3	7.3	7.9	7.4	7.1	6.8	6.2	6.6	6.1	5.6
Hungary	13.5	12.3	11.8		10.2	9.7	9.0	7.4	7.0	6.3	6.2	6.1	6.1	7.0	7.1
Ireland	15.4	14.2	12.2	11.5	9.9	7.7	5.7	4.3	4.1	4.7	5.0	4.9	4.6	4.6
Italy	7.4	8.3	8.6	8.7	8.7	8.8	8.4	7.8	7.0	6.7	6.5	6.3	6.1	5.4
Japan	2.4	2.8	3.1	3.3	3.4	4.2	4.8	4.9	5.2	5.5	5.5	4.9	4.6	4.3
Korea	3.3	2.8	2.3	2.4	2.8	7.8	7.4		5.0	4.5	3.7	3.8	3.9	4.0	3.8
Luxembourg	2.2	2.6	2.0	2.2	2.0	1.9	1.8	1.8	1.7	2.1	3.0	3.7	3.5	3.5
Netherlands	5.4	6.0	5.5	4.7	3.7	2.9	2.3	2.2	1.8	2.5	3.5	4.3	4.4	3.5
New Zealand	10.1	8.5	6.2	6.1	6.6	7.5	7.0	6.1	5.3	5.0	4.3	3.5	3.4	3.5
Norway	7.3	6.6	5.7	4.7	3.9	3.1	3.4	3.6	3.7	4.1	4.9	4.8	4.8	3.6
Poland	14.5	15.1	13.8	12.3		9.1	8.5	11.8	14.4	16.9	19.1	18.9	18.2	16.6	12.9
Portugal	4.8	6.1	6.5	6.5	6.1		4.1	4.0	3.2	3.2	4.1	5.5	5.8	6.7	6.5
Slovak Republic	..	13.3	12.5	10.2	11.1		12.2	16.3	19.0	19.8	18.6	17.4	17.4	15.4	12.2
Spain	15.5	16.2	14.8	14.3	13.1	11.2	9.0	7.9	7.5	8.1	8.2	8.0	7.1	6.3
Sweden	10.7	10.8	9.7	10.1	10.2	8.4	6.6	5.9	5.2	5.3	6.0	6.5	7.4		6.9
Switzerland	3.3	3.4	3.0	3.6	4.3	3.2	2.6	2.2	2.0	3.0	3.9	4.0	3.9	..
United Kingdom	12.1	11.0	9.9	9.2	7.6	6.8	6.5	5.8	5.5	5.6	5.5	5.0	5.2	5.7
United States	7.2		6.2	5.6	5.4	4.9	4.4	4.1		3.9	4.8	5.9	6.3	5.6	5.1	4.6
EU15 total	9.1	9.4	8.9	9.1	8.8	8.2	7.5	6.7	6.4	6.9	7.4	7.5	7.6	7.1
OECD total	..	7.3	6.8	6.8	6.4	6.4	6.2	5.8	6.1	6.7	6.9	6.7	6.4	5.9
Russian Federation	..	..	9.7	10.0	12.1	13.5	13.2	10.8	9.3	8.1	8.5	8.0	7.3	7.5

StatLink http://dx.doi.org/10.1787/274203436078

Unemployment rates: men

As a percentage of male civilian labour force, average 1996-2006 or latest available period

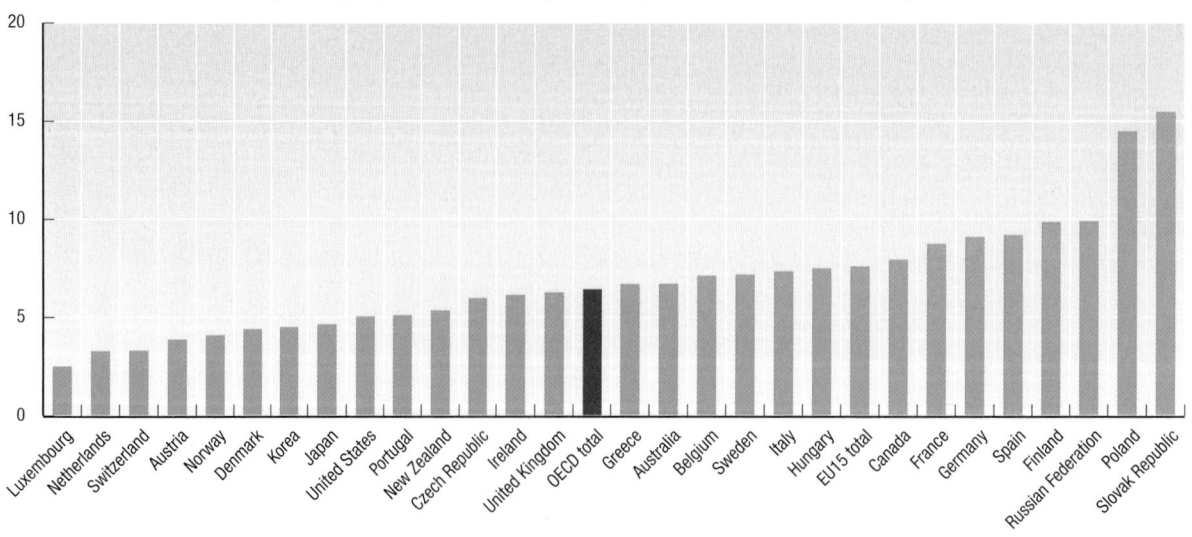

StatLink http://dx.doi.org/10.1787/268468683710

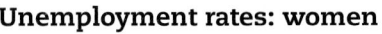

Unemployment rates: women
As a percentage of female civilian labour force

	1993	1994	1995	1996	1997	1998	1999	2000	2001	2002	2003	2004	2005	2006
Australia	9.8	9.0	7.9	7.9	8.1	7.5	6.8	6.2	6.5	6.2	6.0	5.6	5.2	5.0
Austria	5.1	5.0	5.0	5.3	5.4	5.4	4.7	4.3	4.2	4.4	4.7	5.3	5.5	5.2
Belgium	11.4	12.7	12.7	12.5	11.9	11.6	10.3	8.5	7.5	8.6	8.9	9.5	9.5	9.3
Canada	10.7	9.8	9.1	9.3	8.9	8.0	7.3	6.7	6.9	7.1	7.2	6.9	6.5	6.1
Czech Republic	5.4	5.2	4.8	4.7	5.9	8.1	10.3	10.3	9.7	9.0	9.9	9.9	9.8	8.9
Denmark	9.8	8.5	8.1	7.5	6.2	6.0	5.7	4.8	5.0	5.0	6.1	6.0	5.3	4.5
Finland	14.2	14.9	15.0	14.8	13.0	11.9	10.8	10.5	9.7	9.1	8.9	9.0	8.6	8.1
France	13.0	13.6	13.1	13.5	13.3	12.9	12.2	10.9	10.0	9.8	10.6	10.6	10.7	10.4
Germany	8.9	9.4	9.0	9.2	9.8	9.3	8.4	7.5	7.4	7.9	8.7	9.1	10.0	9.4
Greece	13.6	13.7	13.8	15.4	14.8	16.9	18.1	17.1	16.1	15.6	15.0	16.2	15.3	13.6
Hungary	10.4	9.4	8.7	8.8	8.1	7.8	6.3	5.6	5.0	5.4	5.6	6.1	7.4	7.8
Ireland	16.0	14.6	12.5	11.8	9.9	7.3	5.6	4.2	3.8	4.1	4.3	4.0	4.0	4.1
Italy	13.9	14.6	15.3	15.2	15.3	15.4	14.8	13.6	12.2	11.5	11.3	10.5	10.0	8.8
Japan	2.6	3.0	3.2	3.4	3.4	4.0	4.5	4.5	4.7	5.1	4.9	4.4	4.2	3.9
Korea	2.3	2.0	1.7	1.6	2.3	5.7	5.3	3.6	3.3	2.7	3.3	3.4	3.4	2.9
Luxembourg	3.3	4.1	4.3	4.2	3.9	4.0	3.3	3.1	2.5	3.7	4.7	7.1	5.8	6.3
Netherlands	7.5	7.9	8.1	7.7	6.6	5.0	4.4	3.6	2.8	3.1	3.9	4.9	5.0	4.4
New Zealand	8.8	7.6	6.3	6.1	6.6	7.4	6.5	5.8	5.3	5.3	5.0	4.4	4.0	4.1
Norway	5.7	5.3	5.1	4.8	4.2	3.3	3.1	3.2	3.4	3.6	4.0	4.0	4.4	3.4
Poland	18.5	19.0	17.3	16.2	13.0	12.2	15.2	18.1	19.8	20.9	20.4	19.9	19.1	14.9
Portugal	6.7	8.0	8.2	8.2	7.7	6.3	5.2	4.9	5.0	6.0	7.2	7.6	8.7	9.0
Slovak Republic	..	14.1	13.8	12.7	12.8	13.2	16.4	18.6	18.7	18.7	17.8	19.2	17.2	14.7
Spain	23.5	25.4	24.6	23.8	22.6	21.1	18.1	16.0	14.8	15.7	15.3	14.3	12.2	11.6
Sweden	7.3	7.8	7.8	9.0	9.5	8.0	6.8	5.3	4.5	4.6	5.2	6.1	7.2	7.1
Switzerland	4.7	4.5	4.1	4.2	4.1	4.0	3.5	3.2	3.4	3.4	4.5	4.9	5.1	..
United Kingdom	7.8	7.2	6.7	6.3	5.8	5.3	5.2	4.8	4.4	4.5	4.3	4.2	4.3	4.9
United States	6.6	6.0	5.6	5.4	5.0	4.6	4.3	4.1	4.7	5.6	5.7	5.4	5.1	4.6
EU15 total	11.2	11.6	11.4	11.4	11.3	10.7	9.9	8.9	8.3	8.5	8.8	8.9	8.9	8.5
OECD total	..	8.1	7.8	7.8	7.5	7.4	7.2	6.7	6.8	7.2	7.3	7.2	7.0	6.5
Russian Federation	..	..	9.2	9.3	11.5	13.0	12.9	10.4	8.6	7.6	8.0	7.5	7.0	6.8

StatLink ⫘ http://dx.doi.org/10.1787/274216717605

Unemployment rates: women
As a percentage of female civilian labour force, average 1996-2006 or latest available period

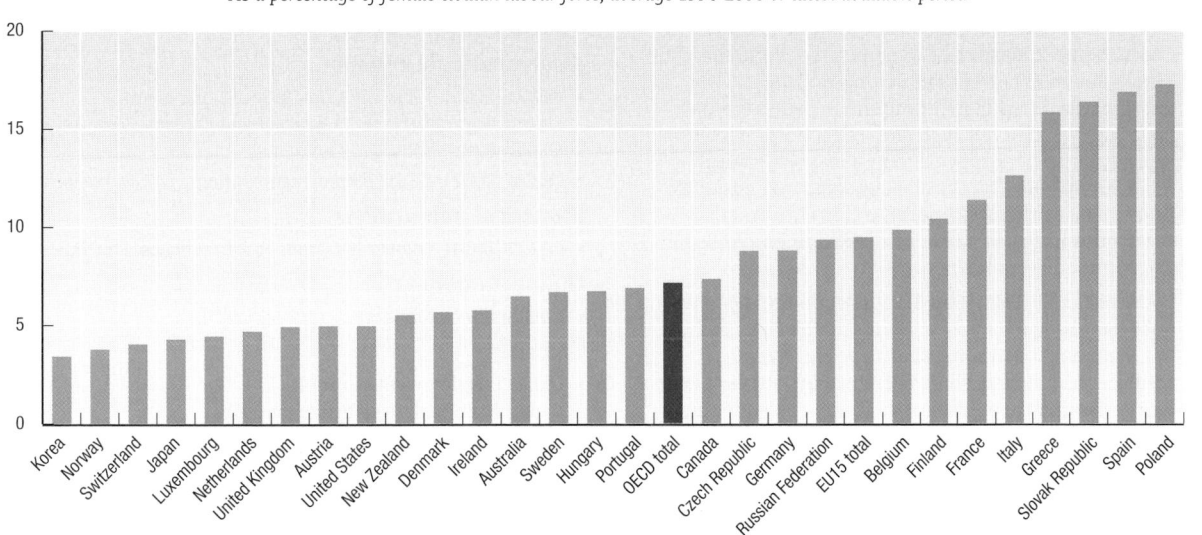

StatLink ⫘ http://dx.doi.org/10.1787/268473046608

LONG-TERM UNEMPLOYMENT

Clearly, long-term unemployment is of particular concern to policy makers. Quite apart from the mental stress caused to the unemployed and their families, high rates of long-term unemployment indicate that labour markets are operating inefficiently and, in countries which pay generous unemployment benefits, the existence of long-term unemployment is a significant burden on government finances.

Definition

Long-term unemployment is conventionally defined either as those unemployed for 6 months or more or, as here, those unemployed for 12 months or more. The ratios calculated here show the proportion of these long-term unemployed among all unemployed.

Unemployment is defined in most OECD countries in accordance with the ILO Guidelines. Unemployment is usually measured by household labour force surveys and the unemployed are defined as those persons who report that they have worked in gainful employment for less than one hour in the previous week, who are available for work and who have taken actions to seek employment in the previous four weeks. The ILO Guidelines specify the kinds of actions that count as seeking work.

Comparability

All OECD countries use the ILO Guidelines for measuring unemployment, but the operational definitions used in national labour force surveys vary slightly in Iceland and Turkey. Unemployment levels are also likely to be affected by changes in the survey design and/or the survey conduct, but unemployment rates are likely to be fairly consistent over time.

In comparing rates of long-term unemployment, it is important to bear in mind differences in institutional arrangements between countries. Rates of long-term unemployment will generally be higher in countries where unemployment benefits are relatively generous and are available for long periods of unemployment. In countries where the benefits are low and of limited duration, unemployed persons will more quickly lower their salary expectations or consider taking jobs that are in other ways less attractive than those which they formerly held.

Long-term trends

In 2006, rates of long-term unemployment varied from 10% or less in Korea, Mexico, New Zealand, Iceland, Canada and United States, to 55% or more in the Czech Republic, Belgium, Germany, Greece and the Slovak Republic. Lower rates of long-term unemployment are generally found in countries that have enjoyed relatively high rates of economic growth in recent years. There appears to be a two-way causal relationship here – on the one hand, jobs are easier to find in a fast growing economy and, on the other, economies may grow faster by making unemployment an unattractive proposition.

Over the period 1993-2006, long-term unemployment rates have been relatively stable for the OECD as a whole, but there have been some sharp rises in several countries and equally sharp falls in others. Rates of long-term unemployment have more than doubled in the Czech Republic and Japan. On the other hand, since 1993, the share of long-term unemployed has more than halved in Australia, Korea and New Zealand.

Source
• OECD (2007), *Labour Force Statistics*, OECD, Paris.

Further information
Analytical publications
• OECD (2002), "The Ins and Outs of Long-term Unemployment", *OECD Employment Outlook*, Chapter 4, OECD, Paris, pp. 187-243.
• OECD (2007), *OECD Employment Outlook*, OECD, Paris.

Statistical publications
• OECD (2004), *Quarterly Labour Force Statistics*, OECD, Paris.

Online databases
• *Employment Statistics.*

Websites
• OECD Employment Outlook, *www.oecd.org/els/employmentoutlook.*
• OECD Labour Statistics Database, *www.oecd.org/statistics/labour.*
• OECD Employment Data, *www.oecd.org/els/employment/data.*

Long-term unemployment

Persons unemployed for 12 months or more as a percentage of total unemployed

	1993	1994	1995	1996	1997	1998	1999	2000	2001	2002	2003	2004	2005	2006
Australia	36.7	36.1	32.0	28.5	31.2	29.7	28.3	25.5	22.0	22.3	21.3	20.5	17.7	17.8
Austria	..	18.4	29.1	24.9	27.5	30.3	29.2	25.8	23.3	19.2	24.5	27.6	25.3	27.3
Belgium	53.0	58.3	62.4	61.3	60.5	61.7	60.5	56.3	51.7	49.6	46.3	49.6	51.6	55.6
Canada	16.5	17.9	16.8	16.8	16.1	13.8	11.7	11.2	9.5	9.6	10.0	9.5	9.6	8.7
Czech Republic	18.5	22.3	31.2	31.3	30.5	31.2	37.1	48.8	52.7	50.7	49.9	51.8	53.6	55.2
Denmark	25.2	32.1	27.9	26.5	27.2	26.9	20.5	20.0	22.2	19.7	19.9	22.6	25.9	20.4
Finland	30.6	..	37.6	34.5	29.8	27.5	29.6	29.0	26.2	24.4	24.7	23.4	24.9	24.8
France	34.2	38.5	42.5	39.6	41.4	44.2	40.4	42.6	37.6	33.8	42.9	41.6	42.5	44.0
Germany	40.3	44.3	48.7	47.8	50.1	52.6	51.7	51.5	50.4	47.9	50.0	51.8	54.0	57.2
Greece	50.9	50.5	51.4	56.7	55.7	54.9	55.3	56.4	52.8	52.7	56.3	54.8	53.7	55.6
Hungary	33.5	41.3	50.6	54.4	51.3	49.8	49.5	49.0	46.6	44.8	42.2	45.1	46.1	46.1
Iceland	12.2	15.1	16.8	19.8	16.3	16.1	11.7	11.8	12.5	11.1	8.1	11.2	13.3	7.3
Ireland	59.1	64.3	61.6	59.5	57.0	..	55.3	..	33.1	29.4	35.5	34.3	34.3	34.3
Italy	57.7	61.5	63.6	65.6	66.3	59.6	61.4	61.3	63.4	59.2	58.2	49.7	52.2	52.9
Japan	15.6	17.5	18.1	19.3	21.8	20.3	22.4	25.5	26.6	30.8	33.5	33.7	33.3	33.0
Korea	2.6	5.4	4.4	3.8	2.6	1.5	3.8	2.3	2.3	2.5	0.6	1.1	0.8	1.1
Luxembourg	31.6	29.6	23.2	27.6	34.6	31.3	32.3	22.4	28.4	27.4	24.7	21.0	26.4	..
Mexico	..	..	1.5	2.2	1.8	0.8	1.5	1.2	1.0	0.9	0.9	1.1	2.3	2.5
Netherlands	52.4	49.4	46.8	50.0	49.1	47.9	43.5	..	..	26.7	29.2	32.5	40.1	45.2
New Zealand	33.3	32.7	25.7	20.8	19.3	19.3	20.9	19.3	16.7	14.5	13.5	11.7	9.4	7.1
Norway	27.2	28.8	24.2	14.2	12.4	8.3	7.1	5.3	5.5	6.4	6.4	9.2	9.5	14.1
Poland	39.1	40.4	40.0	39.0	38.0	37.4	34.8	37.9	43.1	48.4	49.7	47.9	52.2	50.4
Portugal	43.5	43.4	50.9	53.1	55.6	44.7	41.2	42.9	38.1	35.5	32.8	43.2	48.6	51.8
Slovak Republic	..	42.6	54.1	52.6	51.6	51.3	47.7	54.6	53.7	59.8	61.1	60.6	68.1	73.1
Spain	50.1	56.2	57.1	55.9	55.7	54.3	51.2	47.6	44.0	40.2	39.8	37.7	32.6	29.5
Sweden	15.8	25.7	27.8	30.1	33.4	33.5	30.1	26.4	22.3	21.0	17.8	18.9	14.1	14.2
Switzerland	20.3	29.0	33.6	25.6	28.2	34.8	39.6	29.0	29.9	21.8	26.1	33.5	39.0	39.1
Turkey	46.8	45.9	36.4	44.3	41.6	40.3	28.2	21.1	21.3	29.4	24.4	39.2	39.6	35.8
United Kingdom	42.5	45.4	43.6	39.8	38.6	32.7	29.6	28.0	27.8	22.9	22.8	21.4	22.4	22.1
United States	11.5	12.2	9.7	9.5	8.7	8.0	6.8	6.0	6.1	8.5	11.8	12.7	11.8	10.0
EU15 total	44.1	48.4	50.3	49.4	50.2	49.2	47.5	46.9	45.3	41.5	43.4	42.4	43.5	44.2
OECD total	32.0	35.5	34.0	34.2	35.0	33.1	31.7	31.4	29.5	29.4	30.9	31.8	32.7	32.2
Russian Federation	..	..	29.7	32.6	38.2	40.7	47.0	46.2	39.2	39.2	37.6	39.0	38.5	41.7

StatLink http://dx.doi.org/10.1787/274261407254

Long-term unemployment

Persons unemployed for 12 months or more as a percentage of total unemployed, 2006 or latest available year

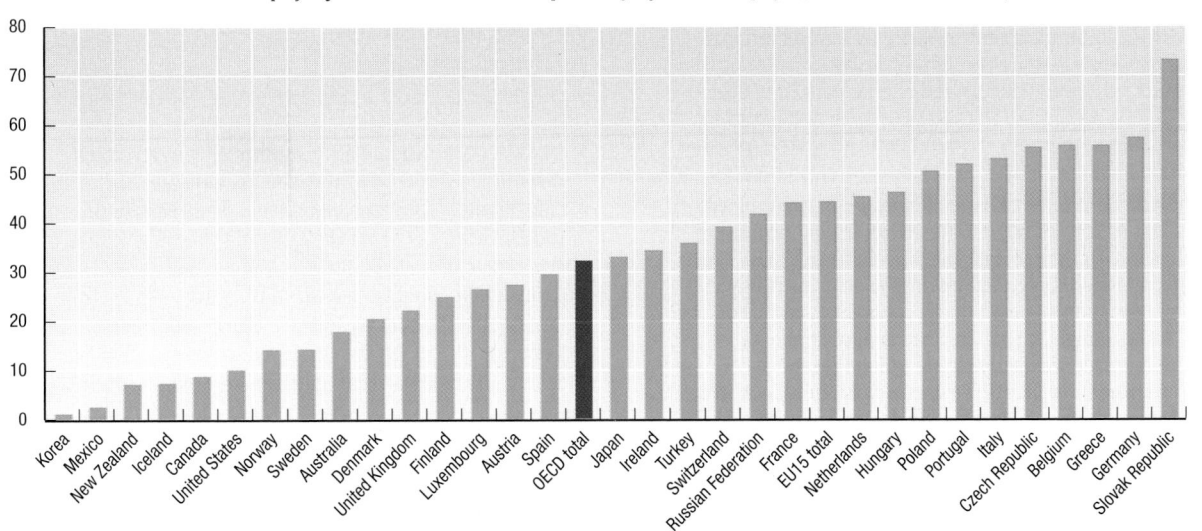

StatLink http://dx.doi.org/10.1787/268502020154

REGIONAL UNEMPLOYMENT

Unemployment rates vary significantly among OECD countries but large international differences hide even larger differences among regions. In 2004, regional differences in unemployment rates were above 10 percentage points in one third of OECD countries.

Definition

Unemployed persons are defined as those who report that they are without work, that they are available for work and that they have taken active steps to find work in the last four weeks. The ILO Guidelines specify what actions count as active steps to find work and these include answering vacancy notices, visiting factories, construction sites and other places of work, and placing advertisements in the press as well as registering with labour offices.

The unemployment rate is defined as the number of unemployed persons as a percentage of the labour force, where the latter consists of unemployed and employed persons.

When unemployment is high, some persons become discouraged and stop looking for work. They are then excluded from the labour force so that the unemployment rate may fall, or stop rising, even though there has been no underlying improvement in the labour market.

The Gini index offers an accurate picture of regional disparities. It looks not only at the regions with the highest and the lowest rates of unemployment but also at the differences among all regions. The index ranges between 0 and 1: the higher its value, the larger the regional disparities. Regional disparities tend to be underestimated when the size of regions is large.

Comparability

As for the other regional statistics, the comparability of unemployment rates is affected by differences in the meaning of the word region (see Regional population) and the different geography of rural and urban communities (see Regional GDP), both within and among countries.

Overview

In 2004, Italy and Iceland were the countries with the largest disparity in unemployment rates with a Gini index equal to 0.34. According to this index, regional disparities were also large in Germany, Belgium, Canada, and the Slovak Republic. In most other countries, regional disparities were close to the OECD average (0.18). Only in Sweden, the Netherlands, Ireland and Norway did unemployment rates reflect a more even regional pattern.

The percentages of the labour force located in regions where unemployment rates are above the national average reveal the share of the national workforce that is affected by regional disparities in unemployment rates. In 2004, 48% of the OECD labour force was based in regions with unemployment rates above the national rate.

Significant international differences in unemployment rates hide even larger differences among regions. In Poland, Germany, Italy, the Slovak Republic and Spain differences in regional unemployment rates were greater than 18 percentage points. In Canada, Finland, Turkey, Belgium and the Czech Republic these differences were smaller but still large (above 10 percentage points). Only in Mexico, Ireland, Korea, the Netherlands and Norway did unemployment rates reflect a more even regional pattern.

Source

- *OECD Regional Database.*

Further information
Analytical publications

- OECD (2001), *OECD Territorial Outlook, 2001 Edition*, OECD, Paris.
- OECD (2003), *Geographic Concentration and Territorial Disparity in OECD Countries*, OECD, Paris.
- OECD (2005), *Local Governance and the Drivers of Growth*, OECD, Paris.
- OECD (2007), *Higher Education and Regions: Globally Competitive, Locally Engaged*, OECD, Paris.
- OECD (2007), *OECD Regions at a Glance: 2007 Edition*, OECD, Paris.
- Spiezia, V. (2003), *OECD Statistics Brief*, OECD, Paris.

Websites

- OECD Regional Database, *www.oecd.org/gov/territorialindicators*.

Unemployment rate

*As a percentage of the labour force,
2004 or latest available year*

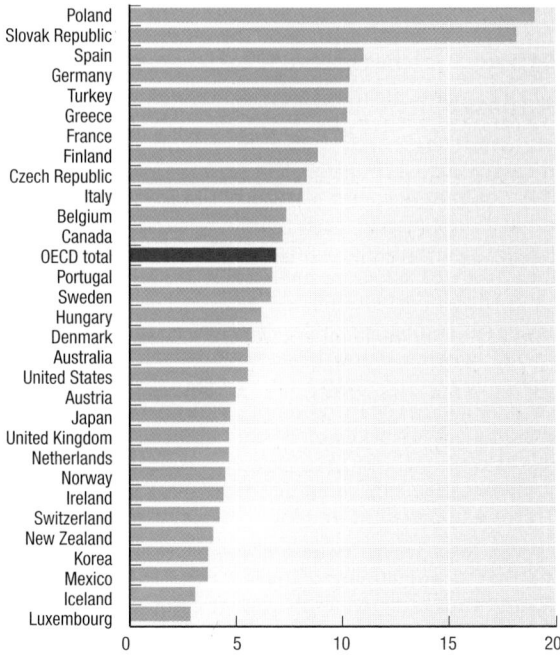

Percentage of the total labour force living in regions with an unemployment rate above the national average

2004 or latest available year

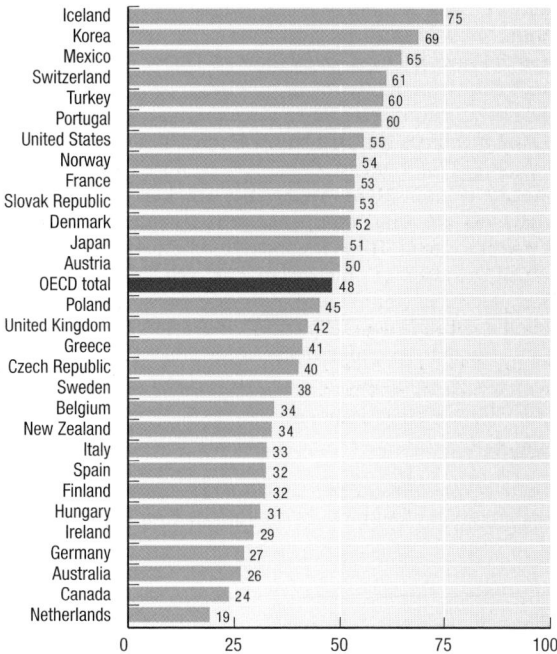

Variation of regional unemployment rates

*Minimum and maximum regional rates, as a percentage
of national rates, 2004 or latest available year*

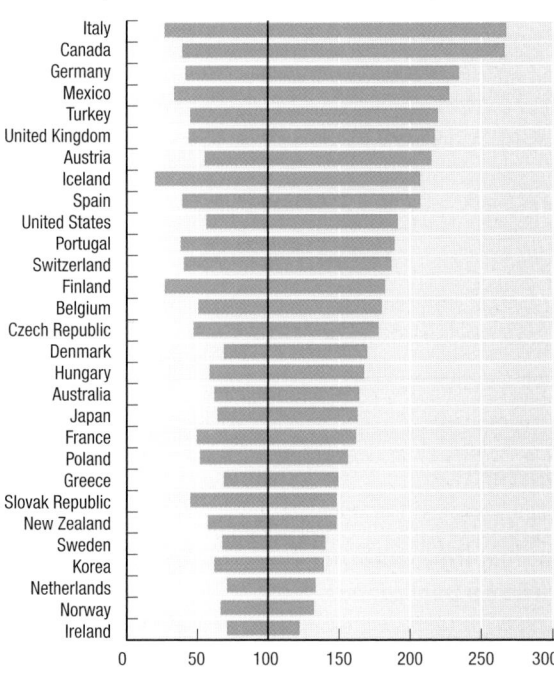

Gini index of regional disparities in unemployment rates

2004 or latest available year

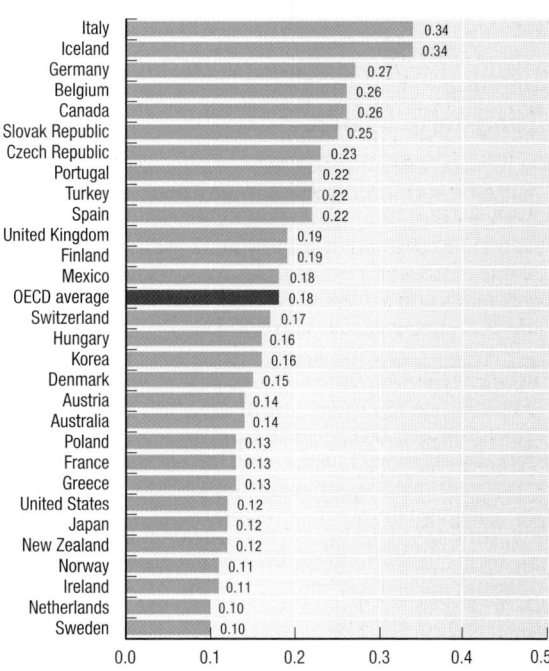

StatLink http://dx.doi.org/10.1787/268505141256

LABOUR COMPENSATION

Labour compensation per unit labour input shows the average compensation received by employees of businesses, either per hour worked or on an annual basis per employee. Annual growth rates based on data in national currency show relative changes over time in labour compensation across countries. Adjusting by purchasing power parity (PPP) converts all countries data to a common currency allowing meaningful cross country comparisons of data in levels to be made. The country data can be interpreted as the quantity of equivalent goods and services that could be purchased for the compensation received for labour services rendered. The data presented here are an output of the *OECD System of Unit Labour Cost and Related Indicators* which produces annual and quarterly unit labour cost and related indicators (*e.g.*, labour compensation per unit labour input, labour productivity) according to a specific methodology to ensure data are comparable across all OECD countries.

Definition

Labour compensation per unit labour input is defined as compensation of employees divided by total hours worked by employees of businesses (Australia, Austria, Canada, Denmark, France, Germany, Greece, Hungary, Italy, Korea, Norway, Slovak Republic, Spain and Sweden) or total employees (all other countries). The adjustment to PPP US dollars series is based on the PPP for private consumption.

Comparability

Every effort has been made to ensure that data are comparable across countries. The primary data source is the OECD National Accounts database within which data are compiled on a similar basis across countries according to the *1993 System of National Accounts*. Therefore cross country comparisons of labour compensation per employee or per hour in US dollars PPP adjusted levels can be used for static analysis (*i.e.* comparison of levels across countries at a point in time) whereas growth rates based on the national currency series are useful for comparing evolution over time. Ideally, cross country comparisons are best made from the US dollars PPP adjusted labour compensation per hour series as comparability of levels across countries for the per employee series can suffer from different proportions of full-time and part-time employees across countries.

However, even when hours are used it should be kept in mind that no adjustment is made for the skill composition of hours. Thus, differences in average compensation across countries will also reflect differences in the skill composition of employed persons.

Long-term trends

At the total economy level, based on the PPP adjusted labour compensation per employee data it is evident that over the last 13 years employees from the United States and Luxembourg have been, on average, the most highly compensated for their labour services, and in general the gap between these countries and the rest of the OECD member countries has widened.

In the period observed for the PPP adjusted labour compensation per employee only four countries recorded annual average growth above 5%, namely the Czech Republic, Greece, Poland and the Slovak Republic. This higher growth rate however, has not helped employees compensated in these countries reduce the gap significantly between them and employees compensated in the top 10 countries, since employee compensation in these top 10 countries are also growing at an annual average growth above 3%.

Source

• *Main Economic Indicators.*

Further information

Statistical publications

• OECD (2007), *Main Economic Indicators*, OECD, Paris.

Labour compensation per unit labour input, total economy
Annual growth in percentage

	1993	1994	1995	1996	1997	1998	1999	2000	2001	2002	2003	2004	2005	2006
Australia	2.2	1.5	4.3	5.5	3.6	3.1	3.1	3.9	5.0	3.1	4.1	4.0	4.4	..
Austria	4.5	4.1	4.6	0.3	0.5	2.8	3.7	2.9	1.5	2.1	1.4	1.0	2.6	2.8
Belgium	4.6	4.4	1.4	1.4	3.4	1.3	3.5	2.0	3.6	3.8	1.7	1.9	1.9	3.2
Canada	1.1	-0.1	1.6	1.5	5.6	2.9	2.2	5.2	3.0	2.2	3.1	2.3	4.9	..
Czech Republic	..	..	..	16.7	8.6	8.4	8.4	6.2	7.9	7.4	8.8	5.7	4.7	6.2
Denmark	2.4	3.8	3.3	4.8	1.8	3.1	2.8	3.2	3.9	4.5	4.1	2.4	2.2	3.1
Finland	0.5	3.4	4.1	2.6	1.6	4.5	2.2	3.7	4.7	1.8	2.8	3.6	3.8	2.8
France	3.0	1.7	3.5	1.7	2.3	2.3	2.4	5.1	3.1	6.1	3.2	1.6	3.5	..
Germany	5.4	3.2	4.7	2.7	1.6	1.3	2.0	3.3	2.4	2.1	2.0	0.1	0.6	1.3
Greece	..	..	..	10.3	16.1	4.2	4.1	5.5	6.7	8.2	6.3	6.3	5.7	3.1
Hungary	..	..	..	20.6	19.1	13.9	4.0	15.9	18.5	12.2	11.1	11.5	7.1	3.0
Ireland	..	..	..	4.3	5.0	4.7	4.5	8.0	7.5	5.5	6.4	6.4	5.0	4.5
Italy	3.5	4.0	4.1	4.8	4.9	-2.5	2.1	2.2	4.1	2.9	2.9	2.8	3.6	3.2
Japan	0.8	1.4	1.6	0.6	1.5	-0.1	-1.1	0.4	-0.5	-1.6	-1.4	-1.3	0.2	..
Korea	13.0	12.6	14.7	12.9	6.5	8.4	0.1	2.4	7.4	6.3	9.6	5.0	5.5	3.5
Luxembourg	5.7	3.9	1.3	1.9	2.6	0.9	4.0	5.3	3.5	3.1	2.2	3.9	3.8	4.5
Mexico	..	..	..	21.3	22.6	20.7	20.6	16.2	11.0	5.5	6.8	3.6	..	..
Netherlands	2.8	2.1	1.2	1.5	2.4	4.0	3.4	4.6	4.9	4.3	3.4	3.4	1.0	2.2
New Zealand	3.7	2.3	1.6	2.9	3.7	-0.6	-0.6	3.3	4.2	3.9	4.6	4.4	3.1	..
Norway	1.6	3.3	4.6	4.7	5.2	7.1	5.5	6.1	7.6	5.4	4.8	2.8	4.6	5.9
Poland	33.0	40.4	34.0	27.3	20.9	15.9	12.1	11.7	10.4	1.4		3.2	3.9	3.6	..
Portugal	..	..	..	6.1	6.0	5.3	5.4	6.4	4.0	3.6	3.5	2.6	..	..
Slovak Republic	..	..	..	9.6	15.9	14.9	6.3	11.9	6.2	13.1	13.1	8.3	3.0	6.6
Spain	7.3	3.7	3.7	3.9	2.1	1.6	1.9	2.8	3.9	3.5	3.7	3.1	3.4	3.1
Sweden	..	3.6	2.4	6.3	4.6	2.6	0.8	8.5	5.7	4.5	4.3	2.4	4.1	3.2
United Kingdom	3.6	3.1	3.6	3.4	4.1	6.8	4.7	5.4	4.9	3.7	4.7	4.2	4.4	4.4
United States	3.5	2.8	3.3	3.2	3.8	5.9	4.9	5.2	2.6	2.7	3.1	4.1	3.2	4.4
Euro area	4.1	3.0	3.3	2.8	0.1	0.7	2.6	2.5	2.6	2.6	2.3	2.1	1.8	2.2
Major Seven	3.1	2.5	3.1	2.6	3.2	3.4	3.0	4.0	2.4	2.2	2.3	2.5	2.7	3.9

StatLink http://dx.doi.org/10.1787/274268586135

Labour compensation per unit labour input, total economy
Average annual growth in percentage, 1995-2006 or latest available period

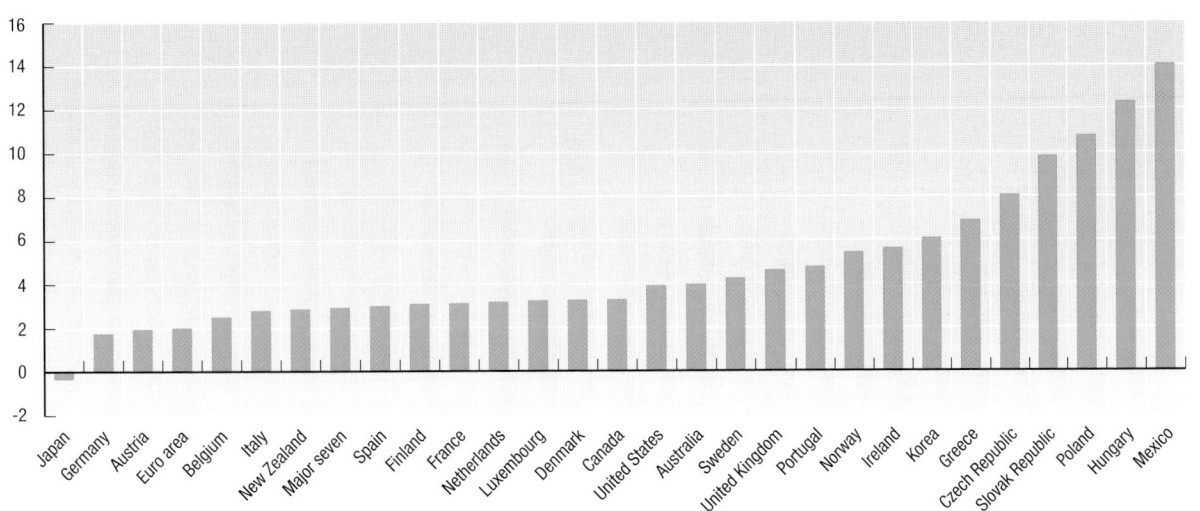

StatLink http://dx.doi.org/10.1787/268545073440

Labour compensation per employee, total economy
US dollars calculated using PPPs

	1993	1994	1995	1996	1997	1998	1999	2000	2001	2002	2003	2004	2005	2006
Australia	24 215.9	24 885.6	25 988.0	27 730.5	28 602.5	29 429.4	30 713.5	31 736.0	32 239.7	32 612.9	33 089.2	..	..	..
Austria	29 533.8	30 484.5	31 411.2	31 900.4	32 277.6	33 441.5	34 349.9	35 895.0	35 683.0	36 971.4	38 176.3	39 012.9	40 180.7	41 685.9
Belgium	33 568.1	35 010.6	35 725.4	36 370.4	37 517.1	37 164.6	38 876.9	41 245.9	42 699.5	45 160.9	44 333.6	45 378.2	46 192.4	47 797.9
Canada	26 001.6	26 467.7	27 100.3	27 806.6	29 009.2	29 741.5	30 451.7	31 806.4	32 752.4	32 784.5	33 624.5	35 103.0	36 961.6	..
Czech Republic	..	..	11 388.6	12 589.7	12 815.5	12 886.3	13 915.4	14 682.8	16 090.6	16 779.3	18 727.9	19 578.7	20 643.7	21 977.9
Denmark	23 914.9	24 065.4	25 014.3	26 150.1	27 173.2	28 528.7	29 318.4	30 397.8	30 916.9	32 564.7	32 590.7	34 026.1	34 800.3	..
Finland	21 880.5	23 029.2	24 272.5	25 109.9	25 633.0	26 621.1	27 448.4	28 618.3	29 328.9	30 134.6	30 733.0	32 741.8	33 851.8	35 380.4
France	28 408.7	29 017.0	30 003.5	30 781.1	31 879.8	32 711.9	34 015.0	35 716.0	37 594.1	39 169.5	38 379.5	39 950.1	41 818.0	43 316.1
Germany	27 983.4	28 695.5	29 971.3	30 684.9	30 991.1	31 281.6	32 187.3	32 795.6	33 534.1	34 168.3	35 338.5	36 167.2	36 216.5	36 901.7
Greece	..	..	18 608.7	19 193.6	20 943.1	20 973.1	21 964.8	23 288.5	25 606.7	28 447.8	28 425.6	29 591.2	30 887.9	32 721.2
Hungary	..	..	14 293.7	14 288.1	14 940.4	15 135.4	14 620.8	15 611.8	17 260.8	18 989.4	19 885.9	21 131.8	22 303.5	22 870.3
Ireland	..	..	25 935.4	26 861.2	27 118.7	28 093.1	28 320.5	29 518.5	30 851.8	31 098.4	33 211.7	35 693.1	37 525.8	39 358.1
Italy	28 109.6	28 387.3	28 551.6	29 504.8	30 855.0	30 464.5	31 018.3	31 735.4	32 261.9	32 100.8	33 030.5	33 886.4	34 869.5	35 833.3
Japan	23 154.0	23 861.8	24 809.7	25 498.4	25 965.4	26 106.7	26 386.7	27 996.8	28 763.0	29 694.5	30 619.1	31 220.0	33 013.1	..
Korea	18 348.0	19 175.7	21 185.1	22 844.5	22 802.1	22 520.2	22 612.8	22 520.6	23 381.9	23 855.2	25 287.0	26 136.5	27 389.4	28 387.7
Luxembourg	36 560.0	37 780.8	38 352.0	39 565.8	39 837.7	40 812.2	43 173.8	45 781.8	46 923.8	49 145.3	50 345.2	52 755.4	54 532.3	56 981.3
Mexico	..	..	7 852.1	7 442.1	7 961.3	8 049.1	8 653.5	9 380.9	9 921.5	10 131.3	10 486.2	10 464.7	..	..
Netherlands	27 506.6	27 945.5	28 275.1	28 893.5	29 460.8	30 737.4	31 749.3	33 863.7	34 872.9	36 503.9	36 492.3	38 535.1	39 227.8	40 498.4
New Zealand	22 088.6	22 779.1	23 090.6	23 690.7	24 554.1	24 165.8	24 261.1	24 504.1	25 489.1	25 763.0	26 484.8	28 038.4	28 252.6	..
Norway	21 847.9	22 818.0	23 574.0	25 129.6	26 019.7	27 357.7	28 600.1	29 758.9	31 122.6	32 690.4	34 306.0	36 213.7	38 029.0	39 921.9
Poland	9 209.2	9 558.2	10 292.7	11 299.8	12 165.2	12 879.8	13 782.9	14 444.3	15 713.9	16 106.0	16 601.1	17 238.0	17 302.6	..
Portugal	..	..	16 360.3	17 213.0	17 918.7	18 157.4	19 353.8	20 537.4	21 227.9	21 537.0	22 663.5	23 041.2	..	..
Slovak Republic	..	8 285.8	9 339.5	9 768.2	11 044.1	11 916.1	11 766.3	12 367.5	13 345.5	14 387.2	14 316.5	15 048.1	16 001.0	17 184.0
Spain	25 782.2	26 021.2	26 281.2	26 997.1	27 675.6	28 257.8	28 752.9	29 701.0	30 998.9	32 401.5	32 323.6	32 294.2	32 441.2	33 121.7
Sweden	22 473.4	23 647.2	24 102.0	26 198.3	27 408.9	28 122.0	28 927.8	31 884.0	32 705.5	33 530.6	34 655.7	36 786.1	38 068.1	..
United Kingdom	23 036.0	23 734.3	24 319.9	25 283.2	26 383.2	27 493.5	28 629.1	31 205.9	33 314.3	34 165.0	35 787.5	38 006.2	38 448.8	40 201.9
United States	33 803.4	34 749.8	35 897.0	37 045.2	38 438.8	40 698.2	42 673.9	44 882.6	46 070.9	47 317.9	48 780.6	50 804.8	52 441.6	54 747.8
Euro area	28 232.0	29 117.5	30 003.6	30 685.4	31 300.1	31 738.8	32 253.4	33 426.1	34 440.7	35 520.7	36 429.5	37 419.5	38 397.6	..
OECD total	25 877.6	26 601.8	27 430.4	28 264.1	29 147.8	30 141.7	31 303.0	32 893.1	33 991.9	34 872.6	35 851.2	..	..	..

StatLink ᵐˢ⅃ http://dx.doi.org/10.1787/274317476540

Labour compensation per employee, total economy
Average annual growth in percentage, 1995-2006 or latest available period

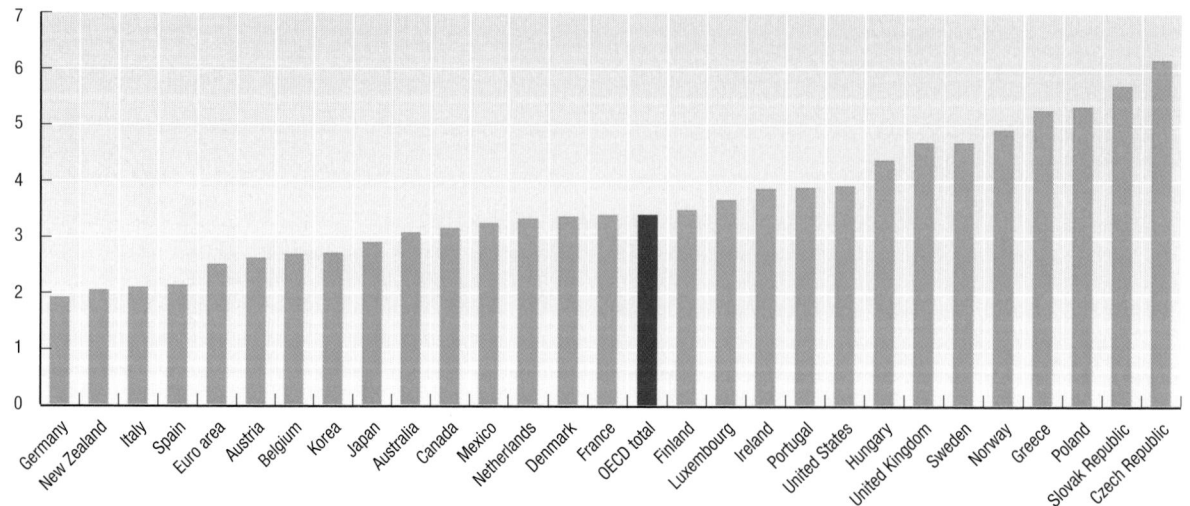

StatLink ᵐˢ⅃ http://dx.doi.org/10.1787/268550265554

Labour compensation per hour, total economy
US dollars calculated using PPPs

	1993	1994	1995	1996	1997	1998	1999	2000	2001	2002	2003	2004	2005	2006
Australia	..	13.8	14.4	15.2	15.8	16.2	16.9	17.4	18.0	18.3	18.6	19.5	20.1	..
Austria	16.7	17.3	18.1	18.2	18.4	19.1	19.9	21.0	20.9	21.7	22.3	22.7	23.4	24.3
Canada	14.8	15.0	15.3	15.6	16.5	17.0	17.3	18.1	18.7	18.9	19.5	20.1	21.3	..
Denmark	15.9	16.4	17.0	17.9	18.3	19.0	19.4	20.0	20.2	21.4	21.5	22.3	22.6	23.4
Finland	13.4	14.0	14.7	15.2	15.5	16.2	16.7	17.5	18.0	18.5	18.9	20.1	20.9	21.8
France	17.9	18.4	19.3	19.7	20.5	21.2	22.0	23.7	25.2	26.9	26.5	27.1	28.4	..
Germany	18.9	19.5	20.6	21.4	21.8	22.1	22.9	23.6	24.4	25.0	26.0	26.5	26.7	27.3
Greece	..	..	9.0	9.4	10.5	10.4	10.7	11.3	12.4	13.8	13.8	14.5	15.1	15.5
Hungary	..	..	7.2	7.2	7.4	7.5	7.2	7.7	8.7	9.5	10.1	10.8	11.3	11.6
Italy	17.0	17.2	17.2	17.6	18.5	18.2	18.5	18.9	19.5	19.5	20.1	20.6	21.3	22.1
Korea	7.0	7.4	8.1	8.8	9.0	9.2	9.1	9.0	9.4	9.7	10.5	11.0	11.7	12.2
Norway	15.0	15.7	16.4	17.5	18.2	19.1	20.0	21.0	22.4	23.8	25.2	26.2	27.5	29.1
Slovak Republic	..	..	5.2	5.5	6.3	6.9	6.7	7.1	7.6	8.5	8.9	9.3	9.7	10.3
Spain	..	..	15.8	16.1	16.5	16.8	17.1	17.6	18.4	19.3	19.4	19.5	19.8	20.2
Sweden	14.2	14.6	14.8	16.0	16.7	17.1	17.5	19.5	20.2	21.0	22.0	23.1	24.1	25.2

StatLink ⧉ http://dx.doi.org/10.1787/274323126247

Labour compensation per hour, total economy
Average annual growth in percentage, 1995-2006 or latest available period

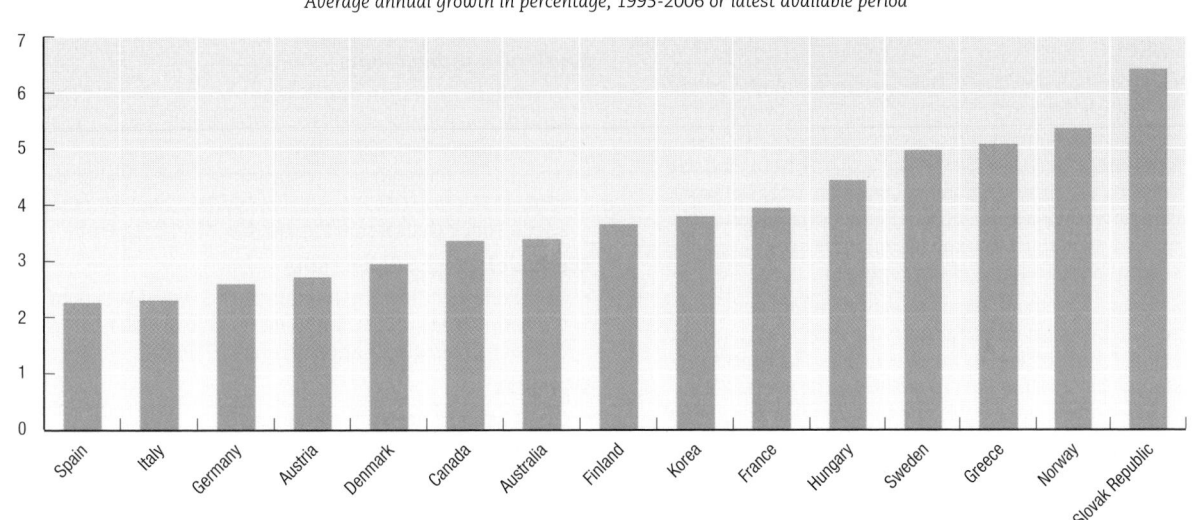

StatLink ⧉ http://dx.doi.org/10.1787/268566317605

HOURS WORKED

Governments of some OECD countries have pursued policies to make it easier for parents to reconcile work and family, and some of these policies also tend to reduce working time. Examples include the extension of annual paid leave, maternity/parental leave and workers' options for working part-time schedules or, albeit less frequently, the reduction of the full-time workweek.

Definition

The average hours worked is calculated as the total numbers of hours worked over the year divided by the average numbers of people in employment.

Employment is generally measured through household labour force surveys and, in accordance with the ILO Guidelines, employed persons are defined as those aged 15 years or over who report that they have worked in gainful employment for at least one hour in the previous week.

Estimates of the hours actually worked are also based on household labour force surveys in most countries, while the rest use establishment surveys, administrative sources or a combination of sources. They include regular work hours of full-time and part-time workers, over-time (paid and unpaid), hours worked in additional jobs and time not worked because of public holidays, annual paid leave, time spent on illness and maternity leave, strikes and labour disputes, bad weather, economic conditions and several other minor reasons.

Comparability

National statisticians and the OECD secretariat work to ensure that these data are as comparable as possible, but they are based on a range of different sources of varying reliability. For example, for several EU countries, the estimates are made by the OECD using results from the *Spring European Labour Force Survey*. The results reflect a single observation in the year and the survey data have to be supplemented by information from other sources for hours not worked due to public holidays and annual paid leave. Annual working hours reported for the remaining countries are provided by national statistical offices and are estimated using the best available sources. The data are intended for comparisons of trends over time and are not fully suitable for inter-country comparisons because of differences in their sources and other uncertainties about their international comparability.

Data cover dependent and self-employed as well as full-time and part-time employment.

Long-term trends

In the large majority of OECD countries, hours worked have fallen over the period from 1993 to 2006. However, this decline was not particularly large in most countries, as compared to the decline in earlier decades and some of the decline in average hours between these two years may reflect transitory business cycle effects, since labour markets generally were more buoyant in 1992 (near the end of a long expansion in many OECD countries) than in 2005.

The average hours worked per year per employed person fell from in 1993 to in 2006; this is equivalent to a reduction in hours worked of more than one 40-hour workweek. The table shows that working hours fell in a majority of countries; hours increased in only Denmark, Hungary, Mexico and Sweden. Reductions in hours worked were most marked in, Ireland, Korea, Luxembourg, France and Germany.

Although one should exercise caution when comparing across countries, it is clear from the table and chart that actual hours worked in the Czech Republic, Greece, Hungary, Korea and Poland are above the average for OECD countries as a whole and that actual hours worked are relatively low in Belgium, France, Germany, the Netherlands and Norway.

Source
- OECD (2007), *OECD Employment Outlook*, OECD, Paris.

Further information
Analytical publications
- Durand, M., J. Martin and A. Saint-Martin (2004), "The 35-hour week: Portrait of a French exception", *OECD Observer, No. 244, September 2004*, OECD, Paris.
- Evans, J., D. Lippoldt and P. Marianna (2001), *Trends in Working Hours in OECD Countries*, OECD Labour Market and Social Policy Occasional Papers, No. 45, OECD, Paris.

Methodological publications
- OECD (2004), "Clocking In (and Out): Several Facets of Working Time", *OECD Employment Outlook: 2004 Edition*, Chapter 1, see also Annex I.A1, OECD, Paris.

Websites
- OECD Labour Statistics Database, *www.oecd.org/statistics/labour*.
- OECD Employment Data, *www.oecd.org/els/employment/data*.

Average hours actually worked

Hours per year per person in employment

	1993	1994	1995	1996	1997	1998	1999	2000	2001	2002	2003	2004	2005	2006
Australia	1 757	1 771	1 780	1 777	1 768	1 769	1 755	1 777	1 748	1 727	1 730	1 728	1 719	1 714
Austria	..	..	1 647	1 664	1 668	1 664	1 638	1 632	1 630	1 632	1 641	1 653	1 656	1 659
Belgium	1 646	1 646	1 674	1 646	1 660	1 672	1 581	1 554	1 577	1 579	1 575	1 549	1 565	1 571
Canada	1 763	1 780	1 775	1 784	1 767	1 767	1 769	1 768	1 762	1 744	1 734	1 752	1 738	1 738
Czech Republic	2 064	2 043	2 064	2 066	2 067	2 075	2 088	2 092	2 000	1 980	1 972	1 986	2 002	1 997
Denmark	1 531	1 494	1 499	1 495	1 512	1 528	1 539	1 554	1 562	1 556	1 552	1 558	1 574	1 584
Finland	1 755	1 775	1 776	1 775	1 771	1 761	1 765	1 750	1 734	1 728	1 720	1 724	1 718	1 721
France	1 682	1 675	1 651	1 655	1 649	1 637	1 630	1 591	1 578	1 536	1 530	1 555	1 559	1 564
Germany	1 550	1 547	1 534	1 518	1 509	1 503	1 492	1 473	1 458	1 445	1 439	1 442	1 437	1 436
Greece	2 199	2 165	2 154	2 129	2 096	2 093	2 139	2 152	2 092	2 072	2 071	2 067	2 074	2 052
Hungary	1 899	2 032	2 039	2 034	2 060	2 052	2 067	2 061	2 019	2 026	1 997	1 996	1 994	1 989
Iceland	1 828	1 813	1 832	1 860	1 839	1 817	1 873	1 885	1 847	1 812	1 807	1 810	1 794	1 794
Ireland	1 883	1 883	1 875	1 882	1 832	1 753	1 725	1 719	1 709	1 695	1 671	1 668	1 654	1 640
Italy	1 863	1 857	1 859	1 873	1 863	1 880	1 876	1 861	1 843	1 831	1 826	1 826	1 815	1 800
Japan	1 905	1 898	1 884	1 892	1 865	1 842	1 810	1 821	1 809	1 798	1 799	1 787	1 775	1 784
Korea	2 667	2 651	2 658	2 648	2 592	2 496	2 502	2 520	2 506	2 465	2 434	2 394	2 354	2 357
Luxembourg	1 732	1 709	1 719	1 691	1 678	1 672	1 669	1 662	1 646	1 634	1 614	1 585	1 570	1 604
Mexico	1 821	..	1 857	1 902	1 927	1 878	1 922	1 888	1 864	1 888	1 857	1 849	1 909	1 883
Netherlands	1 419	1 411	1 391	1 421	1 414	1 400	1 381	1 372	1 372	1 348	1 363	1 362	1 375	1 391
New Zealand	1 854	1 849	1 842	1 833	1 821	1 824	1 838	1 830	1 817	1 817	1 813	1 827	1 810	1 787
Norway	1 507	1 505	1 488	1 483	1 478	1 476	1 473	1 455	1 429	1 414	1 399	1 417	1 421	1 407
Poland	..	..	..	..	..	..	..	1 988	1 974	1 979	1 984	1 983	1 994	1 985
Portugal	1 850	1 838	1 897	1 848	1 812	1 799	1 812	1 765	1 769	1 767	1 742	1 763	1 752	1 758
Slovak Republic	..	1 854	1 879	1 840	1 834	1 798	1 808	1 811	1 799	1 746	1 673	1 708	1 741	1 749
Spain	1 816	1 816	1 815	1 811	1 813	1 834	1 817	1 815	1 817	1 798	1 800	1 799	1 769	1 764
Sweden	1 582	1 621	1 626	1 635	1 639	1 638	1 647	1 625	1 603	1 580	1 562	1 585	1 588	1 583
Switzerland	1 704	1 725	1 702	1 674	1 662	1 669	1 690	1 685	1 646	1 629	1 639	1 629	1 659	1 659
Turkey	..	..	..	..	..	..	..	..	..	..	..	1 918	1 918	1 918
United Kingdom	1 726	1 740	1 743	1 742	1 740	1 734	1 723	1 711	1 714	1 696	1 677	1 672	1 676	1 669
United States	1 825	1 833	1 840	1 832	1 842	1 843	1 844	1 832	1 811	1 807	1 797	1 800	1 795	1 797
EU15 total	1 697	1 696	1 691	1 689	1 683	1 682	1 672	1 655	1 647	1 630	1 625	1 630	1 627	1 625
OECD total	1 836	1 712	1 840	1 842	1 838	1 825	1 821	1 812	1 796	1 787	1 779	1 779	1 778	1 777

StatLink http://dx.doi.org/10.1787/274371410400

Average hours actually worked

Hours per year per person in employment, 2006

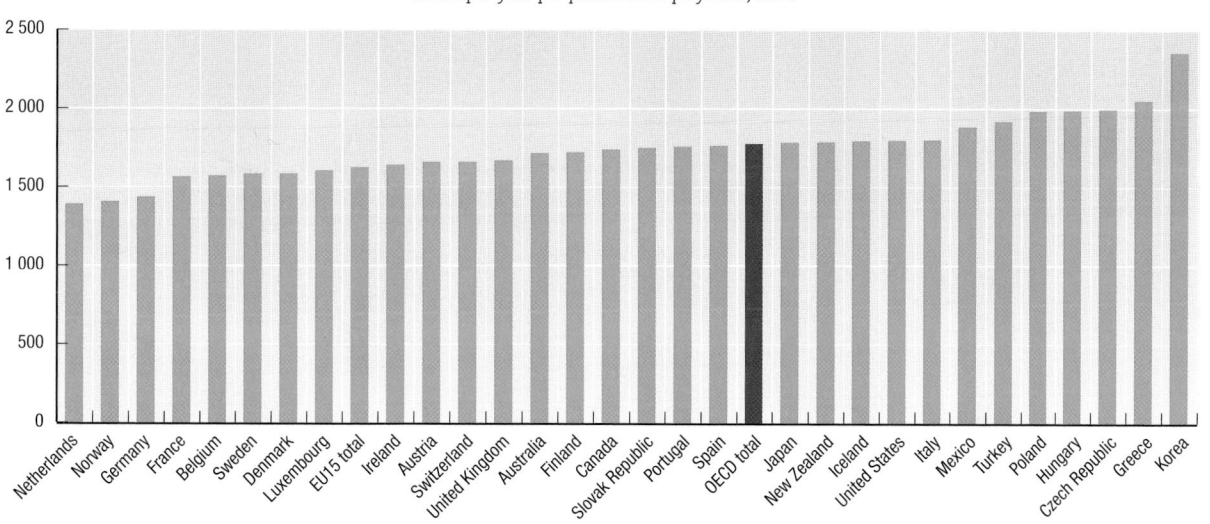

StatLink http://dx.doi.org/10.1787/268611353076

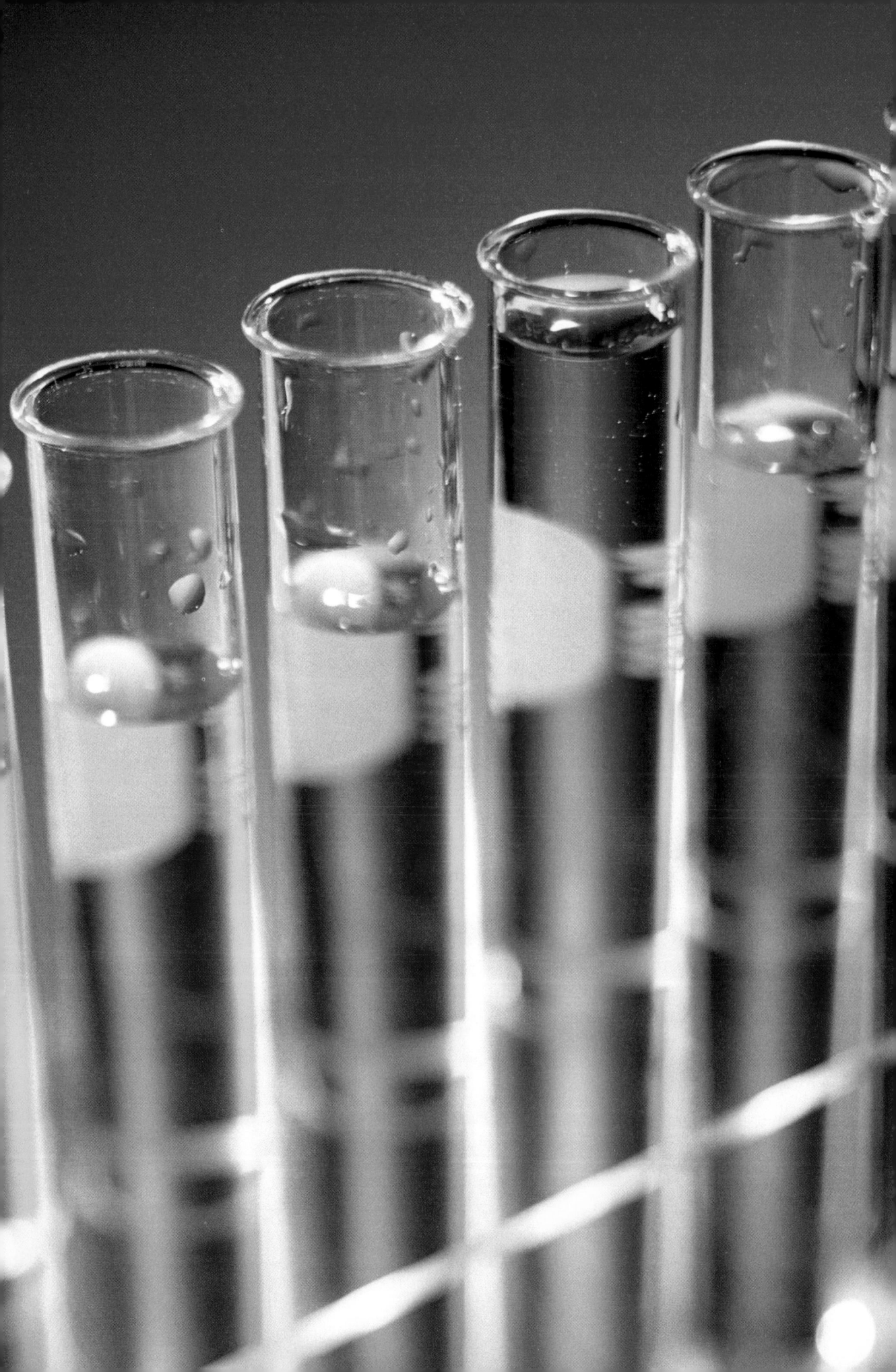

SCIENCE AND TECHNOLOGY

RESEARCH AND DEVELOPMENT (R&D)
EXPENDITURE ON R&D
INVESTMENT IN KNOWLEDGE
RESEARCHERS
PATENTS

ICT
SIZE OF THE ICT SECTOR
INVESTMENT IN ICT
COMPUTER AND INTERNET ACCESS BY HOUSEHOLDS

COMMUNICATIONS
EXPORTS OF INFORMATION AND COMMUNICATIONS EQUIPMENT
TELEPHONE ACCESS

EXPENDITURE ON R&D

Expenditure on research and development (R&D) is a key indicator of government and private sector efforts to obtain competitive advantage in science and technology. In 2005, research and development amounted to 2.3% of GDP for the OECD as a whole.

Definition

Research and development (R&D) comprise creative work undertaken on a systematic basis in order to increase the stock of knowledge, including knowledge of man, culture and society, and the use of this stock of knowledge to devise new applications. R&D is a term covering three activities: basic research, applied research, and experimental development. Basic research is experimental or theoretical work undertaken primarily to acquire new knowledge of the underlying foundation of phenomena and observable facts, without any particular application or use in view. Applied research is also original investigation undertaken in order to acquire new knowledge. It is, however, directed primarily towards a specific practical aim or objective. Experimental development is systematic work, drawing on existing knowledge gained from research and/or practical experience, that is directed to producing new materials, products or devices, to installing new processes, systems and services, or to improving substantially those already produced or installed.

The main aggregate used for international comparisons is gross domestic expenditure on R&D (GERD). This consists of the total expenditure (current and capital) on R&D by all resident companies, research institutes, university and government laboratories, etc. It excludes R&D expenditures financed by domestic firms but performed abroad.

Long-term trends

Since 2000, R&D expenditure relative to GDP (R&D intensity) has increased in Japan, and it has decreased slightly in the United States.

In 2004 and 2005, Sweden, Finland, and Japan were the only three OECD countries in which the R&D-to-GDP ratio exceeded 3%, well above the OECD average of 2.3%. Since the mid-1990s, R&D expenditure (in real terms) has been growing the fastest in Iceland and Turkey, both with average annual growth rates above 10%.

R&D expenditure for China has been growing even faster than GDP, resulting in a rapidly increasing R&D intensity, growing from 0.9% in 2000 to 1.4% in 2006.

Comparability

The R&D data shown here have been compiled according to the guidelines of the Frascati Manual. It should, however, be noted that over the period shown, several countries have improved the coverage of their surveys of R&D activities in the services sector (Japan, Netherlands, Norway and United States) and in higher education (Finland, Greece, Japan, Netherlands, Spain and the United States). Other countries, including especially Italy, Japan and Sweden, have worked to improve the international comparability of their data. Some of the changes shown in the table reflect these methodological improvements as well as the underlying changes in R&D expenditures.

For Korea, social sciences and the humanities are excluded from the R&D data. For the United States, capital expenditure is not covered.

Data for Brazil and India are not completely according to Frascati Manual guidelines, and were compiled from national sources. Data for Brazil, India and South Africa are underestimated, as are the data for China before 2000.

Source
- OECD (2007), *Main Science and Technology Indicators*, OECD, Paris.

Further information

Analytical publications
- OECD (2006), *OECD Science, Technology and Industry Outlook 2006*, OECD, Paris.
- OECD (2007), *OECD Science, Technology and Industry: Scoreboard 2007*, OECD, Paris.
- OECD (2007), *The Space Economy at a Glance*, OECD, Paris.

Statistical publications
- OECD (2007), *OECD Science, Technology and R&D Statistics on CD-ROM*, OECD, Paris.

Methodological publications
- OECD (2003), *Frascati Manual 2002: Proposed Standard Practice for Surveys on Research and Experimental Development*, OECD, Paris.

Online databases
- STAN: *OECD Structural Analysis Statistics – online database*, ANBERD: R&D Expenditure in Industry.

Websites
- OECD Science, Technology and Industry, *www.oecd.org/sti*.

Gross domestic expenditure on R&D
As a percentage of GDP

	1993	1994	1995	1996	1997	1998	1999	2000	2001	2002	2003	2004	2005	2006
Australia	..	1.53	..	1.61	..	1.47	..	1.51	..	1.69	..	1.78	..	..
Austria	1.44	1.51	1.54	1.59	1.69	1.77	1.88	1.91	2.03	2.12	2.23	2.22	2.41	2.45
Belgium	1.66	1.65	1.67	1.77	1.83	1.86	1.94	1.97	2.08	1.94	1.89	1.87	1.86	1.85
Canada	1.68	1.73	1.70	1.65	1.66	1.76	1.80	1.92	2.09	2.04	2.01	2.01	1.98	1.97
Czech Republic	..	..	0.95	0.97	1.08	1.15	1.14	1.21	1.20	1.20	1.25	1.25	1.41	1.54
Denmark	1.72	..	1.82	1.84	1.92	2.04	2.18	..	2.39	2.51	2.58	2.50	2.45	2.43
Finland	2.14	2.28	2.26	2.52	2.70	2.86	3.16	3.34	3.30	3.36	3.43	3.45	3.48	3.45
France	2.38	2.32	2.29	2.27 |	2.19	2.14	2.16 |	2.15	2.20	2.23	2.17 |	2.15	2.13	2.12
Germany	2.28	2.18	2.19	2.19	2.24	2.27	2.40	2.45	2.46	2.49	2.52	2.49	2.48	2.51
Greece	0.36	.. |	0.38	..	0.39	..	0.52	..	0.51	..	0.50	0.48	0.51	0.50
Hungary	0.95 |	0.87	0.71	0.63	0.70	0.66	0.67	0.78	0.92	1.00	0.93 |	0.88	0.94	1.00
Iceland	1.33	1.37	1.53	..	1.83	2.01	2.30	2.68	2.96	2.97	2.82	..	2.78	..
Ireland	1.16	1.25	1.26	1.30	1.27	1.23	1.18	1.12	1.10	1.10	1.18	1.25	1.26	1.32
Italy	1.10	1.02	0.97	0.99 |	1.03	1.05	1.02	1.05	1.09	1.13	1.11	1.10	1.10	..
Japan	2.65	2.60	2.71 |	2.81	2.87	3.00	3.02	3.04	3.12	3.17	3.20	3.17	3.33	..
Korea	2.12	2.32	2.37	2.42	2.48	2.34	2.25	2.39	2.59	2.53	2.63	2.85	2.98	..
Luxembourg	..	..	..	..	..	..	..	1.65	..	1.66	1.66	1.61	..	..
Mexico	0.22	0.29	0.31	0.31	0.34	0.38	0.43	0.37	0.39	0.44	0.43 |	0.47	0.50	..
Netherlands	1.91 |	1.95	1.97 |	1.98	1.99	1.90	1.96	1.82	1.80	1.72	1.76	1.78	1.73	..
New Zealand	1.01	..	0.95	..	1.09	..	1.00	.. |	1.14	..	1.19	..	1.17	..
Norway	1.70	.. |	1.69	..	1.63	..	1.64	..	1.59	1.66	1.71	1.59	1.52	1.49
Poland	0.76	0.70 |	0.63	0.65	0.65	0.67	0.69	0.64	0.62	0.56	0.54	0.56	0.57	0.56
Portugal	0.58	0.56	0.54	0.57	0.59	0.65	0.71	0.76	0.80	0.76	0.74	0.77	0.81	..
Slovak Republic	1.35 |	0.89	0.92	0.90 |	1.07	0.78	0.65	0.65	0.63	0.57	0.58	0.51	0.51	0.49
Spain	0.86	0.79	0.79	0.81	0.80	0.87	0.86	0.91	0.91	0.99	1.05	1.06	1.12	..
Sweden	3.15	.. |	3.32	..	3.51	..	3.62	..	4.25	..	3.95	3.71 |	3.89	3.82
Switzerland	..	..	..	2.65	..	..	..	2.53	..	..	..	2.90	..	..
Turkey	0.44	0.36	0.38	0.45	0.49	0.50	0.63	0.64	0.72	0.66	0.61	0.67	0.79	..
United Kingdom	2.05	2.01	1.95	1.87	1.81	1.80	1.87	1.86	1.83	1.83	1.79	1.73	1.78	..
United States	2.52	2.42	2.51	2.55	2.58 |	2.62	2.66	2.74	2.76	2.66	2.66	2.59	2.62	2.62
EU27 total	..	..	1.66	1.66	1.66	1.67	1.72	1.73	1.76	1.76	1.75	1.73	1.74	..
OECD total	2.11	2.06 |	2.07	2.10	2.12	2.15	2.18	2.22	2.27	2.23	2.24	2.21	2.25	..
Brazil	..	..	0.87	0.77	..	..	..	1.01	1.05	1.00	0.97	0.91	..	..
China	0.70	0.64	0.57	0.57	0.64	0.65	0.76 |	0.90	0.95	1.07	1.13	1.23	1.33	1.43
India	0.71	0.65	0.63	0.65	0.70	0.72	0.74	0.77	0.75	0.73	0.71	0.69	..	..
Russian Federation	0.77	0.84	0.85	0.97	1.04	0.95	1.00	1.05	1.18	1.25	1.28	1.15	1.07	1.08
South Africa	0.61	..	..	..	0.60	..	..	..	0.73	..	0.80	0.86	0.92	..

StatLink http://dx.doi.org/10.1787/274374238001

Gross domestic expenditure on R&D
As a percentage of GDP, 2006 or latest available year

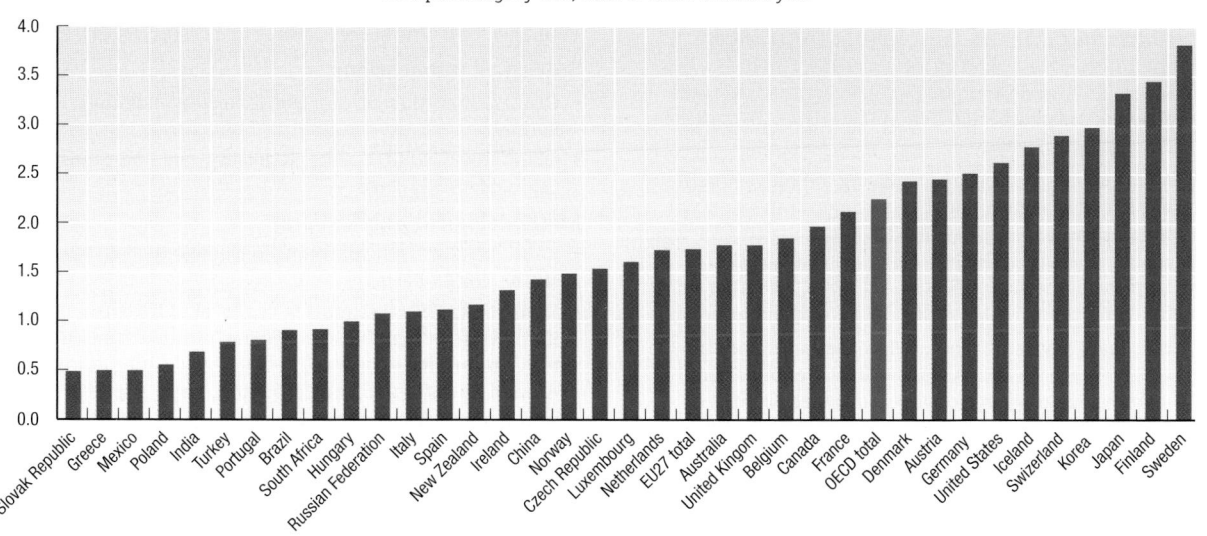

StatLink http://dx.doi.org/10.1787/268663601088

INVESTMENT IN KNOWLEDGE

"Investment in knowledge" is a synthetic indicator designed to compare member countries' expenditures on their "knowledge base" which are aimed at bringing future returns.

Definition

Investment in knowledge is defined and calculated as the sum of expenditure on R&D, on total higher education (public and private) and on software. Simple summation of the three components would lead to overestimation of the investment in knowledge owing to overlaps (R&D and software, R&D and education, software and education). Therefore, data reported here have been adjusted to exclude the overlaps between components.

Note that as the term is used here, "investment" has a broader connotation than its usual meaning in economic statistics. It includes current expenditures, such as on education and R&D, as well as capital outlays, such as purchases of software and construction of school buildings.

Comparability

The OECD is the source of the data on R&D, education and software. In previous years, the software component of investment in knowledge was estimated from a private source. However, the OECD has recently developed a capital services database, which includes software investment data. Software data from the OECD's capital services database are used here, and the figures reported here differ from those of previous years.

Note that OECD total excludes Australia, Austria and Greece from the group of reporting countries; EU15 total excludes Greece from the group of reporting countries.

Long-term trends

In 2004, investment in knowledge amounted to 4.9% of GDP in the OECD area. It exceeds the OECD average in the United States (6.6%), Sweden (6.4%), Finland (5.9%), Japan (5.3%) and Denmark (5.1%). In contrast, it is less than 2.5% in Ireland and Italy and less than 2% of GDP in Portugal and Greece.

Most OECD countries are increasing their investment in the knowledge base. For all reporting countries except Ireland, the ratio of investment in knowledge to GDP was higher in 2004 (or 2003) than in 1997. Further, the increase in the United States and Japan is sharper than in the EU countries for which data is available.

For Japan, Sweden, France, the Netherlands and the United Kingdom, increases in software expenditure were the major source of increased investment in knowledge. In the United States and Belgium, higher education was the main driver of the expansion of investment in knowledge. R&D was the main source of increase in Denmark, Finland, Canada, Spain, Germany, Portugal, Greece, Australia and Austria.

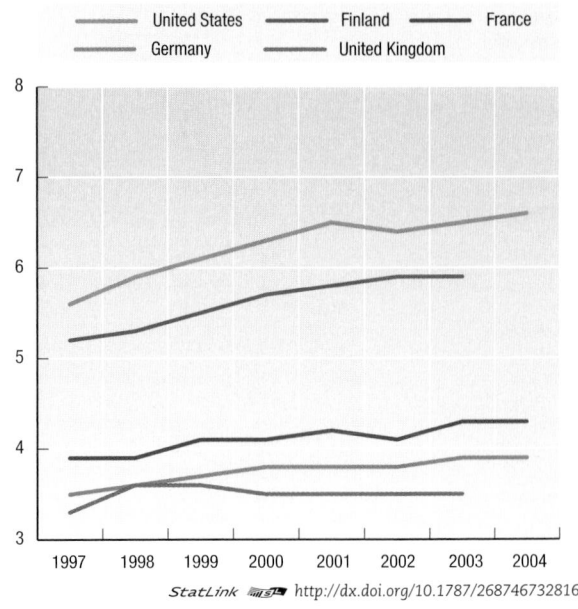

Investment in knowledge for selected countries

As a percentage of GDP

— United States — Finland — France
— Germany — United Kingdom

StatLink http://dx.doi.org/10.1787/268746732816

Source

- OECD (2007), *OECD Science, Technology and Industry: Scoreboard 2007*, OECD, Paris.

Further information

Analytical publications

- Ahmad, N. (2003), *Measuring Investment in Software*, OECD Science, Technology and Industry Working Papers, No. 2003/6, OECD, Paris.
- OECD (2006), *Innovation and Knowledge-Intensive Service Activities*, OECD, Paris.
- OECD (2007), *The Space Economy at a Glance*, OECD, Paris.

Statistical publications

- OECD (2007), *Main Science and Technology Indicators*, OECD, Paris.
- OECD (2007), *OECD Science, Technology and R&D Statistics on CD-ROM*, OECD, Paris.

Methodological publications

- Kahn, M. (2001), "Investment in Knowledge", *STI Review No. 27*, OECD, Paris.
- Kahn, M. (2005), "Estimating the level of Investment in Knowledge across OECD countries", *Intellectual Capital for Community – Nations, Regions, and Cities* edited by Ahmed Bounfor and Leif Edvinsson, Elsevier Butterworth-Heinemann, Amsterdam; Boston.

Websites

- OECD Measuring Science and Technology, *www.oecd.org/sti/measuring-scitech*.
- OECD Science, Technology and Industry Scoreboard, *www.sourceoecd.org/scoreboard*.

Investment in knowledge

As a percentage of GDP

	1997	1998	1999	2000	2001	2002	2003	2004
Australia	..	3.6	..	3.9	..	4.0	3.9	3.9
Austria	..	3.1	..	..	..	3.3	3.4	..
Belgium	..	2.6	3.5	3.6	3.8	3.5	3.4	..
Canada	3.9	4.0	4.6	4.6	4.9	..	4.5	4.5
Denmark	3.8	4.5	4.7	4.7	5.1	5.3	5.1	..
Finland	5.2	5.3	5.5	5.7	5.8	5.9	5.9	..
France	3.9	3.9	4.1	4.1	4.2	4.1	4.3	4.3
Germany	3.5	3.6	3.7	3.8	3.8	3.8	3.9	3.9
Greece	1.7	..	1.7	..	1.9	..	1.9	..
Ireland	2.6	2.5	2.6	2.6	2.5	2.3	2.3	..
Italy	2.0	2.1	2.2	2.2	2.4	2.4	2.4	..
Japan	4.1	4.4	4.5	4.6	4.8	4.9	5.1	5.3
Netherlands	3.5	3.6	3.9	3.7	3.8	3.6	3.7	..
Portugal	1.5	1.6	1.7	1.8	1.8	1.7	1.7	..
Spain	2.2	2.3	2.4	2.5	2.6	2.6	2.7	2.7
Sweden	5.6	..	6.2	..	6.9	..	6.4	..
United Kingdom	3.3	3.6	3.6	3.5	3.5	3.5	3.5	..
United States	5.6	5.9	6.1	6.3	6.5	6.4	6.5	6.6
EU15 total	3.2	..	3.5	..	3.6	..	3.6	..
OECD total	4.2	..	4.7	..	4.9	..	4.9	..

StatLink ⟨⟩ http://dx.doi.org/10.1787/274582752121

Investment in knowledge

As a percentage of GDP, 2004 or latest available year

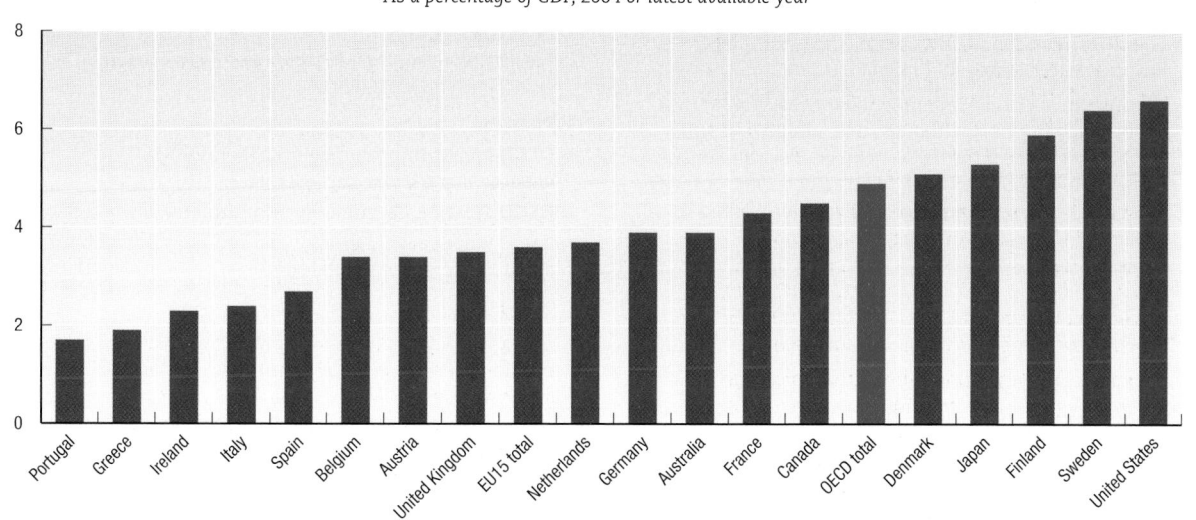

StatLink ⟨⟩ http://dx.doi.org/10.1787/268703568655

RESEARCHERS

Researchers are the central element of the research and development system. In 2005, approximately 3.9 million persons in the OECD area were employed in research and development and approximately two-thirds of these were engaged in the business sector.

Definition

Researchers are defined as professionals engaged in the conception and creation of new knowledge, products, processes, methods and systems as well as those who are directly involved in the management of projects. They include researchers working in both civil and military research in government, universities, research institutes as well as in the business sector.

Comparability

The number of researchers is expressed in full-time equivalent (FTE) on R&D (i.e. a person working half-time on R&D is counted as 0.5 person-year) and includes staff engaged in R&D during the course of one year. The data have been compiled on the basis of the methodology of the Frascati Manual, but comparability over time is affected to some extent by improvements in the coverage of national R&D surveys and efforts by countries to improve the international comparability of their data.

For the United Kingdom and the United States, the total researchers figures beginning 1999 and 2000 respectively are OECD estimates. Also for the United States, data since 1985 exclude military personnel.

Data for Brazil and India are not completely according to Frascati Manual guidelines, and were compiled from national sources. Data for Brazil and South Africa are underestimated, as are the data for China before 2000.

Long-term trends

In 2005, there were about 7.4 researchers per thousand employees in the OECD area, compared with 5.9 per thousand in 1995. The number of researchers has steadily increased over the last two decades. Among the major OECD regions, Japan has the highest number of researchers relative to total employment, followed by the United States and the European Union.

Finland, Sweden, Japan, and New Zealand have the highest number of research workers per thousand persons employed. Rates are also high in the United States, Denmark and Norway. Among the OECD countries, research workers per thousand employees are low in Mexico, Turkey and Italy.

Among the major non-member countries, growth has been steady in China, although, at 1.5 in 2005, it still remains well below the OECD average. The rate for the Russian Federation has been falling since 1994, but was still close to 7 researchers per thousand employed in 2005.

Source

- OECD (2007), *Main Science and Technology Indicators*, OECD, Paris.

Further information

Analytical publications

- OECD (2007), *OECD Science, Technology and Industry: Scoreboard 2007*, OECD, Paris.

Statistical publications

- OECD (2007), *OECD Science, Technology and R&D Statistics on CD-ROM*, OECD, Paris.

Methodological publications

- OECD (2003), *Frascati Manual 2002: Proposed Standard Practice for Surveys on Research and Experimental Development*, OECD, Paris.

Websites

- OECD Measuring Science and Technology, *www.oecd.org/sti/measuring-scitech*.
- OECD Science, Technology and Industry, *www.oecd.org/sti*.
- OECD Science, Technology and Industry Scoreboard, *www.sourceoecd.org/scoreboard*.

Researchers

Per thousand employed, full-time equivalent

	1993	1994	1995	1996	1997	1998	1999	2000	2001	2002	2003	2004	2005	2006
Australia	..	7.0	..	7.3	..	7.3	..	7.3	..	7.8	..	8.4	..	..
Austria	3.3	..	..	..	..	4.7	..	..	..	5.8	..	6.3	6.9	7.2
Belgium	5.5	5.9	6.0	6.5	6.7	7.0	7.4	7.5	7.8	7.4	7.5	7.8	7.9	8.0
Canada	5.7	6.4	6.4	6.6	6.7	6.7	6.7	7.2	7.6	7.5	7.5	7.8	..	..
Czech Republic	..	..	2.3	2.5	2.4	2.5	2.7	2.8	3.0	3.0	3.2	3.3	4.9	5.2
Denmark	5.3	..	6.1	6.3	6.5	..	6.9	..	7.0	9.2	9.1	9.5	10.2	10.2
Finland	7.4	..	8.2	..	12.3	13.9	14.5	15.2	15.8	16.4	17.7	17.3	16.5	16.6
France	6.5	6.6	6.7	6.8	6.8	6.7	6.8	7.1	7.2	7.5	7.7	8.0	8.2	..
Germany	..	..	6.2	6.1	6.3	6.3	6.6	6.6	6.7	6.8	6.9	7.0	7.2	7.2
Greece	2.0	..	2.3	..	2.6	..	3.4	..	3.3	..	3.5	..	4.2	4.2
Hungary	3.1	3.1	2.9	2.9	3.1	3.2	3.3	3.8	3.8	3.9	3.9	3.8	4.1	4.5
Ireland	4.1	4.3	4.5	4.8	5.0	5.1	4.9	5.0	5.1	5.3	5.5	5.9	5.9	6.0
Italy	3.4	3.5	3.5	3.5	3.0	2.9	2.9	2.9	2.9	3.0	2.9	3.0	3.4	..
Japan	7.9	8.1	8.3	9.2	9.3	9.8	10.0	9.9	10.4	10.1	10.6	10.6	11.0	..
Korea	..	..	4.9	4.8	4.8	4.7	4.9	5.1	6.3	6.4	6.8	6.9	7.9	..
Luxembourg	..	..	..	..	..	..	..	6.2	..	..	6.7	6.8	7.3	..
Mexico	0.5	0.5	0.6	0.6	0.6	0.6	0.6	..	..	..	0.9	1.1	1.2	..
Netherlands	4.6	4.9	4.8	4.9	5.1	5.1	5.1	5.2	5.5	4.6	4.5	5.1	4.9	..
New Zealand	5.3	..	4.7	..	6.2	..	6.2	..	9.1	..	10.4	..	10.5	..
Norway	7.2	..	7.5	..	7.9	..	7.9	..	8.6	..	9.1	9.1	9.2	..
Poland	..	3.0	3.2	3.3	3.4	3.4	3.6	3.5	3.7	3.8	4.5	4.7	4.7	4.5
Portugal	2.2	2.3	2.5	2.7	2.9	3.0	3.2	3.3	3.5	3.7	4.0	4.0	4.1	..
Slovak Republic	..	4.9	4.6	4.6	4.7	4.8	4.5	4.9	4.7	4.5	4.7	5.2	5.2	5.5
Spain	3.2	3.6	3.5	3.7	3.8	4.0	3.9	4.7	4.7	4.8	5.2	5.5	5.7	..
Sweden	7.2	..	8.2	..	9.2	..	9.6	..	10.6	..	11.1	11.3	12.7	12.7
Switzerland	..	..	..	5.6	..	..	..	6.4	..	..	..	6.1	..	..
Turkey	0.7	0.7	0.8	0.9	0.9	0.9	0.9	1.1	1.1	1.1	1.6	1.6	1.8	..
United Kingdom	4.8	4.9	5.2	5.1	5.1	5.5	5.6	5.4	5.6	5.8	5.9	5.7	5.8	..
United States	8.2	..	8.1	..	8.8	..	9.3	9.3	9.5	9.7	9.9	10.0	9.7	..
EU27 total	..	..	4.8	4.7	4.9	4.9	5.1	5.1	5.3	5.5	5.6	5.7	6.0	..
OECD total	5.4	5.9	5.9	6.1	6.2	6.4	6.5	6.6	6.8	6.9	7.2	7.2	7.4	..
Brazil	..	..	..	..	..	..	..	0.8	0.9	0.9	1.0	1.0	..	..
China	0.7	0.8	0.8	0.8	0.8	0.7	0.7	1.0	1.0	1.1	1.2	1.2	1.5	1.6
India	..	..	..	..	..	..	..	0.3	..	..	..	..	..	..
Russian Federation	..	9.1	9.2	8.5	8.2	7.7	7.8	7.8	7.9	7.5	7.4	7.1	6.8	6.8
South Africa	..	..	..	..	..	..	..	..	1.2	..	1.3	1.6	1.5	..

StatLink http://dx.doi.org/10.1787/274600808805

Researchers

Per thousand employed, full-time equivalent, 2006 or latest available year

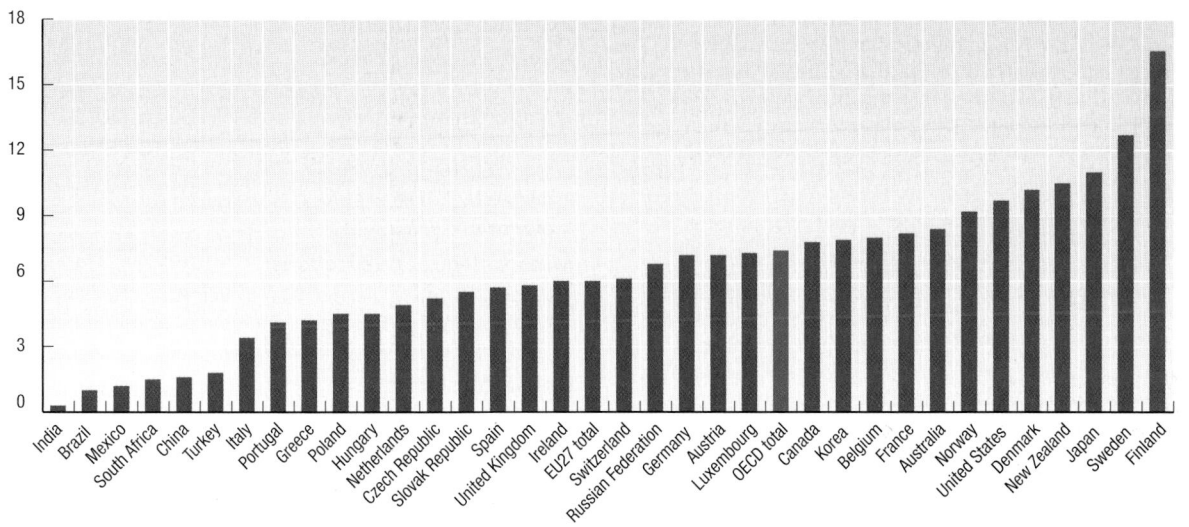

StatLink http://dx.doi.org/10.1787/268814257284

PATENTS

Patent-based indicators provide a measure of the output of a country's R&D, i.e. its inventions. The methodology used for counting patents can influence the results. Simple counts of patents filed at a national patent office are affected by various kinds of limitations, such as weak international comparability (home advantage for patent applications) and highly heterogeneous patent values. The OECD has developed *triadic patent families*, which are designed to capture all important inventions only and to be internationally comparable.

Definition

A patent family is defined as a set of patents taken in various countries (i.e. patent offices) to protect the same invention. Triadic patent families are a set of patents taken at all three of these major patent offices – the European Patent Office (EPO), the Japan Patent Office (JPO) and the United States Patent and Trademark Office (USPTO).

Triadic patent family counts are attributed to the country of residence of the inventor and to the date when the patent was first registered.

Comparability

The concept of triadic patent families has been developed in order to improve the international comparability and quality of patent-based indicators. Indeed, only patents applied in the same set of countries are included in the family: home advantage and influence of geographical location are therefore eliminated. Furthermore, patents included in the family are typically of higher value: patentees only take on the additional costs and delays of extending protection to other countries if they deem it worthwhile.

Share of countries in triadic patent families
Percentage, Year 2005

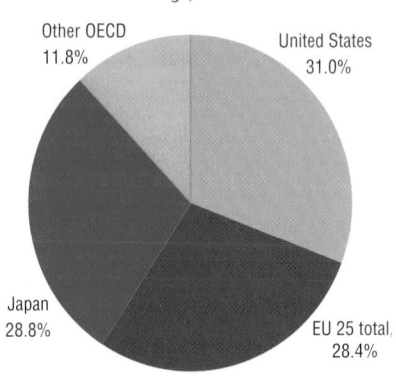

StatLink http://dx.doi.org/10.1787/268866601751

Long-term trends

Growth during the second half of the 1990s was at a steady 7% a year on average until 2000. The beginning of the 21st century was marked by a slowdown, with patent families increasing by 2% a year on average. The United States, the European Union and Japan show a similar trend, with a stronger deceleration in Japan after 2000.

About 53 000 triadic patent families were filed worldwide in 2005, a sharp increase from less than 35 000 in 1995. The United States accounts for 31% of patent families, a loss of around 3 percentage points from its level in 1995 (34.4%); the relative proportion of patent families originating from Europe has also tended to decrease, losing more than 4 percentage points between 1995 and 2005 (to 28.4% in 2005). In contrast, Japan's share in triadic patent families gained almost 2 percentage points to reach nearly 29% in 2005.

When triadic patent families are normalised using total population, Japan, Switzerland, Germany, the Netherlands and Sweden appear as the five most innovative countries in 2005. Ratios for Finland, Israel, Korea, Luxembourg and the United States are above the OECD average (44). Japan has the highest number of patent families per million population (119), followed by Switzerland (107). One of the largest increases between 1995 and 2005, from 7 to 65 patent families per million inhabitants, occurred in Korea. By size, China has less than 0.4 patent families per million population.

Source

• OECD (2007), *Compendium of Patent Statistics 2007*, OECD, Paris.

Further information

Analytical publications

• Lichtenberg, F. and S. Virabhak (2002), *Using Patents Data to Map Technical Change in Health-Related Areas*, OECD Science, Technology and Industry Working Papers, No. 2002/16, OECD, Paris.

• OECD (2006), *OECD Reviews of Innovation Policy – Switzerland*, OECD, Paris.

Methodological publications

• Dernis, H. and M. Khan (2004), *Triadic Patent Families Methodology*, OECD Science, Technology and Industry Working Papers, No. 2004/2, OECD, Paris.

Online databases

• OECD Patent Database.

Websites

• OECD Intellectual Property Rights, *www.oecd.org/sti/ipr*.

• OECD Work on Patents, *www.oecd.org/sti/ipr-statistics*.

OECD FACTBOOK 2008 – ISBN 978-92-64-04054-0 – © OECD 2008

Triadic patent families

Number

	1992	1993	1994	1995	1996	1997	1998	1999	2000	2001	2002	2003	2004	2005
Australia	180	192	227	221	220	261	309	324	398	389	397	409	425	414
Austria	145	171	209	215	210	250	264	241	259	270	274	281	288	301
Belgium	290	328	343	369	346	411	385	394	366	337	337	340	358	333
Canada	273	286	355	382	438	556	590	631	609	599	686	712	766	820
Czech Republic	7	8	5	3	11	11	14	11	8	13	14	15	15	15
Denmark	131	156	177	180	217	211	266	234	238	228	227	233	222	220
Finland	224	243	342	305	346	426	422	423	358	325	254	259	268	264
France	1 628	1 694	1 864	1 878	2 093	2 112	2 245	2 308	2 277	2 257	2 354	2 407	2 440	2 463
Germany	3 849	4 007	4 358	4 737	5 338	5 499	6 069	6 255	6 236	6 223	6 112	6 176	6 283	6 266
Greece	6	2	4	1	13	10	11	12	9	6	9	12	10	13
Hungary	18	22	19	25	23	32	17	36	34	31	27	37	39	37
Iceland	-	1	3	4	7	4	5	7	10	3	8	7	5	5
Ireland	24	18	31	27	26	36	40	63	42	50	46	48	51	59
Italy	572	627	619	601	679	712	636	637	662	693	663	703	706	716
Japan	8 154	8 454	8 234	9 429	10 379	10 649	11 232	12 740	14 709	13 642	13 922	14 428	15 347	15 239
Korea	120	161	213	324	324	416	487	663	820	1 027	1 383	2 018	2 583	3 158
Luxembourg	9	14	7	13	14	14	21	19	17	21	15	22	27	24
Mexico	6	6	5	13	10	13	9	12	10	13	14	17	17	20
Netherlands	613	594	670	710	792	794	899	1 028	1 169	1 409	1 220	1 203	1 215	1 184
New Zealand	26	12	21	20	32	39	45	51	58	45	60	73	67	64
Norway	71	71	83	86	73	89	92	110	111	92	107	102	109	111
Poland	5	11	4	5	9	9	4	9	9	8	12	10	10	11
Portugal	4	3	1	3	4	6	8	7	4	6	7	9	7	9
Slovak Republic	2	2	1	2	1	4	4	3	2	2	3	3	3	3
Spain	64	71	83	87	86	99	120	126	150	164	168	167	200	201
Sweden	513	501	628	669	773	835	743	730	605	593	662	596	606	652
Switzerland	705	699	707	724	770	763	763	752	796	782	773	794	802	801
Turkey	-	2	2	2	2	3	7	4	5	9	10	12	17	27
United Kingdom	1 297	1 366	1 468	1 499	1 600	1 547	1 671	1 678	1 650	1 640	1 681	1 637	1 601	1 588
United States	10 544	10 379	10 947	12 020	12 904	14 544	14 218	15 516	15 664	15 417	16 020	16 037	15 916	16 368
OECD total	29 478	30 103	31 630	34 554	37 740	40 354	41 598	45 020	47 287	46 296	47 467	48 766	50 402	51 386
Brazil	13	21	11	15	16	27	27	32	34	42	45	45	53	59
China	16	15	17	19	22	40	42	62	90	122	195	253	312	433
India	6	8	6	12	17	28	40	49	54	90	115	128	124	132
Russian Federation	40	29	48	51	46	53	70	55	53	53	48	50	50	49
South Africa	31	33	20	24	27	35	37	29	36	29	32	32	30	33
World	29 814	30 453	31 990	34 960	38 261	40 994	42 391	45 782	48 145	47 235	48 495	49 975	51 677	52 864

StatLink http://dx.doi.org/10.1787/274614371216

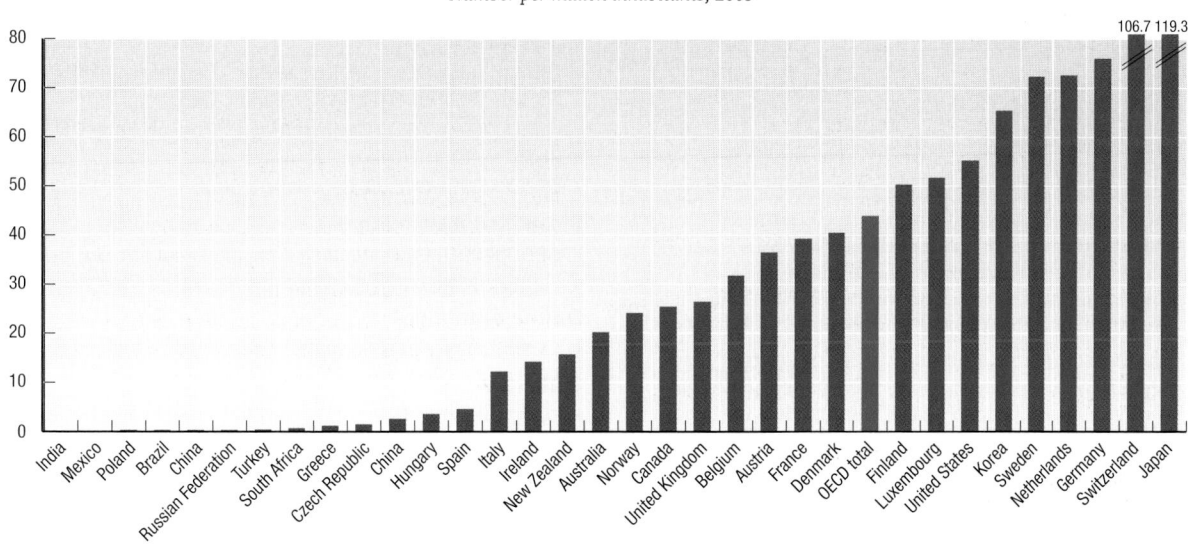

Triadic patent families

Number per million inhabitants, 2005

StatLink http://dx.doi.org/10.1787/268860884713

SIZE OF THE ICT SECTOR

Information and communication technologies (ICT) have been at the heart of economic changes for more than a decade. ICT-producing sectors play an important role, notably by contributing to rapid technological progress and productivity growth.

Definition

In 1998, the OECD countries reached agreement on an industry-based definition of the ICT sector based on Revision 3 of the International Standard Industrial Classification (ISIC Rev. 3). The principles underlying the definition are the following.

For manufacturing industries, the products of a candidate industry must be intended to fulfill the function of information processing and communication including transmission and display, must use electronic processing to detect, measure and/or record physical phenomena or control a physical process.

For services industries, the products of a candidate industry must be intended to enable the function of information processing and communication by electronic means.

Comparability

The existence of a widely accepted definition of the ICT sector is the first step towards making comparisons across time and countries possible. However, the definition is not as yet consistently applied and data provided by member countries have been combined with different data sources to estimate ICT aggregates compatible with national accounts totals. For this reason, statistics presented here may differ from figures contained in national reports and in previous OECD publications.

Long-term trends

The ICT sector grew strongly in OECD countries over the 1990s. For the 1995-2003 period the share of ICT services has grown most in the Ireland, Finland, Hungary and Sweden. In 2003, Finland's ICT manufacturing sector's share of manufacturing value added represented 22% of total manufacturing value added. In 2003, the ICT manufacturing sector represented between 1.2% and 22.2% of total manufacturing value added in OECD countries. The average share for the 25 OECD countries for which data are available was about 6.5%.

The Telecommunication services sector is largest, as a percentage of business services value added, in Hungary, Portugal, Australia and Finland. It is smallest in Greece, Korea and the Netherlands.

Source
- OECD (2007), *OECD Science, Technology and Industry: Scoreboard 2007*, OECD, Paris.

Further information
Analytical publications
- OECD (2003), *ICT and Economic Growth: Evidence from OECD countries, industries and firms*, OECD, Paris.
- OECD (2005), *Guide to Measuring the Information Society*, OECD, Paris.
- OECD (2006), *OECD Information Technology Outlook 2006*, OECD, Paris.
- OECD (2006), *OECD Reviews of Risk Management Policies – Norway: Information Security*, OECD, Paris.
- OECD (2007), *OECD Communications Outlook 2007*, OECD, Paris.
- OECD (2007), *OECD e-Government Studies*, OECD, Paris.

Statistical publications
- OECD (2004), *Understanding Economic Growth A Macro-level, Industry-level, and Firm-level Perspective*, OECD, Paris.

Online databases
- *Telecommunications Database*.

Websites
- OECD Science, Technology and Industry, *www.oecd.org/sti*.
- OECD Telecommunications and Internet Policy, *www.oecd.org/sti/telecom*.

Share of ICT in value added

Year 2003

	Share of ICT manufacturing in total manufacturing value added		Share of ICT services in total business services value added		
	ICT manufacturing	Percentage point change 1995-2003	Telecomminucation services	Other ICT services	Percentage point change 1995-2003
Australia	3.3	..	4.9	4.4	..
Austria	6.6	-0.7	3.1	6.6	0.9
Belgium	3.4	-0.6	3.3	6.5	1.5
Canada	4.4	-1.9	4.2	4.7	1.5
Czech Republic	4.3	1.3	4.6	1.9	0.2
Denmark	4.9	0.5	2.9	6.9	0.1
Finland	22.2	13.4	4.7	6.5	3.3
France	5.4	-1.3	2.9	6.6	1.0
Germany	5.2	0.3	3.7	4.0	1.6
Greece	1.2	0.2	0.4	6.0	0.5
Hungary	7.8	3.0	6.8	4.1	3.3
Ireland	9.7	-7.1	2.7	10.7	6.9
Italy	4.0	-0.2	2.7	5.2	1.1
Japan	12.5	-0.3	3.2	2.2	1.0
Korea	20.2	4.2	0.5	8.0	1.8
Mexico	5.9	0.7	3.2	1.1	0.3
Netherlands	6.0	-1.2	2.1	8.8	1.5
New Zealand	1.5	..	..	..	..
Norway	4.6	0.3	3.4	6.2	1.7
Portugal	4.1	4.1	5.8	4.3	0.4
Slovak Republic	3.2	-0.1	4.3	1.7	0.5
Spain	2.4	-1.3	4.5	3.7	1.0
Sweden	4.2	-3.5	3.5	7.8	2.9
United Kingdom	6.7	-1.6	4.0	7.9	1.6
United States	8.1	-1.1	4.2	6.9	1.4
OECD total	6.5	0.3	3.6	5.5	1.6

StatLink http://dx.doi.org/10.1787/274620321533

Share of ICT in value added

Share of ICT manufacturing and ICT services value added, 2003

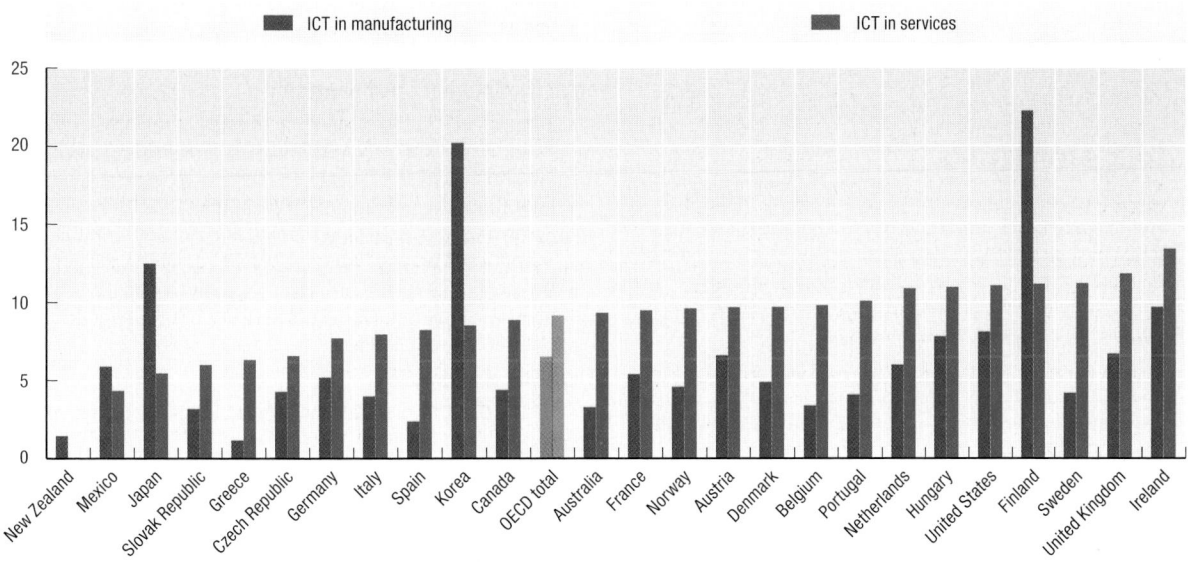

StatLink http://dx.doi.org/10.1787/268880111213

INVESTMENT IN ICT

Investment in physical capital is important for growth. It is a way to expand and renew the capital stock and enable new technologies to enter the production process. Information and communication technology (ICT) has been the most dynamic component of investment in recent years.

Definition

Investment is defined in accordance with the 1993 *System of National Accounts*. It covers the acquisition of equipment and computer software that is used in production for more than one year. ICT has three components: information technology equipment (computers and related hardware), communications equipment and software. Software includes acquisition of pre-packaged software, customised software and software developed in-house.

The investment shares shown in the table and graph are percentages of each country's gross fixed capital formation, excluding residential construction.

Comparability

Correct measurement of ICT investment in both nominal and volume terms is crucial for estimating the contribution of ICT to economic growth and performance. Data availability and measurement of ICT investment based on national accounts (SNA 93) vary considerably across OECD countries, especially as regards measurement of investment in software, deflators applied, breakdown by institutional sector and temporal coverage.

In the national accounts, expenditure on ICT products is considered investment only if the products can be physically isolated (*i.e.* ICT embodied in equipment is considered not as investment but as intermediate consumption). This means that ICT investment may be underestimated and the order of magnitude of the underestimation may differ depending on how

intermediate consumption and investment are treated in each country's accounts. In particular, it is only very recently that expenditure on software has started being treated as investment in the national accounts, and methodologies still vary across countries. The difficulties of measuring software investment are also linked to the ways in which software can be acquired, *e.g.* via rental and licences or embedded in hardware. Moreover, software is often developed on own account. To tackle the specific problems relating to software in the national accounts, a joint OECD-EU task force on the measurement of software in the national accounts has developed recommendations concerning the capitalisation of software. These are now being implemented by OECD member countries.

Note that ICT components that are incorporated in other products, such as motor vehicles or machine tools, are included in the value of those other products and are excluded from ICT investment as defined here.

Source

- *OECD Productivity Database.*

Further information

Analytical publications

- OECD (2003), *ICT and Economic Growth: Evidence from OECD countries, industries and firms*, OECD, Paris.
- OECD (2006), *OECD Information Technology Outlook 2006*, OECD, Paris.
- OECD (2007), *OECD Communications Outlook 2007*, OECD, Paris.
- OECD (2007), *OECD Science, Technology and Industry: Scoreboard 2007*, OECD, Paris.

Statistical publications

- OECD (2007), *National Accounts of OECD Countries*, OECD, Paris.
- OECD (2007), *STAN Industry Structural Analysis Database on CD-Rom*, OECD, Paris.

Methodological publications

- Ahmad, N. (2003), *Measuring Investment in Software*, OECD Science, Technology and Industry Working Papers, No. 2003/6, OECD, Paris.
- Lequillier, F. *et al.* (2003), *Report of the OECD Task Force on Software Measurement in the National Accounts*, OECD Statistics Working Papers, No. 2003/1, OECD, Paris.
- Schreyer, P., P.-E. Bignon and J. Dupont (2003), *OECD Capital Services Estimates*, OECD Statistics Working Papers, No. 2003/6, OECD, Paris.

Online databases

- *STAN: OECD Structural Analysis Statistics – online database.*

Websites

- OECD Productivity Database, *www.oecd.org/statistics/productivity*.
- OECD Compendium of Productivity Indicators, *www.oecd.org/statistics/productivity/compendium*.

Long-term trends

ICT shares in total non-residential investment doubled, and in some cases, even quadrupled between 1980 and 2000 but then started to decrease, following the bursting of the dot-com bubble. In 2006, ICT shares remain particularly high in the United States, the United Kingdom, Korea and Netherlands.

Software has been the fastest growing component of ICT investment. In many countries, its share in non-residential investment multiplied several times between 1980 and 2006.

In 2006, software's share in total investment is highest in Denmark, Finland, France, Sweden, the United Kingdom and the United States.

Shares of ICT investment in non-residential gross fixed capital formation

As a percentage of total non-residential gross fixed capital formation, total economy

	1993	1994	1995	1996	1997	1998	1999	2000	2001	2002	2003	2004	2005	2006
Australia	18.4	18.7	19.1	19.8	21.0	20.9	22.5	26.0	24.7	23.9	22.9	21.6	..	..
Austria	10.2	10.8	11.3	10.8	11.2	12.6	13.5	13.4	14.0	14.5	13.1	12.4	11.9	..
Belgium	15.9	16.9	18.0	18.4	19.4	21.5	21.7	24.2	23.3	20.3	19.9	20.1	..	..
Canada	16.9	16.4	16.8	18.0	17.5	18.8	19.9	20.6	20.2	19.2	18.8	18.1	16.5	15.8
Denmark	21.3	21.3	19.7	18.5	19.8	19.5	21.6	19.9	19.2	22.0	22.0	22.0	22.1	..
Finland	17.1	18.2	19.9	17.5	17.5	18.7	19.4	19.5	17.9	18.5	20.1	19.2	21.2	..
France	12.5	13.1	13.9	15.5	17.5	18.7	19.9	19.2	20.5	19.2	18.6	17.6	17.6	17.8
Germany	13.2	13.0	13.3	14.1	14.5	15.3	16.6	17.5	17.8	17.0	15.3	14.9	15.2	14.9
Greece	13.2	11.7	10.0	10.9	11.0	12.4	11.7	12.8	14.3	11.5	10.8	10.9	..	..
Ireland	6.9	7.6	10.3	11.1	9.4	10.8	9.9	10.0	9.8	8.5	7.7	8.1	7.5	7.7
Italy	12.1	12.7	12.2	12.8	13.9	13.3	13.0	13.8	12.9	11.6	10.8	10.6	10.5	10.7
Japan	9.3	9.3	10.5	12.7	12.9	13.8	15.1	15.9	15.8	14.5	15.6	15.9	..	..
Korea	..	..	9.8	10.3	11.0	12.2	15.0	17.9	16.8	15.6	13.4	12.5	..	..
Netherlands	15.8	16.3	15.6	16.1	17.7	18.7	18.9	19.7	19.9	19.1	20.0	21.4	22.1	..
New Zealand	14.4	14.4	13.9	13.6	14.6	17.8	16.8	19.7	17.1	15.2	15.0	14.3	14.2	14.7
Norway	8.1	8.8	9.2	9.3	9.4	9.2	10.5	11.0	11.5	11.6	11.0	..	..	..
Portugal	10.7	11.4	12.2	12.2	12.0	13.0	13.4	12.4	13.1	11.9	13.6	12.9	12.7	..
Spain	12.6	12.9	12.5	14.6	14.5	14.7	14.9	14.7	13.7	12.3	11.1	11.2	10.9	10.5
Sweden	25.7	24.7	24.1	23.3	24.8	27.1	28.7	31.3	28.7	26.3	24.7	24.3	25.6	25.0
Switzerland	14.6	15.7	14.6	15.0	16.6	16.9	17.9	17.3	17.5	18.5	18.6	18.9	..	..
United Kingdom	18.5	20.2	22.3	24.3	23.3	24.9	26.7	29.3	28.5	27.0	24.9	25.8	26.4	..
United States	23.8	23.8	24.7	25.6	27.1	27.6	29.8	31.7	30.4	29.4	29.1	28.5	27.4	26.5

StatLink ⊞ http://dx.doi.org/10.1787/274652847771

Shares of ICT investment in non-residential gross fixed capital formation

As a percentage of total non-residential gross fixed capital formation, total economy, 2006 or latest available year

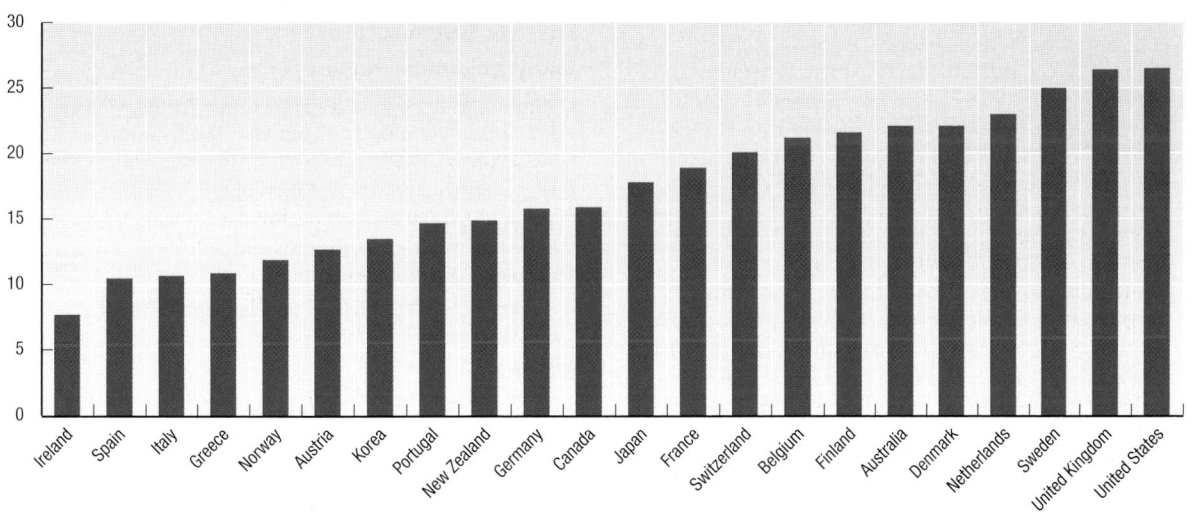

StatLink ⊞ http://dx.doi.org/10.1787/268886140144

COMPUTER AND INTERNET ACCESS BY HOUSEHOLDS

Computers are increasingly present in homes in OECD countries, both in countries that already have high penetration rates and in those where adoption has lagged.

Definition

The table shows the number of households that reported having at least one personal computer in working order in their household. The second part of the table shows the percentage of households who reported that they had access to the Internet. In almost all cases this access is via a personal computer either using a dial-up, ADSL or cable broadband access.

Comparability

Over a very short period, national statistical offices have made great progress in providing indicators of the use of information and communication technology. From an international perspective, the major drawback of official statistics on ICT use is that they remain based on different standards and measure rapidly changing behaviour at different points in time. Most countries use existing surveys, such as labour force, time use, household expenditure or general social surveys. Others rely on special surveys.

Another issue for international comparability is the choice between households and individuals as the survey unit. Household surveys generally provide information on both the household and the individuals in the household. Person-based data typically provide information on the number of individuals with access to a technology, those using the technology, the location at which they use it and the purpose of use.

Statistics on ICT use by households may run into problems of international comparability because of structural differences in the composition of households. On the other hand, statistics on individuals may use different age groups, and age is an important determinant of ICT use. Household- and person-based measures yield different figures in terms of levels and growth rates. Such differences complicate international comparisons and make benchmarking exercises based on a single indicator of Internet access or use misleading, since country rankings change according to the indicator used.

The OECD has addressed issues of international comparability by developing a model survey on ICT use in households/by individuals. The model survey is designed to be flexible; it uses modules addressing different topics so that additional components can be added as technologies reflecting usage practices and policy interests change. The ICT access and use by households and individuals model survey is available on the OECD website.

Long-term trends

Penetration rates are highest in, Denmark, Iceland, Sweden, Japan, the Netherlands, Korea, Luxembourg, Germany and Norway 75 % or more of households had access to a home computer by 2006. On the other hand, shares in Turkey, Mexico, Greece and the Czech Republic were below 40%. Between 2001 and 2006, the percentages of households with access to a home computer increased particularly sharply in Japan, the United Kingdom and Germany.

The picture with regard to Internet access is similar. In Korea, Iceland, the Netherlands, Denmark, Sweden and Switzerland, more than 75% of households had Internet access by 2006. In Turkey, Mexico and Greece, on the other hand, less than one quarter of the households had Internet access by 2006.

Source

- OECD (2007), *OECD Science, Technology and Industry: Scoreboard 2007*, OECD, Paris.
- Eurostat (2005), Eurostat community survey on ICT usage in households and by individuals, May 2005, Eurostat, Luxembourg.

Further information

Analytical publications

- OECD (2004), *Access Pricing in Telecommunications*, OECD, Paris.
- OECD (2006), *OECD Information Technology Outlook 2006*, OECD, Paris.
- OECD (2007), *OECD Communications Outlook 2007*, OECD, Paris.

Statistical publications

- OECD (2005), *OECD Telecommunications Database*, CD-ROM, OECD, Paris.

Websites

- OECD Science, Technology and Industry, *www.oecd.org/sti*.
- OECD Telecommunications and Internet Policy, *www.oecd.org/sti/telecom*.

Households with access to home computers and the Internet

	Percentage of households with access to a home computer						Percentage of households with access to the Internet					
	2001	2002	2003	2004	2005	2006	2001	2002	2003	2004	2005	2006
Australia	58.0	61.0	66.0	67.0	70.0	..	42.0	46.0	53.0	56.0	60.0	..
Austria	..	49.2	50.8	58.6	63.1	66.8	..	33.5	37.4	44.6	46.7	52.3
Belgium	..	..	..	..	..	57.5	..	..	..	..	50.2	54.0
Canada	59.9	64.1	66.6	68.7	72.0	..	49.9	54.3	56.9	59.8	64.3	..
Czech Republic	..	27.8	23.8	..	30.0	39.0	..	..	14.8	19.4	19.1	29.3
Denmark	69.6	72.2	78.5	79.3	83.8	84.8	59.0	55.6	64.2	69.4	74.9	78.7
Finland	52.9	54.5	57.4	57.0	64.0	71.1	39.5	44.3	47.4	50.9	54.1	64.7
France	32.4	36.6	45.7	49.8	..	56.4	18.1	23.0	31.0	33.6	..	40.9
Germany	53.0	61.0	65.2	68.7	69.9	76.8	36.0	46.1	54.1	60.0	61.6	67.1
Greece	..	25.3	28.7	29.0	32.6	36.7	..	12.2	16.3	16.5	21.7	23.1
Hungary	..	..	..	31.9	42.3	49.5	..	..	..	14.2	22.1	32.3
Iceland	..	..	..	85.7	89.3	84.4	..	..	..	80.6	84.4	83.0
Ireland	..	..	42.2	46.3	54.9	58.5	..	..	35.6	39.7	47.2	50.0
Italy	..	39.9	47.7	47.4	45.7	47.6	..	33.7	32.1	34.1	38.6	40.0
Japan	58.0	71.7	78.2	77.5	80.5	..	..	48.8	53.6	55.8	57.0	60.5
Korea	76.9	78.6	77.9	77.8	78.9	79.6	63.2	70.2	68.8	86.0	92.7	94.0
Luxembourg	..	52.6	58.0	67.3	74.5	77.1	..	39.9	45.4	58.6	64.6	70.2
Mexico	11.6	15.2	..	18.0	18.4	20.5	6.1	7.4	..	8.7	9.0	10.1
Netherlands	..	69.0	70.8	..	77.9	80.0	..	58.0	60.5	..	78.3	80.3
New Zealand	47.0	..	..	..	..	71.6	37.4	..	..	..	..	64.5
Norway	..	..	71.2	71.5	74.2	75.3	..	..	60.5	60.1	64.0	68.8
Poland	..	..	..	36.1	40.1	45.3	..	..	..	26.0	30.4	35.9
Portugal	39.0	26.8	38.3	41.3	42.5	45.4	18.0	15.1	21.7	26.2	31.5	35.2
Slovak Republic	..	..	..	39.0	46.7	50.1	..	..	..	23.0	23.0	26.6
Spain	..	..	47.1	52.1	54.6	56.9	..	17.4	27.5	33.6	35.5	39.1
Sweden	69.2	..	..	..	79.7	82.5	53.3	..	..	..	72.5	77.4
Switzerland	62.2	65.4	68.9	70.6	..	..	54.7	61.9	66.4	69.8	73.5	76.8
Turkey	..	..	..	10.2	12.2	..	..	..	..	7.0	7.7	..
United Kingdom	49.0	57.9	63.2	65.3	70.0	71.4	40.0	49.7	55.1	55.9	60.2	62.6
United States	56.2	..	61.8	..	..	..	50.3	..	54.6	..	..	..
Brazil	..	..	..	..	18.6	22.1	..	..	..	..	13.7	16.9
Russian Federation	..	..	..	20.0	26.0	33.0	..	..	..	27.3	25.0	28.5

StatLink http://dx.doi.org/10.1787/274673214225

Households with access to a home computer
As a percentage of all households, 2006 or latest available year

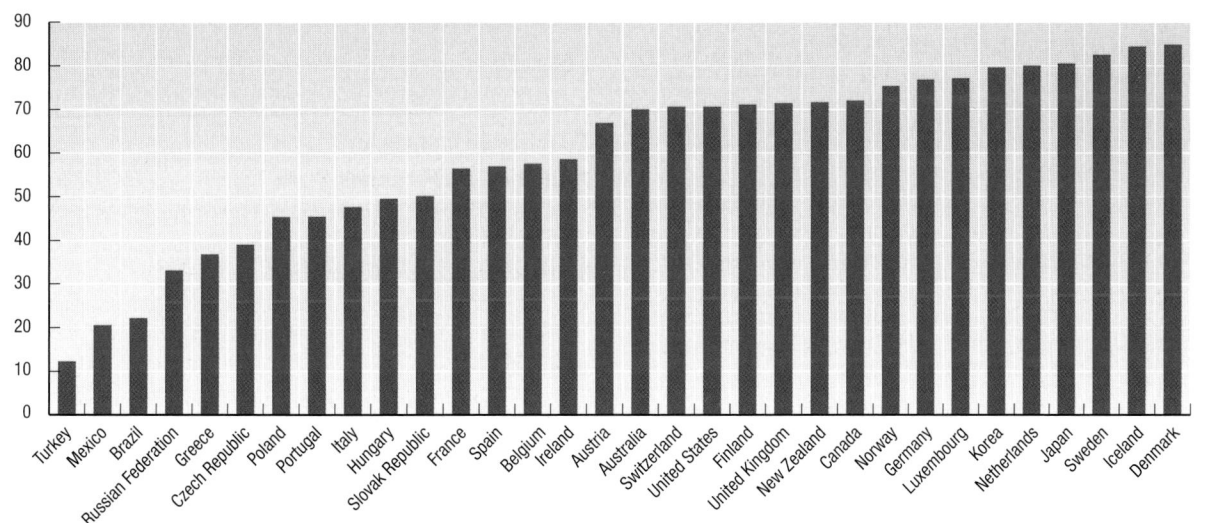

StatLink http://dx.doi.org/10.1787/268888864704

EXPORTS OF INFORMATION AND COMMUNICATIONS EQUIPMENT

Exports of ICT goods accounted for much of the growth in trade over the past decade. In all OECD countries, they grew more rapidly than total manufacturing exports. This is especially the case for high-technology exports.

Definition

The OECD has developed a commodity-based definition of the ICT sector based on the CPC (Central Product Classification) and the Harmonised System (HS). The definition of ICT goods includes the following broad categories: telecommunications equipment; computer and related equipment; electronic components; audio and video equipment; and other ICT goods.

Comparability

The data for this table are taken from the statistics on international trade. These are compiled according to internationally agreed standards and are generally considered to be of good comparability.

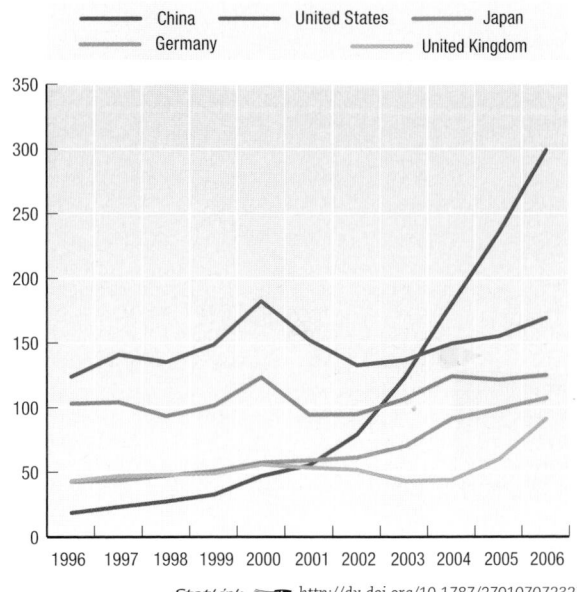

Exports of ICT equipment
Billion US dollars

China — United States — Japan — Germany — United Kingdom

StatLink http://dx.doi.org/10.1787/270107072327

Long-term trends

Growth of exports of ICT has been particularly high for the countries that started with a low base in 1996 – Hungary, the Slovak Republic, the Czech Republic, Poland and Iceland. Germany and especially Korea stand out as countries which started the period with substantial ICT exports and which have seen them grow rapidly between 1996 and 2006.

By the end of the period, the OECD countries could be divided into three groups – United States, Japan, Germany, United Kingdom and Korea with high exports of ICT goods, a middle group consisting of the Netherlands, Mexico, France, Ireland and Hungary and the remainder with relatively low values of ICT exports. As noted above, however, some of these, such as the four Central European countries, are rapidly increasing the value of their ICT exports.

Among the five non-member countries, growth of ICT exports has been slow and steady for all except China which has experienced spectacular growth in exports of ICT goods. Between 1996 and 2006, the value of ICT exports from China have been growing at an average rate of 36% per year and since 2004, China's ICT exports has surpassed those of the United States.

Sources
- *ITCS International Trade by Commodity Statistics.*

Further information
Analytical publications
- OECD (2006), *OECD Information Technology Outlook 2006*, OECD, Paris.

Methodological publications
- OECD (2003), A proposed classification of ICT goods, OECD, Paris, *www.oecd.org/dataoecd/5/61/22343094.pdf.*

Websites
- OECD Key ICT indicators, *www.oecd.org/sti/ictindicators.*

Exports of ICT equipment
Million US dollars

	1996	1997	1998	1999	2000	2001	2002	2003	2004	2005	2006
Australia	2 180	2 282	1 873	1 830	2 068	1 983	1 762	1 948	2 128	2 262	2 238
Austria	3 270	3 568	4 074	4 111	5 018	5 237	5 846	6 627	7 861	8 134	8 465
Belgium	..	8 344	9 373	9 548	11 434	11 814	10 561	12 488	13 581	14 620	13 655
Canada	13 875	14 913	14 573	15 728	22 626	15 011	12 018	12 016	14 222	16 615	18 047
Czech Republic	894	962	1 513	1 339	2 128	3 201	4 790	5 922	9 104	9 778	13 498
Denmark	3 154	3 805	3 862	4 016	4 177	4 060	5 435	5 136	5 823	7 102	6 778
Finland	5 935	6 920	8 656	9 343	11 555	9 414	9 789	11 085	11 563	14 557	14 640
France	25 892	28 155	32 257	32 084	35 689	30 455	27 827	28 209	32 328	33 182	38 120
Germany	42 812	43 700	47 517	50 793	57 452	59 083	61 433	70 349	91 452	99 127	107 388
Greece	182	219	257	315	481	381	397	456	585	525	700
Hungary	663	3 294	4 761	5 943	7 776	7 510	8 938	11 967	16 983	17 277	19 353
Iceland	2	3	4	5	12	9	13	17	18	25	16
Ireland	13 265	16 224	18 637	23 644	26 349	29 732	27 260	22 565	23 673	24 933	24 521
Italy	13 047	11 711	11 890	11 777	12 842	12 825	11 435	12 549	14 659	15 162	15 386
Japan	103 213	104 239	93 612	101 473	123 548	94 696	95 015	106 655	124 242	121 474	125 089
Korea	34 316	36 248	33 906	45 061	61 525	46 793	55 021	66 545	86 099	87 163	88 544
Luxembourg	..	..	..	1 102	1 114	1 552	1 300	1 103	1 229	1 390	1 143
Mexico	16 422	20 369	24 678	30 432	38 267	38 058	36 324	35 906	41 336	43 870	53 462
Netherlands	24 899	31 926	31 584	35 396	41 218	34 543	31 593	45 505	58 305	64 748	70 049
New Zealand	232	290	299	280	286	273	314	365	464	494	509
Norway	1 301	1 432	1 513	1 502	1 430	1 525	1 345	1 471	1 670	1 858	2 173
Poland	648	917	1 295	1 242	1 424	1 738	2 154	2 652	3 341	4 123	6 124
Portugal	1 371	1 357	1 465	1 781	1 893	2 065	2 012	2 716	2 899	3 184	3 907
Slovak Republic	..	310	386	409	464	574	624	1 032	1 896	3 200	5 518
Spain	4 969	5 115	5 683	6 055	6 137	6 161	5 897	7 615	8 218	8 280	8 547
Sweden	11 407	12 513	13 224	13 720	16 579	9 353	10 251	11 374	14 807	15 818	16 475
Switzerland	4 143	3 919	4 090	4 337	4 712	4 301	3 730	4 237	4 947	5 690	5 512
Turkey	496	647	1 043	924	1 103	1 188	1 714	2 125	3 096	3 395	1 718
United Kingdom	43 116	47 039	48 019	48 964	55 865	53 396	51 657	43 052	43 848	59 755	91 282
United States	123 802	140 814	135 108	148 465	182 262	152 150	132 614	136 631	149 273	154 917	169 027
OECD total	495 502	538 124	545 778	611 620	737 431	639 080	619 068	670 316	789 649	842 660	931 882
Brazil	..	1 176	1 190	1 479	2 513	2 640	2 420	2 332	2 290	4 038	4 396
China	18 584	23 194	27 419	32 663	46 996	55 305	79 377	123 303	180 422	235 167	298 993
India	659	545	317	444	714	880	939	1 262	1 205	1 424	1 742
Russian Federation	..	917	609	755	799	1 009	942	896	1 137	1 157	1 519
South Africa	..	..	..	..	521	545	493	615	761	798	968

StatLink http://dx.doi.org/10.1787/274688374172

Exports of ICT equipment
Million US dollars, 2006

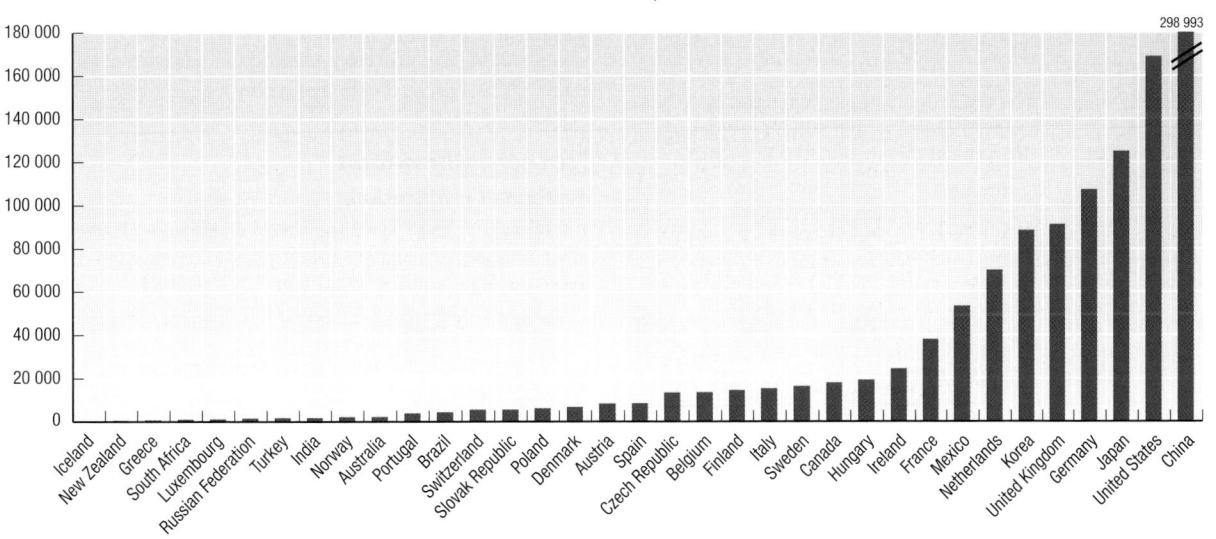

StatLink http://dx.doi.org/10.1787/270046424882

TELEPHONE ACCESS

The number of telephone connections – more precisely the number of fixed and mobile telecommunications access paths – has increased dramatically in OECD countries. This is associated both with growing use of the Internet and, particularly in recent years, with the growing popularity of cellular mobile telephones.

Definition

For the OECD member countries, total communication access paths are the total of fixed lines (standard analogue access lines and ISDN lines) plus the number of DSL, cable modem subscribers and mobile telephone subscribers. For Brazil, China, India, Russian Federation and South Africa, total communication access paths are the sum of main telephone lines in operation, ISDN lines, DSL and cable modem subscribers and cellular mobile telephone subscribers.

Long-term trends

Access to communications networks continues to expand in all OECD countries. At the end of 2005, the total number of fixed and mobile telecommunications paths had increased to more than 1.5 billion. This represented a 8.8% increase over 2004 and an average increase of more than 8.5% in each year since 1997.

Growth was not occurring across all access paths. The number of cellular mobile communication subscribers continues to climb. An additional 97 million mobile subscribers were added in 2005. By way of contrast, some segments of the fixed connection market have begun to decrease. The number of fixed access lines decreased in both 2003, 2004 and 2005 and will most likely continue to do so over the coming years.

By 2005, all but two OECD countries – Mexico and Turkey – had more than one telecommunications access path per inhabitant and seventeen countries reported more than one and a half per inhabitant – Spain, Austria, Australia, Portugal, New Zealand, Germany, the Netherlands, Greece, Norway, Switzerland, Finland, United Kingdom, Denmark, Italy, Sweden, Iceland and Luxembourg.

Among the five non-OECD countries shown here, growth has been spectacular in China, which had less than one access path per 100 inhabitants in 1991 but 60 in 2005. The Russian Federation has now the highest number of paths per 100 inhabitants among these countries. In spite of steady growth over the period, there were only about 13 access paths per 100 inhabitants in India in 2005.

A growing trend toward liberalisation, and the consequent use of prepaid cards in competitive markets, has helped drive the growth of mobile communications in both OECD and non-OECD countries. In 2004 the total number of cellular mobile users in non-member countries overtook the total for the OECD area.

Comparability

For OECD countries, the data are collected according to agreed definitions and are highly comparable. The data shown for the five large non-OECD countries were partly collected according to the OECD definitions and partly provided by the International Telecommunications Union (ITU). The definition used by the ITU is slightly narrower than that used by the OECD, although data reported for the two sets of countries can be regarded as broadly comparable.

Mobile cellular subscribers
OECD and non-OECD share in the world total, 1996-2005

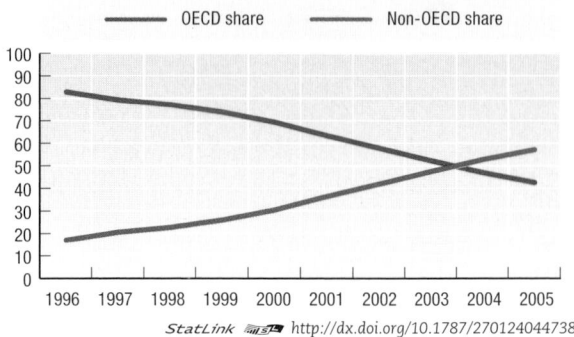

StatLink ⬛⬛ http://dx.doi.org/10.1787/270124044738

Sources

- ITU (2006), *World Telecommunications Indicators Database.*
- OECD (2007), *OECD Communications Outlook 2007*, OECD, Paris.

Further information
Analytical publications

- Caspary, G. and D. O'Connor (2003), *Providing Low-cost Information Technology Access to Rural Communities in Developing Countries: What Works? What Pays?*, OECD Development Centre Working Papers, No. 229, OECD, Paris.
- OECD (2006), *OECD Information Technology Outlook 2006*, OECD, Paris.

Websites

- OECD Telecommunications and Internet Policy, *www.oecd.org/sti/telecom.*

OECD FACTBOOK 2008 – ISBN 978-92-64-04054-0 – © OECD 2008

Telephone access
Number of telecommunication access paths per 100 inhabitants

	1992	1993	1994	1995	1996	1997	1998	1999	2000	2001	2002	2003	2004	2005
Australia	51.2	53.7	55.5	62.3	72.9	76.8	81.1	86.5	96.5	111.5	120.6	129.6	140.5	152.6
Austria	46.4	48.1	49.8	51.6	54.0	59.4	72.2	97.7	120.2	126.1	128.3	133.7	145.7	152.2
Belgium	43.1	44.3	46.1	48.3	51.8	59.1	63.6	76.5	100.0	121.0	128.3	135.1	143.0	149.2
Canada	60.9	62.9	65.9	57.1	72.5	76.7	82.5	86.5	96.7	106.9	111.3	116.9	122.9	129.2
Czech Republic	17.7	19.1	21.1	19.0	29.3	36.8	45.7	55.9	80.3	104.0	117.8	127.8	137.2	147.5
Denmark	62.2	65.9	69.8	77.2	86.9	87.2	96.8	109.4	124.4	137.7	148.7	156.4	166.7	175.0
Finland	61.4	53.5	54.4	55.5	84.8	97.5	112.6	121.7	131.7	141.2	148.9	153.0	158.0	168.3
France	52.1	53.5	55.0	57.8	57.8	63.3	70.4	84.4	97.9	109.4	112.6	119.5	127.7	136.7
Germany	45.5	48.7	52.6	53.7	57.0	59.6	66.3	77.4	107.2	118.7	123.7	131.8	145.8	156.2
Greece	42.8	45.2	48.4	51.1	54.7	59.1	70.1	87.6	107.1	125.8	137.3	145.1	151.1	163.2
Hungary	12.7	15.2	18.8	24.1	30.6	37.5	44.1	51.2	65.3	82.9	100.9	112.5	121.5	128.3
Iceland	59.5	61.0	64.0	67.2	74.6	81.6	96.8	120.3	134.4	141.6	154.0	163.4	168.1	179.5
Ireland	32.5	34.3	36.8	40.1	46.5	54.9	68.2	86.9	96.3	114.8	121.9	128.9	137.8	148.5
Italy	43.1	44.7	47.1	50.7	55.3	65.1	79.8	96.7	117.5	133.8	137.8	147.3	159.1	175.1
Japan	47.9	49.0	51.6	58.5	71.2	80.2	87.0	94.1	102.0	109.3	117.3	125.0	130.9	134.8
Korea	36.3	38.8	41.7	45.6	50.8	60.4	75.1	98.3	113.1	126.7	136.4	134.9	140.7	143.0
Luxembourg	52.8	55.3	58.5	62.7	70.9	77.8	83.8	98.4	125.7	155.0	163.4	177.9	206.2	225.5
Mexico	8.2	9.1	10.1	10.5	10.7	11.7	13.9	19.2	26.8	35.6	40.5	45.6	55.3	65.5
Netherlands	49.8	51.3	53.0	55.5	59.0	69.3	70.8	95.8	123.1	125.3	128.7	139.9	162.4	161.5
New Zealand	47.0	48.0	53.0	56.7	58.8	65.1	79.1	86.0	102.2	108.5	111.6	121.0	135.6	153.2
Norway	59.5	62.7	68.8	78.6	85.4	94.3	102.6	114.6	125.8	132.7	138.1	144.8	159.8	165.0
Poland	10.3	11.5	13.1	15.0	17.5	21.5	26.9	34.8	46.2	58.0	67.7	77.2	93.3	107.3
Portugal	30.6	33.8	36.5	39.2	43.8	53.3	68.8	84.2	102.3	114.7	120.3	135.5	140.8	153.1
Slovak Republic	15.5	16.8	18.9	21.1	23.7	29.6	37.2	43.0	55.4	68.6	80.4	92.6	103.5	103.7
Spain	35.7	37.1	38.4	40.7	46.9	51.6	59.2	80.3	103.7	116.8	135.2	139.1	138.7	151.2
Sweden	76.2	77.5	83.7	91.0	96.8	104.5	115.2	126.8	141.4	151.8	161.0	171.2	172.2	177.5
Switzerland	63.4	65.3	67.1	69.6	68.0	74.9	83.0	100.6	122.2	130.7	139.0	147.9	154.2	165.3
Turkey	16.3	20.6	22.5	23.7	24.1	27.8	32.3	40.2	49.6	54.4	60.7	66.4	75.7	89.0
United Kingdom	47.9	50.8	54.3	58.6	63.0	65.7	76.0	94.7	114.2	130.3	137.2	143.9	159.1	172.4
United States	59.7	62.1	65.9	70.9	65.6	71.1	76.4	82.6	90.8	94.7	100.3	103.7	112.6	122.8
OECD average	43.1	45.2.	48.0	51.6	53.8	59.3	66.2	76.7	90.0	99.2	105.9	111.8	121.0	130.6
Brazil	7.2	7.4	8.2	9.2	10.9	13.2	16.4	23.7	31.6	38.3	42.2	48.5	61.7	73.0
China	1.0	1.5	2.4	3.7	5.0	6.7	8.9	12.1	18.2	25.2	32.5	42.4	52.1	60.0
India	0.8	0.9	1.1	1.3	1.6	2.0	2.4	2.9	3.6	4.4	5.3	6.6	8.7	12.9
Russian Federation	15.4	15.8	16.2	16.9	17.6	19.4	20.3	22.0	24.1	28.0	36.4	49.7	77.7	111.3
South Africa	9.2	9.4	10.3	11.1	12.4	15.2	19.3	24.1	29.6	34.5	40.2	46.6	54.9	82.2

StatLink http://dx.doi.org/10.1787/274730311351

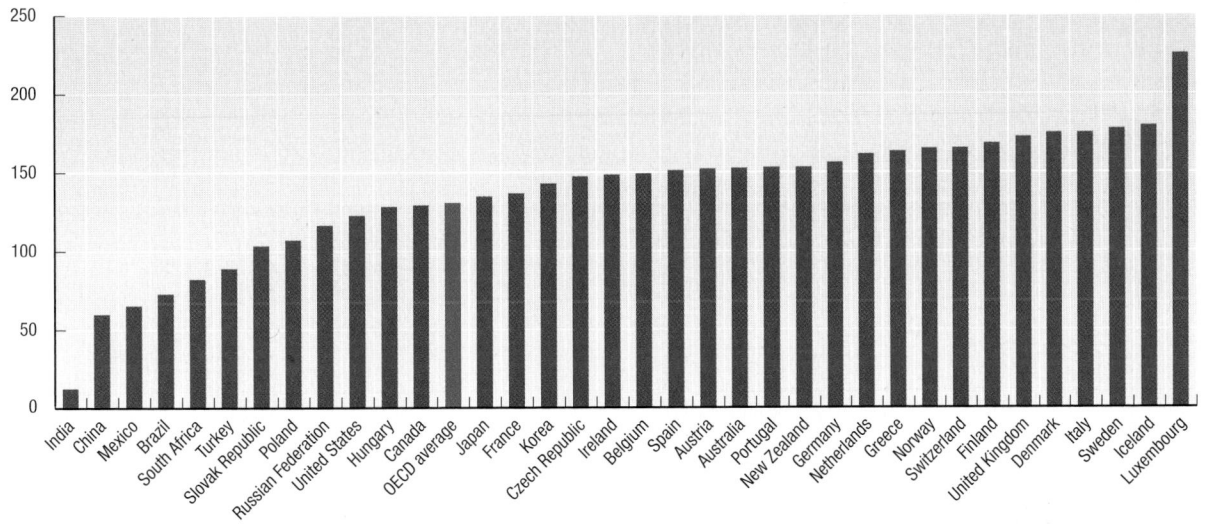

Telephone access
Number of telecommunication access paths per 100 inhabitants, 2005

StatLink http://dx.doi.org/10.1787/270121077856

ENVIRONMENT

WATER AND NATURAL RESOURCES
WATER CONSUMPTION

FISHERIES

AIR AND LAND
EMISSIONS OF CARBON DIOXIDE (CO_2)

MUNICIPAL WASTE

NUTRIENT USE IN AGRICULTURE

WATER CONSUMPTION

Freshwater resources are of major environmental and economic importance. Their distribution varies widely among and within countries. In arid regions, freshwater resources may at times be limited to the extent that demand for water can be met only by going beyond sustainable use in terms of quantity.

Freshwater abstractions, particularly for public water supplies, irrigation, industrial processes and cooling of electric power plants, exert a major pressure on water resources, with significant implications for the quantity and quality of water resources. Main concerns relate to the inefficient use of water and to its environmental and socio-economic consequences: low river flows, water shortages, salinisation of freshwater bodies in coastal areas, human health problems, loss of wetlands, desertification and reduced food production.

Definition

Water abstractions refer to freshwater taken from ground or surface water sources, either permanently or temporarily, and conveyed to the place of use. If the water is returned to a surface water source, abstraction of the same water by the downstream user is counted again in compiling total abstractions.

Mine water and drainage water are included. Water used for hydroelectricity generation is an *in situ* use and is excluded.

Comparability

It should be borne in mind that the definitions and estimation methods employed by member countries may vary considerably and may have changed over time. In general, data availability and quality is best for abstractions for public supply, representing about 15% of the total water abstracted in OECD countries.

Long-term trends

Most OECD countries increased their water abstractions over the 1960s and 1970s in response to demand by the agricultural and energy sectors. Since the 1980s, some countries have stabilised their abstractions through more efficient irrigation techniques, the decline of water-intensive industries (*e.g.* mining, steel), increased use of cleaner production technologies and reduced losses in pipe networks. More recently, this stabilisation partly reflects consequences of droughts while population growth continues to drive increases in public supply.

At world level, it is estimated that water demand rose by more than double the rate of population growth in the last century, with agriculture being the largest user of water.

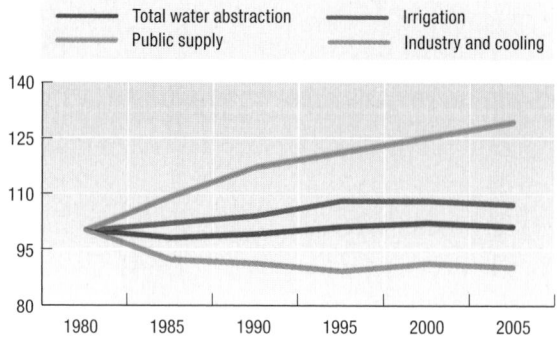

Water abstractions in OECD countries
Year 1980 = 100

- Total water abstraction
- Public supply
- Irrigation
- Industry and cooling

StatLink ᵐˢᵖ http://dx.doi.org/10.1787/270202384435

Sources

- OECD (2005), *OECD Environmental Data Compendium 2004*, updates from the 2004 OECD/Eurostat Questionnaire on the State of the Environment, OECD, Paris.
- OECD (2006), *Environment at a Glance: OECD Environmental Indicators*, OECD, Paris.

Further information

Analytical publications

- OECD, WHO (2003), *Assessing Microbial Safety of Drinking Water: Improving Approaches and Methods*, OECD, Paris.
- OECD (2003), *Social Issues in the Provision and Pricing of Water Services*, OECD, Paris.
- OECD (2003), *Water: Performance and Challenges in OECD Countries*, OECD Environmental Performance Reviews, OECD, Paris.
- OECD (2006), *China in the Global Economy – Environment, Water Resources and Agricultural Policies: Lessons from China and OECD Countries*, OECD, Paris.
- OECD (2006), *Environmental Performance Reviews – Water: the experience in OECD countries*, OECD, Paris.
- OECD (2006), *Financing Water and Environment Infrastructure: The Case of Eastern Europe, the Caucasus and Central Asia*, OECD, Paris.
- OECD (2006), *OECD Trade Policy Studies – Liberalisation and Universal Access to Basic Services: Telecommunications, Water and Sanitation, Financial Services, and Electricity*, OECD, Paris.
- OECD (2006), *Water and Agriculture: Sustainability, Markets and Policies*, OECD, Paris.

Websites

- OECD Environmental Indicators, *www.oecd.org/env/indicators*.
- OECD Water Supply and Sanitation Sector Reform, *www.oecd.org/env/water*.

Water abstractions

	Total gross abstractions Million m³					Per capita abstractions m³/capita
	1980	1985	1990	1995	2000	2005 or latest available year	2005 or latest available year
Australia	10 900	14 600	..	24 071	21 703	18 767	930
Austria	3 342	3 580	3 807	3 449	3 668	3 816	470
Belgium	..	..	..	8 255	7 546	6 749	650
Canada	37 594	42 383	45 096	42 214	..	42 214	1 420
Czech Republic	3 622	3 679	3 623	2 743	1 918	2 028	200
Denmark	1 205	..	1 261	887	726	668	120
Finland	3 700	4 000	2 347	2 586	2 346	2 319	450
France	30 972	34 887	37 687	40 671	32 715	33 164	560
Germany	42 206	41 216	47 873	43 374	40 590	35 557	430
Greece	5 040	5 496	7 030	8 695	..	8 695	830
Hungary	4 805	6 267	6 293	5 976	6 621	5 818	580
Iceland	108	112	167	165	163	165	570
Ireland	1 070	..	..	1 176		1 176	330
Italy	..	..	..	..	41 982	41 982	730
Japan	86 000	87 198	88 889	89 078	87 148	86 210	680
Korea	17 510	18 580	20 570	23 670	26 020	26 193	550
Luxembourg	..	67	59	57	60	60	140
Mexico	56 003	..	..	73 672	70 428	75 431	730
Netherlands	9 198	9 349	7 984	6 507	8 937	8 937	560
New Zealand	..	..	..	..	5 410	5 410	1 410
Norway	..	2 025	..	2 420	3 245	3 391	750
Poland	15 131	16 409	15 164	12 924	11 994	11 548	300
Portugal	10 500	..	8 600	10 849	8 808	8 808	860
Slovak Republic	2 232	2 061	2 116	1 386	1 171	1 064	200
Spain	39 920	46 250	36 900	33 288	37 071	36 992	900
Sweden	4 106	2 970	2 968	2 725	2 688	2 676	300
Switzerland	2 589	2 646	2 665	2 571	2 564	2 518	350
Turkey	16 200	19 400	28 073	33 482	43 650	44 849	620
United Kingdom	13 514	11 533	12 052	12 117	15 022	13 649	250
United States	517 720	467 335	468 620	470 514	476 800	476 800	1 730
OECD total	993 300	974 200	987 700	998 600	1 011 900	1 007 700	890
China	..	..	..	..	..	563 298	432

StatLink http://dx.doi.org/10.1787/274783786017

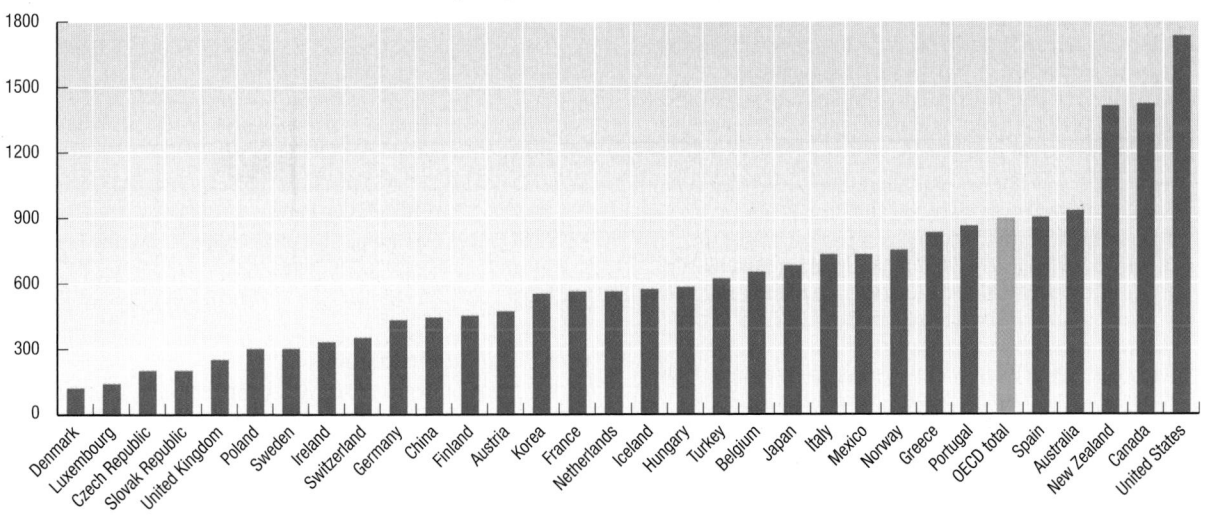

Water abstractions
m³ per capita, 2005 or latest available year

StatLink http://dx.doi.org/10.1787/270150856211

FISHERIES

Fisheries make an important contribution to sustainable incomes, employment opportunities and overall food protein intake. On the other hand, overfishing of some species in some areas is threatening stocks with depletion. In certain countries, including at least two OECD countries – Iceland and Japan – fish is the main source of protein intake.

Definition

The figures refer to the tonnage of landed catches of marine fish, and to cultivated fish and crustaceans taken from inland waters and sea tanks. Landed catches of marine fish for each country cover landings in both foreign and domestic ports. The table distinguishes between marine capture fisheries and aquaculture because of their different production systems and growth rates.

Comparability

The time series presented are relatively comprehensive and consistent across the years, but some of the variation over time may reflect changes in national reporting systems. In one case, the data shown are estimated by the OECD Secretariat.

Fish landings in domestic and foreign ports

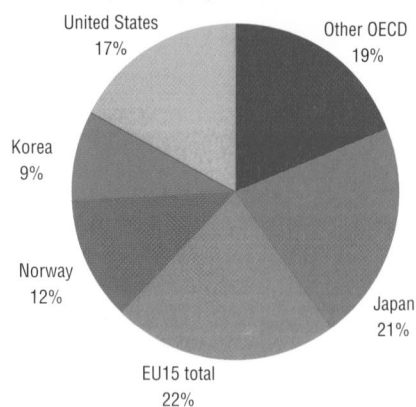

As a percentage of OECD total, 2005

United States 17%
Other OECD 19%
Korea 9%
Norway 12%
Japan 21%
EU15 total 22%

StatLink http://dx.doi.org/10.1787/270226032811

Long-term trends

Total global marine capture production according to FAO data reached 93.8 million tonnes in 2005, of which the relative contribution by OECD countries was 23%. Japan, the United States, Norway and Korea were the largest contributors with 67% of total OECD production. Despite this, total marine capture by OECD countries continued their overall downward trend, decreasing by an average of 3% from a decade ago. As a result, the relative contribution of OECD countries to total marine capture production dropped from 26% (in 1995) to 23% (in 2005), although this is an increase from 21% in 2002. Denmark, Greece and Japan suffered the largest decrease in marine capture production. A few countries did, however, increase captures – Canada, Australia and New Zealand all raised their tonnages by an average of 1% or more per year between 1995 and 2005.

Total OECD aquaculture production increased by an average of 1.3% a year between 1995 and 2005. Worldwide, the aquaculture sector has growth by an average of 8.8% since 1970. OECD countries contributed over 11% of total world aquaculture production in 2005. High rates of growth continued in Canada, Ireland and Norway while the United States and Japan registered a slight decrease. EU aquaculture production increased by almost 2% a year over the same period. Aquaculture contributed 20% to total OECD fisheries production in 2005 compared to 43% globally.

Source

- OECD (2007), *Review of Fisheries in OECD Countries: Vol. 2 – Country Statistics, 2002-2004, 2006 Edition*, OECD, Paris.

Further information

Analytical publications

- OECD (2003), *Liberalising Fisheries Markets: Scope and Effects*, OECD, Paris.
- OECD (2003), *The Costs of Managing Fisheries*, OECD, Paris.
- OECD (2004), *Fish Piracy: Combating Illegal, Unreported and Unregulated Fishing*, OECD, Paris.
- OECD (2005), *Why Fish Piracy Persists: The Economics of Illegal, Unreported and Unregulated Fishing*, OECD, Paris.
- OECD (2006), *Financial Support to Fisheries: Implications for Sustainable Development*, OECD, Paris.
- OECD (2006), *The Development Dimension – Fishing for Coherence: Proceedings of the Workshop on Policy Coherence for Development in Fisheries*, OECD, Paris.
- OECD (2006), *Using Market Mechanisms to Manage Fisheries: Smoothing the Path*, OECD, Paris.
- OECD (2007), *Structural Change in Fisheries: Dealing with the Human Dimension*, OECD, Paris.
- OECD (2007), *The Human Side of Fisheries Adjustment*, OECD, Paris.

Statistical publications

- OECD (2005), *Review of Fisheries in OECD Countries: Volume 1: Policies and Summary Statistics, 2005 Edition*, OECD, Paris.

Websites

- OECD Fisheries, *www.oecd.org/agr/fish*.

Marine capture and aquaculture production
Thousand tonnes

	Fish landings in domestic and foreign ports							Aquaculture						
	1995	2000	2001	2002	2003	2004	2005	1995	2000	2001	2002	2003	2004	2005
Australia	201	185	187	187	215	231	237	24	37	40	44	44	51	48
Austria	-	-	-	-	-	-	-	4	..	..	..	..	..	..
Belgium	29	27	27	26	24	24	22	2	2	2	2	..	..	..
Canada	854	1 008	1 060	1 042	1 088	1 452	1 020	66	127	153	177	157	145	145
Czech Republic	-	-	-	-	-	-	-	19	19	20	19	20	19	20
Denmark	2 025	1 524	1 501	1 433	1 028	1 090	913	45	44	42	37	38	43	39
Finland	106	92	96	95	76	89	77	17	15	16	15	13	13	14
France	616	682	665	690	695	663	606	281	267	253	250	240	244	244
Germany	241	194	179	182	222	223	246	40	45	43	50	64	57	57
Greece	153	93	91	94	90	91	90	33	88	95	101	102	98	110
Hungary	-	-	-	-	-	-	-	9	..	..	..	..	..	..
Iceland	1 603	1 930	1 942	2 132	1 981	1 730	1 669	4	4	5	3	6	8	8
Ireland	379	291	305	281	195	306	282	27	41	54	53	63	59	61
Italy	301	387	339	304	312	288	268	225	228	264	260	192	233	234
Japan	7 450	5 092	4 814	4 495	4 743	4 515	4 466	1 390	1 292	1 311	1 385	1 306	1 261	1 257
Korea	2 322	2 090	2 142	1 867	1 831	1 752	1 829	1 017	667	668	794	844	938	1 057
Mexico	1 222	1 193	1 251	1 295	1 303	1 246	1 246	158	46	75	71	70	80	80
Netherlands	463	404	404	467	391	379	413	84	92	92	92	..	52	68
New Zealand	567	536	501	512	688	633	633	69	87	76	76	87	94	105
Norway	2 701	2 894	2 862	2 923	2 702	2 671	2 546	278	492	511	554	584	637	657
Poland	241	200	207	204	160	174	136	25	32	34	33	32	35	36
Portugal	242	172	173	181	182	163	157	5	8	8	8	8	7	7
Slovak Republic	-	-	-	-	-	-	-	..	1	1	1	1	1	1
Spain	1 075	1 002	941	747	774	687	717	224	312	313	328	313	362	273
Sweden	379	341	308	284	281	262	248	8	6	8	6	7	7	7
Switzerland	-	-	-	-	-	-	-	1	..	..	..	..	..	..
Turkey	577	461	484	523	463	505	380	22	79	67	61	79	94	118
United Kingdom	912	748	738	685	575	654	670	92	144	150	150	212	202	152
United States	4 783	4 245	4 434	4 407	4 402	4 492	3 641	413	373	371	393	420	408	408
EU15 total	6 920	5 957	5 734	5 474	4 845	4 918	4 710	1 087	1 290	1 339	1 346	1 271	1 396	1 287
OECD total	29 442	25 791	25 587	24 612	24 420	24 319	21 267	4 567	4 544	4 671	4 922	4 901	5 147	5 206
Russian Federation	..	4 289	3 833	3 456	3 426	3 174	..	..	205	236	268	289	302	..

StatLink 🔗 http://dx.doi.org/10.1787/274846318837

Fish landings in domestic and foreign ports
Average annual growth in percentage, 1995-2005 or latest available period

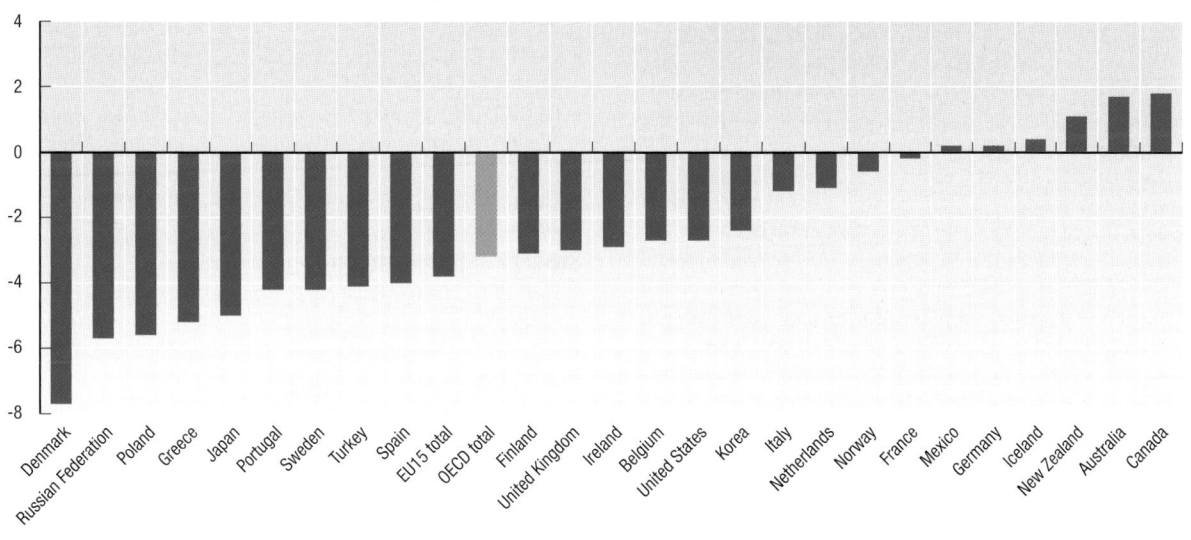

StatLink 🔗 http://dx.doi.org/10.1787/270216170344

EMISSIONS OF CARBON DIOXIDE (CO_2)

Carbon dioxide (CO_2) makes up the largest share of "greenhouse gases". The addition of man-made greenhouse gases to the atmosphere disturbs the earth's radiative balance. This is leading to an increase in the earth's surface temperature and to related effects on climate, sea level rise and world agriculture.

Definition

The table refers to emissions of CO_2 from burning oil, coal and gas for energy use. Carbon dioxide also enters the atmosphere from burning wood and waste materials and from some industrial processes such as cement production. Emissions of CO_2 from these sources are a relatively small part of global emissions and are not included in these statistics. The *Revised 1996 IPCC Guidelines for National Greenhouse Gas Inventories* (see below) provide a fuller, technical definition of how CO_2 emissions have been estimated for this table. The forecasts provided in the table refer to the Reference Scenario of the *World Energy Outlook*.

Long-term trends

Global emissions of carbon dioxide have risen by 92%, or on average 1.9% per year, since 1971, and are projected to rise by another 54% by 2030, or by 1.8% per year. In 1971, the current OECD countries were responsible for 66% of the total. As a consequence of rapidly increasing emissions in the developing world, the OECD contribution to the total fell to 48% in 2005, but this is expected to fall to 36% by 2030. By far, the largest increases in non-OECD countries occurred in Asia, where emissions in China have risen by 5.6% per annum between 1971 and 2005. The use of coal in China increased levels of CO_2 by 3.5 billion tonnes over the 34-year period.

Two significant downturns can be seen in OECD CO_2 emissions, following the oil shocks of the mid-1970s and early 1980s. Emissions from the economies in transition declined over the last decade, helping to offset the OECD increases between 1990 and the present. However, this decline did not stabilise global emissions as emissions in developing countries grew.

Disaggregating the emissions data shows substantial variations within individual sectors. Between 1971 and 2005, the combined share of electricity and heat generation and transport shifted from one-half to two-thirds of global emissions.

Fossil fuel shares in overall emissions changed slightly during the period. The relative weight of coal in global emissions has remained at approximately 40% since the early 1970s. The share of natural gas has increased from 15% in 1971 to 20% in 2005. Oil's share decreased from 49% to 40%. Fuel switching and the increasing use of non-fossil energy sources reduced the CO_2/total primary energy supply (TPES) ratio by 7% over the past 34 years.

Comparability

These emissions estimates are affected by the quality of the underlying energy data. For example, some countries, both OECD and non-OECD, have trouble reporting information on bunker fuels and incorrectly define bunkers as fuel used abroad by their own ships and planes. Since emissions from bunkers are excluded from the national totals, this affects the comparability across countries. On the other hand, since the estimates have been made using the same method and emission factors for all countries, in general, the comparability across countries is quite good.

Sources

- IEA (2007), *CO_2 Emissions from Fuel Combustion : 1971/2005: 2007 Edition*, IEA, Paris.
- IEA (2007), *World Energy Outlook 2007: China and India Insights*, IEA, Paris.

Further information

Analytical publications

- ECMT (2007), *Cutting Transport CO_2 Emissions: What Progress?*, ECMT, Paris.
- IEA (2006), *Energy Technology Perspectives: Scenarios and Strategies to 2050*, IEA, Paris.
- IEA (2007), *Climate Policy Uncertainty and Investment Risk*, IEA, Paris.
- IEA (2007), *Energy Security and Climate Policy – Assessing Interactions*, IEA, Paris.
- IEA (2007), *Legal Aspects of Storing CO_2: Update and Recommendations*, IEA, Paris.
- IEA (2007), *Tracking Industrial Energy Efficiency and CO_2 Emissions*, IEA, Paris.
- OECD (2004), *Can Cars Come Clean? Strategies for Low-Emission Vehicles*, OECD, Paris.
- OECD (2006), *Climate Change in the European Alps: Adapting Winter Tourism and Natural Hazards Management*, OECD, Paris.
- OECD (2006), *The Political Economy of Environmentally Related Taxes*, OECD, Paris.

Statistical publications

- IEA (2007), *Energy Balances of Non-OECD Countries*, IEA, Paris.
- IEA (2007), *Energy Balances of OECD Countries*, IEA, Paris.

Methodological publications

- WMO, UNEP, OECD, IEA (1996), *Revised 1996 IPCC Guidelines for National Greenhouse Gas Inventories*, IPCC/OECD/IEA, Paris.

Online databases

- *CO_2 Emissions from Fuel Combustion*.

CO₂ emissions from energy use

Million tonnes

	1971	1990	1995	1996	1997	1998	1999	2000	2001	2002	2003	2004	2005	2030
Australia	143	260	280	296	311	327	334	339	342	347	348	355	377	..
Austria	49	58	60	65	64	65	63	64	68	70	75	76	77	..
Belgium	118	109	115	121	119	121	118	119	120	112	120	115	112	..
Canada	340	429	461	477	493	498	509	530	523	532	555	550	549	..
Czech Republic	151	154	121	125	121	115	108	118	118	115	118	119	118	..
Denmark	56	51	58	71	61	57	54	50	52	51	56	51	48	..
Finland	40	55	57	63	61	57	56	54	59	63	72	67	55	..
France	435	355	357	371	364	387	380	379	387	379	387	387	388	..
Germany	984	968	881	904	875	867	836	831	851	836	846	850	813	..
Greece	25	71	73	76	79	84	83	88	90	90	94	94	96	..
Hungary	62	71	59	60	57	58	58	56	56	56	58	57	58	..
Iceland	1	2	2	2	2	2	2	2	2	2	2	2	2	..
Ireland	22	31	33	35	36	39	40	41	44	43	42	42	44	..
Italy	295	398	411	407	411	422	422	426	427	434	453	451	454	..
Japan	743	1 058	1 141	1 155	1 150	1 119	1 157	1 172	1 157	1 194	1 203	1 201	1 214	1 182
Korea	51	227	362	390	415	359	393	425	438	444	454	464	449	..
Luxembourg	15	11	8	8	8	7	8	8	8	9	10	11	11	..
Mexico	97	293	310	316	329	350	343	357	356	360	368	374	389	..
Netherlands	130	158	172	179	175	174	169	174	179	179	185	186	183	..
New Zealand	14	21	24	26	29	29	31	32	34	34	36	34	35	..
Norway	24	29	33	34	36	37	39	34	34	33	36	36	37	..
Poland	298	349	333	348	338	315	305	293	292	281	292	296	296	..
Portugal	15	40	49	47	49	54	61	60	59	63	59	60	63	..
Slovak Republic	39	57	41	41	42	40	39	37	39	38	39	38	38	..
Spain	121	207	236	225	243	251	271	286	288	304	312	330	342	..
Sweden	83	53	58	64	57	59	57	54	53	55	56	54	51	..
Switzerland	39	41	42	42	41	43	43	42	43	42	44	44	45	..
Turkey	42	129	155	172	181	182	181	203	184	194	204	210	219	..
United Kingdom	627	558	528	543	520	524	518	522	542	526	540	540	530	..
United States	4 297	4 850	5 109	5 290	5 436	5 485	5 530	5 701	5 623	5 653	5 712	5 792	5 817	6 891
EU27 total	..	4 101	3 879	3 991	3 906	3 902	3 831	3 842	3 927	3 896	4 014	4 021	3 976	4 176
OECD total	9 357	11 092	11 569	11 954	12 105	12 126	12 209	12 497	12 469	12 541	12 774	12 885	12 910	15 067
Brazil	91	193	239	258	276	284	295	305	314	313	306	323	329	..
China	800	2 211	2 986	3 160	3 100	3 156	3 046	3 038	3 084	3 309	3 830	4 547	5 060	11 448
India	199	587	780	823	866	869	934	968	978	1 008	1 033	1 110	1 147	3 314
Russian Federation	..	2 189	1 589	1 562	1 451	1 433	1 473	1 513	1 516	1 503	1 538	1 529	1 544	1 973
South Africa	174	255	277	286	299	310	291	299	284	295	321	338	330	..
World	14 112	21 024	21 808	22 512	22 663	22 819	22 981	23 487	23 599	24 076	25 090	26 320	27 136	41 905

StatLink http://dx.doi.org/10.1787/274861083225

World CO₂ emissions from energy use, by region

Million tonnes

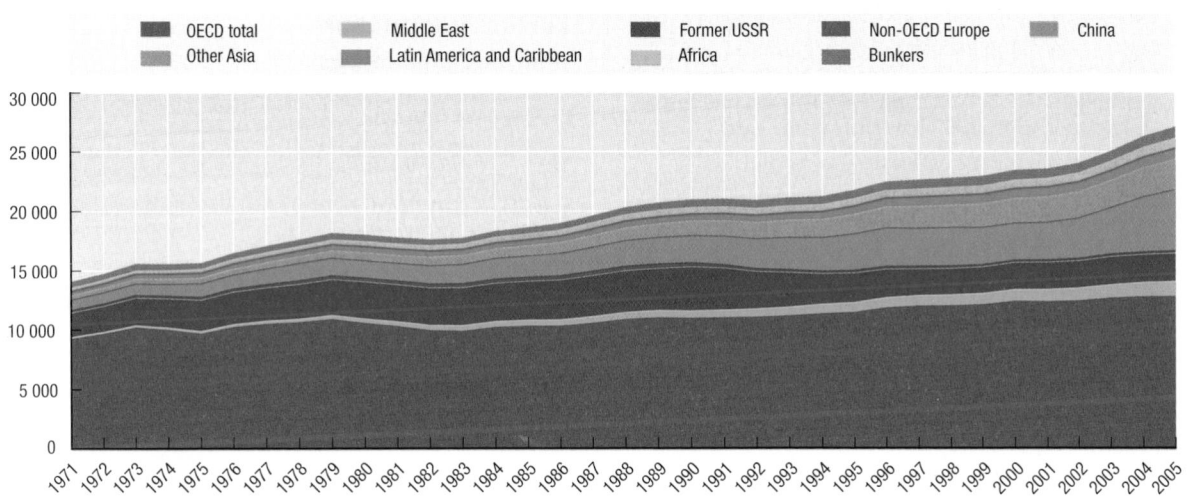

StatLink http://dx.doi.org/10.1787/270306230215

MUNICIPAL WASTE

The amount of municipal waste generated in a country is related to the rate of urbanisation, the types and patterns of consumption, household revenue and lifestyles. While municipal waste is only one part of total waste generated, its management and treatment often absorbs more than one third of the public sector's financial efforts to abate and control pollution.

The main environmental concerns relate to the potential impact from inappropriate waste management on human health and the environment (soil and water contamination, air quality, land use and landscape).

Kilogrammes of municipal waste per capita – or "waste generation intensities" – are broad indicators of potential environmental pressure. They should be complemented with information on waste management practices and costs, and on consumption levels and patterns.

Definition

Municipal waste is waste collected and treated by or for municipalities. It covers waste from households, including bulky waste, similar waste from commerce and trade, office buildings, institutions and small businesses, yard and garden waste, street sweepings, the contents of litter containers, and market cleansing waste. The definition excludes waste from municipal sewage networks and treatment, as well as municipal construction and demolition waste.

Comparability

The definition of municipal waste and the surveying methods used vary from country to country.

The main problems relate to the coverage of household-like waste from commerce and trade, and of separate waste collections, carried out by private companies.

Data for Canada and New Zealand refer to household waste only.

OECD total does not include the Czech Republic, Hungary, Korea, Poland and the Slovak Republic. Per capita value covers all OECD countries.

Long-term trends

The quantity of municipal waste generated in the OECD area (thirty countries) has been rising since 1980 and exceeded 650 million tonnes in recent years (560 kg per capita). Generation intensity – i.e. kilogrammes per capita – has risen mostly in line with private final consumption expenditure and GDP, but there has been a slowdown in the rate of growth in recent years.

The amount of municipal waste also depends on national waste management practices. Only a few countries have succeeded in reducing the quantity of solid waste to be disposed of. In most countries for which data are available, increased affluence, associated with economic growth and changes in consumption patterns, tends to generate higher rates of waste per capita.

Sources

- OECD (2005), *OECD Environmental Data Compendium 2004*, OECD, Paris.
- OECD (2006), *Environment at a Glance: OECD Environmental Indicators*, OECD, Paris.
- OECD (2008), *OECD Environmental Outlook to 2030*, OECD, Paris.

Further information

Analytical publications

- OECD (2004), *Addressing the Economics of Waste*, OECD, Paris.
- OECD (2004), *Economic Aspects of Extended Producer Responsibility*, OECD, Paris.
- OECD (2004), *Toward Waste Prevention Performance Indicators*, OECD, Paris.

Websites

- OECD Environmental Indicators, *www.oecd.org/env/indicators*.
- OECD Waste Prevention and Management, *www.oecd.org/env/waste*.

Municipal waste generation

	Total amount generated Thousand tonnes					Generation intensities kg/capita
	1980	1985	1990	1995	2000	2005 or latest available year	2005 or latest available year
Australia	10 000	..	12 000	..	13 200	13 200	690
Austria	..	..	3 204	3 476	4 250	4 588	560
Belgium	2 763	3 055	3 436	4 615	4 783	4 847	460
Canada	..	..	8 925	7 030	11 279	13 375	420
Czech Republic	..	2 600	..	3 200	3 434	2 954	290
Denmark	2 046	2 430	..	2 960	3 546	3 990	740
Finland	..	..	..	2 109	2 600	2 450	470
France	..	..	26 220	28 253	31 232	33 963	540
Germany	..	..	..	44 390	50 132	49 563	600
Greece	2 500	3 000	3 000	3 200	4 447	4 853	440
Hungary	..	..	5 500	4 752	4 552	4 632	460
Iceland	..	..	..	114	130	153	520
Ireland	640	1 100	..	1 848	2 279	3 050	740
Italy	14 041	15 000	20 000	25 780	28 959	31 677	540
Japan	43 995	43 450	50 441	50 694	52 362	51 607	400
Korea	..	20 994	30 646	17 438	16 950	18 252	380
Luxembourg	128	131	224	240	285	321	710
Mexico	..	..	21 062	30 510	30 733	36 088	340
Netherlands	7 050	6 933	7 430	8 469	9 769	10 178	620
New Zealand	880	..	1 140	1 431	1 541	1 541	400
Norway	1 700	1 968	2 000	2 722	2 755	3 498	760
Poland	10 055	11 087	11 098	10 985	12 226	9 354	250
Portugal	1 980	2 350	3 000	3 855	4 531	5 009	470
Slovak Republic	..	1 901	1 600	1 620	1 707	1 468	270
Spain	..	..	..	20 076	26 505	27 593	650
Sweden	2 510	2 650	3 200	3 555	3 796	4 347	480
Switzerland	2 790	3 398	4 101	4 200	4 728	4 855	650
Turkey	12 000	18 000	22 315	27 234	30 617	31 352	440
United Kingdom	..	..	27 100	28 900	33 954	35 077	580
United States	137 568	149 189	186 167	193 869	215 578	222 863	750
OECD total	367 000	397 000	479 000	526 000	586 000	614 000	560
Brazil	..	..	..	..	..	58 000	340
China	..	..	..	..	..	155 768	120
India	..	..	..	..	..	108 000	100
Russian Federation	..	..	..	..	..	50 000	340
South Africa	..	..	..	..	..	20 000	430

StatLink ⬛🖳 http://dx.doi.org/10.1787/274862546854

Municipal waste generation

kg per capita, 2005 or latest available year

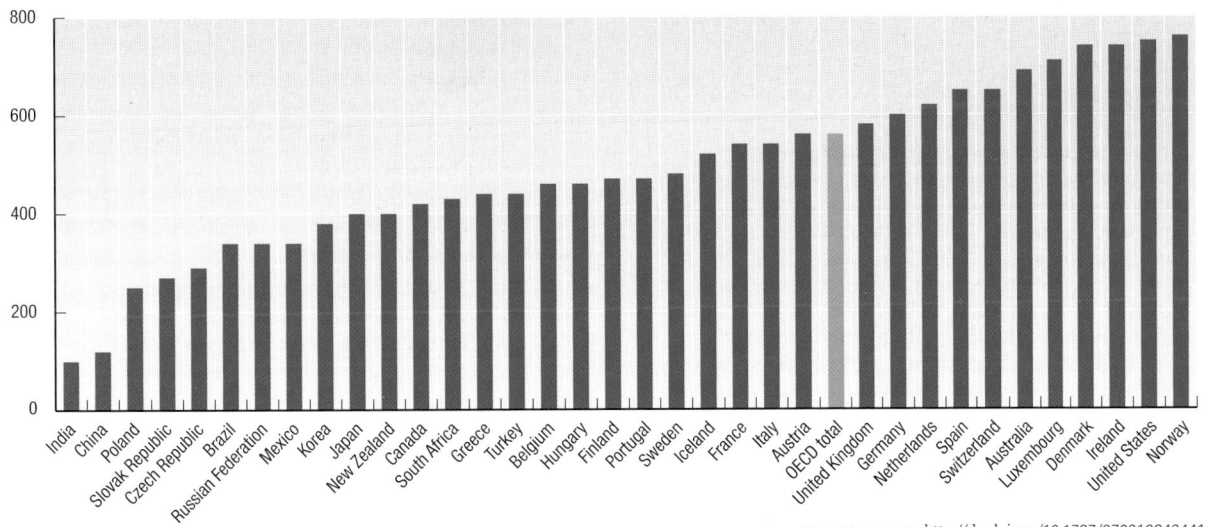

StatLink ⬛🖳 http://dx.doi.org/10.1787/270310843441

NUTRIENT USE IN AGRICULTURE

Inputs of nutrients, such as nitrogen and phosphorus, are important in farming systems as they are critical in raising plant productivity, and a nutrient deficiency can impair soil fertility. A build up of surplus nutrients in excess of crop and forage needs can lead to losses representing a possible cause of economic inefficiency in nutrient use and also a source of potential environmental harm, in terms of water pollution (*e.g.* eutrophication of water), and air pollution (*e.g.* ammonia), while the sustainability of phosphorus resources is a concern as world reserves are diminishing.

Definition

Gross nutrient balances are calculated as the difference between the total quantity of nutrient inputs entering an agricultural system, and the quantity of nutrient outputs leaving the system. This calculation can be used as a proxy to reveal the status of environmental pressures, such as declining soil fertility in the case of a nutrient deficit, or for a nutrient surplus the risk of polluting soil, water and air.

Comparability

The nutrient balance indicators are expressed in terms of the kilograms of nutrient surplus (deficit) per hectare of agricultural land per annum, and in terms of changes in the physical quantities (tonnes) of nutrient surpluses (deficits). The former is an intensity indicator and the latter provide an indication of the trend and level of potential physical pressure of nutrient surpluses into the environment.

The main elements in the OECD gross nutrient (nitrogen and phosphorus) balance

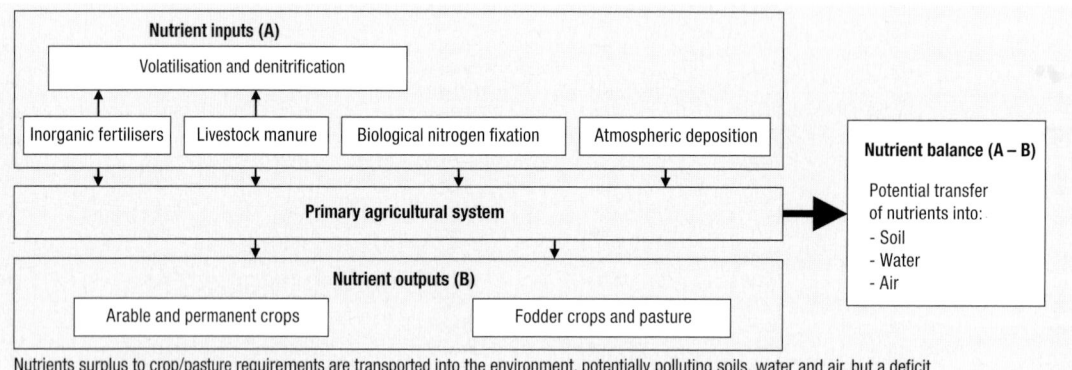

Nutrients surplus to crop/pasture requirements are transported into the environment, potentially polluting soils, water and air, but a deficit of nutrients in soils can also occur to the detriment of soil fertility and crop productivity.

Long-term trends

The decrease in nutrient balance surpluses has contributed to reduced pressures on soil, water and air, although a third of OECD countries registered an increase in surpluses. Rising or large nitrogen surpluses are commonly a result of the intensification of livestock production, since the growth in the use of inorganic nitrogen fertilisers has been limited in most countries. Where adoption of nutrient management plans has been high, this has had an impact in reducing surpluses, but there is further potential to reduce nutrients to levels that are not environmentally damaging. In most countries there is considerable variation in the level and trends of regional nutrient balances around national averages.

Source

• OECD (2008), *Environmental Performance of OECD Agriculture since 1990*, OECD, Paris.

Further information

Analytical publications

• OECD (1999), *Environmental Indicators for Agriculture: Concepts and Framework, Volume 1*, OECD, Paris.

• OECD (1999), *Environmental Indicators for Agriculture: Issues and Design – "The York Workshop", Volume 2*, OECD, Paris.

• OECD (2007), *Environmental Indicators for Agriculture: Volume 3*, OECD, Paris.

• OECD (2008), *Environmental Performance of OECD Agriculture since 1990*, OECD, Paris.

Methodological publications

• OECD (2007), *OECD Nitrogen Balance Handbook*, only available online at website below, OECD, Paris.

• OECD (2008), *OECD Phosphorus Balance Handbook*, only available online at website below, OECD, Paris.

Online databases

• *OECD Nitrogen Balance Database.*

Websites

• OECD Agri-Environmental Indicators, *www.oecd.org/agr/env/indicators.htm.*

Gross agricultural nutrient balances

Balance expressed as kg nutrient per hectare of total agricultural land

	Nitrogen			Phosphorus		
	Average 1990-1992	Average 2002-2004	% Change	Average 1990-1992	Average 2002-2004	% Change
Australia	16	17	5	1	1	35
Austria	66	48	−27	7	3	−61
Belgium	255	184	−28	41	23	−45
Canada	19	35	85	1	1	137
Czech Republic	77	70	−9	10	2	−84
Denmark	178	127	−29	17	11	−33
Finland	83	55	−34	20	8	−60
France	63	54	−16	13	4	−71
Germany	145	113	−22	16	4	−75
Greece	32	15	−52	8	4	−49
Hungary	21	37	74	−4	−1	..
Iceland	7	7	−5	2	1	−21
Ireland	76	83	9	10	6	−35
Italy	33	39	16	14	11	−22
Japan	180	171	−5	65	51	−21
Korea	213	240	13	47	48	2
Luxembourg	229	129	−44	48	11	−77
Mexico	27	22	−18	2	1	−53
Netherlands	345	229	−34	38	19	−49
New Zealand	31	46	46	6	14	136
Norway	92	77	−16	15	13	−13
Poland	49	48	−2	5	3	−43
Portugal	42	47	13	15	15	5
Slovak Republic	80	46	−43	15	1	−96
Spain	32	33	5	6	8	23
Sweden	57	48	−16	5	2	−65
Switzerland	77	76	−1	12	5	−55
Turkey	37	28	−24	9	5	−40
United Kingdom	56	43	−23	15	13	−13
United States	34	37	7	3	3	13
EU15 total	113	83	−26	18	10	−48
OECD total	88	74	−17	16	10	−37

StatLink ⫘ http://dx.doi.org/10.1787/274874233644

Gross agricultural nitrogen and phosphorus balances

Change in averages 1990-92 to 2002-04 expressed as tonnes of nutrients

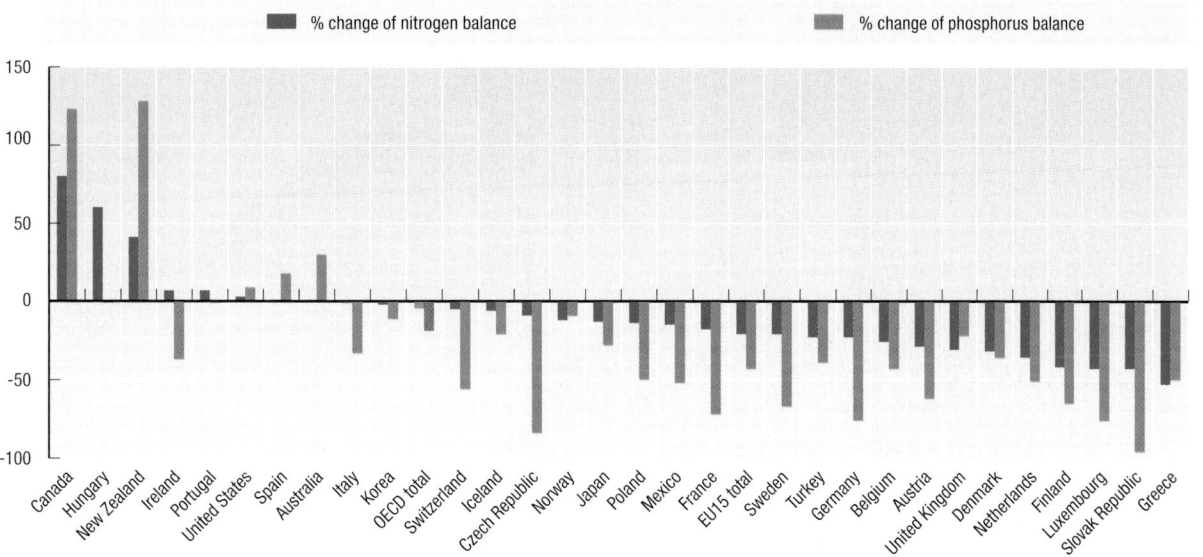

StatLink ⫘ http://dx.doi.org/10.1787/270316550388

EDUCATION

OUTCOMES
INTERNATIONAL STUDENT ASSESSMENT
TRENDS IN TERTIARY GRADUATION RATES
TERTIARY ATTAINMENT

EXPENDITURE ON EDUCATION
EXPENDITURE ON TERTIARY EDUCATION
RELATIVE EARNINGS OF GRADUATES
PUBLIC AND PRIVATE EDUCATION EXPENDITURE

INTERNATIONAL STUDENT ASSESSMENT

How effective are school systems at providing young people with a solid foundation of knowledge and skills that will equip them for life and learning beyond school? OECD's Programme for International Student Assessment (PISA) assesses student knowledge and skills in science, mathematics and reading at age 15, *i.e.* towards the end of compulsory education.

PISA 2006 also assessed the attitudes which students have towards science and the environment, their interest in science, the extent to which they are aware of the life opportunities that possessing science competencies may open, and the science learning opportunities and environment which their schools offer.

Definition

The PISA survey covers science, mathematics and reading. For the 2006 round of PISA, three and a half hours of testing time was in science, two hours for mathematics and one hour for reading. Each student spent two hours on the assessment items.

Scientific literacy is the capacity to use scientific knowledge to identify questions, to acquire new knowledge, to explain scientific phenomena, and to draw evidence-based conclusions about science-related issues.

Mathematical literacy is the capacity to identify and understand the role that mathematics plays in the world, to make well-founded judgments and to use and engage with mathematics in ways that meet the needs of that individual's life as a constructive, concerned and reflective citizen.

Reading literacy is the capacity to understand, use and reflect on written texts, in order to achieve one's goals, to develop one's knowledge and potential and to participate in society.

Comparability

Leading experts in participating countries advise on the scope and nature of the assessments and final decisions on this are taken by OECD governments. Substantial efforts and resources are devoted to achieving cultural and linguistic breadth and balance in the assessment materials and stringent quality assurance mechanisms are applied in translation, sampling and data collection.

Over 400 000 15-year-old students in 57 participating countries were assessed for PISA 2006. Because the results are based on probability samples, it is possible to calculate the standard errors of the estimates and these are shown in the tables.

Overview

The graph "Performance on the science scale in PISA 2006" shows the results for science in terms of differences from the OECD average score (500). As in the 2003 PISA, Finland is the top of the league. For Hungary, Sweden, Poland, Denmark and France the science scores are not significantly different from the OECD average. The table "Mean scores and gender differences on the science scale in PISA 2006" presents also the scores in science by gender. In OECD on average, the boys are doing slightly better than the girls; The results are significantly better for boys in Denmark, Luxembourg, Mexico, the Netherlands, Switzerland and United Kingdom, whereas significantly better results for girls than for boys occur in Greece and Turkey.

The results for mathematics and reading are displayed in the following graphs. Finland and Korea are competing for the top positions in these results. Germany, Sweden, Ireland, France, United Kingdom and Poland are not significantly different from the OECD average in mathematics. The other countries are significantly above or below the OECD average and are indicated in green. In reading, Japan, United Kingdom, Germany, Denmark, Austria and France are not significantly different from the OECD average. In the same way as for mathematics, countries significantly above or below the OECD average are indicated.

In mathematics, females remain at a disadvantage in many countries, with on average 11 score points of difference in favour of males. On the opposite side, in reading, differences in favour of females are observed in all countries. On average across OECD countries, females are 38 score points ahead of their male counterparts.

Sources

- OECD (2001), *PISA Knowledge and Skills for Life – First Results from PISA 2000*, OECD, Paris.
- OECD (2004), *PISA Learning for Tomorrow's World: First Results from PISA 2003*, OECD, Paris.
- OECD (2007), *Pisa 2006: Science, Competencies for tomorrow's World*, OECD, Paris.

Further information

Analytical publications

- OECD (2003), *PISA Literacy Skills for the World of Tomorrow – Further Results from PISA 2000*, OECD, Paris.
- OECD (2005), *PISA Problem Solving for Tomorrow's World: First Measures of Cross-Curricular Competencies from PISA 2003*, OECD, Paris.
- OECD (2006), *Are Students Ready for a Technology-Rich World? What Pisa studies Tell Us*, OECD, Paris.
- OECD (2006), *Where Immigrant Students Succeed: A Comparative Review of Performance and Engagement in PISA 2003*, OECD, Paris.

Methodological publications

- OECD (2006), *Assessing Scientific, Reading and Mathematical Literacy: A Framework for PISA 2006*, OECD, Paris.

Online databases

- *OECD PISA Database.*

Websites

- PISA Website, *www.pisa.oecd.org.*

Mean scores and gender differences on the science scale in PISA 2006

	All students		Males		Females		Difference (males − females)	
	Mean score	S.E.	Mean score	S.E.	Mean score	S.E.	Score difference	S.E.
Australia	527	2.3	527	3.2	527	2.7	0	3.8
Austria	511	3.9	515	4.2	507	4.9	8	4.9
Belgium	510	2.5	511	3.3	510	3.2	1	4.1
Canada	534	2.0	536	2.5	532	2.1	4	2.2
Czech Republic	513	3.5	515	4.2	510	4.8	5	5.6
Denmark	496	3.1	500	3.6	491	3.4	9	3.2
Finland	563	2.0	562	2.6	565	2.4	−3	2.9
France	495	3.4	497	4.3	494	3.6	3	4.0
Germany	516	3.8	519	4.6	512	3.8	7	3.7
Greece	473	3.2	468	4.5	479	3.4	−11	4.7
Hungary	504	2.7	507	3.3	501	3.5	6	4.2
Iceland	491	1.6	488	2.6	494	2.1	−6	3.4
Ireland	508	3.2	508	4.3	509	3.3	0	4.3
Italy	475	2.0	477	2.8	474	2.5	3	3.5
Japan	531	3.4	533	4.9	530	5.1	3	7.4
Korea	522	3.4	521	4.8	523	3.9	−2	5.5
Luxembourg	486	1.1	491	1.8	482	1.8	9	2.9
Mexico	410	2.7	413	3.2	406	2.6	7	2.2
Netherlands	525	2.7	528	3.2	521	3.1	7	3.0
New Zealand	530	2.7	528	3.9	532	3.6	−4	5.2
Norway	487	3.1	484	3.8	489	3.2	−4	3.4
Poland	498	2.3	500	2.7	496	2.6	3	2.5
Portugal	474	3.0	477	3.7	472	3.2	5	3.3
Slovak Republic	488	2.6	491	3.9	485	3.0	6	4.7
Spain	488	2.6	491	2.9	486	2.7	4	2.4
Sweden	503	2.4	504	2.7	503	2.9	1	3.0
Switzerland	512	3.2	514	3.3	509	3.6	6	2.7
Turkey	424	3.8	418	4.6	430	4.1	−12	4.1
United Kingdom	515	2.3	520	3.0	510	2.8	10	3.4
United States	489	4.2	489	5.1	489	4.0	1	3.5
OECD average	500	0.5	501	0.7	499	0.6	2	0.7
OECD total	491	1.2	492	1.4	490	1.3	3	1.3
Brazil	390	2.8	395	3.2	386	2.9	9	2.3
Russian Federation	479	3.7	481	4.1	478	3.7	3	2.7

StatLink http://dx.doi.org/10.1787/274875832073

Performance on the science scale in PISA 2006
Mean scores

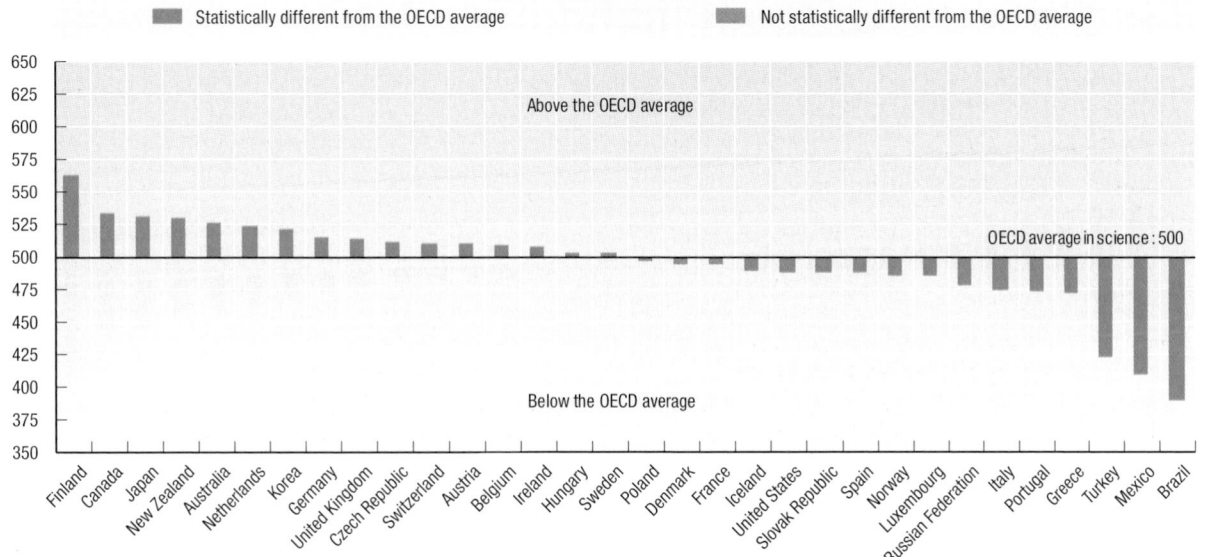

StatLink http://dx.doi.org/10.1787/270431272710

Mean scores and gender differences on the reading scale in PISA 2006

	All students		Males		Females		Difference (males – females)	
	Mean score	S.E.	Mean score	S.E.	Mean score	S.E.	Score difference	S.E.
Australia	513	2.1	495	3.0	532	2.2	–37	3.6
Austria	490	4.1	468	4.9	513	5.5	–45	6.0
Belgium	501	3.0	482	4.1	522	3.5	–40	4.8
Canada	527	2.4	511	2.8	543	2.5	–32	2.3
Czech Republic	483	4.2	463	5.0	509	5.4	–46	6.2
Denmark	494	3.2	480	3.6	509	3.5	–30	3.2
Finland	547	2.1	521	2.7	572	2.3	–51	2.8
France	488	4.1	470	5.2	505	3.9	–35	4.4
Germany	495	4.4	475	5.3	517	4.4	–42	3.9
Greece	460	4.0	432	5.7	488	3.5	–57	5.6
Hungary	482	3.3	463	3.7	503	3.9	–40	4.1
Iceland	484	1.9	460	2.8	509	2.3	–48	3.3
Ireland	517	3.5	500	4.5	534	3.8	–34	4.9
Italy	469	2.4	448	3.4	489	2.8	–41	4.0
Japan	498	3.6	483	5.4	513	5.2	–31	7.7
Korea	556	3.8	539	4.6	574	4.5	–35	5.9
Luxembourg	479	1.3	464	2.0	495	2.1	–32	3.2
Mexico	410	3.1	393	3.5	427	3.0	–34	2.5
Netherlands	507	2.9	495	3.7	519	3.0	–24	3.4
New Zealand	521	3.0	502	3.6	539	3.6	–37	4.6
Norway	484	3.2	462	3.8	508	3.3	–46	3.3
Poland	508	2.8	487	3.4	528	2.8	–40	2.9
Portugal	472	3.6	455	4.4	488	3.5	–33	3.7
Slovak Republic	466	3.1	446	4.2	488	3.8	–42	5.4
Spain	461	2.2	443	2.6	479	2.3	–35	2.1
Sweden	507	3.4	488	4.0	528	3.5	–40	3.2
Switzerland	499	3.1	484	3.2	515	3.3	–31	2.6
Turkey	447	4.2	427	5.1	471	4.3	–44	4.3
United Kingdom	495	2.3	480	3.0	510	2.6	–29	3.5
OECD average	492	0.6	473	0.7	511	0.7	–38	0.8
OECD total	484	1.0	466	1.2	502	1.3	–36	1.4
Brazil	393	3.7	376	4.3	408	3.7	–32	3.0
Russian Federation	440	4.3	420	4.8	458	4.3	–38	3.2

StatLink ⌗ http://dx.doi.org/10.1787/274883325383

Performance on the reading scale in PISA 2006
Mean scores

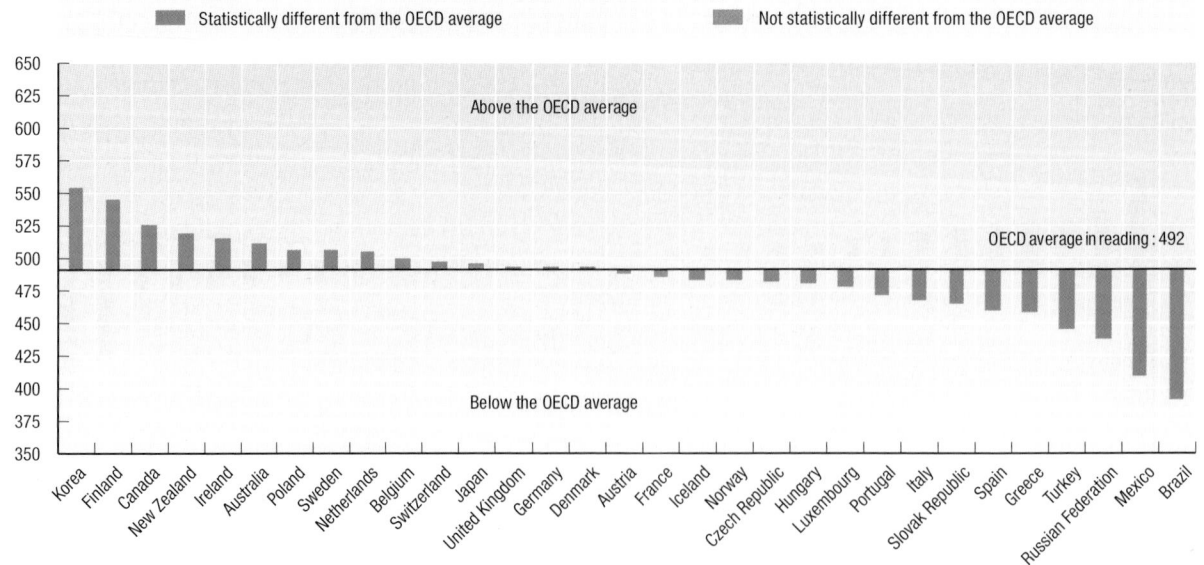

StatLink ⌗ http://dx.doi.org/10.1787/270437717033

Mean scores and gender differences on the mathematics scale in PISA 2006

	All students		Males		Females		Difference (males – females)	
	Mean score	S.E.	Mean score	S.E.	Mean score	S.E.	Score difference	S.E.
Australia	520	2.2	527	3.2	513	2.4	14	3.4
Austria	505	3.7	517	4.4	494	4.1	23	4.7
Belgium	520	3.0	524	4.1	517	3.4	7	4.8
Canada	527	2.0	534	2.4	520	2.0	14	1.9
Czech Republic	510	3.6	514	4.2	504	4.8	11	5.6
Denmark	513	2.6	518	2.9	508	3.0	10	2.8
Finland	548	2.3	554	2.7	543	2.6	12	2.6
France	496	3.2	499	4.0	492	3.3	6	3.7
Germany	504	3.9	513	4.6	494	3.9	20	3.7
Greece	459	3.0	462	4.3	457	3.0	5	4.5
Hungary	491	2.9	496	3.5	486	3.7	10	4.3
Iceland	506	1.8	503	2.6	508	2.2	−4	3.2
Ireland	501	2.8	507	3.7	496	3.2	11	4.1
Italy	462	2.3	470	2.9	453	2.7	17	3.4
Japan	523	3.3	533	4.8	513	4.9	20	7.2
Korea	547	3.8	552	5.3	543	4.5	9	6.3
Luxembourg	490	1.1	498	1.7	482	1.8	17	2.8
Mexico	406	2.9	410	3.4	401	3.1	9	2.6
Netherlands	531	2.6	537	3.1	524	2.8	13	2.8
New Zealand	522	2.4	527	3.1	517	3.6	11	4.7
Norway	490	2.6	493	3.3	487	2.8	6	3.1
Poland	495	2.4	500	2.8	491	2.7	9	2.6
Portugal	466	3.1	474	3.7	459	3.2	15	3.3
Slovak Republic	492	2.8	499	3.7	485	3.5	14	4.6
Spain	480	2.3	484	2.6	476	2.6	9	2.2
Sweden	502	2.4	505	2.7	500	3.0	5	2.9
Switzerland	530	3.2	536	3.3	523	3.6	13	2.7
Turkey	424	4.9	427	5.6	421	5.1	6	4.6
United Kingdom	495	2.1	504	2.6	487	2.6	17	2.9
United States	474	4.0	479	4.6	470	3.9	9	2.9
OECD average	498	0.5	503	0.7	492	0.6	11	0.7
OECD total	484	1.2	489	1.3	478	1.3	12	1.2
Brazil	370	2.9	380	3.4	361	3.0	19	2.8
Russian Federation	476	3.9	479	4.6	473	3.9	6	3.3

StatLink ◻▥ http://dx.doi.org/10.1787/275010842073

Performance on the mathematics scale in PISA 2006
Mean scores

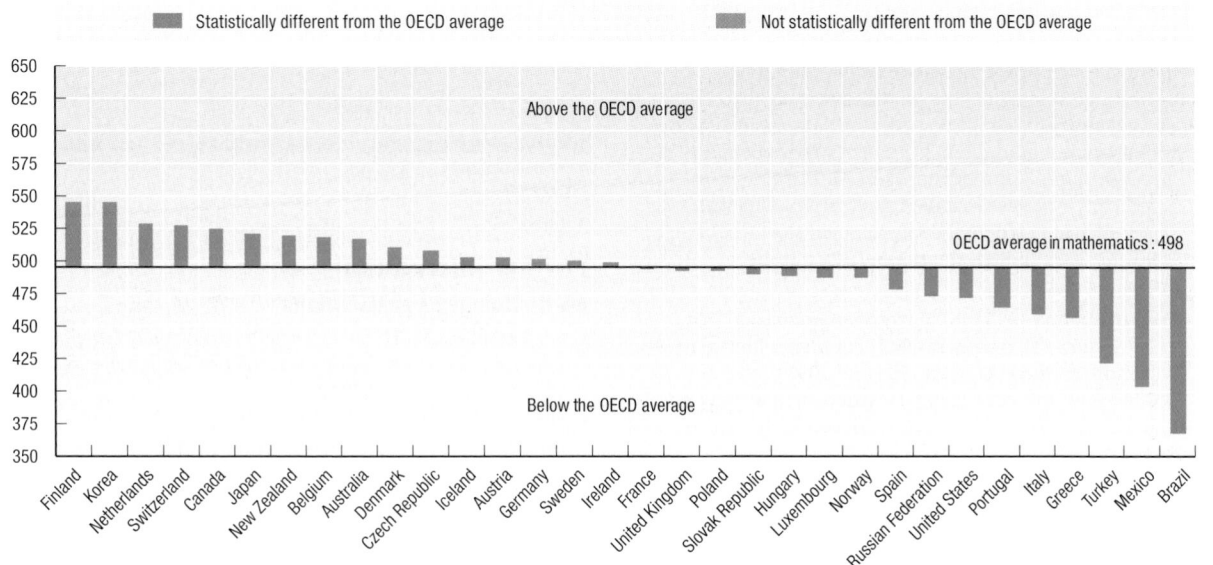

StatLink ◻▥ http://dx.doi.org/10.1787/270443378266

TRENDS IN TERTIARY GRADUATION RATES

Upper secondary graduation is becoming the norm in most countries today. In addition, the majority of students are graduating from upper secondary programmes designed to provide access to tertiary education, which is leading to increased enrolment and graduation in tertiary programmes. Countries with high graduation rates at the tertiary level are also the ones most likely to be developing or maintaining a highly skilled labour force.

Definition

This indicator shows the current tertiary graduate output of educational systems, i.e. the percentage of the population in the typical age cohort for tertiary education that follows and successfully completes tertiary programmes. The indicator only contains the proportion of first-time graduates.

Tertiary education covers a wide range of programmes, but overall serves as an indicator of the rate at which countries produce advanced knowledge. A traditional university degree is associated with completion of "type A" tertiary courses; "type B" generally refers to shorter and often vocationally oriented courses and usually lead to direct labour market access. The indicator also sheds light on the internal efficiency of tertiary educational systems.

Comparability

Graduation rates for first tertiary programmes (tertiary-type A, tertiary-type B and advanced research programmes) are calculated as net graduation rates, as the sum of age-specific graduation rates. Gross graduation rates are presented for those countries that cannot provide such detailed data. In order to calculate gross graduation rates, countries identify the age at which first-time graduation typically occurs.

Data on trends in graduation rate at tertiary level for the years 1995, 2000, 2001, 2002, 2003 and 2004 are based on a special survey carried out in OECD countries and four of the six partner economies in January 2007. The data for the academic year 2004-2005 are based on the UNESCO/OECD/Eurostat data collection on education statistics.

Long-term trends

On average across the 24 OECD countries with comparable data, 36% of persons at the typical age of graduation completed tertiary-type A education in 2005. This figure ranged from around 20% or less in Austria, Germany and Turkey to more than 40% in Australia, Denmark, Finland, Iceland, Italy, the Netherlands, New Zealand, Norway and Poland. These graduation rates tend to be higher in countries where the programmes provided are of shorter duration. On average across OECD countries, the graduation rate for shorter, vocationally oriented programmes represents 9% of the typical age cohort, and 1.3% for programmes leading to advanced research qualifications.

The tertiary-type A graduation rate has known on average a significant increase of more than ten percentage points over the ten last years. In virtually every country for which comparable data are available, tertiary-type A graduation rates increased between 1995 and 2005, often quite substantially. One of the most significant increases in type A graduation rates was reported in Italy where the rate doubled to 41% between 2000 and 2005, though this was largely a result of structural change.

Over the period 1995 to 2005, tertiary graduation rates evolved quite differently in OECD countries. Increase was more marked between 1995 and 2000 than from 2000 to 2005, for some countries (such as New Zealand and Norway). The reverse was observed in the Czech Republic, Greece, Japan and Switzerland, where the increase in graduation rate has occurred mainly in the last five years.

Source

- OECD (2007), *Education at a Glance*, OECD, Paris.

Further information
Methodological publications

- OECD (2004), *OECD Handbook for Internationally Comparative Education Statistics: Concepts, Standards, Definitions and Classifications*, OECD, Paris.
- UIS, OECD and Eurostat (2007), *UOE Data Collection – 2007 Data Collection on Education Systems: Definitions, Explanations and Instructions*, OECD, Paris.

Websites

- OECD Education at a Glance, *www.oecd.org/edu/eag2007*.

Tertiary graduation rates (first-time graduation)

Percentage of tertiary graduates to the population at the typical age of graduation

	Tertiary-type A							Tertiary-type B					
	Typical age of graduation	1995	2000	2002	2003	2004	2005	Typical age of graduation	1995	2000	2002	2003	2004	2005
Australia	20-25	..	36	46	50	47	59	23-29	..	1	..	..	..	..
Austria	23-25	10	15	18	19	20	20	20-22	..	..	..	..	7	8
Canada	22-25	..	28	..	..	..	..	..	..	..	..	..	..	..
Czech Republic	23-24	13	14	15	17	20	25	23-24	6	5	4	4	5	6
Denmark	22-27	25	37	41	43	44	46	21-25	8	10	13	14	11	10
Finland	25-29	20	41	49	48	47	..	21-22	34	7	2	1	..	..
Germany	25-26	14	18	18	18	19	20	21-22	13	11	10	10	10	11
Greece	25	14	15	18	20	24	25	24	5	6	7	9	11	12
Hungary	21-25	..	..	..	..	29	36	21	..	..	..	..	3	4
Iceland	23-25	..	33	41	45	51	56	22-24	..	6	6	7	5	4
Ireland	21	..	30	32	37	39	38	20	..	15	13	19	20	24
Italy	23-25	..	19	25	..	36	41	22-23	..	..	1	..	..	..
Japan	22-24	25	29	33	34	35	36	20	28	29	27	26	26	27
Netherlands	22-23	29	35	37	38	40	42	..	..	..	..	..	..	..
New Zealand	21-24	33	50	46	49	50	51	20	12	17	18	20	21	21
Norway	22-25	26	37	38	39	45	41	20	6	6	5	5	3	2
Poland	24-25	..	34	43	44	45	45	..	..	..	..	..	..	..
Portugal	22-26	15	23	30	33	32	32	21	6	8	7	7	8	9
Slovak Republic	22-25	15	..	23	25	28	30	21-22	1	2	3	2	3	2
Spain	20-22	24	30	32	32	33	33	19	2	8	13	16	17	17
Sweden	23-26	24	28	32	35	37	38	22-23	..	4	4	4	4	5
Switzerland	23-26	9	12	21	22	26	27	23-29	13	14	11	12	12	8
Turkey	22-24	6	9	10	11	11	11	..	..	..	..	..	..	..
United Kingdom	20-21	..	37	37	38	39	39	20-21	..	..	12	14	16	17
United States	22	33	34	32	32	33	34	20	9	8	8	9	9	10
OECD average		20	28	31	33	35	36		10	8	8	9	9	9
Brazil	23	..	10	13	15	..	..	..	..	..	..	..	..	..

StatLink http://dx.doi.org/10.1787/275033578078

Tertiary-type A graduation rates

Percentage of tertiary-type A graduates to the population at the typical age of graduation

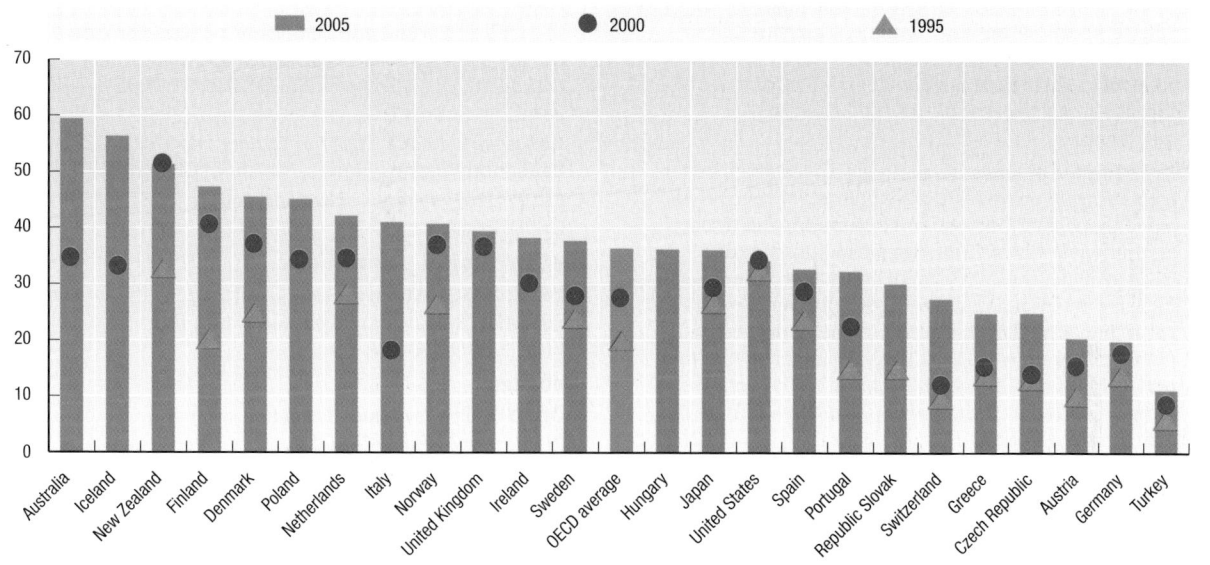

■ 2005   ● 2000   ▲ 1995

StatLink http://dx.doi.org/10.1787/270454337735

TERTIARY ATTAINMENT

The share of the population that has attained qualifications at the tertiary level is a key indicator of how well countries are placed to profit from technological and scientific progress. Differences between tertiary attainment of younger and older age groups is a measure of progress in the provision of higher education.

Definition

For each age group shown, those who have completed tertiary education are shown as a percentage of all persons in that age group. Tertiary education includes both tertiary-type "A programmes", which are largely theoretically-based and designed to provide qualifications for entry to advanced research programmes and professions with high skill requirements, as well as tertiary-type "B programmes" which are classified at the same level of competencies as tertiary-type A programmes but are more occupationally-oriented and lead to direct labour market access. The tertiary attainment profiles are based on the percentage of the population aged 25 to 64 that has completed that level of education.

Comparability

The International Standard Classification of Education (ISCED-97) is used to define the levels of education in a comparable way across countries. See the *OECD Handbook for Internationally Comparative Education Statistics* for a description of ISCED-97 education programmes and attainment levels and their mappings for each country.

Long-term trends

OECD countries have seen significant increases in the proportion of the adult population attaining tertiary education over the last decades. In 2005 for the 25-64 year-old population, 16 countries are grouped together within a range of 10 points between 25 and 35% of the population having attained the tertiary level. Three member countries are performing remarkably high: Canada, Japan and the United States. Conversely, three member countries are significantly below this average percentage in tertiary attainment where less than 13% of the population has attained tertiary qualifications: Italy, Portugal and Turkey.

In the youngest age group, 25 to 34 years old, the OECD country mean for tertiary attainment increased from 20 to over 32% between 1991 and 2005. In three OECD countries – Canada, Japan and Korea – 50% or more of this age group had in 2005 obtained a tertiary qualification.

An indication of longer term trends can be obtained by comparing the current attainment levels of younger and older age cohorts. For instance, comparing the tertiary attainment levels of 25-34 year olds with those of 55-64 year olds indicates that in Korea, there has been an increase in tertiary attainment over the past 30 years of more than 40 percentage points, some 27 percentage points higher than the OECD average increase over this period. In contrast, some OECD countries have only seen marginal increases (USA) or even decreases (Germany) of over the same period.

Source

- OECD (2007), *Education at a Glance*, OECD, Paris.

Further information

Analytical publications

- Blöndal S., S. Field and N. Girouard (2002), *Investment in Human Capital Through Post-Compulsory Education and Training: Selected Efficiency and Equity Aspects*, OECD Economics Department Working Papers, No. 333, OECD, Paris.
- Blöndal, S., S. Field and N. Girouard (2002), "*Investment in Human Capital through Upper-Secondary and Tertiary Education*", OECD Economic Studies, No. 34, 2002/I, OECD, Paris.
- Hansson, B. (2007), *Effects of Tertiary Expansion*, OECD Education Working Papers, No. 10, OECD, Paris.
- OECD (2007), *Reviews of National Policies for Education*, OECD, Paris.

Methodological publications

- OECD (2004), *OECD Handbook for Internationally Comparative Education Statistics: Concepts, Standards, Definitions and Classifications*, OECD, Paris.

Websites

- OECD Centre for Educational Research and Innovation (CERI), *www.oecd.org/edu/ceri*.
- OECD Education at a Glance, *www.oecd.org/edu/eag2007*.

Tertiary attainment for age group 25-64
As a percentage of the population of that age group

	1992	1993	1994	1995	1996	1997	1998	1999	2000	2001	2002	2003	2004	2005
Australia	..	22.5	23.1	24.3	24.8	24.3	25.4	26.7	27.5	29.0	30.8	31.3	30.8	31.7
Austria	6.9	..	7.7	7.9	8.1	10.6	10.9	10.9	13.9	14.1	14.5	14.5		18.3	17.8
Belgium	20.2	..	22.3	24.6	23.9	25.1	25.3	26.7	27.1	27.6	28.1	29.0	30.4	31.0
Canada	30.8	..	34.2	34.9	35.6	37.3	38.1	39.2	40.0	41.6	42.6	44.0	44.6	46.1
Czech Republic	..	..	10.1	10.4	10.4	10.6	10.4	10.8	11.0	11.1	11.9	12.0	12.3	13.1
Denmark	19.2	..	19.6	20.4	20.9	..	25.4	26.5	26.2	28.4	29.6	31.9	32.9	33.5
Finland	25.9	..	26.8	27.7	28.4	29.4	30.2	31.3	32.0	32.3	32.6	33.3	34.2	34.6
France	16.0	17.1	17.8	18.6	19.2	20.0	20.6	21.5	22.0	23.0	24.0	23.3	23.9	24.8
Germany	20.1	..	20.4	22.2	21.8	22.6	23.0	22.9	23.5	23.2	23.4	24.0	24.9	24.6
Greece	..	..	17.9	17.4	18.9	15.5	16.8	17.4	17.5	17.9	18.6	19.2	21.2	21.3
Hungary	..	..	..	..	13.4	12.2	13.2	13.5	14.0	14.0	14.2	15.4	16.7	17.1
Iceland	..	..	..	..	20.8	20.9	21.0	22.4	23.2	24.6	25.6	28.9	29.1	30.5
Ireland	17.0	..	18.6	19.9	22.6	22.8	21.1	20.5	18.5		23.6	24.8	26.3	27.8	29.1
Italy	6.4	..	7.5	7.9	8.1	..	8.6	9.3	9.4	10.0	10.4	10.5	11.6	12.2
Japan	..	..	..	..	..	30.5	30.6	31.8	33.6	34.1	36.6	37.4	38.7	39.9
Korea	16.1	17.5	17.8	18.6	19.6	19.8	22.5	23.1	23.9	25.0	26.0	29.5	30.5	31.6
Luxembourg	..	..	..	18.1	19.0	..	..	18.3	18.3	18.1	18.6	14.3		23.7	26.5
Mexico	..	..	..	11.9	13.2	13.8	13.6	13.4	14.6	15.0	15.3	15.4	16.4	14.9
Netherlands	20.9	..	21.4	22.0	22.5	..	24.2	22.6	23.4	23.2	25.0	27.5	29.5	30.1
New Zealand	23.6	..	23.2	25.3	..	25.8	26.6	27.0	28.0	29.2	29.8	30.9		25.3	27.1
Norway	25.3	..	27.4	28.6	26.9	25.8	27.4	27.5	28.4	30.2	31.0	31.0	31.8	32.7
Poland	..	..	..	9.9	..	10.2	10.9	11.3	11.4	11.9	12.6	14.2	15.7	16.9
Portugal	..	..	10.7	11.0	10.9	..	8.3	8.7	8.9	9.1	9.3	10.8	12.5	12.8
Slovak Republic	..	..	11.3	11.1	11.5	10.5	10.3	10.1	10.4	10.9	11.0	11.8	12.4	13.7
Spain	13.1	..	15.0	16.1	17.5	18.6	19.7	21.0	22.6	23.6	24.4	25.2	26.4	28.2
Sweden	25.8	..	27.0	28.3	27.4	27.5	28.0	28.7	30.1	31.6	32.6	33.4	34.5		29.6
Switzerland	21.0	..	21.4	21.1	21.9	22.2	22.9	23.6	24.2	25.4	25.4	26.9	28.1	28.8
Turkey	4.8	..	7.0	8.4	..	7.6	7.5	8.1	8.3	8.4	9.1	9.7	9.1	9.7
United Kingdom	18.5	..	21.3	21.9	22.3	22.7	23.7	24.8	25.7	26.1	26.9	28.0	29.2	29.6
United States	30.2	..	32.2	33.3	33.9	34.1	34.9	35.8	36.5	37.3	38.1	38.4	39.1	39.0
OECD average	19.0	..	19.2	19.3	20.1	20.8	20.7	21.2	21.8	22.7	23.4	24.3	25.4	26.0
Brazil	..	..	..	..	..	..	..	..	..	..	..	..	7.8	..
Russian Federation	..	..	..	..	..	..	..	..	..	..	..	54.6		

StatLink http://dx.doi.org/10.1787/275047548651

Tertiary attainment for age group 25-64
As a percentage of the population of that age group, 2005 or latest available year

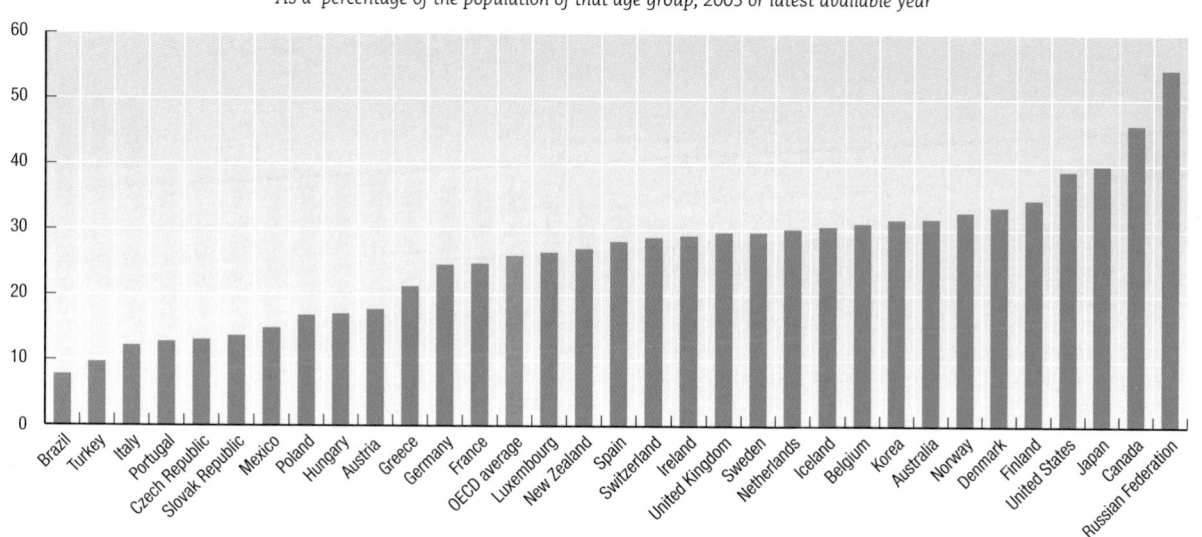

StatLink http://dx.doi.org/10.1787/270458837266

Tertiary attainment for age group 25-34

As a percentage of the population of that age group

	1992	1993	1994	1995	1996	1997	1998	1999	2000	2001	2002	2003	2004	2005
Australia	..	22.8	23.6	24.7	25.3	25.7	28.1	29.0	31.4	33.5	35.8	36.3	36.2	38.1
Austria	7.9	..	8.8	8.7	9.2	12.4	12.5	12.7	15.0	14.3	14.8	15.4 |	20.3	19.7
Belgium	27.2	..	30.0	32.9	32.2	33.1	33.8	34.4	36.0	37.5	37.6	38.9	40.7	40.6
Canada	34.2	..	37.8	39.3	40.6	44.1	45.5	46.8	48.3	50.5	51.2	52.8	53.3	53.8
Czech Republic	..	..	12.5	11.8	11.2	10.9	10.5	10.9	11.2	11.3	12.3	12.1	13.0	14.2
Denmark	19.5	..	19.7	20.3	20.7	..	26.8	28.6	28.9	31.1	32.3	35.1	37.6	39.8
Finland	33.5	..	34.1	35.0	35.2	36.4	36.0	37.4	37.6	38.2	39.2	39.8	38.2	37.5
France	21.6	23.1	24.3	25.4	26.0	27.8	29.6	30.9	32.4	34.2	36.1	37.1	38.1	39.3
Germany	18.8	..	18.7	20.8	20.3	21.0	21.5	21.5	22.3	21.8	21.7	21.8	22.9	22.5
Greece	..	..	25.0	26.0	28.2	22.3	23.7	23.9	23.6	23.3	23.4	23.7	25.3	25.4
Hungary	..	..	..	..	14.3	12.4	13.9	13.7	14.7	14.8	15.0	16.8	18.9	19.6
Iceland	..	..	..	..	23.7	23.0	24.2	27.6	27.8	26.5	28.1	32.8	33.3	35.8
Ireland	21.2	..	24.4	27.2	31.3	32.5	29.5	28.1	25.2 |	33.4	35.2	37.1	39.6	40.6
Italy	6.8	..	7.9	8.2	8.3	..	9.0	10.0	10.4	11.8	12.5	12.7	14.8	16.1
Japan	..	..	..	..	..	45.7	46.1	45.8	47.8	48.5	51.0	51.6	52.6	53.2
Korea	23.9	26.8	27.7	29.2	30.6	30.9	33.8	34.8	36.9	39.2	41.2	46.6	49.1	51.0
Luxembourg	..	..	..	..	..	..	..	21.2	22.9	23.4	22.6	18.8 |	32.4	37.0
Mexico	..	..	..	16.3	17.1	17.3	16.7	16.6	17.4	18.0	18.4	18.7	19.3	18.1
Netherlands	23.6	..	23.9	24.5	25.1	..	27.5	25.1	26.6	26.5	28.3	32.1	34.5	35.4
New Zealand	23.2	..	21.1	24.2	..	25.4	26.4	26.0	27.2	28.5	29.3	32.4 |	28.0	30.8
Norway	28.2	..	30.7	32.1	30.0	29.9	32.8	34.7	34.9	37.9	39.7	39.8	39.2	40.9
Poland	..	..	..	9.9	..	10.3	11.8	12.3	14.2	15.2	16.8	20.4	23.2	25.5
Portugal	..	..	13.2	13.5	14.4	..	11.5	12.2	13.0	14.0	15.0	16.3	18.6	19.1
Slovak Republic	..	..	12.5	11.6	12.4	10.4	11.3	11.1	11.2	11.9	11.9	13.2	14.3	16.3
Spain	22.5	..	25.2	26.6	28.6	30.3	32.0	33.5	.34.1	35.5	36.7	37.5	38.1	39.7
Sweden	26.5	..	27.3	28.6	28.4	29.3	30.7	31.7	33.6	36.9	39.2	40.4	42.3 |	37.3
Switzerland	21.3	..	22.0	21.5	22.5	24.7	25.0	25.9	25.6	25.6	26.7	29.2	30.4	31.0
Turkey	5.6	..	6.6	7.5	..	7.3	7.8	8.7	8.9	9.1	10.5	11.4	10.8	11.8
United Kingdom	20.6	..	23.1	23.3	24.3	24.7	25.9	27.3	28.6	29.5	31.2	33.1	34.9	35.0
United States	30.2	..	32.0	33.6	35.2	35.7	36.2	37.4	38.1	39.1	39.3	38.7	39.0	39.2
OECD average	21.9	..	22.2	22.4	23.8	24.9	24.8	25.3	26.2	27.4	28.4	29.8	31.3	32.2
Brazil	..	..	..	..	..	..	..	..	..	..	..	..	7.9	..
Russian Federation	..	..	..	..	..	..	..	..	..	..	..	56.1	..	..

StatLink http://dx.doi.org/10.1787/275065032051

Tertiary attainment for age group 25-34

As a percentage of the population of that age group, 2005 or latest available year

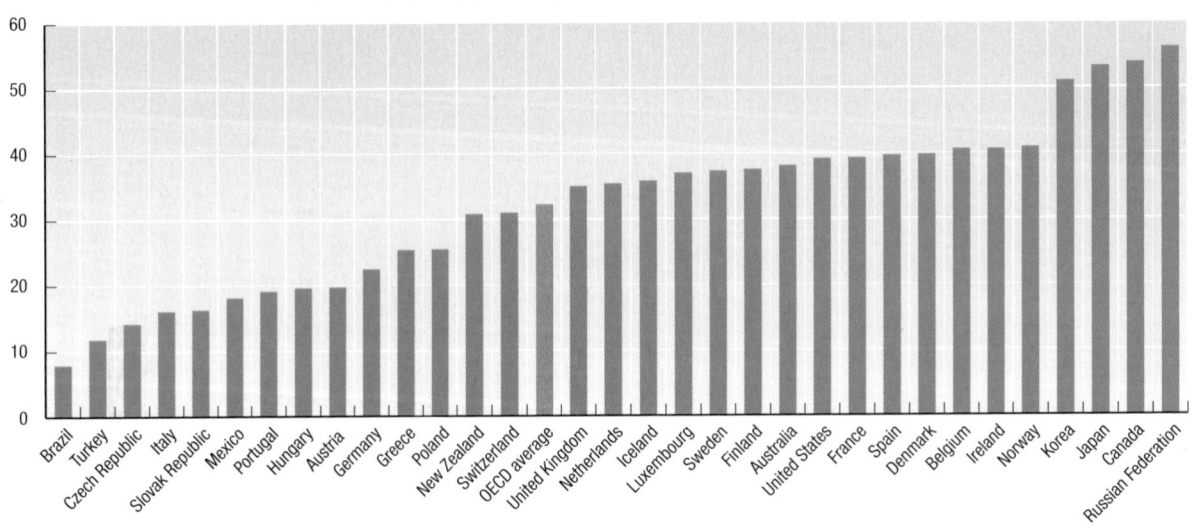

StatLink http://dx.doi.org/10.1787/270461233273

OECD FACTBOOK 2008 – ISBN 978-92-64-04054-0 – © OECD 2008

Tertiary attainment for age group 55-64
As a percentage of the population of that age group

	1992	1993	1994	1995	1996	1997	1998	1999	2000	2001	2002	2003	2004	2005
Australia	..	13.5	14.7	17.2	16.9	17.1	17.0	17.5	19.1	21.1	22.5	23.3	23.0	23.8
Austria	3.3	..	3.6	4.2	4.7	6.3	6.5	6.5	9.9	10.6	11.0	11.3	14.8	14.0
Belgium	9.2	..	11.1	13.1	12.7	13.7	13.8	15.7	16.8	17.1	18.2	18.9	20.0	21.9
Canada	19.2	..	23.0	23.6	25.1	24.3	25.7	27.4	28.3	30.1	32.1	33.8	34.5	36.4
Czech Republic	..	..	7.6	8.3	7.5	7.9	8.5	9.4	9.1	9.3	10.6	10.3	10.2	10.7
Denmark	12.6	..	13.2	13.8	14.3	..	19.3	19.0	18.9	22.2	24.2	25.9	26.8	27.3
Finland	12.8	..	13.9	15.5	17.0	17.9	19.3	20.7	22.7	23.4	23.4	24.2	25.7	26.5
France	7.3	7.9	8.4	8.9	9.6	10.5	11.2	12.4	13.3	14.1	15.2	13.7	14.4	15.5
Germany	15.7	..	16.5	17.5	17.5	18.4	19.3	19.4	20.2	20.2	20.6	21.6	22.8	22.9
Greece	..	..	9.1	7.8	8.4	7.5	7.8	8.1	8.3	8.8	10.1	11.2	12.2	11.9
Hungary	..	..	..	..	8.9	8.5	10.2	11.2	11.8	11.5	12.6	13.8	14.4	14.6
Iceland	..	..	..	..	9.5	11.6	10.8	11.3	13.5	14.8	16.9	16.5	18.4	20.5
Ireland	10.4	..	11.3	11.0	12.6	12.5	11.4	12.6	11.5	13.5	14.3	14.6	15.4	16.7
Italy	3.5	..	4.2	4.4	4.6	..	4.8	5.5	5.5	6.2	6.7	6.9	7.4	8.0
Japan	..	..	..	..	..	13.7	13.2	14.3	15.1	15.1	18.0	19.2	20.6	21.7
Korea	5.9	6.7	6.7	6.8	6.8	6.5	8.3	8.5	8.6	8.9	9.1	9.5	9.7	10.0
Luxembourg	..	..	..	..	..	..	..	12.0	13.0	13.5	14.4	10.2	15.8	18.6
Mexico	..	..	..	4.4	4.6	5.7	4.9	5.7	7.0	7.2	7.2	7.6	8.5	7.9
Netherlands	13.2	..	14.4	14.2	15.6	..	16.9	16.9	17.7	17.4	19.6	21.9	24.0	24.4
New Zealand	17.1	..	17.9	21.1	..	21.2	23.1	23.1	24.2	24.1	26.2	27.4	19.7	21.2
Norway	14.2	..	17.7	18.0	16.9	17.5	18.9	18.8	20.4	21.5	21.7	21.7	23.2	24.0
Poland	..	..	..	8.2	..	9.1	9.9	10.4	9.9	10.2	10.5	11.1	12.2	12.7
Portugal	..	..	5.6	5.9	6.2	..	4.7	4.5	4.7	4.9	4.6	5.6	6.7	7.4
Slovak Republic	..	..	7.0	7.5	7.2	6.1	6.7	6.9	7.8	8.6	8.6	8.9	9.3	10.5
Spain	5.2	..	5.6	6.0	7.1	7.6	8.1	8.7	9.7	10.3	10.5	11.0	12.4	14.5
Sweden	16.5	..	19.4	20.2	18.5	19.3	19.9	21.3	23.0	24.4	25.2	26.3	27.3	24.9
Switzerland	17.0	..	16.9	17.4	16.8	16.5	18.0	17.8	18.3	20.2	21.3	22.0	22.1	22.1
Turkey	1.7	..	4.3	5.9	..	4.6	4.5	5.3	5.9	5.9	6.3	7.3	6.6	7.2
United Kingdom	13.6	..	15.5	16.2	16.9	16.3	17.2	18.5	18.9	19.1	19.8	20.8	22.7	23.8
United States	21.9	..	23.6	24.3	25.6	26.2	27.2	28.0	29.7	30.6	33.2	34.7	36.2	36.9
OECD average	11.6	..	12.1	12.4	12.5	13.1	13.3	13.9	14.8	15.5	16.5	17.0	17.9	18.6
Brazil	..	..	..	..	..	..	..	..	..	..	..	..	3.7	..
Russian Federation	..	..	..	..	..	..	..	..	..	..	..	44.8	..	..

StatLink http://dx.doi.org/10.1787/275108875767

Tertiary attainment for age group 55-64
As a percentage of the population of that age group, 2005 or latest available year

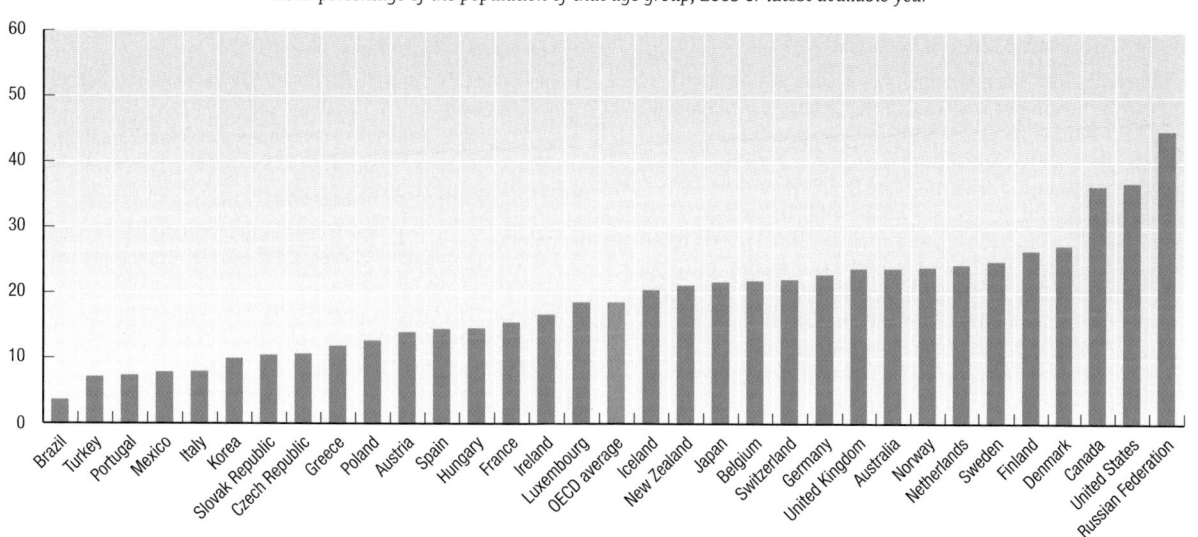

StatLink http://dx.doi.org/10.1787/270468540744

EXPENDITURE ON TERTIARY EDUCATION

Policy makers must balance the importance of improving the quality of educational services with the desirability of expanding access to educational opportunities, notably at the tertiary level. The comparative review of how trends in educational expenditure per student have evolved shows that in many OECD countries the expansion of enrolments, particularly in tertiary education, has not always been paralleled by changes in educational investment.

Definition

The indicator shows direct public and private expenditure on educational institutions in relation to the number of tertiary full-time equivalent students enrolled in these institutions. Public subsidies for students' living expenses have been excluded to ensure international comparability of the data.

Expenditure on education per student is obtained by dividing the total expenditure on educational institutions by the number of full-time equivalents students. Only those educational institutions and programmes are taken into account for which both enrolment and expenditure data are available.

Comparability

Expenditure in national currency for 2004 is converted to US dollars by PPP exchange rates. The PPP exchange rate is used because the market exchange rate is affected by many factors (interest rates, trade policies, expectations of economic growth, etc.) that have little to do with relative purchasing power of currencies in different countries.

The changes in expenditure on educational institutions per student are based on data from 1995 and 2004. The data on expenditure for 1995 were obtained by a special survey updated in 2004. OECD countries were asked to collect the 1995 data according to the definitions and the coverage of a joint UNESCO-OECD-Eurostat data collection programme. All expenditure data have been adjusted to 2004 prices using the GDP price deflator.

Long-term trends

In 2004, the level of expenditure per tertiar.n average in OECD countries was 11 100 USD converted using PPPs. This average masks a considerable variation of spending at tertiary level with one country (Poland) spending less than 5 000 USD per student rising up to a level of spending of more than 21 000 USD in Switzerland and the United States. OECD countries in which most R&D is performed by tertiary educational institutions tend to report higher expenditure per tertiary student than countries in which a large part of R&D is performed in other public institutions or by industry.

On average, for the countries where data are available, expenditure on tertiary education per student increased by 9% over the period 1995 to 2004. Despite this average increase however, there was a decrease in expenditure in six out of 23 OECD countries (the Czech Republic, Hungary, Poland, Portugal, Sweden and the United Kingdom) and in the partner economy Brazil which was largely due to a rapid increase in the number of tertiary students enrolled in the same period. On the other hand, expenditure per tertiary student rose significantly in Greece, Ireland, Mexico, the Slovak Republic and Switzerland despite a significant growth in enrolment of 107, 37, 53, 90 and 31%, respectively.

Source

- OECD (2007), *Education at a Glance*, OECD, Paris.

Further information

Analytical publications

- OECD (2004), *Internationalisation and Trade in Higher Education: Opportunities and Challenges*, OECD, Paris.
- OECD (2004), *Quality and Recognition in Higher Education: The Cross-border Challenge*, OECD, Paris.
- OECD (2006), *Education Policy Analysis: Focus on Higher Education* , OECD, Paris.
- OECD (2007), *Higher Education Management and Policy*, OECD, Paris.
- OECD (2007), *Reviews of National Policies for Education*, OECD, Paris.

Methodological publications

- OECD (2004), *OECD Handbook for Internationally Comparative Education Statistics: Concepts, Standards, Definitions and Classifications*, OECD, Paris.
- UIS, OECD and Eurostat (2007), *UOE Data Collection – 2007 Data Collection on Education Systems: Definitions, Explanations and Instructions*, OECD, Paris.

Websites

- OECD Education at a Glance, *www.oecd.org/edu/eag2007*.

Expenditure per student in tertiary education
Year 2004

	Index of change, year 1995 = 100			Expenditure per student in tertiary education: 2004 constant prices (US dollars)
	Expenditure	Number of students	Expenditure per student	
Australia	132	131	101	14 036
Austria	126	103	122	13 959
Belgium	..	..	..	11 842
Czech Republic	145	210	69	6 752
Denmark	133	107	123	15 225
Finland	128	116	110	12 505
France	..	..	..	10 668
Germany	112	105	107	12 255
Greece	312	207	151	5 593
Hungary	159	218	73	7 095
Iceland	..	..	..	8 881
Ireland	174	137	126	10 211
Italy	144	111	130	7 723
Japan	125	124	101	12 193
Korea	..	150	..	7 068
Mexico	168	153	110	5 778
Netherlands	115	113	101	13 846
New Zealand	109	..	..	8 866
Norway	117	113	103	14 997
Poland	202	224	90	4 412
Portugal	143	146	98	7 741
Slovak Republic	210	190	111	6 535
Spain	162	97	167	9 378
Sweden	144	145	99	16 218
Switzerland	176	131	134	21 966
Turkey	191	106	181	..
United Kingdom	122	130	93	11 484
United States	163	124	132	22 476
OECD average	155	141	109	11 100
Brazil	129	176	73	9 019
Russian Federation	..	..	..	2 562

StatLink ⬚🔗 *http://dx.doi.org/10.1787/275181634101*

Changes in real expenditure on educational institutions in tertiary education
Percentage change 1995-2004

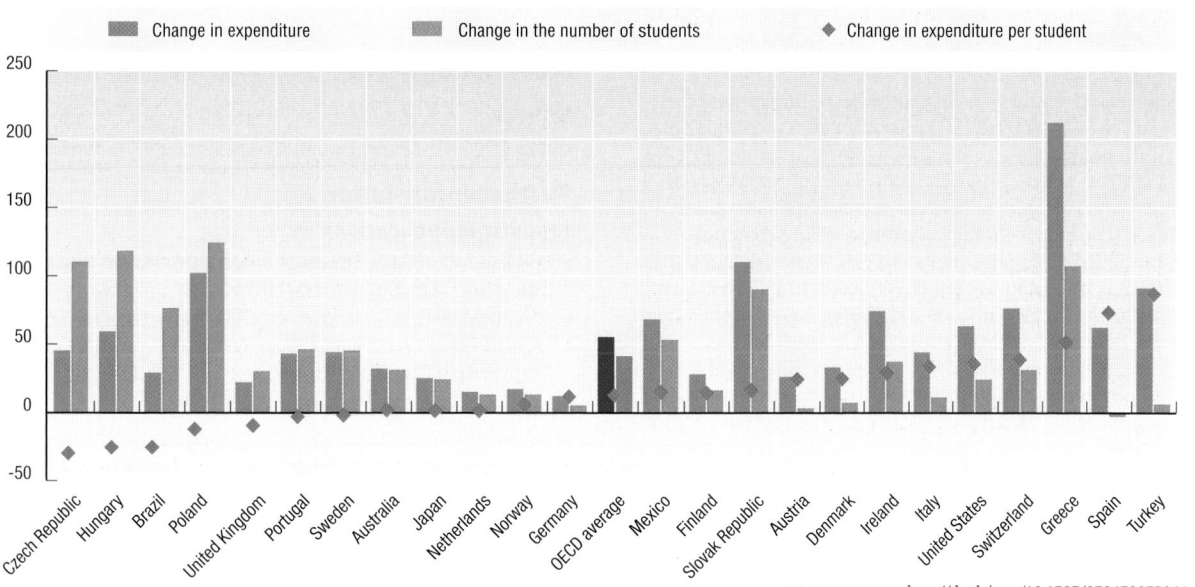

StatLink ⬚🔗 *http://dx.doi.org/10.1787/270472075044*

RELATIVE EARNINGS OF GRADUATES

The relative earnings of the population that has attained qualifications at the tertiary level is a key indicator of the financial return from education. How well countries' salary scales are placed to remunerate higher education investments may also reflect differences in the supply of educational programmes at different levels (or barriers to access to those programmes).

Definition

Relative earnings of those who have completed tertiary education are shown as a percentage of earnings of those who have completed upper secondary or post-secondary non-tertiary education. Tertiary education includes both tertiary-type "A programmes", which are largely theoretically-based and designed to provide qualifications for entry to advanced research programmes and professions with high skill requirements, as well as tertiary-type "B programmes" which are more occupationally-oriented and lead to direct labour market access. The relative earnings profiles are based on the earnings of the population aged 25 to 64.

Long-term trends

In all countries, graduates of tertiary-level education earn substantially more than upper secondary and post-secondary non-tertiary graduates. For 25-to-64-year-olds, financial rewards from tertiary education are particularly high in the Czech Republic, Hungary, Portugal, and the United States for both females and males while in Finland, Italy, and Poland males have a substantial wage premium and in Ireland, Korea, Turkey and the United Kingdom females with tertiary education earn substantially more than their counterparts with upper secondary or post-secondary non-tertiary education. On average, across the countries for which data are available, the average wage premium for completing tertiary education is above 50% both for males and females relative to their counterparts with an upper secondary and post-secondary non-tertiary education.

Trends in relative earnings provide an indication of supply and demand for higher educated individuals in different countries. Increases in earnings premium over time can be seen as an indication of a short supply of tertiary educated individuals relative to the demand from the labour market whereas a falling earnings premium could potentially indicate an excess supply of tertiary educated. A comparison over time for countries with data for 1997 or 1998 and 2004 or 2005 suggests that the demand for tertiary educated individuals still outstrips the supply in most countries. Spain is the only country where a significant drop in the earnings premium has taken place during this period but only for males with tertiary education. Significant increases in the wage premium have taken place in Germany, Hungary, Ireland, and Italy for both males and females and for males in the United States.

Comparability

The International Standard Classification of Education (ISCED-97) is used to define the levels of education. See the OECD Handbook for Internationally Comparative Education Statistics for a description of ISCED-97 education programmes and attainment levels and their mappings for each country.

Earnings data for the Czech Republic, Hungary, Luxembourg, Poland and Portugal exclude part time work. Moreover earnings data for Hungary, Luxembourg, Poland and Portugal exclude part year or seasonal employment. Earnings are considered before income tax except for Belgium and Korea where data are after income tax. The length of the reference period is one week for Australia, New Zealand and the United Kingdom; one month for Belgium, France, Germany, Hungary, Ireland and Portugal; the calendar year for Austria, Canada, the Czech Republic, Denmark, Finland, Italy, Luxembourg, the Netherlands, Norway, Spain and Sweden; and other 12-month period for Korea, Switzerland and the United States.

Source

- OECD (2007), *Education at a Glance 2007*, OECD, Paris.

Further information

Analytical publications

- Hansson, B. (2007), *Effects of Tertiary Expansion*, OECD Education Working Papers, No. 10, OECD, Paris.
- Oliveira Martins, J. et al. (2007), *The Policy Determinants of Investment in Tertiary Education*, OECD Economics Department Working Papers, No. 576, OECD, Paris.

Methodological publications

- OECD (2004), *OECD Handbook for Internationally Comparative Education Statistics: Concepts, Standards, Definitions and Classifications*, OECD, Paris.

Websites

- OECD Education at a Glance, *www.oecd.org/edu/eag2007*.

Trends in relative earnings for age group 25-64 with tertiary education

Upper secondary and post-secondary non-tertiary education = 100

	Males							Females						
	1999	2000	2001	2002	2003	2004	2005	1999	2000	2001	2002	2003	2004	2005
Australia	139	..	142	..	..	..	136	146	..	146	..	..	..	146
Austria	..	..	..	..	..	..	149	..	..	..	..	..	..	156
Belgium	..	128	..	132	132	137	..	..	132	..	139	132	137	..
Canada	144	151	150	143	143	140	..	145	145	149	141	144	146	..
Czech Republic	178	..	..	..	..	193	190	170	..	..	..	..	160	161
Denmark	133	..	132	131	134	133	..	123	..	124	123	127	126	..
Finland	167	..	163	163	160	161	..	145	..	146	146	146	146	..
France	159	..	..	160	151	154	152	145	..	..	148	146	145	142
Germany	138	141	..	140	150	149	151	123	137	..	137	145	148	151
Hungary	238	232	232	245	255	253	253	167	164	164	176	192	190	188
Ireland	..	138	..	141	..	157	..	..	163	..	153	..	170	..
Italy	..	143	..	162	..	183	..	..	137	..	147	..	134	..
Korea	..	..	..	..	127	..	..	..	..	..	..	176	..	..
Luxembourg	..	..	..	149	..	..	..	..	..	..	131	..	..	..
Netherlands	..	..	..	143	..	..	..	..	..	..	155	..	..	..
New Zealand	140	130	130	..	132	136	140	129	136	136	..	132	133	135
Norway	135	..	..	138	129	140	..	135	..	..	140	130	142	..
Poland	..	..	..	..	..	179	..	..	..	..	..	..	151	..
Portugal	180	..	..	..	..	182	..	170	..	..	..	..	177	..
Spain	..	..	138	..	..	132	..	..	..	125	..	..	141	..
Sweden	138	..	141	139	137	135	..	126	..	129	129	128	127	..
Switzerland	134	139	..	136	136	142	140	142	150	..	151	153	160	149
Turkey	..	..	..	..	..	139	..	..	..	..	..	..	164	..
United Kingdom	150	147	147	..	151	150	142	178	183	183	..	180	178	180
United States	167	178	..	178	177	179	183	163	164	..	165	167	166	167

StatLink http://dx.doi.org/10.1787/275237063862

Relative earnings for age group 25-64 with tertiary education

Upper secondary and post-secondary non-tertiary education = 100, 2005 or latest available year

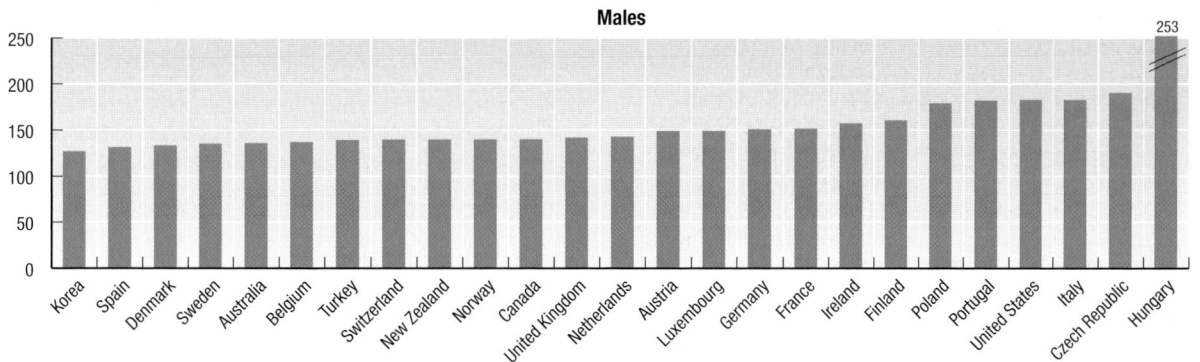

Males

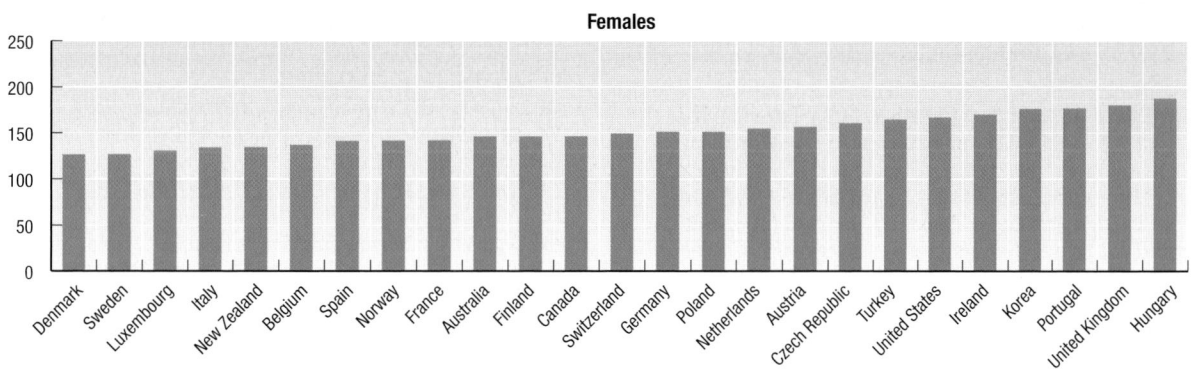

Females

StatLink http://dx.doi.org/10.1787/270484601844

PUBLIC AND PRIVATE EDUCATION EXPENDITURE

Expenditure on education is an investment that can help to foster economic growth, enhance productivity, contribute to personal and social development, and reduce social inequality. The proportion of total financial resources devoted to education is one of the key choices made in each country by governments, enterprises and individual students and their families.

Definition

This indicator covers expenditure on schools, universities and other public and private institutions involved in delivering or supporting educational services. Expenditure on institutions is not limited to expenditure on instructional services but also includes public and private expenditure on ancillary services for students and families, where these services are provided through educational institutions. At the tertiary level, spending on research and development can also be significant and is included in this indicator, to the extent that the research is performed by educational institutions.

In principle, public expenditure includes public subsidies to households attributable for educational institutions and direct expenditure on educational institutions from international sources, and consequently private expenditure is net of public subsidies attributable for educational institutions. However, public subsidies for educational expenditure outside educational institutions (e.g. textbooks purchased by families, private tutoring sought for students, student living costs) are excluded. At the tertiary level, student living costs and forgone earnings can also account for a significant proportion of the costs of education.

Comparability

The broad definition of institutions outlined above ensures that expenditure on services, which are provided in some OECD countries by schools and universities and in others by agencies other than schools, are covered on a comparable basis. Additionally, to ensure comparability over time the data on expenditure for 1995 were obtained by a special survey updated in 2004; expenditure for 1995 was adjusted to the methods and definitions used in the 2004 data collection.

Long-term trends

In 2004, taking into account both public and private sources of funds, OECD countries as a whole spent 6.2% of their collective GDP on their educational institutions. The highest spending on educational institutions can be observed in Denmark, Iceland, Korea and the United States, with more than 7% of GDP. Eight out of 28 OECD countries for which data are available, however, spend less than 5% of GDP on educational institutions.

In all the countries, public and private expenditure on education increased by 7% or more between 1995 and 2004 in real terms. However, the increase in spending on education between 1995 and 2004 tended to fall behind the growth in national income in a third of the OECD countries for which data are available. Most notable differences are observed in Austria, Ireland and Spain where the proportion of GDP spent on education decreased by 0.5 or more in percentage points between 1995 and 2004.

It should be noted that growth in GDP masks the fact that there was a significant increase in real terms in spending on educational institutions in all of the OECD countries from 1995 to 2004. In addition, the size of the school age population shapes the demand for education and training, and national levels of teachers' salaries also affect the share of expenditure on education.

Source

- OECD (2007), *Education at a Glance*, OECD, Paris.

Further information

Analytical publications

- OECD (2006), *Schooling for Tomorrow – Think Scenarios, Rethink Education*, OECD, Paris.
- OECD (2006), *Starting Strong II: Early Childhood Education and Care*, OECD, Paris.

Methodological publications

- OECD (2004), *OECD Handbook for Internationally Comparative Education Statistics: Concepts, Standards, Definitions and Classifications*, OECD, Paris.
- UIS, OECD and Eurostat (2007), *UOE Data Collection – 2007 Data Collection on Education Systems: Definitions, Explanations and Instructions*, OECD, Paris.

Websites

- OECD Education at a Glance, *www.oecd.org/edu/eag2007*.

Expenditure on educational institutions for all levels of education

As a percentage of GDP

	1995			2004		
	Public	Private	Total	Public	Private	Total
Australia	4.5	1.0	5.5	4.3	1.6	5.9
Austria	5.8	0.3	6.1	5.0	0.4	5.4
Belgium	..	..	..	5.8	0.2	6.1
Canada	6.2	0.8	7.0	..	..	..
Czech Republic	4.8	0.3	5.1	4.2	0.6	4.9
Denmark	6.0	0.2	6.2	6.9	0.3	7.2
Finland	6.3	..	6.3	6.0	0.1	6.1
France	..	..	..	5.7	0.4	6.1
Germany	4.4	1.0	5.4	4.3	0.9	5.2
Greece	2.3	..	2.3	3.3	0.2	3.4
Hungary	4.8	0.6	5.3	5.1	0.5	5.6
Iceland	..	..	..	7.2	0.7	8.0
Ireland	4.7	0.5	5.2	4.3	0.3	4.6
Italy	4.7	..	..	4.4	0.5	4.9
Japan	3.6	1.2	4.7	3.5	1.2	4.8
Korea	..	..	..	4.4	2.8	7.2
Mexico	4.6	1.0	5.6	5.2	1.2	6.4
Netherlands	4.6	0.2	4.8	4.6	0.5	5.1
New Zealand	4.8	..	..	5.6	1.3	6.9
Norway	6.0	0.4	6.3	6.2	..	..
Poland	5.2	..	..	5.4	0.6	6.0
Portugal	5.0	..	5.0	5.3	0.1	5.4
Slovak Republic	4.5	0.1	4.6	4.0	0.8	4.8
Spain	4.5	0.8	5.3	4.2	0.6	4.7
Sweden	6.1	0.1	6.2	6.5	0.2	6.7
Switzerland	5.6	0.4	6.0	5.9	..	..
Turkey	2.4	..	2.4	3.8	0.3	4.1
United Kingdom	4.8	0.7	5.5	5.0	1.0	5.9
United States	4.7	1.9	6.6	5.1	2.3	7.4
OECD average	..	..	..	5.0	0.7	5.7
OECD total	..	..	..	4.7	1.4	6.2
Brazil	3.6	..	..	3.9	..	..
Russian Federation	..	..	..	3.6	..	..

StatLink http://dx.doi.org/10.1787/275251867381

Total expenditure on educational institutions for all levels of education

As a percentage of GDP

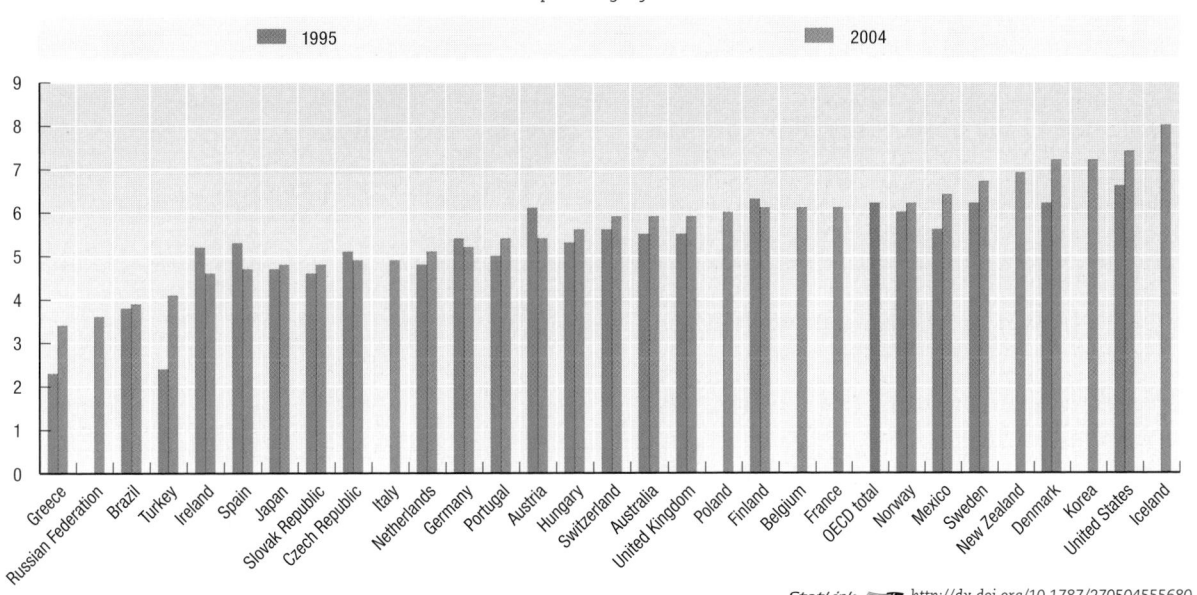

StatLink http://dx.doi.org/10.1787/270504555680

PUBLIC FINANCE

GOVERNMENT DEFICITS AND DEBT
GOVERNMENT DEFICITS
GOVERNMENT DEBT

PUBLIC EXPENDITURE
HEALTH EXPENDITURE
SOCIAL EXPENDITURE
LAW, ORDER AND DEFENCE EXPENDITURE

SUPPORT AND AID
AGRICULTURAL SUPPORT ESTIMATES
GOVERNMENT SUPPORT FOR FISHING
OFFICIAL DEVELOPMENT ASSISTANCE

TAXES
TOTAL TAX REVENUE
TAXES ON THE AVERAGE WORKER

GOVERNMENT DEFICITS

Government deficits or surpluses are commonly assessed using the net borrowing (or net lending) figures of the general government sector in the national accounts. During the period between 1991 and 2005, governments in most OECD countries have recorded deficits but in 2006 half of the OECD countries recorded general government surpluses. Government deficits have to be met by borrowing from residents or foreigners.

Definition

The net borrowing/net lending of the general government is the balancing item of the non-financial accounts (according to the *1993 System of National Accounts*). It is also equal to the difference between total revenue and total expenditure, including capital expenditure (in particular, gross fixed capital formation). The main revenue of general government consists of tax, social contributions, dividends and other property income. The main expenditure items consist of the compensation of civil servants, social benefits, interest on the public debt, subsidies and gross fixed capital formation. A negative figure indicates a deficit.

The data in the table are on a national accounts basis and may differ from the numbers reported to the European Commission under the excessive deficit procedure (EDP) for some EU countries and for some years.

Comparability

Data in this table are based on the 1993 System of National Accounts or on the 1995 European System of Accounts so that all countries are using a common set of definitions. In several OECD countries the accounts for 2000, 2001 or 2002 were affected by the sale of mobile telephone licenses, recorded in national accounts as a negative expenditure (the sale of an asset) thereby reducing the deficit. To ensure comparability very large one-offs were excluded from the data in a few cases (Germany and Netherlands in 1995, Japan in 1998).

Long-term trends

Government deficits are sensitive to the economic cycle as well as to government taxation and spending policies. For the OECD as a whole, deficits as a percentage of GDP reached a peak in 1993 but then fell steadily over the next six years and had turned into surpluses (net lending) at the peak of the economic cycle in 2000. Since then, deficits have been growing and the deficit to GDP ratio had become high in 2003 for most of the larger member countries including France, Germany, the United Kingdom, the United States and, especially, Japan. In 2004-2006 the deficit to GDP ratios were reduced in most countries with the exception of Hungary, Italy, Portugal and the Slovak Republic.

In the run-up to monetary union, EU countries that expected to adopt the Euro followed fiscal policies aimed at reducing government deficits. Deficit reduction policies were successfully implemented in several other countries, including New Zealand since 1994 and Australia, Denmark, Finland and Sweden since 1998. Korea is the only country which has recorded surpluses throughout the period, although Norway has had surpluses in most years since 1990.

Source
- OECD (2007), *OECD Economic Outlook: December No. 82 – Volume 2007 Issue 2*, OECD, Paris.

Further information
Analytical publications
- OECD (2007), *OECD Economic Surveys*, OECD, Paris.

Statistical publications
- OECD (2007), *National Accounts of OECD Countries*, OECD, Paris.

Online databases
- *National Accounts.*
- *OECD Economic Outlook Statistics.*

Websites
- OECD Economic Outlook – Sources and Methods, *www.oecd.org/eco/sources-and-methods*.

Government net borrowing/net lending
As a percentage of GDP

	1993	1994	1995	1996	1997	1998	1999	2000	2001	2002	2003	2004	2005	2006
Australia	-4.4	-4.5	-3.7	-2.4	-0.7	1.6	2.3	0.5	0.1	0.6	1.7	0.9	1.2	1.2
Austria	-4.4	-4.8	-5.7	-4.0	-1.8	-2.4	-2.3	-1.6	-0.1	-0.7	-1.8	-1.3	-1.7	-1.5
Belgium	-7.3	-5.0	-4.4	-3.8	-2.1	-0.8	-0.5	0.1	0.5	0.0	0.0	-0.1	-0.1	0.2
Canada	-8.7	-6.7	-5.3	-2.8	0.2	0.1	1.6	2.9	0.7	-0.1	-0.1	0.8	1.6	1.0
Czech Republic	..	..	-13.4	-3.3	-3.8	-5.0	-3.7	-3.7	-5.7	-6.8	-6.6	-2.9	-3.5	-2.9
Denmark	-3.8	-3.3	-2.9	-1.9	-0.5	0.0	1.4	2.3	1.2	0.2	-0.1	1.9	4.6	4.7
Finland	-8.3	-6.7	-6.2	-3.5	-1.2	1.7	1.6	6.9	5.0	4.1	2.3	2.1	2.5	3.7
France	-6.4	-5.4	-5.5	-4.0	-3.3	-2.6	-1.8	-1.5	-1.6	-3.2	-4.1	-3.6	-3.0	-2.6
Germany	-3.0	-2.3	-3.2	-3.3	-2.6	-2.2	-1.5	1.3	-2.8	-3.6	-4.0	-3.8	-3.4	-1.6
Greece	-11.9	-8.3	-9.1	-6.6	-5.9	-3.8	-3.1	-3.7	-4.4	-4.8	-5.7	-7.2	-5.2	-2.8
Hungary	-6.8	-11.4	-7.7	-6.0	-7.4	-8.5	-5.3	-3.0	-4.1	-8.9	-7.2	-6.4	-7.8	-9.3
Iceland	-4.5	-4.7	-3.0	-1.6	0.0	-0.4	1.1	1.7	-0.7	-2.6	-2.8	0.0	4.9	6.3
Ireland	-2.7	-2.0	-2.1	-0.1	1.4	2.3	2.6	4.7	1.0	-0.4	0.4	1.4	1.2	2.9
Italy	-10.1	-9.1	-7.4	-7.0	-2.7	-3.1	-1.8	-0.9	-3.1	-3.0	-3.5	-3.5	-4.3	-4.5
Japan	-2.4	-4.2	-5.1	-5.1	-4.0	-5.8	-7.4	-7.6	-6.3	-8.0	-7.9	-6.2	-6.4	-2.9
Korea	2.2	2.9	3.8	3.4	3.3	1.6	2.7	5.4	4.6	5.4	0.4	2.5	3.0	3.0
Luxembourg	1.5	2.5	2.4	1.2	3.7	3.4	3.4	6.0	6.1	2.1	0.5	-1.2	-0.1	0.7
Netherlands	-2.8	-3.5	-4.3	-1.9	-1.2	-0.9	0.4	2.0	-0.3	-2.0	-3.1	-1.8	-0.3	0.5
New Zealand	-0.4	3.1	2.9	2.9	1.7	0.1	-0.2	1.6	2.1	3.2	3.8	4.3	4.5	3.8
Norway	-1.4	0.3	3.2	6.3	7.6	3.3	6.0	15.4	13.3	9.2	7.3	11.1	15.2	18.0
Poland	..	..	-4.4	-4.9	-4.6	-4.3	-2.3	-3.0	-5.1	-5.0	-6.3	-5.7	-4.3	-3.8
Portugal	-7.7	-7.4	-5.2	-4.5	-3.4	-3.0	-2.7	-3.0	-4.3	-2.9	-3.0	-3.4	-6.1	-3.9
Slovak Republic	..	-8.7	-3.4	-9.8	-6.2	-5.3	-7.1	-12.2	-6.5	-8.2	-2.8	-2.4	-2.8	-3.7
Spain	-7.3	-6.8	-6.5	-4.9	-3.4	-3.2	-1.4	-1.0	-0.7	-0.5	-0.2	-0.4	1.0	1.8
Sweden	-11.3	-9.2	-7.4	-3.4	-1.7	1.2	1.2	3.8	1.7	-1.5	-1.1	0.6	2.1	2.3
Switzerland	-2.7	-1.9	-1.2	-1.4	-2.4	-1.5	0.0	2.3	0.9	0.1	-1.2	-1.1	0.4	1.1
United Kingdom	-7.9	-6.7	-5.8	-4.1	-2.1	0.1	1.1	4.0	0.9	-1.7	-3.3	-3.3	-3.5	-2.8
United States	-4.9	-3.6	-3.1	-2.2	-0.8	0.4	0.9	1.6	-0.4	-3.8	-4.8	-4.4	-3.6	-2.6
Euro area	-5.7	-4.9	-5.0	-4.2	-2.7	-2.3	-1.4	0.0	-1.8	-2.6	-3.1	-2.9	-2.5	-1.6
OECD total	-4.9	-4.2	-4.0	-3.1	-1.8	-1.3	-0.8	0.2	-1.3	-3.2	-4.0	-3.4	-2.9	-1.8

StatLink 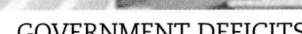 http://dx.doi.org/10.1787/275262656545

Government net borrowing/net lending
As a percentage of GDP, average 2004-2006

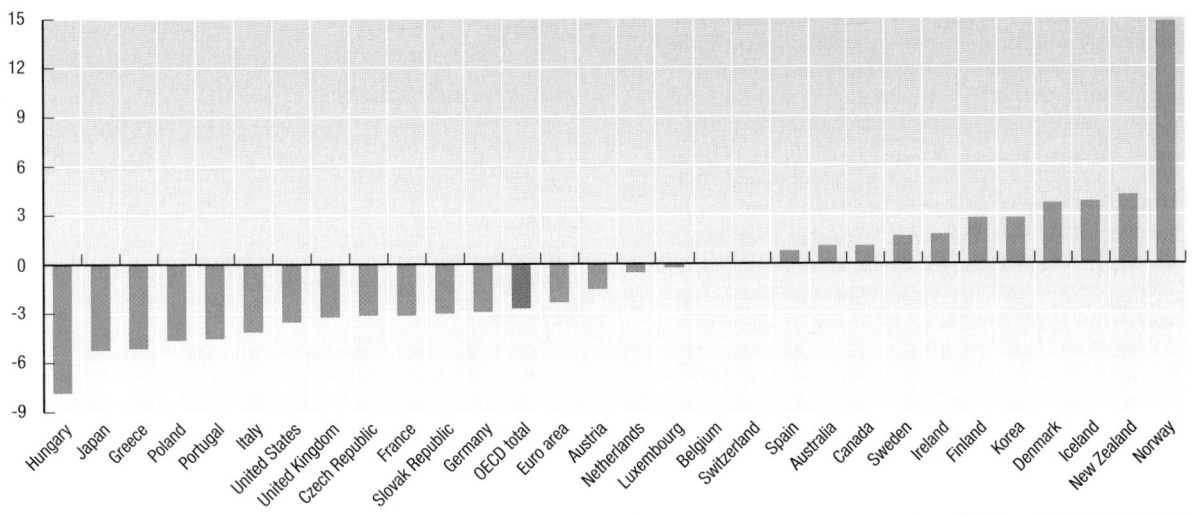

StatLink http://dx.doi.org/10.1787/270532823007

GOVERNMENT DEBT

There are two standard ways to measure the extent of government debt – by reference to gross financial liabilities or by reference to net financial liabilities – the latter being measured as gross financial liabilities minus financial assets. Gross financial liabilities as a percentage of GDP is the most commonly used government debt ratio and is shown here.

Definition

For most countries, gross financial liabilities refer to the liabilities (short and long-term) of all the institutions in the general government sector, as defined in the *1993 System of National Accounts* (SNA) or in the 1995 European System of Accounts (ESA). This definition differs from the definition of debt applied under the Maastricht Treaty essentially in two respects. First, gross debt according to the Maastricht definition excludes trade credits and advances, as well as shares and insurance technical reserves. Second, government bonds are valued at nominal values instead of at market value or issue price plus accrued interest as required by the SNA rules. The United States and Canada also value government bonds at nominal value.

In principle, debts within and between different levels of government are consolidated; a loan from one level of government to another represents both an asset and an equal liability for the government as a whole and so it cancels out (is "consolidated") for the general government sector.

Comparability

The comparability of data can be affected in two ways. First, national differences in implementing SNA/ESA definitions can affect the comparability of government debt across countries. Second, changes in implementing SNA/ESA definitions can affect the comparability of data within a country over time.

Long-term trends

From 1990 to 1996, government gross financial liabilities were rising in most countries. Since then, government debt has been decreasing as a percentage of GDP in many of the 28 countries in the table. There are, however, exceptions: government debt ratios continued to increase particularly fast in Japan and Korea and significantly in France, Germany, Greece and Portugal. Korea's government debt ratio rose by over 8% per year from 1990 to 2006 but this is measured from a very low initial rate and by 2006, Korea's government debt ratio was still among the lowest in the OECD.

In 2006, government debt ratios exceeded 100% in Greece, Italy and Japan and was close to 90% in Belgium. Most countries were in a band between 40% and 70%, with two countries reporting debt ratios of under 20% - Australia and Luxembourg.

Source

- OECD (2007), *OECD Economic Outlook: December No. 82 – Volume 2007 Issue 2*, OECD, Paris.

Further information

Analytical publications

- OECD (2002), *Debt Management and Government Securities Markets in the 21st Century*, OECD, Paris.
- OECD (2006), *Credit Risk and Credit Access in Asia*, OECD, Paris.
- OECD (2007), *OECD Economic Surveys*, OECD, Paris.

Statistical publications

- OECD (2007), *Central Government Debt*, OECD, Paris.
- OECD (2007), *National Accounts of OECD Countries*, OECD, Paris.

Online databases

- *National Accounts.*
- *OECD Economic Outlook Statistics.*

Websites

- OECD Economic Outlook – Sources and Methods, *www.oecd.org/eco/sources-and-methods.*

General government gross financial liabilities

As a percentage of GDP

	1993	1994	1995	1996	1997	1998	1999	2000	2001	2002	2003	2004	2005	2006
Australia	30.6	40.1	41.9	39.1	37.4	32.3	28.0	25.0	22.2	20.1	18.8	17.1	16.8	16.1
Austria	61.5	64.7	69.2	69.6	66.0	67.4	69.9	69.4	70.2	71.7	69.7	69.2	69.5	65.5
Belgium	140.7	137.8	135.3	133.2	128.1	122.9	119.6	113.4	111.8	108.3	103.5	98.5	94.2	90.1
Canada	96.3	98.0	101.6	101.7	96.3	95.2	91.4	82.1	82.7	80.6	76.6	72.4	70.3	68.1
Czech Republic	..	..	..	..	..	..	..	..	..	33.1	34.9	34.7	34.8	34.7
Denmark	85.0	78.9	79.3	76.6	72.1	69.7	64.1	57.1	55.0	55.4	53.6	50.3	42.2	36.0
Finland	57.8	60.8	65.3	66.2	64.5	60.9	54.7	52.3	49.7	49.4	51.2	51.5	48.4	44.9
France	51.0	60.2	62.6	66.3	68.4	70.0	66.5	65.2	63.8	66.8	71.0	73.6	75.4	70.9
Germany	46.3	46.6	55.7	58.9	60.4	62.2	61.5	60.4	59.7	62.1	65.3	68.7	71.1	69.3
Greece	..	..	101.2	103.1	100.0	97.6	101.1	114.9	117.9	116.3	112.5	114.4	112.3	106.0
Hungary	92.0	91.8	88.5	76.1	66.8	65.0	66.2	60.1	59.7	60.9	61.3	65.2	68.6	72.1
Iceland	53.1	55.7	58.9	56.3	53.1	47.9	43.4	41.0	45.9	42.1	40.8	34.4	25.5	30.3
Ireland	..	..	..	..	..	62.2	51.3	40.2	37.4	35.2	34.1	32.8	32.8	29.1
Italy	116.0	120.6	122.2	128.6	130.2	132.6	126.4	121.6	120.8	119.5	117.0	117.5	120.5	118.7
Japan	74.7	80.2	87.6	95.0	101.6	114.3	128.3	136.7	145.1	153.6	159.5	167.1	177.3	179.7
Korea	5.6	5.2	5.5	5.9	7.5	13.1	15.6	16.3	17.4	16.6	18.4	22.6	24.7	27.7
Luxembourg	..	..	9.5	10.1	10.2	11.2	10.0	9.2	8.2	8.5	7.9	8.6	7.7	10.8
Netherlands	96.7	86.7	89.6	88.1	82.2	80.8	71.6	63.9	59.4	60.3	61.4	61.9	61.0	54.7
New Zealand	..	57.4	51.3	44.9	42.3	42.2	39.6	37.4	35.4	33.5	31.4	28.7	27.6	27.2
Norway	40.8	37.3	40.9	36.5	32.0	30.8	30.8	34.1	32.9	40.5	49.2	52.8	49.2	59.6
Poland	..	..	51.6	51.4	48.3	43.8	46.6	42.4	37.4	50.3	50.8	49.7	50.2	53.6
Portugal	..	..	68.8	68.4	67.4	65.2	61.9	60.9	61.8	65.3	65.8	67.9	71.9	71.6
Slovak Republic	..	..	38.0	37.2	38.6	41.0	53.1	57.4	57.1	50.1	48.6	47.6	39.1	35.2
Spain	65.5	64.1	68.8	75.6	74.6	74.4	68.5	66.5	61.9	60.3	55.1	53.2	50.6	46.7
Sweden	79.0	83.3	82.0	85.5	84.2	83.5	74.7	65.7	64.4	61.7	61.1	60.9	61.3	53.9
Switzerland	42.9	45.5	47.7	50.1	52.1	54.9	51.9	52.5	51.3	57.2	57.0	57.9	56.4	56.0
United Kingdom	49.0	47.3	52.2	52.0	52.9	53.3	48.3	45.6	40.8	41.3	41.7	43.8	46.5	46.6
United States	71.9	71.1	70.7	70.0	67.6	64.5	61.0	55.2	55.2	57.6	60.9	62.0	62.4	61.9
Euro area	65.9	69.0	72.3	77.4	79.5	80.1	78.3	75.1	73.7	74.0	75.0	75.8	76.9	74.8
OECD total	66.9	68.3	70.2	72.2	72.4	73.0	72.4	69.6	69.9	71.9	74.1	75.8	77.6	77.1

StatLink 〰🔗 http://dx.doi.org/10.1787/275264344677

General government gross financial liabilities

As a percentage of GDP

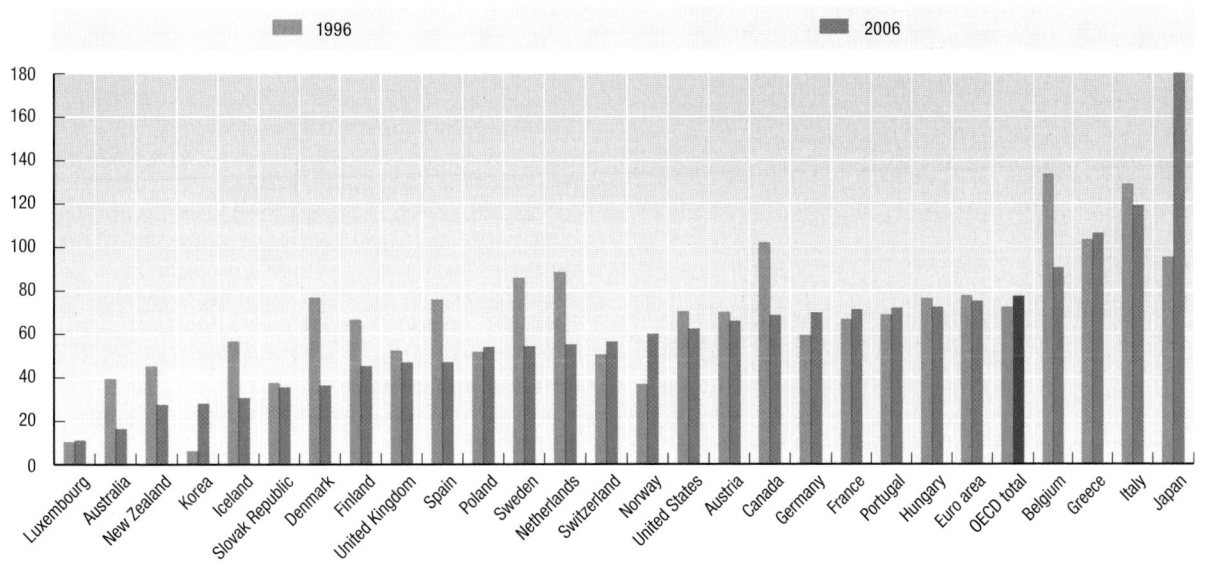

■ 1996   ■ 2006

StatLink 〰🔗 http://dx.doi.org/10.1787/270576206642

HEALTH EXPENDITURE

In most OECD countries, spending on health is a large and growing share of both public and private expenditure. The level of spending as a share of GDP varies widely across countries, reflecting a wide array of market and social factors as well as the diverse financing and organisational structures of the health system in each country.

Long-term trends

In 2005, the average share of GDP that OECD countries devoted to health spending reached 9%. However, this share varied considerably across OECD countries, ranging from around 6% in Korea, Poland and Mexico to 15.3% of GDP for the United States. The number of countries spending more than 10% of their GDP on health goods and services stood at eight in 2005, compared with four in 2000 and two countries in 1995. Concerning public expenditure as a share of GDP, there was an almost three-fold difference between the highest and lowest countries. Public spending on health in France accounted for 8.9% of GDP in 2005, while in Korea, where health care is evenly split between public and private financing, public financing of health was 3.2% of GDP.

Changes over time in the ratio of health expenditure to GDP reflect the combined effect of trends in both GDP and health expenditure. Nearly all OECD countries have experienced an increase in the proportion of the national economy devoted to health over the past ten years. In the United States, Canada and Switzerland, health expenditure growth outpaced by a wide margin economic growth between 2000 and 2003 whith the ratio of health expenditure to GDP stabilising thereafter. On the other hand, the increase in the share of GDP devoted to health has been more modest over the past ten years in Germany and Japan, where low economic growth has been matched by low growth in health spending.

There is a positive association between GDP per capita and health expenditure per capita across OECD countries. The association is stronger among OECD countries with low GDP per capita than among countries with a higher GDP per capita. For countries with similar levels of GDP per capita there are substantial differences in health expenditure. For example, the health spending per capita of Japan and Germany differs considerably with Japan spending less than 75% of the level of Germany.

Recent OECD projections suggest that, depending on the type of scenario, health and long-term care expenditures could increase by between 3.5 to more than 6 percentage points of GDP on average across OECD countries between 2005 and 2050, of which 2 to 4 percentage points for health care. For health care, the impact of population ageing on expenditures is expected to increase over time, but its effect is moderate compared with the impact of non-demographic factors (e.g. higher incomes and diffusion of new treatments and medical products).

Definition

Total expenditure on health measures the final consumption of health goods and services (i.e. current health expenditure) plus capital investment in health care infrastructure. This includes spending by both public and private sources (including households) on medical services and goods, public health and prevention programmes and administration. Excluded are health-related expenditure such as training, research and environmental health.

Comparability

OECD countries are at varying stages of reporting total expenditure on health according to the boundary of health care proposed in the OECD manual A System of Health Accounts (SHA). This means that data reported are at varying levels of comparability. The comparability of health expenditure data has improved over recent years. However, limitations do remain (even among those countries where total expenditure is fairly comparable), due to the fact that data reporting is connected to current administrative records of financing systems. For example, different practices regarding the inclusion of long-term care in health or social expenditure are a major factor affecting data comparability.

The size of a country's GDP and hence its ratio of total health expenditure to GDP can be affected by the retained earnings of foreign companies operating in the country. This is particularly the case for countries such as Ireland.

Source
- OECD (2007), OECD Health Data 2007, OECD, Paris.

Further information

Analytical publications
- OECD (2004), The OECD Health Project: Private Health Insurance in OECD Countries, OECD, Paris.
- OECD (2004), The OECD Health Project: Towards High-Performing Health Systems, OECD, Paris.
- OECD (2005), The OECD Health Project: Health Technologies and Decision Making, OECD, Paris.
- OECD (2006), Sickness, Disability and Work: Breaking the Barriers (Vol. 1): Norway, Poland and Switzerland, OECD, Paris.
- OECD (2007), "The Drivers of Public Expenditure on Health and Long-Term Care: an Integrated Approach", OECD Economic Studies, No. 43, Volume 2006, Issue 2, OECD, Paris.

Statistical publications
- OECD (2007), Health at a Glance 2007: OECD Indicators, OECD, Paris.

Methodological publications
- OECD (2000), A System of Health Accounts, OECD, Paris.

Online databases
- OECD Health Data.

Total and public expenditure on health

As a percentage of GDP

	Public expenditure							Total expenditure						
	1980	1990	2000	2002	2003	2004	2005	1980	1990	2000	2002	2003	2004	2005
Australia	4.3	5.1	6.0	6.2	6.2	6.4	..	6.8	7.5	8.8	9.1	9.2	9.5	..
Austria	5.1	5.1	7.6	7.6	7.7	7.8	7.7	7.5	7.0	10.0	10.1	10.2	10.3	10.2
Belgium	..	..	6.6	6.7	7.2	7.5	7.4	6.3	7.2	8.6	9.0	10.1	10.2	10.3
Canada	5.3	6.6	6.2	6.7	6.8	6.8	6.9	7.0	8.9	8.8	9.6	9.8	9.8	9.8
Czech Republic	..	4.6	5.9	6.4	6.7	6.5	6.4	..	4.7	6.5	7.1	7.4	7.3	7.2
Denmark	7.9	6.9	6.8	7.3	7.7	7.8	7.7	8.9	8.3	8.3	8.8	9.1	9.2	9.1
Finland	5.0	6.2	4.9	5.4	5.6	5.7	5.9	6.3	7.7	6.6	7.0	7.3	7.4	7.5
France	5.6	6.4	7.5	7.9	8.6	8.7	8.9	7.0	8.4	9.6	10.0	10.9	11.0	11.1
Germany	6.6	7.8	8.2	8.4	8.5	8.1	8.2	8.4	9.6	10.3	10.6	10.8	10.6	10.7
Greece	2.8	3.1	4.1	4.6	4.7	4.3	4.3	5.1	5.8	9.3	9.7	10.0	9.6	10.1
Hungary	..	6.3	4.9	5.3	5.9	5.7	..	..	7.0	6.9	7.6	8.3	8.1	..
Iceland	5.5	6.8	7.6	8.3	8.5	8.3	7.9	6.3	7.8	9.3	10.0	10.3	10.0	9.5
Ireland	6.8	4.4	4.6	5.4	5.6	5.8	5.8	8.3	6.1	6.3	7.2	7.3	7.5	7.5
Italy	..	6.1	5.8	6.2	6.2	6.6	6.8	..	7.7	8.1	8.3	8.3	8.7	8.9
Japan	4.7	4.6	6.2	6.5	6.6	6.6	..	6.5	6.0	7.7	8.0	8.1	8.0	..
Korea	1.1	1.6	2.2	2.7	2.8	2.9	3.2	4.1	4.3	4.8	5.3	5.4	5.5	6.0
Luxembourg	4.8	5.0	5.2	6.1	6.8	7.1	7.1	5.2	5.4	5.8	6.8	7.6	7.9	7.9
Mexico	..	2.0	2.6	2.7	2.8	3.0	2.9	..	4.8	5.6	6.2	6.3	6.5	6.4
Netherlands	5.2	5.4	5.0	5.5	..	..	..	7.5	8.0	8.0	8.9	9.1	9.2	..
New Zealand	5.1	5.7	6.0	6.4	6.3	6.7	7.0	5.9	6.9	7.7	8.2	8.0	8.5	9.0
Norway	5.9	6.3	6.9	8.2	8.4	8.1	7.6	7.0	7.6	8.4	9.8	10.0	9.7	9.1
Poland	..	4.4	3.9	4.5	4.4	4.3	4.3	..	4.8	5.5	6.3	6.2	6.2	6.2
Portugal	3.4	3.8	6.4	6.5	7.1	7.2	7.4	5.3	5.9	8.8	9.0	9.7	10.0	10.2
Slovak Republic	..	..	4.9	5.0	5.2	5.3	5.3	..	..	5.5	5.6	5.9	7.2	7.1
Spain	4.2	5.1	5.2	5.2	5.5	5.7	5.9	5.3	6.5	7.2	7.3	7.8	8.1	8.3
Sweden	8.3	7.5	7.1	7.8	7.9	7.7	7.7	9.0	8.3	8.4	9.1	9.3	9.1	9.1
Switzerland	..	4.3	5.8	6.5	6.7	6.8	6.9	7.4	8.3	10.4	11.1	11.5	11.5	11.6
Turkey	1.0	2.2	4.2	5.2	5.4	5.6	5.4	3.3	3.6	6.6	7.4	7.6	7.7	7.6
United Kingdom	5.0	5.0	5.9	6.4	6.7	6.9	7.2	5.6	6.0	7.3	7.7	7.8	8.1	8.3
United States	3.6	4.7	5.8	6.6	6.7	6.8	6.9	8.8	11.9	13.2	14.7	15.2	15.2	15.3
OECD average	4.9	5.1	5.7	6.1	6.4	6.4	6.4	6.6	7.0	7.9	8.5	8.8	8.9	9.0

StatLink http://dx.doi.org/10.1787/275270388145

Expenditure on health

As a percentage of GDP, 2005 or latest available year

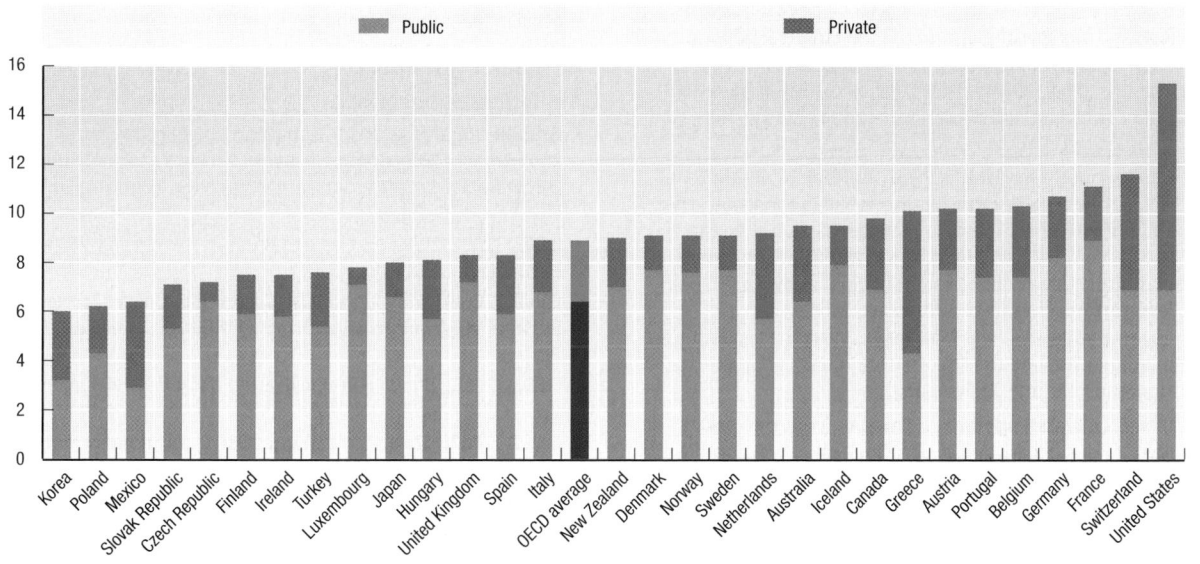

StatLink http://dx.doi.org/10.1787/270584861664

SOCIAL EXPENDITURE

Social expenditures as a percentage of GDP are a measure of the extent to which governments assume responsibility for supporting the standard of living of disadvantaged or vulnerable groups.

Definition

Public social expenditure comprises cash benefits, direct "in-kind" provision of goods and services, and tax breaks with social purposes. To be considered "social", benefits have to address one or more social goals. Benefits may be targeted at low-income households, but they may also be for the elderly, disabled, sick, unemployed, or young persons. Programmes regulating the provision of social benefits have to involve: a) redistribution of resources across households, or b) compulsory participation. Social benefits are regarded as public when general government (that is central, state, and local governments, including social security funds) controls relevant financial flows. The expenditures shown here refer only to public social benefits and exclude similar benefits provided by private charities.

Long-term trends

In 2003, on average, public social expenditure amounted to 21% of GDP, although there are significant cross-country variations. In Sweden, public social spending is about 31% while it is 5-6% in Mexico and Korea.

Changes in gross public social expenditures over time are also significant. Since 1980, gross public social expenditure has increased from about 16% to 21% of GDP in 2003 on average across 28 OECD countries. Experiences differ across OECD countries, but on average public social spending-to-GDP ratios increased most significantly in the early 1980s, early 1990s and, again in the beginning of this millennium, when the average public spending-to-GDP increased by 1% of GDP from 2000 to 2003. In between these decennial turning points spending-to-GDP ratios changed little; during the 1980s the average OECD public social spending to GDP ratio oscillated just below 20% of GDP while during the 1990s it trended downwards after the economic downturn in the early 1990s, but nevertheless remained above 20% of GDP.

It is convenient to divide expenditures according to their social purposes to better analyse policy focus and trends. Broadly speaking, the three biggest groups of social transfers are pensions (on average 8% of GDP), health (6%) and income transfers to the working-age population (5%). Public spending on other social services only exceeds 5% of GDP in the Nordic countries, where the public role in providing services to the elderly, the disabled and families is the most extensive.

Public support for families with children is nearly 2% of GDP on average, but this has increased in most countries since 1980. Family support exceeds 3% of GDP in the Nordic countries and Austria, as they have the most comprehensive public system of child allowances, paid leave arrangements and childcare. Moreover, governments also help families through the tax system; examples include the "quotient familial" in France and "income splitting" in Germany.

Social insurance spending related to work incapacity (disability, sickness and occupational injury benefits) has declined in as many countries as it has increased since 1980. Particularly large declines were found in Belgium and in the Netherlands.

Comparability

For cross-country comparisons, the most commonly used indicator of social support is gross (before tax) public social expenditure related to GDP. Measurement problems do exist, particularly with regard to spending by lower tiers of government, which may be underestimated in some countries. As noted above, similar social benefits provided by private charities are excluded.

Source
- Social Expenditure Database.

Further information
Analytical publications
- Adema, W. and M. Ladaique (2005), *Net Social Expenditure, 2005 Edition: More Comprehensive Measures of Social Support*, OECD Social Employment and Migration Working Papers, No. 29, OECD, Paris.
- OECD (2002-2004), *Babies and Bosses – Reconciling Work and Family Life*, OECD, Paris.
- OECD (2003), *Transforming Disability into Ability: Policies to Promote Work and Income Security for Disabled People*, OECD, Paris.
- OECD (2006), *Starting Strong II: Early Childhood Education and Care*, OECD, Paris.
- OECD (2007), *Society at a Glance: OECD Social Indicators – 2006 Edition*, OECD, Paris.

Websites
- OECD Social and Welfare Statistics, *www.oecd.org/statistics/social*.

Public social expenditure
As a percentage of GDP

	1990	1991	1992	1993	1994	1995	1996	1997	1998	1999	2000	2001	2002	2003
Australia	14.1	15.2	16.2	16.5	16.2	17.1	17.2	17.0	17.0	16.9	17.9	17.4	17.5	17.9
Austria	23.7	23.9	24.5	26.0	26.6	26.6	26.6	25.5	25.4	25.6	25.3	25.4	25.8	26.1
Belgium	25.0	25.8	25.9	27.0	26.5	26.4	26.9	25.8	26.1	25.9	25.3	25.7	26.1	26.5
Canada	18.4	20.6	21.3	21.2	20.2	19.2	18.4	17.7	18.0	17.0	16.7	17.3	17.3	17.3
Czech Republic	16.0	17.3	17.6	18.1	18.1	18.2	18.3	19.1	19.5	20.0	20.3	20.4	21.0	21.1
Denmark	25.5	26.3	26.8	28.6	29.4	28.9	28.2	27.2	27.0	26.8	25.8	26.4	26.9	27.6
Finland	24.5	29.6	33.6	29.9	29.2	27.4	27.1	25.2	23.2	22.8	21.3	21.4	21.9	22.5
France	25.3	26.0	26.6	28.1	28.1	28.3	28.6	28.5	28.7	28.8	27.6	27.5	27.9	28.7
Germany	22.5	23.7	25.7	26.1	26.1	26.6	27.1	26.4	26.3	26.4	26.3	26.3	27.0	27.3
Greece	18.6	18.0	18.1	19.1	19.1	19.3	20.0	20.0	20.6	21.4	21.3	22.3	21.3	21.3
Hungary	..	..	..	..	..	..	..	..	..	21.6	20.6	20.7	21.9	22.7
Iceland	14.0	14.5	15.0	15.3	15.2	15.5	15.2	14.9	14.9	15.4	15.3	15.6	17.3	18.7
Ireland	15.5	16.3	17.1	17.1	16.8	16.3	15.4	14.3	13.4	14.2	13.6	14.4	15.5	15.9
Italy	19.9	20.1	20.7	20.9	20.7	19.8	22.0	22.7	23.0	23.3	23.2	23.3	23.8	24.2
Japan	11.2	11.4	11.9	12.5	13.1	13.9	14.1	14.2	14.9	15.4	16.1	16.8	17.5	17.7
Korea	3.0	2.8	3.1	3.2	3.2	3.5	3.6	3.9	5.5	6.3	5.1	5.5	5.4	5.7
Luxembourg	21.9	22.3	22.7	23.1	22.9	23.8	23.8	22.5	21.6	21.7	20.4	19.8	21.6	22.2
Mexico	3.6	4.0	4.4	4.7	5.2	4.7	4.5	4.5	5.0	5.8	5.8	5.9	6.3	6.8
Netherlands	24.4	24.4	24.9	25.1	23.6	22.8	21.8	21.2	20.6	19.9	19.3	19.5	19.9	20.7
New Zealand	21.8	22.2	22.0	20.3	19.5	19.0	18.9	19.9	20.0	19.3	19.1	18.4	18.4	18.0
Norway	22.6	23.5	24.4	24.3	24.0	23.5	22.7	22.2	24.5	24.6	22.2	23.2	24.6	25.1
Poland	15.1	21.5	25.5	24.9	23.8	23.1	23.3	22.7	21.5	22.2	21.2	22.4	23.0	22.9
Portugal	13.7	14.7	15.5	17.0	17.2	18.1	18.7	18.6	19.0	19.5	20.2	20.9	22.2	23.5
Slovak Republic	..	..	..	..	..	18.9	18.7	18.2	18.2	18.8	18.1	17.8	17.9	17.3
Spain	20.0	20.7	21.8	23.2	22.1	21.5	21.4	20.8	20.7	20.4	20.4	20.2	20.2	20.3
Sweden	30.5	32.1	35.0	36.2	34.9	32.5	32.1	30.7	30.5	30.1	28.8	29.3	30.4	31.3
Switzerland	13.5	14.5	16.0	17.4	17.3	17.5	18.1	18.8	19.0	18.8	18.0	18.7	19.4	20.5
Turkey	7.6	8.2	8.5	8.3	7.9	7.5	9.7	10.8	11.1	13.2	..	..	..	..
United Kingdom	17.2	18.6	20.3	21.0	20.5	20.4	20.1	19.2	19.3	19.0	19.1	20.1	20.1	20.6
United States	13.4	14.4	15.1	15.3	15.3	15.4	15.2	14.9	14.8	14.6	14.6	15.2	16.0	16.2
EU15 average	21.9	22.8	24.0	24.6	24.2	23.9	24.0	23.2	23.0	23.0	22.5	22.8	23.4	23.9
OECD average	17.9	19.0	20.0	20.4	20.1	19.9	20.0	19.6	19.7	19.8	19.4	19.7	20.3	20.7

StatLink http://dx.doi.org/10.1787/275342777042

Public social expenditure
As a percentage of GDP

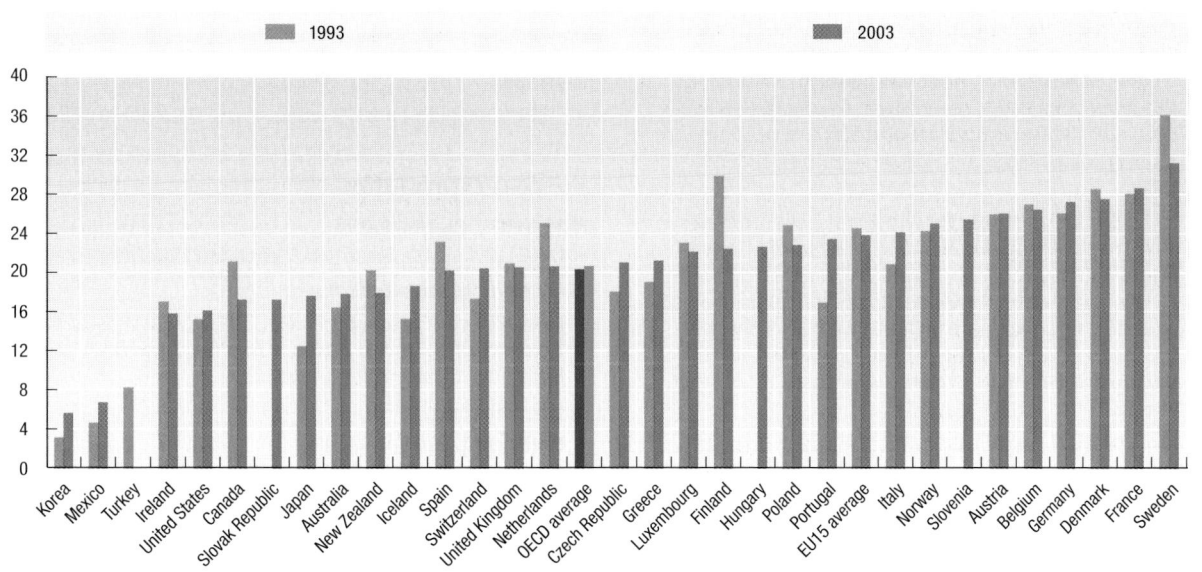

StatLink http://dx.doi.org/10.1787/270622132156

LAW, ORDER AND DEFENCE EXPENDITURE

Two essential tasks of a government are to protect the state from external aggression and maintain law and public order within its frontiers. Over the period considered here, the collapse of the Soviet Union led to a reduction in defence expenditures in many OECD countries, while the terror attacks in the United States led to increases in government expenditures on internal security. The figures shown here reflect these opposing influences.

Definition

The table is taken from national accounts sources, and the data conform to the definitions of the *1993 System of National Accounts*. The expenditures cover all expenditures whether current or capital.

Law and order covers the police forces, intelligence services, prisons and other correctional facilities, the judicial system, and ministries of internal affairs. Note that the figures shown here do not include the costs of government-mandated security arrangements at airports, seaports and other border crossings. Nor, of course, do they include the provision of security in shopping-malls, football matches, concerts and other public gatherings, all of which have certainly increased in recent years.

Comparability

Data are taken from national accounts sources and have been compiled according to the Classification of the *Functions of Government* (COFOG). In general, the data are broadly comparable.

Long-term trends

Within the total, the shares of the two components – law and order and defence – vary considerably between countries with high shares for defence expenditures in the United States, Korea, Norway, Denmark, France and Sweden and high shares for law and order in Iceland, Luxembourg, Ireland, Spain and Belgium. On average, the share of expenditures on law and order has generally been growing faster than defence and now accounts for more than half of the total for the countries shown in the table.

In 2005 – the latest year for which most countries can supply data – expenditure was highest in the United States and the United Kingdom, and lowest in Luxembourg, Iceland and Ireland. In the majority of countries the shares of expenditures on defence, law and order in GDP have been falling since 1995 with particularly large falls in Norway, Sweden, Ireland and France.

Source

- OECD (2007), *National Accounts of OECD Countries*, OECD, Paris.

Further information

Analytical publications

- OECD (2004), *The Security Economy*, OECD, Paris.

Methodological publications

- UN, OECD, IMF, Eurostat (eds.) (1993), *System of National Accounts 1993*, United Nations, Geneva, Paragraph XVIII.9, *http://unstats.un.org/unsd/sna1993*.

Online databases

- *National Accounts*.

Law, order and defence expenditure
As a percentage of GDP

	1993	1994	1995	1996	1997	1998	1999	2000	2001	2002	2003	2004	2005	2006
Austria	..	..	2.5	2.5	2.5	2.4	2.4	2.4	2.3	2.3	2.3	2.3	2.3	2.3
Belgium	3.0	3.0	2.9	2.9	2.8	2.8	2.8	2.7	2.8	2.9	2.9	2.8	2.7	..
Czech Republic	..	..	4.5	4.1	4.1	3.7	4.0	4.1	3.8	3.7	4.2	3.5	4.1	..
Denmark	2.9	2.9	2.8	2.7	2.7	2.7	2.6	2.5	2.6	2.6	2.6	2.7	2.6	2.6
Finland	3.5	3.7	3.5	3.6	3.4	3.2	3.0	2.9	2.8	2.7	2.9	3.1	3.2	..
France	..	..	3.8	3.8	3.7	3.5	3.4	3.2	3.3	3.4	3.3	3.3	3.3	..
Germany	3.2	3.1	3.0	3.0	2.9	2.9	2.9	2.8	2.8	2.9	2.8	2.8	2.7	..
Hungary	..	..	..	..	..	..	..	..	3.2	3.8	3.4	3.4	3.3	..
Iceland	..	..	..	..	1.6	1.5	1.5	1.5	1.5	1.5	1.6	1.5	1.5	1.5
Ireland	3.1	3.0	2.7	2.6	2.5	2.5	2.2	2.1	2.1	2.0	1.9	2.1	2.1	..
Italy	3.5	3.4	3.2	3.2	3.1	3.1	3.1	3.1	3.0	3.2	3.4	3.4	3.5	..
Japan	..	..	..	2.3	2.3	2.3	2.4	2.4	2.4	2.4	2.4	2.4	2.3	..
Korea	..	..	4.1	4.2	4.1	4.2	4.0	3.9	3.8	3.8	3.8	3.8	4.1	..
Luxembourg	1.3	1.3	1.3	1.3	1.4	1.3	1.1	1.1	1.2	1.3	1.3	1.3	1.3	1.2
Netherlands	..	..	3.3	3.3	3.1	3.0	3.1	3.0	3.1	3.2	3.3	3.2	3.1	..
New Zealand	..	..	..	..	..	..	..	..	..	..	2.9	2.7	3.0	..
Norway	3.9	3.9	3.5	3.4	3.3	3.4	3.3	2.9	2.9	3.2	3.1	2.9	2.6	..
Poland	..	..	..	..	..	..	..	..	..	2.8	2.9	2.6	2.8	..
Portugal	..	..	..	..	..	..	3.2	3.3	3.2	3.3	3.4	3.4	3.4	..
Slovak Republic	..	..	..	..	..	..	..	..	..	..	3.7	2.3	..	..
Spain	..	..	..	..	..	..	3.0	2.9	3.0	3.0	2.9	2.9	2.9	..
Sweden	..	..	3.8	3.9	3.7	3.7	3.8	3.6	3.5	3.5	3.4	3.2	3.0	..
United Kingdom	6.0	5.7		5.3	4.9	4.9	4.7	4.6	4.8	4.7	4.8	5.1	5.0	5.1	..
United States	6.5	6.1	5.9	5.7	5.4	5.3	5.2	5.2	5.4	5.8	6.1	6.3	6.3	6.4

StatLink 🔗 http://dx.doi.org/10.1787/275348465471

Law, order and defence expenditure
As a percentage of GDP

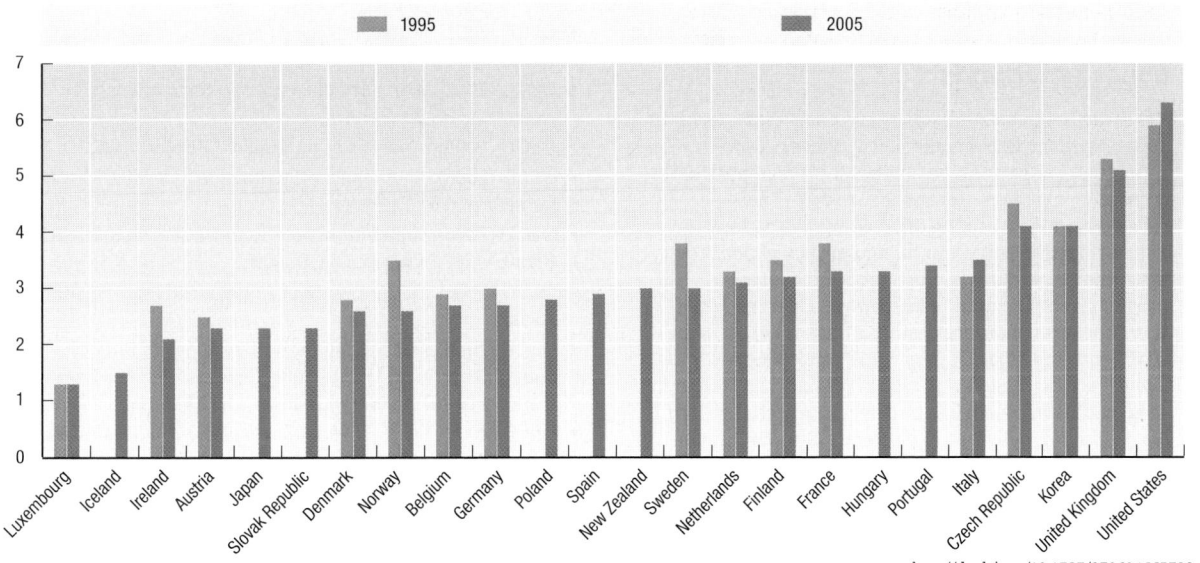

StatLink 🔗 http://dx.doi.org/10.1787/270624665722

AGRICULTURAL SUPPORT ESTIMATES

During the mid-1980s, when the Uruguay Round of agricultural trade negotiations was getting underway, the OECD undertook to measure and codify support to the farm sector arising from agricultural policies. This led to the development of the producer support estimate (PSE), an indicator that is available on a timely and comprehensive basis for all 30 of the OECD's member countries (the European Union is treated as a single entity) and selected non-members. The measure includes budgetary transfers financed by taxpayers but also includes the implicit tax on consumers that arises from agricultural policies – border protection, and administered pricing – that raise farm prices above the levels that would otherwise prevail. The measure is agreed by OECD member countries and is widely recognised as the only available internationally comparable indicator.

Definition

The OECD PSE is an indicator of the annual monetary value of gross transfers from consumers and taxpayers to agricultural producers, measured at the farmgate level, arising from policy measures that support agriculture, regardless of their nature, objectives or impacts on farm production or income. It can be expressed as a total monetary amount, but is more usually quoted as a percentage of gross farm receipts (%PSE). This is the measure used here.

Comparability

Continuous efforts are made to ensure consistency in the treatment and completeness of coverage of policies in all OECD countries through the annual preparation of the Monitoring and Evaluation report. Each year, the provisional estimates are subject to review and approval by representatives of OECD's member countries, as are all methodological developments. The %PSE is the most appropriate and widely used measure to compare support across countries, commodities and time.

Long-term trends

There are large and increasing differences in the levels of support among OECD countries. Producer support estimates as a percentage of gross farm receipts (%PSE) currently range from almost zero to 66%. These differences reflect among other things, variations in policy objectives, different historical uses of policy instruments, and the varying pace and degrees of progress in agricultural policy reform. Over the longer term, the level of producer support has fallen in most OECD countries. The average %PSE in 2004-06 at 29% is lower than the 1986-88 average of 38% and has fallen in most countries. There has also been some change in the way support is delivered to the sector. Support known to be the most distorting in terms of production and trade is less dominant than in the past – 70% of total support during the 2004-2006 period compared to over 90% in 1986-1988.

In the table, data are not shown for individual EU member countries. Austria, Finland and Sweden are included in the EU15 from 1995. The Czech Republic, Hungary, Poland and the Slovak Republic, together with the 6 EU members which are not members of the OECD, are included in the EU25 from 2004. The OCDE total includes the Czech Republic, Hungary, Poland and the Slovak Republic for the entire period but excludes the 6 EU members not members of the OECD.

Agricultural producer support estimate for selected countries

As a percentage of value of gross farm receipts

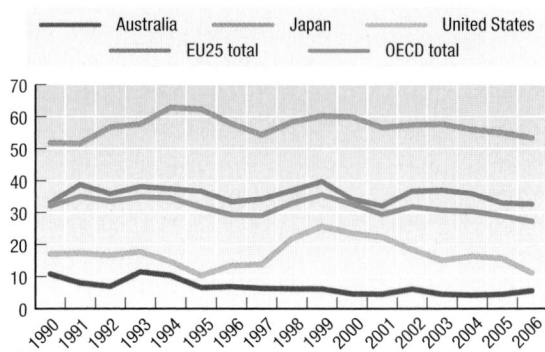

StatLink ⟶ http://dx.doi.org/10.1787/270663210320

Source

- OECD (2007), *Agricultural Policies in OECD Countries: Monitoring and Evaluation 2007*, OECD, Paris.

Further information

Analytical publications

- OECD, FAO (2007), *OECD-FAO Agricultural Outlook 2007-2016*, OECD, Paris.
- OECD (2001), *Market Effects of Crop Support Measures*, OECD, Paris.
- OECD (2002), *Agricultural Policies in China after WTO Accession*, OECD, Paris.
- OECD (2004), *Analysis of the 2003 CAP Reform*, OECD, Paris.
- OECD (2005), *Environmentally Harmful Subsidies: Challenges for Reform*, OECD, Paris.
- OECD (2006), *Agricultural Policies in OECD Countries: At a Glance – 2006 Edition*, OECD, Paris.
- OECD (2006), *OECD Review of Agricultural Policies*, OECD, Paris.
- OECD (2006), *OECD Sustainable Development Studies – Subsidy Reform and Sustainable Development: Economic, Environmental and Social Aspects*, OECD, Paris.
- OECD (2007), *OECD Sustainable Development Studies: Subsidy Reform and Sustainable Development: Political Economy Aspects*, OECD, Paris.

Methodological publications

- OECD (2002), *Methodology for the Measurement of Support and Use in Policy Evaluation*, OECD, Paris.

Agricultural producer support estimate by country

As a percentage of value of gross farm receipts

	1993	1994	1995	1996	1997	1998	1999	2000	2001	2002	2003	2004	2005	2006
Australia	11.4	10.3	6.5	6.8	6.3	6.1	6.1	4.6	4.5	6.1	4.4	4.2	4.4	5.5
Canada	24.3	20.7	19.6	15.6	14.4	16.8	18.0	19.9	15.9	21.2	24.5	20.8	21.9	22.7
Iceland	64.7	61.5	59.1	57.1	59.2	70.5	71.6	66.7	63.0	66.5	65.7	64.8	67.4	66.4
Japan	57.6	62.7	62.2	57.8	54.3	58.3	60.1	59.8	56.5	57.4	57.6	55.9	54.9	53.3
Korea	72.7	73.0	72.0	64.1	63.0	56.5	65.4	66.5	60.7	64.4	61.0	62.7	63.1	63.3
Mexico	30.5	22.6	-4.9	4.9	14.4	17.2	14.4	20.4	15.3	23.1	18.5	10.8	14.3	17.4
New Zealand	0.7	1.3	1.5	1.0	1.1	1.0	0.9	0.5	0.7	0.4	0.9	0.9	1.4	0.8
Norway	69.1	69.8	65.3	66.2	69.2	71.1	72.0	67.1	66.5	74.7	71.7	67.4	66.4	64.8
Switzerland	71.5	73.1	64.9	68.6	69.8	71.6	75.9	70.4	68.3	71.1	68.8	67.8	66.9	62.6
Turkey	23.4	14.3	13.0	15.7	25.0	26.4	22.4	20.8	3.4	21.1	28.8	25.7	26.6	20.1
United States	17.7	14.7	10.3	13.4	13.8	21.8	25.6	23.5	22.3	18.5	15.0	16.3	15.7	11.1
EU25 total	38.0	37.3	36.5	33.2	34.1	36.8	39.7	34.0	31.9	36.6	36.9	35.8	32.8	32.5
OECD total	34.8	34.4	31.6	29.2	29.0	32.8	35.5	32.5	29.4	31.7	30.6	30.3	28.8	27.1
Brazil	..	..	-7.7	-3.4	-4.4	4.0	-0.8	4.4	3.4	3.8	4.7	3.6	5.9	..
China	-13.1	0.9	6.3	1.9	1.9	1.4	-2.1	4.0	6.5	7.2	9.9	6.8	8.4	..
Russian Federation	-28.7	-4.1	13.7	18.5	27.0	19.0	0.8	4.6	14.3	18.0	15.9	19.3	15.5	..
South Africa	..	12.3	16.8	8.7	11.9	8.6	8.4	5.6	1.8	8.0	7.0	8.0	9.0	..

StatLink http://dx.doi.org/10.1787/275353782282

Agricultural producer support estimate by country

As a percentage of value of gross farm receipts

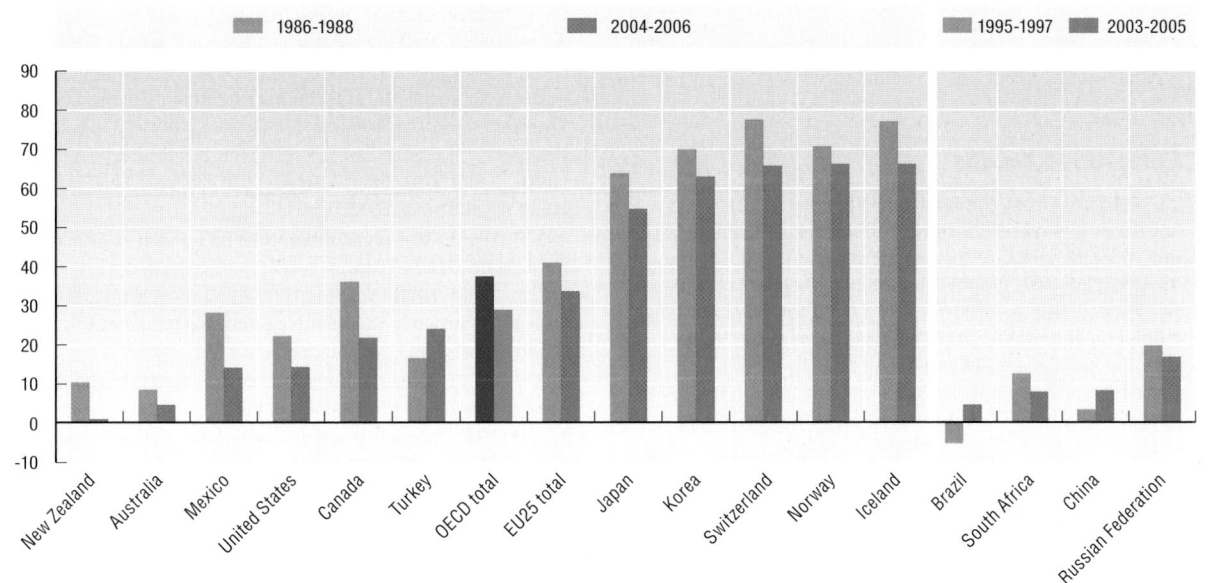

StatLink http://dx.doi.org/10.1787/270635075246

GOVERNMENT SUPPORT FOR FISHING

Catches from sea fishing have been declining due to falling stocks as a result of over-fishing, and because of national and international measures to preserve remaining fish resources. This has been particularly marked in the Northern Hemisphere and has led governments in many OECD countries to provide financial support to the fishing industry.

Definition

The time series, "Government financial transfers (GFT)", provides an indicator of the financial support received by the fisheries sector. GFT consists of direct revenue enhancing transfers (direct payments), transfers that reduce operating costs, and costs of general services provided to the fishing industry. General services consist mainly of fishery protection services but also include the costs of local area weather forecasting and the costs of navigation and satellite surveillance systems designed to assist fishing fleets.

Comparability

The data are relatively comprehensive and consistent across the years although some year-to-year variations must be interpreted with caution as they may reflect changes in national statistical systems. Note too that the general services provided by governments may contain large and irregular capital investments. For example, the GFTs for Greece in 2001 and, in particular, for 2002, include the implementation cost of a satellite control system.

GFT to fishing for selected countries
Million US dollars

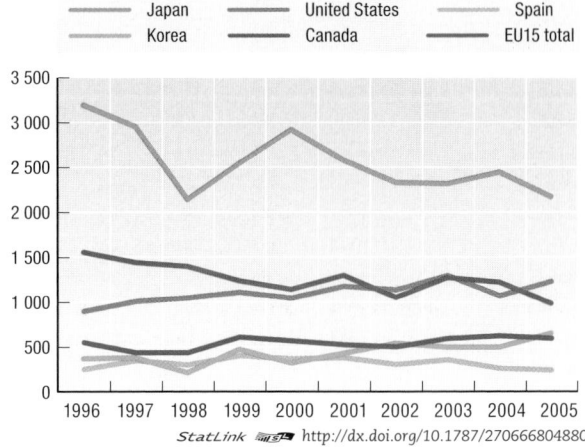

StatLink ⬛🔗 http://dx.doi.org/10.1787/270666804880

Source

• OECD (2007), *Review of Fisheries in OECD Countries: Vol. 2 – Country Statistics, 2002-2004, 2006 Edition*, OECD, Paris.

Further information

Analytical publications

• Cox, A. (2003), *OECD Work on Defining and Measuring Subsidies in Fisheries*, OECD, Paris.
• Cox, A. (2004), *Subsidies and Deep-Sea Fisheries Management: Policy Issues and Challenges*, OECD, Paris.
• Cox, A. and C. Schmidt (2003), *Subsidies in the OECD Fisheries Sector: A Review of Recent Analysis and Future Directions*, background paper for the FAO Expert Consultation on Identifying, Assessing and Reporting on Subsidies in the Fishing Industry, Rome, 3-6 December 2002.
• Flatten, O. and P. Wallis (2000), *Government Financial Transfers to Fishing Industries in OECD Countries*, OECD, Paris.
• OECD (2000), *Transition to Responsible Fisheries: Economic and Policy Implications*, OECD, Paris.
• OECD (2005), *Environmentally Harmful Subsidies: Challenges for Reform*, OECD, Paris.
• OECD (2006), *OECD Sustainable Development Studies – Subsidy Reform and Sustainable Development: Economic, Environmental and Social Aspects*, OECD, Paris.
• OECD (2006), *Financial Support to Fisheries: Implications for Sustainable Development*, OECD, Paris.
• OECD (2007), *Structural Change in Fisheries: Dealing with the Human Dimension*, OECD, Paris.
• OECD (2007), *The Human Side of Fisheries Adjustment*, OECD, Paris.

Websites

• OECD Fisheries, *www.oecd.org/agr/fish*.

Long-term trends

Overall transfers to the fishing industry in OECD countries have been fluctuating at around USD 6 billion over the last decade. This represents around 18% of the value of the total catch from capture fisheries. Japan is the largest spender, contributing 37% of total OECD transfers, although this number has been decreasing over the last decade. The majority of GFTs are for fisheries management, research and enforcement (38% of total GFTs in OECD countries) and infrastructure expenditure (39%). The remaining spending consists of vessel decommissioning schemes (7%), income support (5%), access agreements (3%), vessel construction and modernization (3%) and other cost reducing transfers and direct payments for general services (5%).

Government financial transfers to fishing
Thousand US dollars

	1996	1997	1998	1999	2000	2001	2002	2003	2004	2005
Australia	37 391	41 230	..	..	82 272	75 902	78 038	95 558	95 560	46 299
Belgium	4 970	4 949	..	4 473	6 849	2 830	1 607	1 668	6 328	8 613
Canada	545 301	433 309	..	606 443	564 497	521 355	497 771	589 975	618 787	591 000
Czech Republic	..	..	..	269	241	223	235	..	..	..
Denmark	85 771	82 030	90 507	27 765	16 316	..	68 769	37 659	28 505	58 108
Finland	28 978	26 198	26 888	19 236	13 908	16 510	16 025	20 231	19 397	24 817
France	158 203	140 807	..	71 665	166 147	141 786	155 283	179 740	236 811	126 194
Germany	81 567	63 215	16 488	31 276	29 834	28 988	28 208	7 343	6 088	4 350
Greece	52 308	46 958	26 908	43 030	87 315	86 957	88 334	119 045	35 500	61 013
Iceland	43 770	38 678	36 954	39 763	41 978	28 310	28 955	48 348	55 705	64 326
Ireland	112 673	98 880	..	143 184	..	..	63 632	64 960	..	..
Italy	162 625	91 811	..	200 470	217 679	231 680	159 630	149 270	170 055	119 239
Japan	3 186 363	2 945 785	2 135 946	2 537 536	2 913 149	2 574 086	2 323 601	2 310 744	2 437 934	2 165 198
Korea	367 793	378 994	211 927	471 556	320 449	428 313	538 695	495 280	495 280	649 387
Mexico	14 201	16 808	..	..	..	..	..	177 000	114 000	..
Netherlands	39 927	35 849	..	..	1 389	12 779	12 443	6 569	5 218	13 685
New Zealand	37 241	40 397	29 412	29 630	27 273	15 126	18 981	38 325	50 134	32 197
Norway	172 694	163 437	153 046	180 962	104 564	99 465	156 340	139 200	142 315	149 521
Poland	8 148	7 927	..	..	..	..	..	..	..	..
Portugal	71 847	65 077	..	28 674	25 578	25 066	24 899	26 930	26 930	32 769
Spain	246 473	344 581	296 642	399 604	364 096	376 614	301 926	353 290	256 569	238 151
Sweden	62 320	53 452	26 960	31 053	25 186	22 505	24 753	30 650	34 422	36 603
Turkey	28 665	15 114	..	1 277	26 372	17 721	16 167	16 300	59 500	98 072
United Kingdom	115 359	128 066	90 833	75 968	81 394	73 738	..	82 691	87 487	90 000
United States	891 160	1 002 580	1 041 000	1 103 100	1 037 710	1 169 590	1 130 810	1 290 440	1 064 400	1 222 500
EU15 total	1 549 000	1 435 000	1 392 000	1 232 000	1 136 000	1 293 000	1 047 000	1 267 000	1 215 000	978 790
OECD total	6 555 748	6 266 132	4 183 511	6 046 934	6 154 196	5 949 544	5 735 102	6 281 216	6 046 925	5 832 042

StatLink http://dx.doi.org/10.1787/275367125357

Government financial transfers to fishing
Average annual growth in percentage, 1996-2005 or latest available period

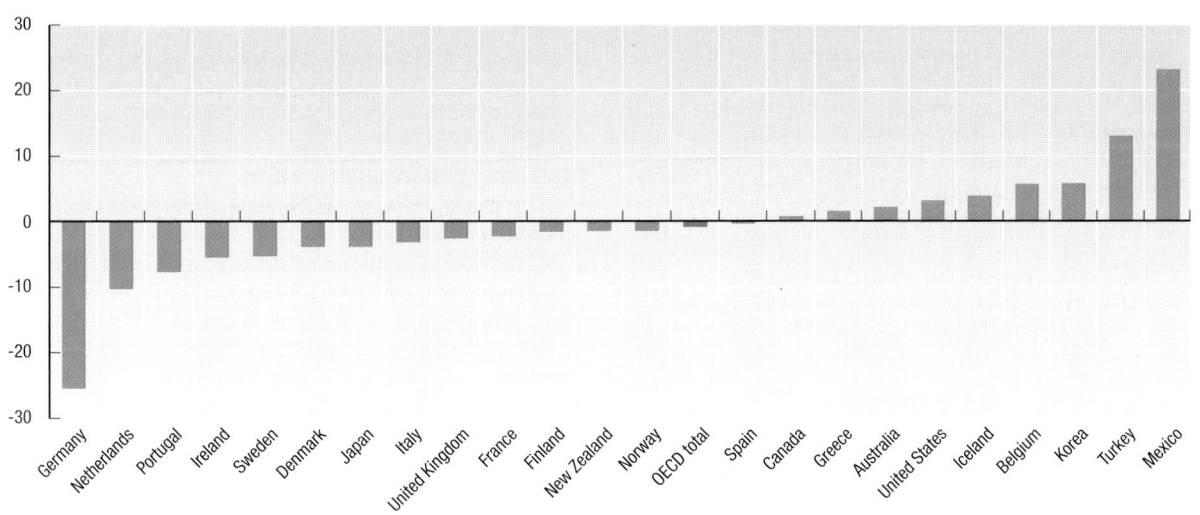

StatLink http://dx.doi.org/10.1787/270666130113

OFFICIAL DEVELOPMENT ASSISTANCE

The promotion of economic and social development in non-member countries has been a principal objective of the OECD since its foundation. The share of national income devoted to official development assistance (ODA) is widely regarded as a test of a country's commitment to international development, and there is a long-standing United Nations target for developed countries to devote 0.7% of their gross national income (GNI) to ODA. The tables in this section show total ODA as shares of GNI as well as the geographical distribution of bilateral ODA.

Definition

Official development assistance is defined as government aid to developing countries designed to promote the economic development and welfare of recipient countries. Loans and credits for military purposes are excluded. The aid may be provided bilaterally, from donor to recipient, or it may be channeled through a multilateral development agency such as the United Nations or the World Bank.

Aid includes grants, "soft" loans, and the provision of technical assistance. Soft loans are those where the grant element is at least 25%. ODA is usually measured on a net basis, *i.e.* after subtracting loan repayments from the gross aid flows. Data on the geographical distribution of aid are presented on a gross basis to show the level of new aid provided during the period.

The OECD maintains a list of developing countries and territories, and only aid to these countries counts as ODA. The list is periodically updated and currently contains over 150 countries or territories which had per capita incomes of less than USD 10 066 in 2004 (by comparison, per capita income in OECD countries averaged over USD 35 000 in that year). Note that of the 30 member countries of the OECD, only the 22 shown in the table are members of the Development Assistance Committee (DAC), along with the European Commission.

Comparability

Statistics on ODA are compiled according to a set of directives drawn up by the DAC and each country's statistics are subject to regular peer reviews by other DAC members. Data for Greece are available only since 1996 as Greece joined the DAC in 1999. From 1990 to 1992 inclusive, forgiveness of non-ODA debt was reportable as a part of a country's ODA but was excluded from the DAC total.

Long-term trends

The DAC total shown in the graph is the weighted average of total ODA provided by DAC members as a percentage of their total GNI; it amounted to 0.31% in 2006. The unweighted average, measuring "average country effort", was 0.46% in 2006. The decline since 1990 in both the weighted and unweighted averages was halted in 1999 and then reversed as DAC members increased their aid following the commitments they made at the Monterrey 2002 Financing for Development Conference.

ODA shares of GNI declined to their lowest point in 1997 but since 2002 have been increasing again, reaching a peak in 2005, due to debt relief. 2006 marked the first fall in ODA in real terms since 1997, though the level is still the highest recorded with the exception of 2005. While ODA is expected to fall back slightly again in 2007 as debt relief for Nigeria and Iraq tapers off, it is expected that other types of aid should then increase as donors move to fulfill their more recent pledges.

Source

*   *Development Assistance Committee Aid Statistics.*

Further information

Analytical publications

*   OECD (2005), The Development Dimension, *The Development Effectiveness of Food Aid: Does Tying Matter?*, OECD, Paris.
*   OECD (2006), The Development Dimension, *The Development Dimension – Aid for Trade: Making it Effective*, OECD, Paris.
*   OECD (2007), *Development Aid at a Glance 2007, Statistics by Region*, OECD, Paris.
*   OECD (2007), *Financing Development: Aid and Beyond*, OECD, Paris.
*   OECD (2008), *OECD Journal on Development: Development Co-operation – 2007 Report – Efforts and Policies of the Members of the Development Assistance Committee*, Volume 9, Issue 1, OECD, Paris.

Statistical publications

*   OECD (2008), *International Development Statistics on CD-ROM*, OECD, Paris.
*   OECD (2008), *Geographical Distribution of Financial Flows to Aid Recipients 2002/2006: 2008 Edition*, OECD, Paris.

Online databases

*   *International Development Statistics, www.oecd.org/dac/stats/idsonline.*

Websites

*   Development Assistance Committee Aid Statistics, *www.oecd.org/dac/stats.*
*   OECD, Calculation of the Grant Element of Loans, *www.oecd.org/dataoecd/15/0/31738575.pdf.*

Net official development assistance
As a percentage of gross national income

	1993	1994	1995	1996	1997	1998	1999	2000	2001	2002	2003	2004	2005	2006
Australia	0.35	0.34	0.34	0.27	0.27	0.27	0.26	0.27	0.25	0.26	0.25	0.25	0.25	0.30
Austria	0.11	0.17	0.27	0.23	0.24	0.22	0.24	0.23	0.34	0.26	0.20	0.23	0.52	0.47
Belgium	0.39	0.32	0.38	0.34	0.31	0.35	0.30	0.36	0.37	0.43	0.60	0.41	0.53	0.50
Canada	0.45	0.43	0.38	0.32	0.34	0.30	0.28	0.25	0.22	0.28	0.24	0.27	0.34	0.29
Denmark	1.03	1.03	0.96	1.04	0.97	0.99	1.01	1.06	1.03	0.96	0.84	0.85	0.81	0.80
Finland	0.45	0.31	0.31	0.33	0.32	0.31	0.33	0.31	0.32	0.35	0.35	0.37	0.46	0.40
France	0.63	0.62	0.55	0.48	0.44	0.38	0.38	0.30	0.31	0.37	0.40	0.41	0.47	0.47
Germany	0.35	0.33	0.31	0.32	0.28	0.26	0.26	0.27	0.27	0.27	0.28	0.28	0.36	0.36
Greece	..	..	0.15	0.15	0.14	0.15	0.15	0.20	0.17	0.21	0.21	0.16	0.17	0.17
Ireland	0.20	0.25	0.29	0.31	0.31	0.30	0.31	0.29	0.33	0.40	0.39	0.39	0.42	0.54
Italy	0.31	0.27	0.15	0.20	0.11	0.20	0.15	0.13	0.15	0.20	0.17	0.15	0.29	0.20
Japan	0.27	0.29	0.27	0.20	0.21	0.27	0.27	0.28	0.23	0.23	0.20	0.19	0.28	0.25
Luxembourg	0.35	0.40	0.36	0.44	0.55	0.65	0.66	0.71	0.76	0.77	0.81	0.83	0.86	0.89
Netherlands	0.82	0.76	0.81	0.81	0.81	0.80	0.79	0.84	0.82	0.81	0.80	0.73	0.82	0.81
New Zealand	0.25	0.24	0.23	0.21	0.26	0.27	0.27	0.25	0.25	0.22	0.23	0.23	0.27	0.27
Norway	1.01	1.05	0.86	0.83	0.84	0.89	0.88	0.76	0.80	0.89	0.92	0.87	0.94	0.89
Portugal	0.28	0.34	0.25	0.21	0.25	0.24	0.26	0.26	0.25	0.27	0.22	0.63	0.21	0.21
Spain	0.28	0.28	0.24	0.22	0.24	0.24	0.23	0.22	0.30	0.26	0.23	0.24	0.27	0.32
Sweden	0.99	0.96	0.77	0.84	0.79	0.72	0.70	0.80	0.77	0.84	0.79	0.78	0.94	1.02
Switzerland	0.33	0.36	0.34	0.34	0.34	0.32	0.35	0.34	0.34	0.32	0.39	0.41	0.44	0.39
United Kingdom	0.31	0.31	0.29	0.27	0.26	0.27	0.24	0.32	0.32	0.31	0.34	0.36	0.47	0.51
United States	0.15	0.14	0.10	0.12	0.09	0.10	0.10	0.10	0.11	0.13	0.15	0.17	0.23	0.18
DAC total	0.30	0.29	0.26	0.25	0.22	0.23	0.22	0.22	0.22	0.23	0.25	0.26	0.33	0.31
of which: EU members	0.43	0.41	0.37	0.37	0.33	0.33	0.31	0.32	0.33	0.35	0.35	0.35	0.44	0.43

StatLink ᵍ http://dx.doi.org/10.1787/275443820107

Net official development assistance
As a percentage of gross national income

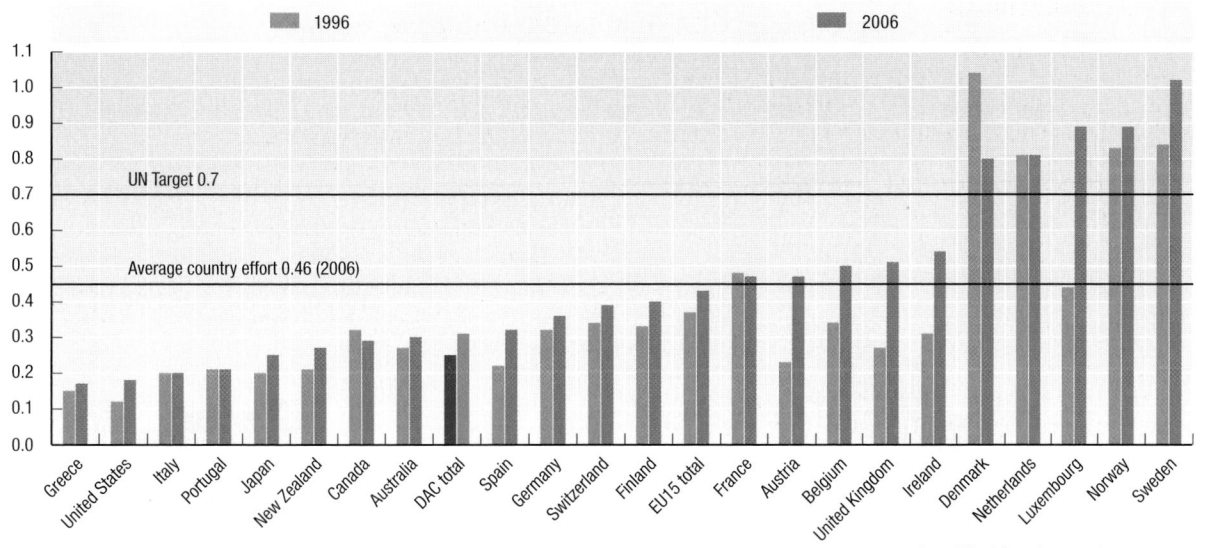

StatLink ᵍ http://dx.doi.org/10.1787/270676476461

Major recipients by region of total gross bilateral ODA from DAC countries
Million US dollars, 3-year averages

	1992-1994		1995-1997		1998-2000
Sub-Saharan Africa	11 918	Sub-Saharan Africa	10 623	Sub-Saharan Africa	9 100
Mozambique	908	Mozambique	706	Mozambique	748
Tanzania	788	Côte d'Ivoire	626	Tanzania	737
Côte d'Ivoire	759	Tanzania	597	Côte d'Ivoire	483
Zambia	641	Ethiopia	464	Uganda	454
Cameroon	571	Senegal	428	Ghana	408
Somalia	543	Uganda	417	Zambia	394
Ethiopia	509	Cameroon	416	South Africa	390
Kenya	482	Kenya	415	Senegal	383
Senegal	477	Zambia	411	Cameroon	365
Zimbabwe	393	Madagascar	369	Ethiopia	359
Middle East and North of Africa	7 608	Middle East and North of Africa	5 318	Middle East and North of Africa	3 877
Egypt	3 296	Egypt	1 826	Egypt	1 503
Israel	1 691	Israel	989	Morocco	489
Morocco	629	Morocco	505	Jordan	367
Algeria	381	Jordan	390	Palestinian Administered Areas	323
Jordan	329	Algeria	261	Tunisia	265
South and Central Asia	4 622	South and Central Asia	4 597	South and Central Asia	4 489
India	1 696	India	1 656	India	1 483
Bangladesh	919	Bangladesh	813	Bangladesh	813
Pakistan	800	Pakistan	661	Pakistan	586
Sri Lanka	385	Sri Lanka	403	Sri Lanka	369
Nepal	270	Nepal	254	Nepal	232
Far East Asia and Oceania	10 311	Far East Asia and Oceania	9 705	Far East Asia and Oceania	9 754
Indonesia	2 439	China	2 107	Indonesia	2 203
China	2 414	Indonesia	1 884	China	2 105
Philippines	1 606	Philippines	1 122	Thailand	1 093
Thailand	778	Thailand	970	Viet Nam	1 013
Viet Nam	487	Viet Nam	593	Philippines	957
Europe	1 793	Europe	1 564	Europe	2 264
States Ex-Yugoslavia Unspecified	962	Bosnia	618	Bosnia	584
Turkey	458	Turkey	408	Serbia	453
Albania	123	Albania	103	Turkey	305
Latin America and Caribbean	5 754	Latin America and Caribbean	5 717	Latin America and Caribbean	5 100
El Salvador	494	Bolivia	547	Peru	481
Bolivia	491	Nicaragua	530	Bolivia	404
Peru	479	Peru	415	Nicaragua	376
Mexico	415	Brazil	329	Brazil	361
Nicaragua	408	Mexico	300	Honduras	306

StatLink http://dx.doi.org/10.1787/275466631858

Gross bilateral ODA from DAC countries by region
Million US dollars

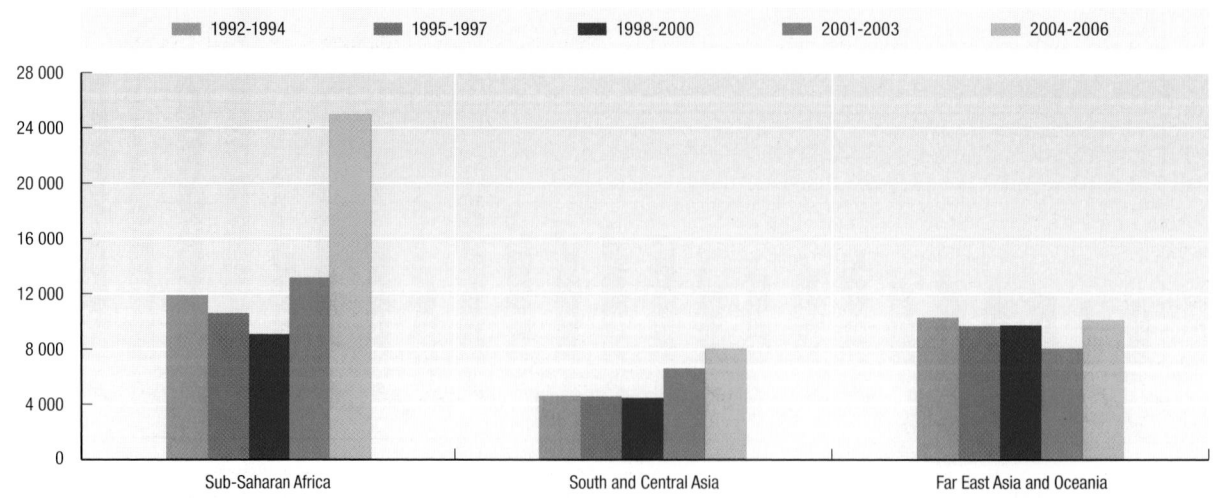

StatLink http://dx.doi.org/10.1787/270761150741

OECD FACTBOOK 2008 – ISBN 978-92-64-04054-0 – © OECD 2008

Major recipients by region of total gross bilateral ODA from DAC countries (cont.)

Million US dollars, 3-year averages

	2001-2003		2004-2006
Sub-Saharan Africa	13 172	Sub-Saharan Africa	24 973
Congo, Democratic Republic	1 889	Nigeria	5 940
Mozambique	1 066	Sudan	1 278
Tanzania	963	Congo, Democratic Republic	1 265
Ethiopia	641	Zambia	1 150
Cameroon	628	Ghana	1 146
Côte d'Ivoire	523	Ethiopia	1 105
Uganda	497	Cameroon	1 010
Ghana	446	Tanzania	1 002
Zambia	432	Mozambique	822
South Africa	416	Uganda	797
Middle East and North of Africa	4 675	Middle East and North of Africa	16 255
Egypt	1 298	Iraq	11 586
Iraq	760	Egypt	1 199
Jordan	687	Morocco	707
Morocco	476	Palestinian Administered Areas	643
Palestinian Administered Areas	394	Jordan	506
South and Central Asia	6 636	South and Central Asia	8 069
India	1 639	Afghanistan	2 091
Pakistan	1 336	India	1 715
Afghanistan	848	Bangladesh	856
Bangladesh	792	Pakistan	848
Sri Lanka	396	Sri Lanka	719
Far East Asia and Oceania	8 077	Far East Asia and Oceania	10 128
China	1 920	China	2 558
Indonesia	1 581	Indonesia	2 016
Philippines	1 014	Viet Nam	1 368
Viet Nam	880	Philippines	1 039
Thailand	818	Thailand	767
Europe	2 813	Europe	2 928
Serbia	1 135	Serbia	862
Turkey	357	Turkey	447
Bosnia	337	Bosnia	305
Latin America and Caribbean	5 408	Latin America and Caribbean	6 669
Bolivia	679	Colombia	723
Colombia	587	Bolivia	705
Peru	582	Nicaragua	701
Nicaragua	535	Peru	609
Brazil	369	Honduras	585

StatLink http://dx.doi.org/10.1787/275466631858

Gross bilateral ODA from DAC countries by region

Million US dollars

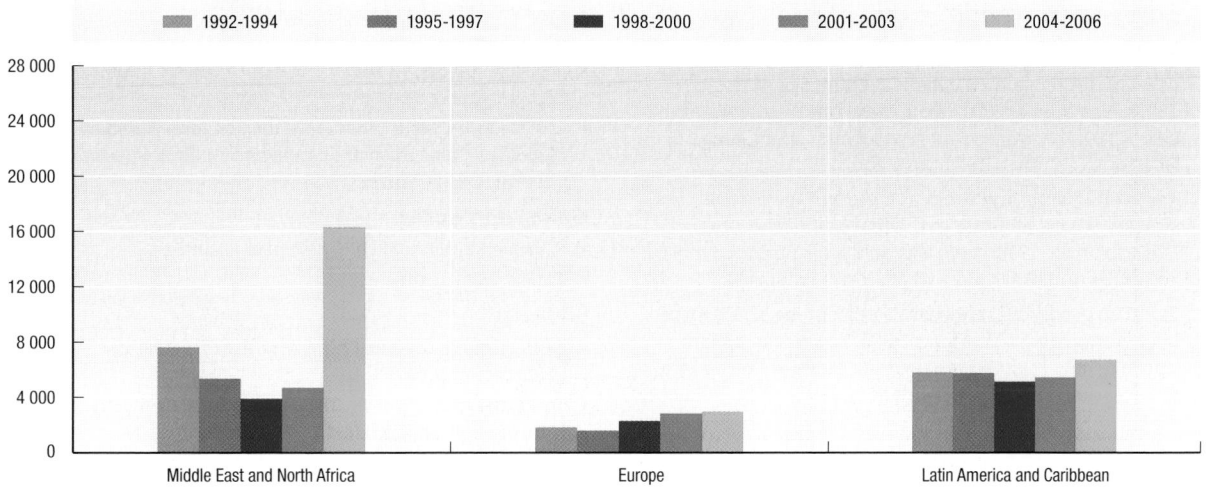

StatLink http://dx.doi.org/10.1787/270763547658

TOTAL TAX REVENUE

Total tax revenue as a percentage of GDP indicates the share of a country's output that is collected by the government through taxes. It can thus be regarded as one measure of the degree to which the government controls the economy's resources. Taxes on incomes and profits as a percentage of GDP represents the amount of resources collected by government directly from the incomes of people and companies. Taxes on goods and services as a percentage of GDP represents the amount of resources the government collects from people as they spend their income on goods and services.

Definition

Taxes are defined as compulsory, unrequited payments to general government. They are unrequited in the sense that benefits provided by government to taxpayers are not normally in proportion to their payments.

Taxes on incomes and profits cover taxes levied on the net income or profits (gross income minus allowable tax reliefs) of individuals and enterprises. They also cover taxes levied on the capital gains of individuals and enterprises, and gains from gambling.

Taxes on goods and services covers all taxes levied on the production, extraction, sale, transfer, leasing or delivery of goods, and the rendering of services, or on the use of goods or permission to use goods or to perform activities. They consist mainly of value added and sales taxes.

Note that the sum of taxes on goods and services and taxes on income and profits do not equal total tax revenues, which also includes payments by employers and employees made under compulsory social security schemes as well as payroll taxes, taxes related to the ownership and transfer of property, and other taxes.

Comparability

The data are collected in a way that makes them as internationally comparable as possible. Country representatives have agreed on the definition of each type of tax and how they should be measured in all OECD countries, and they are then responsible for submitting data that conform to these rules. The rules are set out in "The OECD Interpretative Guide" at the end of each edition of *Revenue Statistics*.

Source

- OECD (2007), *Revenue Statistics 1965-2006 – 2007 Edition*, OECD, Paris.

Further information

Analytical publications

- OECD (2004), *Recent Tax Policy Trends and Reforms in OECD Countries*, OECD Tax Policy Studies, No. 9, OECD, Paris.
- OECD (2005), *Consumption Tax Trends: VAT/GST and Excise rates, Trends and Administration Issues*, 2005 Edition, OECD, Paris.
- OECD (2006), *OECD Tax Policy Studies – No. 15 Encouraging Savings through Tax-Preferred Accounts*, OECD, Paris.
- OECD (2006), *The Political Economy of Environmentally Related Taxes*, OECD, Paris.

Statistical publications

- OECD (2007), *Taxing Wages 2005/2006: 2006 Edition*, OECD, Paris.

Methodological publications

- *Electronic Model Tax Convention (eMTC)*, www.sourceoecd.org/reference/modeltax.
- OECD (1992-2005), *Model Tax Convention on Income and on Capital*, yearly updates, OECD, Paris.
- OECD (2005), *Model Tax Convention on Income and on Capital Model Tax Convention on Income and on Capital*, condensed version, OECD, Paris.

Online databases

- *Revenue Statistics of OECD Member Countries*.
- *Taxing Wages Statistics*.

Websites

- OECD Centre for Tax Policy and Administration, www.oecd.org/ctp.
- Tax Administration in OECD Countries: Comparative Information Series (2004), www.oecd.org/ctp/ta.

Long-term trends

Total tax revenue as a percentage of GDP followed a slow upward trend in almost all OECD countries during the 1990s. However, in 2000, the upward trend stopped, and, since 2001, the average tax revenues as a percentage of GDP for OECD countries have stabilised.

Taxes on income and profit as a percentage of GDP showed no overall trend in the first half of the 1990s. However, from 1996, there was an upward trend in most countries until 2000, after which it has stabilised.

Taxes on goods and services as a percentage of GDP have been remarkably stable since 1992. There was a slight upward trend in the first half of the 1990s, followed by a stabilisation.

Total tax revenue
As a percentage of GDP

	1993	1994	1995	1996	1997	1998	1999	2000	2001	2002	2003	2004	2005	2006
Australia	26.9	28.0	28.8	29.4	29.2	30.0	30.5	31.1	29.6	30.5	30.7	31.1	30.9	..
Austria	41.9	41.7	41.1	42.4	43.9	43.9	43.5	42.6	44.6	43.6	43.1	42.8	42.1	41.9
Belgium	43.3	43.6	43.6	44.0	44.5	45.2	45.2	44.9	44.9	45.0	44.6	44.8	45.4	44.8
Canada	35.4	35.2	35.6	35.9	36.7	36.7	36.4	35.6	34.8	33.7	33.7	33.6	33.4	33.4
Czech Republic	40.4	38.9	37.5	36.0	36.3	34.9	35.8	35.3	35.6	36.3	37.3	38.3	37.8	36.7
Denmark	47.7	48.7	48.8	49.2	48.9	49.3	50.1	49.4	48.4	47.8	48.0	49.3	50.3	49.0
Finland	44.4	46.9	45.7	47.0	46.3	46.1	45.8	47.2	44.6	44.6	44.0	43.4	44.0	43.5
France	42.4	42.8	42.9	44.1	44.4	44.2	45.1	44.4	44.0	43.4	43.2	43.5	44.1	44.5
Germany	37.0	37.2	37.2	36.5	36.2	36.4	37.1	37.2	36.1	35.4	35.5	34.8	34.8	35.7
Greece	24.1	24.3	25.2	31.2	26.4	27.9	28.7	29.7	28.7	29.0	28.1	27.1	27.3	27.4
Hungary	45.7	43.3	41.3	39.6	38.0	37.8	38.1	38.0	38.0	37.8	37.5	37.6	37.2	37.1
Iceland	31.1	30.6	31.2	32.3	32.2	35.5	38.1	38.1	36.3	35.8	37.2	38.3	41.4	..
Ireland	34.0	34.6	32.0	32.1	31.4	31.3	31.5	31.7	29.5	28.2	28.8	30.2	30.6	31.7
Italy	42.2	40.2	40.1	41.8	43.2	41.7	42.5	42.3	42.0	41.4	41.8	41.1	41.0	42.7
Japan	27.1	26.3	26.8	26.8	27.2	26.8	26.3	27.0	27.3	26.2	25.7	26.3	27.4	..
Korea	19.0	19.4	19.4	20.0	21.0	21.1	21.5	23.6	24.1	24.4	25.3	24.6	25.5	26.8
Luxembourg	36.5	36.8	37.1	37.6	39.3	39.4	38.3	39.1	39.7	39.2	38.5	37.9	38.6	36.3
Mexico	17.7	17.2	16.7	16.7	17.5	16.6	17.3	18.5	18.8	18.1	19.0	19.0	19.9	20.6
Netherlands	45.0	43.0	41.5	40.9	40.9	39.1	40.1	39.7	38.2	37.5	36.9	37.4	39.1	39.5
New Zealand	36.0	36.5	36.6	34.8	35.0	33.4	33.4	33.6	33.0	34.4	34.3	35.5	37.8	36.5
Norway	39.4	40.8	40.9	40.8	41.5	42.4	42.7	42.6	42.9	43.1	42.3	43.3	43.7	43.6
Poland	38.8	36.9	36.2	36.1	35.2	34.6	32.3	31.6	33.6	34.6	34.1	33.4	34.3	..
Portugal	29.3	30.1	31.7	32.6	32.7	32.9	33.9	34.1	33.8	34.5	34.7	33.8	34.8	35.4
Slovak Republic	..	..	..	..	..	36.6	34.3	32.9	31.7	32.0	33.2	31.6	31.6	29.6
Spain	32.8	32.9	32.1	31.9	32.9	33.2	34.1	34.2	33.8	34.2	34.2	34.7	35.8	36.7
Sweden	46.6	46.8	48.1	50.0	51.2	51.7	52.1	52.6	50.7	48.9	49.4	49.9	50.7	50.1
Switzerland	26.7	27.2	27.8	28.3	27.9	28.9	29.1	30.5	30.1	30.1	29.4	29.1	29.7	30.1
Turkey	22.7	22.2	22.6	25.4	27.9	28.4	31.3	32.3	35.1	31.1	32.8	31.3	32.3	32.5
United Kingdom	32.9	33.5	34.7	34.6	35.1	36.2	36.6	37.3	37.0	35.5	35.2	35.6	36.5	37.4
United States	27.1	27.5	27.9	28.3	28.7	29.3	29.4	29.9	28.8	26.5	25.9	26.0	27.3	28.2
EU15 average	38.7	38.9	38.8	39.7	39.8	39.9	40.3	40.4	39.7	39.2	39.1	39.1	39.7	39.8
OECD average	35.0	34.9	34.9	35.4	35.6	35.7	36.0	36.2	35.9	35.4	35.5	35.5	36.2	..

StatLink http://dx.doi.org/10.1787/275468386544

Total tax revenue
As a percentage of GDP

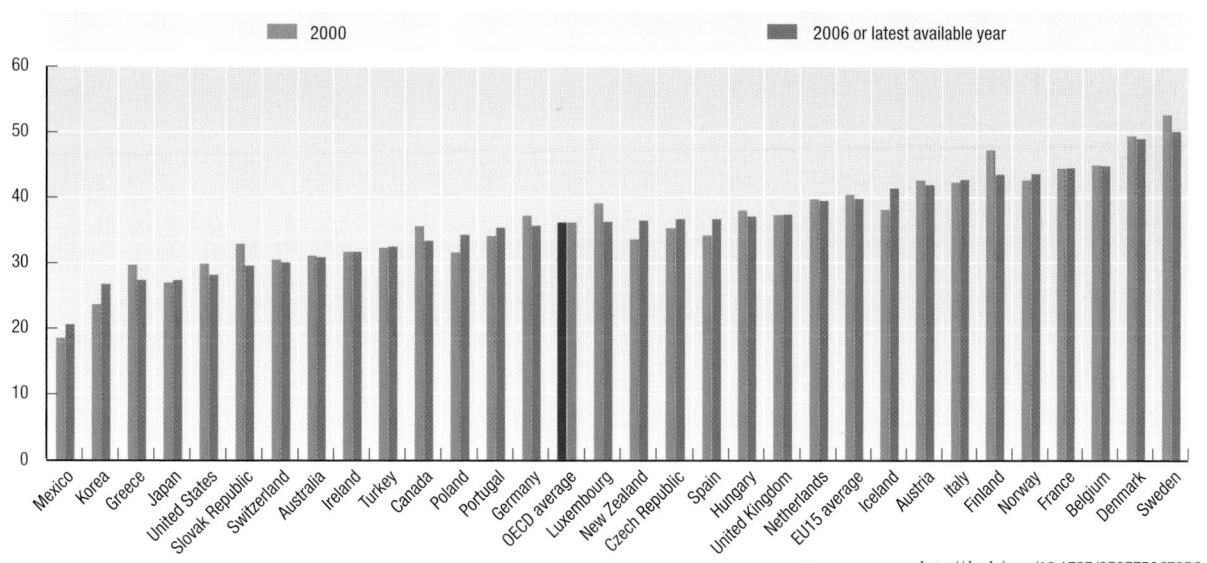

StatLink http://dx.doi.org/10.1787/270775267356

Taxes on income and profits
As a percentage of GDP

	1993	1994	1995	1996	1997	1998	1999	2000	2001	2002	2003	2004	2005	2006
Australia	14.6	15.2	15.9	16.6	16.5	17.7	18.3	18.1	16.7	17.2	17.3	18.2	18.2	..
Austria	11.3	10.3	10.9	11.9	12.7	12.9	12.5	12.2	14.0	13.0	12.8	12.6	12.0	12.2
Belgium	15.7	16.0	16.6	16.6	17.0	17.5	17.1	17.3	17.5	17.3	16.9	17.0	17.4	16.9
Canada	15.7	15.8	16.5	16.9	17.9	17.7	18.1	17.8	16.7	15.4	15.4	15.7	15.9	16.3
Czech Republic	10.3	9.7	9.4	8.1	8.7	8.1	8.3	8.0	8.6	9.0	9.5	9.6	9.1	8.6
Denmark	29.1	30.0	30.1	30.2	29.8	29.4	29.6	29.8	28.7	28.5	28.8	29.8	30.7	29.3
Finland	15.0	16.4	16.5	18.2	17.7	18.1	17.8	20.3	18.2	18.1	17.0	16.8	16.8	16.6
France	6.9	7.0	7.0	7.4	8.1	10.2	10.8	11.1	11.2	10.4	10.0	10.2	10.4	10.8
Germany	11.4	11.0	11.3	10.5	10.2	10.7	11.1	11.2	10.4	9.9	9.8	9.5	9.8	10.8
Greece	4.6	5.3	5.6	5.5	5.9	7.1	7.3	8.1	7.0	7.0	6.5	6.5	7.0	6.5
Hungary	9.5	9.1	8.6	8.7	8.3	8.4	8.9	9.2	9.7	10.0	9.3	8.9	8.8	9.0
Iceland	10.1	10.2	10.6	11.3	11.5	13.5	14.9	15.4	15.9	15.9	16.7	16.9	18.8	..
Ireland	13.6	14.1	12.7	13.1	13.1	12.9	13.1	13.3	12.2	11.1	11.4	12.0	11.8	11.0
Italy	15.6	14.0	14.2	14.5	15.3	13.6	14.4	14.0	14.3	13.4	12.9	12.9	12.9	14.0
Japan	11.5	10.3	10.3	10.2	10.1	9.0	8.4	9.4	9.1	8.0	7.9	8.4	9.3	10.2
Korea	5.7	5.9	6.2	6.0	5.5	6.4	5.3	6.8	6.4	6.2	7.1	6.9	7.5	7.9
Luxembourg	13.5	13.9	14.6	14.9	15.6	15.1	13.9	14.1	14.3	14.3	14.0	12.6	13.3	12.7
Mexico	5.5	5.2	4.1	4.0	4.6	4.7	5.0	5.0	5.2	5.2	5.0	4.7	4.8	5.2
Netherlands	14.7	12.0	10.9	11.1	10.7	10.3	10.2	10.0	10.1	10.2	9.4	9.2	10.8	10.9
New Zealand	21.1	22.3	22.4	20.7	20.9	19.4	19.4	20.2	19.5	20.5	20.4	21.7	23.8	22.6
Norway	13.3	14.2	14.3	14.8	15.7	15.7	16.0	19.2	19.3	18.8	18.5	20.1	21.5	21.7
Poland	12.3	11.3	11.1	10.6	10.4	10.2	9.9	9.7	9.5	9.6	6.0	5.9	6.4	..
Portugal	8.1	7.9	7.9	8.6	8.7	8.6	9.1	9.6	9.1	8.9	8.4	8.3	8.5	8.5
Slovak Republic	..	..	..	..	..	9.4	8.4	7.0	6.9	6.8	6.8	5.7	5.7	5.7
Spain	9.8	9.3	9.4	9.2	9.8	9.4	9.6	9.7	9.5	10.0	9.6	9.8	10.5	11.3
Sweden	19.1	19.9	18.9	19.6	20.2	20.1	21.1	21.5	19.2	17.5	18.2	19.0	19.8	19.7
Switzerland	12.0	12.5	12.0	12.4	12.0	12.6	12.2	13.4	12.7	13.0	12.6	12.6	13.2	13.7
Turkey	7.3	6.6	6.4	6.7	7.6	9.4	9.8	9.5	10.1	7.7	7.8	6.7	7.0	7.0
United Kingdom	11.6	12.0	12.8	12.7	13.0	14.1	14.1	14.6	14.7	13.5	12.9	13.1	14.0	14.9
United States	12.1	12.3	12.8	13.5	14.0	14.4	14.6	15.1	14.1	11.7	11.2	11.4	12.7	13.7
EU15 average	13.3	13.3	13.3	13.6	13.8	14.0	14.1	14.4	14.0	13.5	13.2	13.3	13.7	13.7
OECD average	12.4	12.4	12.4	12.6	12.8	12.9	13.0	13.3	13.0	12.6	12.3	12.4	13.0	..

StatLink http://dx.doi.org/10.1787/275471216110

Taxes on income and profits
As a percentage of GDP

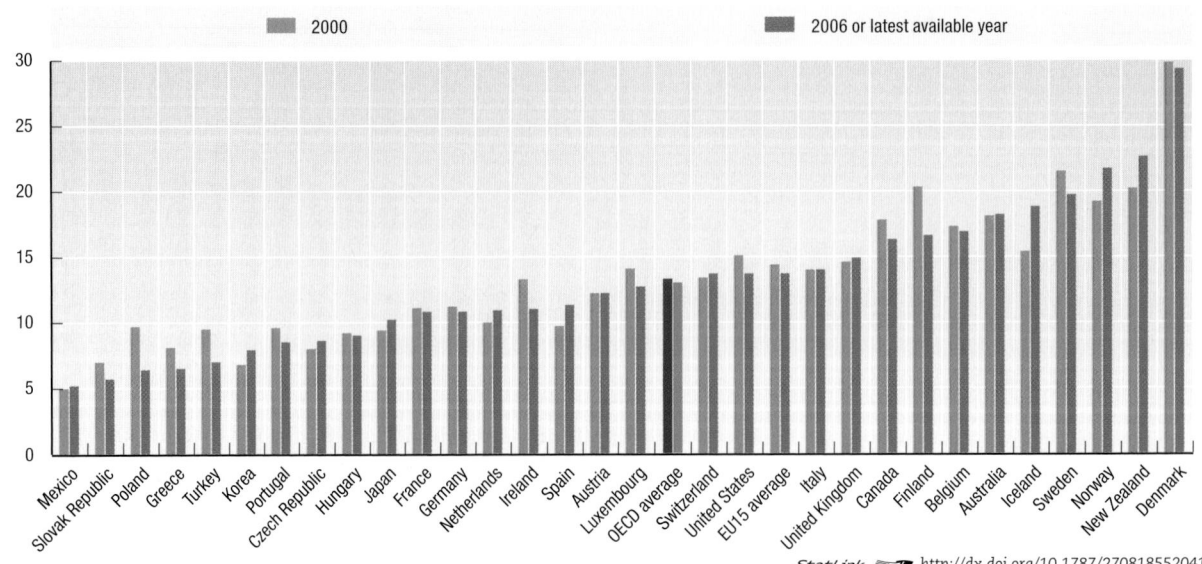

■ 2000   ■ 2006 or latest available year

StatLink http://dx.doi.org/10.1787/270818552041

OECD FACTBOOK 2008 – ISBN 978-92-64-04054-0 – © OECD 2008

Taxes on goods and services
As a percentage of GDP

	1993	1994	1995	1996	1997	1998	1999	2000	2001	2002	2003	2004	2005	2006
Australia	7.9	8.2	8.4	8.2	8.0	8.2	8.0	8.9	8.9	9.2	9.1	8.9	8.6	..
Austria	12.3	12.9	11.5	11.9	12.3	12.3	12.4	12.0	12.1	12.3	12.1	12.1	12.0	11.6
Belgium	11.2	11.4	11.2	11.5	11.7	11.1	11.5	11.4	11.0	11.1	11.0	11.2	11.5	11.5
Canada	9.4	9.2	9.0	9.0	9.0	9.1	8.8	8.6	8.8	8.9	8.9	8.7	8.5	8.1
Czech Republic	13.5	13.0	12.1	11.8	11.3	10.8	11.5	11.2	10.8	10.8	11.1	11.9	11.8	11.2
Denmark	15.0	15.5	15.7	16.1	16.1	16.4	16.5	15.9	15.9	16.0	15.8	16.1	16.2	16.3
Finland	14.0	14.4	13.8	13.9	14.5	14.1	14.2	13.7	13.2	13.5	14.1	13.8	13.8	13.6
France	11.2	11.6	11.7	12.2	12.0	11.9	12.0	11.4	11.1	11.1	11.0	11.1	11.2	11.1
Germany	10.3	10.7	10.4	10.3	10.1	10.0	10.4	10.5	10.4	10.3	10.5	10.2	10.1	10.2
Greece	11.0	10.5	10.4	10.6	10.8	10.4	10.6	10.5	10.9	10.6	10.0	9.6	9.4	10.7
Hungary	17.0	16.0	16.8	16.1	14.9	14.7	15.3	15.4	14.7	14.2	14.8	15.3	14.8	14.5
Iceland	15.5	15.0	15.2	15.6	15.3	16.8	17.8	17.1	14.9	14.3	15.0	15.8	16.7	..
Ireland	13.0	13.2	12.7	12.7	12.3	12.2	12.1	12.2	11.0	11.1	11.0	11.4	11.6	11.6
Italy	10.9	11.4	10.9	10.8	11.2	11.5	11.7	11.8	11.2	11.2	10.7	10.8	10.8	11.1
Japan	4.1	4.2	4.2	4.3	4.7	5.3	5.4	5.2	5.3	5.3	5.2	5.3	5.3	5.2
Korea	8.3	8.4	8.4	8.8	9.0	8.0	8.6	9.0	9.5	9.5	9.4	8.9	8.8	8.7
Luxembourg	10.0	10.2	9.9	9.8	10.4	10.5	10.4	10.6	10.5	10.6	10.6	11.3	11.1	10.0
Mexico	8.3	8.1	9.0	9.3	9.4	8.3	8.6	9.8	9.7	8.9	10.0	10.5	11.3	11.5
Netherlands	11.0	11.3	11.3	11.6	11.3	11.3	11.7	11.5	11.8	11.6	11.7	12.0	12.4	12.3
New Zealand	12.9	12.3	12.2	12.2	12.2	12.1	12.1	11.6	11.8	12.1	12.1	12.0	12.1	12.0
Norway	15.1	15.7	15.8	15.5	15.4	15.8	15.6	13.5	13.3	13.3	12.9	12.7	12.2	12.0
Poland	13.2	13.2	12.8	12.9	12.0	11.9	12.1	11.5	11.2	12.3	12.3	12.4	12.6	..
Portugal	12.5	13.5	12.9	13.2	12.8	13.1	13.3	12.8	12.9	13.2	13.3	13.3	13.6	14.2
Slovak Republic	..	..	..	..	..	12.3	12.1	11.9	11.1	11.5	11.9	12.2	12.5	11.4
Spain	8.8	9.3	9.2	9.3	9.5	9.8	10.2	10.1	9.7	9.6	9.7	9.8	10.0	9.8
Sweden	12.7	12.1	13.3	12.9	13.0	12.9	12.8	12.9	12.9	13.1	13.2	13.0	13.2	13.1
Switzerland	5.3	5.3	6.1	6.0	6.0	6.2	6.7	6.8	7.0	6.8	6.9	6.9	7.0	7.0
Turkey	7.2	8.3	8.5	9.7	10.3	10.2	11.2	13.6	14.1	14.6	16.2	14.9	15.9	15.7
United Kingdom	11.6	11.8	12.2	12.3	12.2	11.9	12.1	11.9	11.6	11.5	11.5	11.4	11.1	10.9
United States	5.0	5.1	5.0	4.9	4.9	4.9	4.8	4.8	4.7	4.7	4.7	4.7	4.8	4.7
EU15 average	11.7	12.0	11.8	11.9	12.0	12.0	12.1	11.9	11.7	11.8	11.7	11.8	11.9	11.9
OECD average	11.0	11.1	11.1	11.2	11.1	11.1	11.4	11.3	11.1	11.1	11.2	11.3	11.4	..

StatLink ᴍˢᴸ *http://dx.doi.org/10.1787/275611683612*

Taxes on goods and services
As a percentage of GDP

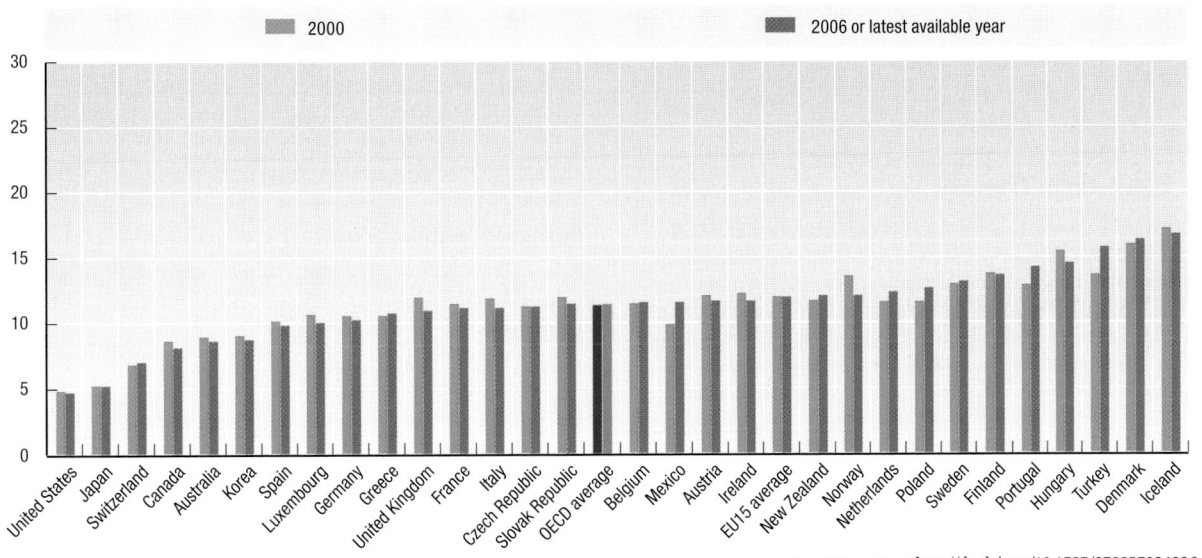

StatLink ᴍˢᴸ *http://dx.doi.org/10.1787/270857034236*

TAXES ON THE AVERAGE WORKER

This series, taxes on a single average worker, measures the difference between the salary cost of a single average worker to their employer and the amount of disposable income (net wage) that the worker receives. This "tax wedge" represents the extent to which the tax system discourages employment.

Definition

The taxes included in the measure are personal income taxes, employees' social security contributions and employers' social security contributions. For the few countries that have them, it also includes payroll taxes. The amount of these taxes paid in relation to employing one average worker is expressed as a percentage of their labour cost (gross wage plus employers' social security contributions and payroll tax).

An average worker is defined as somebody who earns the average income of full-time workers of the country concerned in sectors C-K of the International Standard Industrial Classification (ISIC). The average worker is single, meaning that he or she does not receive any tax relief in respect of a spouse, unmarried partner or child.

Comparability

The types of taxes included in the measure are fully comparable across countries, as they are based on common definitions agreed by all OECD countries and published in *Revenue Statistics*.

The income levels of the workers are different in each country, but they are each equal to the average income of full-time workers in ISIC sectors C-K. Thus, they can be regarded as income levels that correspond to comparable types of work in each country. Before 2000, the wage measure only covered full-time manual workers in manufacturing.

The information on the average worker's income level is supplied by the ministries of finance in all OECD countries and is based on national statistical surveys. The amount of taxes paid by the single worker is calculated by applying the tax laws of the country concerned. Thus, the tax rates are the result of a modeling exercise rather than direct observation of taxes actually paid.

Data for Australia from 1996 include payroll taxes. Data for earlier years are not available on the same basis.

Long-term trends

On average, the taxes on an average worker increased until 1997 and have since declined, in both the European Union and the OECD as a whole. However, there are important differences between countries. The countries that have experienced an overall increase in the taxes on an average worker since 2000 include Japan Mexico and the Netherlands. Countries that have experienced an overall decline include Australia, Denmark, Finland, Ireland, Luxembourg and the Slovak Republic.

Source

- OECD (2007), *Taxing Wages 2005/2006: 2006 Edition*, OECD, Paris.

Further information

Analytical publications

- Immervoll, H. (2004), *Average and Marginal Effective Tax Rates Facing Workers in the EU: A Micro-Level Analysis of Levels, Distributions and Driving Factors*, OECD Social Employment and Migration Working Papers, No. 19, OECD, Paris.
- OECD (2006), *OECD Tax Policy Studies – No. 15 Encouraging Savings through Tax-Preferred Accounts*, OECD, Paris.
- OECD (2006), *OECD Tax Policy Studies: No. 11: The Taxation of Employee Stock Options*, OECD, Paris.
- OECD (2007), *Benefits and Wages: OECD Indicators*, OECD, Paris.

Statistical publications

- OECD (2007), *Revenue Statistics 1965-2006 – 2007 Edition*, OECD, Paris.

Websites

- OECD Benefits and Wages, *www.oecd.org/els/social/workingincentives*.
- OECD Centre for Tax Policy and Administration, *www.oecd.org/ctp*.
- OECD Tax Policy Analysis, *www.oecd.org/ctp/tpa*.

Taxes on the average worker
As a percentage of labour cost

	1993	1994	1995	1996	1997	1998	1999	2000	2001	2002	2003	2004	2005	2006
Australia	..	..	..	29.3	29.6	30.2	30.4	30.6	27.3	27.7	28.0	28.0	28.3	28.1
Austria	40.0	39.7	41.2	41.5	45.6	45.8	45.9	47.3	46.9	47.1	47.4	48.1	47.9	48.1
Belgium	54.6	54.6	56.3	56.4	56.6	56.8	56.9	57.1	56.7	56.3	55.7	55.4	55.4	55.4
Canada	30.8	31.4	31.5	32.1	32.3	31.7	31.1	33.2	32.0	32.1	32.0	32.0	31.9	32.1
Czech Republic	42.6	42.8	43.2	42.6	42.9	42.8	42.7	42.7	42.6	42.9	43.2	43.5	43.8	42.6
Denmark	47.0	45.2	45.2	44.8	45.2	43.7	44.5	44.3	43.6	42.6	41.3	41.1	41.3
Finland	49.3	50.5	51.2	50.3	48.9	48.8	47.4	47.8	46.4	45.9	45.0	44.5	44.6	44.1
France	..	51.6	49.1	49.7	48.7	47.6	48.1	49.6	49.8	49.8	49.8	49.9	50.1	50.2
Germany	46.4	48.3	50.2	51.2	52.3	52.2	51.9	54.0	53.0	53.5	54.2	53.2	52.4	52.5
Greece	35.3	35.1	35.6	35.8	35.8	36.1	35.7	38.4	38.1	37.7	37.7	39.5	40.4	41.2
Hungary	..	..	51.4	52.0	52.0	51.6	50.7	54.6	55.8	53.7	50.8	51.8	51.1	51.0
Iceland	22.0	22.9	23.1	24.5	24.4	25.9	26.0	26.1	26.9	28.4	29.2	29.4	29.0	28.6
Ireland	40.0	38.4	36.9	36.1	33.9	33.0	32.4	28.9	25.8	24.5	24.2	25.0	23.5	23.1
Italy	49.2	49.9	50.3	50.8	51.5	47.5	47.2	46.4	46.0	46.0	45.0	45.4	45.4	45.2
Japan	21.2	21.6	19.5	19.4	20.7	19.6	24.0	24.8	24.9	30.5	27.4	27.3	27.7	28.8
Korea	..	..	6.9	6.3	12.4	14.7	16.1	16.4	16.4	16.1	16.3	17.2	17.3	18.1
Luxembourg	34.9	35.1	34.3	34.5	35.2	33.8	34.6	38.6	37.0	34.2	34.7	35.1	35.9	36.5
Mexico	26.6	26.5	27.2	25.4	20.8	21.9	14.1	12.6	13.2	15.8	16.8	15.3	14.7	15.0
Netherlands	45.7	45.6	44.8	43.8	43.6	43.5	44.3	39.7	37.2	37.4	37.1	38.8	38.9	44.4
New Zealand	24.0	24.3	24.5	22.3	21.6	20.0	19.4	19.4	19.4	19.5	19.7	20.0	20.4	20.9
Norway	36.8	36.9	37.5	37.6	37.4	37.5	37.3	38.6	39.2	38.6	38.1	38.1	37.2	37.3
Poland	44.1	..	44.7	44.7	43.9	43.2	43.0	43.2	42.9	42.9	43.1	43.4	43.5	43.7
Portugal	33.3	34.1	33.7	33.8	33.9	33.8	33.4	37.3	36.4	36.6	36.8	36.8	36.3	36.3
Slovak Republic	..	..	..	..	..	..	..	41.8	42.8	42.5	42.9	42.5	38.3	38.5
Spain	38.0	38.8	38.5	38.8	39.0	39.0	37.5	38.6	38.8	39.1	38.5	38.7	38.9	39.1
Sweden	45.6	46.8	49.3	50.2	50.7	50.7	50.5	50.1	49.1	47.8	48.2	48.4	48.1	47.9
Switzerland	28.7	28.7	30.6	30.4	30.0	30.0	29.8	30.0	30.1	30.1	29.7	29.4	29.5	29.7
Turkey	40.0	36.1	35.3	38.3	40.7	39.8	30.3	40.4	43.6	42.5	42.2	42.8	42.8	42.8
United Kingdom	32.6	33.3	33.4	32.6	32.0	32.0	30.8	32.2	31.9	32.0	33.5	33.6	33.7	33.9
United States	31.2	31.2	31.0	31.1	31.1	31.0	31.1	29.5	29.4	29.2	29.0	29.0	28.9	28.9
EU15 average	42.3	43.1	43.3	43.4	43.5	43.0	42.7	43.4	42.4	42.0	42.0	42.2	42.2	42.6
OECD average	37.6	38.0	37.7	37.5	37.7	37.4	36.8	37.8	37.4	37.4	37.3	37.4	37.2	37.5

StatLink ⟨≡⟩ http://dx.doi.org/10.1787/275613070451

Taxes on the average worker
As a percentage of labour cost

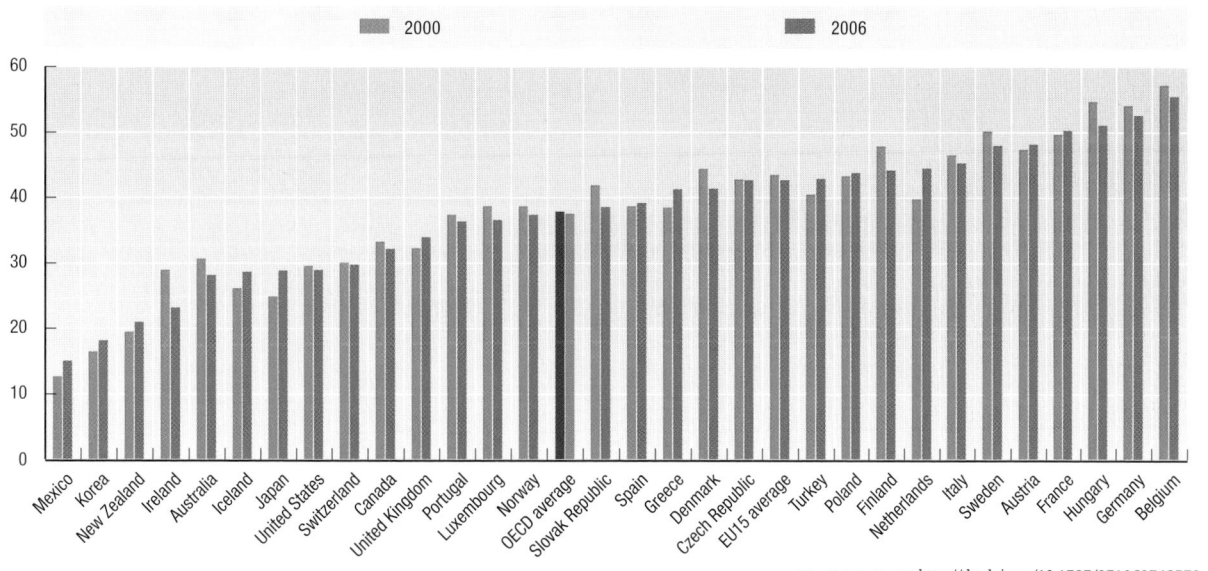

StatLink ⟨≡⟩ http://dx.doi.org/10.1787/271060748570

QUALITY OF LIFE

HEALTH
LIFE EXPECTANCY
INFANT MORTALITY
OBESITY

LEISURE
TOURISM: HOTEL NIGHTS
RECREATION AND CULTURE

SOCIETY
YOUTH INACTIVITY
INCOME INEQUALITY
PRISON POPULATION

TRANSPORT
ROAD NETWORK
ROAD MOTOR VEHICLES AND ROAD FATALITIES

LIFE EXPECTANCY

Life expectancy at birth remains one of the most frequently quoted indicators of health status.

Gains in life expectancy in OECD countries in recent decades, reflecting sharp reductions in mortality rates, can be attributed to a number of factors, including rising living standards, improved lifestyle and better education, as well as greater access to quality health services. Other factors, such as better nutrition, sanitation and housing also played a role, particularly in countries with developing economies.

It is difficult to estimate the relative contribution of the numerous non-medical and medical factors that might affect variations in life expectancy over time and across countries. Higher national income (as measured by GDP per capita) is generally associated with higher life expectancy at birth across OECD countries, although the relationship is less pronounced at higher levels of income.

Definition

Life expectancy measures how long on average people would live based on a given set of age-specific death rates. However, the actual age-specific death rates of any particular birth cohort cannot be known in advance. If age-specific death rates are falling (as has been the case over the past decades in OECD countries), actual life spans will be higher than life expectancy calculated with current death rates.

Comparability

Each country calculates its life expectancy according to methodologies that can vary somewhat. These differences in methodology can affect the comparability of reported life expectancy estimates, as different methods can change a country's estimates by a fraction of a year.

Long-term trends

On average across OECD countries, life expectancy at birth for the whole population reached 78.6 years in 2005, a full ten years greater than in 1960. In one-third of OECD countries, life expectancy at birth exceeded 80 years in 2005. The country with the highest life expectancy was Japan, with a life expectancy for women and men combined of 82.1 years. At the other end of the scale, life expectancy in OECD countries was the lowest in Turkey, followed by Hungary. However, while life expectancy in Hungary has increased only modestly since 1960, it has increased sharply in Turkey, rapidly catching up with the OECD average.

The gender gap in life expectancy stood at 5.7 years on average across OECD countries in 2005, with life expectancy reaching 75.7 years among men and 81.4 years among women. This gender gap increased by half-a-year on average across countries between 1960 and 2005. But this result hides different trends between earlier and later decades. While the gender gap in life expectancy increased substantially in many countries during the 1960s and the 1970s, it narrowed during the past 25 years, reflecting higher gains in life expectancy among men than among women in most OECD countries. The narrowing of the gender gap in life expectancy over the past 25 years can been attributed at least partly to the narrowing of differences in risk-increasing behaviours, such as smoking, between men and women, accompanied by sharp reductions in mortality rates from cardio-vascular diseases among men.

Source

- OECD (2007), *OECD Health Data 2007*, OECD, Paris.

Further information

Analytical publications

- OECD (2002), *Measuring Up: Improving Health System Performance in OECD Countries*, OECD, Paris.
- OECD (2003), *A Disease-based Comparison of Health Systems: What is Best and at what Cost?*, OECD, Paris.
- OECD (2004), *The OECD Health Project: Towards High-Performing Health Systems*, OECD, Paris.

Statistical publications

- OECD (2007), *Health at a Glance 2007: OECD Indicators*, OECD, Paris.
- OECD (2007), *Society at a Glance: OECD Social Indicators – 2006 Edition*, OECD, Paris.

Online databases

- *OECD Health Data.*

Websites

- OECD Health Data, *www.oecd.org/health/healthdata*.

Life expectancy at birth: total
Number of years

	1960	1970	1980	1990	1995	2000	2001	2002	2003	2004	2005
Australia	70.9	70.8	74.6	77.0	77.9	79.3	79.7	80.0	80.3	80.6	80.9
Austria	68.7	70.0	72.6	75.5	76.6	78.1	78.6	78.8	78.8	79.3	79.5
Belgium	70.6	71.0	73.4	76.1	76.8	77.8	78.1	78.2	78.3	78.5	78.7
Canada	71.3	72.9	75.3	77.6	78.1	79.3	79.6	79.7	79.9	80.2	..
Czech Republic	70.7	69.6	70.3	71.5	73.2	75.0	75.3	75.4	75.4	75.8	76.0
Denmark	72.4	73.3	74.3	74.9	75.3	76.9	77.0	77.2	77.5	77.6	77.9
Finland	69.0	70.8	73.4	74.9	76.5	77.6	78.1	78.2	78.5	78.8	78.9
France	70.3	72.2	74.3	76.9	77.9	79.0	79.2	79.4	79.4	80.3	80.3
Germany	69.6	70.4	72.9	75.2	76.5	78.0	78.4	78.3	78.6	78.6	79.0
Greece	69.9	72.0	74.5	77.1	77.7	78.0	78.5	78.7	78.9	79.1	79.3
Hungary	68.0	69.2	69.1	69.4	69.9	71.7	72.3	72.6	72.6	72.8	72.8
Iceland	72.9	74.3	76.7	78.0	78.0	80.1	80.2	80.6	81.2	81.0	81.2
Ireland	70.0	71.2	72.9	74.9	75.7	76.5	77.1	77.8	78.3	..	79.5
Italy	69.8	72.0	74.0	76.9	78.1	79.6	79.8	79.9	79.7	..	80.4
Japan	67.8	72.0	76.1	78.9	79.6	81.2	81.5	81.8	81.8	82.1	82.1
Korea	52.4	62.2	65.9	71.4	73.5	76.0	76.4	77.0	77.4	78.0	78.5
Luxembourg	69.4	70.3	72.5	75.4	76.6	78.0	78.0	78.2	78.0	..	79.3
Mexico	57.5	60.9	67.2	71.2	72.7	74.1	74.4	74.6	74.9	75.2	75.5
Netherlands	73.5	73.7	75.9	77.0	77.5	78.0	78.3	78.4	78.6	79.2	79.4
New Zealand	71.3	71.5	73.2	75.4	77.1	78.7	78.7	78.7	79.6	79.6	79.6
Norway	73.6	74.2	75.8	76.6	77.8	78.7	78.9	79.0	79.6	79.9	80.1
Poland	67.8	70.0	70.2	70.7	72.0	73.9	74.3	74.6	74.7	75.0	75.1
Portugal	64.0	67.5	71.5	73.9	75.2	76.6	76.9	77.2	77.4	77.8	78.2
Slovak Republic	70.6	69.8	70.6	71.0	72.4	73.3	73.6	73.8	73.9	74.1	74.0
Spain	69.8	72.0	75.6	76.8	77.9	79.2	79.5	79.6	80.3	80.5	80.7
Sweden	73.1	74.7	75.8	77.6	78.8	79.7	79.9	79.9	80.2	80.6	80.6
Switzerland	71.6	73.8	76.2	77.4	78.5	79.8	80.2	80.4	80.6	81.2	81.3
Turkey	48.3	54.2	58.1	66.1	67.9	70.5	70.6	70.8	71.0	71.2	71.4
United Kingdom	70.8	71.9	73.2	75.7	76.6	77.8	78.1	78.2	78.5	78.9	79.0
United States	69.9	70.9	73.7	75.3	75.7	76.8	77.1	77.2	77.5	77.8	..
OECD average	68.5	70.3	72.7	74.9	75.9	77.3	77.6	77.8	78.0	78.4	78.6
Brazil	..	..	62.6	66.6	68.5	70.4	70.7	71.0	71.3	71.6	71.9
China	..	..	..	..	..	..	..	..	..	..	73.0
Russian Federation	..	..	..	..	64.5	65.3	65.2	65.0	64.9	65.3	65.3

StatLink http://dx.doi.org/10.1787/275627145125

Life expectancy at birth: total
Number of years

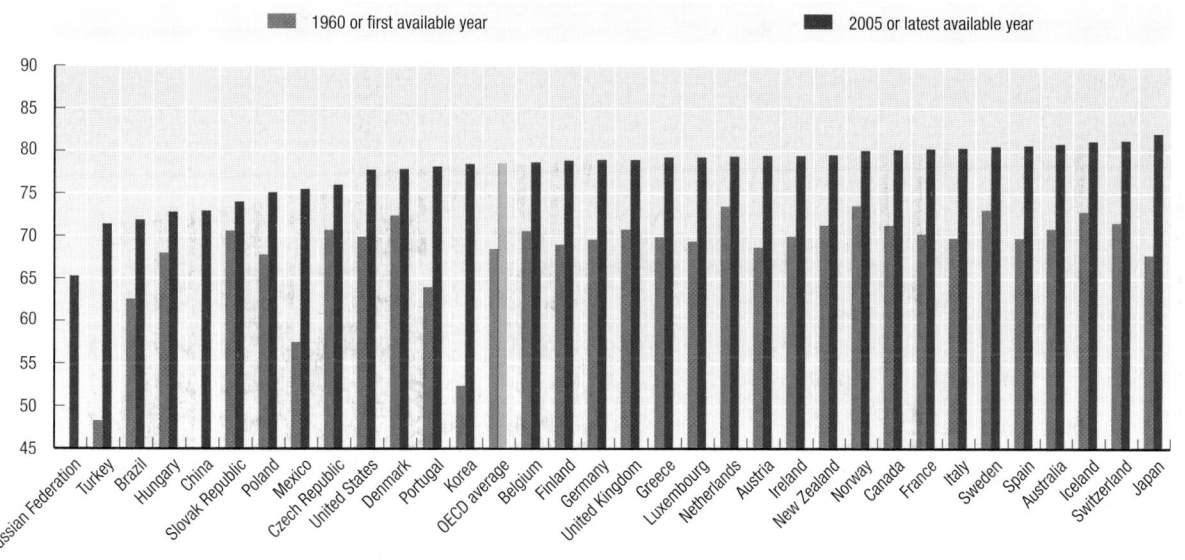

■ 1960 or first available year   ■ 2005 or latest available year

StatLink http://dx.doi.org/10.1787/271080301538

Life expectancy at birth: men
Number of years

	1960	1970	1980	1990	1995	2000	2001	2002	2003	2004	2005
Australia	67.9	67.4	71.0	73.9	75.0	76.6	77.0	77.4	77.8	78.1	78.5
Austria	65.4	66.5	69.0	72.2	73.3	75.1	75.6	75.8	75.9	76.4	76.7
Belgium	67.7	67.8	70.0	72.7	73.4	74.6	74.9	75.1	75.3	75.6	75.8
Canada	68.4	69.3	71.7	74.4	75.1	76.7	77.0	77.2	77.4	77.8	..
Czech Republic	67.9	66.1	66.8	67.6	69.7	71.6	72.1	72.1	72.1	72.6	72.9
Denmark	70.4	70.7	71.2	72.0	72.7	74.5	74.7	74.8	75.1	75.2	75.6
Finland	65.5	66.5	69.2	70.9	72.8	74.2	74.6	74.9	75.1	75.3	75.5
France	67.0	68.4	70.2	72.8	73.9	75.3	75.5	75.8	75.9	76.7	76.7
Germany	66.9	67.2	69.6	72.0	73.3	75.0	75.5	75.4	75.7	75.7	76.2
Greece	67.3	70.1	72.2	74.6	75.0	75.5	75.9	76.2	76.5	76.6	76.8
Hungary	65.9	66.3	65.5	65.1	65.3	67.4	68.1	68.4	68.4	68.6	68.6
Iceland	70.7	71.2	73.7	75.4	75.9	78.4	78.1	78.7	79.7	79.2	79.2
Ireland	68.1	68.8	70.1	72.1	72.9	73.9	74.5	75.2	75.8	..	77.1
Italy	67.2	69.0	70.6	73.6	74.9	76.6	76.7	76.8	76.8	..	77.6
Japan	65.3	69.3	73.4	75.9	76.4	77.7	78.1	78.3	78.4	78.6	78.6
Korea	51.1	58.7	61.8	67.3	69.6	72.3	72.8	73.4	73.9	74.5	75.1
Luxembourg	66.5	67.1	69.1	72.3	73.0	74.8	75.2	74.9	75.0	..	76.2
Mexico	55.8	58.5	64.1	68.3	70.0	71.6	71.9	72.1	72.4	72.7	73.0
Netherlands	71.5	70.8	72.5	73.8	74.6	75.5	75.8	76.0	76.2	76.9	77.2
New Zealand	68.7	68.3	70.0	72.4	74.4	76.3	76.3	76.3	77.5	77.5	77.5
Norway	71.3	71.0	72.3	73.4	74.8	76.0	76.2	76.4	77.1	77.5	77.7
Poland	64.9	66.6	66.0	66.2	67.6	69.7	70.2	70.4	70.5	70.7	70.8
Portugal	61.2	64.2	67.7	70.4	71.6	73.2	73.5	73.8	74.2	74.5	74.9
Slovak Republic	68.4	66.7	66.8	66.6	68.4	69.1	69.5	69.8	69.9	70.3	70.1
Spain	67.4	69.2	72.5	73.3	74.3	75.8	76.1	76.2	76.9	77.2	77.4
Sweden	71.2	72.2	72.8	74.8	76.2	77.4	77.6	77.7	77.9	78.4	78.4
Switzerland	68.7	70.7	72.8	74.0	75.3	76.9	77.4	77.8	78.0	78.6	78.7
Turkey	46.3	52.0	55.8	63.8	65.6	68.1	68.2	68.4	68.6	68.8	68.9
United Kingdom	67.9	68.7	70.2	72.9	74.0	75.4	75.7	75.9	76.2	76.7	76.9
United States	66.6	67.1	70.0	71.8	72.5	74.1	74.4	74.5	74.8	75.2	..
OECD average	66.0	67.2	69.3	71.6	72.7	74.3	74.6	74.9	75.2	75.6	75.7
Brazil	..	..	59.6	62.8	64.8	66.7	67.0	67.3	67.6	67.9	68.1
Russian Federation	..	..	..	..	58.1	59.0	58.9	58.7	58.6	58.9	58.9

StatLink ⟨⟨⟩ http://dx.doi.org/10.1787/275648340687

Life expectancy at birth: men
Number of years, 2005 or latest available year

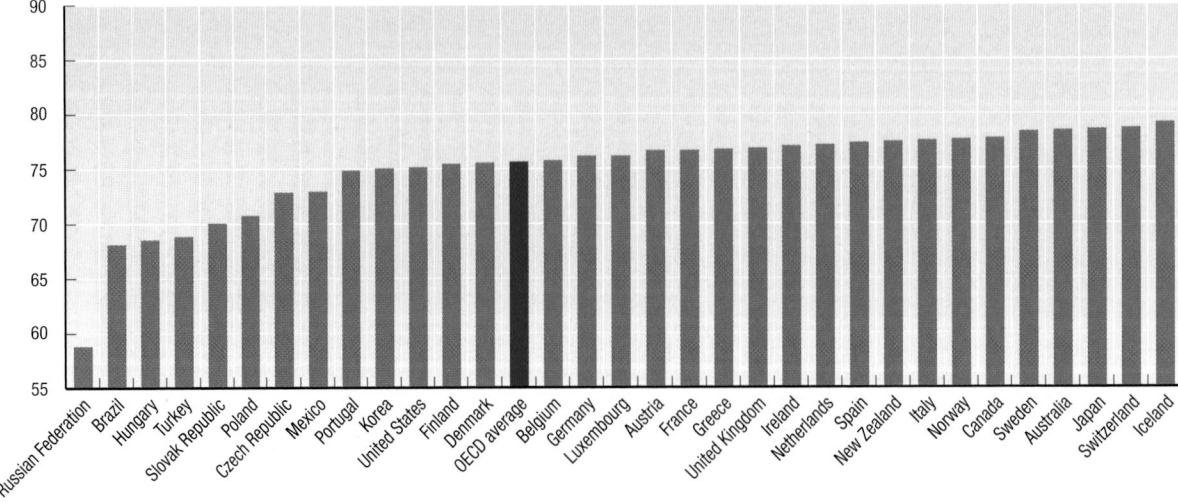

StatLink ⟨⟨⟩ http://dx.doi.org/10.1787/271116608026

Life expectancy at birth: women
Number of years

	1960	1970	1980	1990	1995	2000	2001	2002	2003	2004	2005
Australia	73.9	74.2	78.1	80.1	80.8	82.0	82.4	82.6	82.8	83.0	83.3
Austria	71.9	73.4	76.1	78.8	79.9	81.1	81.5	81.7	81.6	82.1	82.2
Belgium	73.5	74.2	76.8	79.4	80.2	80.9	81.2	81.2	81.3	81.5	81.6
Canada	74.2	76.4	78.9	80.8	81.1	81.9	82.1	82.1	82.4	82.6	..
Czech Republic	73.4	73.0	73.9	75.4	76.6	78.4	78.5	78.7	78.7	79.0	79.1
Denmark	74.4	75.9	77.3	77.7	77.8	79.3	79.3	79.5	79.9	79.9	80.2
Finland	72.5	75.0	77.6	78.9	80.2	81.0	81.5	81.5	81.8	82.3	82.3
France	73.6	75.9	78.4	80.9	81.8	82.7	82.9	83.0	82.9	83.8	83.8
Germany	72.4	73.6	76.1	78.4	79.7	81.0	81.3	81.2	81.4	81.4	81.8
Greece	72.4	73.8	76.8	79.5	80.3	80.5	81.0	81.1	81.3	81.5	81.7
Hungary	70.1	72.1	72.7	73.7	74.5	75.9	76.4	76.7	76.7	76.9	76.9
Iceland	75.0	77.3	79.7	80.5	80.0	81.8	82.2	82.5	82.7	82.7	83.1
Ireland	71.9	73.5	75.6	77.6	78.4	79.1	79.6	80.3	80.7	..	81.8
Italy	72.3	74.9	77.4	80.1	81.3	82.5	82.8	82.9	82.5	..	83.2
Japan	70.2	74.7	78.8	81.9	82.9	84.6	84.9	85.2	85.3	85.6	85.5
Korea	53.7	65.6	70.0	75.5	77.4	79.6	80.0	80.5	80.8	81.4	81.9
Luxembourg	72.2	73.4	75.9	78.5	80.2	81.1	80.7	81.5	81.0	..	82.3
Mexico	59.2	63.2	70.2	74.1	75.3	76.5	76.8	77.1	77.4	77.6	77.9
Netherlands	75.4	76.5	79.2	80.1	80.4	80.5	80.7	80.7	80.9	81.4	81.6
New Zealand	73.9	74.6	76.3	78.3	79.7	81.1	81.1	81.1	81.7	81.7	81.7
Norway	75.8	77.3	79.2	79.8	80.8	81.4	81.5	81.5	82.0	82.3	82.5
Poland	70.6	73.3	74.4	75.2	76.4	78.0	78.3	78.7	78.8	79.2	79.4
Portugal	66.8	70.8	75.2	77.4	78.7	80.0	80.3	80.5	80.5	81.0	81.4
Slovak Republic	72.7	72.9	74.3	75.4	76.3	77.4	77.7	77.7	77.8	77.8	77.9
Spain	72.2	74.8	78.6	80.3	81.5	82.5	82.8	82.9	83.6	83.7	83.9
Sweden	74.9	77.1	78.8	80.4	81.4	82.0	82.1	82.1	82.5	82.7	82.8
Switzerland	74.5	76.9	79.6	80.7	81.7	82.6	83.0	83.0	83.1	83.7	83.9
Turkey	50.3	56.3	60.3	68.3	70.2	72.8	73.0	73.2	73.4	73.6	73.8
United Kingdom	73.7	75.0	76.2	78.5	79.2	80.2	80.4	80.5	80.7	81.1	81.1
United States	73.1	74.7	77.4	78.8	78.9	79.5	79.8	79.9	80.1	80.4	..
OECD average	71.0	73.3	76.0	78.2	79.1	80.3	80.5	80.7	80.9	81.2	81.4
Brazil	..	..	65.7	70.4	72.3	74.3	74.6	74.9	75.2	75.5	75.8
Russian Federation	..	..	..	..	71.6	72.3	72.2	71.9	71.8	72.3	72.4

StatLink 🔗 http://dx.doi.org/10.1787/275658262653

Life expectancy at birth: women
Number of years, 2005 or latest available year

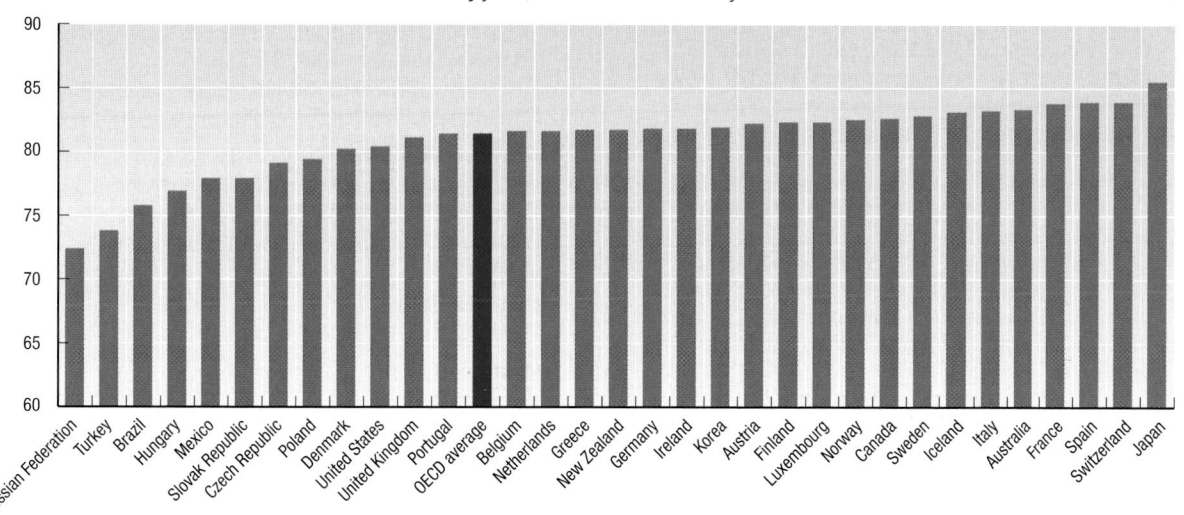

StatLink 🔗 http://dx.doi.org/10.1787/271124617544

INFANT MORTALITY

Numerous studies have taken infant mortality rates as a health outcome to examine the effect of a variety of medical and non-medical determinants of health. The infant mortality rate, the rate at which babies of less than one year of age die, reflects the effect of economic and social conditions on the health of mothers and newborns as well as the effectiveness of health systems. The fact that some countries with a high level of health expenditure do not necessarily exhibit low levels of infant mortality has led to the conclusion that more health spending is not necessarily required to obtain better results. A body of research suggests that many factors beyond the quality and efficiency of the health system, such as income inequality, social environment, and individual lifestyles and attitudes, influence infant mortality rates.

Definition

The infant mortality rate is the number of deaths of children under one year of age expressed per 1 000 live births. Neonatal mortality refers to the death of children under 28 days.

Comparability

Some of the international variation in infant and neonatal mortality rates may be due to variations among countries in registering practices of premature infants (whether they are reported as live births or fetal deaths). In several countries, such as in the United States, Canada, Japan and the Nordic countries, very premature babies with relatively low odds of survival are registered as live births, which increases mortality rates compared with other countries that do not register them as live births.

Long-term trends

All OECD countries have achieved remarkable progress in reducing infant mortality rates from the levels of 1970, when the average was approaching 30 deaths per 1 000 live births. The OECD average in 2005 stood at 5.5 deaths per 1 000 live births, which equates to a reduction of over 80% since 1970. Portugal has seen its infant mortality rate reduced by over 90% since 1970, moving from the country with the highest rate in Europe to one with an infant mortality rate among the lowest in the OECD in 2005. Large reductions in infant mortality rates have also been observed in Korea. On the other hand, the reduction in infant mortality rates has been slower in the Netherlands and the United States.

Around two-thirds of the deaths that occur during the first year of life are neonatal deaths (i.e. during the first four weeks). Congenital malformations, prematurity and other conditions arising during pregnancy are the principal factors contributing to neonatal mortality in developed countries. With an increasing number of women deferring childbearing and the rise in multiple births linked with fertility treatments, the number of pre-term births has tended to increase. In a number of higher-income countries, this has contributed to a leveling-off of the downward trend in infant mortality rates over the past few years. For deaths beyond a month (post neonatal mortality), there tends to be a greater range of causes – the most common being SIDS (sudden infant death syndrome), birth defects, infections and accidents.

Source

- OECD (2007), *OECD Health Data 2007*, OECD, Paris.

Further information

Analytical publications

- OECD (2004), *The OECD Health Project: Towards High-Performing Health Systems*, OECD, Paris.
- OECD (2004), *The OECD Health Project: Towards High-Performing Health Systems – Policy Studies*, OECD, Paris.

Statistical publications

- OECD (2006), *Economic Valuation of Environmental Health Risks to Children*, OECD, Paris.
- OECD (2007), *Health at a Glance 2007: OECD Indicators*, OECD, Paris.

Online databases

- *OECD Health Data.*

Websites

- OECD Health Data, *www.oecd.org/health/healthdata.*

Infant mortality
Deaths per 1 000 live births

	1970	1980	1990	1995	2000	2001	2002	2003	2004	2005
Australia	17.9	10.7	8.2	5.7	5.2	5.3	5.0	4.8	4.7	5.0
Austria	25.9	14.3	7.8	5.4	4.8	4.8	4.1	4.5	4.5	4.2
Belgium	21.1	12.1	6.5	5.9	4.8	4.5	4.4	4.3	4.3	3.7
Canada	18.8	10.4	6.8	6.1	5.3	5.2	5.4	5.3	5.3	5.4
Czech Republic	20.2	16.9	10.8	7.7	4.1	4.0	4.1	3.9	3.7	3.4
Denmark	14.2	8.4	7.5	5.1	5.3	4.9	4.4	4.4	4.4	4.4
Finland	13.2	7.6	5.6	3.9	3.8	3.2	3.0	3.1	3.3	3.0
France	18.2	10.0	7.3	4.9	4.4	4.5	4.1	4.0	3.9	3.6
Germany	22.5	12.4	7.0	5.3	4.4	4.3	4.2	4.2	4.1	3.9
Greece	29.6	17.9	9.7	8.1	5.4	5.1	5.1	4.0	4.1	3.8
Hungary	35.9	23.2	14.8	10.7	9.2	8.1	7.2	7.3	6.6	6.2
Iceland	13.3	7.8	5.8	6.0	3.0	2.7	2.3	2.4	2.8	2.3
Ireland	19.5	11.1	8.2	6.4	6.2	5.7	5.0	5.3	4.6	4.0
Italy	29.0	14.6	8.2	6.2	4.5	4.6	4.3	3.9	4.1	4.7
Japan	13.1	7.5	4.6	4.3	3.2	3.1	3.0	3.0	2.8	2.8
Korea	45.0	17.0	10.0	7.7	6.2	..	5.3	..	..	..
Luxembourg	25.0	11.4	7.3	5.6	5.1	5.8	5.1	4.9	3.9	2.6
Mexico	79.4	51.0	36.2	27.6	23.3	22.4	21.4	20.5	19.7	18.8
Netherlands	12.7	8.6	7.1	5.5	5.1	5.4	5.0	4.8	4.4	4.9
New Zealand	16.7	13.0	8.4	6.7	6.1	5.3	5.6	4.9	5.6	5.1
Norway	12.7	8.1	6.9	4.0	3.8	3.9	3.5	3.4	3.2	3.1
Poland	36.7	25.5	19.3	13.6	8.1	7.7	7.5	7.0	6.8	6.4
Portugal	55.5	24.2	11.0	7.5	5.5	5.0	5.0	4.1	3.8	3.5
Slovak Republic	25.7	20.9	12.0	11.0	8.6	6.2	7.6	7.9	6.8	7.2
Spain	28.1	12.3	7.6	5.5	4.4	4.1	4.1	3.9	4.0	4.1
Sweden	11.0	6.9	6.0	4.1	3.4	3.7	3.3	3.1	3.1	2.4
Switzerland	15.1	9.1	6.8	5.0	4.9	5.0	5.0	4.3	4.2	4.2
Turkey	145.0	117.5	55.4	43.0	28.9	27.8	26.7	28.7 |	24.6	23.6
United Kingdom	18.5	12.1	7.9	6.2	5.6	5.5	5.2	5.3	5.0	5.1
United States	20.0	12.6	9.2	7.6	6.9	6.8	7.0	6.9	6.8	..
OECD average	28.7	17.8	11.0	8.4	6.7	6.4	6.1	6.0	5.7	5.5
Brazil	..	69.1	47.0	37.9	30.1	29.2	28.4	27.5	26.6	25.8
China	..	..	..	..	..	..	..	..	..	24.3
Russian Federation	..	..	..	18.1	15.3	14.6	13.3	12.4	11.6	11.0

StatLink ⬛⬛⬛ http://dx.doi.org/10.1787/275672465188

Infant mortality
Deaths per 1 000 live births, 2005 or latest available year

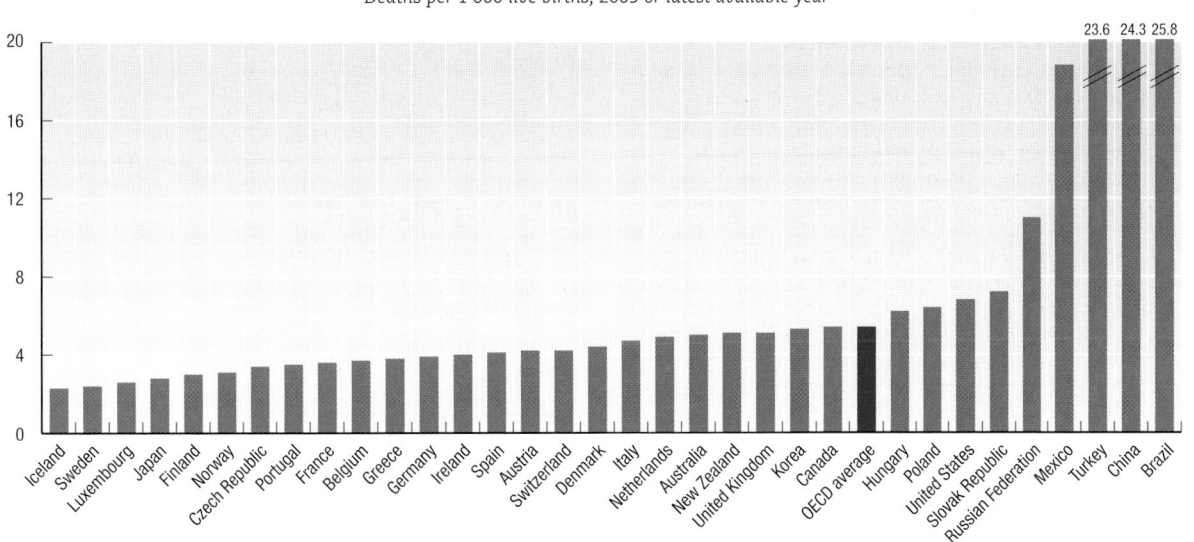

StatLink ⬛⬛⬛ http://dx.doi.org/10.1787/271130730173

OBESITY

Obesity is a known risk factor for numerous health problems, including hypertension, high cholesterol, diabetes, cardiovascular diseases, respiratory problems (asthma), musculoskeletal diseases (arthritis) and some forms of cancer. At an individual level, several factors can lead to obesity, including excessive calorie consumption, lack of physical activity, genetic predisposition and disorders of the endocrine system.

Because obesity is associated with higher risks of chronic illnesses, it is linked to significant additional health care costs.

Definition

The most frequently used measure of overweight and obesity is based on the body mass index (BMI), which is a single number that evaluates an individual's weight status in relation to height (weight/height^2, with weight in kilograms and height in meters). Based on the WHO current classification, adults with a BMI between 25 and 30 are defined as overweight, and those with a BMI over 30 as obese.

Comparability

The BMI classification may not be suitable for all ethnic groups, who may have equivalent levels of risk at lower BMI (for example, Asians) or higher BMI. The thresholds for adults are also not suitable to measure overweight and obesity among children.

For most countries, data on obesity are self-reported through population-based health interview surveys. The exceptions are Australia, the Czech Republic (2005), Luxembourg, New Zealand, the United Kingdom and the United States, where the data are derived from health examinations whereby actual measures are taken of people's height and weight. These differences in data collection methodologies seriously limit data comparability. Estimates from health examinations are generally higher and more reliable than those coming from health interviews.

Long-term trends

Half or more of the adult population is now defined as either being overweight or obese in no less than 15 OECD countries: Mexico, the United States, the United Kingdom, Australia, Greece, New Zealand, Luxembourg, Hungary, the Czech Republic, Canada, Germany, Portugal, Finland, Spain and Iceland. By comparison, overweight and obesity rates are much lower in the OECD's two Asian countries (Japan and Korea) and in some European countries (France and Switzerland), although overweight and obesity rates are also increasing in these countries. Focusing only on obesity, the prevalence of obesity among adults varies from a low of 3% in Japan and Korea to over 30% in the United States and Mexico.

Based on consistent measures of obesity over time, the rate of obesity has more than doubled over the past twenty years in the United States, while it has almost tripled in Australia and more than tripled in the United Kingdom. The obesity rate in many Western European countries has also increased substantially over the past decade.

In all countries, more men are overweight than women, but in almost half of OECD countries, more women are obese than men. Taking overweight and obesity together, the rate for women exceeds that for men in only two countries – Mexico and Turkey.

Source

- OECD (2007), *OECD Health Data 2007*, OECD, Paris.

Further information

Analytical publications

- OECD (2004), *The OECD Health Project: Towards High-Performing Health Systems*, OECD, Paris.
- OECD (2004), *The OECD Health Project: Towards High-Performing Health Systems – Policy Studies*, OECD, Paris.

Statistical publications

- OECD (2007), *Health at a Glance 2007: OECD Indicators*, OECD, Paris.

Online Databases

- *OECD Health Data*.

Websites

- OECD Health Data, *www.oecd.org/health/healthdata*.
- Session on Obesity and Health at the OECD Forum 2004, *www.oecd.org/forum2004*.

Overweight and obese population aged 15 and above

As a percentage of population aged 15 and above, 2005 or latest available year

	Females			Males			Total		
	Overweight	Obese	Overweight and obese	Overweight	Obese	Overweight and obese	Overweight	Obese	Overweight and obese
Australia	28.2	21.4	49.6	45.3	21.9	67.2	36.7	21.7	58.4
Austria	21.3	9.1	30.4	54.3	9.1	63.4	37.0	9.1	46.1
Belgium	24.4	13.4	37.8	38.7	11.9	50.6	31.4	12.7	44.1
Canada	24.7	19.0	43.7	39.3	17.0	56.3	31.9	18.0	49.9
Czech Republic	29.0	17.0	46.0	42.0	18.0	60.0	35.0	17.0	52.0
Denmark	26.4	11.8	38.2	40.9	11.0	51.9	33.2	11.4	44.6
Finland	26.6	13.5	40.1	44.8	14.9	59.7	35.0	14.1	49.2
France	19.6	9.3	29.0	31.1	9.8	40.5	25.1	9.5	34.6
Germany	28.7	12.8	41.5	43.5	14.4	57.9	36.0	13.6	49.6
Greece	29.9	18.2	48.1	41.1	26.0	67.1	35.2	21.9	57.1
Hungary	29.8	18.0	47.8	38.7	19.6	58.3	34.0	18.8	52.8
Iceland	28.0	12.4	40.4	44.6	12.4	57.0	35.9	12.4	48.3
Ireland	25.0	12.0	37.0	41.0	14.0	55.0	34.0	13.0	47.0
Italy	26.2	9.7	35.9	43.9	10.2	54.0	34.7	9.9	44.6
Japan	16.9	3.2	20.1	24.5	2.8	27.3	20.3	3.0	23.3
Korea	23.7	3.3	27.0	30.3	3.7	34.0	27.0	3.5	30.5
Luxembourg	25.4	18.5	43.9	41.1	18.8	59.9	34.6	18.6	53.3
Mexico	36.6	34.7	71.3	42.6	23.7	66.4	39.1	30.2	69.2
Netherlands	28.2	11.4	39.6	40.5	9.9	50.4	34.2	10.7	44.9
New Zealand	28.4	21.7	50.2	42.1	20.1	62.2	35.2	20.9	56.2
Norway	26.0	8.0	34.0	43.0	9.0	52.0	34.0	9.0	43.0
Poland	26.6	12.5	39.1	39.5	12.6	52.1	32.8	12.5	45.3
Portugal	31.8	14.0	45.8	42.3	11.4	53.7	36.8	12.8	49.6
Slovak Republic	24.9	15.6	40.5	42.0	15.2	57.2	32.2	15.4	47.6
Spain	27.6	13.4	40.9	43.5	12.9	56.3	35.3	13.1	48.4
Sweden	25.9	10.3	36.2	40.7	11.1	51.8	33.3	10.7	44.0
Switzerland	21.8	7.5	29.3	37.5	7.9	45.4	29.4	7.7	37.1
Turkey	28.9	14.5	43.4	33.6	9.7	43.3	31.6	12.0	43.4
United Kingdom	32.1	24.2	56.3	42.6	22.1	64.7	37.0	23.0	60.0
United States	28.6	33.2	61.8	39.7	31.1	70.8	34.1	32.2	66.3

StatLink http://dx.doi.org/10.1787/275676256538

Obese population aged 15 and above

As a percentage of population aged 15 and above, 2005 or latest available year

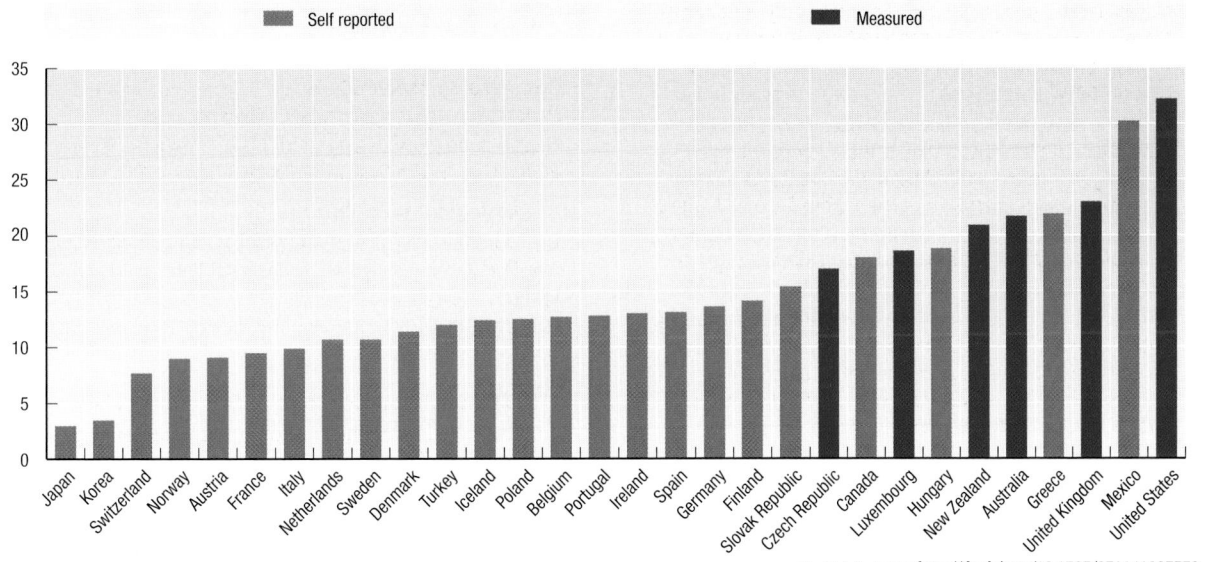

StatLink http://dx.doi.org/10.1787/271141387770

TOURISM: HOTEL NIGHTS

Arrivals of non-resident tourists in accommodation (hotel or similar establishments) is one of the standard measures of international tourism activity. It excludes domestic tourism.

Definition

This statistic refers to the number of non-residents who arrive in a hotel or similar establishment such as apartment-hotels, motels, roadside inns, beach hotels, residential clubs, boarding houses, and similar accommodation providing limited hotel services. Note that arrivals of non-resident tourists do not show the number of travellers. When a person visits the same country several times a year, each visit is counted as a separate arrival and if a person visits several countries during the course of a single trip, his/her arrival in each country is recorded as a separate arrival. Same day visitors are excluded as are tourists who stay with friends or relatives.

Comparability

Several OECD countries cannot provide statistics on "arrivals of non-resident tourists in hotels or similar establishments". For those countries, the statistics presented here are "arrivals of non-residents at national borders". Canada, China, India, Ireland and the United States report the number of non-resident tourist arrivals at their national borders; a tourist is a visitor who intends to stay for at least one night. The figures for Japan, Korea and New Zealand include the number of non-resident visitor arrivals at their national borders; a visitor includes overnight (tourist) and same day visitors. Australia (1990-1997 visitors and 1998-2006 tourists) and South Africa (1990-1994 visitors and 1995-2006 tourists) time series present mixed indicators.

Long-term trends

Over the last decade, the United States recorded the largest number of arrivals in hotels and similar establishments followed by China, France, Italy and Spain. Arrivals grew at 6% per year or more in Iceland, China, Spain, India, Japan, the Russian Federation and Turkey. The lowest rates of increase (less than 1% per year) were recorded in Norway, Denmark, Canada, the United Kingdom and the United States.

The UN World Tourism Organization (UNWTO) forecasts that international arrivals will reach over 1.56 billion by the year 2020. East Asia and the Pacific, South Asia, the Middle East, and Africa are forecasted to record growth at rates of over 5% per year, compared with the world average of 4.1%. The more mature tourism regions, Europe and the Americas, are expected to show lower than average growth rates. Europe will maintain the highest share of world arrivals, although there will be a decline from 60% of world arrivals in 1995 to 46% by 2020.

OECD member countries (eight out of ten of the main tourism destinations in the world are OECD countries) represent around 60% of international arrivals; this share of the world market will slightly decrease in the future due to new emerging destinations. However, the importance of the tourism economy in the OECD area continues to increase. Tourism now accounts for between 2 and 12 per cent of GDP, between 3 and 11 per cent of employment, and on average about 30% of service exports in OECD member countries.

Sources

- *The Statistical Office of the European Communities (Eurostat).*
- *World Tourism Organization (UNWTO).*

Further information

Analytical publications

- OECD (2006), *Climate Change in the European Alps: Adapting Winter Tourism and Natural Hazards Management*, OECD, Paris.
- OECD (2006), *Innovation and Growth in Tourism*, OECD, Paris.
- OECD (2008), *Tourism in OECD Countries 2008: Trends and Policies*, OECD, Paris.

Statistical publications

- Eurostat (2007), *Panorama on Tourism*, European Commission, Luxembourg.
- Eurostat (2007), *Tourism Statistics Pocket book*, European Commission, Luxembourg.
- UNWTO, *Tourism 2020 Vision*, UNWTO, Madrid.
- UNWTO (2007), *Yearbook of Tourism Statistics*, UNWTO, Madrid.

Methodological publications

- UN, Eurostat, OECD, UNWTO (2001), *Tourism Satellite Account: Recommended Methodological Framework*, OECD, Paris.
- UN, UNWTO (1994), *Recommandation on Tourism Statistics*, UN, New York.

Websites

- OECD, *www.oecd.org/cfe/tourism.*
- Eurostat, *http://ec.europa.eu/eurostat.*
- World Tourism Organization, *www.world-tourism.org.*

Arrivals of non-resident tourists staying in hotels and similar establishments
Thousands

	1993	1994	1995	1996	1997	1998	1999	2000	2001	2002	2003	2004	2005	2006
Australia	2 996	3 362	3 726	4 165	4 318	3 825	4 109	4 530	4 435	4 420	4 354	4 774	5 020	5 064
Austria	13 032	12 878	12 464	12 533	12 329	12 803	12 755	13 240	13 279	13 487	13 748	14 075	14 542	14 947
Belgium	3 719	3 947	4 138	4 469	4 710	4 859	4 983	5 163	5 117	5 323	5 261	5 385	5 409	5 665
Canada	15 105	15 972	16 932	17 286	17 669	18 870	19 411	19 627	19 679	20 057	17 534	19 145	18 770	18 265
Czech Republic	..	2 448	2 891	3 696	4 013	4 067	4 141	3 863	4 439	4 314	4 485	5 346	5 686	5 781
Denmark	..	..	..	1 307	1 317	1 305	1 268	1 347	1 310	1 284	1 294	1 363	1 350	1 356
Finland	1 447	1 633	1 587	1 537	1 618	1 655	1 613	1 751	1 774	1 796	1 800	1 825	1 828	2 045
France	26 270	27 121	27 018	27 096	29 625	32 339	34 267	36 474	35 097	36 093	32 520	33 988	35 003	32 506
Germany	12 071	12 269	12 683	13 042	13 745	14 457	14 965	16 719	15 754	15 672	15 979	17 620	18 761	20 630
Greece	6 209	6 659	6 250	5 973	6 785	7 276	7 229	7 767	6 997	6 654	6 574	6 313	7 143	7 548
Hungary	..	2 122	2 116	2 202	2 188	2 472	2 401	2 604	2 669	2 659	2 599	2 951	3 140	3 009
Iceland	..	..	..	311	354	400	431	451	465	513	569	615	643	714
Ireland	3 888	4 309	4 818	5 289	5 587	6 064	6 403	6 646	6 353	6 476	6 764	6 953	7 333	8 001
Italy	17 919	21 074	23 467	24 929	25 133	25 927	26 530	28 797	29 138	29 340	28 174	29 916	30 870	34 057
Japan	3 410	3 468	3 345	3 837	4 218	4 106	4 438	4 757	4 772	5 239	5 212	6 138	6 728	7 334
Korea	3 331	3 580	3 753	3 684	3 908	4 250	4 660	5 322	5 147	5 347	4 753	5 818	6 023	6 155
Luxembourg	507	492	496	461	508	525	580	589	577	599	581	613	667	673
Mexico	5 174	5 159	6 718	7 491	8 155	8 157	9 501	9 867	9 410	7 869	8 556	9 972	10 691	9 689
Netherlands	3 778	4 456	4 797	4 999	6 163	7 432	7 550	7 738	7 445	7 433	6 930	7 601	8 081	8 567
New Zealand	1 157	1 323	1 409	1 529	1 497	1 485	1 607	1 787	1 909	2 045	2 104	2 334	2 366	2 409
Norway	2 556	2 830	2 880	2 746	2 702	2 829	2 857	2 787	2 686	2 561	2 439	2 556	2 656	2 841
Poland	2 315	2 540	2 792	3 020	2 919	2 695	1 982	2 505	2 488	2 536	2 701	3 385	3 723	3 738
Portugal	3 372	3 809	4 000	4 069	4 314	4 974	4 911	5 119	4 934	5 060	4 906	5 201	5 355	5 883
Slovak Republic	536	680	735	758	660	701	767	836	927	1 041	1 043	1 094	1 203	1 292
Spain	12 914	15 310	16 286	17 008	18 250	20 199	26 799	27 150	27 012	26 611	27 249	27 620	29 029	34 412
Sweden	1 629	1 830	1 995	2 091	2 143	2 304	2 320	2 465	2 586	2 577	2 552	2 610	2 736	2 867
Switzerland	7 225	7 358	6 946	6 730	7 039	7 185	7 154	7 821	7 455	6 868	6 530	..	7 229	7 863
Turkey	4 072	3 716	4 617	6 440	9 382	7 539	4 805	6 789	8 769	9 859	8 983	10 962	12 937	11 883
United Kingdom	14 259	14 927	17 118	16 890	17 110	16 304	17 019	17 019	17 019	14 176	14 397	13 172	17 009	18 322
United States	45 779	44 753	43 490	46 636	47 875	46 377	48 510	51 237	46 927	43 581	41 218	46 086	49 206	50 978
Brazil	1 402	1 529	1 709	2 266	2 419	3 854	3 754	3 868	3 331	3 536	2 633	3 068	3 215	..
China	18 982	21 070	20 034	22 765	23 770	25 073	27 047	31 229	33 167	36 803	32 970	41 761	46 809	..
India	1 765	1 886	2 124	2 288	2 374	2 359	2 482	2 649	2 537	2 384	2 726	3 457	3 919	4 447
Russian Federation	..	..	5 311	5 496	6 489	6 282	7 102	7 410	3 215	3 231	3 101	3 275	3 438	4 416
South Africa	3 358	3 897	4 488	4 915	4 976	5 732	5 890	5 872	5 787	6 430	6 505	6 678	7 369	8 396

StatLink ᎎᏏ᠍Ꮮ http://dx.doi.org/10.1787/275707387207

Arrivals of non-resident tourist staying in hotels and similar establishments
Average annual growth in percentage, 1996-2006 or latest available period

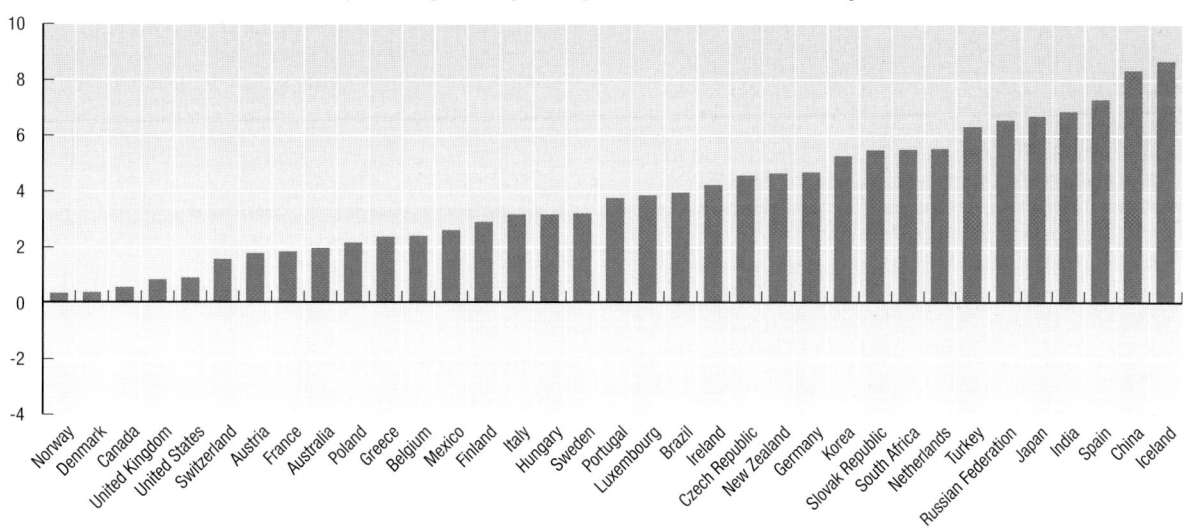

StatLink ᎎᏏ᠍Ꮮ http://dx.doi.org/10.1787/271202003416

RECREATION AND CULTURE

In general, percentages of GDP spent on recreation and culture are positively correlated with per capita income – the richer the country, the higher the percentage expenditure on culture and recreation – but there are some striking exceptions. Ireland (rich) spends relatively little on recreation and culture while the Czech Republic (poor) spends a rather high share.

Definition

Household expenditure on recreation and culture includes purchases of audio-visual, photographic and computer equipment; CDs and DVDs; musical instruments; camper vans; caravans; sports equipment; toys; domestic pets and related products; gardening tools and plants; newspapers; tickets to sporting matches, cinemas and theatres; and spending on gambling (including lottery tickets) less any winnings. It excludes expenditures on restaurants, hotels, and travel and holiday homes but includes package holidays.

Government expenditures include administration of sporting, recreational and cultural affairs as well as the maintenance of zoos, botanical gardens, public beaches and parks; support for broadcasting services and, where present, support for religious, fraternal, civic, youth and other social organisations (including the operation and repair of facilities and payment to clergy and other officers). Also included are grants to artists and arts companies. Capital outlays such as the construction of sports stadiums, public swimming pools, national theatres, opera houses and museums are included.

Comparability

The data in these tables are all taken from the OECD's national accounts database and are compiled according to a common set of definitions.

Long-term trends

In most countries, household expenditures on recreation and culture have remained fairly stable at around 5% of GDP over the last decade. Notable exceptions were New Zealand, the Slovak Republic and the United Kingdom where household expenditures grew much faster than average. In some countries, notably Ireland, Poland and the Netherlands, expenditures declined considerably as shares of GDP. By the end of the period, household expenditures were well above the OECD average in the United Kingdom, New Zealand, Australia and Austria and much below it in Mexico and Ireland.

Data on government expenditures on recreation, culture and religion are available for fewer countries. In most of these countries, government expenditure amounts to between 0.5 and 2% of GDP. By the end of the period, government expenditures were much higher than average in Luxembourg, Hungary, Denmark and (particularly) Iceland and below 0.5% of GDP in Japan and the United States. Over the period covered, they have grown quite rapidly in Korea, Belgium, and France but have fallen in Sweden and Norway.

The third table shows the combination of private and public expenditures on recreation and culture. As shares of GDP they are between 5 and 7% in most countries but somewhat higher in Iceland, the United Kingdom, New Zealand and Austria, and substantially lower in Ireland and Korea.

Source

- OECD (2007), *National Accounts of OECD Countries*, OECD, Paris.

Further information

Analytical publications

- OECD (2005), *Culture and Local Development*, OECD, Paris.

OECD FACTBOOK 2008 – ISBN 978-92-64-04054-0 – © OECD 2008

Household expenditure on recreation and culture
As a percentage of GDP

	1993	1994	1995	1996	1997	1998	1999	2000	2001	2002	2003	2004	2005	2006
Australia	6.7	6.9	7.2	7.2	7.3	7.3	7.2	7.3	7.1	7.2	7.2	7.1	6.9	..
Austria	6.7	6.6	6.4	6.5	6.5	6.7	6.9	6.9	6.9	6.9	6.8	6.7	6.6	6.5
Belgium	..	..	4.8	4.9	5.0	5.0	5.1	5.2	5.2	4.8	4.8	4.7	4.7	4.7
Canada	5.3	5.5	5.5	5.6	5.6	5.7	5.7	5.7	5.7	5.8	5.7	5.6	5.5	..
Czech Republic	..	..	5.5	5.8	6.4	6.3	6.2	6.1	6.2	6.0	6.2	6.0	5.9	5.6
Denmark	5.1	5.1	5.1	5.3	5.3	5.3	5.2	5.2	5.1	5.1	5.3	5.4	5.3	..
Finland	5.4	5.3	5.3	5.6	5.4	5.4	5.4	5.4	5.3	5.3	5.5	5.5	5.7	5.7
France	4.8	4.8	4.8	4.8	4.8	4.9	5.0	5.1	5.1	5.2	5.2	5.2	5.2	5.2
Germany	5.2	5.1	5.1	5.2	5.3	5.4	5.5	5.6	5.6	5.4	5.3	5.3	5.3	5.2
Hungary	..	..	..	..	..	..	..	4.1	4.2	4.2	4.2	4.2	4.3	4.3
Iceland	6.3	7.1	7.2	7.1	6.6	6.7	7.0	7.1	6.9	6.9	6.7	6.5	6.5	6.3
Ireland	..	..	4.0	4.1	3.7	3.4	3.1	3.4	3.4	3.0	3.0	3.1	3.1	..
Italy	4.3	4.3	4.2	4.3	4.3	4.4	4.5	4.5	4.4	4.3	4.2	4.3	4.1	4.1
Japan	..	..	..	5.6	5.8	5.8	5.8	6.1	6.2	6.2	6.2	6.2	6.1	..
Korea	4.0	4.2	4.3	4.2	4.0	3.4	3.6	4.1	4.2	4.4	4.0	3.6	3.7	3.7
Luxembourg	..	..	3.9	3.9	3.9	4.0	3.7	3.6	3.8	3.9	3.6	3.5	3.4	3.1
Mexico	2.3	2.2	1.9	1.8	1.9	2.0	2.0	2.0	2.0	1.9	1.9	2.0	..	..
Netherlands	5.4	5.3	5.2	5.3	5.3	5.5	5.6	5.5	5.4	5.3	5.1	5.0	4.8	4.8
New Zealand	5.7	6.1	6.3	6.5	6.7	6.9	7.0	7.2	7.1	..	..	..	..	..
Norway	5.1	5.2	5.4	5.5	5.4	5.8	5.8	5.2	5.3	5.5	5.6	5.5	5.1	..
Poland	..	..	4.8	5.3	5.1	5.3	5.1	5.2	4.6	4.5	4.6	4.6	4.0	..
Portugal	..	..	3.6	3.9	4.0	4.0	4.1	4.2	4.1	4.1	4.1	4.2	..	..
Slovak Republic	..	..	4.0	4.2	4.2	4.3	4.6	4.7	5.4	5.2	4.8	4.7	5.0	4.9
Spain	..	..	5.2	5.3	5.3	5.6	5.7	5.7	5.7	5.6	5.5	5.5	5.5	..
Sweden	5.2	5.1	5.0	5.0	5.1	5.3	5.5	5.6	5.6	5.5	5.5	5.4	5.3	..
Switzerland	5.4	5.4	5.4	5.3	5.3	5.2	5.2	5.1	5.1	5.1	5.1	5.0	4.9	4.7
United Kingdom	6.4	6.4	6.8	7.0	7.1	7.3	7.4	7.3	7.3	7.5	7.5	7.7	7.7	..
United States	5.7	5.9	6.1	6.2	6.2	6.2	6.3	6.4	6.4	6.4	6.4	6.4	6.4	6.4

StatLink http://dx.doi.org/10.1787/275710187238

Household expenditure on recreation and culture
As a percentage of GDP, 2005

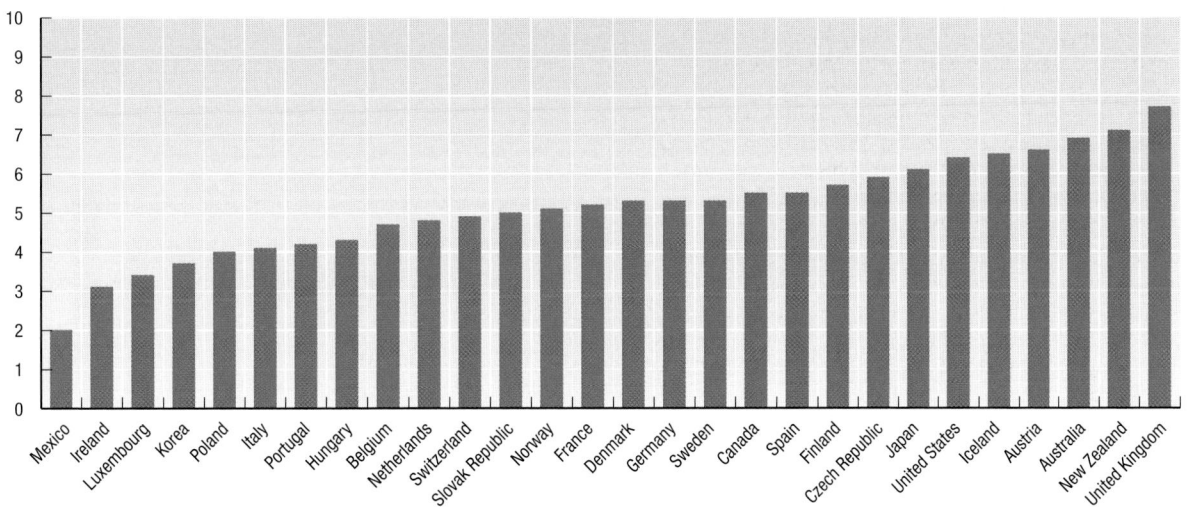

StatLink http://dx.doi.org/10.1787/271205205545

Government expenditure on recreation and culture

As a percentage of GDP

	1993	1994	1995	1996	1997	1998	1999	2000	2001	2002	2003	2004	2005	2006
Austria	..	..	1.2	1.1	1.1	1.1	1.1	1.0	1.1	1.0	1.0	1.0	0.9	1.0
Belgium	0.9	0.9	0.9	0.9	0.9	0.9	0.9	1.0	1.0	1.3	1.2	1.3	1.3	..
Czech Republic	..	..	1.2	1.3	1.1	1.1	1.0	1.0	1.1	1.3	1.3	1.2	1.2	..
Denmark	1.6	1.7	1.6	1.7	1.6	1.6	1.6	1.6	1.6	1.6	1.6	1.8	1.6	1.6
Finland	1.3	1.2	1.3	1.4	1.4	1.3	1.2	1.2	1.2	1.2	1.2	1.2	1.2	..
France	..	..	1.1	1.1	1.1	1.1	1.2	1.1	1.2	1.3	1.4	1.4	1.5	..
Germany	0.8	0.8	0.8	0.8	0.7	0.7	0.7	0.7	0.7	0.7	0.7	0.6	0.6	..
Hungary	..	..	..	..	..	..	..	..	1.6	1.8	1.8	1.8	1.6	..
Iceland	..	..	..	..	2.4	2.9	3.0	3.2	3.0	3.3	3.6	3.7	3.4	3.7
Ireland	0.4	0.5	0.4	0.5	0.4	0.5	0.5	0.5	0.6	0.6	0.5	0.5	0.5	..
Italy	0.8	0.8	0.8	0.9	0.9	0.9	0.9	0.9	0.8	0.8	0.8	0.9	0.8	..
Japan	..	..	..	0.2	0.2	0.2	0.2	0.2	0.2	0.2	0.2	0.2	0.2	..
Korea	..	..	0.4	0.4	0.5	0.6	0.6	0.7	0.7	0.6	0.8	0.8	0.8	..
Luxembourg	1.5	1.5	1.5	1.6	1.7	1.7	1.8	1.6	1.7	1.8	1.9	2.0	2.2	1.7
Netherlands	..	..	1.2	1.2	1.1	1.1	1.1	1.4	1.4	1.5	1.5	1.4	1.4	..
New Zealand	..	..	..	..	..	..	..	..	..	..	1.3	1.3	1.1	..
Norway	1.5	1.4	1.3	1.2	1.2	1.2	1.2	1.1	1.1	1.2	1.2	1.1	1.1	..
Poland	..	..	..	..	..	..	..	..	..	..	1.1	1.0	1.0	1.0	..
Portugal	..	..	..	..	..	..	1.2	1.1	1.1	1.1	1.1	1.1	1.1	..
Slovak Republic	..	..	..	..	..	..	..	..	..	..	1.1	1.2	..	..
Spain	..	..	..	..	..	..	1.4	1.4	1.4	1.4	1.4	1.4	1.4	..
Sweden	..	..	1.8	1.9	1.8	1.8	1.8	1.1	1.1	1.1	1.1	1.0	1.1	..
United Kingdom	1.0	1.0	0.9	0.9	0.8	0.8	1.0	1.0	1.0	1.0	0.9	0.9	0.9	..
United States	0.3	0.3	0.3	0.3	0.3	0.3	0.3	0.3	0.3	0.3	0.3	0.3	0.3	0.3

StatLink http://dx.doi.org/10.1787/275713744403

Government expenditure on recreation and culture

As a percentage of GDP, 2005

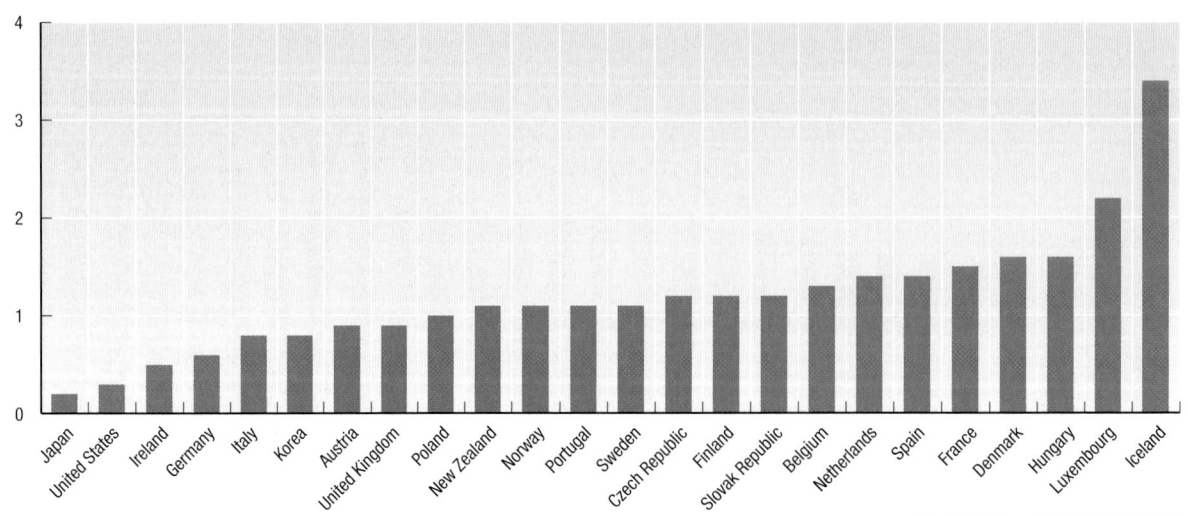

StatLink http://dx.doi.org/10.1787/271208648807

OECD FACTBOOK 2008 – ISBN 978-92-64-04054-0 – © OECD 2008

Household and government expenditure on recreation and culture
As a percentage of GDP

	1993	1994	1995	1996	1997	1998	1999	2000	2001	2002	2003	2004	2005	2006
Austria	..	..	7.6	7.7	7.7	7.8	8.0	7.9	8.0	7.9	7.8	7.6	7.6	7.5
Belgium	..	..	5.6	5.7	5.9	5.9	6.1	6.2	6.1	6.1	6.0	6.0	6.0	..
Czech Republic	..	..	6.6	7.2	7.5	7.4	7.2	7.1	7.3	7.3	7.5	7.2	7.1	..
Denmark	6.7	6.8	6.8	6.9	6.9	6.8	6.8	6.7	6.7	6.7	6.9	7.2	6.9	..
Finland	6.6	6.5	6.6	7.0	6.8	6.7	6.6	6.6	6.5	6.5	6.7	6.7	6.9	..
France	..	..	5.9	5.9	5.9	6.1	6.1	6.2	6.3	6.5	6.6	6.7	6.7	..
Germany	6.0	5.9	5.9	5.9	6.0	6.1	6.2	6.3	6.3	6.1	6.0	6.0	5.9	..
Hungary	..	..	..	..	..	..	..	..	5.8	6.0	6.1	5.9	5.9	..
Iceland	..	..	..	..	9.0	9.6	10.0	10.3	9.9	10.1	10.2	10.2	9.8	9.9
Ireland	..	..	4.5	4.6	4.1	3.9	3.6	3.9	3.9	3.6	3.5	3.7	3.7	..
Italy	5.0	5.1	5.0	5.2	5.2	5.3	5.4	5.3	5.2	5.1	5.0	5.1	4.9	..
Japan	..	..	..	5.8	6.0	6.0	6.0	6.3	6.4	6.4	6.4	6.3	6.2	..
Korea	..	..	4.7	4.6	4.5	4.0	4.3	4.8	4.9	5.0	4.8	4.4	4.5	..
Luxembourg	..	..	5.4	5.5	5.6	5.7	5.5	5.2	5.4	5.7	5.5	5.5	5.5	4.9
Netherlands	..	..	6.4	6.5	6.5	6.6	6.8	6.9	6.8	6.8	6.6	6.4	6.2	..
Norway	6.7	6.6	6.6	6.7	6.6	7.0	7.0	6.2	6.4	6.7	6.8	6.6	6.2	..
Poland	..	..	..	..	..	..	..	..	..	5.5	5.6	5.6	5.0	..
Portugal	..	..	..	..	..	..	5.3	5.2	5.2	5.3	5.2	5.3	..	..
Slovak Republic	..	..	..	..	..	..	..	..	..	..	5.9	5.8	..	..
Spain	..	..	..	..	..	..	7.1	7.1	7.1	7.0	6.9	6.9	6.9	..
Sweden	..	..	6.8	6.9	6.9	7.1	7.3	6.6	6.7	6.5	6.5	6.4	6.4	..
United Kingdom	7.3	7.4		7.7	7.8	7.9	8.2	8.4	8.3	8.3	8.5	8.5	8.6	8.6	..
United States	6.0	6.2	6.4	6.5	6.5	6.5	6.6	6.7	6.7	6.7	6.7	6.7	6.7	6.7

StatLink http://dx.doi.org/10.1787/275745206374

Expenditure on recreation and culture
As a percentage of GDP, 2005

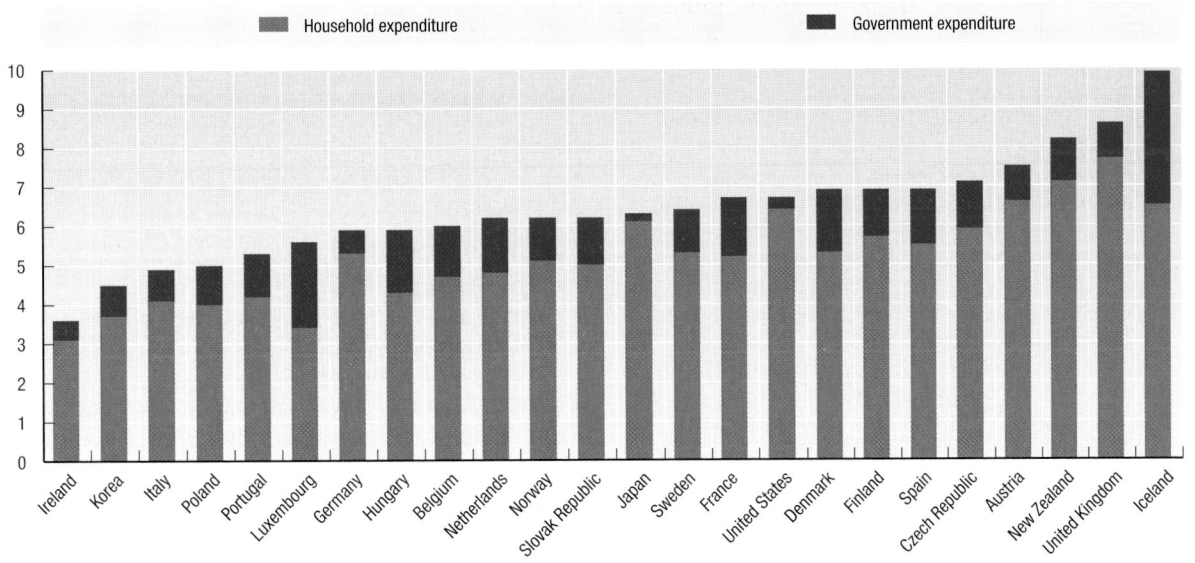

StatLink http://dx.doi.org/10.1787/271237288245

YOUTH INACTIVITY

If young people are not in employment and not at school, there are good reasons to be concerned about their current well-being and their future prospects. Low educational attainments and the growing importance of educational attainment for successful integration into the workforce make it difficult for those leaving school without adequate qualifications to move into jobs with good career prospects. The shares of young persons who are neither in employment nor in education is an indicator of those who are candidates to later become the "socially excluded" – persons with incomes below or at the poverty-line and who lack the skills to improve their economic situation.

Definition

The indicator presents the proportion of youths aged 15 to 19 who are not in education, training or employment as a percentage of the total number of all in that age group. Youths in education include those attending part-time as well as full-time education, but exclude those in non-formal education and educational activities of very short duration. Employment is defined according to the ILO Guidelines and covers all those who have worked for monetary gain for at least one hour in the week previous to the enquiry date.

Comparability

Standard definitions are specified for both "being in education" and "being in employment" and countries try to apply these criteria correctly. The main problem of comparability is that in some countries, youths performing compulsory military service are neither recorded as being in employment nor in education; they are therefore included in the numerator of the ratio although they could reasonably be considered to be both in training and in employment. However, in countries where there is still conscription, the duration of military services is quite short and reallocation of military conscripts to the employment/ education category would not much change the figures given here.

Long-term trends

On average, across the countries for which data are available, 7.3% of male and 8.3% of female teenagers were neither in school nor at work in 2005. Differences across countries are large: in Netherlands, Poland, and Sweden less than 4% of the females were in this situation and in Denmark, Germany, Netherlands, and Poland less than 4% of the males were neither in school or work. The situation is substantially worse in Italy where this share exceeded 10% and in Turkey where over 20% is neither in school nor in work.

For the OECD as a whole, there has been a decline in the percentages of all teenagers who are neither in employment nor education, but the decline has been most marked for females. Improved labour market conditions in general and the fact that young people, and particularly females, spend more time in education than they did a decade ago has contributed to this.

Several features of the labour markets and training systems affect the ease of transition from school to work. OECD reviews of youths' transition from school to work have identified Nordic and English-speaking countries as those where this process is smoother than in countries in Continental and Southern Europe countries. Beyond waste of human capital and risks of marginalisation in the labour markets, delays in settling into jobs will lead many youths to live longer with their parents and defer the formation of independent families, further compounding fertility declines.

Source

- OECD (2007), *Education at a Glance 2007: OECD Indicators*, OECD, Paris.

Further information

Analytical publications

- OECD (2000), *From Initial Education to Working Life: Making Transitions Work*, OECD, Paris.
- OECD (2007), *Jobs for Youth*, OECD, Paris.
- OECD (2007), *OECD Employment Outlook*, OECD, Paris.
- OECD (2007), *Society at a Glance: OECD Social Indicators – 2006 Edition*, OECD, Paris.

Websites

- OECD Education at a Glance, *www.oecd.org/edu/eag2007*.
- Youth Employment Summit, *www.yesweb.org*.

Youths aged between 15 and 19 who are not in education nor in employment

As percentage of persons in that age group

	Males							Females						
	1995	2000	2001	2002	2003	2004	2005	1995	2000	2001	2002	2003	2004	2005
Australia	9.2	6.4	7.9	6.9	6.4	7.6	7.1	10.6	7.3	7.2	7.2	7.2	7.4	7.7
Austria	..	..	..	8.1	5.8	7.2	7.6	..	..	..	4.4	5.4	7.5	6.2
Belgium	9.9	6.7	6.0	7.3	6.9	5.8	5.9	11.2	6.3	6.4	6.4	7.4	3.9	6.6
Canada	7.6	7.8	6.9	7.3	7.5	8.4	6.5	7.7	6.6	5.6	5.9	6.2	6.6	5.8
Czech Republic	6.0	7.3	6.4	5.8	5.4	5.0	5.5	6.9	8.5	7.3	6.3	6.2	6.4	5.1
Denmark	1.9	1.9	4.7	2.4	3.3	1.9	3.5	4.1	3.6	2.7	2.4	1.7	2.3	5.2
Finland	..	..	..	..	6.5	5.4	5.6	..	..	..	..	6.0	6.4	4.9
France	2.3	3.4	3.4	3.7	..	6.2	6.8	2.7	3.2	3.5	3.2	..	4.5	5.5
Germany	..	5.2	4.9	4.3	4.7	3.5	3.8	..	6.3	5.3	5.1	4.8	3.7	5.0
Greece	6.7	6.9	5.6	5.2	9.0	8.7	9.5	14.1	11.2	9.7	7.5	10.1	11.3	10.0
Hungary	11.8	8.6	8.8	8.3	6.6	6.6	6.3	9.7	8.6	7.8	7.8	6.9	5.8	6.5
Iceland	14.8	..	..	..	..	..	..	14.8	..	..	..	..	..	..
Ireland	..	4.5	4.3	5.2	5.3	9.6	4.8	..	4.3	3.9	4.5	5.0	10.3	4.0
Italy	..	12.2	12.1	10.8	9.1	11.1	10.9	..	14.1	13.0	10.3	9.4	10.9	11.4
Japan	5.0	7.3	6.5	8.3	9.0	8.1	7.6	9.3	10.3	10.5	10.6	10.7	10.4	9.9
Luxembourg	7.3	..	..	..	..	..	..	8.8	..	..	4.3	..	4.0	..
Mexico	12.0	7.6	7.2	7.4	8.1	7.6	..	34.4	29.0	28.2	27.4	27.8	26.3	..
Netherlands	..	3.8	2.9	4.0	4.7	3.5	3.8	..	3.6	4.4	3.7	4.1	3.4	3.8
New Zealand	..	..	..	..	..	..	8.4	..	..	..	..	..	..	8.6
Poland	7.3	5.0	6.2	3.5	3.8	3.0	2.2	5.1	4.0	5.4	2.6	2.7	2.1	1.2
Portugal	8.7	6.2	5.4	7.7	8.2	9.0	8.1	9.6	9.2	9.5	6.8	9.4	10.6	8.8
Slovak Republic	17.4	27.8	27.9	17.7	15.2	8.6	5.6	14.3	24.7	24.9	13.5	9.9	7.1	7.0
Spain	11.2	7.7	6.6	6.9	7.3	7.3	8.3	11.9	8.2	7.3	7.5	7.4	7.9	8.8
Sweden	8.0	4.7	5.4	5.9	5.1	6.4	6.0	3.2	2.4	3.1	3.3	3.4	3.2	3.3
Switzerland	22.9	7.3	6.4	5.8	7.1	7.6	7.6	25.5	8.5	7.2	5.8	8.8	6.8	6.8
Turkey	14.3	17.8	19.2	21.7	22.6	24.7	25.8	41.6	46.5	47.0	45.6	44.3	47.1	50.1
United Kingdom	..	8.2	8.3	8.2	9.7	9.0	9.7	..	7.9	8.0	8.9	9.2	9.0	9.0
United States	6.4	6.8	6.9	6.4	..	6.5	5.9	9.3	7.3	8.0	7.5	..	7.3	6.3
OECD average	9.5	7.9	7.8	7.4	7.7	7.5	7.3	12.7	10.5	10.3	8.7	9.3	8.9	8.3

StatLink ᵐˢ⃞ http://dx.doi.org/10.1787/275745325013

Youths aged between 15 and 19 who are not in education nor in employment

As a percentage of persons in that age group, 2005

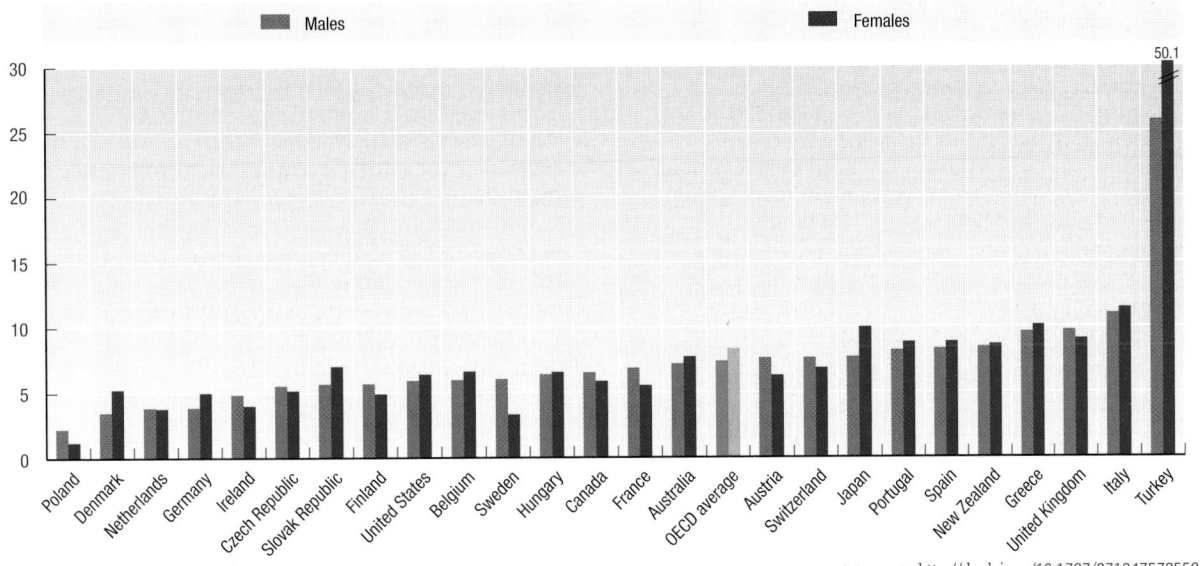

StatLink ᵐˢ⃞ http://dx.doi.org/10.1787/271247578558

INCOME INEQUALITY

The distribution of incomes within a country is important for at least two reasons. Inequalities may create incentives for people to improve their situation through work, innovation or acquiring new skills. On the other hand, crime, poverty and social exclusion are often seen as linked to inequalities of income distribution.

Definition

Income is here defined as *household disposable income*, broadly following the definitions of the *1993 System of National Accounts*. It consists of earnings from work, property income such as interest and dividends, and pensions and other social security benefits; income taxes and social security contributions paid by households are deducted.

The equality of disposable incomes among individuals is measured here by the *Gini Coefficient*. This is a common measure of equality and ranges from 0 in the case of "perfect equality" (each share of the population gets the same share of income) to 100 in the case of "perfect inequality" (all income goes to the share of the population with the highest income). Household income is adjusted to take account of household size. See Sources, below, for a detailed definition of the Gini Coefficient and of the adjustment for household size.

Comparability

"2000" data refer to the year 2000 in all countries except for Australia, Austria and Greece (1999); for Germany, Luxembourg, New Zealand and Switzerland (2001); and for the Czech Republic, Mexico and Turkey (2002). "Mid-1990s" data refer to the year 1995 in all countries except for Austria (1993); for Australia, Denmark, France, Germany, Greece, Ireland, Japan, Mexico and Turkey (1994); and for the Czech Republic and New Zealand (1996). "Mid-1980s" data refer to the year 1983 in Austria, Belgium, Denmark and Sweden; 1984 in Australia, France, Italy and Mexico; 1985 in Canada, Japan, the Netherlands, Spain and the United Kingdom; 1986 in Finland, Luxembourg, New Zealand and Norway; 1987 in Ireland and Turkey; 1988 in Greece; and 1989 in the United States.

Data were provided by national experts using common definitions. In many cases, however, countries have had to make several adjustments to their source data. Small changes between periods and small differences across countries are usually not significant.

Long-term trends

There is considerable variation in levels of income inequality across OECD countries. For years around 2000, the Gini coefficient of income inequality is lowest in Denmark and Sweden, and highest in Mexico and Turkey – the two OECD countries with lowest per capita income. On average, across the 20 countries for which data are available since the mid-1980s, the Gini coefficient of income inequality increased from 29 to 31 but this increase may be within the margin of error for statistics on income distribution. The safest conclusion is that, for these 20 countries as a whole, there was little or no change.

There were, however, some striking changes for several countries when years around 2000 are compared with the mid-1980s. Household income distribution became markedly more equal in Spain and Ireland, and there were smaller reductions in inequality in Australia, Denmark and France.

At the other end of the scale, the Gini coefficients increased (greater inequality) by 10-20% in Norway, Japan, Italy and the United Kingdom and by over 20% in Sweden, New Zealand and Finland. Note, however, that despite the large increase in Sweden, the Gini coefficient is still one of the lowest in the OECD area.

Source

- Förster, M. and M. Mira d'Ercole (2005), *Income Distribution and Poverty in OECD Countries in the Second Half of the 1990s*, OECD Social Employment and Migration Working Papers, No. 22, OECD, Paris.

Further information

Analytical publications

- Jomo, K.S. (2001), *Globalisation, Liberalisation, Poverty and Income Inequality in Southeast Asia*, OECD Development Centre Working Papers, No. 185, OECD, Paris.
- Kayizzi-Mugerwa, S. (2001), *Globalisation, Growth and Income Inequality: The African Experience*, OECD Development Centre Working Papers, No. 186, OECD, Paris.
- OECD (2004), *Income Disparities in China: An OECD Perspective*, OECD, Paris.
- OECD (2005), *Extending Opportunities: How Active Social Policy Can Benefit Us All*, OECD, Paris.
- OECD (2007), *Society at a Glance: OECD Social Indicators – 2006 Edition*, OECD, Paris.
- Uchimura, H. (2005), *Impact of Changes in Social Institutions on Income Inequality in China*, OECD Development Centre Working Papers, No. 243, OECD, Paris.

Websites

- OECD Social and Welfare Statistics, *www.oecd.org/statistics/social*.

OECD FACTBOOK 2008 – ISBN 978-92-64-04054-0 – © OECD 2008

Distribution of household disposable income among individuals

Measured by Gini coefficients

	Mid-1980s	Mid-1990s	2000
Australia	31.2	30.5	30.5
Austria	23.6	23.8	25.2
Canada	28.7	28.3	30.1
Czech Republic	..	25.7	26.0
Denmark	22.8	21.3	22.5
Finland	20.7	22.8	26.1
France	27.6	27.8	27.3
Germany	..	28.3	27.7
Greece	33.6	33.6	34.5
Hungary	..	29.4	29.3
Ireland	33.1	32.4	30.4
Italy	30.6	34.8	34.7
Japan	27.8	29.5	31.4
Luxembourg	24.7	25.9	26.1
Mexico	45.1	52.0	48.0
Netherlands	23.4	25.5	25.1
New Zealand	27.0	33.1	33.7
Norway	23.4	25.6	26.1
Poland	..	38.9	36.7
Portugal	..	35.9	35.6
Spain	36.7	33.9	32.9
Sweden	19.9	21.1	24.3
Switzerland	..	..	26.7
Turkey	43.5	49.1	43.9
United Kingdom	28.6	31.2	32.6
United States	33.8	36.1	35.7
OECD average	29.3	30.9	31.0

StatLink http://dx.doi.org/10.1787/275755833115

Distribution of household disposable income among individuals

Measured by Gini coefficients

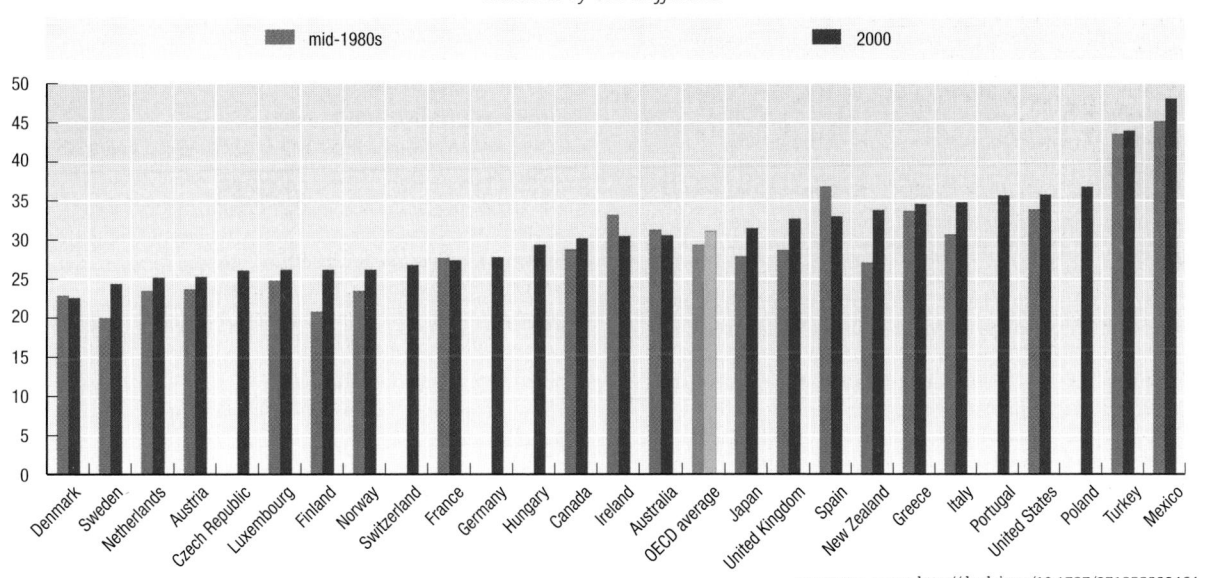

StatLink http://dx.doi.org/10.1787/271258802464

PRISON POPULATION

Crime causes great suffering to victims and their families, but the costs associated with imprisonment can also be considerable. These costs are normally justified by reference to a combination of three societal "needs": to inflict retribution; to deter others from behaving in a similar way; and to prevent re-offending. The size of the prison population depends on the level of crime, the legislative measures and the efficiency of the enforcement measures.

Definition

Not everyone in prison has been found guilty of a crime, especially those awaiting trial or adjudication. The indicator here considers the total prison population, including pre-trial detainees and remand prisoners.

Comparability

The indicator here considers the total prison population, including pre-trial detainees and remand prisoners, per 100 000 of national population. This information has been collected by the International Centre for Prison Studies, every 3 years or so since 1992.

Additional comparative information is available from the above source, such as shares in total prison population of pre-trial detainees/remand prisoners, female prisoners, young prisoners, foreign prisoners, and occupancy levels in percentage (based on official prison capacity).

Long-term trends

Over the last fifteen years, most OECD countries have experienced a continuous rise in their prison population rates. On average, across the 30 OECD countries, this rate has increased from a level of 100 persons per 100 000 unit of the total population in the early 1990s to around 130 persons in 2004. The prison population rate is highest in the United States, where more than 700 per 100 000 population were in prison in 2004: such level is three to four times higher than the second highest OECD country (Poland), and has increased rapidly. This increase extends to most other OECD countries. Since 1992, the prison population rate has more than doubled in the Netherlands, Mexico, Japan, the Czech Republic, Luxembourg, Spain and the United Kingdom, while it appears to have declined only in Canada, Iceland and Korea.

There are large differences across countries in the make-up of the prison population. On average, one in four prisoners is a pre-trial detainee or a remand prisoner, but these two categories account for a much higher share of the prison population in Turkey, Mexico and Luxembourg. Women and youths (aged below 18) account, on average, for 5% and 2% of the prison population respectively. A much larger share of prisoners is accounted for by foreigners (close to 20% of all prisoners, on average), with this share exceeding 40% of the total in Luxembourg, Switzerland, as well as Australia, Austria, Belgium and Greece. In several countries, the rapid rise in the prison population has stretched beyond the receptive capacity of existing institutions; occupancy levels are above 100% in more than half of OECD countries, and above 125% in Greece, Hungary, Italy, Spain and Mexico.

Source

• Walmsley, R. (2005), *World Prison Population List (sixth edition)*, International Center for Prison Studies, London, *www.prisonstudies.org*.

Further information
Analytical publications

• OECD (2007), *Society at a Glance: OECD Social Indicators – 2006 Edition*, OECD, Paris.
• UN Office on Drugs and Crime (2004), *United Nations Surveys on Crime Trends and the Operations of Criminal Justice Systems (ninth survey)*, UNODC, Vienna, *www.unodc.org/unodc/crime_cicp_surveys.html*.

Websites

• OECD Social and Welfare Statistics, *www.oecd.org/statistics/social*.
• United Nations Office on Drugs and Crime, *www.unodc.org*.

Prison population rate
Number per 100 000 inhabitants

	1992	1995	1998	2001	2004
Australia	89.0	96.0	107.0	116.0	120.0
Austria	87.0	77.0	86.0	85.0	96.5
Belgium	71.0	75.0	81.0	85.0	88.0
Canada	123.0	131.0	126.0	116.0	107.0
Czech Republic	123.0	181.0	209.0	210.0	169.0
Denmark	66.0	66.0	64.0	59.0	70.0
Finland	65.0	59.0	50.0	59.0	66.0
France	84.0	89.0	86.0	78.0	91.0
Germany	71.0	81.0	96.0	96.0	96.0
Greece	61.0	56.0	68.0	79.0	82.0
Hungary	143.0	124.0	132.0	152.0	163.0
Iceland	101.0	119.0	103.0	110.0	39.0
Ireland	61.0	57.0	71.0	78.0	85.0
Italy	81.0	87.0	85.0	95.0	97.0
Japan	37.0	37.0	40.0	48.0	58.0
Korea	130.0	136.0	152.0	133.0	121.0
Luxembourg	89.0	114.0	92.0	80.0	121.0
Mexico	98.0	102.0	133.0	164.0	177.5
Netherlands	49.0	66.0	85.0	95.0	123.0
New Zealand	129.0	128.0	146.0	157.0	168.0
Norway	58.0	55.0	57.0	59.0	65.0
Poland	153.0	163.0	148.0	183.0	210.0
Portugal	93.0	124.0	146.0	131.0	129.0
Slovak Republic	119.0	138.0	138.0	129.0	165.0
Spain	90.0	102.0	114.0	117.0	138.0
Sweden	63.0	65.0	60.0	68.0	81.0
Switzerland	79.0	80.0	85.0	71.0	81.0
Turkey	54.0	82.0	102.0	89.0	100.0
United Kingdom	90.1	100.2	124.5	124.4	138.7
United States	505.0	600.0	669.0	685.0	725.0
OECD average	102.1	113.0	121.8	125.0	132.4
Brazil	74.0	92.0	102.0	133.0	183.0
China	..	101.0	115.0	111.0	118.0
India	..	..	28.0	30.0	30.0
Russian Federation	487.0	622.0	688.0	638.0	587.0
South Africa	282.0	280.0	387.0	409.0	333.0

StatLink http://dx.doi.org/10.1787/275761175242

Prison population rate
Number per 100 000 inhabitants, 2004

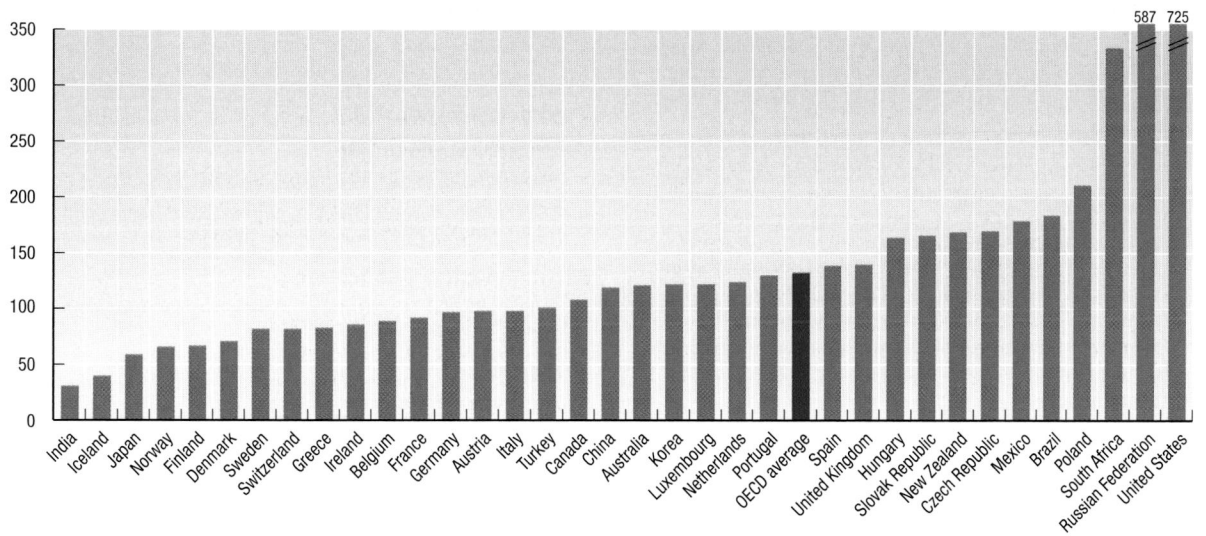

StatLink http://dx.doi.org/10.1787/271280416364

ROAD NETWORK

Motorways impact on the quality of life in several ways. Primarily, they make journeys by passenger cars both safer and easier. On the other hand, motorways may detract from the quality of life of those who live near them, and their construction may have harmful effects on the environment.

Definition

A motorway is defined as a road, specially designed and built for motor traffic, which does not serve properties bordering on it, and which:

- is provided, except at special points or temporarily, with separate carriageways for the two directions of traffic, separated from each other, either by a dividing strip not intended for traffic, or exceptionally by other means ;

- does not cross at level with any road, railway or tramway track, or footpath ;

- is especially sign-posted as a motorway and is reserved for specific categories of road motor vehicles.

In calculating the length of motorways, entry and exit lanes are included irrespectively of the location of the sign-posts. Urban motorways are also included.

Comparability

The data on motorways are regarded as broadly comparable for most countries. However, the figures for Canada are expressed in two-lane equivalent kilometers, the figures for Mexico refer to toll roads only, and Spain classifies some express roads as motorways although they do not exactly meet the definition given above. For some countries, the data are reported for financial rather than calendar years.

Long-term trends

Motorway networks have been growing in all OECD countries for which data are available.

OECD countries fall into three groups when the annual growth rates are considered. There are five countries where motorway networks have been growing at 6% or more each year during the latest years: Korea, Poland, Portugal, Ireland and Greece. These countries had relatively small networks at the beginning of the period so that rapid growth was easy to achieve. There is a middle group which recorded growth rates between 2 and 6% each year; this group includes Japan, France and the Scandinavian countries. At the lower end, there are nine OECD countries plus Russian Federation with growth rates of less than 2% per year; this group includes Canada, Germany, the Netherlands and the United States, where the motorway network was already mature at the beginning of the period, having been built up over several decades.

The size of a country's motorway network is generally correlated with a country's size, but the United Kingdom and Turkey are exceptions in having relatively small motorway networks, while in Germany, France and Spain the motorway networks are extensive relative to their size, whether size is defined by population or by surface area.

Source

- ITF (2006), *Trends in the Transport Sector*, ITF, Paris.

Further information

Analytical publications

- ECMT (2006), *ECMT Annual Report 2005*, ECMT, Paris.
- OECD (2006), *Decoupling the Environmental Impacts of Transport from Economic Growth*, OECD, Paris.

Methodological publications

- UNECE, ECMT, Eurostat (2003), *Glossary for Transport Statistics*, ECMT, Paris.

Websites

- International Transport Forum, *www.internationaltransportforum.org*.

Length of the motorway network
Kilometres

	1993	1994	1995	1996	1997	1998	1999	2000	2001	2002	2003	2004	2005	2006
Austria	1 567	1 589	1 596	1 607	1 613	1 613	1 634	1 633	1 644	1 644	1 670	1 677	1 677	1 678
Belgium	1 665	1 666	1 666	1 674	1 679	1 682	1 691	1 702	1 727	1 729	1 729	1 747	1 747	1 763
Canada	15 983	15 983	15 983	15 983	15 983	15 983	15 983	15 983	16 600	16 900	16 900	16 900	16 900	16 900
Czech Republic	356	390	425	487	487	499	499	499	518	518	518	546	564	564
Denmark	737	786	796	825	900	902	922	953	971	1 009	1 270	1 278	1 278	1 340
Finland	337	388	394	431	444	473	512	549	591	603	653	653	653	693
France	7 645	8 030	8 247	8 596	8 864	9 303	9 626	9 766	10 068	10 223	10 379	10 486	10 843	10 843
Germany	11 080	11 143	11 190	11 190	11 246	11 309	11 427	11 515	11 712	11 786	12 037	12 044	12 174	12 363
Greece	..	..	..	..	..	357	444	636	742	742	880	880	880	880
Hungary	269	293	335	365	382	448	448	448	448	533	542	569	569	569
Ireland	51	68	70	70	70	94	94	103	125	125	176	192	192	192
Italy	6 352	6 401	6 473	6 473	6 473	6 473	6 478	6 478	6 478	6 478	6 478	6 478	6 478	6 478
Japan	5 054	5 410	5 410	5 932	6 114	6 402	6 455	6 617	6 851	6 915	7 196	7 296	7 383	7 383
Korea	..	..	..	..	..	2 107	2 425	2 477	2 567	3 060	3 486	3 489	3 415	3 415
Luxembourg	100	121	123	115	118	118	114	114	115	126	135	146	147	147
Netherlands	2 167	2 178	2 208	2 222	2 236	2 250	2 268	2 265	2 281	2 281	2 308	2 342	2 342	2 342
New Zealand	156	156	156	156	156	156	184	226	167	169	169	171	172	172
Norway	512	524	527	560	570	570	589	606	636	629	664	664	664	664
Poland	231	245	246	258	264	268	317	358	398	405	405	552	552	662
Portugal	579	587	687	710	797	1 252	1 441	1 482	1 659	1 835	1 835	1 835	1 835	1 835
Slovak Republic	198	198	198	215	219	292	295	296	296	302	313	316	316	316
Spain	6 577	6 485	6 962	7 295	7 750	8 569	8 893	9 049	9 571	9 739	10 286	10 286	10 286	10 286
Sweden	1 044	1 145	1 262	1 350	1 428	1 437	1 484	1 501	1 507	1 544	1 591	1 700	1 700	1 740
Switzerland	..	..	..	..	1 258	1 262	1 267	1 270	1 305	1 342	1 351	1 341	1 357	1 361
Turkey	1 070	1 167	1 246	1 493	1 500	1 528	1 726	1 749	1 851	1 851	1 851	1 851	1 851	1 851
United Kingdom	2 756	2 839	3 200	3 200	3 300	3 300	3 400	3 500	3 610	3 611	3 611	3 753	3 748	3 783
United States	73 274	73 274	73 274	73 274	73 274	88 915	89 232	89 426	89 996	89 848	91 287	91 287	91 287	91 287
China	..	..	..	..	..	..	..	..	1 698 000	1 765 200	1 809 800	1 870 700	3 345 200	3 457 000
Russian Federation	..	..	..	..	..	29 000	29 000	29 000	29 000	29 260	29 260	29 260	29 260	29 260

StatLink http://dx.doi.org/10.1787/275802057784

Growth of the motorway network
Average annual growth in percentage, 1993-2006 or latest period available

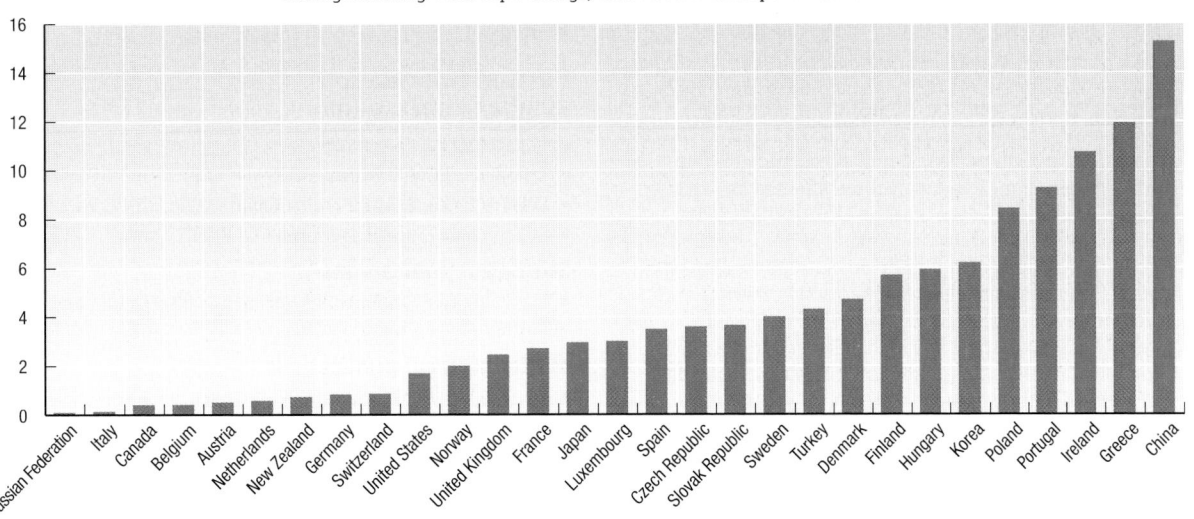

StatLink http://dx.doi.org/10.1787/271300854011

ROAD MOTOR VEHICLES AND ROAD FATALITIES

The number of road motor vehicles is high and rising among OECD countries, and reducing road accidents is a concern in all countries. The tables in this section show the numbers of road motor vehicles per thousand inhabitants and two indicators of road safety – the number of road fatalities per million inhabitants and the number of road fatalities per million vehicles.

Definition

A road motor vehicle is a vehicle running on wheels and intended for use on roads with an engine providing its sole means of propulsion and which is normally used for carrying persons or goods or for drawing, on the road, vehicles used for the carriage of persons or goods. Thus buses, coaches, freight vehicles and motor cycles are included as well as passenger motor cars. Motor vehicles running on rails are excluded.

Road fatality means any person killed immediately or dying within 30 days as a result of a road accident.

Comparability

Road motor vehicles are attributed to the countries where they are registered while deaths are attributed to the countries in which they occur. As a result, ratios of fatalities to million inhabitants and of fatalities to million vehicles cannot strictly be interpreted as indicating the proportion of a country's population that is at risk of suffering a fatal road accident or the likelihood of a vehicle registered in a given country being involved in a fatal accident. In practice, however, this is not considered to be a serious problem because discrepancies between the numerators and denominators tend to cancel out.

The numbers of vehicles entering the existing stock is usually accurate but information on the numbers of vehicles withdrawn from use is less certain.

Long-term trends

In 2006, ratios of motor vehicles to population range from 778 per thousand inhabitants in Portugal to 86 in Turkey. Over the periods shown in the table, ratios of vehicles to population increased in all countries except in the United States. Sharp increases of this ratio occurred in Portugal, Iceland, Greece and Poland.

In 2006, road fatalities per million inhabitants ranged from over 230 per million inhabitants in Russian Federation to 49 in Sweden. Over the periods shown in the table, rates have decreased in all countries except in Iceland and in the Russian Federation with particularly sharp falls in Portugal, New Zealand and France.

Road fatality rates per million inhabitants are an ambiguous indicator of road safety since the number of accidents depends to a great extent on the number of vehicles in each country. The last chart shows the number of fatalities per million vehicles together with fatalities per million inhabitants. Both ratios refer to 2006. Rates per million vehicles are affected by driving habits, traffic legislation and the effectiveness of its enforcement, road design and other factors over which governments may exercise control. In 2006, fatality rates per million vehicles were less than 100 in Switzerland, Norway and Sweden, but exceeded 400 in Slovak Republic, Turkey and 1 100 in Russian Federation. Note that low fatality rates per million inhabitants may be associated with very high fatality rates per million vehicles. For example, a country with a small vehicle population may show a low fatality rate per million inhabitants but a high fatality rate per vehicle.

Source

- ITF (2006), *Trends in the Transport Sector*, ITF, Paris.

Further information

Analytical publications

- ECMT (2004), *Road Safety Performance: National Peer Review: Lithuania*, ECMT, Paris.
- ECMT (2006), *ECMT Annual Report 2005*, ECMT, Paris.
- ECMT (2006), *Speed Management*, ECMT, Paris.

Statistical publications

- ECMT (2003), *Statistical Report on Road Accidents*, ECMT, Paris.

Methodological publications

- UNECE, ECMT, Eurostat (2003), *Glossary for Transport Statistics*, ECMT, Paris.

Websites

- International Transport Forum, *www.internationaltrasportforum.org*.

Road motor vehicles
Per thousand inhabitants

	1993	1994	1995	1996	1997	1998	1999	2000	2001	2002	2003	2004	2005	2006
Australia	..	..	603	599	591	626	629	623	625	634	643	653	665	659
Austria	515	528	543	495	509	529	544	555	563	535	542	553	554	547
Belgium	454	464	487	494	482	490	500	511	517	520	525	531	528	540
Canada	595	569	565	565	564	583	568	574	573	582	585	586	580	590
Czech Republic	434	455	333	383	383	369	373	373	383	394	409	417	431	430
Denmark	373	374	386	398	406	411	420	421	425	428	432	434	441	451
Finland	425	422	427	434	436	451	465	476	481	488	503	523	541	534
France	509	518	520	526	532	548	559	573	583	587	598	604	604	595
Germany	478	523	540	547	551	556	564	570	582	589	593	597	603	592
Greece	271	283	298	313	328	351	378	406	428	450	454	478	503	521
Hungary	232	239	253	257	262	255	261	270	283	300	317	334	341	342
Iceland	457	433	453	467	554	574	609	636	688	694	709	745	732	719
Ireland	295	305	318	348	367	387	409	425	442	445	458	458	439	433
Italy	562	562	573	581	586	603	622	632	656	660	678	677	678	666
Japan	507	520	537	566	575	580	586	592	596	600	604	605	604	612
Korea	..	..	..	..	..	254	236	237	243	243	256	263	269	268
Luxembourg	580	580	625	669	675	671	666	693	719	728	736	751	740	727
Netherlands	419	426	430	443	450	464	461	478	496	504	516	523	528	495
New Zealand	645	649	658	654	636	643	659	679	684	688	699	719	737	735
Norway	461	465	474	467	491	498	503	511	516	521	527	538	545	562
Poland	210	222	232	246	261	272	286	309	325	347	357	375	378	412
Portugal	439	438	501	533	569	610	654	698	711	756	748	773	780	778
Slovak Republic	248	247	213	217	232	245	253	259	265	272	280	250	250	250
Spain	422	419	447	464	481	502	526	541	557	567	561	602	573	591
Sweden	444	442	447	450	456	468	481	494	497	500	504	502	513	512
Switzerland	487	492	498	504	511	518	528	536	545	551	558	565	568	573
Turkey	61	64	68	97	105	111	116	124	92	94	88	87	86	86
United Kingdom	441	439	428	448	458	474	486	493	516	533	526	543	536	538
United States	725	719	771	783	784	792	765	754	759	766	776	769	761	755
Russian Federation	98	111	124	139	145	154	161	174	182	191	194	194	194	195

StatLink http://dx.doi.org/10.1787/275802543058

Road motor vehicles
Per thousand inhabitants

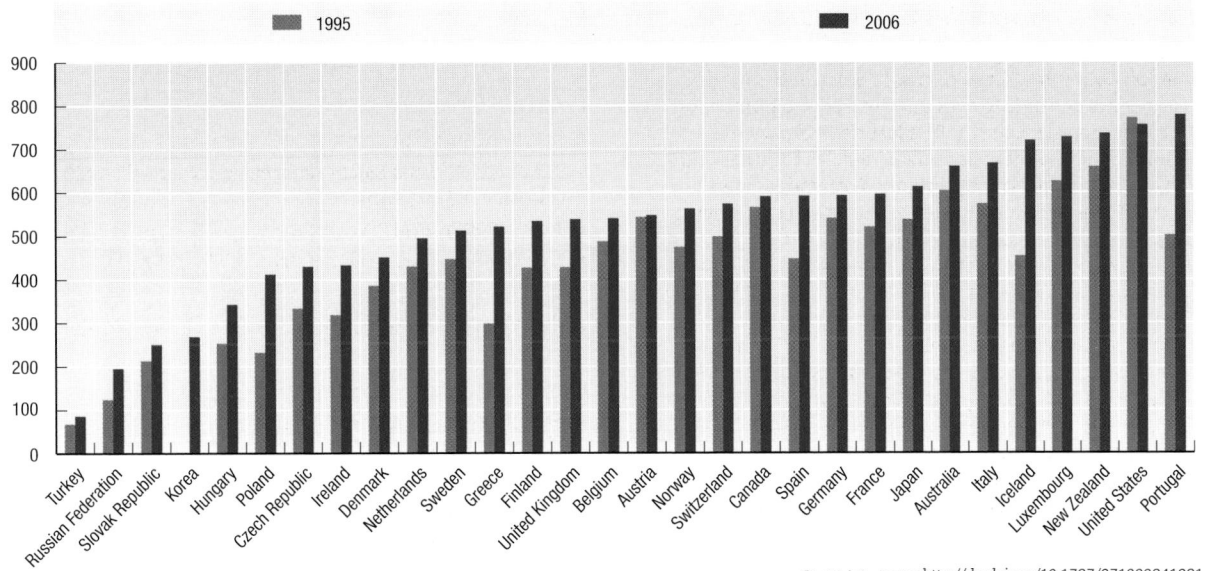

StatLink http://dx.doi.org/10.1787/271323841281

Road fatalities
Per million inhabitants

	1993	1994	1995	1996	1997	1998	1999	2000	2001	2002	2003	2004	2005	2006
Australia	111	109	111	108	95	94	93	95	90	87	82	79	81	78
Austria	161	167	150	127	137	121	135	122	119	118	114	108	94	89
Belgium	165	167	148	134	134	147	136	143	144	131	117	112	104	102
Canada	125	111	113	103	101	97	98	95	90	93	87	85	91	..
Czech Republic	147	158	154	152	155	132	141	145	130	140	142	136	126	104
Denmark	108	105	111	98	93	94	97	93	80	86	80	68	61	56
Finland	96	94	86	79	85	78	83	76	83	80	73	72	72	64
France	157	147	144	138	136	143	136	129	130	121	96	87	88	77
Germany	123	121	116	107	104	95	95	91	85	83	80	71	65	62
Greece	176	183	195	206	201	207	201	193	178	159	145	151	150	149
Hungary	163	152	155	135	137	136	130	118	122	141	131	129	127	130
Iceland	91	44	90	37	55	98	75	113	84	101	80	79	64	104
Ireland	122	113	122	125	129	124	110	110	107	96	84	94	84	87
Italy	124	123	122	115	116	118	116	115	117	117	105	98	94	89
Japan	106	102	100	93	89	95	92	93	89	85	78	75	70	65
Korea	..	..	..	..	..	226	232	218	171	152	151	136	132	..
Luxembourg	196	166	169	170	142	134	133	172	159	140	118	109	101	78
Netherlands	82	84	86	76	74	73	75	73	67	66	67	54	50	50
New Zealand	172	164	162	141	144	132	134	121	118	103	115	107	99	95
Norway	65	65	70	58	69	79	68	76	61	68	61	56	49	52
Poland	165	175	179	165	189	183	174	163	143	152	148	150	143	138
Portugal	240	222	242	241	222	213	200	186	161	165	148	124	118	104
Slovak Republic	120	127	130	119	154	160	125	120	116	116	121	113	111	113
Spain	163	143	147	139	142	150	144	143	135	129	128	115	89	94
Sweden	72	67	65	61	61	60	65	67	65	63	59	53	49	49
Switzerland	104	97	98	87	83	84	81	82	75	70	74	69	55	50
Turkey	108	97	97	86	81	76	69	58	45	62	56	62	62	62
United Kingdom	70	67	66	65	65	62	62	62	63	63	62	57	55	55
United States	156	156	159	158	158	154	153	149	148	149	147	146	147	143
Russian Federation	250	239	221	199	188	198	203	203	213	228	248	241	237	230

StatLink ᴍᴮ *http://dx.doi.org/10.1787/275867644073*

Road fatalities
Per million inhabitants

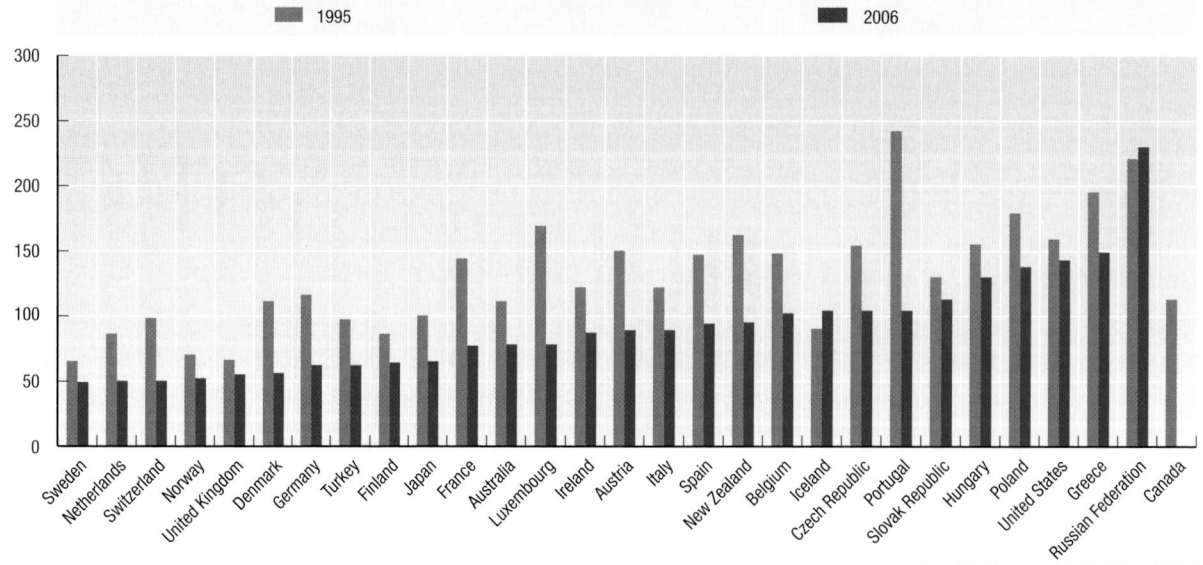

StatLink ᴍᴮ *http://dx.doi.org/10.1787/271343353835*

OECD FACTBOOK 2008 – ISBN 978-92-64-04054-0 – © OECD 2008

Road fatalities
Per million vehicles

	1993	1994	1995	1996	1997	1998	1999	2000	2001	2002	2003	2004	2005	2006
Australia	..	..	183.9	179.9	161.5	149.5	147.8	152.2	143.2	137.7	126.8	121.3	121.1	118.2
Austria	311.9	315.5	277.0	257.1	269.0	228.1	247.7	219.3	210.9	220.5	211.2	195.7	168.8	162.0
Belgium	362.2	359.8	293.6	270.2	278.0	299.9	272.7	280.5	279.0	251.0	223.1	210.5	197.1	188.8
Canada	209.5	195.8	200.1	182.1	178.9	166.2	172.2	166.1	156.3	160.5	149.6	145.7	156.4	..
Czech Republic	339.6	348.2	461.4	404.4	404.4	358.5	379.5	388.4	338.9	356.2	347.2	325.6	292.7	241.9
Denmark	288.6	280.6	287.1	245.6	228.2	228.0	230.5	221.0	189.1	201.1	185.7	157.4	138.6	124.9
Finland	224.5	223.2	202.2	181.2	195.4	171.7	179.4	160.6	173.2	163.4	144.3	137.6	133.5	119.8
France	307.4	284.1	277.7	262.7	255.5	261.1	242.6	226.0	223.1	206.1	160.5	144.4	145.0	129.7
Germany	257.1	230.6	214.1	195.5	188.9	170.9	167.7	159.9	145.5	140.8	135.2	118.5	107.8	104.4
Greece	715.1	704.4	656.3	630.7	622.4	591.3	531.7	476.0	414.4	354.2	320.2	315.5	297.2	285.8
Hungary	702.7	635.7	613.5	523.9	523.3	532.8	498.9	436.5	430.1	469.6	414.1	384.7	372.1	379.3
Iceland	198.3	205.1	198.3	79.4	100.0	170.9	123.5	177.8	121.8	145.0	112.2	106.5	88.0	144.2
Ireland	414.8	371.0	384.3	359.5	350.9	319.7	269.5	258.0	242.3	215.8	183.6	205.0	190.8	201.8
Italy	207.2	205.1	198.5	185.5	184.7	195.4	186.5	181.9	179.0	177.1	155.2	144.3	139.2	134.1
Japan	209.7	196.4	186.3	163.9	155.0	163.1	157.6	156.8	149.8	141.6	130.0	123.8	115.6	105.7
Korea	..	..	..	..	..	891.8	983.4	919.8	702.9	624.1	586.9	518.0	491.2	..
Luxembourg	329.0	320.3	263.6	257.1	195.8	199.3	200.0	248.4	221.5	192.0	160.6	145.0	136.1	107.1
Netherlands	194.6	197.5	200.8	171.3	165.1	157.0	162.0	152.6	135.7	130.5	129.7	103.7	94.7	100.0
New Zealand	267.4	253.4	246.7	216.0	225.7	205.3	202.6	177.6	172.8	149.4	164.6	148.9	133.7	129.0
Norway	141.5	140.1	147.6	124.2	139.6	159.1	134.9	148.1	117.7	131.1	116.5	104.2	88.9	92.8
Poland	783.6	789.0	770.4	668.7	723.6	672.0	609.3	526.6	440.5	438.9	413.5	398.6	377.3	333.7
Portugal	479.1	444.3	419.5	452.1	390.7	349.7	305.3	265.7	226.9	217.6	197.9	160.4	151.4	134.1
Slovak Republic	441.4	477.7	577.9	527.8	629.9	651.8	492.3	463.2	435.8	426.4	432.7	451.7	445.8	451.7
Spain	385.8	347.8	327.8	300.7	295.6	298.7	273.1	264.5	242.3	227.1	228.2	190.8	155.3	159.5
Sweden	162.8	151.7	144.7	134.9	134.0	128.2	136.2	134.7	131.6	125.3	117.3	106.4	95.0	96.2
Switzerland	213.1	196.7	196.1	172.6	161.9	161.8	154.2	153.2	137.5	127.2	133.2	122.4	96.7	86.9
Turkey	..	..	..	886.6	770.8	680.5	596.4	469.4	482.4	656.4	636.0	710.1	725.6	725.6
United Kingdom	153.5	147.0	148.5	140.6	137.1	131.4	126.9	125.1	122.1	118.3	117.2	104.4	103.4	101.6
United States	214.7	217.3	206.1	202.2	201.0	194.7	200.0	197.2	195.1	194.9	190.0	189.8	192.5	189.0
Russian Federation	2 555.6	2 166.2	1 785.3	1 427.9	1 294.2	1 285.9	1 261.4	1 165.4	1 172.1	1 195.9	1 280.8	1 241.4	1 221.6	1 177.2

StatLink http://dx.doi.org/10.1787/276040610450

Road fatalities
2006 or latest available year

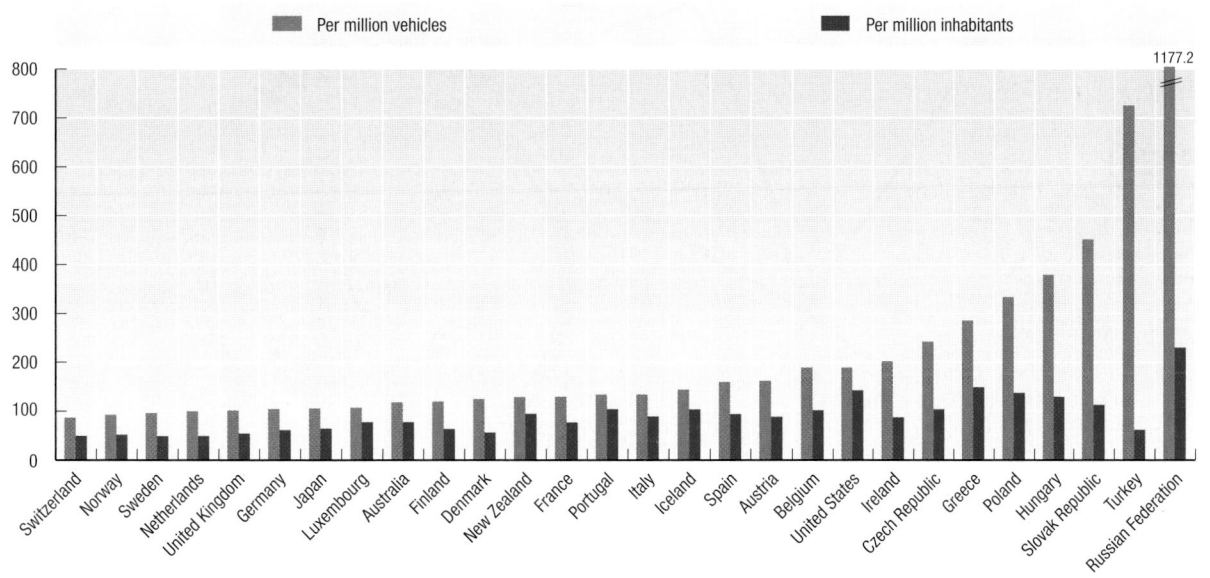

StatLink http://dx.doi.org/10.1787/271357750126

SPECIAL FOCUS

PRODUCTIVITY

INTRODUCTION

ECONOMY-WIDE INDICATORS OF PRODUCTIVITY GROWTH
GROWTH IN GDP PER CAPITA
LABOUR PRODUCTIVITY GROWTH
MULTI-FACTOR PRODUCTIVITY
GROWTH ACCOUNTS FOR OECD COUNTRIES

PRODUCTIVITY LEVELS
INCOME AND PRODUCTIVITY LEVELS
HISTORICAL INCOME AND PRODUCTIVITY LEVELS
LABOUR PRODUCTIVITY AND FIRM-SIZE HETEROGENEITY

PRODUCTIVITY GROWTH BY INDUSTRY
CONTRIBUTION OF KEY ACTIVITIES TO AGGREGATE PRODUCTIVITY GROWTH
PRODUCTIVITY GROWTH IN MANUFACTURING
PRODUCTIVITY GROWTH IN SERVICES

IMPACT OF LABOUR PRODUCTIVITY ON UNIT LABOUR COSTS
UNIT LABOUR COSTS, LABOUR PRODUCTIVITY AND LABOUR COMPENSATION

INTRODUCTION

Productivity isn't everything, but in the long run it is almost everything. A country's ability to improve its standard of living over time depends almost entirely on its ability to raise its output per worker.

Paul Krugman, *The Age of Diminishing Expectations* (1994)

Productivity is commonly defined as a ratio between the output volume and the volume of inputs. In other words, it measures how efficiently production inputs, such as labour and capital, are being used in an economy to produce a given level of output. Productivity is considered a key source of economic growth and competitiveness and, as such, is basic statistical information for many international comparisons and country performance assessments. For example, productivity data are used to investigate the impact of product and labour market regulations on economic performance. Productivity growth constitutes an important element for modelling the productive capacity of economies. It also allows analysts to determine capacity utilisation, which in turn allows one to gauge the position of economies in the business cycle and to forecast economic growth. In addition, production capacity is used to assess demand and inflationary pressures.

There are different measures of productivity and the choice between them depends on the purpose of the productivity measurement and/or data availability. One of the most widely used measures of productivity is Gross Domestic Product (GDP) per hour worked. This measure captures the use of labour inputs better than just output per employee. Generally, the default source for total hours worked is the OECD's National Accounts database, though for a number of countries other sources have to be used. Despite the progress and efforts in this area, the measurement of hours worked still suffers from a number of statistical problems. Namely, different concepts and basic statistical sources are used across countries, which can impair international comparability. In principle, the measurement of labour inputs should also take into account differences in workers' educational attainment, skills and experience. Accordingly, the OECD has started to develop adjusted labour input measures. In some cases, there are important differences between unadjusted and adjusted time profiles of labour inputs.

To take account of the role of capital inputs, an appropriate measure is the flow of productive services that can be drawn from the cumulative stock of past investments (such as machinery and equipment). These services are estimated by the OECD using the rate of change of the "productive capital stock", which takes into account wear and tear, retirements and other sources of reduction in the productive capacity of fixed capital assets. The price of capital services per asset is measured as their rental price. In principle, the latter could be directly observed if markets existed for all capital services. In practice, however, rental prices have to be imputed for most assets, using the implicit rent that capital goods' owners "pay" to themselves (or the "user costs of capital").

After computing the contributions of labour and capital to output, the so-called multi-factor productivity (MFP) can be derived. It measures the residual growth that cannot be explained by the rate of change in the services of labour, capital and intermediate outputs, and is often interpreted as the contribution to economic growth made by factors such as technical and organisational innovation.

Against this background, this section presents a broad overview of productivity indicators in four areas. International comparisons of economy-wide indicators of productivity growth are presented in the first part. The second part presents international comparisons of income and productivity levels, including a measure of productivity heterogeneity by enterprise size classes. Thirdly, productivity growth indicators by industry and services are examined. Finally, the impact of labour productivity on unit labour costs is discussed.

Unless noted otherwise, GDP refers to the total economy.

GROWTH IN GDP PER CAPITA

Gross Domestic Product (GDP) per capita measures economic activity or income per person and is one of the core indicators of economic performance. GDP per capita is a rough measure of average living standards or economic well-being. Per capita GDP growth can be broken down into a part which is due to labour productivity growth (measured as GDP per hour worked) and a part which is due to increased labour utilisation (measured as hours worked per capita). Growing labour utilisation can have considerable impacts on the growth of GDP per capita. A slowing or declining rate of labour utilisation combined with high labour productivity growth can be indicative of a greater use of capital and/or of a decreasing employment of low-productivity workers.

Definition

The indicator hereafter is calculated using GDP and population estimates published in the OECD Annual National Accounts database. For zone aggregates, GDP estimates have been converted to constant US dollars, using 2000 constant Purchasing Power Parities (PPPs). Series on hours were mostly derived from the OECD Annual National Accounts; when this source was not available the OECD Employment Outlook was used instead.

Comparability

All OECD countries follow the *1993 System of National Accounts*, except for Turkey that is using the *1968 System of National Accounts*. Hours worked correspond to actual hours worked, although methods to derive actual hours worked may vary somewhat between countries.

In the chart on this page which shows the long-time period 1970-2006, OECD total does not include the Czech Republic, Hungary, Poland and the Slovak Republic; while in the chart on the right page which shows the short-time period 2001-2006, OECD total does not include Poland and Turkey.

Growth in GDP per capita
Percentage change, annual rate

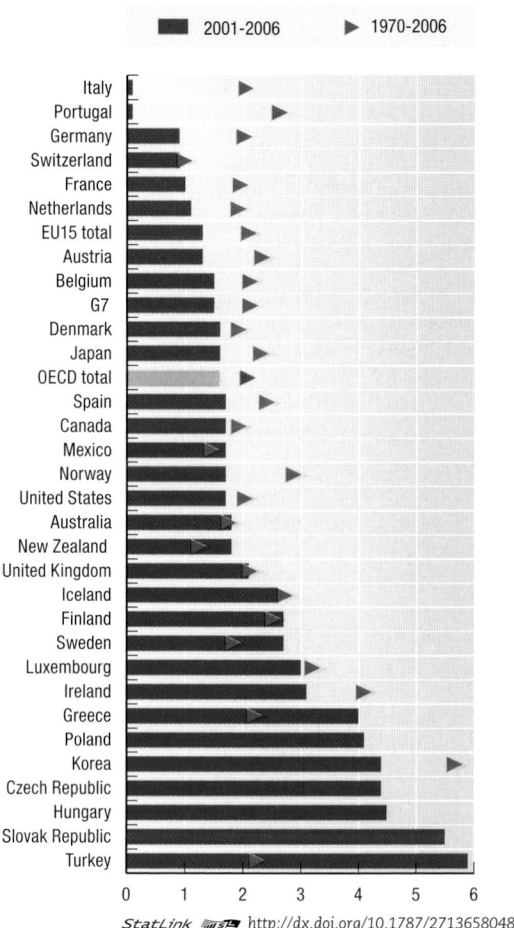

StatLink ⟶ http://dx.doi.org/10.1787/271365804844

Long-term trends

Over the period 1970-2006, growth in GDP per capita has been above 2% in most OECD countries, but significantly more in some countries, notably Ireland and Korea for which the average growth rate went over 4%. In the second half of the 1990s, Hungary, Ireland, Korea, Poland and the Slovak Republic experienced high rates of growth in GDP per capita. More recently, many OECD countries have experienced a deceleration in their income growth relative to long-term trends, notably Italy and Portugal.

Since the beginning of the new millennium, many European countries have decreased in the rate of labour utilisation, which was also accompanied by a sharp decline in labour productivity growth. In contrast, the Czech Republic, Japan and the Slovak Republic experienced a pick-up in both labour utilisation and labour productivity growth. Noteworthy, the estimates shown here are not adjusted for differences in the business cycle; cyclically adjusted estimates might show a somewhat different pattern.

Sources
- *Annual National Accounts.*
- *OECD Productivity Database.*

Further information
Statistical publications
- OECD Compendium of Productivity Indicators, *www.oecd.org/statistics/productivity.*

Methodological publications
- OECD (2001), *Measuring Productivity – OECD Manual Measurement of Aggregate and Industry-level Productivity Growth*, OECD, Paris, *www.sourceoecd.org/9264187375.*
- Pilat, D. and P. Schreyer (2004), "The OECD Productivity Database – An Overview", *International Productivity Monitor*, No. 8, Spring, CSLS, Ottawa, pp. 59-65.

Websites
- *www.oecd.org/statistics/productivity.*
- *www.oecd.org/statistics/productivity/compendium.*

Contribution of labour productivity and labour utilisation to GDP per capita

Percentage change 2001-2006, annual rate

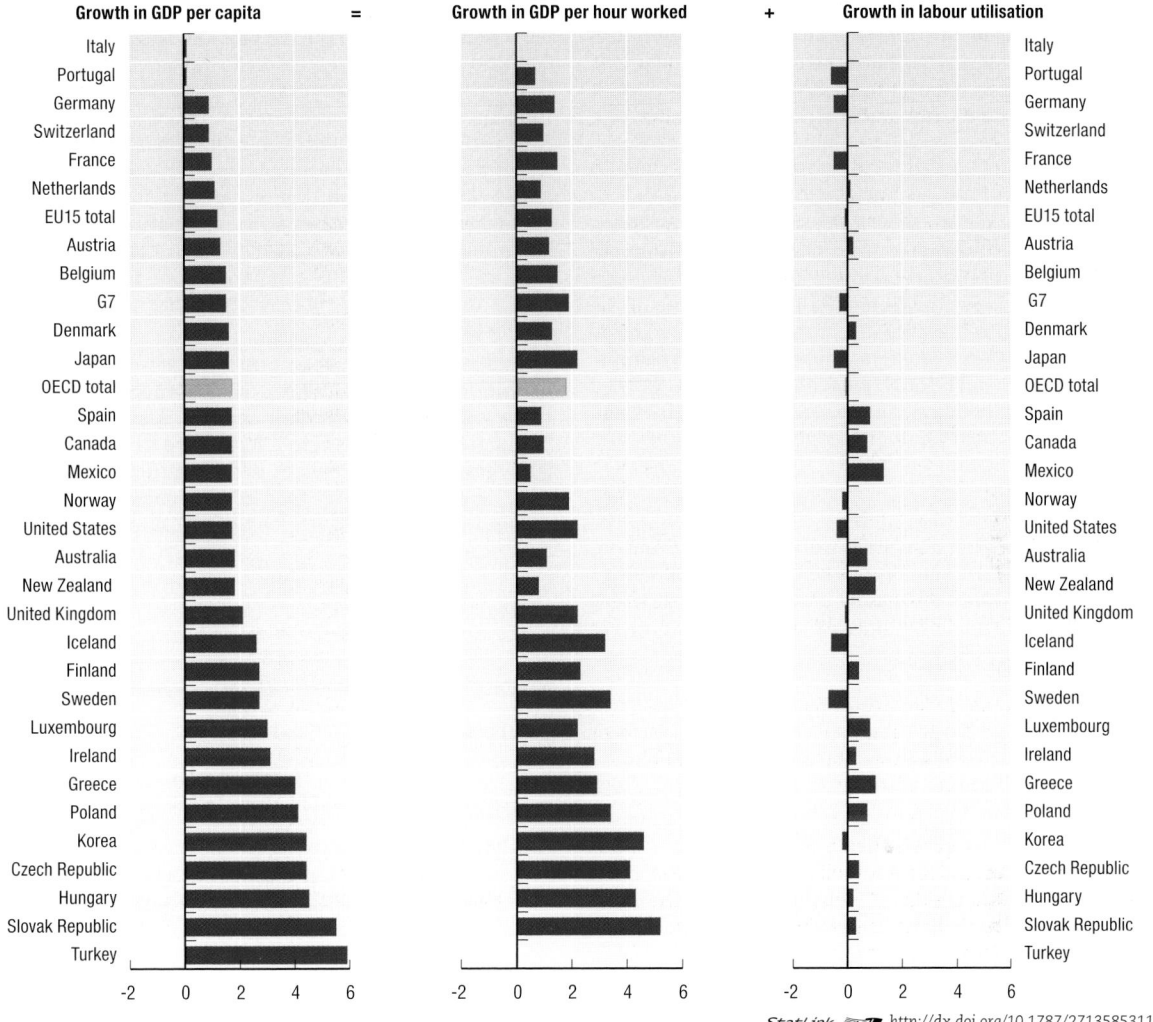

StatLink http://dx.doi.org/10.1787/271358531140

LABOUR PRODUCTIVITY GROWTH

Productivity growth is measured by relating changes in output to changes in one or more inputs to production. The most common productivity measure is labour productivity, which links changes in output to changes in labour input. It is a key economic indicator and it is closely associated with standards of living.

Definition

The output measures used for calculations are Gross Domestic Product estimates from OECD Annual National Accounts database, based on the *1993 System of National Accounts*. Labour input measures used are estimates of the hours actually worked. They reflect regular hours worked by full-time and part-time workers, paid and unpaid overtime, hours worked in additional jobs and time not worked because of public holidays, annual paid leaves, strikes and labour disputes, bad weather, economic conditions and other reasons.

Comparability

OECD and National statisticians work together to ensure that the data on hours actually worked are as comparable as possible, though they are based on a range of different sources of varying reliability. In most countries, the data are taken from household labour force surveys, while the rest use establishment surveys, administrative sources or a combination of sources. One problem is that for several EU countries, the estimates are made by the OECD using results from the *Spring European Labour Force Survey*. The results reflect a single observation in the year, and the survey data have to be supplemented by information from other sources for hours not worked due to public holidays and annual paid leave. Annual working hours reported for the remaining countries are provided by national statistical offices and are estimated using the best available sources. In general, the data are best used for comparisons of trends over time rather than for inter-country comparisons of the level of productivity.

Although the GDP estimates are based on common definitions, the methods used by most countries to estimate value added in government services assume that labour productivity growth is zero. This means that countries with large government sectors or with government sectors that were growing during the period considered will, by assumption, have lower growth in GDP per hour worked than other countries.

Note that in the chart, OECD total excludes Poland and Turkey.

Sources
- *OECD Productivity Database.*

Further information
Analytical publications
- Ahmad, N., F. Lequiller, P. Marianna, D. Pilat, P. Schreyer and A. Wölfl (2003), *Comparing Labour Productivity Growth in the OECD Area: The Role of Measurement*, OECD Science, Technology and Industry Working Papers, No. 2003/14, OECD, Paris.

Methodological publications
- OECD (2001), "The Measurement of Productivity: What Do the Numbers Mean?", *Measuring Productivity – OECD Manual Measurement of Aggregate and Industry-level Productivity Growth*, OECD, Paris, Chapter 3, pp. 29-61.
- OECD (2004), "Clocking In (and Out): Several Facets of Working Time", *OECD Employment Outlook: 2004 Edition*, Chapter 1, see also Annex I.A1, OECD, Paris.
- Pilat, D. and P. Schreyer (2004), "The OECD Productivity Database – An Overview", *International Productivity Monitor*, No. 8, Spring, CSLS, Ottawa, pp. 59-65.
- Schreyer, P. and D. Pilat (2001), "Measuring Productivity", *OECD Economic Studies*, OECD, Paris.
- Van Ark, B. (2004), *"The Measurement of Productivity: What Do the Numbers Mean?"*, *Fostering Productivity – Patterns, Determinants and Policy Implications*, G. Gelauff, L. Klomp, S. Raes and T. Roelandt (eds.), Elsevier, Amsterdam; Boston, Chapter 3, pp. 29-61.

Websites
- *www.oecd.org/statistics/productivity.*
- *www.oecd.org/statistics/productivity/compendium.*

Long-term trends

Labour productivity growth varies considerably among OECD countries. For example, in the first half of the 2000s, labour productivity growth in Hungary, Korea and the Slovak Republic ranged from 4.3 to 5.2% to a growth rate of less than 0.5% in Italy and Mexico.

In a number of OECD countries, labour productivity growth accelerated in the second half of the 1990s but slowed again in the first half of the new millennium. Between 2001-2006 and 1995-2000, the Czech Republic and Hungary were the only countries that experienced a significant acceleration of growth in GDP per hour worked while over the same period, Australia, Ireland, Mexico and Portugal saw a strong deceleration in labour productivity growth.

The rates shown here are not adjusted for differences in the business cycle; cyclically adjusted estimates might show a somewhat different pattern.

GDP per hour worked

Annual growth in percentage

	1971	1980	1985	1995	1997	1998	1999	2000	2001	2002	2003	2004	2005	2006
Australia	1.9	0.4	2.2	0.8	3.4	3.4	2.5	−1.2	3.9	1.8	2.3	0.7	−0.1	0.5
Austria	..	..	..	..	0.7	2.5	3.2	2.7	0.3	0.9	0.7	1.4	1.0	1.9
Belgium	3.5	5.7	0.9	−0.8	2.1	−0.6	1.9	3.4	−2.1	1.5	1.2	3.9	−0.6	1.2
Canada	2.8	0.6	1.2	1.4	4.1	1.8	2.5	2.9	1.0	1.5	0.3	0.4	2.1	0.8
Czech Republic	..	..	..	4.0	−1.0	0.4	4.2	3.5	6.5	2.3	5.3	3.3	4.4	4.6
Denmark	4.7	−1.0	2.5	1.7	0.8	−0.4	0.8	2.1	−0.6	0.9	1.9	1.7	1.3	0.8
Finland	4.8	3.2	3.1	2.0	2.9	3.6	1.1	3.6	2.0	1.0	2.1	3.0	1.8	3.2
France	5.2	2.2	2.9	2.7	2.2	2.6	1.7	3.6	0.9	3.1	1.3	0.6	1.8	0.9
Germany	4.3	0.9	2.3	2.5	2.5	1.2	1.4	2.6	1.8	1.5	1.2	0.5	1.3	2.4
Greece	..	..	0.2	1.7	5.7	−0.6	1.2	3.9	7.9	2.8	2.3	3.8	1.7	3.7
Hungary	..	..	..	4.6	3.1	3.4	0.0	4.1	5.8	3.9	4.2	5.4	4.2	3.4
Iceland	9.4	2.9	−0.2	−4.0	5.9	3.4	−2.6	1.6	4.2	3.3	2.9	7.6	4.6	−2.4
Ireland	4.5	3.9	2.0	4.8	8.3	4.3	5.7	4.8	3.3	4.9	3.7	1.3	1.6	2.2
Italy	4.4	1.9	2.1	2.9	2.1	−0.4	1.0	2.4	0.8	−0.7	−1.2	0.7	0.4	1.0
Japan	4.1	2.3	5.1	2.6	2.3	0.3	3.0	2.8	1.6	2.4	1.7	3.2	2.1	1.2
Korea	..	..	3.8	5.7	5.0	2.9	7.0	3.3	2.3	5.7	4.5	4.4	4.5	3.4
Luxembourg	..	..	1.0	−1.8	3.5	2.3	3.4	3.1	−1.9	1.6	1.5	4.4	3.0	0.2
Mexico	..	..	..	−6.5	−0.3	4.9	0.3	6.1	1.2	−2.8	2.3	1.2	−1.0	2.6
Netherlands	4.5	0.8	−0.3	2.3	1.6	2.3	3.4	2.3	−0.1	1.3	−0.3	3.2	0.3	0.0
New Zealand	2.7	1.1	−1.8	0.1	1.7	0.8	2.9	0.9	1.8	1.7	1.3	−0.5	0.2	1.1
Norway	5.8	2.0	2.9	3.2	2.7	0.1	1.2	3.9	3.4	2.2	3.1	2.0	1.4	0.8
Poland	..	..	..	..	..	..	..	..	4.1	4.2	4.7	4.0	0.7	3.1
Portugal	..	..	..	1.7	4.5	2.7	1.3	4.4	0.0	0.3	1.3	0.4	1.1	0.2
Slovak Republic	..	..	..	4.1	7.1	6.0	2.4	2.4	3.3	7.5	6.6	3.6	2.5	5.2
Spain	4.2	5.8	3.9	0.8	0.3	−0.2	0.1	0.1	0.7	0.6	0.9	0.7	1.0	1.3
Sweden	2.6	1.3	0.9	1.9	3.4	2.0	1.8	3.2	0.4	3.4	3.1	3.2	3.3	2.9
Switzerland	2.7	3.0	1.8	1.6	2.8	0.8	−0.8	2.8	1.9	1.0	−0.6	0.4	2.6	1.4
United Kingdom	4.9	0.9	0.3	1.5	1.3	2.6	2.3	3.2	1.3	2.3	2.9	2.5	0.7	2.4
United States	3.8	0.0	1.8	0.1	1.6	2.0	2.4	2.3	2.0	2.9	3.0	2.4	1.5	1.0
EU15 total	..	..	..	..	2.1	1.3	1.6	2.7	1.1	1.4	1.1	1.3	1.1	1.7
G7	4.1	0.9	2.5	1.5	2.1	1.7	2.5	2.7	1.7	2.3	2.1	2.1	1.6	1.3
OECD total	..	..	..	..	1.9	2.3	2.2	2.6	1.7	1.8	2.2	2.0	1.4	1.4

StatLink ᵃᵐˢˡ᷈ http://dx.doi.org/10.1787/276056348835

Growth in GDP per hour worked

Average annual growth in percentage, 1995-2000 and 2001-2006

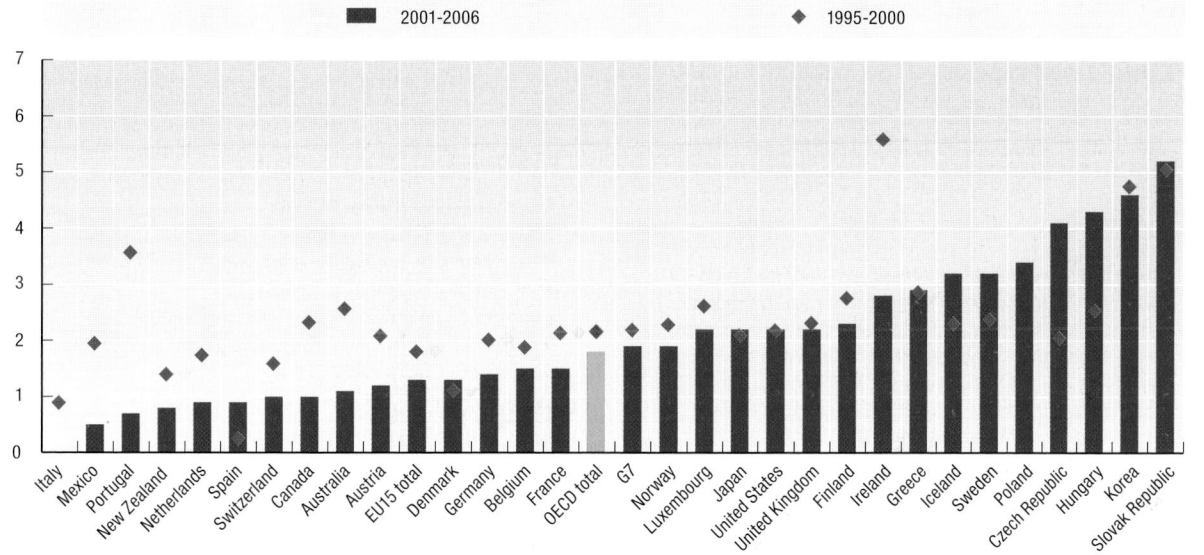

StatLink ᵃᵐˢˡ᷈ http://dx.doi.org/10.1787/271420512642

MULTI-FACTOR PRODUCTIVITY

Growth accounting typically involves breaking down the growth of gross domestic product (GDP) into three components – the contribution of labour, the contribution of capital and multi-factor productivity (MFP).

MFP is the change in GDP that cannot be explained by changes in the quantities of capital and labour that are made available to generate GDP. MFP is sometimes described as disembodied technological progress, because it is the increase in GDP that is not embodied in the amounts of either labour or capital. MFP growth comes from more efficient use of labour and capital inputs, for example through improvements in the management of production processes, organisational change or more generally, innovation. Growth in MFP is a significant factor in explaining the long-term growth of real GDP.

Definition

MFP growth is measured by deducting from output growth the growth of labour and capital inputs. Turned around, the same relation can be used to explain output growth by the contribution of labour and capital inputs, and by MFP growth.

In these calculations, the growth rates of labour and capital inputs are weighted with their share in total costs. Thus, the contribution of labour to GDP growth is measured as the speed with which labour input grows, multiplied by the relative importance of labour captured by its share in total costs. The growth contributions of capital or of certain types of capital are measured in a similar way so that the growth contribution always reflects two effects, the growth rate of the input and its relative importance in production.

Comparability

The growth accounts for OECD countries are based on the OECD Productivity Database where the main problems of consistency of data sources and comparability across countries are addressed.

Output is measured as real GDP, compiled according to the *1993 System of National Accounts*, although there may be some differences in how countries convert current price GDP to real GDP. Labour input is measured as total hours actually worked, and capital input is measured as the flow of capital services, based on an identical method for all countries.

Since MFP is obtained as a residual – *i.e.* that part of GDP growth that is left over when the growth contributions of labour and capital inputs have been deducted – MFP necessarily contains any errors or differences in methods between countries that exist in measuring GDP and labour and capital inputs. Some differences in methods between countries, for example with regard to prices of information and communication technology capital, have been corrected because the OECD uses a standard method for these types of capital goods.

It must also be emphasised that the data used here relate to the total economy and therefore include the government sector. Measuring output and productivity for the government sector is difficult and statistical practices as well as the size of the government sector may vary between countries. This should be kept in mind when interpreting the present series.

In the charts, data for Australia, Belgium, Japan and Switzerland refer to 1985-2004, data for Denmark, Finland, Netherlands, and the United Kingdom refer to 1985-2005, data for Spain refer to 1990-2006, data for Germany refer to 1991-2006, data for Switzerland refer to 1995-2004, and data for Austria and Portugal refer to 1995-2005.

Source
- *OECD Productivity Database.*

Further information
Analytical publications
- OECD (2003), *The Sources of Economic Growth in OECD Countries*, OECD, Paris.
- OECD (2004), *Understanding Economic Growth A Macro-level, Industry-level, and Firm-level Perspective*, OECD, Paris.
- OECD (2007), *OECD Science, Technology and Industry: Scoreboard 2007*, OECD, Paris.

Methodological publications
- OECD (2001), *Measuring Productivity – OECD Manual Measurement of Aggregate and Industry-level Productivity Growth*, OECD, Paris.
- Schreyer, P., P.-E. Bignon and J. Dupont (2003), *OECD Capital Services Estimates*, OECD Statistics Working Papers, No. 2003/6, OECD, Paris.

Websites
- *www.oecd.org/statistics/productivity.*
- *www.oecd.org/statistics/productivity/compendium.*

Long-term trends

Multi-factor productivity growth was one of the factors that helped strengthen growth in Belgium, Japan, Sweden, the United Kingdom and the United States in the recent years (2001-2006) compared with the longer period 1985-2006. In other countries, including Austria, Australia, Denmark, Finland, France, Germany, Ireland, Italy, the Netherlands, New Zealand, Portugal and Switzerland, MFP growth slowed down in the recent years (2001-2006) compared to the longer period 1985-2006, sometimes significantly as in the case of Ireland, Italy, New Zealand and Portugal. MFP growth was negative in the recent years (2001-2006) in Italy but positive in the long term period 1985-2006.

Multi-factor productivity

Annual growth in percentage

	1993	1994	1995	1996	1997	1998	1999	2000	2001	2002	2003	2004	2005	2006
Australia	2.2	0.4	0.8	3.3	2.5	2.8	1.7	−1.5	2.7	0.9	1.5	0.0	..	..
Austria	..	..	..	1.0	0.4	2.1	2.6	2.1	−0.3	0.3	0.2	1.1	0.9	..
Belgium	1.2	3.0	−0.6	1.6	1.8	−0.8	1.4	2.6	−2.1	1.1	0.9	3.2	..	..
Canada	0.5	1.7	0.9	−0.3	3.0	1.1	1.8	2.1	0.0	0.9	−0.3	0.1	1.4	0.3
Denmark	0.4	5.2	1.1	1.4	0.3	−1.0	0.1	1.4	−1.2	−0.2	0.7	1.0	0.9	..
Finland	3.0	3.7	2.0	2.1	3.0	3.3	1.1	3.3	1.6	0.8	1.6	2.8	1.5	..
France	0.1	1.8	2.0	0.0	1.5	2.0	1.1	2.7	0.2	2.0	0.7	0.4	1.2	0.5
Germany	0.3	2.2	1.7	1.4	1.7	0.7	0.8	1.9	1.0	0.6	0.5	0.4	0.9	2.1
Ireland	1.6	2.1	4.8	4.0	8.3	4.3	5.7	4.7	2.8	4.2	2.9	1.2	1.6	2.2
Italy	0.7	3.1	2.2	−0.9	1.3	−0.8	0.4	1.7	0.1	−1.4	−1.6	0.2	−0.3	0.6
Japan	1.1	0.4	1.5	1.0	1.2	−1.2	1.2	2.0	0.5	1.4	1.2	2.7	..	..
Netherlands	1.8	2.4	1.7	−1.5	1.3	1.5	2.6	0.1	−0.5	0.8	−0.7	2.0	0.2	..
New Zealand	2.1	1.5	0.1	0.5	0.9	−0.2	2.5	0.2	1.3	1.4	0.7	−0.6	−0.6	0.3
Portugal	..	..	..	3.6	3.5	1.9	0.5	3.2	−0.7	−0.3	0.3	0.1	0.7	..
Spain	0.7	1.8	0.3	0.2	−0.1	−0.5	−0.4	−0.4	−0.1	−0.1	0.2	0.1	0.3	0.4
Sweden	0.4	2.1	1.5	0.5	2.3	1.4	1.2	2.1	−0.4	2.9	2.6	3.0	3.0	2.3
Switzerland	−0.3	−0.1	0.4	1.0	1.7	0.3	−1.2	2.1	0.8	0.1	−1.1	0.4	..	..
United Kingdom	2.2	2.2	1.0	1.1	0.7	1.4	1.1	2.0	0.4	1.3	2.1	1.9	0.1	..
United States	0.1	0.8	−0.3	1.7	1.0	1.2	1.5	1.3	0.8	2.0	2.4	2.1	1.2	0.7

StatLink ⛓ http://dx.doi.org/10.1787/276058872138

Multi-factor productivity

Average annual growth in percentage, 1985-2006 and 2001-2006 (or closest comparable periods)

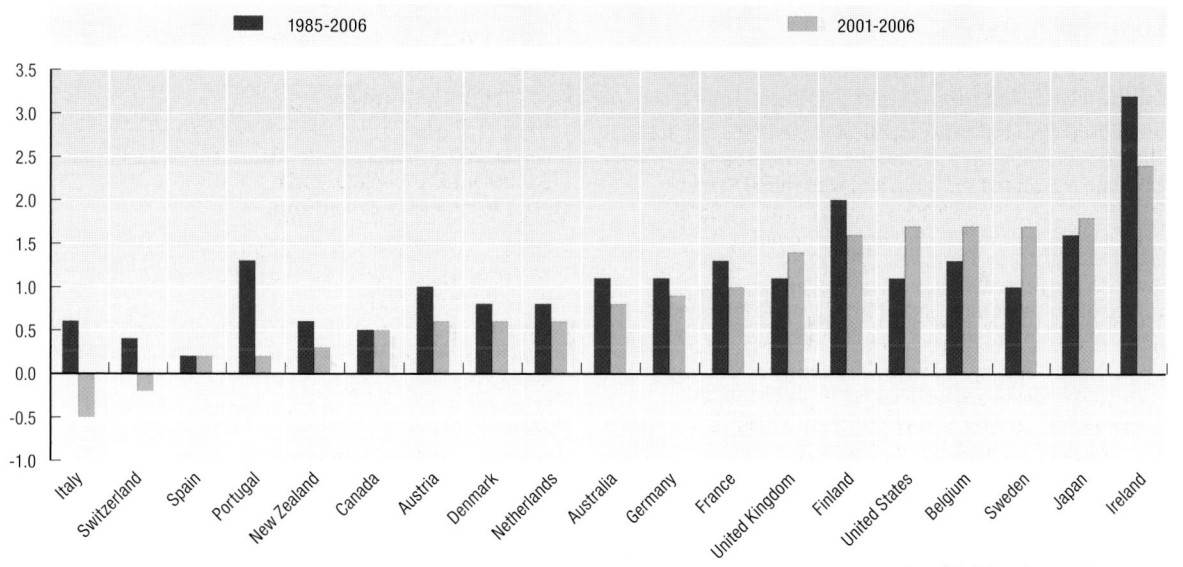

StatLink ⛓ http://dx.doi.org/10.1787/271464318560

GROWTH ACCOUNTS FOR OECD COUNTRIES

Economic growth can be increased by increasing the amount and types of labour and capital used in production, and by attaining greater overall efficiency in how these factors of production are used together, *i.e.* higher multi-factor productivity. Growth accounting involves breaking down growth of GDP into the contribution of labour input, capital input and MFP.

Definition

The growth accounting approach is based on the micro-economic theory of production and directly related to the calculation of multi-factor productivity (MFP) growth. MFP growth is measured by deducting from output growth the growth of labour and capital inputs. Turned around, the same relation can be used to explain output growth by the rates of change of labour and capital inputs and by MFP growth.

In these calculations, the growth rate of labour and capital inputs is weighted with their share in total costs. Thus, the contribution of labour to GDP growth is measured as the speed with which labour input grows, multiplied by the relative importance of labour captured by its share in total costs. The growth contributions of capital or of certain types of capital are measured in a similar way so that the growth contribution always reflects two effects, the growth rate of the input and its relative importance in production.

Comparability

The role of information and communication technologies (ICT) for growth in GDP and MFP is analysed thanks to the differentiation between ICT and non-ICT capital. ICT related capital include hardware, communication and software. Non-ICT capital include transport equipment and non residential construction, products of agriculture, metal products and machinery other than hardware and communication equipment, and other products of non-residential gross fixed capital formation.

Long-term trends

From 1985 to 2006, GDP growth in most OECD countries was for a large part driven by growth in capital and MFP. In many countries, growth in capital accounted for around one third of GDP growth from 1985 to 2006. Over the same period, ICT capital services represented between 0.2 and 0.6 percentage point of growth in GDP. ICT accounts for the bulk of capital's contribution to GDP growth in Australia, Denmark, France, New Zealand, Sweden, the United Kingdom and the United States; its contribution was more modest in Italy and Finland and even smaller in Austria and Ireland. From 1985 to 2006, MFP growth was also an important source of growth of GDP in Finland, Belgium, Ireland, and Japan but its contribution was very small in Canada, Italy, New Zealand, Spain and Switzerland. Growth in labour input was also important for a few countries over 1985-2006, notably Australia, Canada, Ireland, the Netherlands, Spain and the United States.

The appropriate measure for capital input with the growth accounting framework is the flow of productive services that can be drawn from the cumulative stock of past investments in capital assets. These services are estimated by the OECD using the rate of change of the "productive capital stock". This measure takes into account wear and tear and retirements, *i.e.*, reductions in the productive capacity of the fixed assets. The price of capital services for each type of asset is measured as their rental price. In principle, the latter could be directly observed if markets existed for capital services. In practice, however, rental prices have to be imputed for most assets, using the implicit rent that capital goods' owners "pay" themselves (or "user costs of capital").

The measure of total hours worked is an incomplete measure of labour input because it does not account for changes in the skill composition of workers over time, such as educational attainment, and work experience. Adjustment for such attributes would provide a more accurate indication of the contribution of labour to production. In the absence of these adjustments, as is the case in the series shown here, more rapid output growth due to a rise in skills of the labour force are captured by the MFP residual, and not attributed to labour. This should be kept in mind when interpreting rates of MFP growth.

In the charts, data for Australia, Belgium, Japan and Switzerland refers to 1985-2004, data for Denmark, Finland, Netherlands, and the United Kingdom refers to 1985-2005, data for Spain refers to 1990-2006, data for Germany refers to 1991-2006, data for Switzerland refers to 1995-2004, and data for Austria and Portugal refers to 1995-2005.

Source
• *OECD Productivity Database.*

Further information

Analytical publications
• OECD (2003), *The Sources of Economic Growth in OECD Countries*, OECD, Paris.
• OECD (2004), *Understanding Economic Growth A Macro-level, Industry-level, and Firm-level Perspective*, OECD, Paris.
• OECD (2007), *OECD Science, Technology and Industry: Scoreboard 2007*, OECD, Paris.

Methodological publications
• OECD (2001), *Measuring Productivity – OECD Manual Measurement of Aggregate and Industry-level Productivity Growth*, OECD, Paris.
• Schreyer, P. (2004), "Capital Stocks, Capital Services and Multi-factor Productivity Measures", *OECD Economic Studies No. 37, 2003/2*, OECD, Paris, pp. 163-184.
• Schreyer, P., P.-E. Bignon and J. Dupont (2003), *OECD Capital Services Estimates*, OECD Statistics Working Papers, No. 2003/6, OECD, Paris.

Websites
• *www.oecd.org/statistics/productivity.*
• *www.oecd.org/statistics/productivity/compendium.*

Contributions to GDP growth

Average annual growth in percentage, 1985-2006

	Labour input	ICT capital	Non-ICT capital	Multi-factor productivity	GDP growth
Australia	1.13	0.57	0.46	1.12	3.25
Austria	0.48	0.20	0.18	1.00	1.85
Belgium	0.19	0.44	0.24	1.34	2.21
Canada	1.16	0.41	0.67	0.51	2.72
Denmark	0.14	0.52	0.45	0.83	1.94
Finland	−0.22	0.34	0.29	1.96	2.35
France	0.18	0.44	0.34	1.24	2.19
Germany	−0.31	0.35	0.28	1.05	1.35
Ireland	1.72	0.18	0.63	3.21	5.65
Italy	0.32	0.25	0.55	0.60	1.72
Japan	−0.43	0.39	0.53	1.61	2.08
Netherlands	0.92	0.41	0.38	0.96	2.65
New Zealand	0.87	0.44	0.40	0.63	2.32
Portugal	0.28	0.36	0.49	1.25	2.36
Spain	1.49	0.35	0.89	0.21	2.91
Sweden	0.23	0.48	0.33	1.01	2.04
Switzerland	0.29	0.41	0.38	0.45	1.54
United Kingdom	0.43	0.58	0.43	1.14	2.57
United States	1.03	0.49	0.36	1.09	2.94

StatLink ᵐˢ᪲ http://dx.doi.org/10.1787/276076835308

Contributions to GDP growth

Average annual growth in percentage, 1985-2006

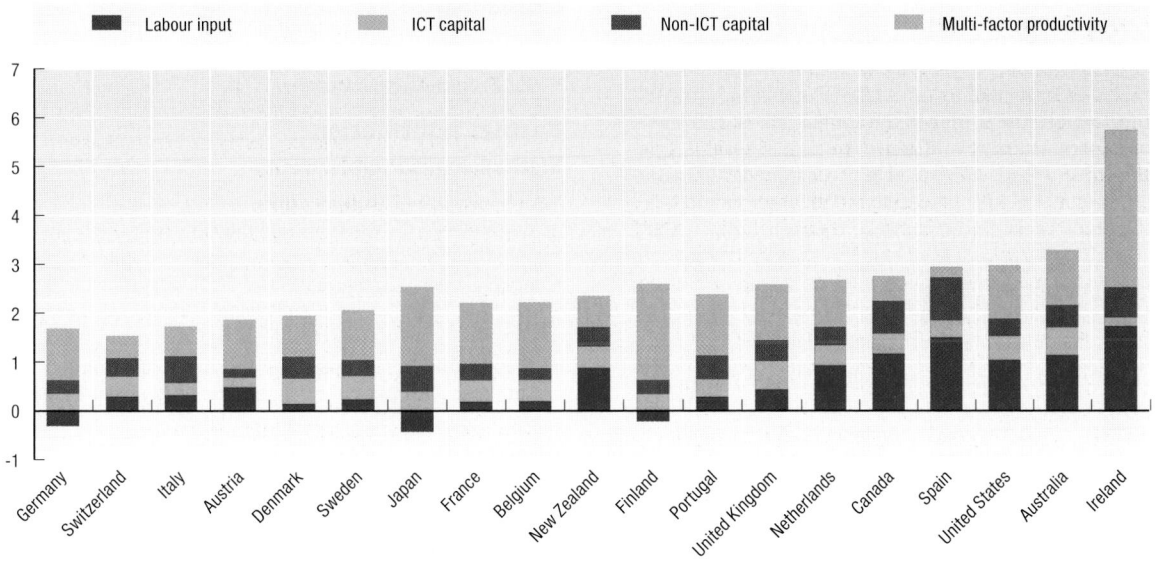

StatLink ᵐˢ᪲ http://dx.doi.org/10.1787/271471520427

INCOME AND PRODUCTIVITY LEVELS

Together with the analysis of growth rates, the levels of GDP per capita and GDP per hour worked are essential to assess the state of the convergence or divergence of economic performances across countries.

Definition

The differences in income levels can be decomposed into differences in labour productivity levels, measured as GDP per hour worked, and differences in the extent of labour utilisation, measured as the number of hours worked per capita. In countries with low levels of GDP per capita, the gaps in labour productivity levels are typically the most significant factor in determining differences in income. The estimates shown here are based on official OECD GDP converted to a common currency using OECD Purchasing Power Parities (PPPs) for 2006.

Comparability

Comparisons of income and productivity levels across countries require several demanding conditions. First, they require comparable data on output. All OECD countries, except Turkey, have implemented the *1993 System of National Accounts*. For this reason, the output level in Turkey is likely to be understated relative to other OECD countries. Other differences, such as the measurement of software investment, can also affect the comparability of GDP across countries, although these differences are usually quite small. Second, in a number of countries, employment data are derived from labour force surveys which may not be entirely consistent with the national accounts. This reduces the comparability of labour utilisation levels across countries. The measure of labour inputs also requires hours worked which are derived either from labour force surveys or from business surveys. Several OECD countries estimate hours worked from a combination of these sources or integrate these sources in a system of labour accounts, which is comparable to the national accounts. The OECD Productivity Database uses consistent estimates of employment and hours worked. Nonetheless, the cross-country comparability of hours worked remains somewhat limited, generating a margin of uncertainty in estimates of productivity levels. The third problem relates to the conversion of output from national currency into a common unit. Market exchange rates cannot be used directly, as they are volatile and reflect other factors, such as capital and trade flows. The preferred alternative is to use Purchasing Power Parities (PPPs), which measure the relative prices of the same basket of consumption goods in different countries.

GDP for Turkey is based on the *1968 System of National Accounts*.

Overview

In 2006, GDP per capita in OECD countries ranged from over USD 39 000 in Ireland, Luxembourg, Norway and the United States to less than USD 17 000 in Mexico, Poland and Turkey. On average, income levels were about 70% of that of the United States, Norway is a notable exception with its GDP per capita 14% above that of the United States.

Relative to the United States, most OECD countries had higher levels of GDP per hour worked than GDP per capita because their levels of labour utilisation were substantially lower than in the United States. This owes to disparities in working hours but also, in several countries, to high unemployment and low participation of the working-age population in the labour market.

The difference between income and productivity levels was largest in European countries. For example, in Belgium, Ireland and the Netherlands, while productivity levels in 2006 surpassed that of the United States, income levels were considerably lower.

In several non-EU countries, such as Canada, Japan, New Zealand and Switzerland, labour utilisation in 2006 was higher than in the United States, notably in Iceland and Korea, mainly owing to relatively long working hours and high rates of labour force participation.

Sources

• *OECD Productivity Database.*

Further information

Methodological publications

• OECD (2001), *Measuring Productivity – OECD Manual Measurement of Aggregate and Industry-level Productivity Growth*, OECD, Paris.
• OECD (2004), "Clocking In (and Out): Several Facets of Working Time", *OECD Employment Outlook: 2004 Edition*, Chapter 1, see also Annex I.A1, OECD, Paris.
• Pilat, D. and P. Schreyer (2004), "The OECD Productivity Database – An Overview", *International Productivity Monitor*, No. 8, Spring, CSLS, Ottawa, pp. 59-65.

Websites

• *www.oecd.org/statistics/productivity.*
• *www.oecd.org/statistics/productivity/compendium.*

Income and productivity levels

Percentage point differences with respect to the United States, 2006

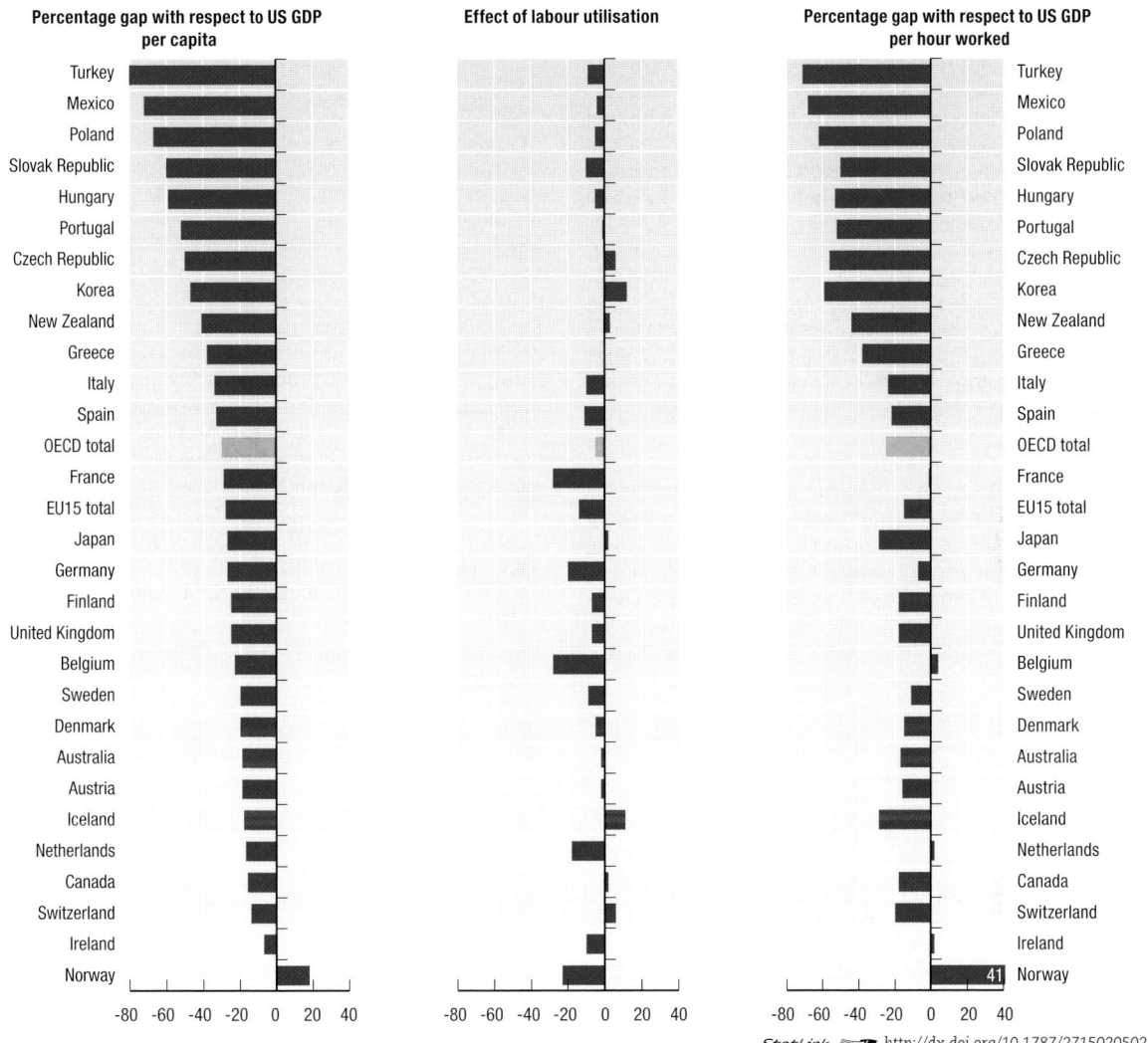

StatLink ⫶ *http://dx.doi.org/10.1787/271502050227*

HISTORICAL INCOME AND PRODUCTIVITY LEVELS

The process of "catch-up" in average income implies that less advanced economies should experience faster growth in output per capita, typically by adopting the practices of more advanced economies, notably as regards capital, technology and labour utilisation. While less developed countries may grow more rapidly at the beginning of the catching-up process, their economic growth rates are expected to decline over time as their income levels come closer to those of the more advanced countries.

Definition

For each country, the rate of "catch-up" vis-à-vis the United States is calculated as the difference between the average annual compounded growth rate of its GDP per capita level over the period and the average annual compounded growth rate of the United States' GDP per capita level over the same period.

Comparability

Comparisons of income and productivity levels for a particular year are derived from the time series of Gross Domestic Product (GDP), population, employment and hours worked of the OECD Productivity Database. For some countries, GDP and population data were also derived from Angus Maddison (2001), *The World Economy: A Millennial Perspective*, OECD Development Centre, OECD, Paris.

Calculations are based on GDP measures converted from national currencies to US dollars using 2006 Purchasing Power Parities.

Levels of GDP per capita

Catch-up and convergence in OECD income levels relative to the United States

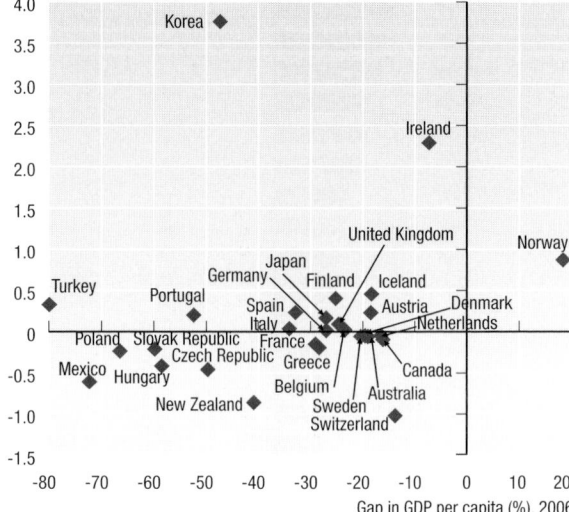

StatLink ⌨ http://dx.doi.org/10.1787/271581457461

Long-term trends

Since the 1970s, GDP per capita and labour productivity have broadly converged in the OECD area. Over the period 1973-2006, Ireland and Korea had the highest rates of catch-up in GDP per capita with 2.3% and 3.8% per year, respectively. More advanced economies that started with relatively high income levels in the 1970s have had lower rates of catch-up, even stagnated or recently have diverged vis-à-vis the United States; this was also the case for less advanced economies such as Eastern European countries, Mexico and Turkey.

Estimates of levels of GDP per hour worked display slightly different patterns. Since the beginning of the new millennium, several European countries have surpassed the United States in terms of average labour productivity levels. Only Australia, Canada, Mexico and New Zealand did not catch-up vis-à-vis the United States' productivity levels.

Sources
• *OECD Productivity Database.*

Further information

Statistical publications
• Maddison, Angus (2003), *The World Economy: Historical Perspectives*, OECD, Paris.

Methodological publications
• OECD (2001), *Measuring Productivity – OECD Manual Measurement of Aggregate and Industry-level Productivity Growth*, OECD, Paris.

Websites
• *www.oecd.org/statistics/productivity.*
• *www.oecd.org/statistics/productivity/compendium.*

Income and productivity levels relative to the United States

United States = 100

	GDP per capita							GDP per hour worked						
	1973	1985	1990	1995	2004	2005	2006	1973	1985	1990	1995	2004	2005	2006
Australia	83	80	76	80	82	82	81	80	85	81	84	84	83	83
Austria	76	80	82	83	81	81	81	72	..	91	90	83	83	84
Belgium	76	76	78	79	77	76	77	84	102	107	114	106	104	104
Canada	87	88	85	82	84	84	84	87	89	85	87	81	82	82
Czech Republic	58	56	51	46	46	48	50	..	..	..	39	41	43	44
Denmark	82	83	79	82	79	79	80	73	85	89	96	85	85	85
Finland	66	70	73	64	72	73	75	54	65	72	79	80	80	82
France	74	75	76	75	72	71	71	73	93	100	104	99	99	99
Germany	73	75	77	79	73	72	73	70	84	90	98	92	92	93
Greece	66	59	55	54	60	61	62	..	57	56	55	61	61	62
Hungary	47	45	39	33	40	41	41	..	..	..	40	44	46	47
Iceland	70	81	80	73	80	83	82	63	72	77	66	71	73	71
Ireland	45	49	55	64	91	92	93	46	65	73	83	101	101	102
Italy	65	71	74	74	68	66	66	70	82	87	91	77	76	76
Japan	69	74	81	81	73	73	73	47	58	67	71	70	71	71
Korea	16	25	33	44	50	51	53	10	19	26	32	38	40	41
Luxembourg	121	115	141	151	172	174	178	..	..	..	..	..	..	143
Mexico	34	34	29	27	27	27	28	45	..	39	35	32	31	32
Netherlands	85	79	81	83	83	83	83	88	108	106	113	104	103	102
New Zealand	78	68	61	61	60	60	59	69	61	64	63	57	56	56
Norway	89	110	105	116	118	118	118	93	121	126	140	141	141	141
Poland	36	31	25	26	32	32	33	..	..	..	..	38	37	38
Portugal	45	40	48	49	49	48	48	40	..	44	50	49	49	48
Slovak Republic	43	41	37	32	36	38	40	..	..	..	37	48	48	50
Spain	62	57	63	63	67	67	67	62	90	89	93	78	78	78
Sweden	81	79	78	74	78	78	80	78	80	80	84	85	87	89
Switzerland	120	105	104	95	86	86	86	96	99	96	87	79	80	80
Turkey	18	18	19	19	19	19	20	..	..	..	..	..	..	29
United Kingdom	73	69	72	73	76	75	75	67	75	76	82	82	81	82
United States	100	100	100	100	100	100	100	100	100	100	100	100	100	100

StatLink http://dx.doi.org/10.1787/276082813320

GDP per hour worked relative to the United States

United States = 100

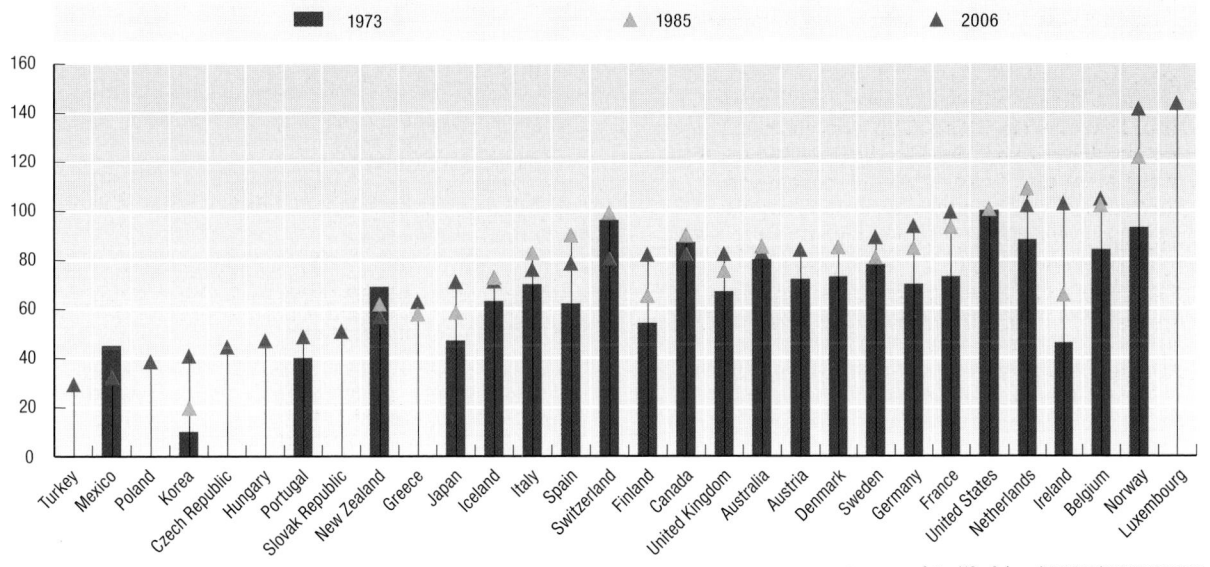

StatLink http://dx.doi.org/10.1787/271574855515

LABOUR PRODUCTIVITY AND FIRM-SIZE HETEROGENEITY

Differences in labour productivity across business enterprises of different sizes can be illustrated by showing normalised labour productivity figures in the manufacturing sector according to employment size class.

Definition

Labour productivity is calculated as the ratio of value added to the number of persons engaged, with the exception of the United States, for which it is the ratio of turnover to the number of employees and new zealand, for which it is the ratio of value added to the number of employees. The normalised labour productivity figures shown here are calculated as labour productivity in a given size class as a percentage of the labour productivity across enterprises in all size classes.

Comparability

The size class breakdown used provides for the best comparability across countries given the varying data collection practices across countries. For some countries slightly different conventions are needed. The data for Mexico refer to the following size classes: "0-10", "11-20", "21-50", "51-250" and "251+". Data shown for "20-49" actually refer to "20-99" for the United States; data shown for "50-249" actually refer to "50-199" for Australia, Korea and Turkey, and "100-499" for the United States; data shown for "250+" actually refer to "200+" for Australia, Korea, and Turkey, and "500+" for the United States.

For Ireland, only enterprises whith 3 or more persons engaged are reflected, while the data for Japan, Korea and Turkey do not include establishments whith fewer than 4, 5 and 10 persons engaged respectively.

The data shown refer to 2005 for all countries except for Turkey (2001), The United States (2002), Mexico and New Zealand (2003), the Czech Republic, Japan and Norway (2004).

Overview

For every country, the highest labour productivity is observed in the biggest enterprise size class, possibly reflecting more intensive capital investment by larger businesses or indicating economies of scale.

For the majority of countries (about 75 %), labour productivity increases monotonically with size class. Interestingly in Denmark, the Slovak republic and, to a lesser extent, the United Kingdom and the United States, labour productivity across small and medium-size enterprises seems significantly more homogeneous than in other countries but this in part reflects the result of averaging throughout the manufacturing sector. At the ISIC 2-digit level, for example, the picture is more heterogeneous.

Source

- *Structural Business Demographic Statistics, OECD database.*

Further information

Analytical publications

- Ahmad, N., F. Lequiller, P. Marianna, D. Pilat, P. Schreyer and A. Wölfl (2003), *Comparing Labour Productivity Growth in the OECD Area: The Role of Measurement*, OECD Science, Technology and Industry Working Papers, No. 2003/14, OECD, Paris.
- OECD (2001), *OECD Science, Technology and Industry Scoreboard: Towards a Knowledge-based Economy 2001 Edition*, D.4., OECD, Paris.
- OECD (2003), *OECD Science, Technology and Industry: Scoreboard 2003*, Section D and Annex 1, OECD, Paris.

Statistical publications

- OECD (2006), *Structural and Demographic Business Statistics: 1996-2003, 2006 Edition*, OECD, Paris.

Methodological publications

- OECD (2001), *Measuring Productivity – OECD Manual Measurement of Aggregate and Industry-level Productivity Growth*, OECD, Paris.

Websites

- *www.oecd.org/statistics/productivity/compendium.*

Normalised labour productivity in manufacturing

As a percentage of total average, breakdown by size-class of enterprise, 2005

	1-9	10-19	20-49	50-249	250+
Australia	68.0	61.3	73.5	86.4	139.5
Austria	58.7	64.8	73.6	92.0	126.5
Belgium	47.2	60.1	72.5	90.9	132.0
Czech republic	56.1	66.2	77.6	90.5	130.6
Denmark	78.0	72.9	83.0	93.4	116.7
Finland	72.5	68.3	69.2	82.1	121.9
France	59.1	73.3	81.0	86.0	126.0
Germany	49.8	58.1	74.3	88.7	122.5
Hungary	29.7	47.3	55.2	73.6	156.3
Ireland	30.0	28.1	31.6	67.8	154.7
Italy	54.0	81.6	99.0	122.1	146.2
Japan	42.9	55.4	65.8	97.8	157.8
Korea	41.3	50.9	59.3	88.0	189.8
Luxembourg	68.0	61.2	65.0	90.9	113.2
Mexico	21.9	47.4	58.2	89.0	141.7
Netherlands	46.2	73.7	76.2	94.0	146.5
Norway	64.9	75.1	84.7	98.7	123.9
Poland	35.0	58.2	60.6	75.9	162.1
Portugal	49.3	66.6	79.8	105.4	191.6
Slovak republic	90.0	72.7	71.9	76.7	117.6
Spain	53.4	67.7	77.6	101.4	165.5
Sweden	47.1	70.1	77.9	85.7	127.7
Turkey		32.7	46.7	69.9	130.6
United Kingdom	74.5	74.4	81.4	90.1	122.0
United States	54.1	46.8	53.8	68.3	129.8

StatLink ⧉ http://dx.doi.org/10.1787/276122477188

Normalised labour productivity in manufacturing

As a percentage of total average, breakdown by size-class of enterprise, 2005

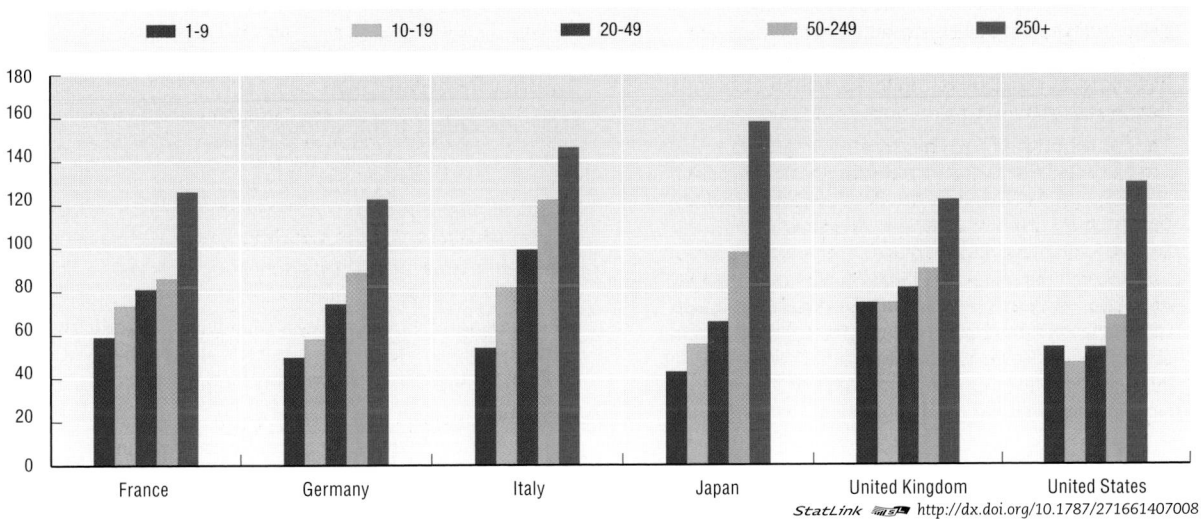

StatLink ⧉ http://dx.doi.org/10.1787/271661407008

CONTRIBUTION OF KEY ACTIVITIES TO AGGREGATE PRODUCTIVITY GROWTH

A breakdown of productivity growth by economic activity can highlight industries that are particularly important for overall productivity performance.

Definition

Labour productivity growth can be calculated as the difference between the rate of growth of output or value added and the rate of growth of labour input. Calculating a sector's contribution to aggregate productivity growth requires a number of simple steps, as explained in the OECD Productivity Manual. First, the aggregate rate of change in value added is a share-weighted average of the industry-specific rate of change in value added, with weights reflecting the current price share of each industry in current price value added. On the input side, aggregation of industry-level labour input is achieved by weighting the growth rates of total employment (National Accounts detailed series on hours worked by industry are not available for many across OECD countries) with each industry's share in total labour compensation. Aggregate labour productivity growth can then be calculated as the difference between the aggregate growth in value added and the aggregate growth in labour input. An industry's contribution to aggregate labour productivity growth is therefore the difference between its contribution to total value added and total labour input. If value added and labour shares are the same, total labour productivity growth is a simple weighted average of industry-specific labour productivity growth.

Similar approaches can be followed when production, instead of value added, is used as the output measure.

"Market services" refers to ISIC Rev. 3 service activities 50 to 74. Further details are available in the indicator on productivity growth in services.

Comparability

For the graphs, the contributions have been scaled so that the sum of the absolute contributions equals 100. Therefore, irrespective of countries' actual total labour productivity growth, the relative contributions of the different sectors can be compared. Difficulties in measuring output and productivity in services sectors should also be taken into consideration when interpreting the results.

In charts, for Japan data do not refer to 1995-2000 but to 1996-2000; data do not refer to 2000-06 for New Zealand but to 2000-02; 2000-03 for Australia; 2000-04 for Portugal and Sweden; 2000-05 for Canada, France, Hungary, Spain and the United States.

Long-term trends

Over the period 2000-2006, "market services" accounted for the bulk of labour productivity growth in many OECD countries. Namely, in Greece, Luxembourg, New-Zealand, Norway, the United Kingdom and the United States, "market services" accounted for over 55% of aggregate labour productivity growth. However, the highest aggregate labour productivity growth performances can still be attributed to the manufacturing sector. This was the case in the Czech Republic, Finland, Korea, the Slovak Republic and Sweden.

The contribution of "market services" to labour productivity growth has increased between 1995-2000 and 2000-2006 in Belgium, the Czech Republic, France, Luxembourg and New Zealand. This growing contribution of market services is sometimes linked to an increasing share in total value added, but in the Czech Republic, Japan and New Zealand, for example, it also reflects faster labour productivity growth in the market service sector. However, in several other countries, labour productivity growth in market services has slowed down in the most recent years.

Sources
- *Annual National Accounts.*
- *OECD Productivity Database.*

Further information
Methodological publications
- OECD (2001), *Measuring Productivity – OECD Manual Measurement of Aggregate and Industry-level Productivity Growth*, OECD, Paris.
- OECD (2004), "Clocking In (and Out): Several Facets of Working Time", *OECD Employment Outlook: 2004 Edition*, Chapter 1, see also Annex I.A1, OECD, Paris.
- Pilat, D. and P. Schreyer (2004), "The OECD Productivity Database – An Overview", *International Productivity Monitor*, No. 8, Spring, CSLS, Ottawa, pp. 59-65.

Websites
- *www.oecd.org/statistics/productivity/compendium.*

Contributions of key activities to growth of value added per person employed

Percentage points, 2000-2006 or latest available year

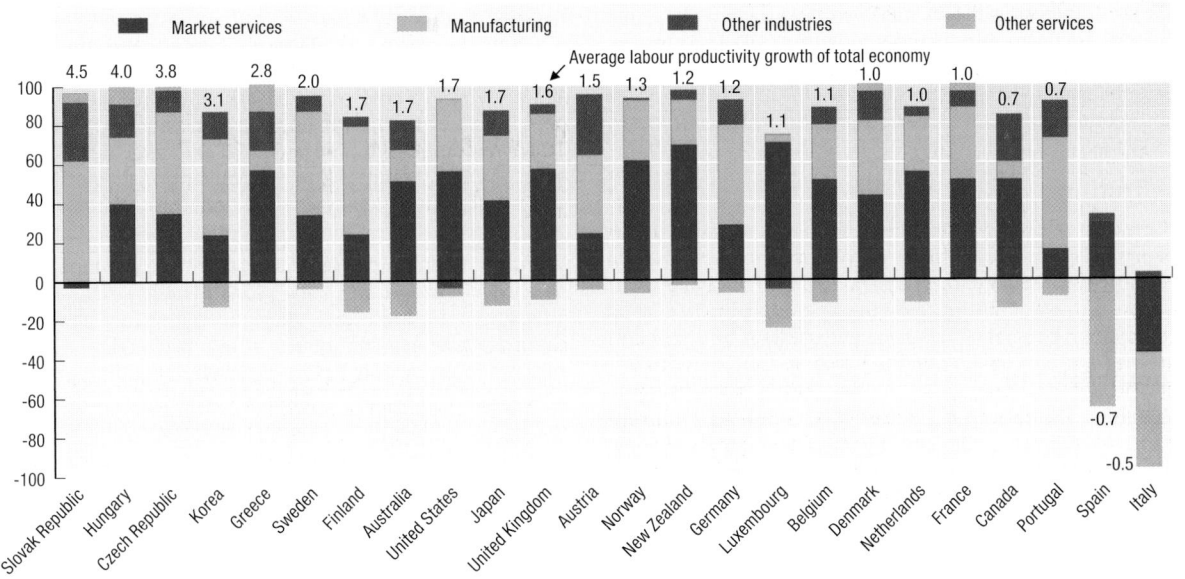

StatLink http://dx.doi.org/10.1787/271713228802

Contributions of key activities to growth of value added per person employed

Percentage points, 1995-2000 or earliest available year

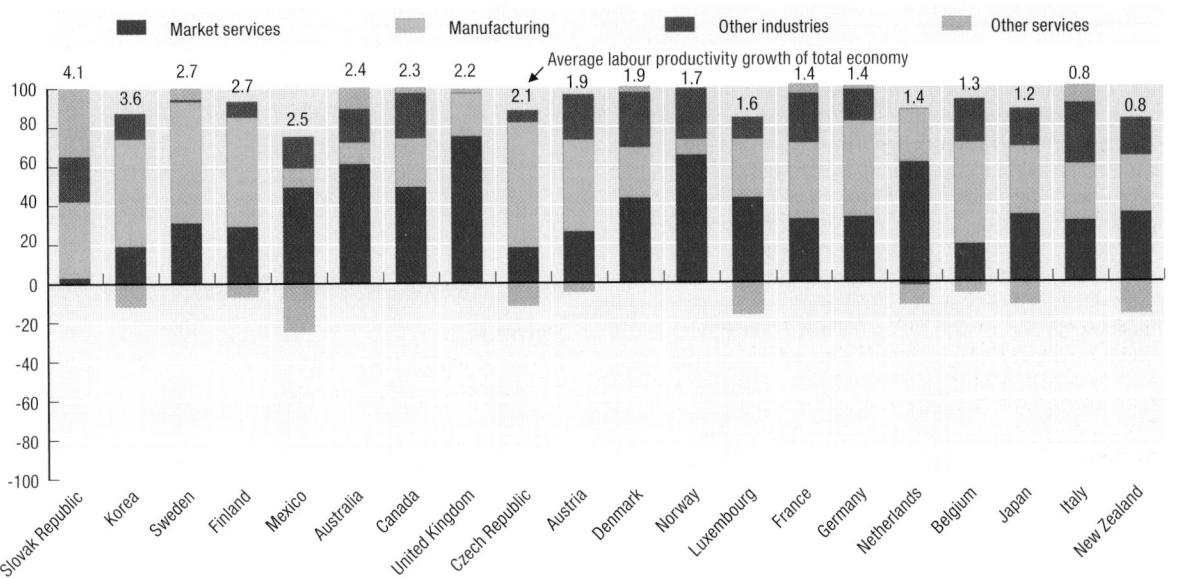

StatLink http://dx.doi.org/10.1787/271718681888

PRODUCTIVITY GROWTH IN MANUFACTURING

The manufacturing sector has historically been the main driver of aggregate productivity growth in OECD countries. While its contribution to aggregate productivity growth has become less important in recent years, particularly in some OECD countries, it still shows strong performance in many industries.

Definition

In the indicator presented here, for each manufacturing industry, labour productivity growth is calculated as the difference between the rate of growth of the industry's value added and the rate of growth of the industry's total employment (number of persons engaged).

Comparability

Examining the role of ICT-producing sectors in economic growth is heavily influenced by measurement problems, both regarding outputs and inputs. The key measurement problem for the manufacturing of ICT goods on both the output and input side concerns prices, in particular how to statistically capture significant quality improvements associated with technological advances in goods such as computers and semi-conductors. The use of so-called hedonic deflators is generally considered as the best way to address these problems. Several countries currently use hedonic methods to deflate output in the computer industry (*e.g.* Canada, Denmark, France, Sweden and the United States), however, these countries do not use exactly the same method. Some countries, such as the United States, apply their own hedonic deflator, others apply the United States hedonic deflator adjusted for exchange rates, and yet other OECD countries apply conventional methods to account for quality change when deriving deflators.

Adjusting for these methodological differences in computer deflators for the purpose of a cross-country comparison is difficult, since there are considerable cross-country differences in industrial specialisation. Only few OECD countries produce computers, where price falls have been very rapid; many only produce peripheral equipment, such as computer terminals. Similar differences in industry composition exist in Radio, Television and Communication Equipment (ISIC 32), which includes the semi-conductor industry. The differences in the composition of output are typically larger than in computer investment, where standardised approaches have been applied (*e.g.* Schreyer *et al.* 2003).

In charts, for Japan data do not refer to 1995-2000 but to 1996-2000; data do not refer to 2000-2005 but to 2000-2004 for Canada, Portugal and Sweden; 2001-2005 for Poland.

Long-term trends

For most OECD countries, manufacturing productivity growth was slower during 2000-2005 than in the period 1995-2000 with the exception of a few countries such as Japan, Norway, the Slovak Republic and the United Kingdom. Notable reductions in the growth of manufacturing productivity in recent years have occurred in Austria, Canada, Italy and Korea, possibly reflecting a strong structural shift in the manufacturing sector in these countries. Within manufacturing, large differences can be observed. High- and medium-high technology industries, such as electrical and optical equipment and transport equipment, have typically experienced relatively high rates of productivity growth while low-technology manufacturing industries, such as textiles, have tended to generate slightly lower rates of productivity growth. However, growth rates for the textiles industry remained quite high in 2000-2005 for some OECD countries, including Czech Republic, France, Norway, the United Kingdom and the United States – important in the face of increasing imports of low cost textiles from developing countries.

Manufacture of electrical and optical equipment is one of the industries with the highest rates of productivity growth, despite some slowing down since late 1990s. During the period 2000-2005 some OECD countries sustained annual productivity growth in this sector of over 10%, including the Czech Republic, Finland, Hungary, Japan, Sweden and the United States.

Sources
- *Annual National Accounts.*
- *OECD STAN database for structural analysis.*

Further information
Methodological publications
- OECD (2001), *Measuring Productivity – OECD Manual Measurement of Aggregate and Industry-level Productivity Growth*, OECD, Paris.
- Pilat, D. et al. (2006), *The Changing Nature of Manufacturing in OECD Economies*, OECD Science, Technology and Industry Working Papers, No. 2006/9, OECD, Paris.
- Triplett, J. (2004), *Handbook on Hedonic Indexes and Quality Adjustments in Price Indexes: Special Application to Information Technology Products*, OECD Science, Technology and Industry Working Papers, No. 2004/9, OECD, Paris.

Websites
- *www.oecd.org/statistics/productivity/compendium.*

Value added per person employed

Percentage change, annual rate

Total manufacturing

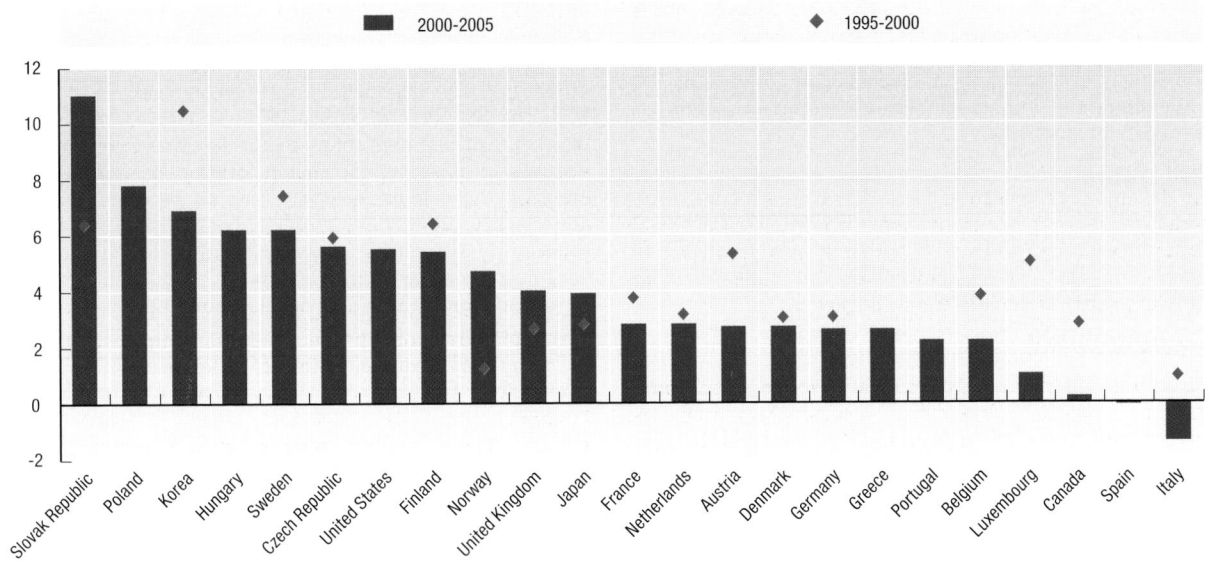

StatLink http://dx.doi.org/10.1787/271772787380

Textiles and textile products

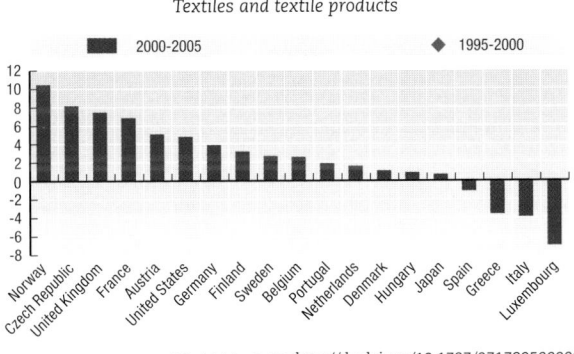

StatLink http://dx.doi.org/10.1787/271782532220

Basic metals and fabricated metal products

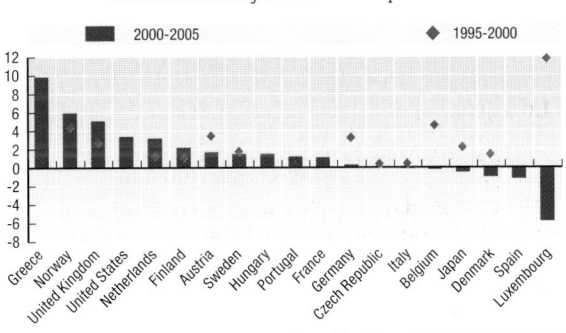

StatLink http://dx.doi.org/10.1787/271806855415

Electrical and optical equipment

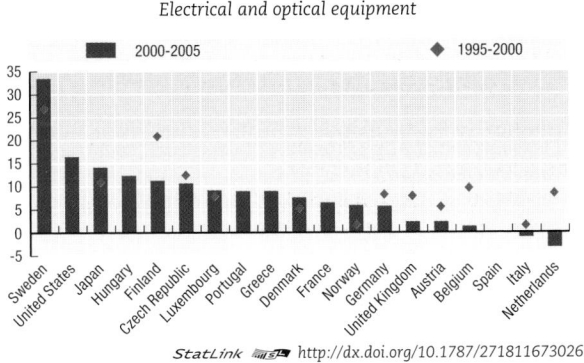

StatLink http://dx.doi.org/10.1787/271811673026

Transport equipment

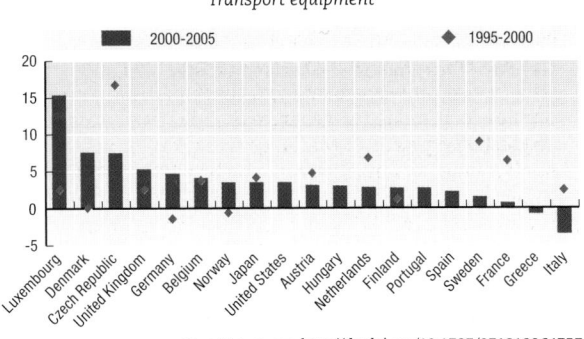

StatLink http://dx.doi.org/10.1787/271813364757

PRODUCTIVITY GROWTH IN SERVICES

Measuring productivity in services tends to be more challenging than measuring productivity in goods production. However, as the service sector now accounts for over 70% of OECD aggregate GDP and employment, and continues to grow, it is increasingly important to understand the impact of different services sectors on aggregate productivity.

Definition

For each service sector, labour productivity growth is calculated as the difference between the rate of growth of value added and the rate of growth of total employment (number of persons engaged).

Comparability

Measuring output and productivity growth in many services is not straightforward. What exactly does a lawyer or economist produce? How can the changing pricing schemes of telecommunications providers be compared over time? And how should one measure the "quantity" of health services provided by hospitals? These and similar questions arise when statisticians attempt to measure the output of service industries and the difficulty of this task is hard to overstate.

Generally, it is more difficult for services than for goods to separate changes in volumes and prices. Characteristics of goods can normally be identified and changes in quantities and qualities are, in principle, measurable. However for services, even quantitative changes are often hard to measure, let alone quality change.

"Market services" here refers to ISIC Rev.3 service activities 50 to 74. In other words, it is an activity based proxy and excludes those industries that tend to be dominated by non-market production such as health, education and community and social services. Note that no adjustments have been made to remove estimates of household rentals (actual and imputed), which has no labour input associated, from value added – current practice when calculating labour productivity by major economic activity in OECD's System of Unit Labour Costs (ULC) Indicators. Also, since the ULC data set uses hours worked, rather than persons engaged, as a measure of labour input wherever possible, estimates of productivity growth of market services here may differ from those presented in the section focussing on ULCs.

In the charts, for Japan, total market services do not include hotels and restaurants (ISIC 55) and data refer to 1996-2000 instead of 1995-2000; 2000-2004 is used instead of 2000-2005 for Canada, Portugal and Sweden; 2001-2005 for Poland.

Long-term trends

Several OECD countries experienced reduced growth in total market service labour productivity during the period 2000-05 compared to 1995-2000. The most notable falls occurred in Mexico, Portugal, the Slovak Republic and Switzerland. Countries that experienced a marked increase included Belgium, the Czech Republic, Hungary, Ireland and Japan. Productivity growth in market services continued to be very small in Italy and Spain.

The variation across services sectors and across countries is considerable. The services sectors with the highest rate of productivity growth tend to be those that invest more in ICT and have more highly skilled workforces. Sometimes labeled "Knowledge-intensive services", these include industries such as post and telecommunications (ISIC 64); finance and insurance; and certain other business services such as computer services (ISIC 72).

Labour productivity in the hotels and restaurants sector seems to have declined considerably across OECD countries with few exceptions. However, the steep falls are partly due to the effect of using persons employed as a measure of labour input rather than hours worked – there are significant numbers of part-time workers in this sector. For most of those countries where hours worked data are available, estimated productivity still declines but to a lesser degree. It is also worth noting that any increase in the quality of output may not be captured in such services.

Sources

- *Annual National Accounts.*
- *OECD STAN database for structural analysis.*

Further information

Methodological publications

- Ahmad, N. *et al.* (2003), *Comparing Labour Productivity Growth in the OECD Area: The Role of Measurement*, OECD Science, Technology and Industry Working Papers, No. 2003/14, OECD, Paris.
- OECD (2001), *Measuring Productivity – OECD Manual Measurement of Aggregate and Industry-level Productivity Growth*, OECD, Paris.
- OECD (2005), *Enhancing the Performance of the Services Sector*, OECD, Paris.
- Wölfl, A. (2003), *Productivity Growth in Service Industries: An Assessment of Recent Patterns and the Role of Measurement*, OECD Science, Technology and Industry Working Papers, No. 2003/7, OECD, Paris.
- Wölfl, A. (2005), *The Service Economy in OECD Countries:*, OECD Science, Technology and Industry Working Papers, No. 2005/3, OECD, Paris.

Websites

- *www.oecd.org/statistics/productivity/compendium.*

Value added per person employed

Percentage change, annual rate

Total market services

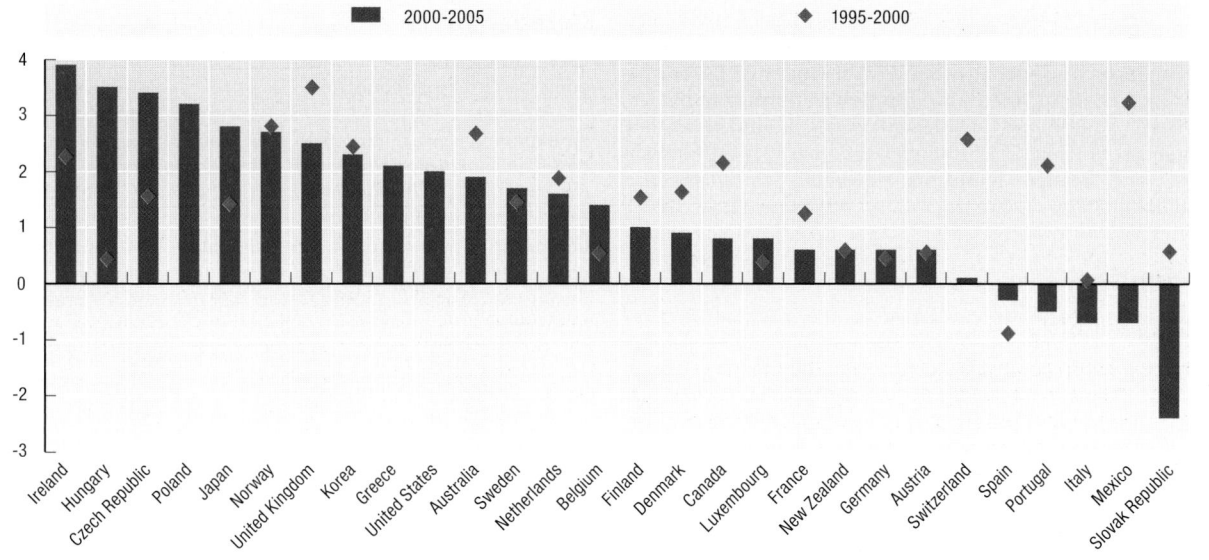

StatLink ᵐˢˡ http://dx.doi.org/10.1787/271843748221

Wholesale and retail trade

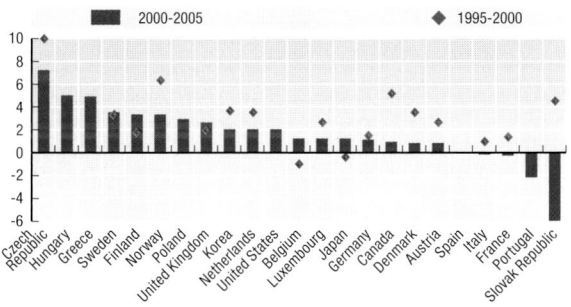

StatLink ᵐˢˡ http://dx.doi.org/10.1787/271858210624

Hotels and restaurants

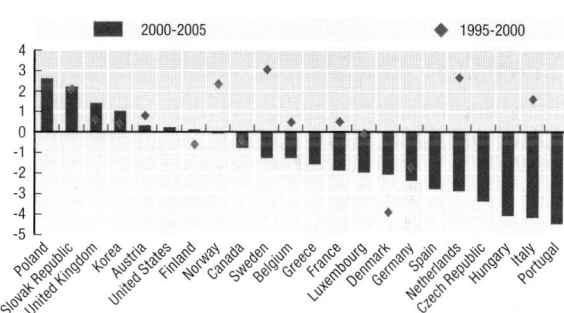

StatLink ᵐˢˡ http://dx.doi.org/10.1787/272053367442

Transport, storage and communication

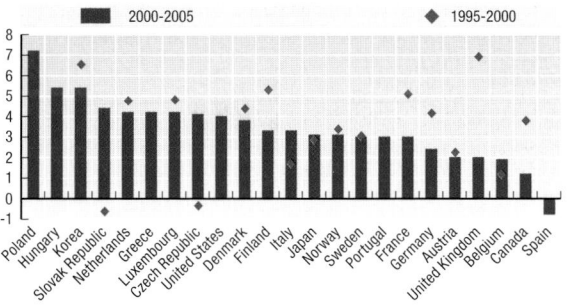

StatLink ᵐˢˡ http://dx.doi.org/10.1787/272074828166

Finance and insurance

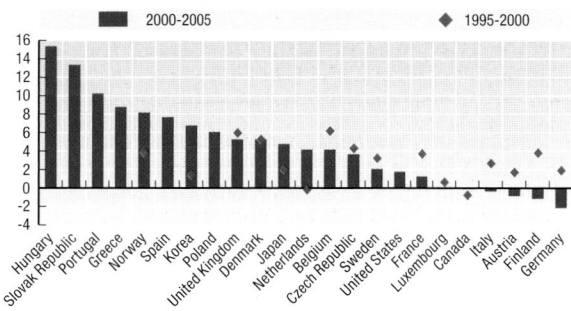

StatLink ᵐˢˡ http://dx.doi.org/10.1787/272184622734

UNIT LABOUR COSTS, LABOUR PRODUCTIVITY AND LABOUR COMPENSATION

Unit labour costs measure the average cost of labour per unit of output. As such, a unit labour cost represents a link between productivity and the cost of labour in producing output. The data presented in this publication are an output of the *OECD System of Unit Labour Cost* and related indicators database which produces annual and quarterly unit labour cost and related indicators according to a specific methodology to ensure data are comparable across OECD countries.

Definition

Unit labour costs are calculated as the quotient of total labour costs and real output, or equivalently as labour compensation per unit labour input divided by labour productivity. Labour compensation per unit labour input is defined as compensation of employees (SNA 93 definition) divided by total hours worked by employees of businesses (or person counts of total employees if data on hours worked are not available). Labour productivity is real output (gross value added) divided by total hours worked by all persons in employment (or counts of total employed persons if data on hours worked are not available). The Business Sector (excluding Agriculture) is defined as the sum of predominantly market orientated industries, namely ISIC Rev. 3 divisions C, D, E, F, G, H, I, and J.

Comparability

Every effort has been made to ensure that data are comparable across countries. The primary data source is the *OECD System of National Accounts* database within which data is expected to be compiled on a similar basis across countries according to the SNA 93. Therefore cross country comparisons of developments in indexes of unit labour costs, labour productivity and labour compensation per unit labour input over time can be made with a strong degree of confidence. In all cases countries were consulted in the initial compilation of annual unit labour costs and related indicators.

The target variable for labour input is total hours worked for both total employment (unit labour cost, and labour productivity) and employees (unit labour cost, and labour compensation per unit labour input) compiled according to the *1993 System of National Accounts*. However, total hours worked are only available for the following countries: Australia, Austria, Canada, Denmark, France, Germany, Greece, Hungary, Italy, Korea, Norway, the Slovak Republic, Spain and Sweden. For the remaining countries (and the Euro area) persons are used for total employment or total employees.

Long-term trends

Business Sector: over the period shown (1993-2006) in the tables and graphs, annual average growth in labour productivity and unit labour costs have shown moderate increases, while labour compensation per unit labour input has shown stronger growth. Only Japan and Finland have recorded negative annual average growth in unit labour costs over this period driven by annual average growth in labour productivity growing faster than labour compensation per unit labour input. Korea, Poland and the Slovak Republic all show average annual growth in labour productivity of 4% or above with all three also having strong annual average growth in labour compensation per unit labour input leading to strong annual average growth in their unit labour costs.

Sources
* *OECD System of Unit Labour Cost Indicators.*

Further information
Analytical publications
* Official Launch of the OECD System of Unit Labour Cost Indicators, *www.oecd.org/std/statisticsnewsletter*. *The OECD Statistics Newsletter*, April 2007, Issue 36.

Statistical publications
* OECD (2007), *Main Economic Indicators*, OECD, Paris.

Online databases
* *OECD System of Unit Labour Cost and Related Indicators.*

UNIT LABOUR COSTS, LABOUR PRODUCTIVITY AND LABOUR COMPENSATION

Unit labour costs, business sector
Annual growth in percentage

	1993	1994	1995	1996	1997	1998	1999	2000	2001	2002	2003	2004	2005	2006
Australia	−0.3	0.3	3.7	1.0	0.7	0.1	1.2	3.9	0.5	0.6	1.9	4.2	3.0	..
Austria	3.6	0.8	0.0	−1.4	0.1	0.4	−0.3	−0.8	1.2	1.1	0.5	−0.7	1.4	−0.3
Belgium	5.1	0.1	−0.1	0.9	−0.1	1.1	2.3	0.6	3.9	1.2	−0.3	−0.1	0.9	1.5
Canada	−0.9	−2.0	1.1	2.2	2.0	1.6	−0.1	1.5	3.0	0.0	2.2	..	..	..
Czech Republic	28.1	15.1	12.0	12.3	11.3	8.9	2.1	2.3	5.2	4.4	3.5	1.1	−2.2	0.2
Denmark	1.6	−2.9	1.3	2.7	1.0	3.9	0.3	−0.3	4.6	3.7	1.7	0.8	1.5	2.4
Finland	−5.9	−3.6	3.4	−0.5	−0.6	1.0	0.2	−0.2	2.8	0.1	0.2	−1.1	1.9	−1.6
France	2.6	−0.7	0.6	1.5	0.5	−0.5	0.3	1.3	2.1	2.7	1.1	1.6	1.4	..
Germany	4.7	0.0	2.0	0.7	−1.6	0.0	0.5	0.1	0.3	0.4	0.4	−1.3	−0.9	−1.9
Greece	..	..	..	8.4	8.2	5.4	1.7	0.3	−1.5	4.4	1.9	3.1	5.8	5.5
Hungary	15.9	10.0	19.7	20.3	13.6	9.0	1.8	12.2	11.2	4.3	5.5	9.4	3.1	..
Iceland	−1.4	1.0	5.0	3.1	2.4	7.5	6.4	5.2	4.8	7.3	1.2	−0.6	6.0	..
Ireland	2.1	2.0	−3.4	−0.6	−0.2	6.3	1.3	4.0	2.3	−2.3	2.5	3.3	4.1	2.4
Italy	1.1	−1.1	1.1	5.1	2.5	−0.6	2.3	−0.8	2.2	4.0	4.5	2.2	3.5	1.6
Japan	1.0	0.2	−1.5	−2.3	−0.5	−0.3	−3.2	−2.5	−2.1	−4.1	−4.5	−4.3	−2.3	..
Korea	7.0	7.0	8.8	6.8	−0.3	1.0	−5.0	−2.0	3.8	0.6	5.8	−0.5	−0.1	−1.1
Luxembourg	2.8	1.0	0.8	3.1	−0.7	−0.9	1.8	3.1	6.2	1.2	1.4	0.8	0.7	1.8
Mexico	13.4	6.1	23.4	19.6	18.5	16.5	15.8	10.1	8.5	4.7	3.1	1.7	..	..
Netherlands	2.3	−0.7	0.5	0.8	1.9	2.3	1.2	2.5	4.7	4.2	1.5	−0.5	−0.6	1.1
New Zealand	−1.2	2.9	1.2	3.5	1.8	0.6	−4.1	−0.1	3.6	1.3	3.9	..	..	..
Norway	−0.4	−1.7	0.9	0.7	3.1	8.3	5.3	1.5	3.1	3.1	0.3	1.2	4.5	8.2
Poland	28.3	30.1	25.0	23.9	17.3	14.4	3.6	3.0	7.9	−4.5	−2.8	−3.1	0.1	..
Portugal	4.1	3.5	−0.7	3.3	1.9	4.2	3.5	2.5	1.9	3.5	2.6	0.7	..	..
Slovak Republic	..	19.9	8.6	1.0	15.2	6.3	5.1	12.8	1.3	7.7	2.5	4.8	2.3	−3.0
Spain	7.4	1.1	2.5	4.3	4.0	2.6	2.3	4.0	3.4	3.0	3.1	2.2	2.2	2.4
Sweden	−4.2	−0.5	−1.1	4.4	0.4	0.9	−2.0	4.4	6.0	−1.1	−1.0	−2.4	−0.3	−0.3
Turkey	59.3	69.0	55.6	91.4	93.4	73.3	88.1	51.3	45.1	29.5	18.2	13.2	7.7	10.5
United Kingdom	−1.0	−1.4	2.0	0.5	2.1	4.4	2.3	2.6	3.4	2.1	2.0	0.6	2.9	1.5
United States	0.6	0.1	2.5	1.8	2.4	3.6	1.6	4.4	1.4	−2.0	−0.5	1.8	1.0	3.8
Euro area	3.5	−0.2	1.2	1.8	−2.0	−0.1	1.5	0.8	1.8	2.1	1.6	0.7	0.9	0.6
Major Seven	1.2	−0.2	1.3	1.0	1.2	1.9	0.6	2.0	1.0	−1.0	−0.3	0.3	0.6	..

StatLink 📊 http://dx.doi.org/10.1787/276128531605

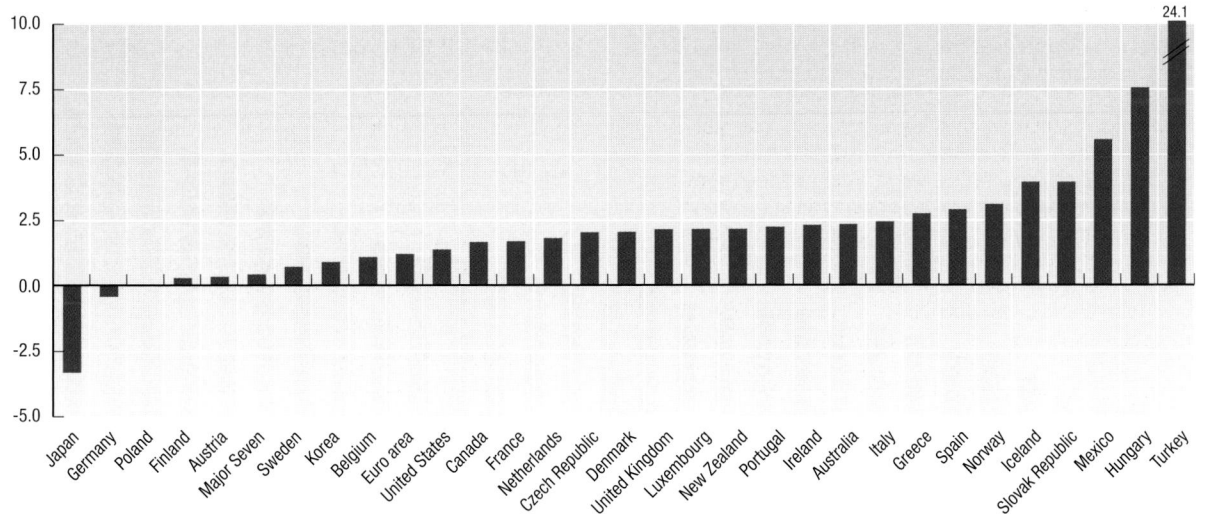

Unit labour costs, business sector
Average annual growth in percentage, 2000-2006 or latest available period

StatLink 📊 http://dx.doi.org/10.1787/272266758118

UNIT LABOUR COSTS, LABOUR PRODUCTIVITY AND LABOUR COMPENSATION

Labour productivity, business sector
Annual growth in percentage

	1993	1994	1995	1996	1997	1998	1999	2000	2001	2002	2003	2004	2005	2006
Australia	2.2	0.5	2.1	3.7	3.6	3.0	1.3	0.3	5.4	2.0	1.5	−0.7	1.1	..
Austria	0.6	3.3	4.0	1.7	1.4	2.6	3.9	4.0	0.6	1.4	1.3	1.7	1.3	3.2
Belgium	−1.4	3.6	1.4	0.4	3.7	−0.3	1.8	1.4	0.1	2.1	2.0	2.2	0.4	1.7
Canada	1.8	2.0	1.5	−0.2	3.2	1.9	2.4	3.6	0.2	1.2	0.7	0.0	2.6	..
Czech Republic	..	..	..	3.9	−1.0	0.3	5.3	4.8	1.9	1.9	4.6	5.1	6.7	6.1
Denmark	0.5	6.9	1.7	1.6	0.9	−1.2	1.7	2.4	−0.5	0.9	2.9	1.1	0.9	0.7
Finland	8.0	8.5	2.1	2.7	2.9	4.0	2.1	4.3	2.6	1.3	2.4	4.7	1.7	4.4
France	1.1	2.5	2.3	0.0	1.8	2.7	1.6	3.9	0.3	2.5	2.1	0.4	2.1	..
Germany	0.7	3.3	2.3	2.2	3.1	1.1	1.2	3.5	2.3	1.8	1.9	1.5	2.0	3.4
Greece	..	..	..	5.0	4.1	−0.3	2.0	5.1	3.6	1.8	4.5	2.8	0.5	0.1
Hungary	..	..	..	2.0	3.4	4.7	−0.5	3.7	4.1	4.7	5.2	4.5	3.9	5.1
Ireland	2.0	2.6	5.8	5.9	5.4	−0.9	4.5	4.3	4.5	6.7	2.2	1.9	1.2	2.2
Italy	1.9	5.2	4.1	−1.1	1.7	−0.9	−0.2	2.9	0.4	−1.1	−1.8	0.0	0.6	1.0
Japan	−0.3	1.3	3.2	2.9	2.0	−0.2	1.8	3.4	1.5	2.9	3.1	4.4	2.9	..
Korea	4.3	5.3	6.4	4.8	5.6	6.3	8.0	5.7	3.0	5.7	5.6	5.0	5.9	4.6
Luxembourg	2.8	3.8	−0.2	−1.2	3.1	1.8	2.0	3.1	−2.7	1.4	0.5	2.7	3.3	3.6
Mexico	..	..	..	3.4	3.9	−3.0	4.0	1.8	−1.3	−0.9	−0.3	1.4	..	..
Netherlands	0.2	3.1	0.4	1.0	0.9	1.6	2.1	2.2	0.2	0.2	2.0	4.2	1.5	1.1
New Zealand	6.0	0.8	−0.7	0.3	1.1	−2.2	3.8	1.9	1.8	1.5	1.3	1.0	−3.6	..
Norway	2.2	5.0	3.4	3.9	2.1	−1.3	0.4	4.4	3.6	2.1	3.3	1.6	0.3	−1.8
Poland	7.4	6.8	4.2	5.6	3.7	1.5	10.4	8.9	1.1	4.1	4.4	6.8	2.9	..
Portugal	1.3	0.5	5.8	3.0	4.1	0.5	1.0	2.7	1.2	−0.4	0.0	1.6	..	..
Slovak Republic	..	..	..	2.4	5.4	8.5	0.1	1.4	3.3	4.5	7.5	3.6	−0.6	8.6
Spain	1.1	2.6	0.5	−1.5	−1.4	−1.0	−0.7	−1.0	0.5	0.4	0.5	0.2	1.1	0.0
Sweden	6.2	4.2	3.6	1.7	5.0	2.7	2.3	4.2	−0.2	5.7	4.7	5.7	4.8	3.9
Switzerland	0.7	1.4	1.6	3.0	2.7	1.5	−1.5	2.0	2.0	2.2	−0.2	0.9	2.3	..
United Kingdom	3.8	4.3	1.6	2.7	1.4	2.6	2.9	3.4	1.2	1.6	2.8	3.6	1.3	2.8
United States	1.1	1.8	0.6	2.4	2.3	3.3	2.9	1.8	1.2	3.2	2.4	3.2	1.7	1.1
Euro area	0.5	3.4	1.9	0.6	1.9	0.8	0.7	1.6	0.5	0.3	0.6	1.3	0.8	1.7
Major Seven	1.0	2.3	1.8	2.0	2.2	1.9	2.2	2.6	1.2	2.4	2.1	2.7	1.9	..

StatLink ᵐˢ▇ http://dx.doi.org/10.1787/276157315844

Labour productivity, business sector
Average annual growth in percentage, 2000-2006 or latest available period

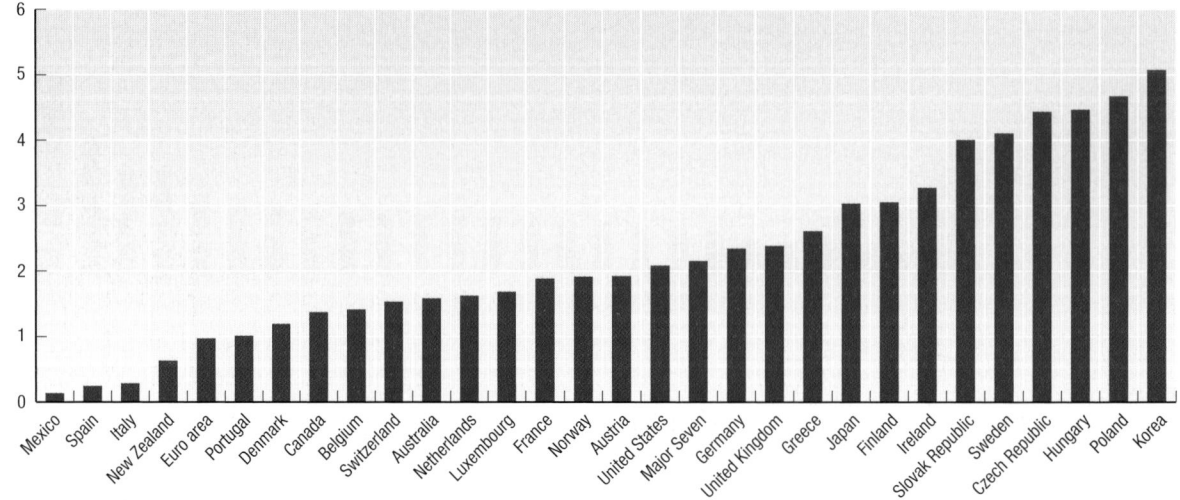

StatLink ᵐˢ▇ http://dx.doi.org/10.1787/272274323024

OECD FACTBOOK 2008 – ISBN 978-92-64-04054-0 – © OECD 2008

UNIT LABOUR COSTS, LABOUR PRODUCTIVITY AND LABOUR COMPENSATION

Labour compensation per unit labour input, business sector

Annual growth in percentage

	1993	1994	1995	1996	1997	1998	1999	2000	2001	2002	2003	2004	2005	2006
Australia	1.8	0.9	6.1	4.6	4.3	3.1	2.6	4.2	5.8	2.6	3.5	3.3	4.2	..
Austria	4.2	4.0	4.0	0.2	1.5	2.9	3.7	3.2	1.9	2.5	1.7	1.0	2.7	3.1
Belgium	3.4	4.0	1.6	1.3	3.6	0.8	4.0	1.8	3.8	3.5	1.6	2.2	1.3	3.2
Canada	0.9	0.1	2.5	1.9	4.9	3.5	2.1	5.1	3.2	1.2	2.8	..	..	..
Czech Republic	..	..	..	16.5	10.0	9.4	7.7	7.1	7.2	6.3	8.4	6.3	4.3	6.2
Denmark	2.1	3.8	3.0	4.3	2.0	2.6	2.1	2.1	4.1	4.6	4.6	1.9	2.4	3.1
Finland	1.7	4.6	5.6	2.3	2.3	5.0	2.3	4.1	5.5	1.4	2.6	3.6	3.6	2.8
France	3.7	1.8	3.0	1.5	2.4	2.2	1.9	5.2	2.3	5.2	3.2	2.0	3.5	..
Germany	5.4	3.3	4.5	3.1	1.5	1.1	1.8	3.7	2.6	2.2	2.4	0.2	1.1	1.6
Greece	..	..	..	14.1	12.1	4.6	3.3	5.4	2.3	6.2	6.6	5.6	6.3	5.3
Hungary	..	..	..	22.5	17.0	13.2	1.7	16.8	15.5	8.4	11.0	14.2	6.9	..
Ireland	..	..	..	5.1	5.0	5.3	5.7	8.2	6.7	4.0	4.7	5.4	5.4	4.6
Italy	3.2	4.2	5.1	4.1	4.1	−1.8	2.1	2.0	2.8	2.7	2.8	2.1	4.0	2.6
Japan	0.7	1.4	1.7	0.5	1.5	−0.5	−1.5	0.7	−0.6	−1.2	−1.6	0.0	0.5	..
Korea	12.8	12.6	15.9	12.7	6.0	9.1	0.5	2.8	6.1	6.8	10.8	5.0	5.7	3.2
Luxembourg	5.6	4.8	0.7	1.8	2.3	0.9	3.9	6.3	3.3	2.5	1.9	3.4	4.0	5.5
Mexico	..	..	..	23.5	23.1	12.9	20.2	12.3	7.4	4.1	3.0	2.8	..	..
Netherlands	2.5	2.4	0.9	1.8	2.7	3.8	3.3	4.7	5.0	4.4	3.5	3.7	0.8	2.2
New Zealand	4.7	3.7	0.4	3.8	2.8	−1.4	−0.6	1.8	5.5	2.7	5.2	..	..	..
Norway	1.7	3.2	4.4	4.5	5.3	6.9	5.7	5.9	6.9	5.3	3.6	2.8	4.9	6.1
Poland	38.2	38.7	30.3	31.0	21.8	16.4	14.4	12.2	8.7	−0.7	1.4	3.6	2.9	..
Portugal	..	..	..	6.5	6.0	4.7	4.5	5.2	3.2	3.1	2.6	2.3	..	..
Slovak Republic	..	..	..	3.6	20.4	15.6	5.2	14.2	5.0	12.7	10.3	8.5	2.3	5.5
Spain	8.8	3.7	2.9	2.8	2.3	1.4	1.2	2.7	3.9	3.3	3.6	2.5	3.3	2.3
Sweden	..	3.7	2.4	6.2	5.3	3.6	0.3	8.7	5.8	4.5	3.6	3.1	4.5	3.6
United Kingdom	2.9	2.9	3.1	2.7	3.7	7.2	5.2	6.0	4.5	3.6	4.6	4.2	4.2	4.4
United States	1.7	1.9	3.1	4.2	4.8	7.0	4.5	6.3	2.6	1.2	1.9	5.1	2.6	4.9
Euro area	4.0	3.3	3.1	2.5	−0.1	0.7	2.1	2.5	2.3	2.4	2.2	2.1	1.7	2.3
Major Seven	2.2	2.1	3.1	3.0	3.5	3.9	2.7	4.6	2.2	1.4	1.8	3.2	2.4	..

StatLink http://dx.doi.org/10.1787/276181136065

Labour compensation per unit labour input, business sector

Average annual growth in percentage, 2000-2006 or latest available period

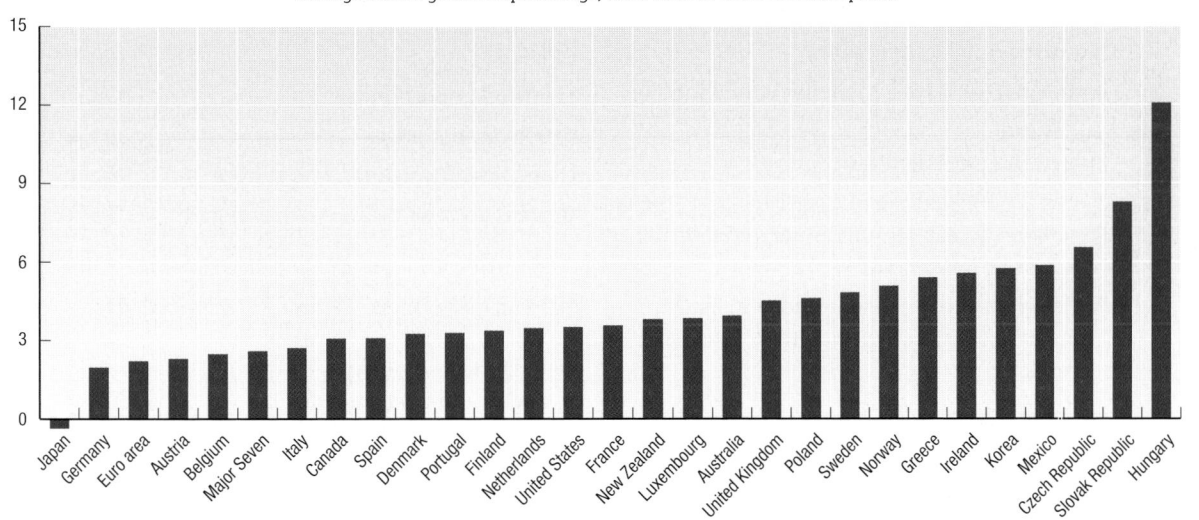

StatLink http://dx.doi.org/10.1787/272307083456

Analytical index

A

Accidents, *see*: Road fatalities   256

Activities of multinationals   84

Ageing societies   18

Agricultural support estimates   216

Agriculture, *see*: Nutrient use in agriculture 184

Agriculture, *see*: Real value added in agriculture, forestry and fishing   57

Agriculture, *see*: Value added by activity   52

Agriculture, producer support, *see*: Agricultural support estimates   216

Aid, *see*: Official development assistance   220

Aquaculture, *see*: Fisheries   178

Aquaculture, *see*: Government support for fishing   218

Arrivals of non-resident tourists staying in hotels and similar establishments   241

Assistance, development, *see*: Official development assistance   220

Average hours actually worked   153

B

Balance of payments   78

Births see: Total fertility rates   15

Borrowing, *see*: Government net borrowing/net lending   207

Brain drain, *see*: Migration and unemployment   26

Broadband access, *see*: Computer and Internet access by households   168

Business services, *see*: Value added in banks, insurance, real estate and other business services   55

C

Carbon dioxide (CO_2), *emission, see*: Emissions of carbon dioxide (CO_2)   180

Cars, *see*: Road motor vehicles   255

Cell phones, *see*: Mobile cellular subscribers 172

Change in relative volume indices of GDP per capita   35

Changes in exchange rates and purchasing power parities   97

Changes in real expenditure on educational institutions in tertiary education   199

Child mortality, *see*: Infant mortality   236

CO_2 emissions from energy use   181

Communications, *see*: Investment in ICT   166

Communications, *see*: Size of the ICT sector 164

Communications, *see*: Value added per person employed: transport, storage and communication   281

Comparative price levels   99

Competitiveness, *see*: Effective exchange rates   100

Computer and internet access by households   168

Consumer Price Indices (CPI)   88

Consumer prices indices, *see*: Relative consumer price indices   102

Contribution of key activities to aggregate productivity growth   276

Contribution of labour productivity and labour utilisation to GDP per capita   263

Contribution of renewables to energy supply   117

Contributions to GDP growth   269

CPI: all items   89

CPI: energy   91

CPI: food   90

Crude oil import prices   123

Crude oil spot prices   123

Culture, *see*: Recreation and culture   242

Current account balance of payments   79

D

DAC countries, *see*: Gross bilateral ODA from DAC countries by region   222

Debt, government, *see*: Government debt   208

Defence, *see*: Law, order and defence expenditure   214

OECD FACTBOOK 2008 – ISBN 978-92-64-04054-0 – © OECD 2008

Deficit, government, *see*: Government deficits 206

Dependency ratio, *see*: Ratio of the inactive elderly population aged 65 and over to the labour force 19

Development assistance, *see*: Official development assistance 220

Differences in GDP when converted to US dollars using exchange rates and PPPs 98

Disposable income, *see*: Distribution of household disposable income among individuals 249

Distribution of elderly population into urban, intermediate and rural regions 21

Distribution of household disposable income among individuals 249

Distribution of the national population into urban, intermediate and rural regions 17

Drop-outs, *see*: Percentage of the total labour force living in regions with an unemployment rate above the national average 147

Dwelling investment, *see*: Investment rates 44

E

Earnings, *see*: Relative earnings of graduates 200

Education, *see*: International student assessment 188

Education, *see*: Public and private education expenditure 202

Education, *tertiary*, *see*: Tertiary attainment 194

Educational attainment of recent immigrants 28

Educational institutions, *see*: Changes in real expenditure on eductional institutions in tertiary education 199

Effective exchange rates 100

Elderly Population by region 20

Electrical equipment, *see*: Value added per person employed: electrical and optical equipment 279

Electricity generation 112

Emissions of Carbon Dioxide (CO_2) 180

Employment in affiliates under foreign control 85

Employment rates by age group 130

Employment rates by gender 126

Employment rates for age group 15-24 131

Employment rates for age group 25-54 132

Employment rates for age group 55-64 133

Employment rates: men 128

Employment rates: total 127

Employment rates: women 129

Energy , *see*: Electricity generation 112

Energy production 118

Energy supply and economic growth 108

Energy supply per capita 110

Energy use, *see*: CO_2 emissions from energy use 181

Enterprises with less than 20 persons engaged 61

Evolution of GDP 40

Evolution of long-term interest rates 94

Evolution of the population 12

Evolution of value added by activity 56

Exchange rates, *see*: Changes in exchange rates and purchasing power parities 97

Exchange rates, *see*: Differences in GDP when converted to US dollars using exchange rates and PPPs 98

Exchange rates, *see*: Nominal effective exchange rates 101

Exchange rates, *see*: Rates of conversion 96

Exchange rates 98

Expenditure on educational institutions for all levels of education 203

Expenditure on health 211

Expenditure on R&D 156

Expenditure on recreation and culture 245

Expenditure on tertiary education 198

Expenditure per student in tertiary education 199

Exports, *see*: Partner countries and regions of OECD merchandise exports 77

Exports , *see*: Trade in services 70

Exports , *see*: Trading partners 74

Exports of goods 69

Exports of ICT equipment 171

Exports of information and communications equipment 170

Exports of services 73

F

FDI flows and stocks 80

Fertility rates, *see*: Total fertility rates 15

Fertility, *Population, see*: Evolution of the population 12

Finance , *see*: Value added per person employed: finance and insurance 281

Financial liabilities, *see*: General government gross financial liabilities 209

Firm size, *see*: Labour productivity and firm-size heterogeneity 274

Fish landings in domestic and foreign ports 178

Fisheries 178

Fishing, *see*: Real value added in agriculture, forestry and fishing 57

Fishing, government transfers, *see*: Government support for fishing 218

Foreign affiliates, *see*: Employment in affiliates under foreign control 85

Foreign direct investment, *see*: Outflows of foreign direct investment 83

Foreign population, *see*: Trends in migration 22

Foreign-born and foreign populations 25

Foreign-born unemployment rate relative to native-born unemployment rate 27

Forestry, *see*: Real value added in agriculture, forestry and fishing 57

G

GDP, *see*: Contributions of key activities to growth of value added per person employed 277

GDP, *see*: Evolution of GDP 40

GDP, *see*: Evolution of value added by activity 56

GDP, *see*: Gross domestic product 33

GDP, *see*: Real GDP growth 41

GDP, *see*: Regional GDP 38

GDP, *see*: Size of GDP 32

GDP, *see*: Value added by activity 52

GDP deflator 49

GDP growth, *see*: Contributions to GDP growth 269

GDP per capita, *see*: Change in relative volume indices of GDP per capita 35

GDP per capita, *see*: Growth in GDP per capita 262

GDP per capita, *see*: Levels of GDP per capita 272

GDP per capita 34

GDP per hour worked 265

GDP per hour worked relative to the United States 273

General government gross financial liabilities 209

GFT to fishing for selected countries 218

Gini index of regional disparities in GDP 39

Gini index of regional disparities in unemployment rates 147

GNI, *see*: Gross and net national income per capita 37

Goods and services, *see*: Trade in goods and services 65

Government debt 208

Government deficits 206

Government expenditure on recreation and culture 244

Government financial transfers to fishing 219

Government net borrowing/net lending 207

Government services, *see*: Value added in business services and in government and personal services 55

Government support for fishing 218

Greenhouse gases, emission, *see*: Emissions of carbon dioxide (CO_2) 180

Gross agricultural nitrogen and phosphorus balances 185

Gross agricultural nutrient balances 185

Gross and net national income per capita 37

Gross bilateral ODA from DAC countries by region 222

Gross domestic expenditure on R&D 157

Gross domestic product 33

Gross fixed capital formation 45

Gross fixed capital formation in housing 47

Gross fixed capital formation in machinery and equipment 46

Gross national income per capita 37

Growth accounts for OECD countries 268

Growth in GDP per capita 262

Growth in GDP per hour worked 265

Growth of the motorway network 253

H

Health expenditure 210

Higher education, *see*: Expenditure on tertiary education 198

Higher education, *see*: Tertiary attainment 194

Higher education, *see*: Trends in tertiary graduation rates 192

Historical income and productivity levels 272

Hotels , *see*: Value added in construction and in transport, trade, hotels and restaurants 54

Hotels , *see*: Value added per person employed: hotels and restaurants 281

Hours worked 152

Household and government expenditure on recreation and culture 245

Household expenditure on recreation and culture 243

Household net saving rates 43

Household saving 42

Households with access to home computers and the internet 169

I

ICT, *see*: Share of ICT in value added 165

ICT sector, *see*: Computer and Internet access by households 168

ICT sector, *see*: Investment in ICT 166

ICT sector, *see*: Size of the ICT sector 164

Immigrant population 24

Immigrants, *see*: Education attainment of recent immigrants 28

Imports, *see*: Partner countries and regions of OECD merchandise imports 76

Imports, *see*: Trade in services 70

Imports, *see*: Trading partners 74

Imports of goods 68

Imports of services 72

Inactivity, *see*: Youth inactivity 246

Incarceration, *see*: Prison population 250

Incidence of part-time employment 135

Income, *see*: Gross national income per capita 37

Income and productivity levels 270

Income and productivity levels relative to the United States 273

Income inequality 248

Income, *disposable*, *see*: Distribution of household disposable income among individuals 249

Index of geographic concentration of elderly population 21

Index of geographic concentration of population 17

Indices of price levels 99

Industry , *see*: Real value added in industry 58

Industry , *see*: Value added by activity 52

Inequality, *see*: Income inequality 248

Infant mortality 236

Inflation 48

Inflows of foreign direct investment 82

Information and communications technology, *see*: Computer and Internet access by households 168

Information and communications technology, *see*: Investment in ICT 166

Information and communications technology, *see*: Size of the ICT sector 164

Insurance, *see*: Value added per person employed: finance and insurance 281

Interest rates, *see*: Long-term interest rates 94

International student assessment 188

Internet access, *see*: Computer and Internet access by households 168

Investment, *see*: Inflows of foreign direct investment 82

Investment in ICT 166

Investment in knowledge 158

Investment rates 44

Investment, foreign, *see*: FDI flows and stocks 80

K

Knowledge, *see*: Investment in knowledge 158

L

Labour compensation per employee,
total economy 150

Labour compensation per hour,
total economy 151

Labour compensation per unit labour input,
business sector 285

Labour compensation per unit labour input,
total economy 149

Labour compensation, total economy 148

Labour costs, *see*: Relative unit labour costs in
manufacturing 103

Labour productivity, *see*: Contribution
of labour productivity and labour
utilisation to GDP per capita 263

Labour productivity and firm-size
heterogeneity 274

Labour productivity growth 264

Labour productivity, business sector 284

Law, order and defence expenditure 214

Lending, *see*: Government net borrowing/
net lending 207

Length of the motorway network 253

Levels of GDP per capita 272

Life expectancy 232

Life expectancy at birth: men 234

Life expectancy at birth: women 235

Literacy, *see*: International student
assessment 188

Long-term interest rates 94

Long-term unemployment 144

M

Machinery investment, *see*: Investment rates 44

Major recipients by region of total bilateral
gross ODA from DAC countries 222

Manufacturing, *see*: Normalised labour
productivity in manufacturing 275

Manufacturing, *see*: Number of employees and
number of enterprises in manufacturing 61

Manufacturing, *see*: PPI: manufacturing 93

Manufacturing, *see*: Productivity growth
in manufacturing 278

Manufacturing, *see*: Relative unit labour costs
in manufacturing 103

Manufacturing, *see*: Value added per person
employed: total manufacturing 279

Marine capture and aquaculture production 179

Market services, *see*: Value added per person
employed: total market services 281

Mean scores and gender differences
on the mathematics scale in PISA 2006 191

Mean scores and gender differences
on the reading scale in PISA 2006 190

Mean scores and gender differences
on the science scale in PISA 2006 189

Metals, *see*: Value added per person employed:
basic metals and metal products 279

Migration, *see*: Net migration rate 23

Migration, *see*: Trends in migration 22

Migration and unemployment 26

Mobile cellular subscribers 172

Mortality, *see*: Infant mortality 236

Motorways, *see*: Length of the motorway
network 253

Multi-factor productivity 266

Multinationals, *see*: Activities
of multinationals 84

Municipal waste 182

N

National GDP per capita 39

National income per capita 36

Net migration rate 23

Net official development assistance 221

Nitrogen and phosphorus balances, *see*:
Gross agricultural nitrogen
and phosphorus balances 185

NNI, *see*: National income per capita 36

Nominal effective exchange rates 101

Normalised labour productivity in
manufacturing 275

Nuclear electricity generation 115

Nuclear energy 114

Number of employees and number
of enterprises in manufacturing 61

Nutrient use in agriculture 184

O

Obese population aged 15 and above	239
Obesity	238
Official development assistance	220
Oil prices	122
Oil production	120
Old people, *see:* Percentage of elderly population by country	21
Optical equipment, *see:* Value added per person employed: electrical and optical equipment	279
Outflows of foreign direct investment	83
Outward and inward FDI stocks	81
Overweight and obese population aged 15 and above	239

P

Partner countries and regions of OECD merchandise exports	77
Partner countries and regions of OECD merchandise imports	76
Partner countries and regions of OECD merchandise trade	75
Part-time employment	134
Patents	162
Percentage of elderly population by country	21
Percentage of the foreign-born labour force and of the native-born labour force aged 25-34 and 25-64 with a tertiary qualification	29
Percentage of the total labour force living in regions with an unemployment rate above the national average	147
Performance on the mathematics scale in PISA	191
Performance on the reading scale in PISA	190
Performance on the science scale in PISA	189
Phones, *see:* Mobile cellular subscribers	172
Phosphorus and nitrogen balances, *see:* Gross agricultural nitrogen and phosphorus balances	185
PISA, *see:* International student assessment	188
PISA, *see:* Mean scores and gender differences on the mathematics scale in PISA 2006	191
PISA, *see:* Mean scores and gender differences on the reading scale in PISA 2006	190
PISA, *see:* Mean scores and gender differences on the science scale in PISA 2006	189
PISA, *see:* Performance on the mathematics scale in PISA	191
Population, *see:* Distribution of the national population into urban, intermediate and rural regions	17
Population, *see:* Immigrant population	24
Population, *see:* Total population	13
Population aged 65 and over	19
Population density, *see:* Range of variation in regional population density	17
Population growth rates	14
PPI, *see:* Producer Price Indices (PPI)	92
PPI: manufacturing	93
PPP, *see:* Rates of conversion	96
PPPs, *see:* Purchasing power parities	97
Price index, *see:* Indices of price levels	99
Price index, *see:* Producer Price Indices (PPI)	92
Price index, *see:* Consumer Price Indices (CPI)	88
Prices, *see:* Comparative price levels	99
Prices, *see:* Producer Price Indices (PPI)	92
Primary energy supply	106
Prison population	250
Private education, *see:* Public and private education expenditure	202
Producer Price Indices (PPI)	92
Production of crude oil	121
Production of crude oil by region	121
Productivity, *see:* Income and productivity levels	270
Productivity, *see:* Labour productivity and firm-size heterogeneity	274
Productivity, *see:* Labour productivity growth	264
Productivity, *see:* Multi-factor productivity	266
Productivity growth, *see:* Contribution of key activities to aggregate productivity growth	276
Productivity growth in manufacturing	278
Productivity growth in services	280
Productivity levels, *see:* Historical income and productivity levels	272
Public and private education expenditure	202
Public social expenditure	213

Purchasing power parities, *see:* Changes in exchange rates and purchasing power parities   97

Purchasing power parities, *see:* Differences in GDP when converted to US dollars using exchange rates and PPPs   98

Purchasing power parities   97

R

R&D, *see:* Expenditure on R&D   156

R&D, *see:* Patents   162

R&D, *see:* Researchers   160

Range of variation in regional population density   17

Rates of conversion   96

Ratio of the inactive elderly population aged 65 and over to the labour force   19

Reading capability, *see:* International student assessment   188

Real GDP growth   41

Real value added in agriculture, forestry and fishing   57

Real value added in industry   58

Real value added in services   59

Recreation and culture   242

Refinery production, *see:* Share of refinery production by product   120

Regional disparities, *see:* Gini index of regional disparities in GDP   39

Regional GDP   38

Regional population   16

Regional unemployment   146

Relative annual growth of exports of goods   69

Relative annual growth of exports of services   73

Relative annual growth of imports of goods   68

Relative annual growth of imports of services   72

Relative consumer price indices   102

Relative earnings for age group 25-64 with tertiary education   201

Relative earnings of graduates   200

Relative unit labour costs in manufacturing103

Renewable energy   116

Renewables , *see:* Contribution of renewables to energy supply   117

Research and development, *see:* Gross domestic expenditure on R&D   157

Researchers   160

Restaurants, *see:* Value added in construction and in transport, trade, hotels and restaurants   54

Restaurants, *see:* Value added per person employed: hotels and restaurants   281

Retail trade, *see:* Value added per person employed: wholesale and retail trade   281

Return on investment in education, *see:* Relative earnings of graduates   200

Road fatalities   256

Road motor vehicles   255

Road motor vehicles and road fatalities   254

Road network   252

S

Savings, *see:* Government debt   208

Savings, *see:* Household saving   42

Science scores, *see:* International student assessment   188

Self-employment   136

Self-employment rates: men   138

Self-employment rates: total   137

Self-employment rates: women   139

Services, *see:* Imports of services   72

Services, *see:* Productivity growth in services   280

Services, *see:* Real value added in services   59

Services trade balance: exports of services minus imports of services   71

Services, exports of, *see:* Trade in services   70

Services, trade balance, *see:* Trade in services   70

Share of ICT in value added   165

Share of national elderly population in the 10% of regions with the largest elderly population   21

Share of national population in the 10% of regions with the largest population   17

Share of refinery production by product   120

Share of total population living in regions with a GDP per capita below the national average   39

Share of trade in GDP   64